THE TIMES
ATLAS OF THE WORLD

COMPACT EDITION

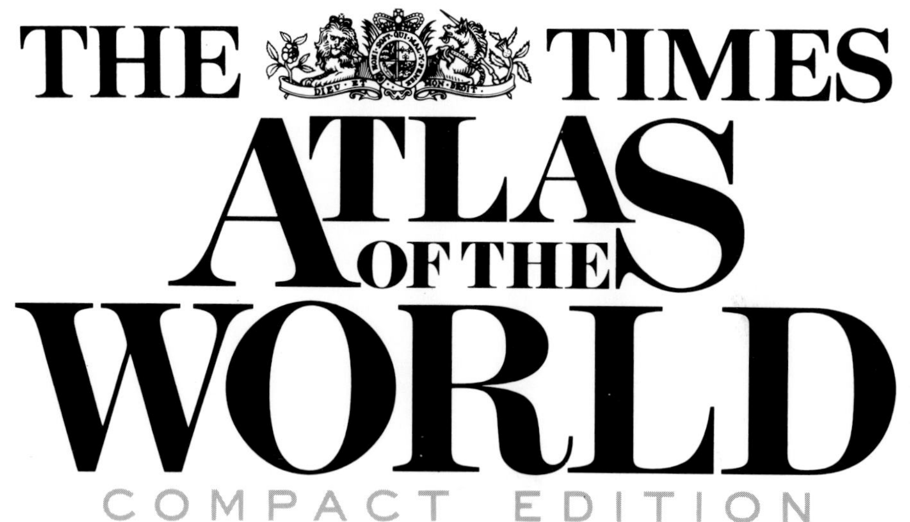

THE TIMES

ATLAS OF THE WORLD

COMPACT EDITION

TIMES BOOKS
HarperCollins*Publishers*

This edition first published 1994 by Times Books
HarperCollins Publishers
77-85 Fulham Palace Road, London W6 8JB

© Times Books and Bartholomew 1994

First published by Batholomew 1991
Revised 1992,1993,1995

ISBN 0 7230 0775 6

Printed in Hong Kong

Details included in this atlas are subject to change without notice. Whilst
every effort is made to keep information up to date the publishers will not be
responsible for any loss, damage or inconvenience caused by inaccuracies in
this atlas. The publishers are always pleased to acknowledge any corrections
brought to their notice, and record their appreciation of the valuable services
rendered in the past by map users in assisting to maintain the accuracy of
their publications.

HH 7817

CONTENTS

World Physical **viii-ix**
World Political **x-xi**
World Time Zones **xii-xiii**
World Environment **xiv-xv**
Key to Symbols **xvi**

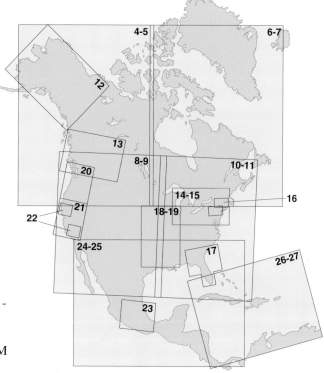

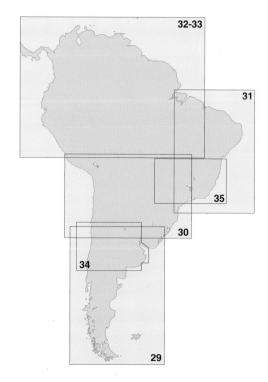

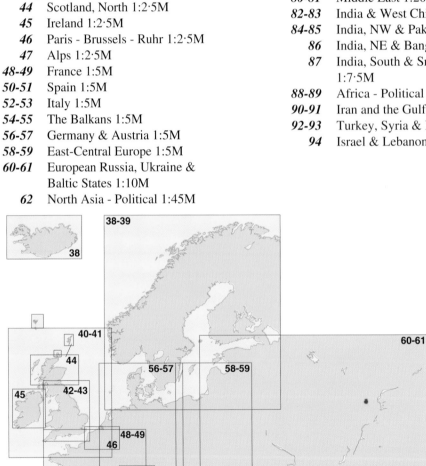

38
38-39
40-41
44
45
42-43
56-57
58-59
60-61
48-49
46
47
50-51
52-53
54-55

96-97
95
98-99
101
100-101

106-107
108-109
110-111

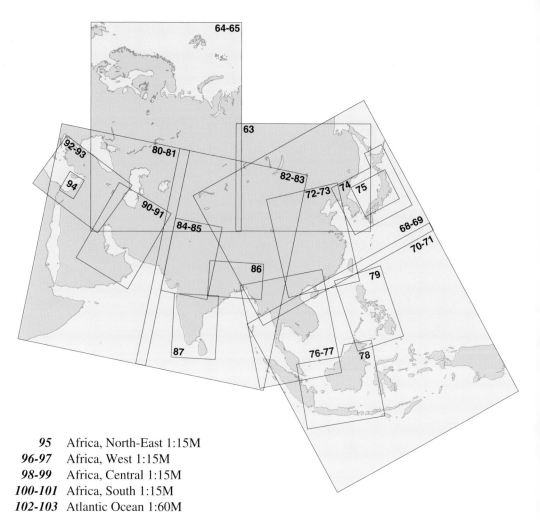

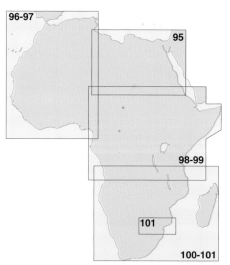

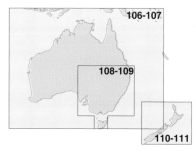

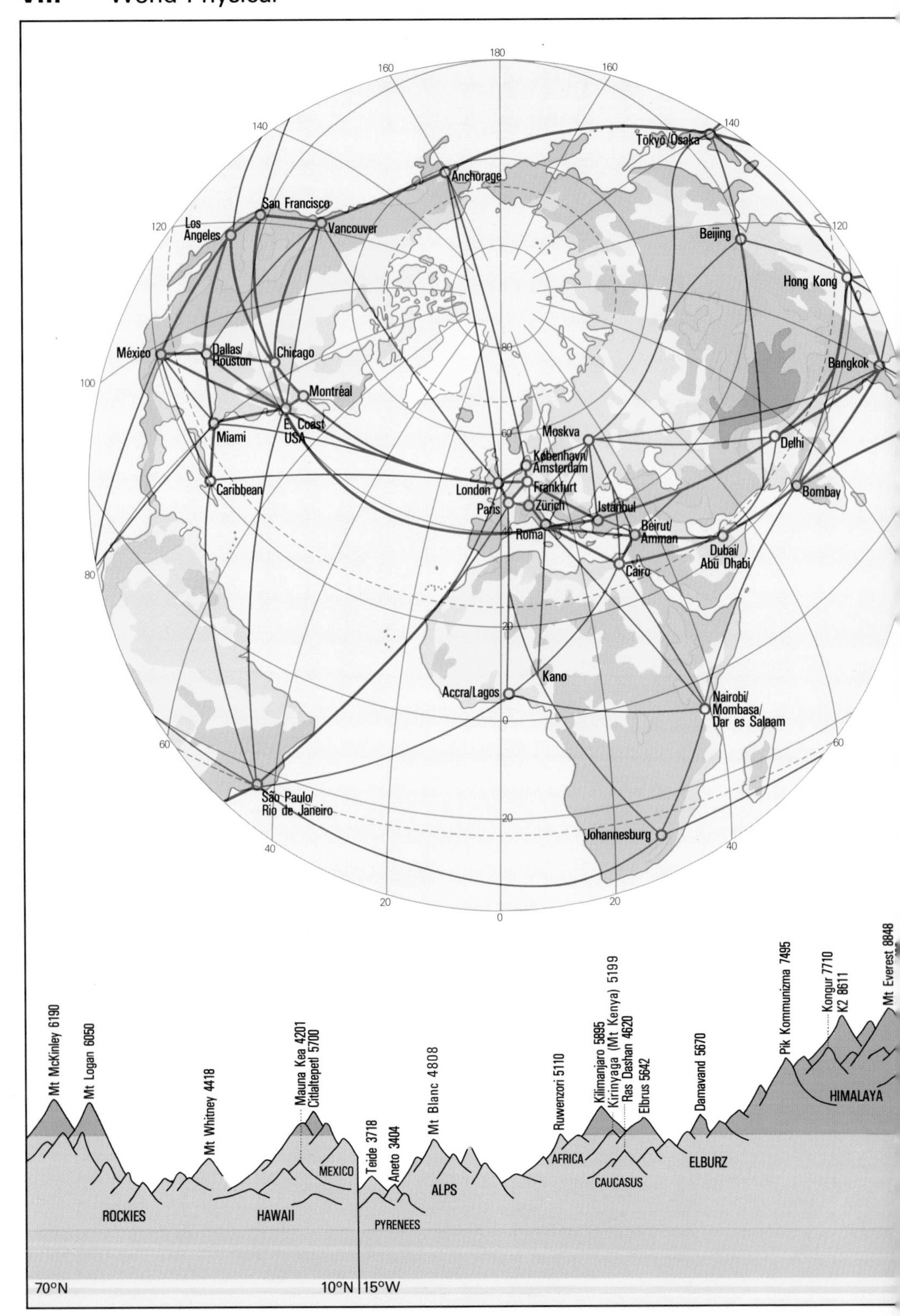

Tōkyō/Ōsaka
Anchorage
San Francisco
Los Angeles
Vancouver
Beijing
Hong Kong
Bangkok
México
Dallas/ Houston
Chicago
Montréal
E. Coast USA
Miami
Caribbean
Moskva
Delhi
København/ Amsterdam
London
Frankfurt
Paris
Zürich
Istanbul
Bombay
Roma
Beirut/ Amman
Dubai/ Abū Dhabi
Cairo
Kano
Accra/Lagos
Nairobi/ Mombasa/ Dar es Salaam
São Paulo/ Rio de Janeiro
Johannesburg
Mt McKinley 6190
Mt Logan 6050
Mt Whitney 4418
Mauna Kea 4201
Citlaltepetl 5700
Teide 3718
Aneto 3404
Mt Blanc 4808
Ruwenzori 5110
Kilimanjaro 5895
Kirinyaga (Mt Kenya) 5199
Ras Dashan 4620
Elbrus 5642
Damavand 5670
Pik Kommunizma 7495
Kongur 7710
K2 8611
Mt Everest 8848
ROCKIES
HAWAII
MEXICO
PYRENEES
ALPS
AFRICA
CAUCASUS
ELBURZ
HIMALAYA
70°N
10°N
15°W

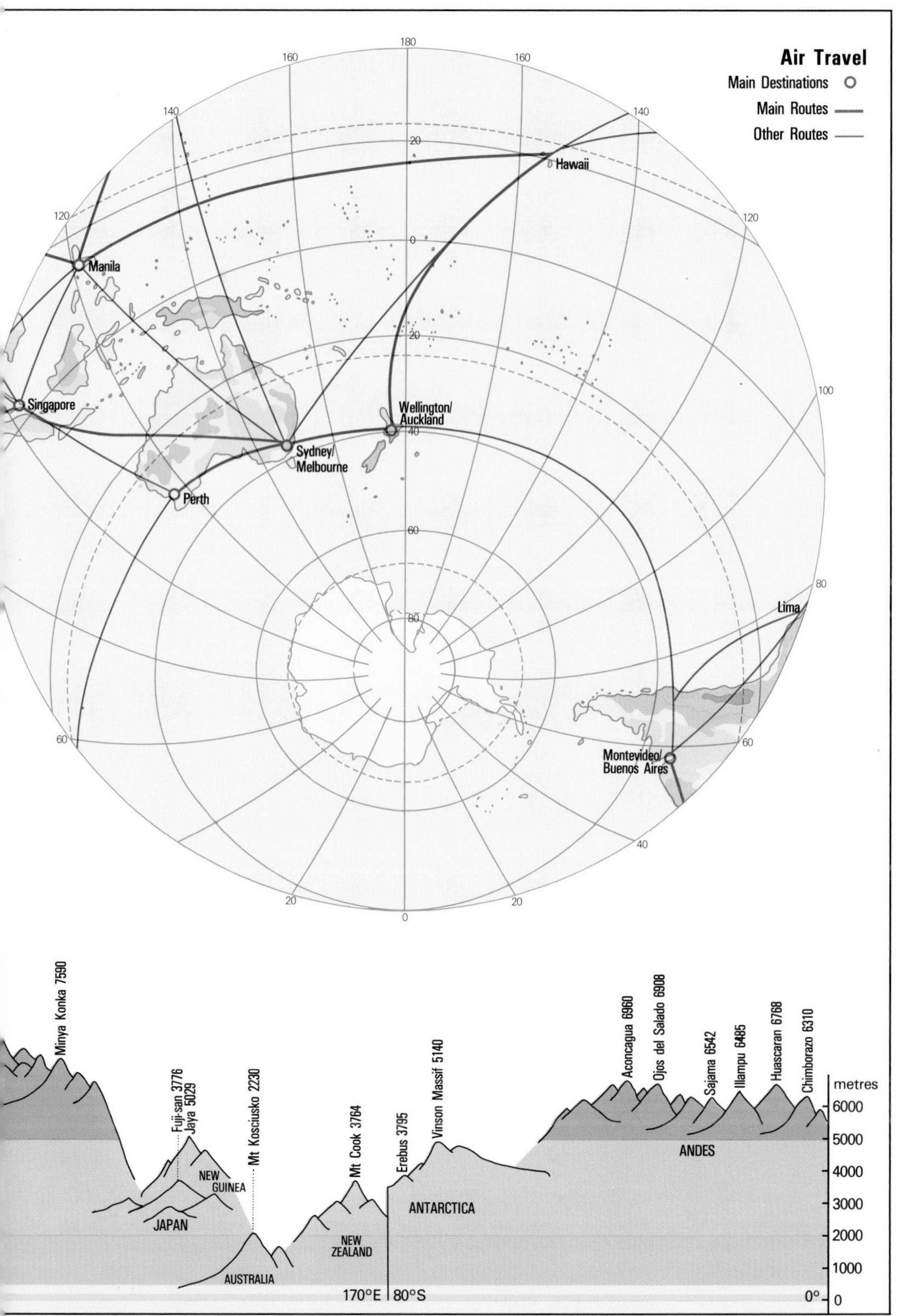
Air Travel
Main Destinations
Main Routes
Other Routes
Hawaii
Manila
Singapore
Wellington/
Auckland
Sydney/
Melbourne
Perth
Lima
Montevideo/
Buenos Aires
Minya Konka 7590
Fuji-san 3776
Jaya 5029
Mt Kosciusko 2230
Mt Cook 3764
Erebus 3795
Vinson Massif 5140
Aconcagua 6960
Ojos del Salado 6908
Sajama 6542
Illampu 6485
Huascaran 6768
Chimborazo 6310
NEW
GUINEA
JAPAN
AUSTRALIA
NEW
ZEALAND
ANTARCTICA
ANDES
170°E
80°S
0°
metres

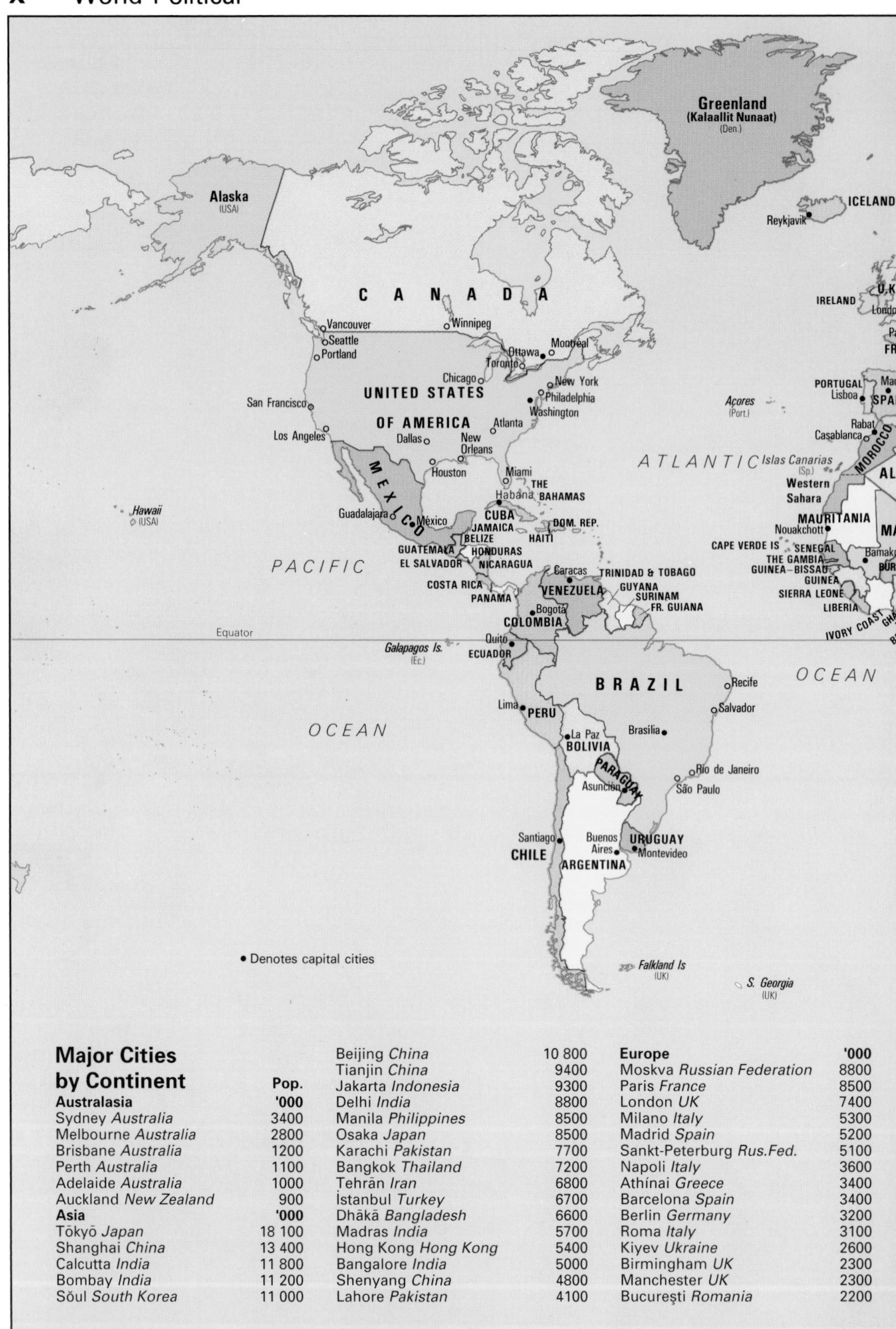

• Denotes capital cities

Major Cities by Continent

Australasia	Pop. '000
Sydney *Australia*	3400
Melbourne *Australia*	2800
Brisbane *Australia*	1200
Perth *Australia*	1100
Adelaide *Australia*	1000
Auckland *New Zealand*	900

Asia	'000
Tōkyō *Japan*	18 100
Shanghai *China*	13 400
Calcutta *India*	11 800
Bombay *India*	11 200
Sŏul *South Korea*	11 000
Beijing *China*	10 800
Tianjin *China*	9400
Jakarta *Indonesia*	9300
Delhi *India*	8800
Manila *Philippines*	8500
Osaka *Japan*	8500
Karachi *Pakistan*	7700
Bangkok *Thailand*	7200
Tehrān *Iran*	6800
İstanbul *Turkey*	6700
Dhākā *Bangladesh*	6600
Madras *India*	5700
Hong Kong *Hong Kong*	5400
Bangalore *India*	5000
Shenyang *China*	4800
Lahore *Pakistan*	4100

Europe	'000
Moskva *Russian Federation*	8800
Paris *France*	8500
London *UK*	7400
Milano *Italy*	5300
Madrid *Spain*	5200
Sankt-Peterburg *Rus.Fed.*	5100
Napoli *Italy*	3600
Athínai *Greece*	3400
Barcelona *Spain*	3400
Berlin *Germany*	3200
Roma *Italy*	3100
Kiyev *Ukraine*	2600
Birmingham *UK*	2300
Manchester *UK*	2300
Bucureşti *Romania*	2200

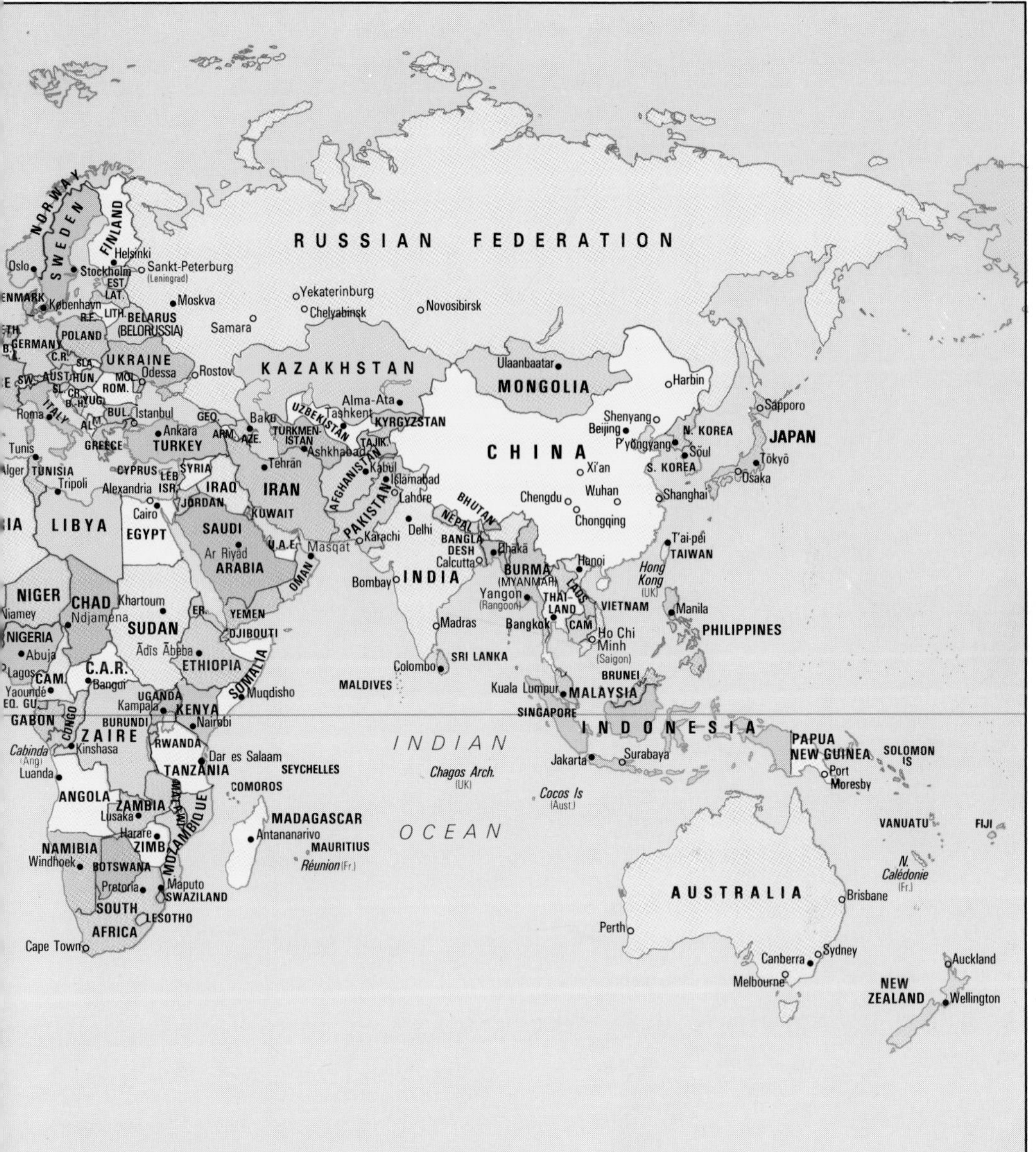

North and Central America	'000	South America	'000	Africa	'000
México *Mexico*	20 200	São Paulo *Brazil*	17 400	Cairo *Egypt*	9000
New York *USA*	16 200	Buenos Aires *Argentina*	11 500	Lagos *Nigeria*	7700
Los Angeles *USA*	11 900	Rio de Janeiro *Brazil*	10 700	Alexandria *Egypt*	3700
Chicago *USA*	7000	Lima *Peru*	6200	Kinshasa *Zaire*	3500
Philadelphia *USA*	4300	Santiago *Chile*	5000	Casablanca *Morocco*	3200
Detroit *USA*	3700	Bogotá *Colombia*	4900	Alger *Algeria*	3000
San Francisco *USA*	3700	Caracas *Venezuela*	4100	Cape Town *South Africa*	2300
Toronto *Canada*	3500	Belo Horizonte *Brazil*	3600	Abidjan *Ivory Coast*	2200
Dallas *USA*	3400	Pôrto Alegre *Brazil*	3100	Tarábulus *Libya*	2100
Guadalajara *Mexico*	3200	Recife *Brazil*	2500	Adîs Ábeba *Ethiopia*	1900
Houston *USA*	3000	Brasília *Brazil*	2400	Khartoum *Sudan*	1900
Monterrey *Mexico*	3000	Salvador *Brazil*	2400	Dar es Salaam *Tanzania*	1700
Montréal *Canada*	3000	Fortaleza *Brazil*	2100	Johannesburg *South Africa*	1700
Washington *USA*	2900	Curitiba *Brazil*	2000	Luanda *Angola*	1700
Boston *USA*	2800	Guayaquil *Ecuador*	1700	Maputo *Mozambique*	1600

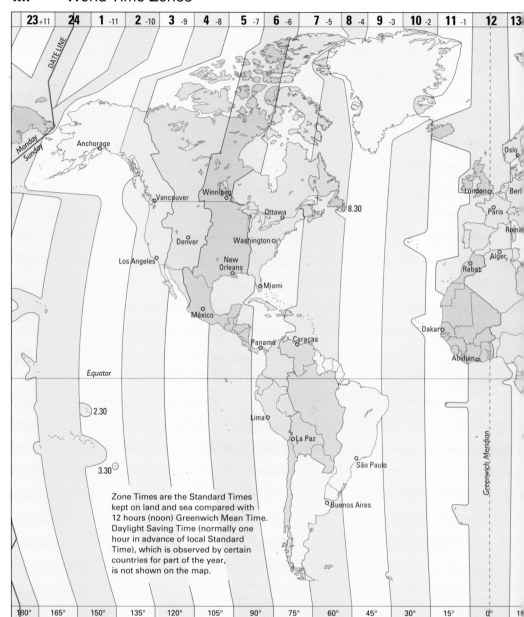

| 23 +11 | 24 | 1 -11 | 2 -10 | 3 -9 | 4 -8 | 5 -7 | 6 -6 | 7 -5 | 8 -4 | 9 -3 | 10 -2 | 11 -1 | 12 | 13 |

DATE LINE

Monday
Sunday

Anchorage

Vancouver

Winnipeg

Ottawa   8.30

Denver   Washington

Los Angeles   New
                 Orleans

              Miami

México

Panamá   Caracas

Equator

2.30

Lima

La Paz

3.30   São Paulo

Zone Times are the Standard Times
kept on land and sea compared with
12 hours (noon) Greenwich Mean Time.
Daylight Saving Time (normally one
hour in advance of local Standard
Time), which is observed by certain
countries for part of the year,
is not shown on the map.

Buenos Aires

Oslo

London   Berl

Paris

Roma

Alger

Rabat

Dakar

Abidjan

Greenwich Meridian

| 180° | 165° | 150° | 135° | 120° | 105° | 90° | 75° | 60° | 45° | 30° | 15° | 0° | 1 |

Journey Times

Sail
(via Cape)
164 days

Steam
(via Cape)
43 days

Steam
(via Suez)
30 days

Supertanker
(via Cape)
28 days

Singapore ←

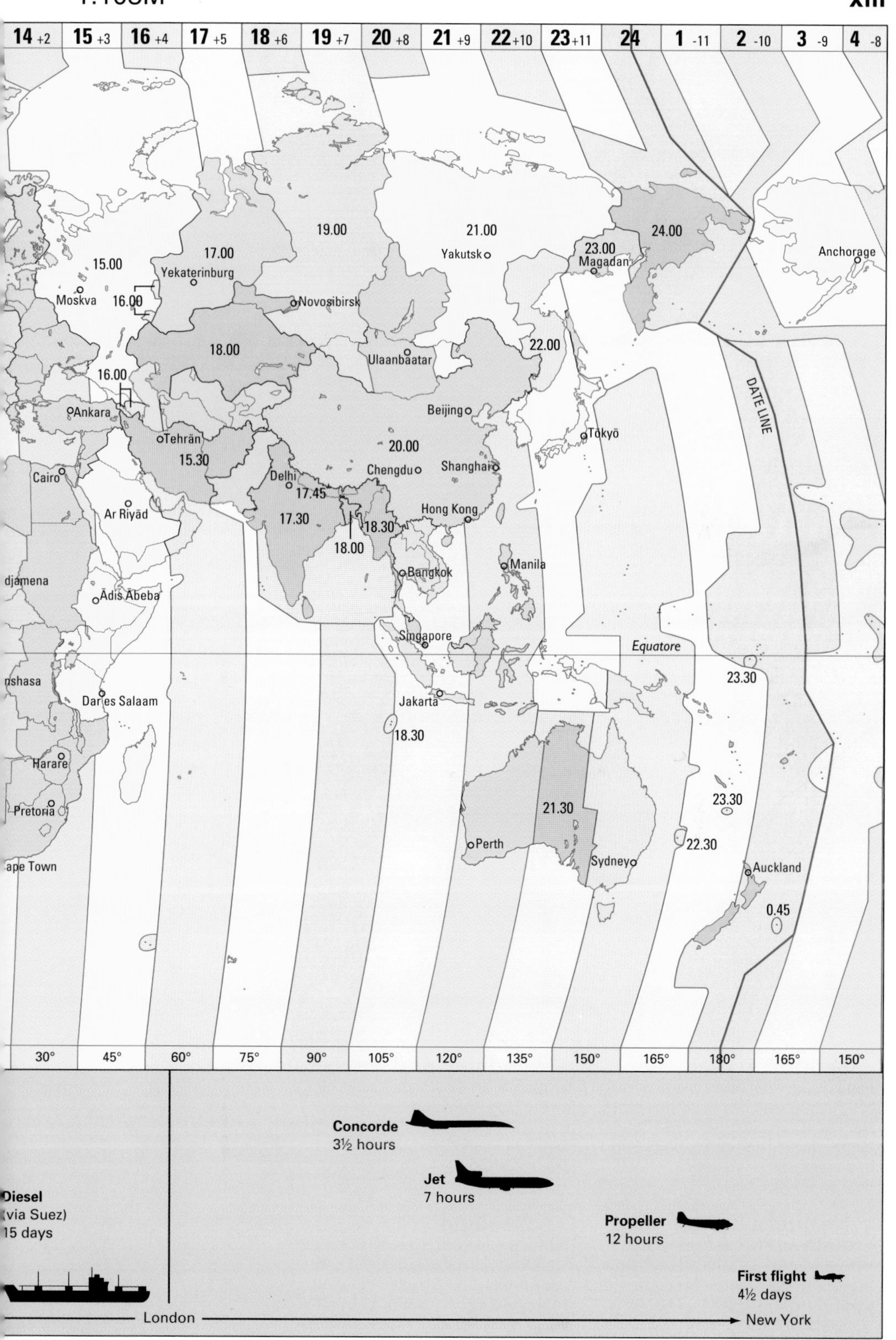

| 14 +2 | 15 +3 | 16 +4 | 17 +5 | 18 +6 | 19 +7 | 20 +8 | 21 +9 | 22 +10 | 23 +11 | 24 | 1 -11 | 2 -10 | 3 -9 | 4 -8 |

15.00
Moskva
16.00

17.00
Yekaterinburg

19.00

Novosibirsk

21.00
Yakutsk

24.00

23.00
Magadan

Anchorage

16.00
Ankara

Tehrän
15.30

18.00

Ulaanbaatar

22.00

DATE LINE

Cairo

Ar Riyād

Delhi
17.45
17.30
18.30
18.00

Chengdu
20.00
Shanghai

Beijing

Hong Kong

Tökyö

djamena

Ädis Abeba

Bangkok

Manila

nshasa

Dar es Salaam

Singapore

Equatore

23.30

Jakarta
18.30

Harare

Pretoria

Perth

21.30

Sydney

22.30

23.30

Auckland

ape Town

0.45

| 30° | 45° | 60° | 75° | 90° | 105° | 120° | 135° | 150° | 165° | 180° | 165° | 150° |

Concorde
3½ hours

Jet
7 hours

Diesel
(via Suez)
15 days

Propeller
12 hours

First flight
4½ days

London → New York

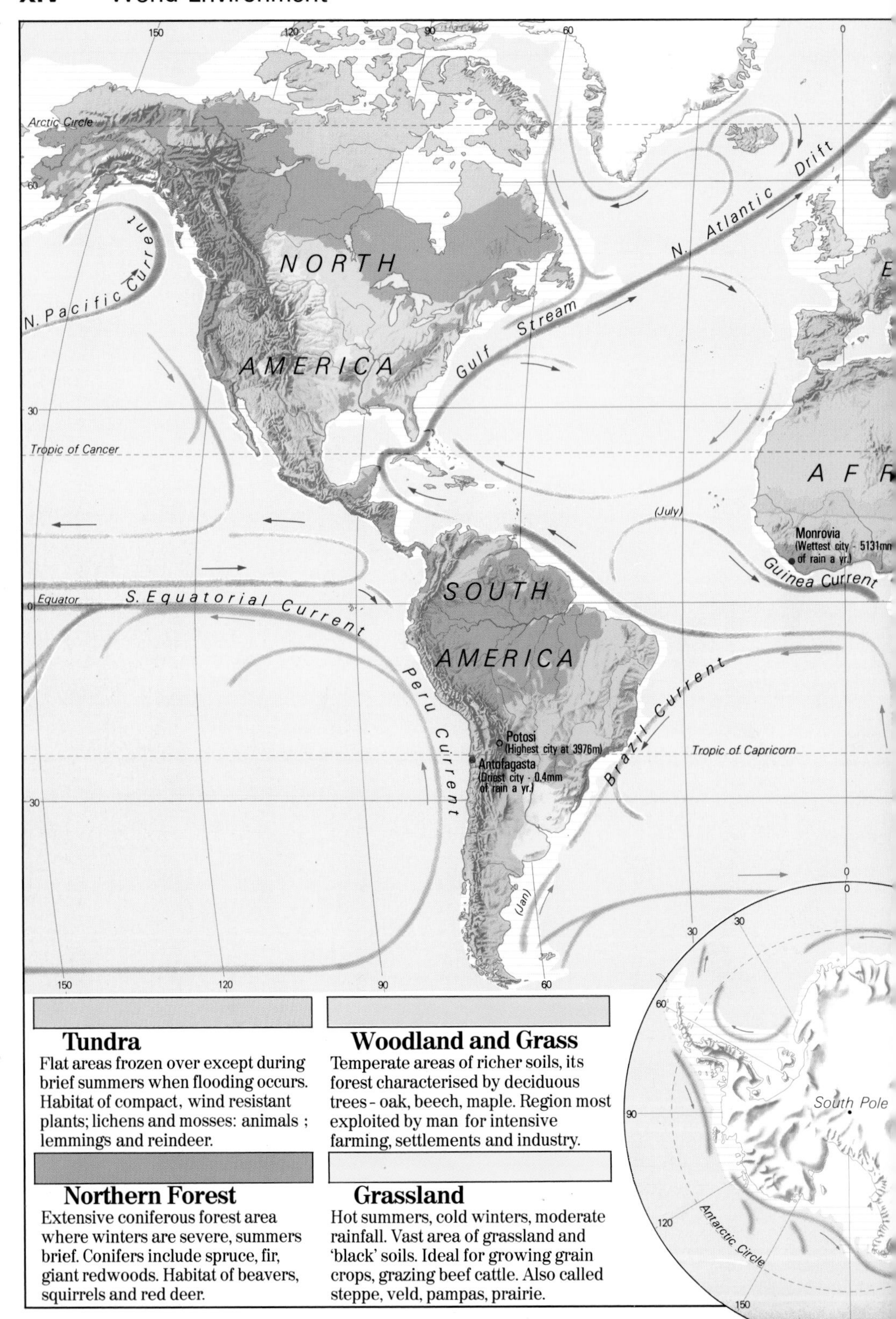

Tundra

Flat areas frozen over except during brief summers when flooding occurs. Habitat of compact, wind resistant plants; lichens and mosses: animals ; lemmings and reindeer.

Woodland and Grass

Temperate areas of richer soils, its forest characterised by deciduous trees - oak, beech, maple. Region most exploited by man for intensive farming, settlements and industry.

Northern Forest

Extensive coniferous forest area where winters are severe, summers brief. Conifers include spruce, fir, giant redwoods. Habitat of beavers, squirrels and red deer.

Grassland

Hot summers, cold winters, moderate rainfall. Vast area of grassland and 'black' soils. Ideal for growing grain crops, grazing beef cattle. Also called steppe, veld, pampas, prairie.

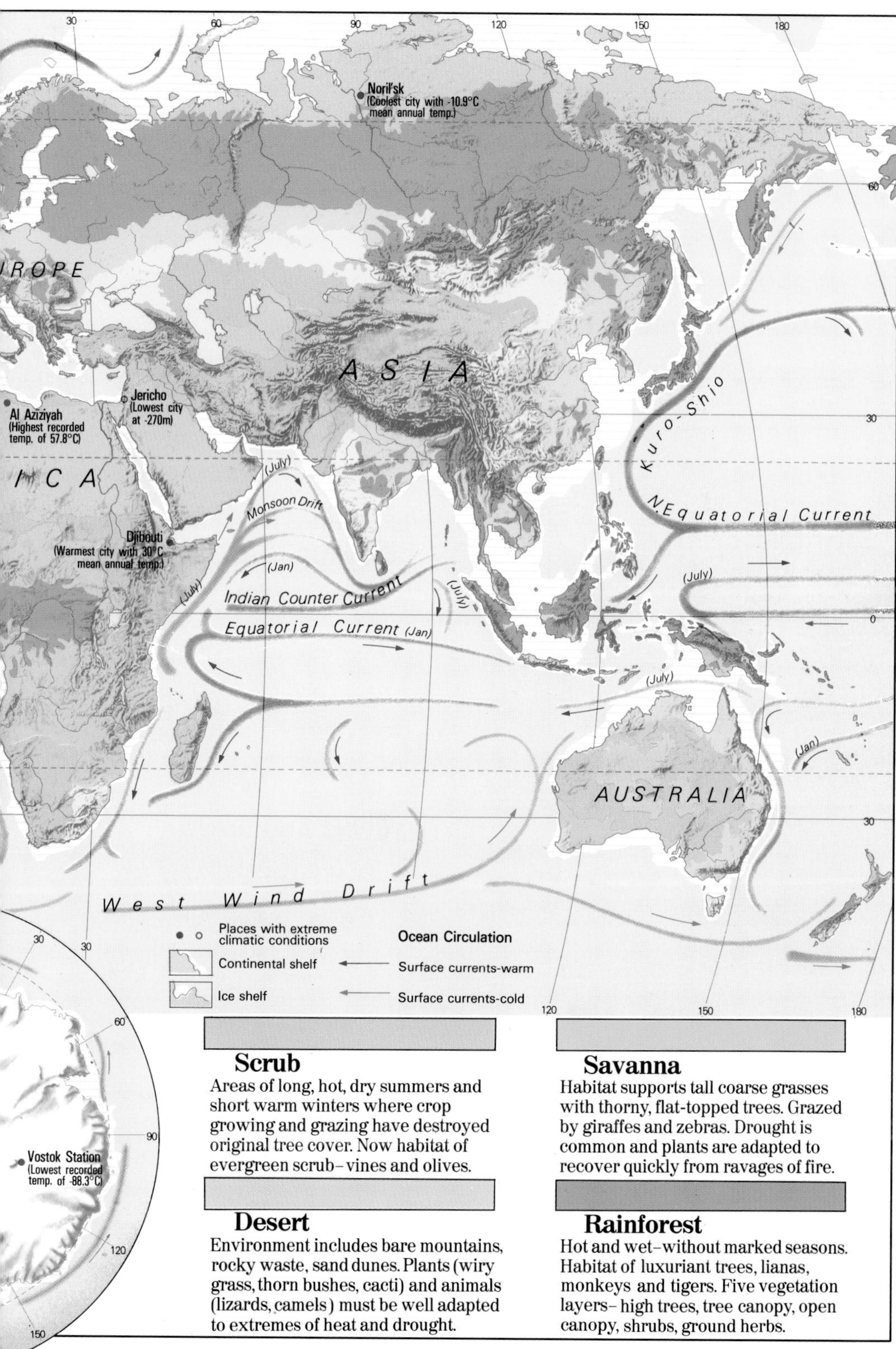

Noril'sk
(Coolest city with -10.9°C
mean annual temp.)

IROPE

60

A S I A

Jericho
(Lowest city
at -270m)

30

Al Aziziyah
(Highest recorded
temp. of 57.8°C)

I C A

Djibouti
(Warmest city with 30°C
mean annual temp.)

Kuro-Shio

(July)

Monsoon Drift

(Jan)

N Equatorial Current

(July)

Indian Counter Current

(July)

Equatorial Current (Jan)

(Jan)

0

30

AUSTRALIA

30

West Wind Drift

(Jan)

Places with extreme
climatic conditions

Ocean Circulation

Continental shelf

Surface currents-warm

Ice shelf

Surface currents-cold

120   150   180

30   30

60

90

Vostok Station
(Lowest recorded
temp. of -88.3°C)

120

150

Scrub

Areas of long, hot, dry summers and
short warm winters where crop
growing and grazing have destroyed
original tree cover. Now habitat of
evergreen scrub–vines and olives.

Desert

Environment includes bare mountains,
rocky waste, sand dunes. Plants (wiry
grass, thorn bushes, cacti) and animals
(lizards, camels) must be well adapted
to extremes of heat and drought.

Savanna

Habitat supports tall coarse grasses
with thorny, flat-topped trees. Grazed
by giraffes and zebras. Drought is
common and plants are adapted to
recover quickly from ravages of fire.

Rainforest

Hot and wet–without marked seasons.
Habitat of luxuriant trees, lianas,
monkeys and tigers. Five vegetation
layers– high trees, tree canopy, open
canopy, shrubs, ground herbs.

BOUNDARIES

————————	International
– – – – –	International under Dispute
▪ ▪ ▪ ▪ ▪ ▪	Cease Fire Line
▬▬▬▬▬	Autonomous or State/ Administrative
– – – –	Maritime (National)
— — — —	International Date Line

COMMUNICATIONS

══════ ━ ━ ━	Motorway/Under Construction
————————	Major/Other Road
– – – – –	Under Construction
· · · · · · ·	Track
=)━━━━(=	Road Tunnel
- - - - - - -	Car Ferry
————————	Main/Other Railway
– – – – –	Under Construction
- - - - - - -	Rail Ferry
→━━━←━	Rail Tunnel
┴┴┴┴┴┴	Canal
⊕ ✈	International/Other Airport

LANDSCAPE FEATURES

 Glacier, Ice Cap

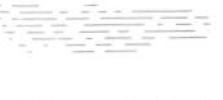

 Marsh, Swamp

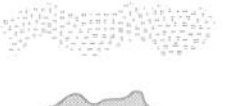

 Sand Desert, Dunes

 Freshwater

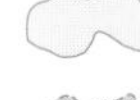

 Saltwater

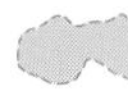

 Seasonal

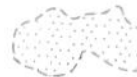

 Salt Pan

OTHER FEATURES

～～～⌇→	River/Seasonal
≍	Pass, Gorge
▨▨▨◢	Dam, Barrage
～～～～	Waterfall, Rapid
————————	Aqueduct
∿∿∿∿∿	Reef
·217 ▲4231	Spot Height, Depth/ Summit, Peak
⌄	Well
△ ▲	Oil/Gas Field
Gas / Oil	Oil/Natural Gas Pipeline
⌐Gembok Nat. Pk ⌐	National Park
∴UR	Historic Site

LETTERING STYLES

CANADA	Independent Nation
FLORIDA	State, Province or Autonomous Region
Gibraltar (U.K.)	Sovereignty of Dependent Territory
Lothian	Administrative Area
LANGUEDOC	Historic Region
Loire ***Vosges***	Physical Feature or Physical Region

TOWNS AND CITIES

Square symbols denote capital cities

▣	⊙	**New York**	Major City
▪	●	**Montréal**	City
☐	○	Ottawa	Small City
▪	•	**Québec**	Large Town
▫	○	St John's	Town
▫	○	Yorkton	Small Town
▫	○	Jasper	Village
			Built-up-area

Depth   Sea Level   Height

0

8000m 6000m 4000m 2000m 200m

200m 500m 1000m 2000m 3000m 4000m 5000m 6000m

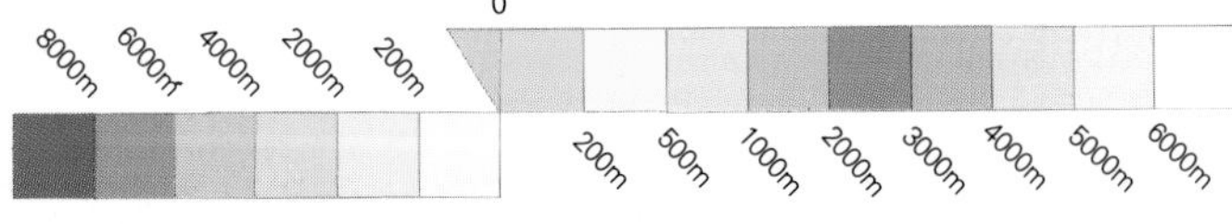

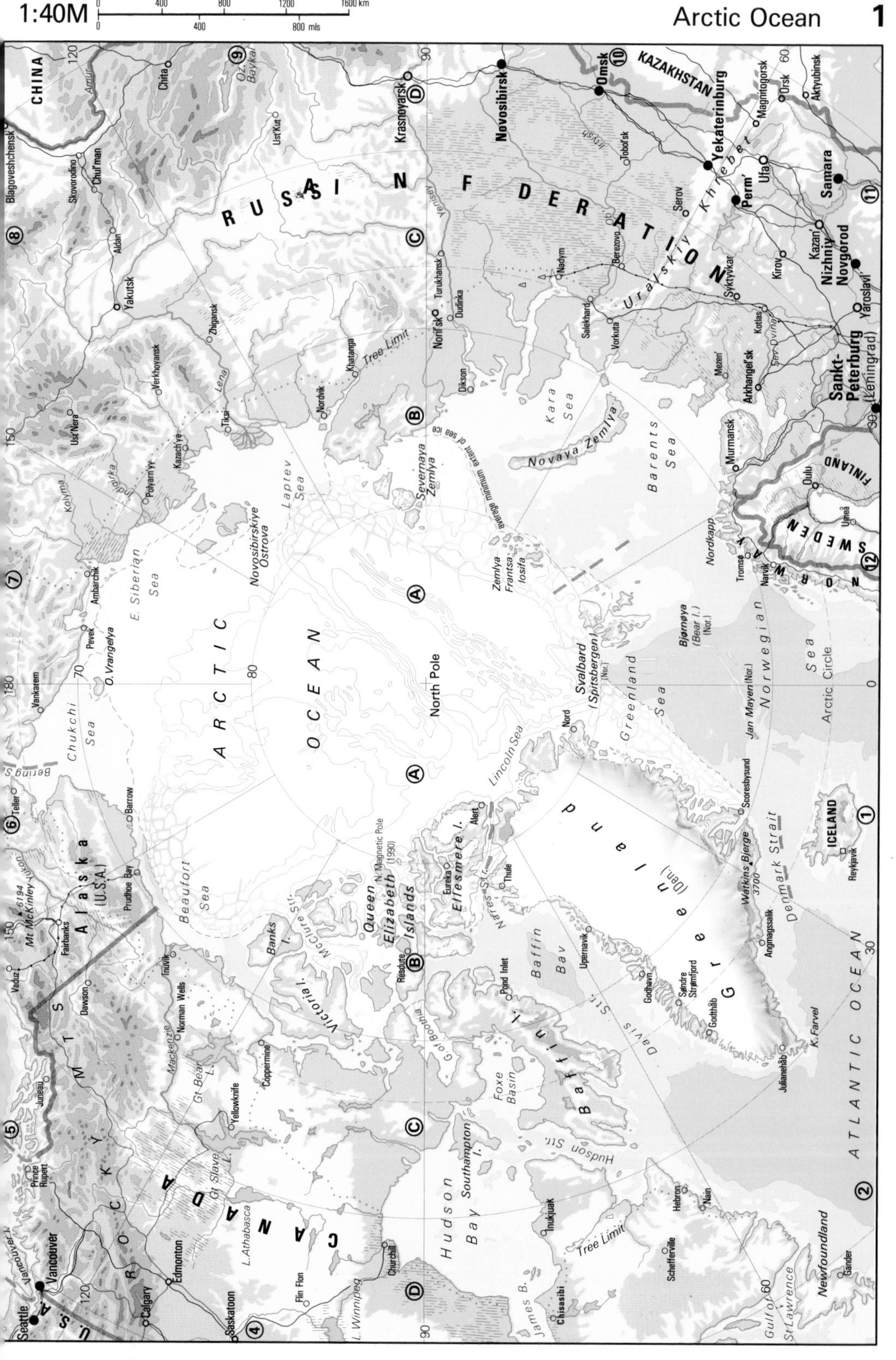
ARCTIC OCEAN
North Pole
RUSSIAN FEDERATION
KAZAKHSTAN
CHINA
FINLAND
SWEDEN
NORWAY
ICELAND
CANADA
Alaska (U.S.A.)
Greenland (Den.)
ATLANTIC OCEAN
Beaufort Sea
Chukchi Sea
E. Siberian Sea
Laptev Sea
Kara Sea
Barents Sea
Greenland Sea
Norwegian Sea
Lincoln Sea
Baffin Bay
Hudson Bay
Foxe Basin
Davis Str.
Denmark Strait
Hudson Str.
Bering S.
Nares Str.
McClure Str.
G. of Boothia
James B.
Gulf of St Lawrence
Arctic Circle
Tree Limit
average minimum extent of sea ice
Novaya Zemlya
Severnaya Zemlya
Zemlya Frantsa Iosifa
Novosibirskiye Ostrova
O. Vrangelya
Svalbard (Spitsbergen) (Nor.)
Bjørnøya (Bear I.) (Nor.)
Jan Mayen (Nor.)
Queen Elizabeth Islands
Ellesmere I.
Banks I.
Victoria I.
Baffin I.
Southampton I.
Newfoundland
N. Magnetic Pole (1990)
Watkins Bjerge 3700
K. Farvel
Mt McKinley 6194
Uralskiy Khrebet
Lena
Yenisey
Kolyma
Indigirka
Irtysh
Sev. Dvina
Amur
Yukon
Mackenzie
Gt Bear L.
Gt Slave L.
L. Athabasca
L. Winnipeg
Oz. Baykal
Novosibirsk
Omsk
Yekaterinburg
Perm'
Samara
Ufa
Kazan'
Nizhniy Novgorod
Yaroslavl'
Sankt-Peterburg (Leningrad)
Murmansk
Arkhangel'sk
Krasnoyarsk
Chita
Yakutsk
Noril'sk
Vancouver
Seattle
Calgary
Edmonton
Saskatoon
Churchill
Reykjavik
Tromsø
Narvik
Nordkapp
Oulu
Umeå
Thule
Alert
Resolute
Barrow
Fairbanks
Dawson
Yellowknife
Godthåb
Scoresbysund
Angmagssalik
Julianehåb

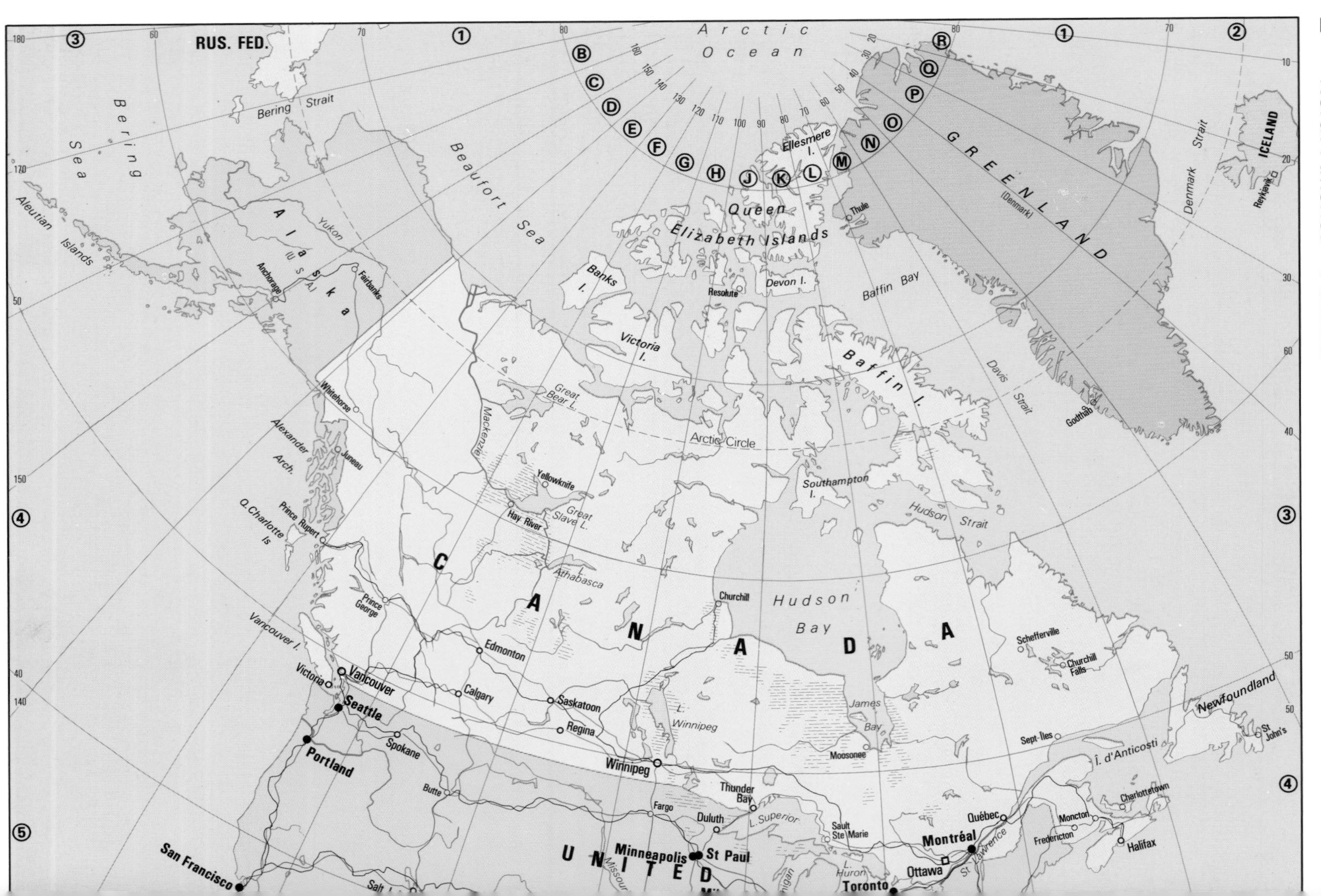
ICELAND
Reykjavik
Denmark Strait
GREENLAND
(Denmark)
Godthåb
Davis Strait
Thule
Baffin Bay
Baffin I.
Hudson Strait
Southampton I.
Arctic Ocean
Ellesmere I.
Queen Elizabeth Islands
Devon I.
Resolute
Banks I.
Victoria I.
Arctic Circle
Beaufort Sea
Great Bear L.
Great Slave L.
Yellowknife
Hay River
Mackenzie
L. Athabasca
Hudson Bay
James Bay
Churchill
Moosonee
L. Winnipeg
Schefferville
Churchill Falls
Sept-Îles
I. d'Anticosti
Newfoundland
St John's
Charlottetown
Halifax
Moncton
Fredericton
Québec
St Lawrence
Montréal
Ottawa
Toronto
Sault Ste Marie
L. Huron
L. Superior
Thunder Bay
Duluth
St Paul
Minneapolis
Fargo
Winnipeg
Regina
Saskatoon
Edmonton
Calgary
Prince George
Butte
Spokane
Vancouver
Seattle
Portland
Victoria
Vancouver I.
Q. Charlotte Is
Prince Rupert
Alexander Arch.
Juneau
Whitehorse
Fairbanks
Yukon
Alaska (U.S.A.)
Anchorage
Bering Strait
Bering Sea
Aleutian Islands
RUS. FED.
CANADA
UNITED

1:35M

| 0 | 250 | 500 | 750 | 1000 | 1250 km |

| 0 | 250 | 500 | 750 mls |

ATLANTIC OCEAN

Bermuda (U.K.)

New York
Philadelphia
Washington
Baltimore
Norfolk
Cleveland
Detroit
L. Erie
Chicago
Indianapolis
Nashville
Memphis
Birmingham
St Louis
Kansas City
Denver
Albuquerque
El Paso
Phoenix
Tucson
San Diego
Los Angeles
Dallas
Fort Worth
San Antonio
Houston
New Orleans
Atlanta
Charleston
Jacksonville
Tampa
Miami

Charleston

STATES OF AMERICA

Colorado
Rio Grande
Chihuahua
Torreón
Monterrey
Mazatlán
Guadalajara
México
Acapulco
Veracruz
Tampico
Mérida

M E X I C O

G. de California
Guadalupe (Mex.)
Is. Revilla Gigedo (Mex.)

Tropic of Cancer

PACIFIC OCEAN

Clipperton (Fr.)

THE BAHAMAS
Nassau

CUBA
Habana
Guantánamo
Kingston
JAMAICA

Gulf of Mexico

BELIZE
Belmopan
GUATEMALA
Guatemala
S.Salvador
EL SALVADOR
HONDURAS
Tegucigalpa
NICARAGUA
Managua
COSTA RICA
S.José
Panamá
PANAMA

HAITI
Port-au-Prince
DOMINICAN REP.
Sto Domingo
Pto Rico (U.S.A)
Netherlands Antilles

CARIBBEAN SEA

DOMINICA
ST LUCIA
ST VINCENT
GRENADA
BAR-BADOS
TRINIDAD & TOBAGO

VENEZUELA
Caracas
Maracaibo
Barranquilla
Sta Marta
Medellín
Bogotá
COLOMBIA
Quito
ECUADOR
PERU

BRAZIL
Negro

I. de Coco (C.R)
Malpelo (Col.)
Galápagos Is (Ecu.)

Equator

Mississippi
Ohio

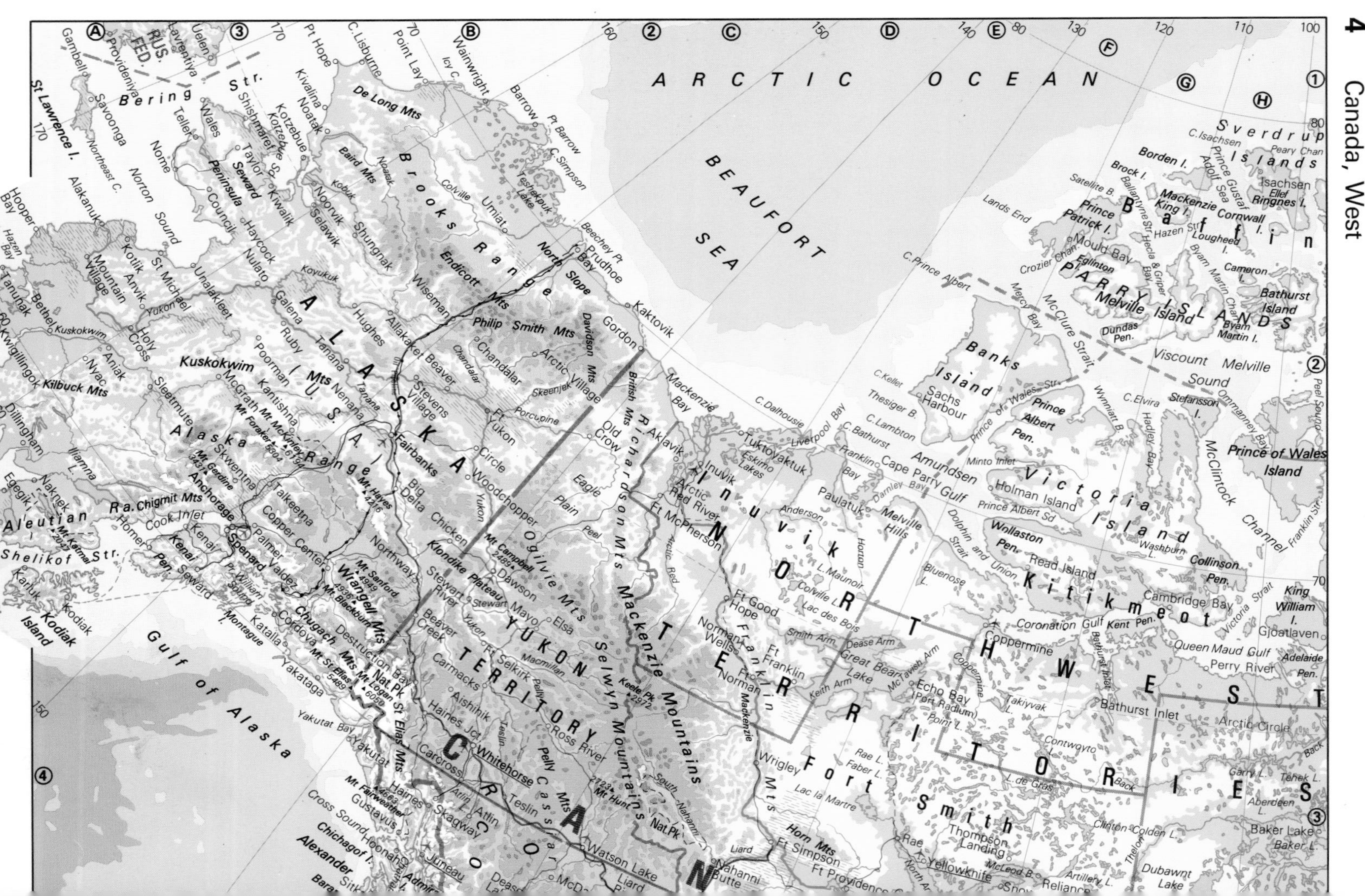
ARCTIC OCEAN
BEAUFORT SEA
Gulf of Alaska
Sverdrup Islands
Isachsen
Ellef Ringnes I.
Prince Gustaf Adolf Sea
Borden I.
Mackenzie King I.
Lougheed
Cameron I.
Bathurst Island
Byam Martin Chan
Byam Martin I.
Brock I.
Ballantyne Str
Hecla & Griper Bay
Prince Patrick I.
Mould Bay
Eglinton
Melville Island
PARRY ISLANDS
Dundas Pen.
Viscount Melville Sound
Peel Sound
Prince of Wales Island
Franklin Str
King William I.
Gjoa Haven
Adelaide Pen.
McClintock Channel
Stefansson I.
Hadley Bay
Wynniatt B.
McClure Strait
Mercy Bay
Banks Island
Sachs Harbour
Prince Albert Pen.
Victoria Island
Holman Island
Prince Albert Sd
Wollaston Pen.
Collinson Pen.
Cambridge Bay
Victoria Strait
Queen Maud Gulf
Perry River
Kent Pen.
Coronation Gulf
Bathurst Inlet
Read Island
Dolphin and Union Strait
Amundsen Gulf
Cape Parry
C. Bathurst
C. Dalhousie
Paulatuk
Horton
Melville Hills
Lands End
C. Prince Albert
Arctic Circle
Baker Lake
Dubawnt Lake
Thelon
Aberdeen L.
Coppermine
Bluenose L.
Great Bear Lake
Echo Bay (Port Radium)
Rae
Yellowknife
Fort Smith
Thompson Landing
Ft Providence
Ft Simpson
Horn Mts
Wrigley
Ft Franklin
Ft Good Hope
Norman Wells
Ft Norman
Franklin Mts
Mackenzie
Tuktoyaktuk
Eskimo Lakes
Inuvik
Aklavik
Arctic Red River
Ft McPherson
Mackenzie Bay
Nahanni Butte
Mackenzie Mountains
Selwyn Mountains
Keele Pk 2972
Mt Hunt 2723
Nat. Pk
Watson Lake
Richardson Mts
British Mts
Old Crow
Eagle Plain
Ogilvie Mts
Mt Campbell 2495
Dawson
Mayo
Elsa
YUKON TERRITORY
Ross River
Pelly Mts
Cassiar
Whitehorse
Teslin
Atlin
Carcross
Skagway
Juneau
Haines
Haines Jct
Carmacks
Ft Selkirk
Stewart River
Beaver Creek
Klondike Plateau
St Elias Mts
Mt Logan 6050
Mt St Elias 5489
Mt Fairweather 4663
Yakutat Bay
Yakutat
Gustavus
Hoonah
Cross Sound
Chichagof I.
Alexander
Kaktovik
Prudhoe Bay
Beechey Pt
Pt Barrow
C. Simpson
Barrow
Teshekpuk Lake
Wainwright
Icy C.
Point Lay
C. Lisburne
Pt Hope
North Slope
Brooks Range
Davidson Mts
Philip Smith Mts
Endicott Mts
De Long Mts
Baird Mts
Umiat
Colville
Arctic Village
Chandalar
Ft Yukon
Circle
Woodchopper
Yukon
Wiseman
Allakaket
Beaver
Stevens Village
Fairbanks
Big Delta
Northway
Mt Hayes 4216
Mt Sanford 4949
Wrangell Mts
Mt Blackburn 4936
Chugach Mts
Destruction Bay
ALASKA
U.S.A.
Alaska Range
Mt McKinley 6194
Mt Foraker 5304
Kantishna
Nenana
Tanana
Hughes
Shungnak
Noatak
Kivalina
Kotzebue
Kotzebue Sd
Noorvik
Selawik
Kiwalik
Shishmaref
Seward Peninsula
Council
Teller
Wales
Nome
Norton Sound
Unalakleet
St Michael
Galena
Ruby
Poorman
McGrath
Kuskokwim Mts
Talkeetna
Copper Center
Palmer
Valdez
Cordova
Katalla
Yakataga
Anchorage
Spenard
Skwentna
Mt Gerdine 3431
Kenai
Kenai Pen.
Seward
Prince William Sound
Montague I.
Cook Inlet
Homer
Chigmit Mts
Iliamna L.
Mt Katmai 2047
Shelikof Str.
Kodiak
Kodiak Island
Karluk
Naknek
Egegik
Dillingham
Kwigillingok
Kilbuck Mts
Bethel
Tanunak
Nyac
Aniak
Holy Cross
Anvik
Sleetmute
Mountain Village
Kotlik
Alakanuk
Hooper Bay
Hazen Bay
Northeast C.
St Lawrence I.
Gambell
Savoonga
Provideniya
Bering Str.
Uelen
Lavrentiya
RUS. FED.
Aleutian Ra.
Inuvik
Kitikmeot
Fort Smith
NORTHWEST TERRITORIES
CANADA

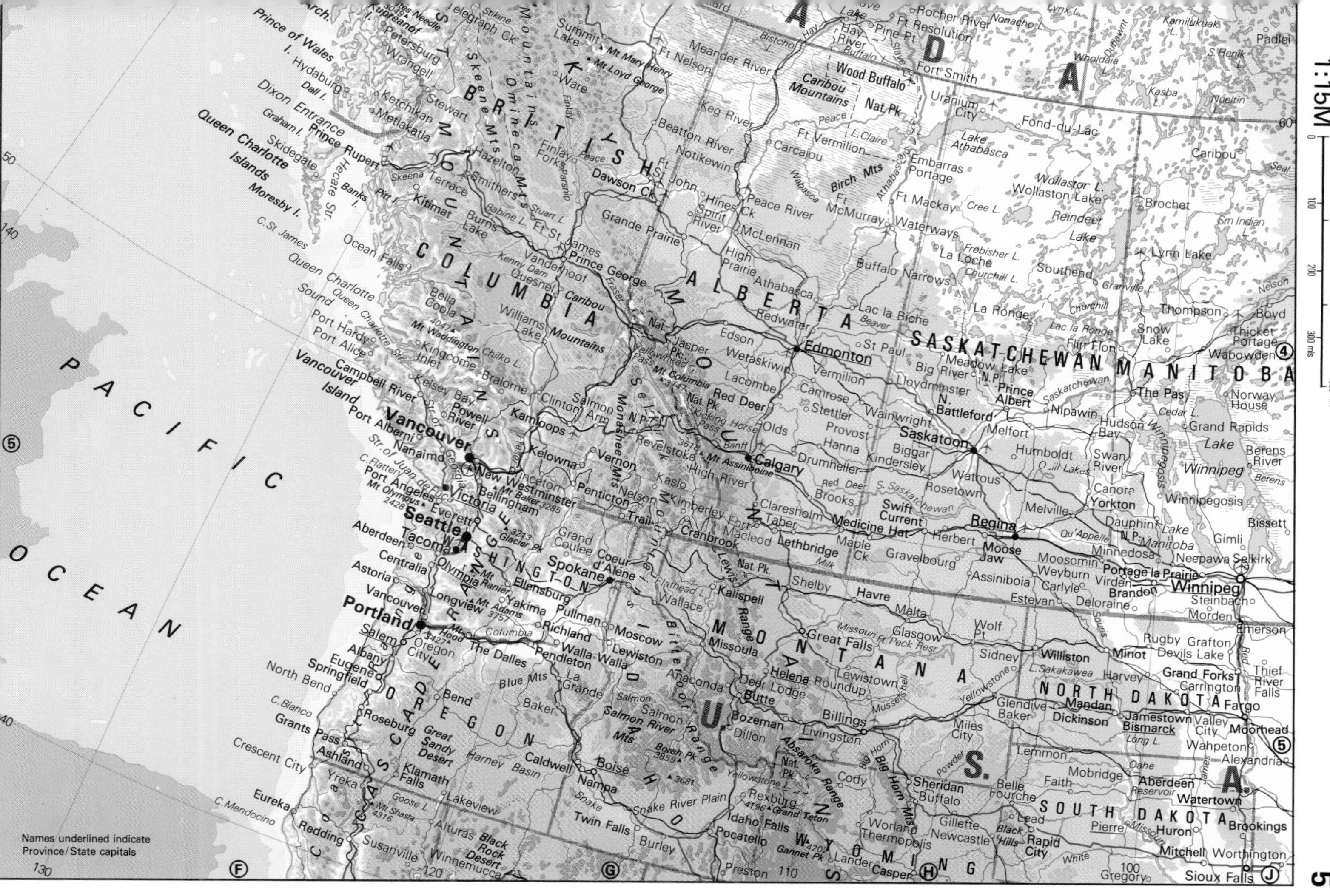
PACIFIC OCEAN
BRITISH COLUMBIA
ALBERTA
SASKATCHEWAN
MANITOBA
WASHINGTON
OREGON
IDAHO
MONTANA
WYOMING
NORTH DAKOTA
SOUTH DAKOTA
Vancouver
Victoria
Seattle
Tacoma
Olympia
Portland
Salem
Spokane
Edmonton
Calgary
Regina
Saskatoon
Winnipeg
Helena
Boise
Bismarck
Pierre
Prince George
Prince Rupert
Kamloops
Kelowna
Lethbridge
Medicine Hat
Billings
Great Falls
Missoula
Butte
Fargo
Sioux Falls
Eureka
Redding
Vancouver Island
Queen Charlotte Islands
Big Horn Mts
Absaroka Range
Lake Athabasca
Lake Winnipeg
Names underlined indicate Province/State capitals

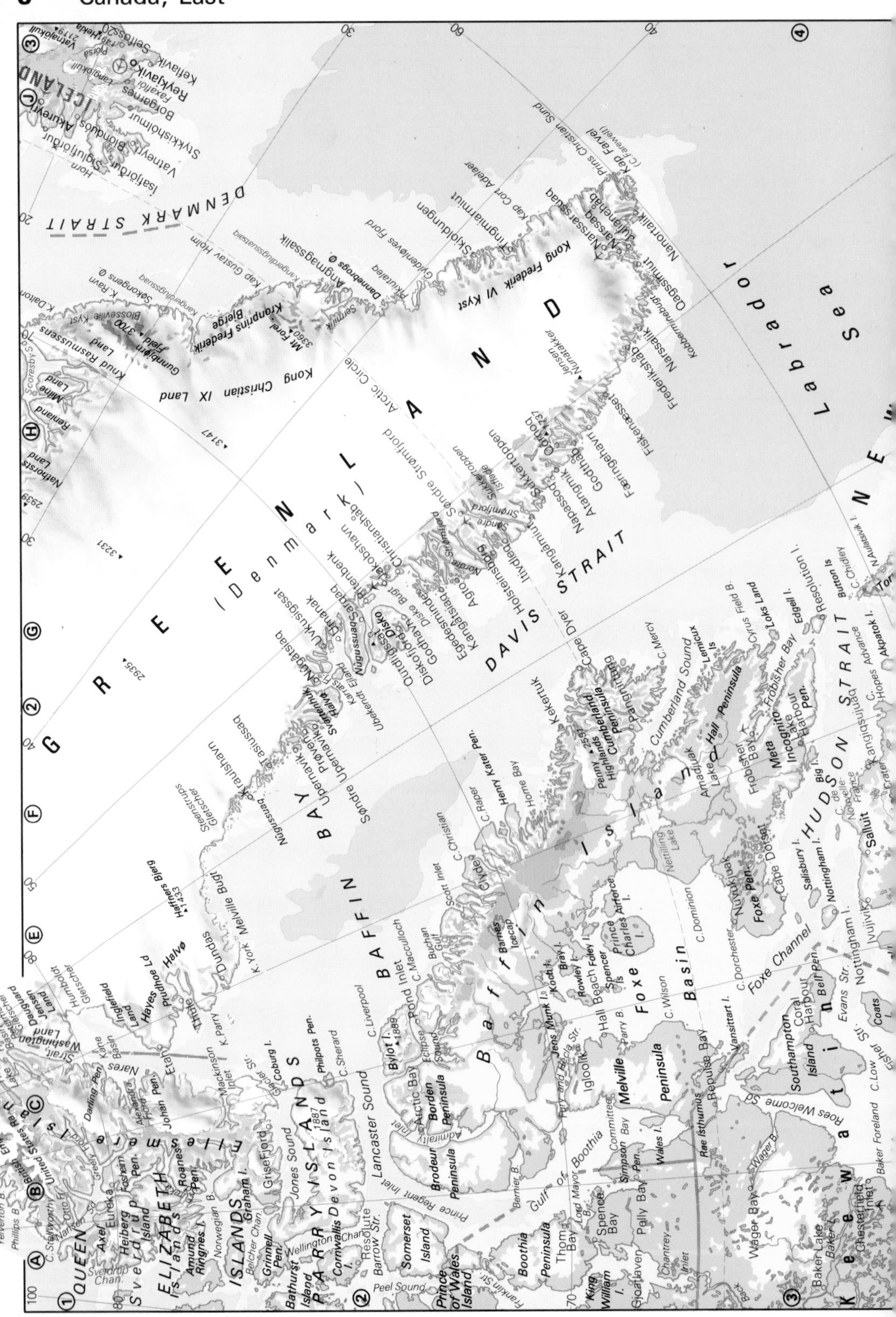
GREENLAND
(Denmark)
BAFFIN BAY
DAVIS STRAIT
DENMARK STRAIT
Labrador Sea
HUDSON STRAIT
Baffin Island
Foxe Basin
Foxe Channel
Lancaster Sound
Jones Sound
Melville Bugt
ICELAND
Reykjavik
Akureyri
Keflavik
Borgarnes
Stykkishólmur
Blönduós
Siglufjördur
Isafjördur
Vatneyri
Kap Farvel
Prins Christian Sund
Nanortalik
Julianehåb
Narssaq
Narssarssuaq
Ivigtut
Frederikshåb
Fiskenæsset
Færingehavn
Godthåb
Sukkertoppen
Holsteinsborg
Egedesminde
Christianshåb
Jakobshavn
Godhavn
Disko
Umanak
Upernavik
Prøven
Thule
Dundas
Angmagssalik
Kong Christian IX Land
Kong Frederik VI Kyst
Gunnbjørn Fjeld
Scoresby Sund
Arctic Circle
Cumberland Sound
Cumberland Peninsula
Frobisher Bay
Hall Peninsula
Meta Incognita Peninsula
Resolution I.
Pangnirtung
Pond Inlet
Bylot I.
Devon Island
Ellesmere Island
Axel Heiberg Island
Sverdrup Islands
QUEEN ELIZABETH ISLANDS
PARRY ISLANDS
Cornwallis I.
Resolute
Bathurst Island
Somerset Island
Prince of Wales Island
Boothia Peninsula
Gulf of Boothia
Melville Peninsula
Igloolik
Repulse Bay
Southampton Island
Coral Harbour
Nottingham I.
Salisbury I.
Salluit
Ivujivik
Kangiqsujuaq
Akpatok I.
Baker Lake
Chesterfield Inlet
Wager Bay
Roes Welcome Sd.
Spence Bay
Pelly Bay
Gjoa Haven
King William I.
Keewatin
Nares Str.
Kane Basin
Hall Basin
Washington Land
Inglefield Land
Prince Charles I.
Air Force I.
Nettilling Lake
Amadjuak Lake
Cape Dorset
Lake Harbour
Clyde
Eureka
Grise Fiord
Arctic Bay
Borden Peninsula
Brodeur Peninsula
Admiralty Inlet
Prince Regent Inlet
Peel Sound
Barrow Str.
Labrador
NEW

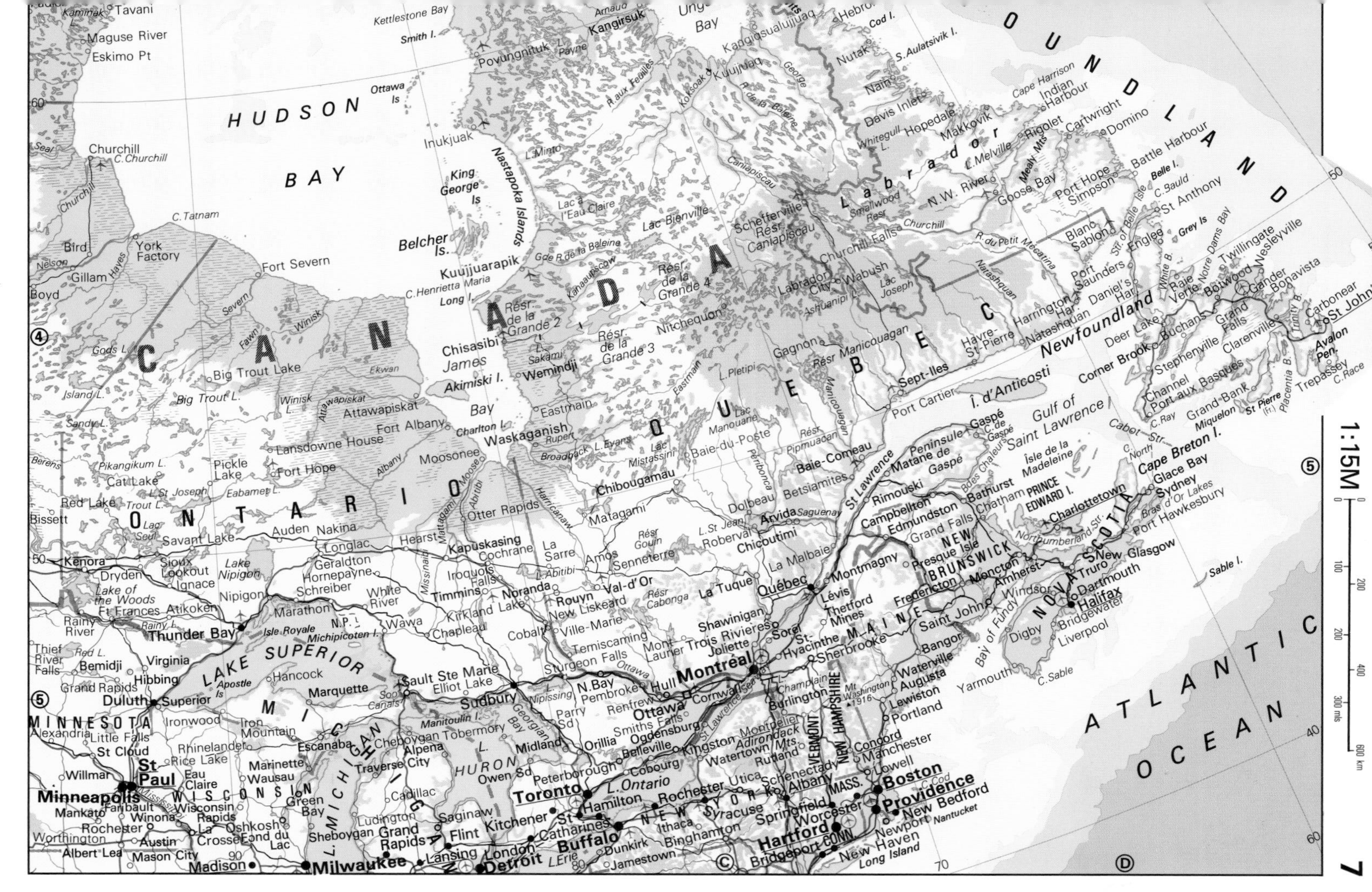

1:15M
0 200 400 600 km
0 100 200 300 mls
HUDSON BAY
C A N A D A
O N T A R I O
Q U E B E C
Labrador
NEWFOUNDLAND
Newfoundland
ATLANTIC OCEAN
LAKE SUPERIOR
L. Ontario
HURON
L. MICHIGAN
Gulf of Saint Lawrence
James Bay
Nastapoka Islands
Belcher Is.
Akimiski I.
Î. d'Anticosti
Cape Breton I.
PRINCE EDWARD I.
NOVA SCOTIA
NEW BRUNSWICK
MAINE
NEW HAMPSHIRE
VERMONT
MASS.
CONN.
NEW YORK
MINNESOTA
WISCONSIN
MICHIGAN
Montréal
Québec
Ottawa
Toronto
Halifax
St John's
Boston
Providence
Hartford
Buffalo
Detroit
Milwaukee
Minneapolis
St Paul
Duluth
Thunder Bay
Sault Ste Marie
Sudbury
Churchill
Kenora
Timmins
Sept-Iles
Chicoutimi
Fredericton
Saint John
Charlottetown
Sydney
Gander

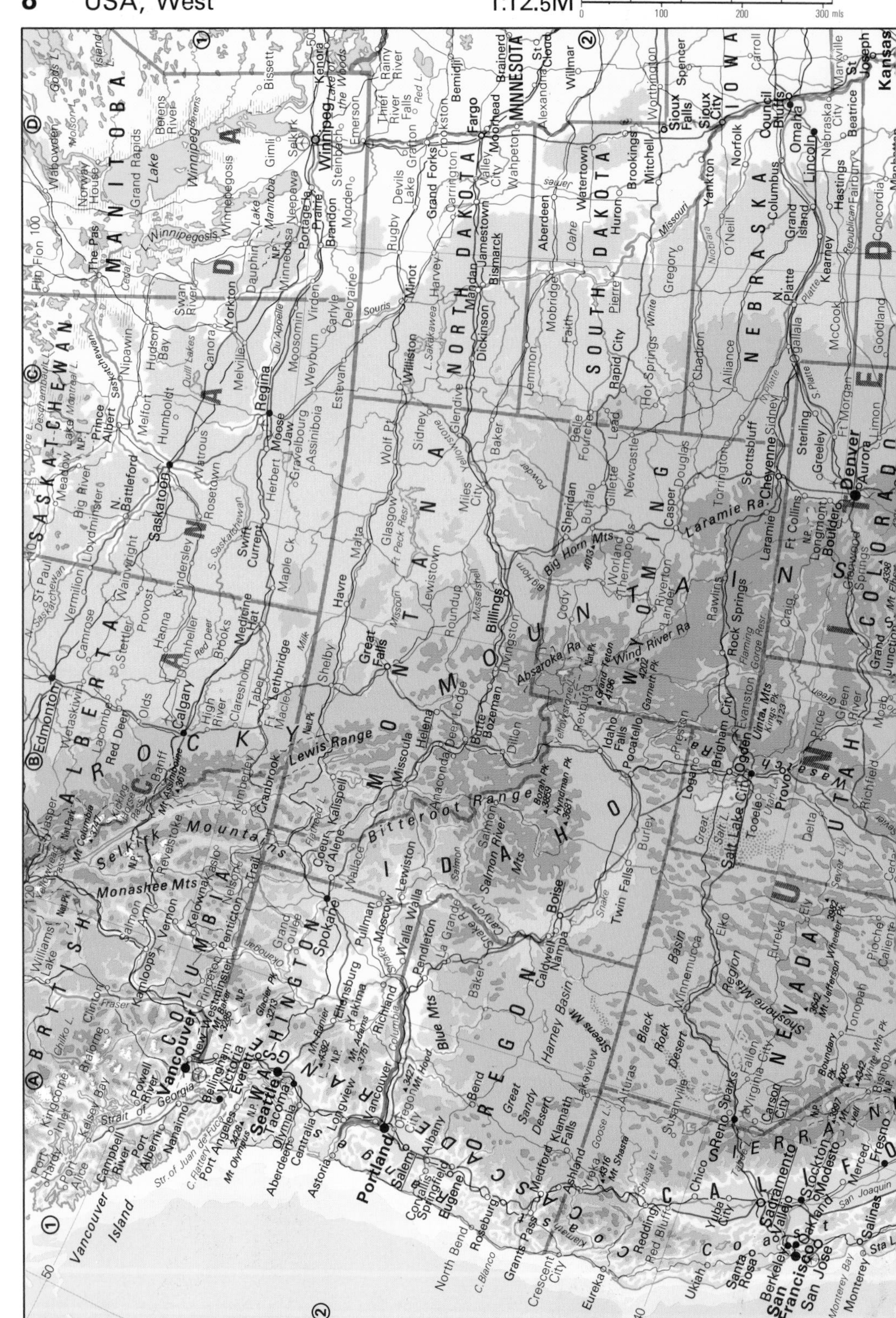

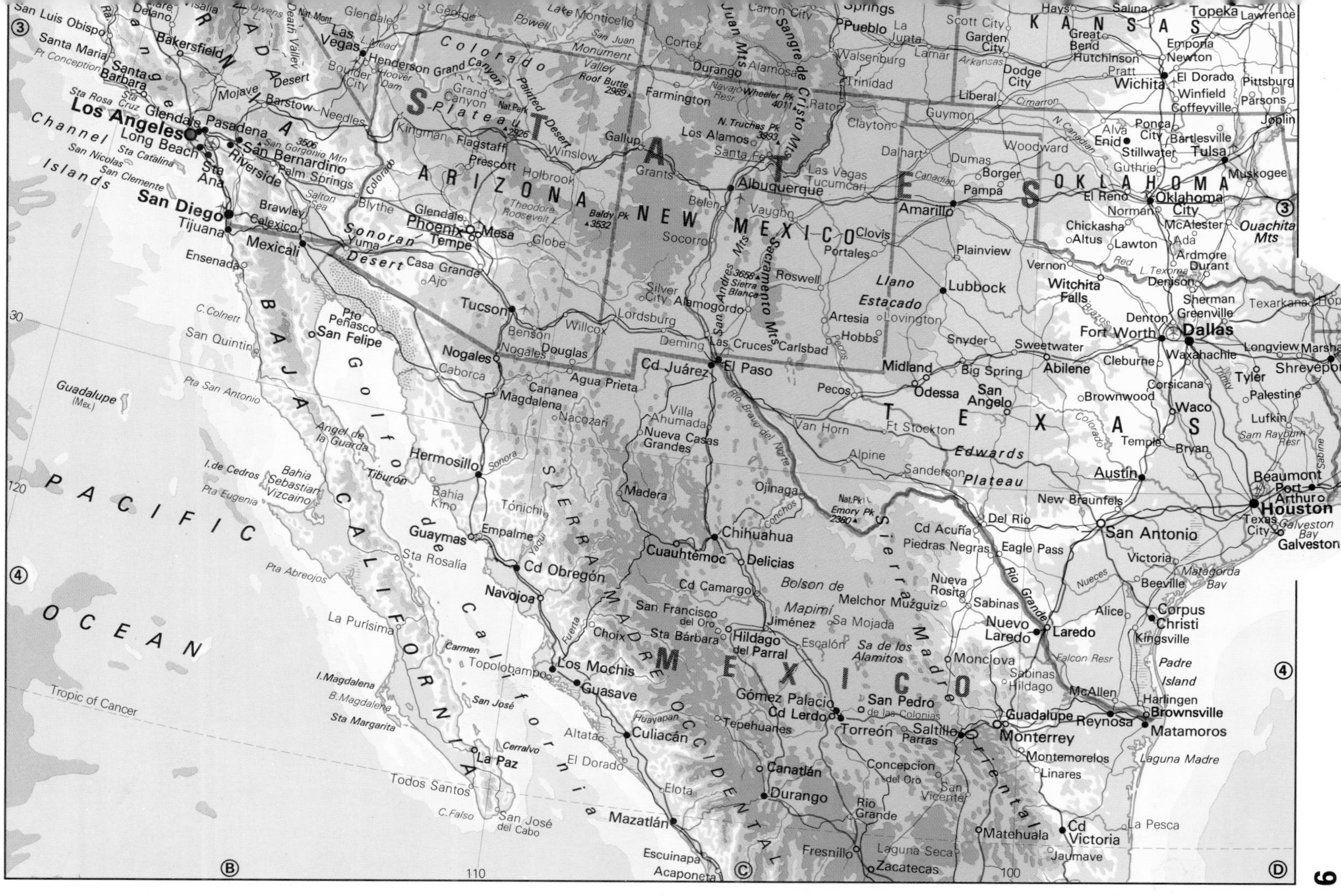
KANSAS
OKLAHOMA
TEXAS
NEW MEXICO
ARIZONA
STATES
MEXICO
BAJA CALIFORNIA
PACIFIC OCEAN
Golfo de California
SIERRA MADRE OCCIDENTAL
Sierra Madre Oriental
Llano Estacado
Edwards Plateau
Colorado Plateau
Sonoran Desert
Painted Desert
Sangre de Cristo Mts
Sacramento Mts
Bolson de Mapimí
Channel Islands
Tropic of Cancer
Los Angeles
San Diego
Tijuana
Mexicali
Phoenix
Tucson
El Paso
Cd Juárez
Albuquerque
Santa Fe
Amarillo
Lubbock
Dallas
Fort Worth
Houston
Austin
San Antonio
Oklahoma City
Tulsa
Wichita
Chihuahua
Hermosillo
Monterrey
Saltillo
Torreón
Durango
Culiacán
Mazatlán
La Paz
Laredo
Nuevo Laredo
Brownsville
Matamoros
Corpus Christi
Galveston
Shreveport
Las Vegas
Bakersfield
San Bernardino
Riverside
Ensenada
Guaymas
Cd Obregón
Los Mochis
Zacatecas
Cd Victoria
Rio Grande
Falcon Resr
Padre Island
Emory Pk 2380
Guadalupe (Mex.)
I. de Cedros
Sta Margarita

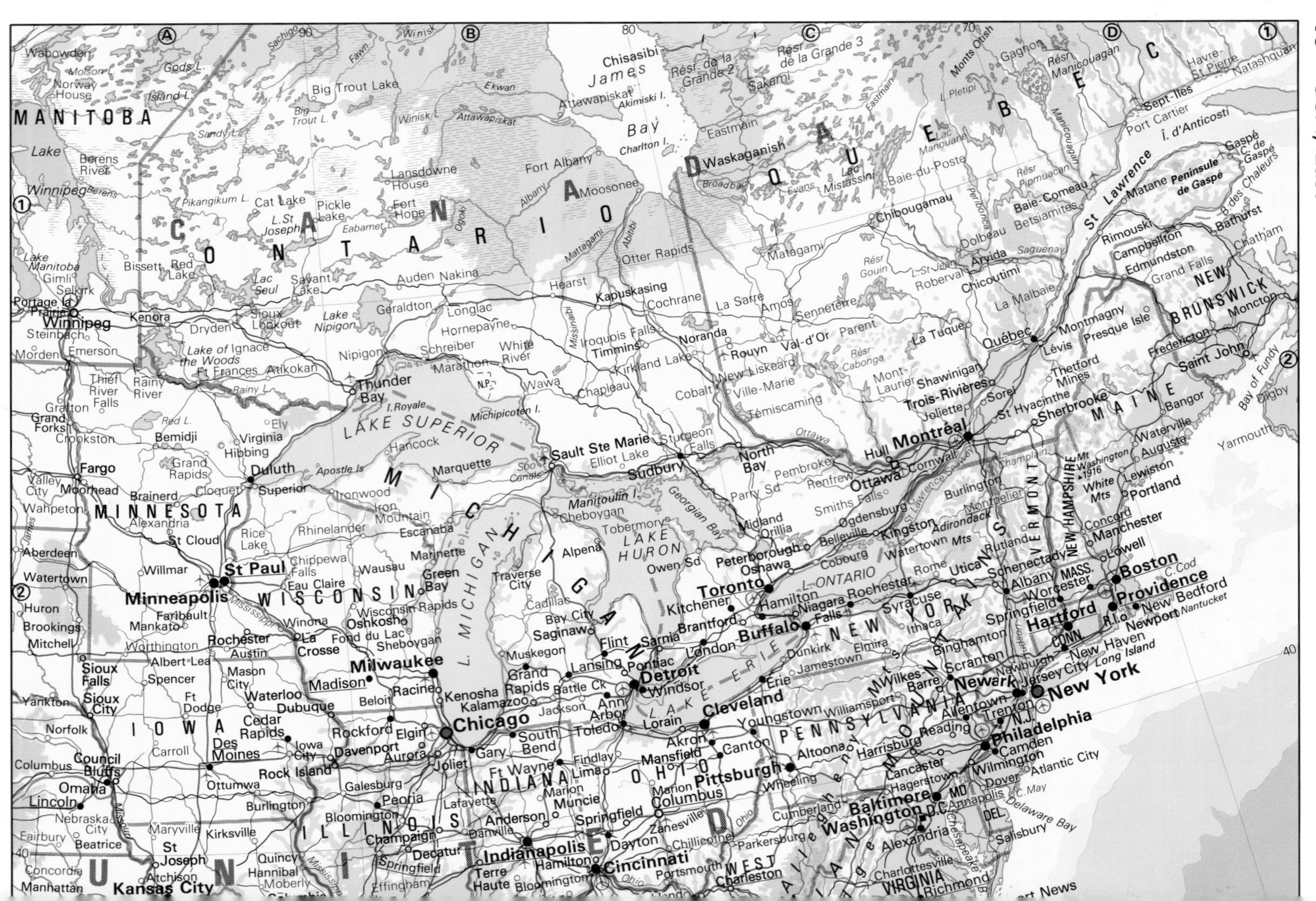
MANITOBA
ONTARIO
QUEBEC
NEW BRUNSWICK
MAINE
VERMONT
NEW HAMPSHIRE
NEW YORK
PENNSYLVANIA
OHIO
INDIANA
ILLINOIS
IOWA
MINNESOTA
WISCONSIN
MICHIGAN
WEST VIRGINIA
VIRGINIA
James Bay
LAKE SUPERIOR
L. MICHIGAN
LAKE HURON
L. ONTARIO
LAKE ERIE
Georgian Bay
Bay of Fundy
Peninsule de Gaspé
Î. d'Anticosti
St Lawrence
Winnipeg
Thunder Bay
Sault Ste Marie
Sudbury
Ottawa
Montréal
Québec
Toronto
Buffalo
Detroit
Cleveland
Pittsburgh
Chicago
Milwaukee
Minneapolis
St Paul
Indianapolis
Cincinnati
Columbus
Philadelphia
Baltimore
Washington
New York
Boston
Providence
Hartford
Newark
Kansas City
Omaha
Des Moines
Duluth
Fargo

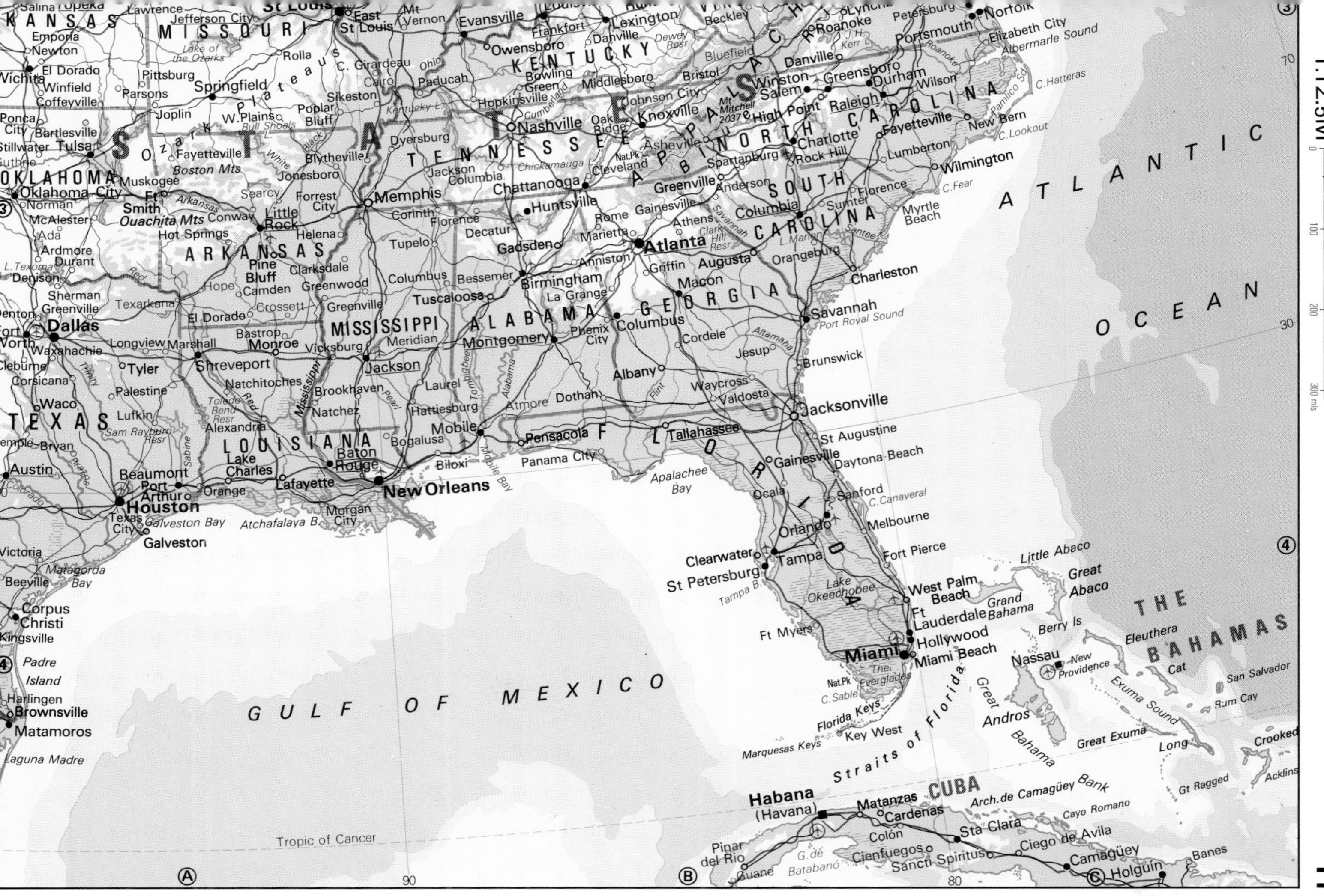

1:12.5M

100 200 300 400 500 km
100   200   300 mls

1:10M

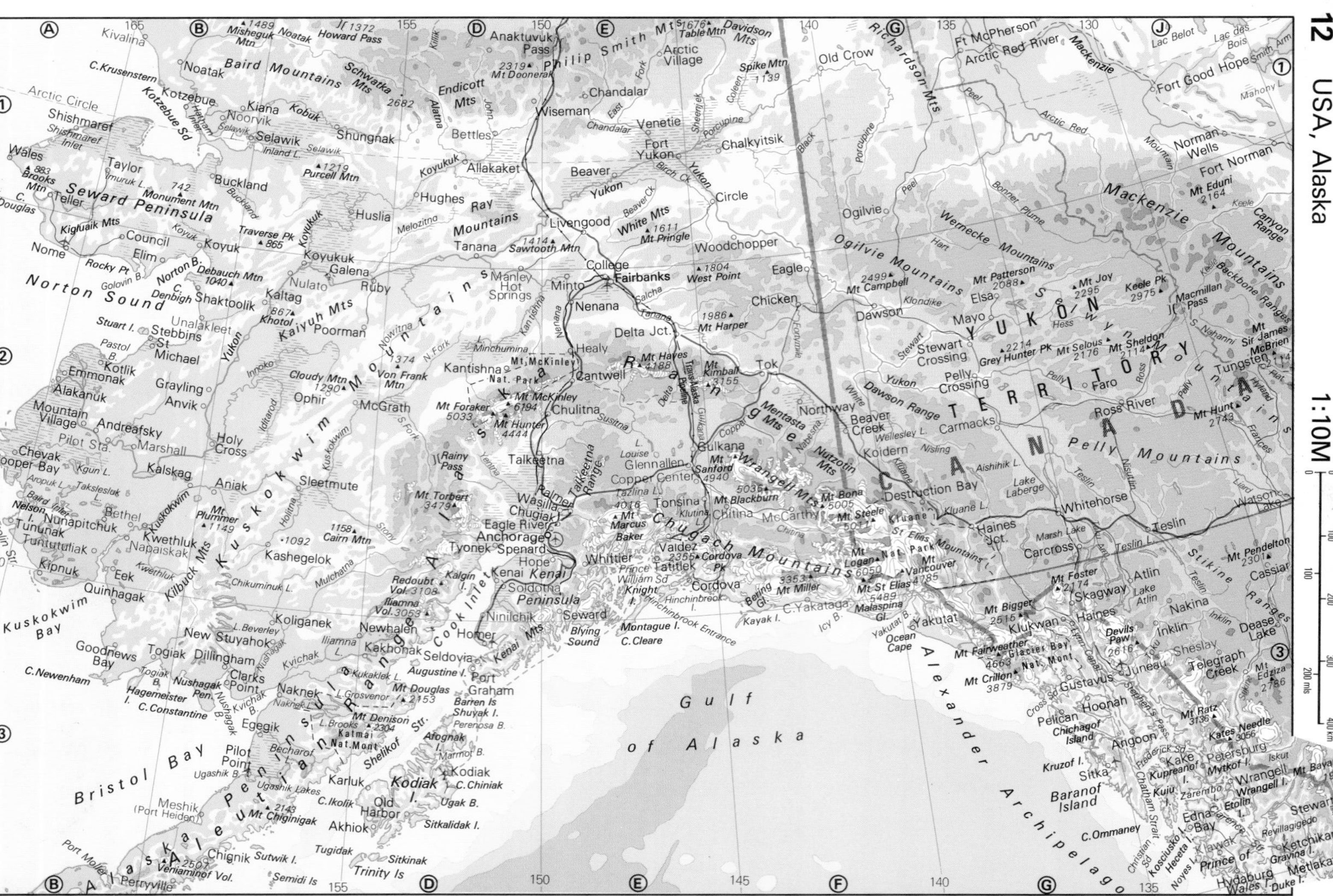
0 100 200 300 400 km
0 100 200 mls
Alexander Archipelago
Gulf of Alaska
Bristol Bay
Norton Sound
Kotzebue Sd
Seward Peninsula
Kenai Peninsula
Alaska Peninsula
Aleutian Range
Kuskokwim Bay
Cook Inlet
Mackenzie Mountains
Ogilvie Mountains
Wernecke Mountains
Richardson Mts
Selwyn Mountains
Pelly Mountains
Cassiar
Stikine Ranges
St Elias Mountains
Chugach Mountains
Wrangell Mts
Kenai Mts
Alaska Range
Kuskokwim Mountains
Kaiyuh Mts
Kilbuck Mts
Baird Mountains
Schwatka Mts
Endicott Mts
Philip Smith Mts
Davidson Mts
White Mts
Ray Mountains
Talkeetna Range
Mentasta Mts
Nutzotin Mts
Dawson Range
Backbone Ranges
Canyon Range
YUKON TERRITORY
CANADA
Mt McKinley 6194
Mt Hunter 4444
Mt Foraker 5033
Mt Hayes 4188
Mt Kimball 3155
Mt Logan 6050
Mt St Elias 5489
Mt Vancouver 4785
Mt Fairweather 4663
Mt Crillon 3879
Mt Sanford 4940
Mt Blackburn 5035
Mt Bona 5005
Mt Steele 5073
Mt Marcus Baker 4016
Mt Torbert 3479
Arctic Circle
Yukon
Kuskokwim
Tanana
Porcupine
Peel
Mackenzie
Koyukuk
Trans-Alaska Pipeline
Anchorage
Fairbanks
Juneau
Whitehorse
Dawson
Nome
Kotzebue
Bethel
Valdez
Cordova
Seward
Homer
Kodiak
Sitka
Skagway
Haines
Yakutat
Wrangell
Petersburg
Dillingham
Tok
Delta Jct.
Glennallen
Talkeetna
Wasilla
Palmer
Kenai
Soldotna
Circle
Fort Yukon
Old Crow
Fort McPherson
Arctic Red River
Fort Good Hope
Norman Wells
Fort Norman
Mayo
Carmacks
Teslin
Atlin
Ross River
Faro
Galena
McGrath
Unalakleet
Nenana
College
Healy
Cantwell
Chitina
Copper Center
Whittier
Gulkana
Tonsina
Chicken
Eagle
Beaver Creek
Destruction Bay
Haines Jct.
Carcross
Dease Lake
Telegraph Creek
Hoonah
Gustavus
Pelican
Angoon
Kake
Metlakatla
Hydaburg
Prince of Wales I.
Baranof Island
Chichagof Island
Kodiak I.
Afognak I.
Montague I.
Kayak I.
Stuart I.
Trinity Is

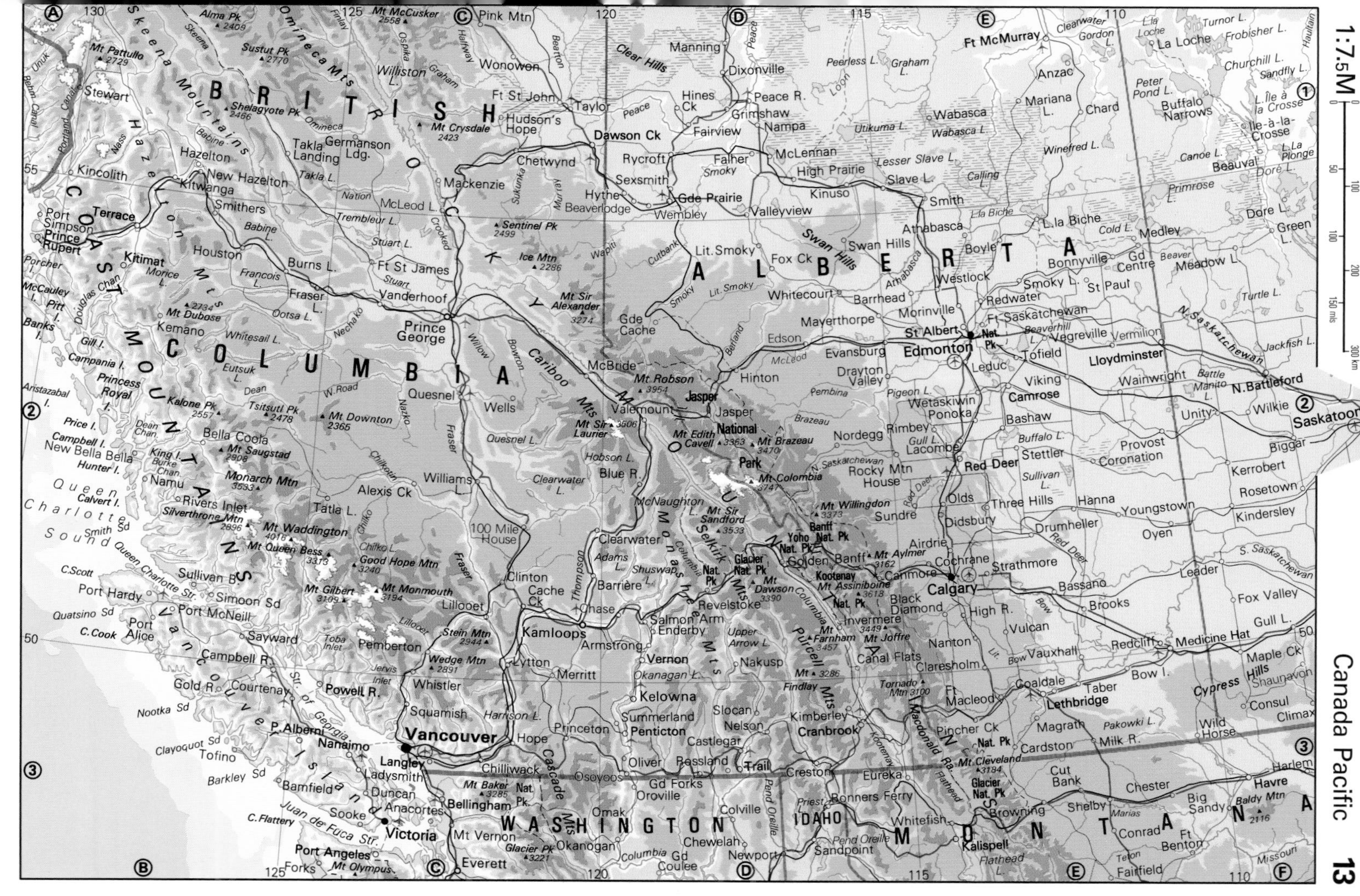
BRITISH COLUMBIA
ALBERTA
WASHINGTON
IDAHO
MONTANA
COAST MOUNTAINS
ROCKY MOUNTAINS
Skeena Mountains
Omineca Mts
Hazelton Mts
Cariboo Mts
Monashee Mts
Selkirk Mts
Purcell Mts
Cascade Mts
Swan Hills
Clear Hills
Cypress Hills
Jasper National Park
Vancouver
Victoria
Edmonton
Calgary
Kamloops
Prince George
Prince Rupert
Kelowna
Vernon
Penticton
Nanaimo
Lethbridge
Medicine Hat
Red Deer
Lloydminster
Saskatoon
N.Battleford
Ft McMurray
Dawson Ck
Ft St John
Gde Prairie
Kitimat
Terrace
Quesnel
Revelstoke
Cranbrook
Trail
Nelson
Banff
Jasper
Golden
Kalispell
Havre
Port Angeles
Everett
Bellingham
Vancouver I.
Queen Charlotte Sound
Str. of Georgia
Juan de Fuca Str.
Mt Robson 3954
Mt Waddington 4016
Mt Columbia 3747
Mt Assiniboine 3618
Mt Baker 3285
Fraser
Columbia
Peace
Athabasca
N. Saskatchewan
S. Saskatchewan
Kootenay
Thompson
Okanagan L.
Williston L.
Lesser Slave L.

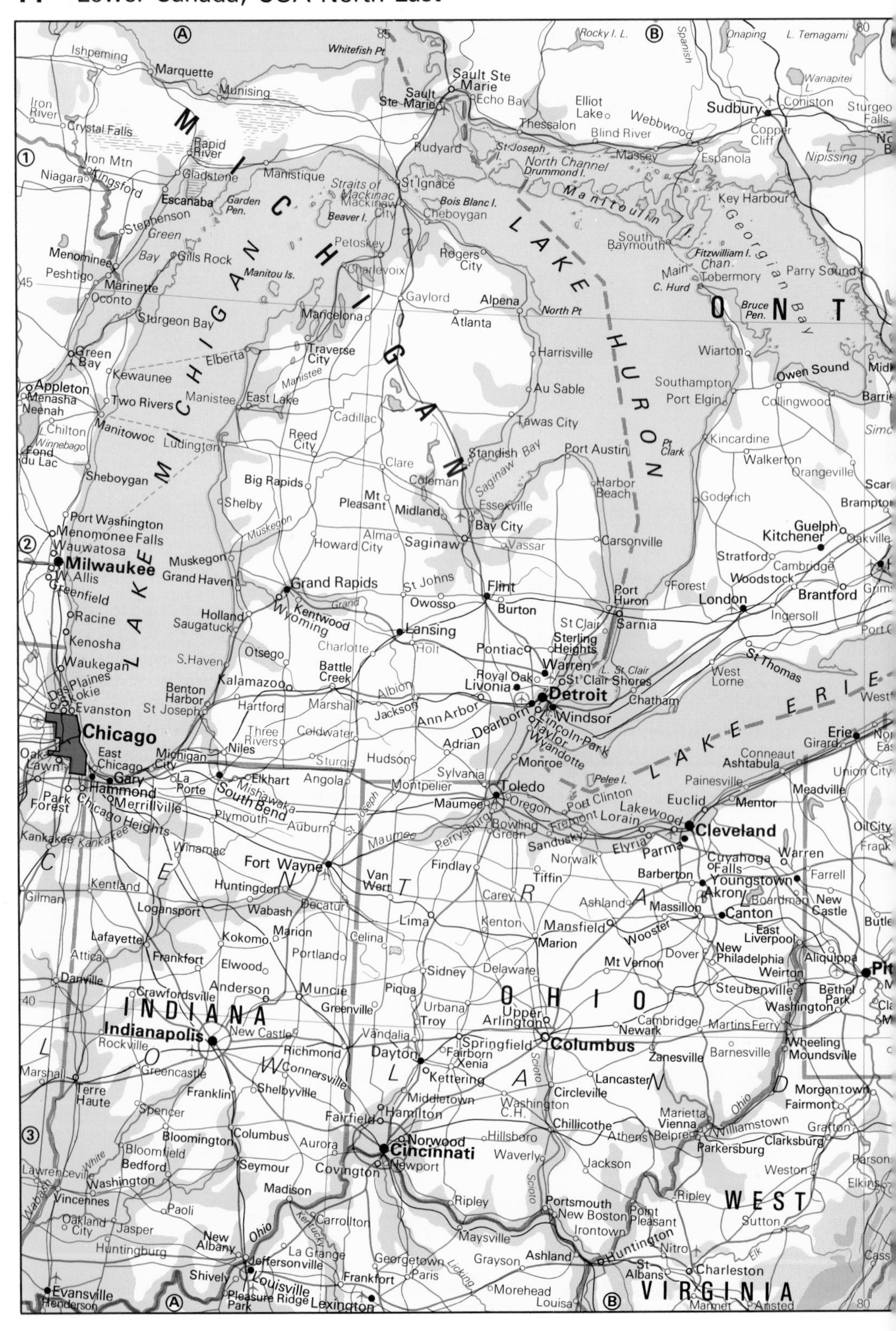
A
B
1
2
3
85
80
45
40
Ishpeming
Marquette
Whitefish Pt
Rocky I. L.
Spanish
Onaping L.
L. Temagami
Wanapitei L.
Sault Ste Marie
Sault Ste Marie
Echo Bay
Elliot Lake
Webbwood
Sudbury
Coniston
Sturgeon Falls
Munising
Iron River
Crystal Falls
Thessalon
Blind River
Copper Cliff
Rapid River
Rudyard
St Joseph I.
North Channel
Drummond I.
Massey
Espanola
L. Nipissing
Iron Mtn
Kingsford
Niagara
Gladstone
Manistique
Straits of Mackinac
St Ignace
Mackinaw City
Manitoulin
Key Harbour
Escanaba
Garden Pen.
Beaver I.
Bois Blanc I.
Cheboygan
Georgian Bay
Stephenson
Green Bay
Menominee
Peshtigo
Marinette
Oconto
Gills Rock
Manitou Is.
Petoskey
Charlevoix
Rogers City
South Baymouth
Fitzwilliam I.
Main Chan.
C. Hurd
Tobermory
Parry Sound
Gaylord
Alpena
North Pt
Bruce Pen.
ONT
Sturgeon Bay
Mancelona
Atlanta
Green Bay
Elberta
Traverse City
Harrisville
Wiarton
Owen Sound
Kewaunee
Appleton
Menasha
Neenah
Two Rivers
Manistee
Manistee
East Lake
Au Sable
Southampton
Port Elgin
Collingwood
Barrie
L. Winnebago
Chilton
Manitowoc
Cadillac
Tawas City
Reed City
Ludington
Kincardine
Fond du Lac
Port Austin
Pt Clark
Clare
Standish
Saginaw Bay
Walkerton
Orangeville
Sheboygan
Big Rapids
Coleman
Harbor Beach
Shelby
Mt Pleasant
Midland
Essexville
Goderich
Brampton
Port Washington
Menomonee Falls
Wauwatosa
Milwaukee
W. Allis
Greenfield
Muskegon
Muskegon
Alma
Howard City
Saginaw
Bay City
Vassar
Carsonville
Guelph
Kitchener
Oakville
Stratford
Cambridge
Grand Haven
Grand Rapids
St Johns
Flint
Forest
Woodstock
Brantford
Grand
Owosso
Port Huron
London
Racine
Holland
Saugatuck
Kentwood
Wyoming
Burton
Ingersoll
Lansing
St Clair
Sarnia
Kenosha
Charlotte
Holt
Sterling Heights
Waukegan
S.Haven
Otsego
Pontiac
Warren
St Thomas
West Lorne
Battle Creek
Royal Oak
L. St Clair
St Clair Shores
Des Plaines
Skokie
Evanston
Benton Harbor
Kalamazoo
Albion
Livonia
Detroit
Chatham
St Joseph
Hartford
Marshall
Jackson
Ann Arbor
Dearborn
Windsor
Lincoln Park
Taylor
Wyandotte
Chicago
Three Rivers
Coldwater
Adrian
Oak Lawn
East Chicago
Michigan City
Niles
Sturgis
Hudson
Monroe
Conneaut
Ashtabula
Erie
Girard
Gary
Hammond
La Porte
Elkhart
Mishawaka
South Bend
Angola
Sylvania
Montpelier
Toledo
Pelee I.
Painesville
Union City
Park Forest
Merrillville
Chicago Heights
Plymouth
Maumee
Oregon
Port Clinton
Euclid
Mentor
Meadville
Auburn
St Joseph
Maumee
Perrysburg
Bowling Green
Fremont
Lorain
Lakewood
Cleveland
Oil City
Kankakee
Kankakee
Winamac
Sandusky
Elyria
Parma
Franklin
Fort Wayne
Findlay
Norwalk
Cuyahoga Falls
Warren
Van Wert
Tiffin
Barberton
Youngstown
Farrell
Kentland
Huntingdon
Akron
Boardman
Gilman
Carey
Ashland
Massillon
Canton
New Castle
Logansport
Wabash
Decatur
Lima
Kenton
Mansfield
Wooster
East Liverpool
Butler
Lafayette
Kokomo
Marion
Celina
Marion
New Philadelphia
Aliquippa
Attica
Frankfort
Portland
Dover
Elwood
Mt Vernon
Weirton
Pittsburgh
Danville
Sidney
Delaware
Steubenville
Bethel Park
Crawfordsville
Anderson
Muncie
Piqua
OHIO
Washington
INDIANA
Greenville
Urbana
Upper Arlington
Cambridge
Newark
Martins Ferry
Troy
Indianapolis
New Castle
Vandalia
Columbus
Rockville
Richmond
Springfield
Scioto
Wheeling
Moundsville
Dayton
Fairborn
Xenia
Zanesville
Barnesville
Marshall
Greencastle
Connersville
Kettering
Lancaster
Terre Haute
Franklin
Shelbyville
Middletown
Circleville
Morgantown
Fairmont
Spencer
Hamilton
Washington C.H.
Marietta
Vienna
Ohio
Williamstown
Fairfield
Chillicothe
Grafton
Bloomington
Columbus
Aurora
Norwood
Cincinnati
Hillsboro
Athens
Belpre
Parkersburg
Clarksburg
Bloomfield
Bedford
White
Waverly
Parsons
Lawrenceville
Washington
Seymour
Covington
Newport
Jackson
Weston
Vincennes
Madison
Elkins
Wabash
Paoli
Ripley
Portsmouth
New Boston
Ripley
WEST
Oakland City
Jasper
Carrollton
Point Pleasant
Sutton
Kentucky
New Albany
Ohio
Irontown
Huntingburg
Maysville
Huntington
Nitro
La Grange
Jeffersonville
Georgetown
Grayson
Ashland
Elk
Cass
Shively
Louisville
Paris
Licking
St Albans
Charleston
Frankfort
Morehead
Evansville
Henderson
Pleasure Ridge Park
Lexington
Louisa
VIRGINIA
Marmet
Amsted
LAKE MICHIGAN
LAKE HURON
LAKE ERIE
MICHIGAN
CENTRAL LOWLAND

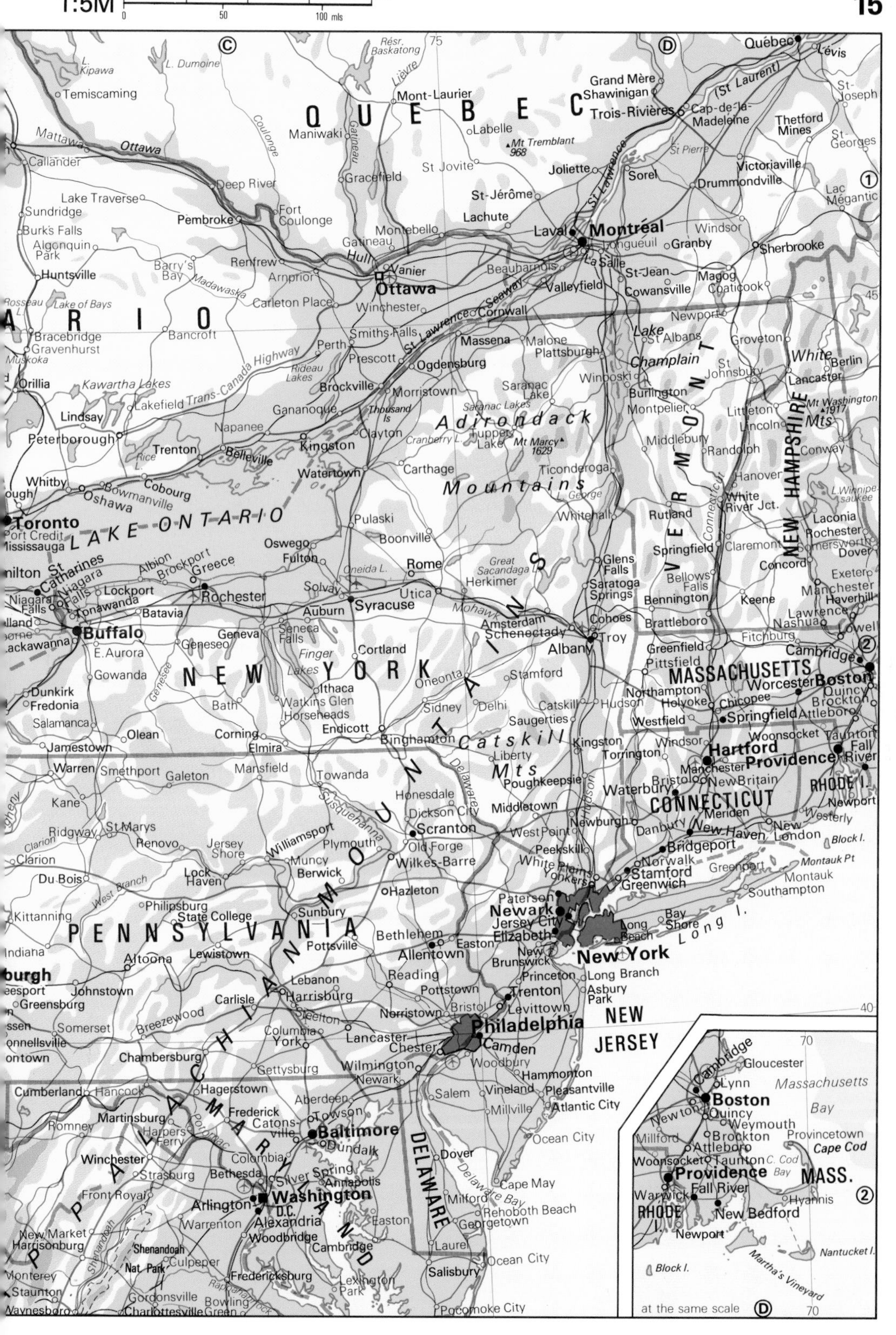

1:5M

0 50 100 150 200 km
0 50 100 mls

© Q U E B E C ©

L. Kipawa
L. Dumoine
Résr. Baskatong
75
Québec
Lévis
St-Joseph
Temiscaming
Maniwaki
Mont-Laurier
Grand Mère
Shawinigan
Trois-Rivières
Cap-de-la-Madeleine
Thetford Mines
St-Georges

Mattawa
Ottawa
Coulonge
Labelle
Mt Tremblant 968
St Pierre
Victoriaville
Lac Mégantic

Callander
Deep River
Gracefield
St Jovite
Joliette
Sorel
Drummondville
①

Lake Traverse
Fort Coulonge
Montebello
St-Jérôme
Lachute
Laval
Montréal
Longueuil
Granby
Sherbrooke

Sundridge
Burk's Falls
Algonquin Park
Pembroke
Renfrew
Gatineau
Hull
Beauharnois
La Salle
St-Jean
Cowansville
Magog
Coaticook

Huntsville
Barry's Bay
Madawaska
Arnprior
Vanier
Seaway
Valleyfield
Cowansville
45

R I O
Rosseau L.
Lake of Bays
Carleton Place
Ottawa
Winchester
Cornwall
Newport
St Albans
White

A R I O
Bracebridge
Gravenhurst
Muskoka
Bancroft
Smiths Falls
Perth
St Lawrence
Massena
Malone
Plattsburgh
Champlain
St Johnsbury
Groveton
Berlin
Lancaster

Orillia
Kawartha Lakes
Lakefield
Rideau Lakes
Trans-Canada Highway
Prescott
Ogdensburg
Saranac Lake
Winooski
Burlington
Montpelier
Middlebury
Mt Washington 1917
Mts

Lindsay
Rice L.
Brockville
Morristown
Thousand Is
Adirondack
Cranberry L.
Tupper Lake
Mt Marcy 1629
Randolph
Conway

Peterborough
Cobourg
Gananoque
Clayton
Watertown
Mountains
Lake George
Ticonderoga
Hanover
L. Winnipesaukee
Laconia

Whitby
Bowmanville
Oshawa
Napanee
Belleville
Kingston
Carthage
Whitehall
Rutland
River Jct.
Rochester
Dover

ough
Toronto
Port Credit
Mississauga
L A K E   O N T A R I O
Pulaski
Boonville
Great Sacandaga
Glens Falls
Saratoga Springs
Springfield
Claremont
Concord
Exeter
Manchester
Haverhill

ilton
St Catharines
Albion
Brockport
Greece
Oswego
Fulton
Rome
Oneida L.
Herkimer
Cohoes
Saratoga Springs
Bennington
Brattleboro
Keene
Nashua
Lawrence
Lowell

Niagara Falls
Tonawanda
Lockport
Batavia
Solvay
Utica
Mohawk
Amsterdam
Schenectady
Troy
Albany
Greenfield
Fitchburg
②

olland
lackawanna
Buffalo
E. Aurora
Geneseo
Geneva
Seneca Falls
Auburn
Syracuse
N E W   Y O R K
Cortland
Oneonta
Stamford
Delhi
Hudson
Pittsfield
Northampton
Holyoke
Chicopee
Worcester
MASSACHUSETTS
Boston
Brockton

Dunkirk
Fredonia
Gowanda
Bath
Finger Lakes
Ithaca
Watkins Glen
Horseheads
Sidney
Catskill
Saugerties
Westfield
Windsor
Springfield
Attleboro

Salamanca
Olean
Corning
Elmira
Endicott
Binghamton
Catskill Mts
Kingston
Torrington
Hartford
Manchester
Providence
Fall River

Jamestown
Warren
Smethport
Galeton
Mansfield
Towanda
Liberty
Middletown
Poughkeepsie
Waterbury
New Britain
Bristol
RHODE I.

Kane
Ridgway
St Marys
Jersey Shore
Honesdale
Dickson City
Scranton
Old Forge
West Point
Newburgh
Danbury
New Haven
New London
Westerly
Newport
Block I.

Du Bois
Renovo
Williamsport
Muncy
Berwick
Wilkes-Barre
White Plains
Peekskill
Bridgeport
Norwalk
Greenport
Montauk Pt
Montauk

Clarion
Lock Haven
Plymouth
Hazleton
Yonkers
Stamford
Greenwich
Southampton

Kittanning
Philipsburg
State College
Sunbury
Paterson
Jersey City
Long Bay
Long I.

urgh
Indiana
Altoona
Lewistown
Bethlehem
Easton
Newark
Elizabeth
New Brunswick
New York
Long Branch
Asbury Park

eesport
Greensburg
Johnstown
P E N N S Y L V A N I A
Lebanon
Harrisburg
Allentown
Pottstown
Princeton
Trenton
Levittown
40

onnellsville
ontown
Somerset
Breezewood
Carlisle
Columbia
York
Reading
Norristown
Bristol
Philadelphia
Camden
N E W   J E R S E Y

Chambersburg
Gettysburg
Lancaster
Chester
Wilmington
Woodbury
Hammonton
Pleasantville

Cumberland
Hancock
Hagerstown
Aberdeen
Salem
Vineland
Atlantic City

Martinsburg
Romney
Frederick
Catonsville
Towson
Baltimore
Dundalk
Ocean City

Winchester
Harpers Ferry
Columbia
Silver Spring
Bethesda
Dover
Cape May

Front Royal
Strasburg
Arlington
Washington D.C.
Annapolis
DELAWARE
Rehoboth Beach
Georgetown

New Market
Harrisonburg
Warrenton
Alexandria
Woodbridge
Cambridge
Milford
Laurel
Ocean City

Staunton
Shenandoah Nat. Park
Culpeper
Fredericksburg
Lexington Park
Salisbury
Pocomoke City

aynesboro
Gordonsville
Charlottesville
Bowling Green
Rappah.
Pocomoke City

A P P A L A C H I A N
M A R Y L A N D
M O U N T A I N S

Inset (at the same scale):
70
Cambridge
Gloucester
Newton
Lynn
Massachusetts Bay
Boston
Quincy
Weymouth
Millford
Attleboro
Brockton
Provincetown
Cape Cod
Woonsocket
Taunton
C. Cod Bay
Providence
MASS.
Warwick
Fall River
Hyannis
RHODE I.
Newport
New Bedford
②
Block I.
Martha's Vineyard
Nantucket I.
at the same scale ©
70

Washington - New York - Boston

1:2.5M

0 25 50 75 100 km
0 25 50 mls

B C 72
Cohoes Watervliet Troy Albany Rensselaer
Cobleskill Richmondville Schoharie Middleburgh
N. Adams Readsboro Hinsdale Winchester Greenville Haverhill Newburyport Methuen Ipswich
Williamstown Adams Mt Greylock 1064 Greenfield Turners Falls Northfield Winchendon Nashua Dracut Lawrence Lowell Gloucester Beverly
Nassau Cheshire Shelburne Falls Millers Falls Athol Gardner Fitchburg Salem Lynn Marblehead
Stamford Ravena Pittsfield S. Deerfield Leominster Clinton
1 Grand Gorge Prattsville Coxsackie Lenox Dalton Amherst Barre Wachusett Res Cambridge Massachusetts
Chatham Lee Northampton Chester Quabbin Resr Waltham Newton Boston
Catskill Catskill Hudson Stockbridge Easthampton Ware Worcester Marlboro Framingham Brookline Quincy Bay
NEW Saugerties Gt Barrington Otis MASSACHUSETTS Holyoke Weymouth
Shandaken Mountains Hudson Berkshire Hills Westfield Chicopee Monson Oxford Norwood Stoughton
Slide Mtn 1281 Ashokan Resr Mt Everett 793 Springfield Southbridge Milford Franklin Brockton
42 Ancram Canaan Thompsonville Webster Mansfield Bridgewater 42
Kingston Millerton Rhinebeck Winsted Windsor Locks Stafford Springs Woonsocket Attleboro Plymouth
Housatonic Windsor Rockville Putnam Central Falls Taunton Middleboro
Liberty YORK Millbrook Hyde Park Amenia Torrington Hartford Storrs Providence Pawtucket Wareham
Ellenville New Paltz Manchester Moosup Cranston Warren Somerset
Monticello Poughkeepsie Bristol New Britain Willimantic Warwick Fall River
Shawangunk Mtn CONNECTICUT RHODE ISLAND Bristol New Bedford
Walden Wappingers Falls Waterbury Southington Colchester Jewett City Falmouth
Otisville Newburgh New Milford Naugatuck Meriden Middletown Norwich Newport Buzzards Bay
Middletown Beacon L. Candlewood Wallingford Uncasville Jamestown Vineyard Haven
Port Jervis Carmel Brewster Hamden Wakefield
Milford Highland Falls West Point Danbury Seymour Deep River Mystic Westerly Rhode Island Sound Martha's Vineyard
Sussex Warwick Bethel Derby New Haven New London
Peekskill Clinton Old Lyme Fishers I. Block Island Sd
2 Hamburg Haverstraw Bridgeport Milford Block Island Nomans Land 2
Franklin Pompton Lakes Suffern New Canaan Stratford Long Island Sound
Newton Nyack Ossining Tarrytown Fairfield Greenport Gardiners I.
Ramsey Norwalk Montauk Pt
Butler White Plains Stamford Greenwich Mattituck Sag Harbor Montauk
Netcong Paterson Yonkers Port Chester Pt Jefferson Riverhead East Hampton
Dover Clifton Huntington Southampton
Morristown Passaic Bronx Kings Park ATLANTIC
NEW E. Orange Newark Manhattan New York Center Moriches OCEAN
Bernardsville Jersey City Queens Bay Shore Sayville Long Island
JERSEY Elizabeth Brooklyn Great South Bay
Somerville B Staten I. Long Beach C 72 D

Milton Bloomsburg 76 Hazleton B Newton Butler White Plains C Port Chester
Lewisburg Danville Catawissa Lehigh Stroudsburg Netcong Yonkers
Sunbury Lansford Bangor Hackettstown Dover Paterson Clifton
Mt Carmel Mahanoy City Lehighton Morristown Passaic
Milroy Middleburg Shamokin Frackville Tamaqua Palmerton Belvidere E. Orange Bronx
676 McClure Minersville Washington Newark New York
Burnham Herndon Pottsville Blue Mtn Whitehall Easton Phillipsburg Bernardsville Jersey City Queens
Lewistown Lykens Tremont Schuylkill Haven Allentown Clinton Brooklyn
Mifflintown Pine Grove Bethlehem Elizabeth
692 Juniata Millersburg Blue Hamburg Emmaus Somerville Staten I. Long Beach
2 Newport PENN. Flemington New Brunswick Perth Amboy Raritan Bay 2
Duncannon Quakertown Lambertville S. Amboy Atlantic Highlands
Dauphin Womelsdorf South River
Harrisburg Lebanon Schuylkill Boyertown Delaware Princeton Red Bank Long Branch
Blue Mtn Palmyra Reading Souderton Hightstown Freehold
Hershey Shillington Lansdale Doylestown
Newville Carlisle Steelton Middletown Pottstown Warminster Morrisville Trenton NEW Asbury Park
Mt Holly Springs Dillsburg Lititz Ephrata Phoenixville Norristown Levittown Bordentown Manasquan
South Mtn Elizabethtown Bristol Lakewood Point Pleasant
Shippensburg Manchester Columbia Lancaster Philadelphia Burlington Lakehurst Breton Woods
Coatesville Willingboro Toms River 40
York Red Lion Parkesburg Downingtown Camden Mt Holly
Susquehanna W. Chester JERSEY Seaside Park
Gettysburg Kennett Square Chester
Hanover Glen Rock Woodbury Barnegat Bay
Waynesboro Littlestown Stewartstown Chatsworth
Emmitsburg Rising Sun Wilmington Penns Grove Atco Barnegat
Newark Glassboro Surf City
Westminster Elkton Woodstown Mullica Tuckerton
Havre de Grace Elk Salem Elmer Hammonton Egg Harbor City Beach Haven
3 Catoctin Mtn Reisterstown Bel Air Aberdeen Vineland Little Egg Harbor
Frederick Towson Cockeysville Middletown Mays Landing Great Bay
Mt Airy MARYLAND Edgewood Cecilton DELAWARE Bridgeton Millville Pleasantville Atlantic City 3
Ellicott City Baltimore Somers Point
Damascus Catonsville Dundalk Smyrna Woodbine Great Egg Harbor
Columbia Port Norris Ocean City
Leesburg Gaithersburg Glen Burnie Chestertown
Rockville Dover Delaware ATLANTIC
Wheaton Laurel Chester Bay Stone Harbor
Potomac Silver Spring College Park Centreville Cape May OCEAN
Bethesda Bowie Queenstown Frederica Wildwood
Arlington Annapolis Greensboro Cape May
Washington Queen Anne Harrington C. May Pt
Fairfax D.C. Mayo Denton Milford
Alexandria A St Michaels 76 Greenwood B C. Henlopen 74 C

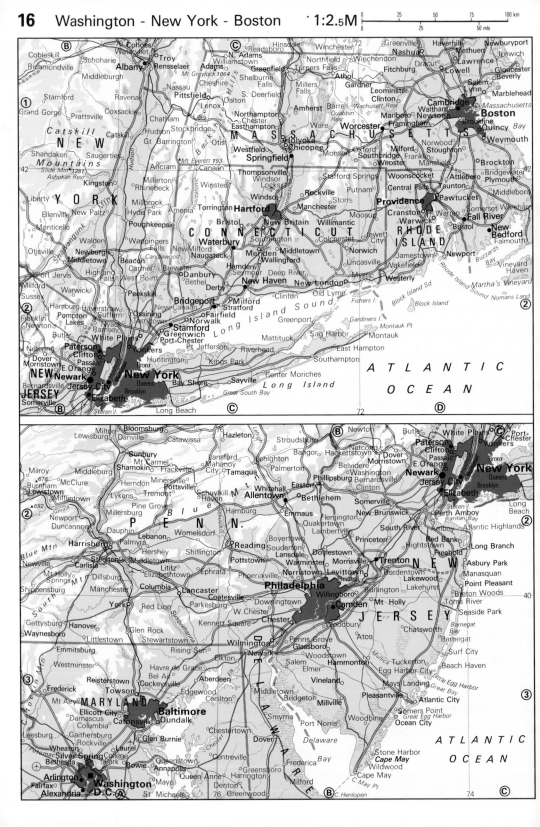

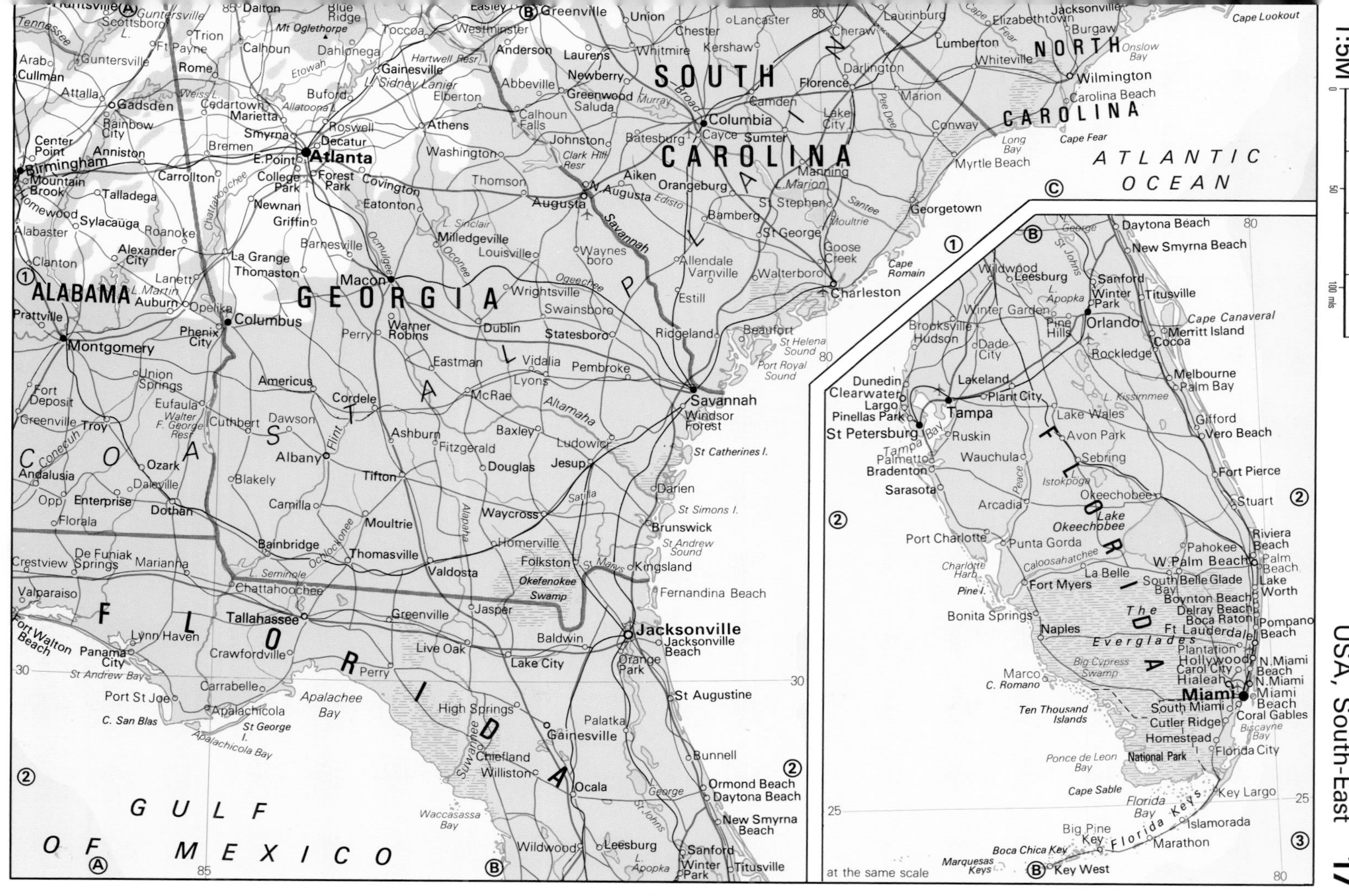

1:5M

50 100 150 200 km
50 100 mls

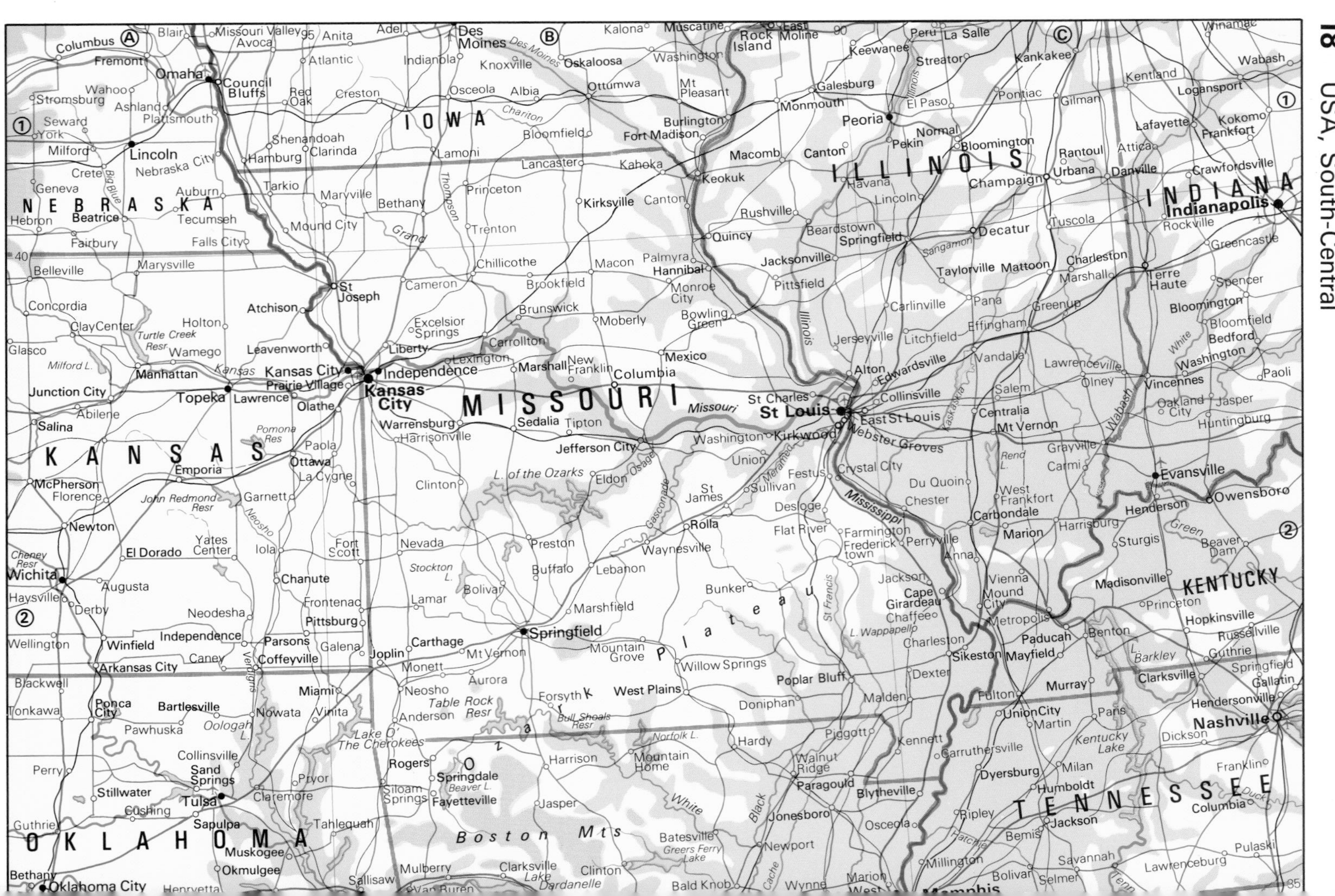
NEBRASKA
IOWA
ILLINOIS
INDIANA
KANSAS
MISSOURI
KENTUCKY
TENNESSEE
OKLAHOMA
Ozark Plateau
Boston Mts
Omaha
Council Bluffs
Lincoln
Des Moines
Peoria
Springfield
Decatur
Champaign
Indianapolis
Terre Haute
Evansville
Owensboro
St Joseph
Kansas City
Independence
Topeka
Columbia
Jefferson City
St Louis
East St Louis
Springfield
Joplin
Wichita
Tulsa
Oklahoma City
Paducah
Cape Girardeau
Nashville
Missouri
Mississippi
Illinois
Wabash
L. of the Ozarks
Table Rock Resr
Kentucky Lake

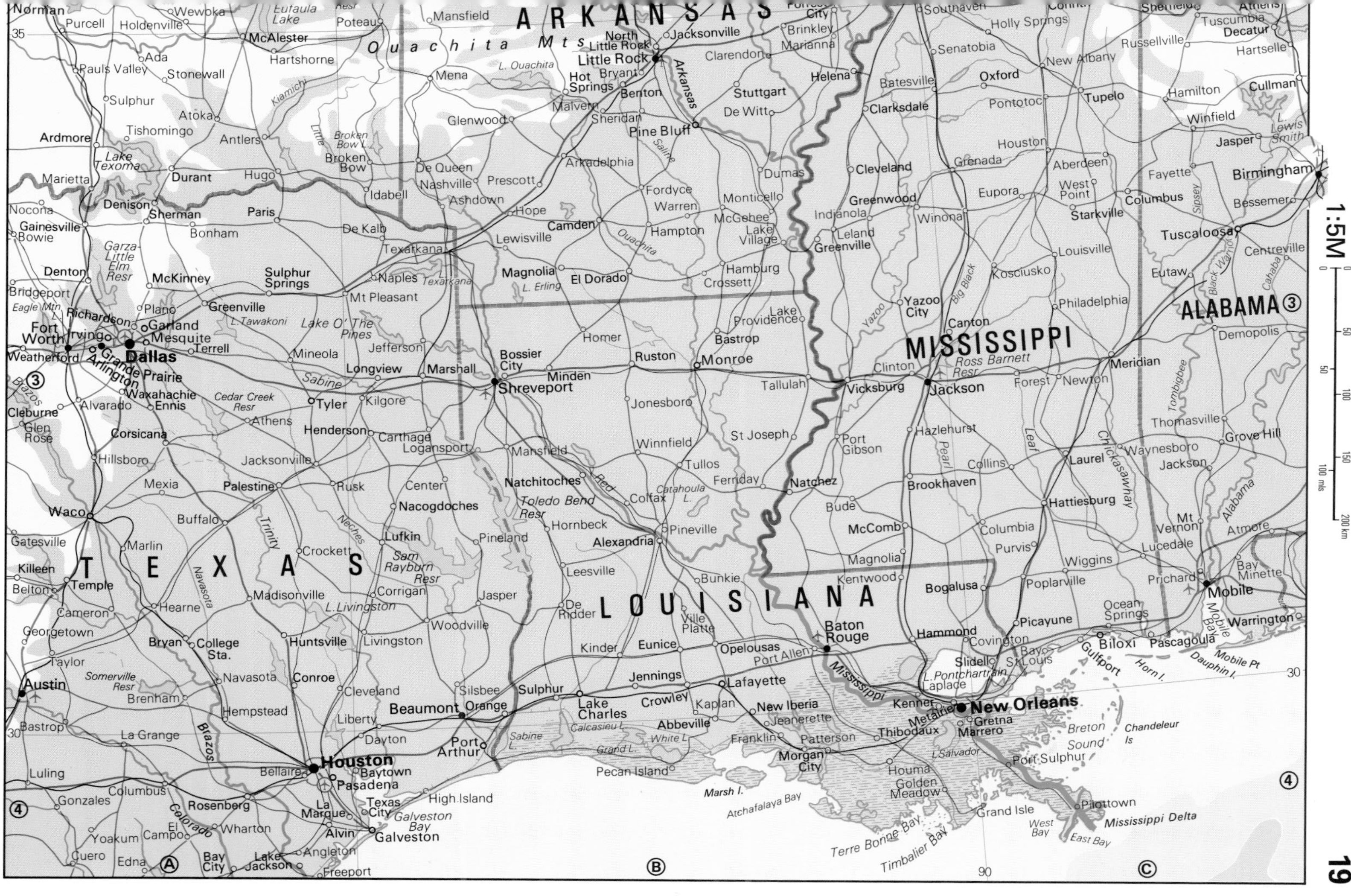

0 50 100 150 200 km
0   50   100 mls

A 125 Parksville Gibsons Vancouver Princeton 120 Keremeos Okanagan Castlegar C Salmo
Port Alberni Horseshoe Bay Hammond Hope Falls Grand Creston
Nanaimo New Mission City Oliver Forks Trail
Vancouver Fraser Osoyoos Metaline
Ladysmith Westmi Blaine Abbotsford C A N A D A 2627 Falls
Bamfield Cowichan Ferndale Chilliwack Mt Ione Bonners
Barkley Sd Duncan Bellingham Oroville Republic Colville Ferry
Port Sidney Mt Baker North Onasket Priest
Renfrew 3285 Cascades Omak Franklin Sandpoint
C. Flattery Victoria Burlington Nat. Mt Logan Okanogan D. Roosevelt Newport Priest Pend
Esquimalt Anacortes Skagit 2733 Park Lake River Oreille
Forks San Juan Is Concrete Okanogan Spirit Lake
Str. of Juan de Fuca Mt Vernon Coeur
Port Angeles Marysville Glacier Peak Brewster Coulee Spokane d'Alene
Olympic Everett 3221 Chelan Banks Wilbur Medical Cheney Kellogg
Nat. Park Edmonds Snohomish L. Chelan L. Lake St Maries
Mt Olympus Monroe Chelan Plummer
2428 Bellevue W A S H I N G T O N
Seattle Renton Wenatchee Odessa
Bremerton Kent Snoqualmie Ephrata Moses Lake Ritzville Colfax Potlatch
Port Orchard Auburn Pass Moscow
Tacoma Yakima Othello Pullman Kendrick
Shelton Puyallup Ellensburg Eltopia Snake Clarkston Lewiston
Hoquiam Olympia Mt Rainier Mount Rainier Naches Selah Sunnyside Richland Dayton
Grays Harb. Aberdeen 4392 Nat. Park Yakima Pasco Walla I D A H O
Willapa B. Raymond Centralia Toppenish Kennewick Walla
South Bend Chehalis Cowlitz Columbia Umatilla Riggins
C. Disappointment Winlock Mt St Helens Mt Adams Goldendale Echo Enterprise He Devil
Longview 2950 3757 Columbia Arlington Pendleton La Grande Mtn 2863
Astoria Rainier Kelso White The Dalles Wallowa
Seaside Woodland Salmon Hood Blue Wallowa Sacajawea 2997 Pk Mts
St Helens Vancouver River Baker
Portland Camas Mountains
Tillamook Hillsboro Gresham Mt Hood Condon Ukiah Unity
Lake Oswego Oregon City 3427 Spray Baker
Newberg Woodburn Mt Wilson Long Creek Midvale
45 McMinnville 1707 45
Lincoln City Salem Dayville Weiser
Stayton Mt Jefferson Madras Payette
Newport Corvallis Idanha 3199 John Day Ontario
Albany Canyon City Unity Vale Nyssa
Yachats Lebanon Redmond Prineville Emmett
Sweet Home Three Sisters Bend Brothers Drewsey
Florence Eugene Springfield 3156 O R E G O N Caldwell
Lowell La Pine Nampa
Reedsport Cottage Grove Oakridge Crescent Burns Murphy
Coos Bay Harney Basin Crane Jordan Snake
C. Blanco N. Bend Oakland High Valley
Myrtle Point Roseburg Desert Silver Lake Harney L. Malheur L.
Port Orford Myrtle Creek Mt Thielsen Owyhee Mts
2 Canyonville 2799 Owyhee
Prospect Crater Mt Scott
Gold Beach Wolf Creek Nat. Pk 2721 Chiloquin
Grants McLoughlin Upper
Central Point Pass 2894 Klamath L. Bly Valley Falls Denio McDermitt
Brookings Medford Ashland Lakeview
Klamath Warner Mts
Hornbrook Falls Dorris Denio Golconda
Pt St George Crescent City Clear L. Resr Willow Ranch Goose L.
Klamath Yreka Upper L. N E V A D A
Klamath Mts Mt Shasta Canby Middle Black Rock Desert Santa Rosa Ra.
4317 Alturas Winnemucca
Dunsmuir Mount Alkali L. Osgood Mts
C A L I F O R N I A Shasta Adin Imlay Battle
Humboldt Bay Arcata Shasta Burney Rye Patch Mountain
Eureka Weaverville Project City Eagle L. Resr Mt Tobin
Fortuna Redding Nat. Pk 3187 2979
C. Mendocino B 120 Susanville C

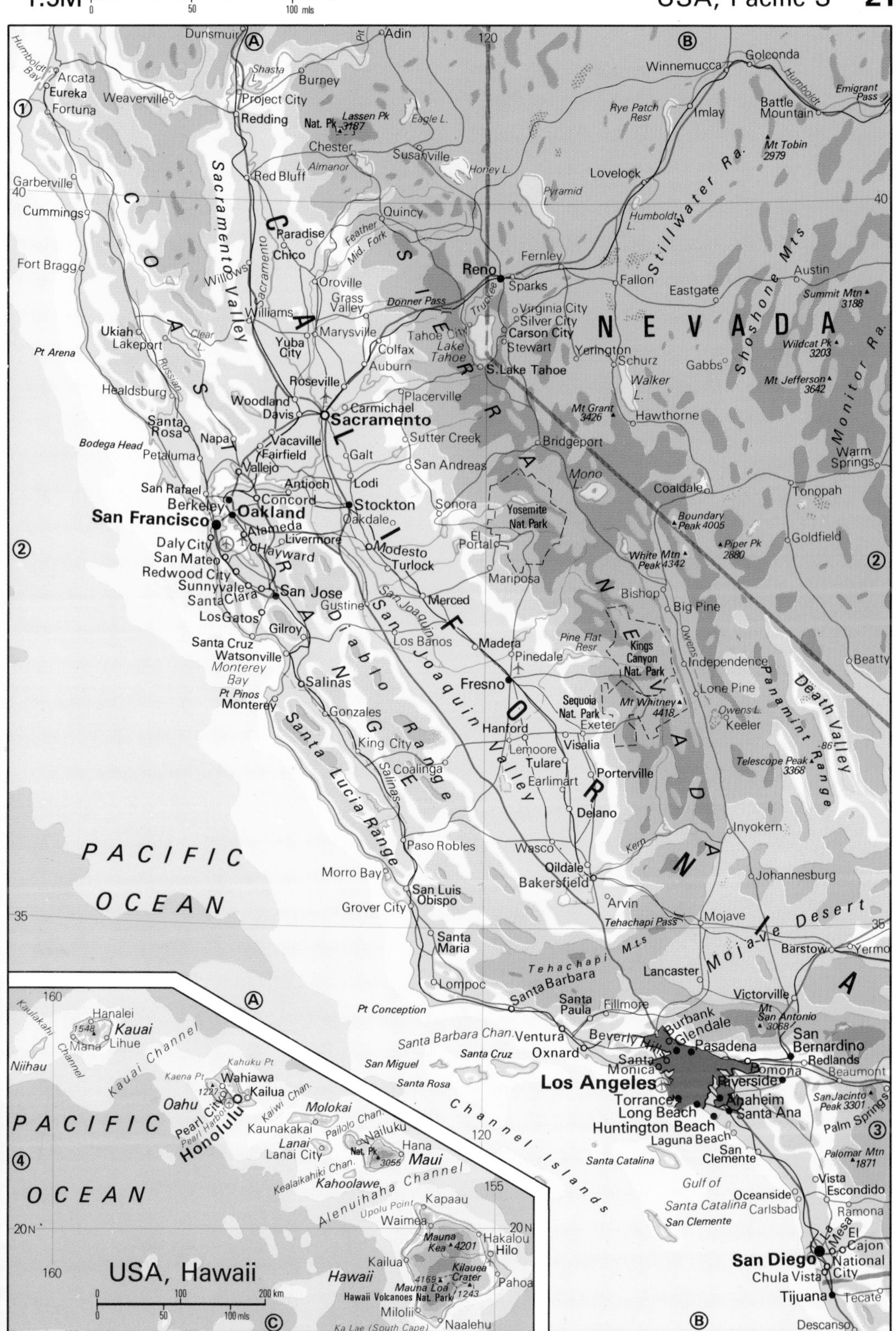

1:5M

0 50 100 150 200 km
0 50 100 mls

PACIFIC OCEAN

N E V A D A

C O A S T

Sacramento Valley

S I E R R A

N E V A D A

C A L I F O R N I A

San Joaquin Valley

Diablo Range

Santa Lucia Range

Mojave Desert

Death Valley

Panamint Range

Monitor Ra.

Shoshone Mts

Stillwater Ra.

Tehachapi Mts

Hawaii inset

USA, Hawaii

0 100 200 km
0 50 100 mls

PACIFIC OCEAN

Kauai Channel

Kauai
Hanalei
Lihue
Mana
1548

Niihau

Oahu
Wahiawa
Kailua
Honolulu
Pearl City
Kahuku Pt
Kaena Pt
1227

Molokai
Kaunakakai

Lanai
Lanai City

Kahoolawe

Maui
Wailuku
Hana
Nat. Pk.
3055

Hawaii
Mauna Kea 4201
Mauna Loa 4165
Kilauea Crater
Hawaii Volcanoes Nat. Park
Hilo
Pahoa
Kapaau
Waimea
Hakalou
Kailua
Naalehu
Ka Lae (South Cape)
Miloli
4243

1:2.5M

0 25 50 75 100 km
0 25 50 mls

Northern map (San Francisco / Central California):

Lytton, Calistoga, Woodland, Folsom, Placerville, Folsom, Camino, Diamond Springs, Markleeville, Topaz L., Healdsburg, L.Berryessa, Forestville, St Helena, Winters, Davis, Carmichael, Sacramento, Highland Pk 3333, Coleville, Santa Rosa, Yountville, Vacaville, Dixon, Plymouth, Sutter Ck, West Pt, Bear Valley, Dardanelle, Devils Gate 2301, Sebastopol, Sonoma, Napa, Elmira, Fairfield, Galt, Jackson, Mokelumne Hill, Arnold, Sonora Pass 2933, Bridgeport, Bridgeport Resr, Petaluma, Novato, Vallejo, S.Pablo B., Pittsburg, Antioch, Isleton, Lodi, Clements, San Andreas, Angels Camp, Murphys, Pinecrest, Excelsior Mtn 3790

S.Pablo B., San Rafael, Mill Valley, Berkeley, Richmond, Concord, Oakley, Stockton, Bellota, Melones Resr, Sonora, Groveland, Mather, Tioga Pass, Mt Dana 3978, Lee Vining, June Lake

Golden Gate, Oakland, Brentwood, Byron, Farmington Resr, Don Pedro Resr, Coulterville, El Portal, Wawona, National Park, Mt Lyell 3997, Mt Ritter 4010

San Francisco, Alameda, San Leandro, Tracy, Ripon, Riverbank, Modesto, L.McClure, Mariposa, Fish Camp, Devil Postpile N.M.

Daly City, S.San Francisco, Hayward, Pleasanton, Livermore, Vernalis, Manteca, Ceres, Modesto, Turlock L., Yosemite, Mammoth Pool Resr

San Mateo, Fremont, Mountain View, Patterson, Turlock, Snelling, Mariposa, Bass Lake, Kaiser Pk 3146, Lakeshore, Huntington L.

Redwood City, Palo Alto, Sunnyvale, Mt Hamilton (Lick Observatory), Newman, Merced, Planada, Raymond, Shaver L.

San Gregorio, Santa Clara, San Jose, Coyote, Gustine, Merced, Mariposa, Fresno, Humphreys, Pine Flat Resr, Patterson Mtn 2489

Pescadero, Los Gatos, Volta, Los Banos, Chowchilla, Berenda, Madera, Friant, Piedra, Kings

Boulder Creek, Morgan Hill, Gilroy, S.Luis Resr, Dos Palos, Firebaugh, Herndon, Clovis, Minkler

Davenport, Soquel, Laveaga Pk 1154, Hollister, Tres Pinos, Mendota, Kerman, Sanger, Reedley, Badger

Santa Cruz, Watsonville, Monterey Bay, San Juan Bautista, Castroville, Salinas, Alisal, Gonzales, Helm, Selma, Kingsburg, Dinuba, Reedley

Pacific Grove, Seaside, Monterey, Carmel, Carmel Valley, Pinnacles N.M., Kingsburg

Southern map (Los Angeles / Southern California):

Sta Ynez, Los Alamos, Buellton, Los Olivos, Big Pine Mtn 2081, Santa Barbara Resr, Gorman, Rosamond L., Helendale, Lompoc, Solvang, L.Cachuma, Lake Hughes, Lancaster, Pt Arguello, Santa Ynez Mts, Ojai, Castaic, Acton, Palmdale, Adelanto, Victorville, Gaviota, Goleta, Carpinteria, Fillmore, Newhall, Wrightwood, Hesperia, Pt Conception, Santa Barbara, Santa Paula, Moorpark, San Fernando, San Gabriel Mts 3068, Mt San Antonio, San Bernardino

San Miguel, Ventura, Oxnard, Camarillo, Burbank, Pasadena, Upland, Colton, Highland, Santa Cruz Chan., Port Hueneme, Los Angeles, Glendale, Hollywood, Monrovia, Pomona, Ontario, Redlands, Santa Rosa, Anacapa Is, Santa Monica, Beverly Hills, Whittier, Riverside, Santa Barbara, Channel Islands, Santa Monica Bay, Inglewood, Torrance, Redondo Beach, Lakewood, Fullerton, Anaheim, Santa Ana, Orange, Corona, Perris, Long Beach, Garden Grove, Costa Mesa, Santiago Pk 1736, Huntington Beach, Newport Beach, Elsinore, Laguna Beach, San Clemente, S.Onofre, Fallbrook, Santa Barbara, Gulf of Santa Catalina, Santa Catalina, Avalon, Oceanside, Vista, San Nicolas, Carlsbad, Encinitas, San Clemente, Del Mar, La Jolla, San Diego

PACIFIC OCEAN

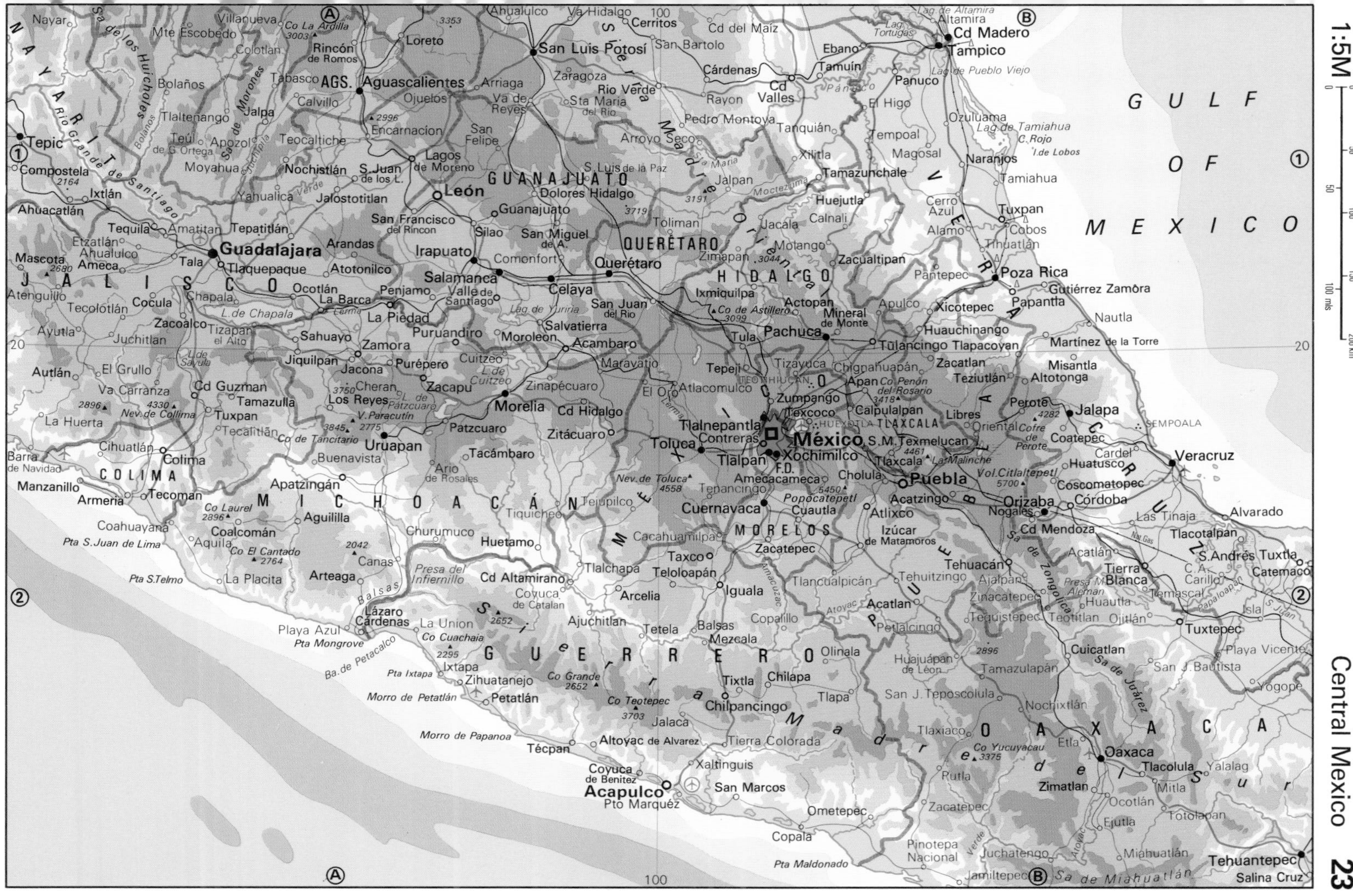
GULF OF MEXICO
Cd Madero
Tampico
Veracruz
Jalapa
Poza Rica
Tuxpan
Orizaba
Córdoba
Puebla
México
Toluca
Cuernavaca
Pachuca
Querétaro
Celaya
Salamanca
Irapuato
León
Guanajuato
San Luis Potosí
Aguascalientes
Guadalajara
Morelia
Uruapan
Colima
Manzanillo
Acapulco
Chilpancingo
Oaxaca
Tehuantepec
Lázaro Cárdenas
Iguala
Taxco
Tlaxcala
Tepic
NAYARIT
JALISCO
GUANAJUATO
QUERÉTARO
HIDALGO
MORELOS
MICHOACÁN
COLIMA
GUERRERO
OAXACA
TLAXCALA
VERACRUZ
Nev. de Toluca 4558
Popocatépetl 5450
Vol. Citlaltépetl 5700
Nev. de Colima 4330
Pta Maldonado
Pta S.Juan de Lima
L. de Chapala

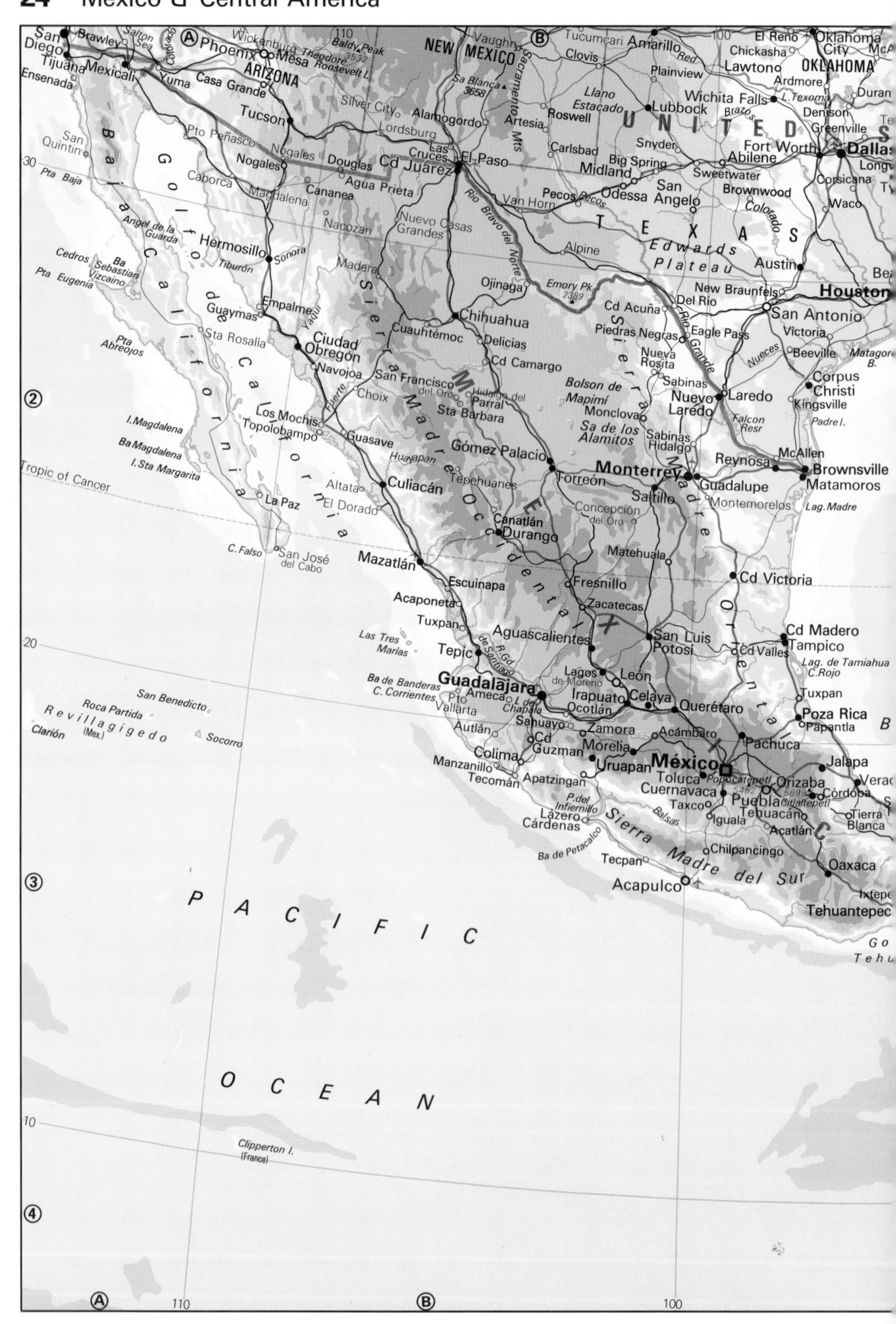
San Diego
Tijuana
Ensenada
Brawley
Salton Sea
Mexicali
Yuma
Colorado
Phoenix
Mesa
ARIZONA
Casa Grande
Tucson
Wickenburg
Baldy Peak
Theodore Roosevelt L.
NEW MEXICO
Vaughn
Sacramento Mts
Sa Blanca 3658
Silver City
Alamogordo
Artesia
Lordsburg
Las Cruces
El Paso
Cd Juárez
Tucumcari
Amarillo
Red
Clovis
Plainview
Llano Estacado
Lubbock
Roswell
Carlsbad
Midland
Big Spring
Odessa
Snyder
Pecos
Van Horn
San Angelo
UNITED S
El Reno
Oklahoma City
Chickasha
Lawton
OKLAHOMA
Ardmore
Wichita Falls
L. Texoma
Durant
Denison
Brazos
Greenville
Fort Worth
Dallas
Abilene
Sweetwater
Brownwood
Corsicana
Longv
Waco
Colorado
TEXAS
Edwards Plateau
Austin
Alpine
Emory Pk 2389
New Braunfels
Houston
San Antonio
Del Rio
Cd Acuña
Eagle Pass
Piedras Negras
Victoria
Beeville
Nueces
Corpus Christi
Kingsville
Padre I.
Matagorda B.
Laredo
Nuevo Laredo
Falcon Resr
McAllen
Reynosa
Brownsville
Matamoros
Lag. Madre
San Quintín
Pta Baja
Pto Peñasco
Nogales
Douglas
Agua Prieta
Caborca
Magdalena
Cananea
Nacozari
Nuevo Casas Grandes
Rio Bravo del Norte
Baja California
Golfo de California
Angel de la Guarda
Hermosillo
Sonora
Tiburón
Cedros
Ba Sebastián Vizcaíno
Pta Eugenia
Guaymas
Empalme
Yaqui
Sta Rosalía
Pta Abreojos
Ciudad Obregón
Navojoa
Madera
Sierra Madre Occidental
Cuauhtémoc
Chihuahua
Ojinaga
Delicias
Cd Camargo
Sierra Madre Oriental
Nueva Rosita
Sabinas
Bolson de Mapimí
Monclova
Sa de los Alamitos
Sabinas Hidalgo
Rio Grande
San Francisco del Oro
Hidalgo del Parral
Sta Barbara
Choix
Fuerte
Los Mochis
Topolobampo
Guasave
I. Magdalena
Ba Magdalena
I. Sta Margarita
Tropic of Cancer
Gómez Palacio
Torreón
Huayapan
Tepehuanes
Monterrey
Guadalupe
Saltillo
Montemorelos
Altata
Culiacán
El Dorado
La Paz
C. Falso
San José del Cabo
Canatlán
Durango
Concepción del Oro
Matehuala
Mazatlán
Escuinapa
Fresnillo
Cd Victoria
Acaponeta
Zacatecas
MEXICO
Tuxpan
Las Tres Marías
Tepic
Aguascalientes
San Luis Potosí
Cd Madero
Tampico
Cd Valles
Lag. de Tamiahua
C. Rojo
R. Gd de Santiago
Ba de Banderas
C. Corrientes
Pto Vallarta
Guadalajara
Ameca
L. de Chapala
Lagos de Moreno
León
Irapuato
Celaya
Querétaro
Ocotlán
Tuxpan
Poza Rica
Papantla
San Benedicto
Roca Partida
Revillagigedo (Mex.)
Clarión
Socorro
Autlán
Sahuayo
Zamora
Acámbaro
Pachuca
Colima
Cd Guzman
Morelia
Uruapan
México
Jalapa
Manzanillo
Tecomán
Apatzingan
Toluca
Popocatepetl 5452
Orizaba
Citlaltepetl 5699
Córdoba
Veracruz
Cuernavaca
Puebla
Taxco
Tehuacán
Tierra Blanca
P. del Infiernillo
Balsas
Iguala
Acatlán
Lázaro Cárdenas
Sierra Madre del Sur
Ba de Petacalco
Chilpancingo
Tecpan
Acapulco
Oaxaca
Ixtepec
Tehuantepec
Go Tehu
PACIFIC OCEAN
Clipperton I. (France)
30
20
10
110
100
A
B
2
3
4

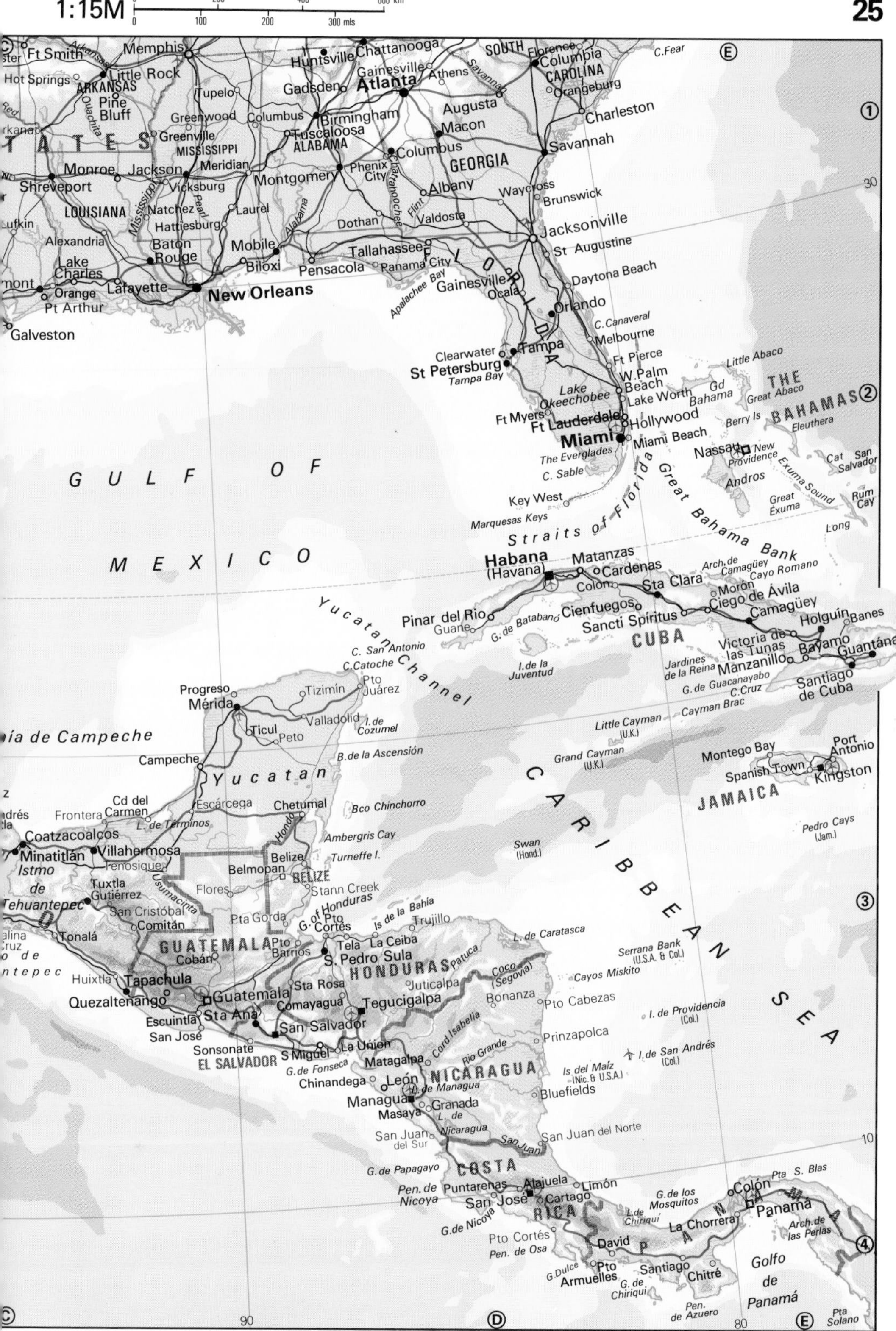

1:15M

200   400   600 km
100   200   300 mls

Ft Smith Memphis Huntsville Chattanooga Gainesville Florence SOUTH Columbia C.Fear
Hot Springs Little Rock ARKANSAS Gadsden Atlanta Athens CAROLINA Orangeburg ①
ATES Pine Bluff Columbus Birmingham Augusta Macon Charleston
Greenwood MISSISSIPPI Tuscaloosa ALABAMA Savannah
Monroe Jackson Meridian Montgomery Phenix City Columbus GEORGIA 30
Shreveport Vicksburg Albany Waycross Brunswick
LOUISIANA Natchez Laurel Dothan Valdosta Jacksonville
Alexandria Hattiesburg Tallahassee St Augustine
Lake Baton Rouge Mobile Pensacola Panama City Gainesville Ocala Daytona Beach
Charles Biloxi Apalachee Bay FLORIDA Orlando C. Canaveral
Orange Lafayette New Orleans Melbourne
Pt Arthur Tampa Clearwater Ft Pierce
Galveston St Petersburg W.Palm Beach Little Abaco
Tampa Bay Lake Lake Worth Great Abaco THE ②
Ft Myers Okeechobee Bahama Gd BAHAMAS
Ft Lauderdale Hollywood Berry Is Eleuthera
Miami Miami Beach Nassau New
The Everglades Providence Cat San Salvador
C. Sable Andros Exuma Sound
Key West Great
Marquesas Keys Exuma Rum Cay
Straits of Florida Long

GULF OF

MEXICO

Habana Matanzas Arch.de Cayo Romano
(Havana) Cardenas Camagüey
Colón Sta Clara Morón Ciego de Ávila
Pinar del Rio Cienfuegos Sancti Spíritus Camagüey
Guane G. de Batabanó CUBA Victoria de Holguín Banes
Yucatan Channel I.de la las Tunas Bayamo Guantánam
C. San Antonio Juventud Jardines Manzanillo
C.Catoche de la Reina C.Cruz Santiago
Pto Manzanayabo de Cuba
Progreso Tizimin Juárez G. de Guacanayabo
Mérida Valladolid I.de Little Cayman Cayman Brac
Ticul Cozumel (U.K.) Port
Ía de Campeche Peto Montego Bay Antonio
B. de la Ascensión Grand Cayman Spanish Town Kingston
Campeche Yucatan (U.K.) JAMAICA
Cd del Escárcega Bco Chinchorro
Frontera Carmen Pedro Cays
Coatzacoalcos I. de Términos Ambergris Cay (Jam.)
Minatitlán Villahermosa Chetumal Turneffe I. Swan ③
Istmo Tenosique Belize (Hond.)
de Tuxtla Belmopan BELIZE
Tehuantepec Gutiérrez Flores Stann Creek
San Cristóbal Usumacinta Pta Gorda G.of Is de la Bahía L. de Caratasca
Comitán Honduras Trujillo
ntepec Tonalá GUATEMALA Pto Tela La Ceiba Serrana Bank
Cobán Barrios S. Pedro Sula (U.S.A. & Col.)
Huixtla Tapachula Sta Rosa HONDURAS Coco Cayos Miskito
Quezaltenango Comayaguá Juticalpa (Segovia)
Escuintla STA ANA Guatemala Tegucigalpa Bonanza Pto Cabezas
San José San Salvador I. de Providencia
Sonsonate EL SALVADOR La Unión Prinzapolca (Col.)
Chinandega S Miguel Matagalpa Cord Isabelia Río Grande I. de San Andrés
G. de Fonseca León NICARAGUA Is del Maíz (Col.)
Managua Masaya Granada (Nic. & U.S.A.)
L. de Managua Bluefields
San Juan L. de San Juan del Norte
del Sur Nicaragua San Juan
Pta S. Blas
G. de Papagayo COSTA Pta
Pen. de Puntarenas Alajuela Limón G. de los Colón Nicoya
Nicoya San José Cartago Mosquitos PANAMA ④
G. de Nicoya RICA La Chorrera Panama
Pto Cortés I. de Arch.de
Pen. de Osa David Chiriquí las Perlas
G.Dulce P Golfo
Pto Santiago de
G. de Armuelles Chitré Panamá
Chiriquí Pen. Pta
de Azuero Solano

CARIBBEAN SEA

Great Bahama Bank

90   D   80   E

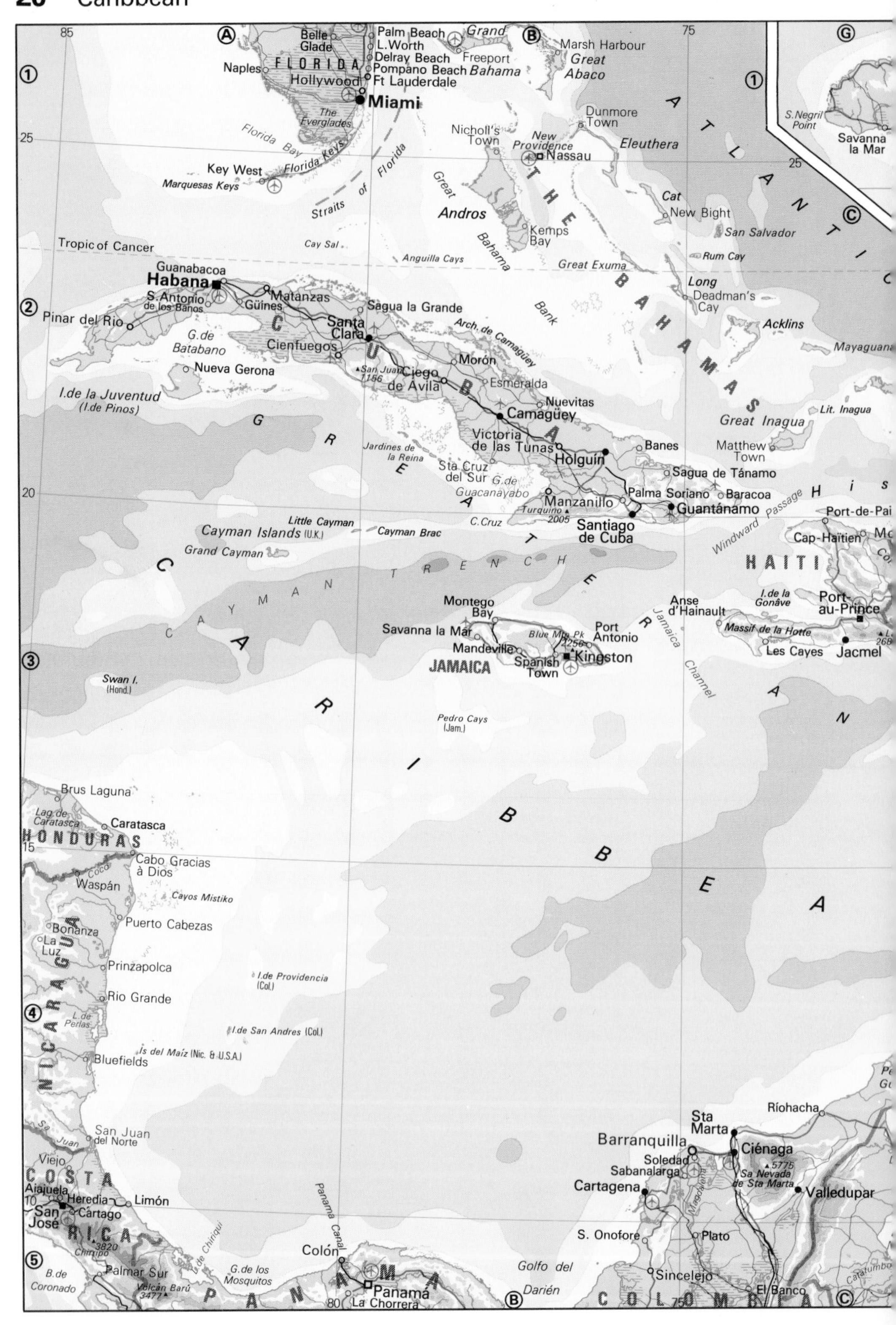

85

Ⓑ 75 Ⓖ

Palm Beach
Belle
Glade
L. Worth
Delray Beach
Pompano Beach
Ft Lauderdale
Naples
Hollywood
Miami
FLORIDA
The
Everglades
Florida Bay

Freeport
Grand
Bahama
Marsh Harbour
Great
Abaco

S. Negril
Point
Savanna
la Mar

①
25

Nicholl's
Town
New
Providence
Dunmore
Town

ATLANTIC

①

Key West
Marquesas Keys
Florida Keys
Straits of Florida

□ Nassau
Eleuthera

25

Cat
New Bight
San Salvador

Ⓒ

Tropic of Cancer
Cay Sal
Anguilla Cays
Andros
Great
Bahama
Kemps
Bay
Great Exuma
Rum Cay

T
H
E

②
Guanabacoa
Habana
S. Antonio
de los Baños
Güines
Matanzas
Sagua la Grande
Arch. de Camagüey
Long
Deadman's
Cay
Acklins

B
A
H
A
M
A
S

Pinar del Rio
G. de
Batabano
Santa
Clara
Cienfuegos
San Juan
1156
Ciego
de Ávila
Morón
Esmeralda
Bank
Mayaguana

I. de la Juventud
(I. de Pinos)
Nueva Gerona
C
U
B
A
Nuevitas
Camagüey
Great Inagua
Lit. Inagua

G
R
E

Jardines de
la Reina
Victoria
de las Tunas
Holguín
Banes
Matthew
Town

20
20

Little Cayman
Cayman Islands (U.K.)
Cayman Brac
Sta Cruz
del Sur
G. de
Guacanayabo
Manzanillo
Turquino ▲ 2005
C. Cruz
Palma Soriano
Sagua de Tánamo
Baracoa
Guantánamo
Port-de-Pai

H
i
s

Windward Passage
Cap-Haïtien
Mo

Grand Cayman
Santiago
de Cuba
H A I T I
Co

C
A
Y
M
A
N
T
R
E
N
C
H

Montego
Bay
Savanna la Mar
Mandeville
Blue Mts Pk
▲ 2256
Port
Antonio
Anse
d'Hainault
I. de la
Gonâve
Port-
au-Prince

③
Swan I.
(Hond.)
JAMAICA
Spanish
Town
Kingston
Massif de la Hotte
Les Cayes
Jacmel
L.
268

C
A
R
I
B
B
E
A
N

Jamaica Channel

Pedro Cays
(Jam.)

Brus Laguna
Lag. de
Caratasca
Caratasca
H O N D U R A S

15
Cabo Gracias
à Dios
Waspán
Cayos Mistiko
Puerto Cabezas
I. de Providencia
(Col.)

④
Bonanza
La
Luz
Prinzapolca
Rio Grande
L. de
Perlas
Is del Maíz (Nic. & U.S.A.)
Bluefields
I. de San Andrés (Col.)

N
I
C
A
R
A
G
U
A

Sta
Marta
Ríohacha

San Juan
del Norte
Barranquilla
Soledad
Sabanalarga
Ciénaga
▲ 5775
Sa Nevada
de Sta Marta
Valledupar

Viejo
C O S T A
Alajuela
Heredia
San
José
Cartago
Limón
R I C A
Chirripó ▲3920
Volcán Barú
3477
Panama Canal
Colón
Cartagena
S. Onofore
Plato

⑤
B. de
Coronado
Palmar Sur
G. de los
Mosquitos
P A N A M Á
Panamá
La Chorrera
80
Golfo del
Darién
Sincelejo
El Banco
C O L O M B I A

Ⓐ
Ⓑ
750
Ⓒ

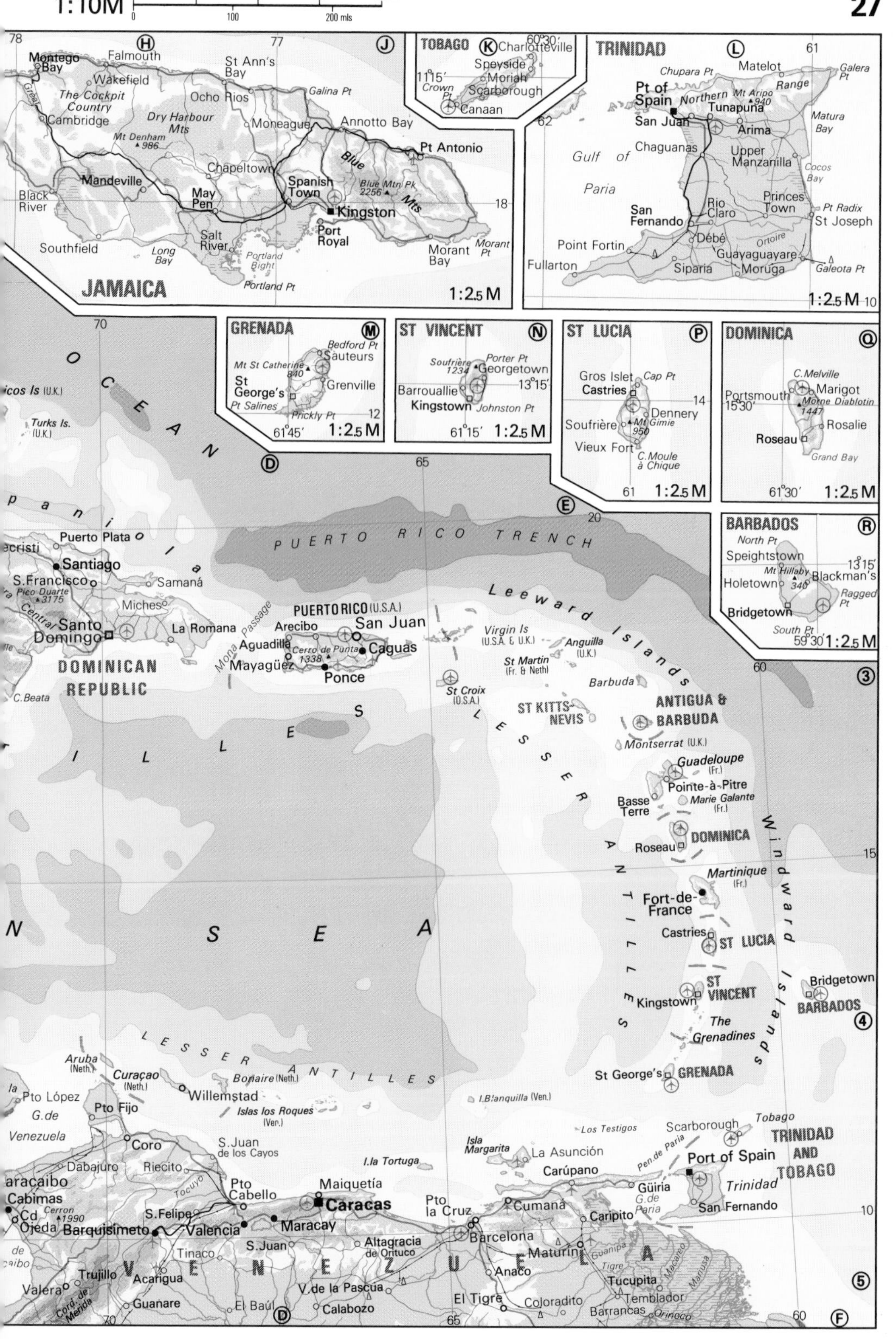

1:10M

100 200 300 400 km
100 200 mls

TOBAGO (K)
60°30'
Charlotteville
Speyside
1115' Moriah
Crown Scarborough
Canaan

TRINIDAD (L) 61
Chupara Pt Matelot
Galera
Pt of Northern Mt Aripo Pt
Spain Tunapuna 940 Range
San Juan Arima
Chaguanas Upper Matura
Manzanilla Bay
Gulf of Cocos
Paria Rio Princes Bay
San Claro Town
Fernando Débé Pt Radix
St Joseph
Point Fortin Siparia Guayaguayare
Fullarton Moruga
Galeota Pt
1:2.5 M-10

JAMAICA
78 (H) 77
Montego Falmouth
Bay
Wakefield St Ann's
Ocho Rios Bay
The Cockpit Galina Pt
Country Moneague
Cambridge Dry Harbour Annotto Bay
Mts Pt Antonio
Mt Denham Chapeltown Blue Blue Mtn Pk
986 Spanish Mts 2256
Mandeville Town
May Kingston 18
Pen Port
Southfield Salt River Royal
Black Long Morant
River Bay Portland Morant Pt
Bight Bay
Portland Pt
1:2.5 M

GRENADA (M)
Bedford Pt
Sauteurs
Mt St Catherine 840
St Grenville
George's
Pt Salines
Prickly Pt 12
61°45' 1:2.5 M
(D) 65

ST VINCENT (N)
Porter Pt
Soufrière Georgetown
1234 13°15'
Barrouallie
Kingstown Johnston Pt
61°15' 1:2.5 M

ST LUCIA (P)
Gros Islet Cap Pt
Castries 14
Dennery
Soufrière Mt
Gimie
950
Vieux Fort
C.Moule
à Chique
61 1:2.5 M

DOMINICA (Q)
C. Melville
Marigot
Portsmouth Morne Diablotin
1530' 1447
Rosalie
Roseau
Grand Bay
61°30' 1:2.5 M

BARBADOS (R)
North Pt
Speightstown 1315'
Holetown Mt Hillaby Blackman's
340
Bridgetown Ragged
Pt
South Pt
59 30' 1:2.5 M

O C E A N

icos Is
(U.K.)
Turks Is.
(U.K.)

P a n i a

P U E R T O R I C O T R E N C H
20
(E)

L e e w a r d I s l a n d s

cristi Puerto Plata
Santiago
S. Francisco
Samaná
Pico Duarte Miches
3175 La Romana
Santo
Domingo
**DOMINICAN
REPUBLIC**
C. Beata

Mona Passage
PUERTO RICO (U.S.A.)
Arecibo San Juan
Aguadilla Caguas
Mayagüez Cerro de Punta
Ponce 1338

Virgin Is. Anguilla
(U.S.A. & U.K.) (U.K.)
St Martin
St Croix (Fr. & Neth)
(U.S.A.) Barbuda
St KITTS
NEVIS **ANTIGUA &
BARBUDA**
Montserrat (U.K.)
Guadeloupe
(Fr.)
Pointe-à-Pitre
Basse Marie Galante
Terre (Fr.)
Roseau **DOMINICA**
15
Martinique
(Fr.)
Fort-de-
France
Castries **ST LUCIA**
Kingstown **ST
VINCENT** Bridgetown
The **BARBADOS**
Grenadines
St George's **GRENADA**

L E S S E R A N T I L L E S

W i n d w a r d I s l a n d s
60 (3)

C A R I B B E A N S E A

Aruba
(Neth.)
Curaçao
(Neth.) Bonaire (Neth.)
la Pto López
G.de Pto Fijo Willemstad
Venezuela Islas los Roques
Coro (Ven.)
Dabajuro S.Juan I.Blanquilla (Ven.)
Riecito de los Cayos
aracaibo I.la Tortuga Los Testigos Tobago
Cabimas Isla Scarborough
Ca Cerrón Maiquetía Margarita La Asunción **TRINIDAD
AND
TOBAGO**
Ojeda 1990 S.Felipe Pto Pen de Paria
Barquisimeto Cabello **Caracas** Pto Carúpano Pto of Spain
Valencia Maracay la Cruz Güiria Trinidad
Tinaco S.Juan Cumaná G.de San Fernando
Trujillo Altagracia Barcelona Paria 10
Valera Acarigua de Orituco Maturín Caripito
Cord. Tinaco V E N E Z U E L A Anaco Tucupita
de Mérida Guanare V.de la Pascua El Tigre Temblador
El Baúl Calabozo Coloradito Barrancas Orinoco
70 (D) 65 60 (F)

1:40M

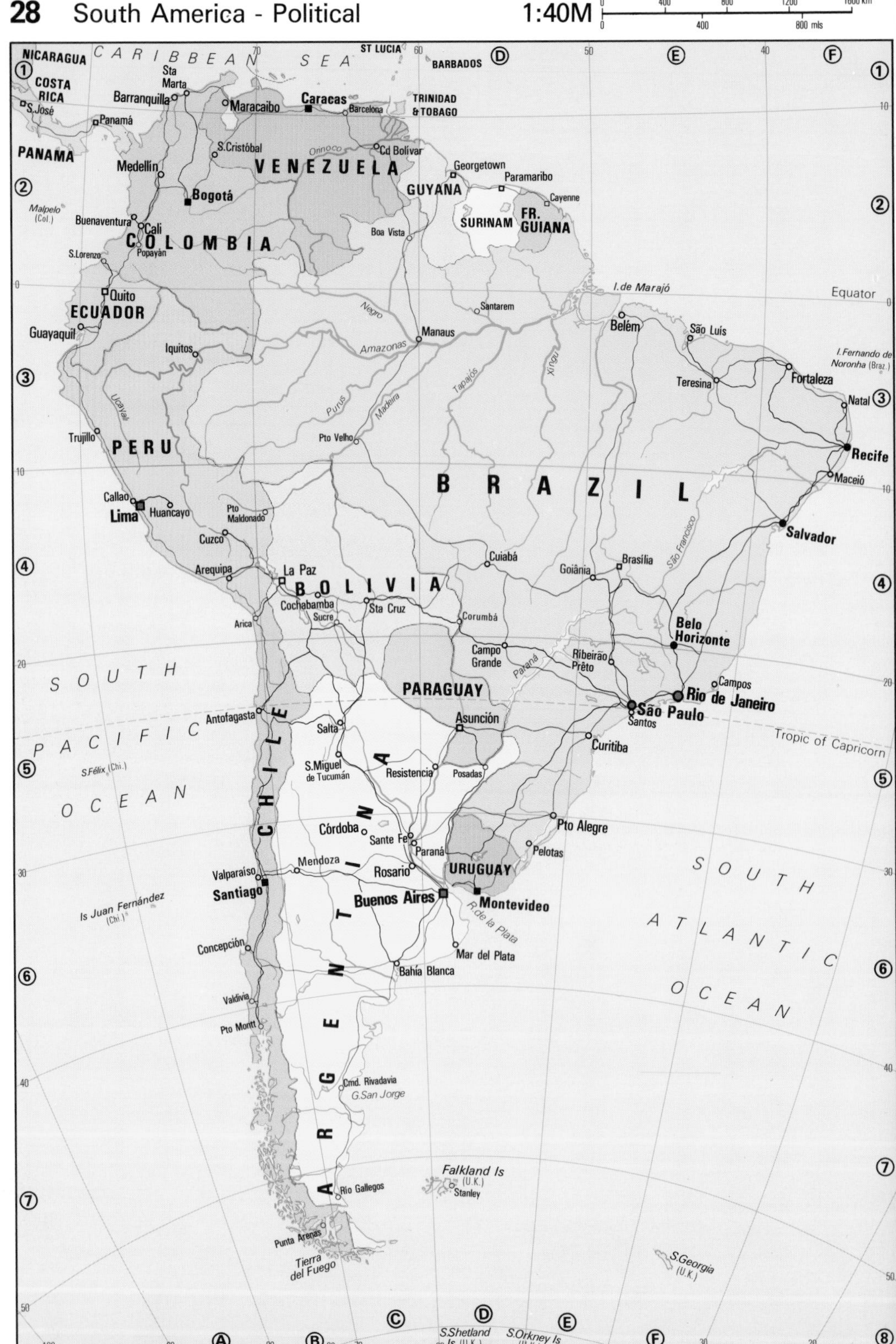

0 400 800 1200 1600 km
0 400 800 mls
CARIBBEAN SEA
NICARAGUA
COSTA RICA
S.José
Panamá
PANAMA
ST LUCIA
BARBADOS
TRINIDAD & TOBAGO
Sta Marta
Barranquilla
Maracaibo
Caracas
Barcelona
Cd Bolívar
Orinoco
S.Cristóbal
Medellín
VENEZUELA
Bogotá
GUYANA
Georgetown
Paramaribo
Cayenne
SURINAM
FR. GUIANA
Malpelo (Col.)
Buenaventura
Cali
Popayán
COLOMBIA
Boa Vista
S.Lorenzo
Quito
ECUADOR
Guayaquil
I.de Marajó
Equator
Negro
Santarem
Belém
São Luís
Manaus
Amazonas
Iquitos
I.Fernando de Noronha (Braz.)
Fortaleza
Teresina
Natal
Xingu
Tapajós
Madeira
Purus
Ucayali
Recife
Trujillo
PERU
Pto Velho
Maceió
BRAZIL
Callao
Lima
Huancayo
Pto Maldonado
Salvador
Cuzco
São Francisco
Cuiabá
Goiânia
Brasília
Arequipa
La Paz
BOLIVIA
Cochabamba
Sucre
Sta Cruz
Corumbá
Arica
Belo Horizonte
Campo Grande
Ribeirão Prêto
Paraná
SOUTH PACIFIC OCEAN
PARAGUAY
Campos
Rio de Janeiro
São Paulo
Santos
Antofagasta
Asunción
Salta
Curitiba
Tropic of Capricorn
S.Miguel de Tucumán
Resistencia
Posadas
S.Félix (Chi.)
CHILE
ARGENTINA
Córdoba
Sante Fe
Paraná
Pto Alegre
Pelotas
Mendoza
Rosario
URUGUAY
Valparaíso
Santiago
Buenos Aires
Montevideo
R.de la Plata
Is Juan Fernández (Chi.)
SOUTH ATLANTIC OCEAN
Concepción
Mar del Plata
Bahía Blanca
Valdivia
Pto Montt
Cmd. Rivadavia
G.San Jorge
Falkland Is (U.K.)
Stanley
Rio Gallegos
Punta Arenas
Tierra del Fuego
S.Georgia (U.K.)
S.Shetland Is (U.K.)
S.Orkney Is (U.K.)

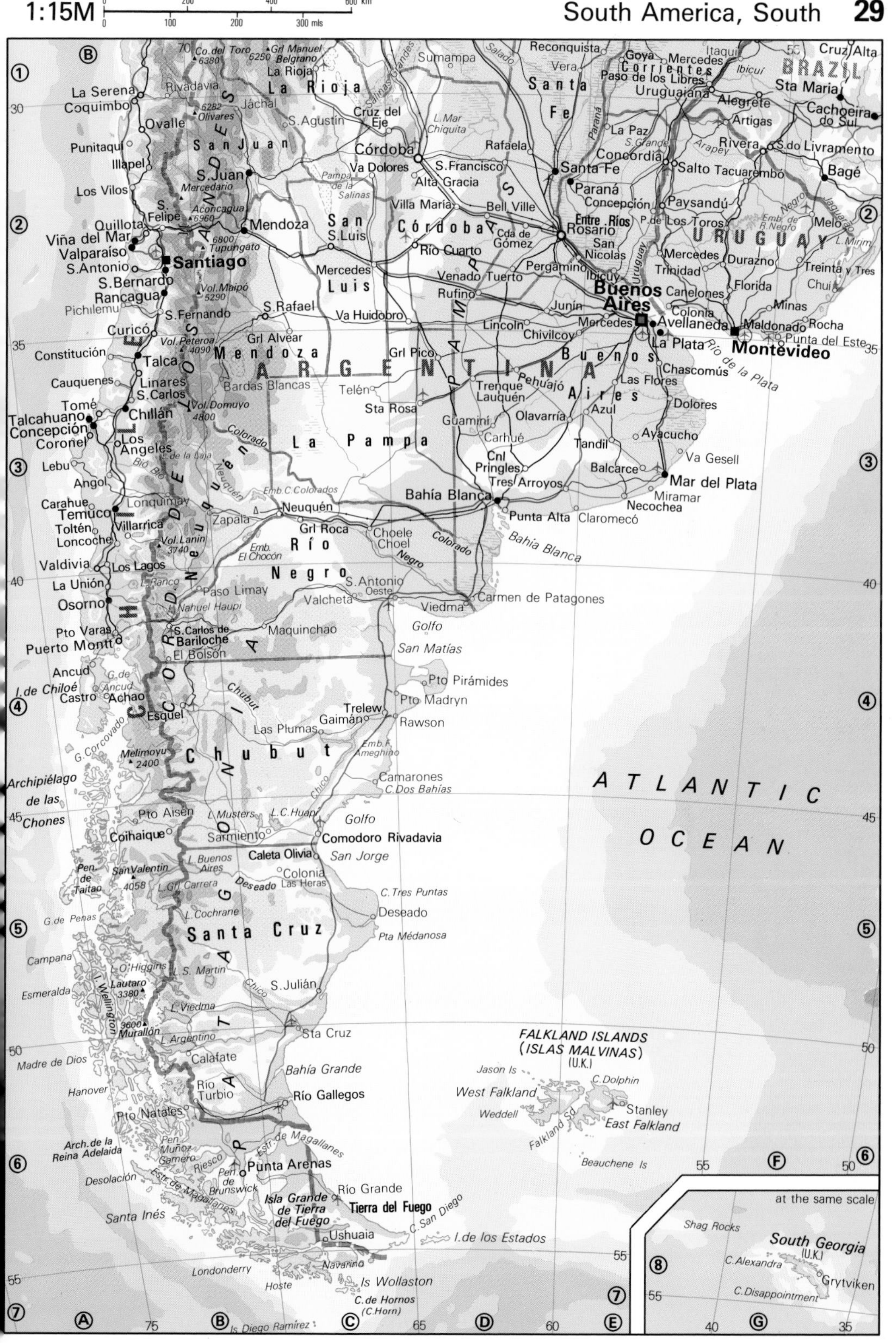

200 400 600 km
100 200 300 mils

ATLANTIC

OCEAN

FALKLAND ISLANDS
(ISLAS MALVINAS)
(U.K.)

at the same scale

South Georgia
(U.K.)

1:15M

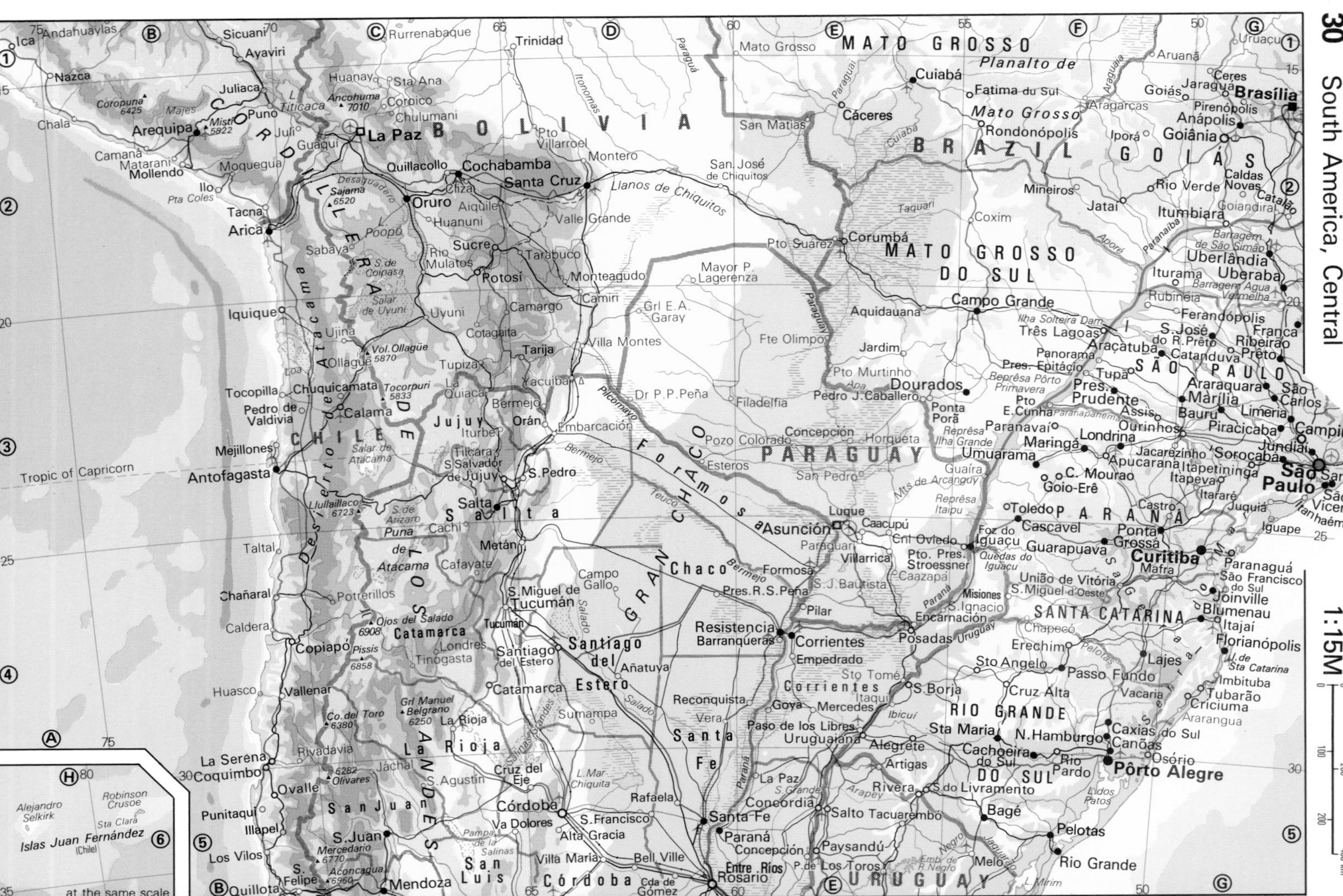
0 200 400 km
0 100 200
MATO GROSSO
Planalto de Mato Grosso
GOIÁS
BRAZIL
MATO GROSSO DO SUL
SÃO PAULO
PARANÁ
SANTA CATARINA
RIO GRANDE DO SUL
PARAGUAY
URUGUAY
BOLIVIA
CHILE
Santa Fe
Córdoba
Santiago del Estero
Corrientes
Salta
Jujuy
Catamarca
La Rioja
San Juan
San Luis
Entre Ríos
Misiones
Chaco
GRAN CHACO
Formosa
CORDILLERA
ANDES
Desierto de Atacama
Llanos de Chiquitos
Brasília
Goiânia
Anápolis
Uberlândia
Uberaba
Campinas
São Paulo
Santos
São Vicente
Ribeirão Prêto
Bauru
Londrina
Maringá
Curitiba
Ponta Grossa
Cascavel
Florianópolis
Blumenau
Joinville
Pôrto Alegre
Pelotas
Rio Grande
Sta Maria
Passo Fundo
Caxias do Sul
Cuiabá
Cáceres
Corumbá
Campo Grande
Dourados
Três Lagoas
Asunción
Concepción
Encarnación
Posadas
Foz do Iguaçu
Resistencia
Corrientes
Rosario
Paraná
Santa Fe
Córdoba
Tucumán
Santiago del Estero
Salta
S.Salvador de Jujuy
Mendoza
S.Juan
La Rioja
Catamarca
Uruguaiana
Paysandú
Salto
Rivera
La Paz
Oruro
Cochabamba
Santa Cruz
Sucre
Potosí
Tarija
Trinidad
Arica
Iquique
Antofagasta
Calama
Copiapó
La Serena
Coquimbo
Arequipa
Tacna
Puno
Tropic of Capricorn
Islas Juan Fernández (Chile)
Robinson Crusoe
Alejandro Selkirk
at the same scale

1:15M

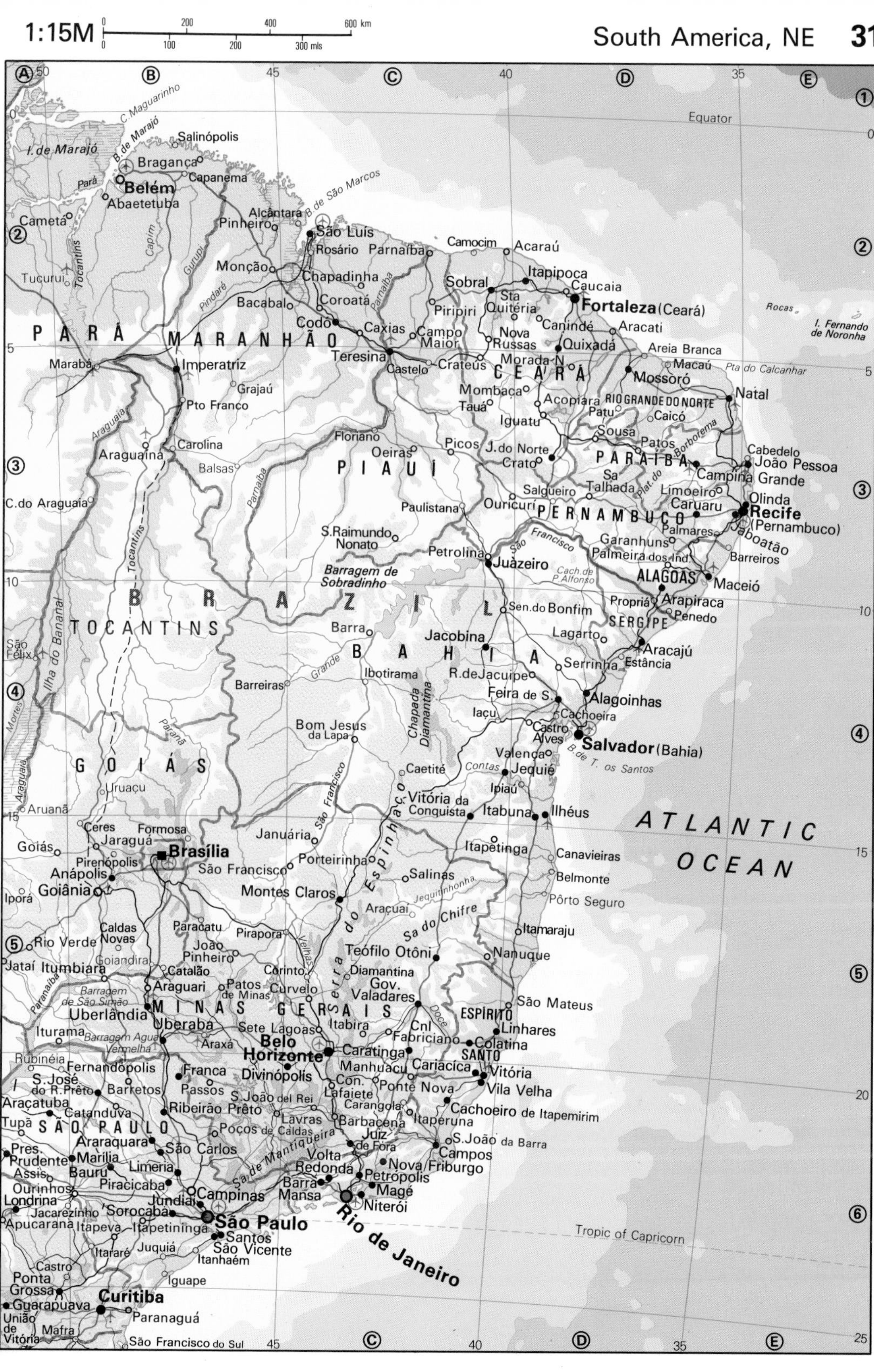

PARÁ

MARANHÃO

CEARÁ

RIO GRANDE DO NORTE

PIAUÍ

PARAÍBA

PERNAMBUCO

ALAGOAS

TOCANTINS

BAHIA

SERGIPE

GOIÁS

Salvador (Bahia)

ATLANTIC

OCEAN

MINAS GERAIS

ESPÍRITO SANTO

SÃO PAULO

Rio de Janeiro

Tropic of Capricorn

Belém
Abaetetuba
Cametá
Tucuruí
Marabá
Imperatriz
Pto Franco
Grajaú
Carolina
Araguaína
Balsas
C.do Araguaiá
São Luís
Rosário
Parnaíba
Alcântara
Pinheiro
Monção
Chapadinha
Bacabal
Coroatá
Codó
Caxias
Teresina
Castelo
Crateús
Floriano
Oeiras
Picos
J. do Norte
Crato
Sobral
Camocim
Acaraú
Itapipoca
Caucaia
Fortaleza (Ceará)
Sta Quitéria
Piripiri
Nova Russas
Campo Maior
Morada-N
Canindé
Aracati
Quixadá
Areia Branca
Mossoró
Macau
Natal
Acopiara
Patu
Caicó
Mombaca
Tauá
Iguatu
S.Raimundo Nonato
Paulistana
Ouricurí
Salgueiro
Sousa
Patos
Cabedelo
João Pessoa
Campina Grande
Olinda
Recife (Pernambuco)
Caruaru
Palmares
Garanhuns
Petrolina
Juàzeiro
Maceió
Arapiraca
Penedo
Propriá
Aracajú
Estância
Jacobina
Lagarto
Serrinha
Feira de S.
Alagoinhas
Cachoeira
Castro Alves
Ibotirama
Iaçu
Ilhéus
Itabuna
Jequié
Ipiaú
Vitória da Conquista
Caetité
Januária
Porteirinha
Salinas
Montes Claros
Canavieiras
Belmonte
Pôrto Seguro
Itamaraju
Nanuque
São Mateus
Teófilo Otôni
Diamantina
Gov. Valadares
Linhares
Colatina
Vitória
Vila Velha
Cachoeiro de Itapemirim
Belo Horizonte
Divinópolis
Barbacena
Juiz de Fora
Campos
Nova Friburgo
Petrópolis
Niterói
São Paulo
Santos
Curitiba

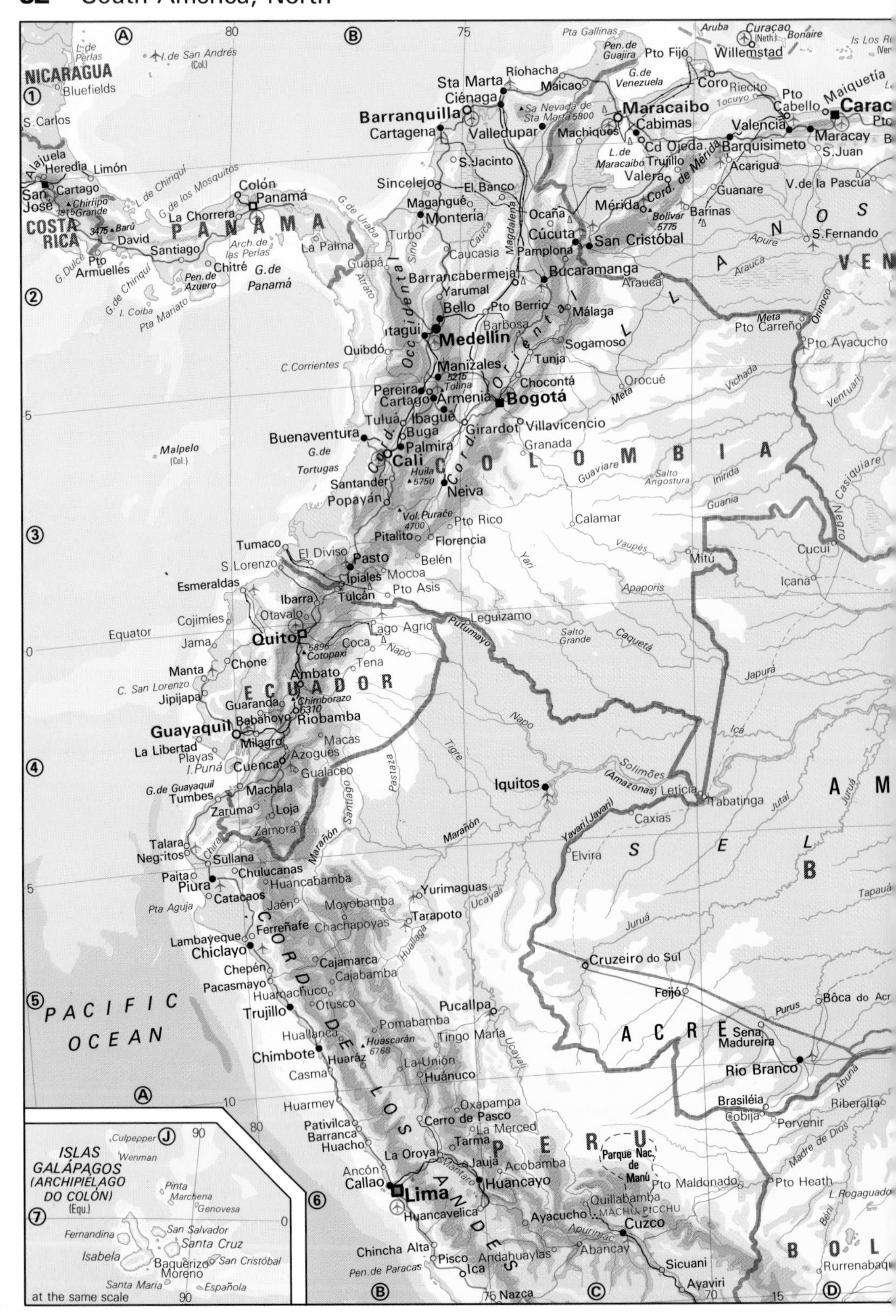

A de Perlas
I. de San Andrés (Col.)
NICARAGUA
① Bluefields
S.Carlos

Pta Gallinas
Aruba Curaçao
(Neth) Bonaire
Willemstad
Is Los R
Pen. de Guajira
Sta Marta Riohacha
Ciénaga Maicao
G. de Venezuela
Pto Fijo
Coro
Riecito
Pto Cabello
Maiquetía
CARAC
Barranquilla
Cartagena Valledupar
Sa Nevada de Sta Marta 5800
Maracaibo Cabimas
Valencia Barquisimeto Maracay S. Juan
Carac
S.Jacinto
Machiques
L. de Maracaibo
Cd Ojeda
Trujillo
Acarigua
V. de la Pascua
Alajuela Heredia Limón
Cartago 3475 Grande
San José 3475 Barú David
COSTA RICA
Santiago
Armuelles
G. Dulce
L. de Chiriquí
G. de los Mosquitos
Colón
Panamá
La Chorrera
PANAMA
Turbo
Sincelejo
Magangué Monteria
El Banco
Valera Mérida
Cúcuta
Ocaña
Bolívar 5775
Barinas
Guanare
S. Fernando
VEN
Pamplona
San Cristóbal
Arauca
Apure
Orinoco
Pto Carreño
Pta Mariato
Arch. de las Perlas
Pen. de Azuero
G. de Panamá
La Palma
Guapá
Sinú
Caucasia
Barrancabermeja
Yarumal
Bucaramanga
Málaga
Barbosa
Sogamoso
LLANOS
Orocué
Vichada
Pto Ayacucho
I. Coiba
Pta Mariato
Quibdó
C. Corrientes
Itagui
Bello
Pto Berrio
Medellin
Manizales
5215
Tunja
Chocontá
Meta
Guaviare
Inírida
Guania
Casiquiare
Negro
Malpelo (Col.)
G. de Tortugas
Buenaventura
Pereira
Cartago
Armenia
Tuluá
Ibagué
Buga
Palmira
Cali
Santander
Popayán
Huila 5750
Neiva
Tolima 5215
Bogotá
Girardot
Villavicencio
Granada
Salto Angostura
Calamar
COLOMBIA
Cucui
Mitú
Icana
Vol. Puracé 4700
Pitalito
Pto Rico
Florencia
Belén
Yari
Vaupés
Apaporis
Icana
PACIFIC OCEAN
Tumaco
El Divisio
Pasto
Ipiales Mocoa
Pto Asis
Putumayo
Leguizamo
Caquetá
Japurá
S.Lorenzo
Esmeraldas
Ibarra
Tulcán
Cojimíes
Otavalo
Equator
Jama
Quito
Coca
Napo
Lago Agrio
Salto Grande
Iça
Manta
Chone
Cotopaxi 5896
Ambato
Tena
C. San Lorenzo
Jipijapa
ECUADOR
Chimborazo 6310
Riobamba
Macas
Napo
Solimões (Amazonas)
Leticia
Tabatinga
AM
Guayaquil
Bebahoyo
Milagro
Azoguez
Gualaceo
Pastaza
Tigre
Iquitos
Caxias
B
La Libertad
Playas
I. Puná
Cuenca
Santiago
Yavari (Javari)
SEL
Guaranda
G.de Guayaquil
Tumbes
Machala
Zaruma
Loja
Zamora
Marañon
Elvira
Juruá
Talara
Negritos
Sullana
Paita
Piura
Chulucanas
Huancabamba
Yurimaguas
Moyobamba
Tarapoto
Ucayali
Huallaga
Juruá
Tapauá
B
Pta Aguja
Catacaos
Jaén
Chachapoyas
Cruzeiro do Sul
ACRE
Lambayeque
Ferreñafe
Chiclayo
Cajamarca
Cajabamba
Feijó
Purus
Bôca do Acr
Chepén
Pacasmayo
Huamachuco
Cajabamba
Pucallpa
Sena Madureira
Rio Branco
Abunã
⑤ PACIFIC OCEAN
Trujillo
Otusco
Pomabamba
Huascarán 6768
Tingo María
ACRE
Brasiléia
Cobija
Riberalta
Chimbote
Huaraz
Casma
La Unión
Huánuco
Huallanca
Rio Branco
Huarmey
Oxapampa
Cerro de Pasco
La Merced
PERU
Brasiléia
Cobija
Porvenir
Madre de Dios
Pativilca
Barranca
Huacho
Tarma
Jauja
Parque Nac. de Manú
Pto Maldonado
Pto Heath
Beni
L. Rogaguado
Ancón
Callao
La Oroya
Huancayo
Acobamba
Quillabamba
MACHU PICCHU
Rurrenabaq
Lima
Huancavelica
Ayacucho
Cuzco
Abancay
Sicuani
BOL
Culpepper
Wenman
Pinta Marchena
Genovesa
Fernandina
Isabela
Santa Cruz
Baquerizo Moreno
San Salvador
San Cristóbal
Santa Maria
Española
Chincha Alta
Pisco
Ica
Pen. de Paracas
Andahuaylas
Nazca
Ayaviri

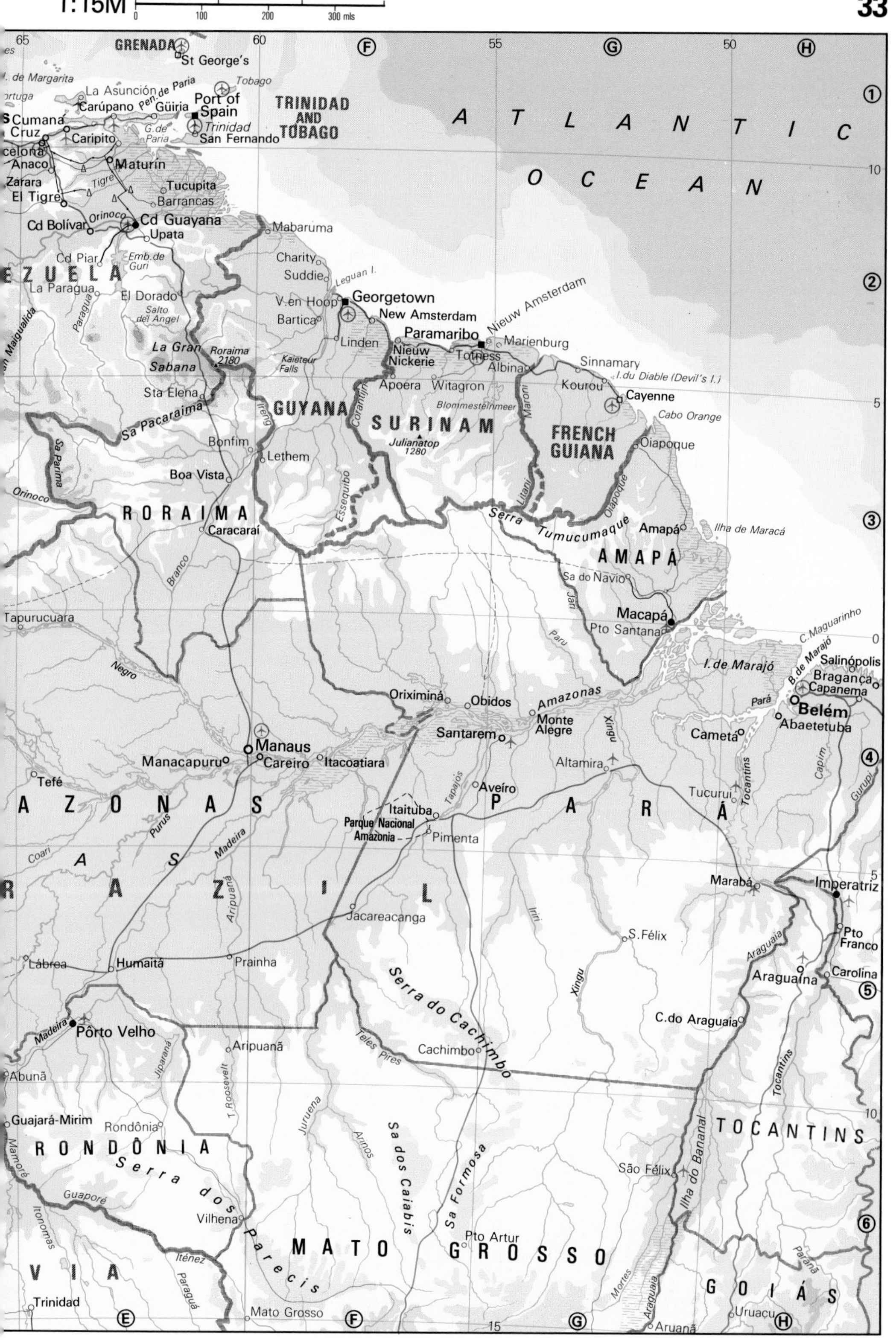

200 400 600 km

100 200 300 mls

ATLANTIC

65 60 Ⓕ 55 Ⓖ 50 Ⓗ

GRENADA ①

St George's

I. de Margarita Tobago

La Asunción Pen. de Paria

Carúpano Güiria Port of

S Cumaná Cruz Port of

Spain

Caripito G. de Paria TRINIDAD

Barcelona Anaco Trinidad AND

Zarara Maturín San Fernando TOBAGO

El Tigre Tucupita 10

Tigre Barrancas ② **O C E A N**

Cd Bolívar Orinoco Mabaruma

Cd Guayana

Cd Piar Emb. de Upata Charity

Guri Suddie Leguan I.

EZUELA El Dorado V-en Hoop Georgetown

La Paragua Salto Bartica New Amsterdam ②

Paraguá del Angel Linden Nieuw Nieuw Amsterdam

La Gran Roraima Kaieteur Nickerie Paramaribo

Sabana 2180 Falls Apoéra Witagron Totness Marienburg

Sta Elena Nieuw Nickerie Albina Sinnamary

Sa Pacaraima GUYANA SURINAM Blommestelnmeer I. du Diable (Devil's I.)

Orinoco Bonfim Lethem Julianatop FRENCH Kourou

Sa Parima 1280 GUIANA Cayenne

Boa Vista 5

Sa Parima Cabo Orange

Orinoco RORAIMA Serra Tumucumaque Oiapoque

Caracaraí Amapá ③

Tapurucuara Branco AMAPÁ Ilha de Maracá

Sa do Navio

Negro Jari C. Maguarinho

Paru Macapá 0

Pto Santana

Oriximiná I. de Marajó Salinópolis

Obidos Amazonas B. de Marajó Bragança

Monte Pará Capanema

Santarem Alegre Xingu Belém

Manacapuru Manaus Cametá Abaetetuba

Tefé Careiro Itacoatiara Altamira Tucuruí ④

AZONAS Tapajós Aveíro PARÁ Tocantins

Coari Purus Itaituba Marabá 5

Lábrea Madeira Parque Nacional Pimenta Imperatriz

Humaitá Amazônia BRAZIL Pto

Prainha Jacareacanga Franco

Araguaia Araguaína Carolina ⑤

Pôrto Velho S. Félix Araguaína

Aripuanã Serra do Cachimbo C. do Araguaía

Abunã Madeira Teles Pires Cachimbo 10

Guajará-Mirim Rondônia Ilha do Bananal TOCANTINS

RONDÔNIA Serra dos Parecis São Félix

Vilhena Sa dos Caiabis

VIA Guaporé MATO GROSSO Pto Artur ⑥

Trinidad Mato Grosso Uruaçu

Iténez Paraguá GOIÁS

Ⓔ Ⓕ 15 Ⓖ Aruanã Ⓗ

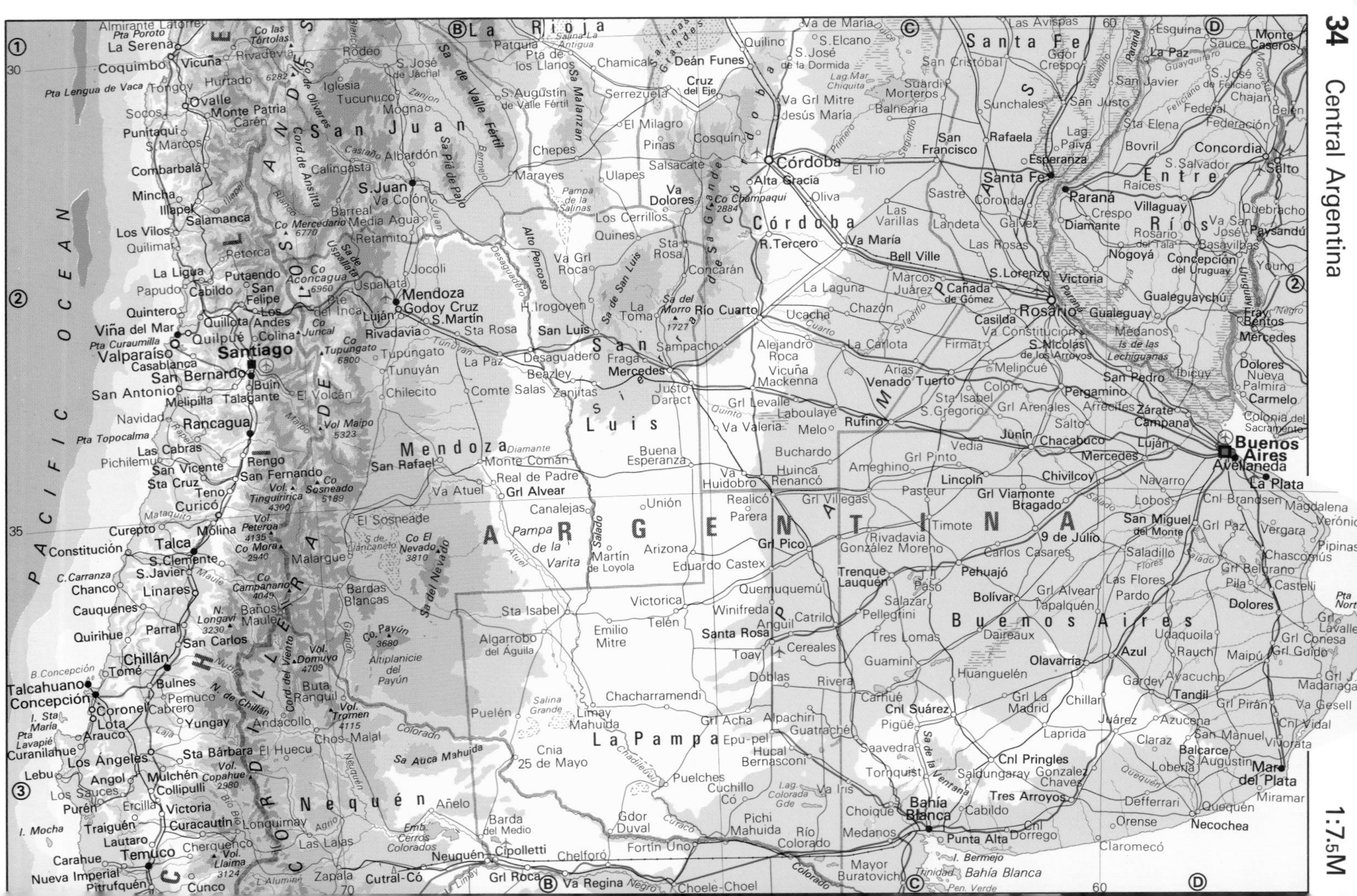
PACIFIC OCEAN
ARGENTINA
CORDILLERA DE LOS ANDES
CHILE
La Rioja
San Juan
Córdoba
Santa Fe
Entre Ríos
San Luis
Mendoza
La Pampa
Buenos Aires
Neuquén
Buenos Aires
Avellaneda
La Plata
Mar del Plata
Monte Caseros
Concordia
Salto
Paysandú
Colonia del Sacramento
Mercedes
Fray Bentos
Gualeguaychú
Concepción del Uruguay
Rosario
Santa Fe
Paraná
Córdoba
Alta Gracia
Va María
Río Cuarto
San Luis
Mendoza
Godoy Cruz
S.Juan
San Rafael
Santiago
Valparaíso
Viña del Mar
Rancagua
Talca
Chillán
Concepción
Talcahuano
Temuco
La Serena
Coquimbo
Santa Rosa
Bahía Blanca
Neuquén
Cipolletti
Tandil
Azul
Olavarría
Necochea
Tres Arroyos
Junín
Pergamino
Rufino
Venado Tuerto
Zárate
Campana
Luján
Chivilcoy
Rafaela
San Francisco
Co Aconcagua 6960
Co Tupungato 6800
Co Mercedario 6770
Vol. Maipo 5323
Vol. Sosneado 5189
Co Champaqui 2884
Co Payún 3680
Vol. Domuyo 4709
Vol. Tromen 4115
Vol. Llaima 3124
Sa de Valle Fértil
Sa de San Luis
Sa de la Ventana
Sa del Nevado
Sa Auca Mahuida
Alto Pencoso
Cord. de Ansilta
Cord. del Viento
Pampa de la Varita
Altiplanicie del Payún
Pta Lengua de Vaca
Pta Topocalma
Pta Curaumilla
I. Mocha
B. Concepción
Bahía Blanca
1:7.5M

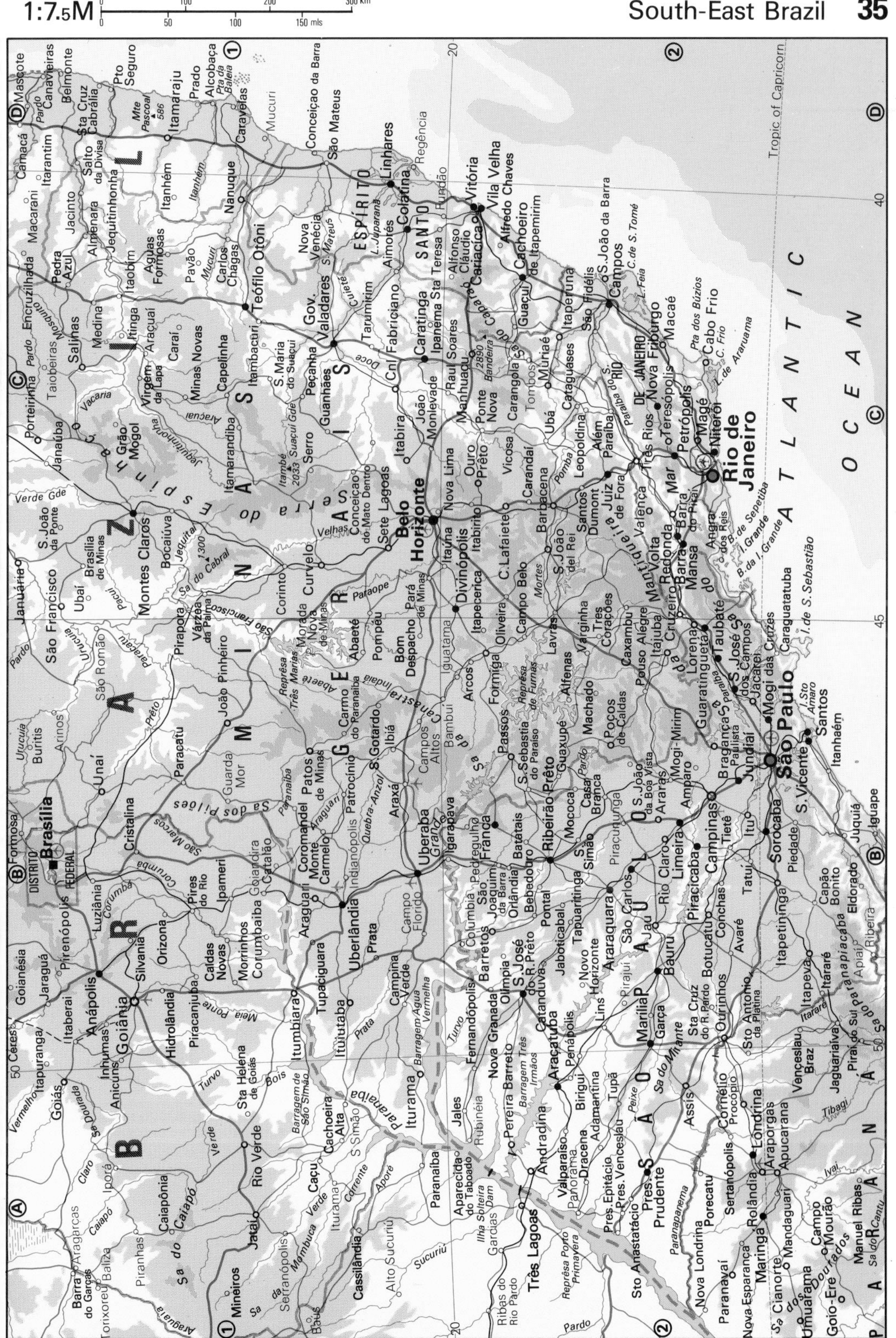
B R A Z I L
M I N A S G E R A I S
ESPÍRITO SANTO
RIO DE JANEIRO
S Ã O P A U L O
P A R A N Á
DISTRITO FEDERAL
A T L A N T I C O C E A N
Tropic of Capricorn
Brasília
Goiânia
Anápolis
Belo Horizonte
Rio de Janeiro
São Paulo
Vitória
Vila Velha
Campos
Niterói
Petrópolis
Juiz de Fora
Santos
Campinas
Ribeirão Prêto
Uberlândia
Uberaba
Montes Claros
Gov. Valadares
Teófilo Otôni
Londrina
Maringá
Bauru
Marília
Pres. Prudente
Sorocaba
Jundiaí
Taubaté
Volta Redonda
Serra do Espinhaço
Serra da Mantiqueira
Serra da Canastra
Represa Três Marias
Represa de Furnas
Paranaíba
São Francisco
Grande
Paraná
Tietê
Paranapanema
Doce
Jequitinhonha
C. Frio
Cabo Frio
I. Grande
I. de S. Sebastião
Itambé 2033
Bandeira 2890

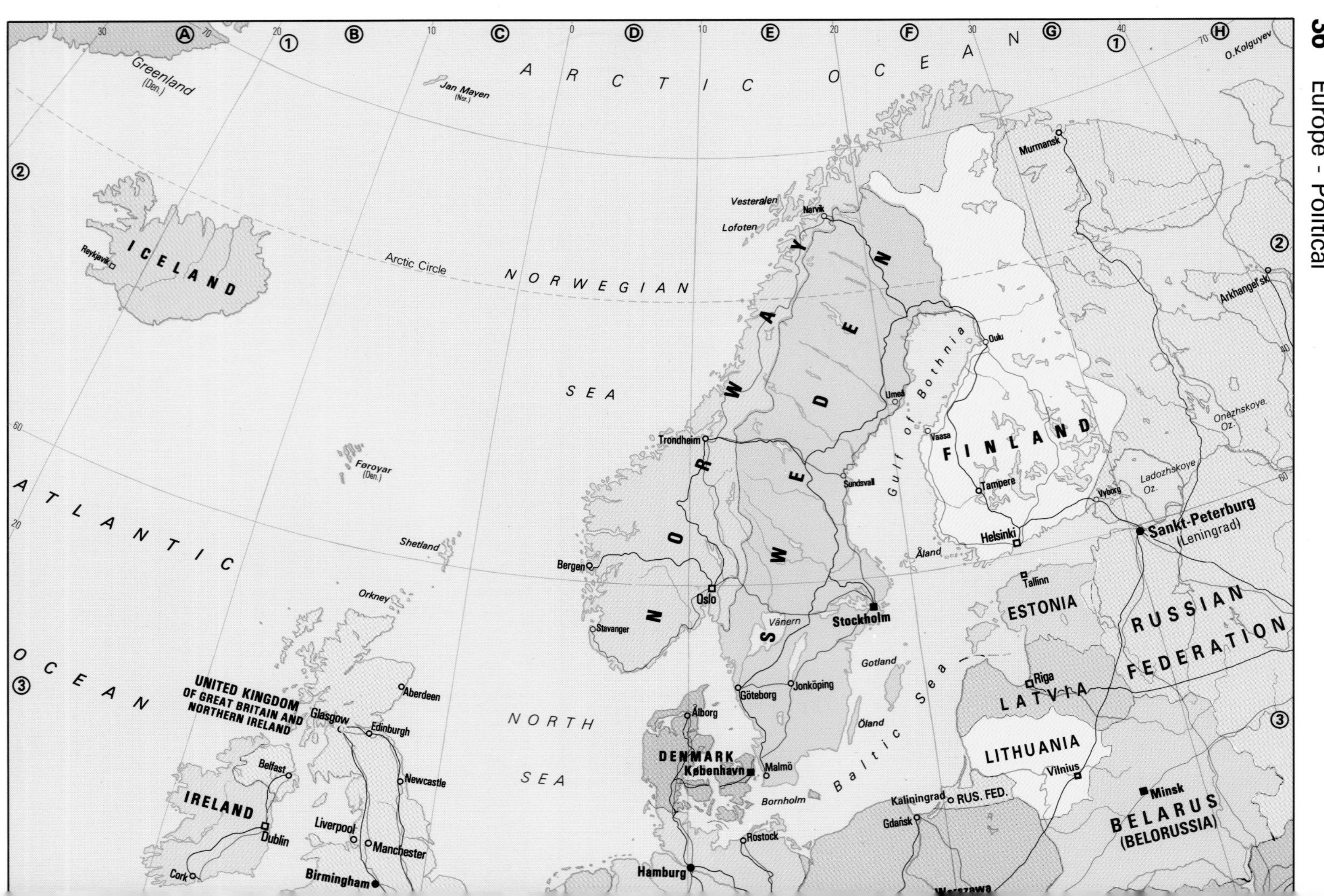
ARCTIC OCEAN
NORWEGIAN SEA
NORTH SEA
ATLANTIC OCEAN
Gulf of Bothnia
Baltic Sea
Arctic Circle
Greenland (Den.)
Jan Mayen (Nor.)
O.Kolguyev
ICELAND
Reykjavík
Føroyar (Den.)
Shetland
Orkney
UNITED KINGDOM OF GREAT BRITAIN AND NORTHERN IRELAND
Aberdeen
Glasgow
Edinburgh
Newcastle
Liverpool
Manchester
Birmingham
IRELAND
Belfast
Dublin
Cork
NORWAY
Vesterålen
Lofoten
Narvik
Trondheim
Bergen
Oslo
Stavanger
SWEDEN
Umeå
Sundsvall
Stockholm
Vänern
Gotland
Öland
Göteborg
Jönköping
Malmö
Bornholm
DENMARK
København
Ålborg
Hamburg
Rostock
Gdańsk
Kaliningrad
RUS. FED.
Warszawa
FINLAND
Oulu
Vaasa
Tampere
Helsinki
Åland
ESTONIA
Tallinn
LATVIA
Riga
LITHUANIA
Vilnius
BELARUS (BELORUSSIA)
Minsk
RUSSIAN FEDERATION
Murmansk
Arkhangel'sk
Onezhskoye Oz.
Ladozhskoye Oz.
Vyborg
Sankt-Peterburg (Leningrad)

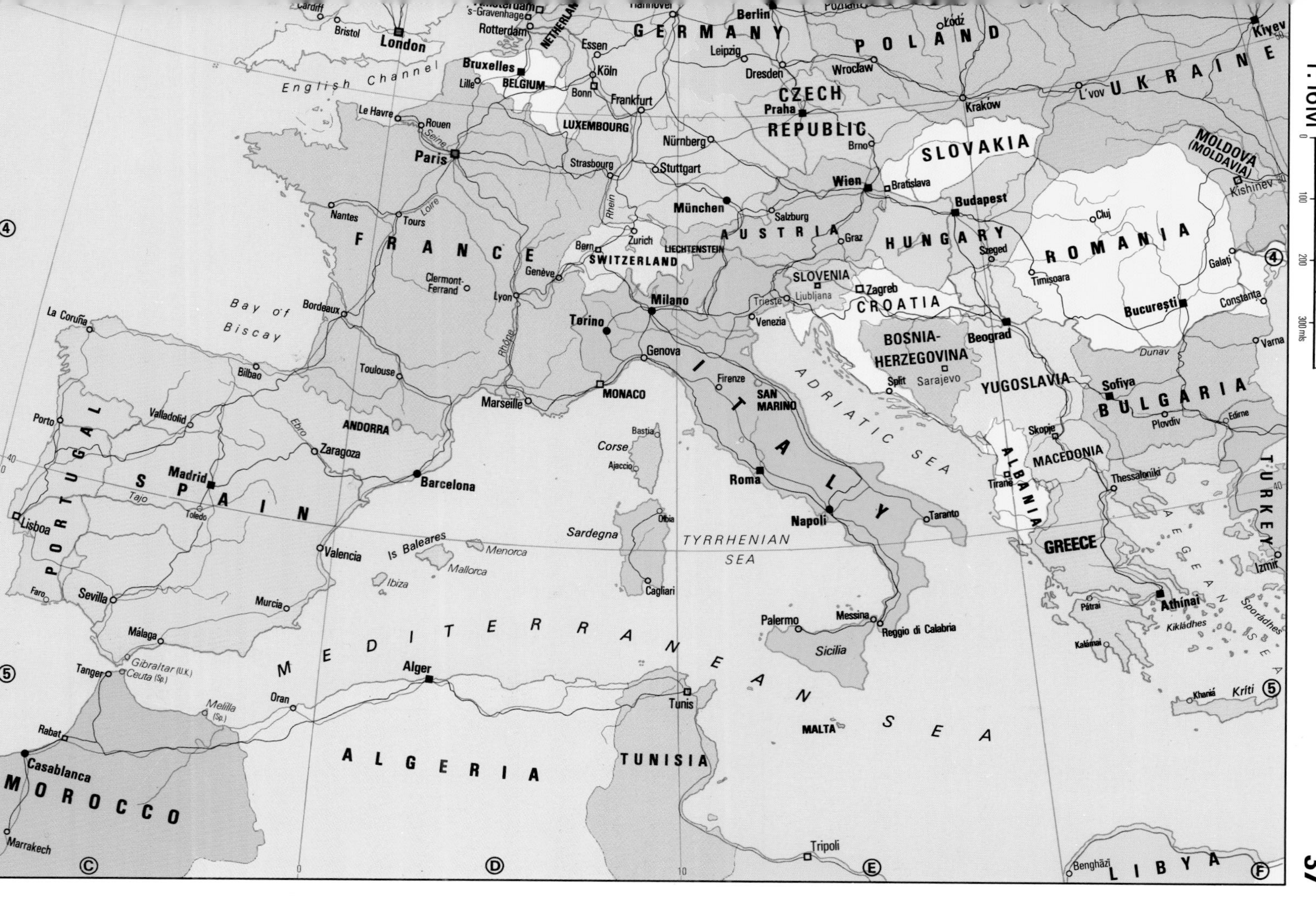

1:16M

0   200   400   600km

0   100   200   300 mls

Cardiff
Bristol
London
's-Gravenhage
Rotterdam
NETHERLANDS
Bruxelles
BELGIUM
Lille
English Channel
Le Havre
Rouen
Seine
Paris
Nantes
Tours
Loire
FRANCE
Clermont-Ferrand
Lyon
Rhône
Genève
Bordeaux
Bay of Biscay
Toulouse
Marseille
MONACO
ANDORRA
GERMANY
Berlin
Leipzig
Dresden
Essen
Köln
Bonn
Frankfurt
LUXEMBOURG
Nürnberg
Strasbourg
Stuttgart
Rhein
München
Zurich
Bern
SWITZERLAND
LIECHTENSTEIN
AUSTRIA
Salzburg
Graz
Wien
Bratislava
POLAND
Łódź
Wrocław
Kraków
CZECH REPUBLIC
Praha
Brno
L'vov
UKRAINE
Kiyev
SLOVAKIA
MOLDOVA (MOLDAVIA)
Kishinev
Budapest
HUNGARY
Szeged
Cluj
ROMANIA
Timișoara
Galați
Constanța
București
Varna
Dunav
SLOVENIA
Ljubljana
Zagreb
CROATIA
Trieste
Venezia
BOSNIA-HERZEGOVINA
Sarajevo
Split
Beograd
YUGOSLAVIA
Sofiya
BULGARIA
Plovdiv
Edirne
Skopje
MACEDONIA
ALBANIA
Tiranë
Thessaloníki
GREECE
Athínai
Pátrai
Kalámai
AEGEAN SEA
Sporádhes
Kikládhes
Khaniá
Kríti
TURKEY
Izmir
ITALY
Milano
Torino
Genova
Firenze
SAN MARINO
Roma
Napoli
Taranto
Reggio di Calabria
Messina
Palermo
Sicilia
ADRIATIC SEA
TYRRHENIAN SEA
Corse
Bastia
Ajaccio
Sardegna
Olbia
Cagliari
La Coruña
Porto
PORTUGAL
Lisboa
Faro
Bilbao
Valladolid
Ebro
Zaragoza
Madrid
SPAIN
Tajo
Toledo
Barcelona
Valencia
Is Baleares
Menorca
Mallorca
Ibiza
Sevilla
Murcia
Málaga
Gibraltar (U.K.)
Ceuta (Sp.)
Tanger
Melilla (Sp.)
MEDITERRANEAN SEA
MALTA
Alger
Oran
Tunis
Rabat
Casablanca
MOROCCO
Marrakech
ALGERIA
TUNISIA
Tripoli
Benghāzī
LIBYA
C
D
E
F
5

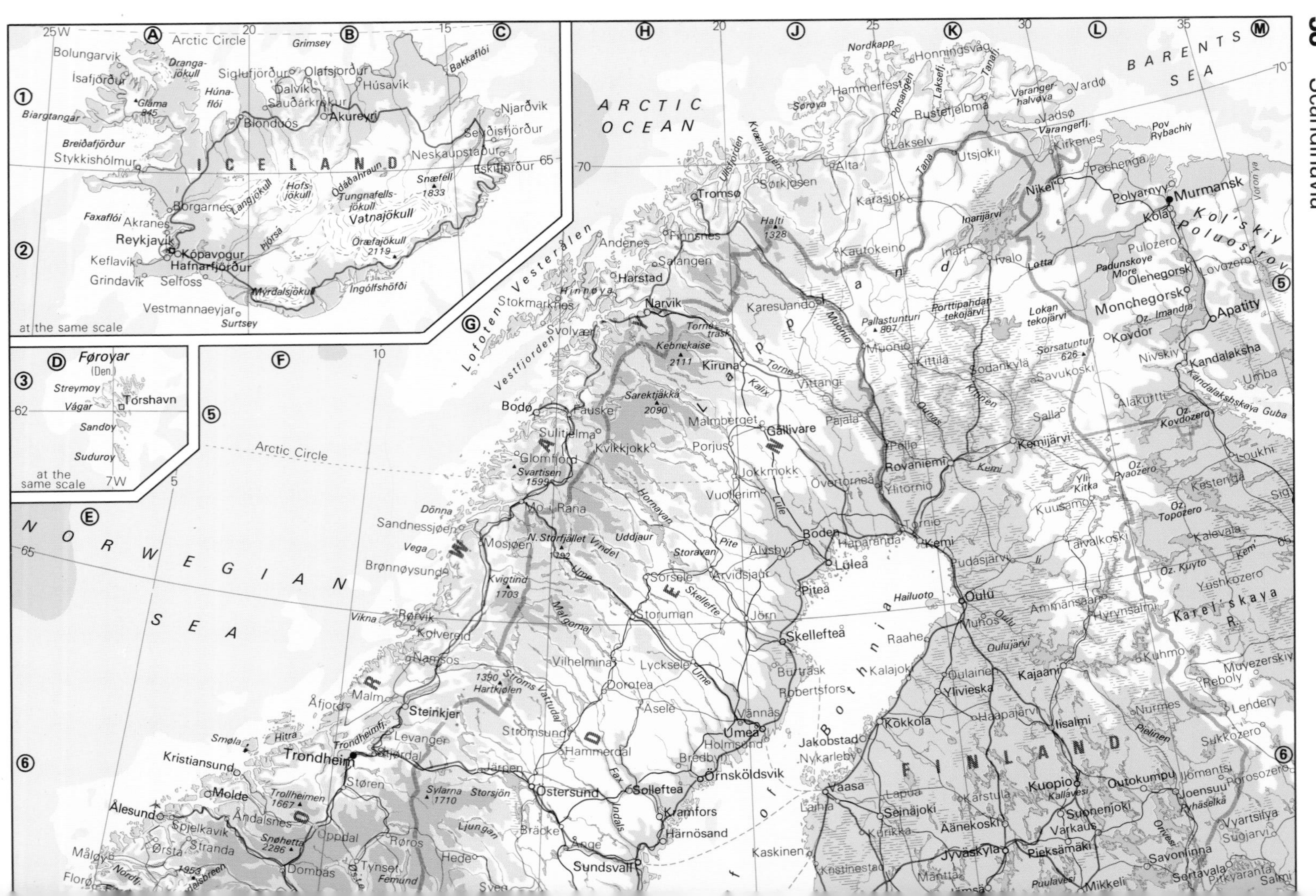
ARCTIC OCEAN
BARENTS SEA
NORWEGIAN SEA
ICELAND
FINLAND
Lapland
Gulf of Bothnia
Lofoten
Vesterålen
Vestfjorden
Kol'skiy Poluostrov
Karel'skaya R.
Arctic Circle
Føroyar (Den.)
Tórshavn
Streymoy
Vágar
Sandoy
Suduroy
at the same scale
Reykjavík
Akureyri
Vatnajökull
Hofsjökull
Mýrdalsjökull
Langjökull
Surtsey
Vestmannaeyjar
Kópavogur
Hafnarfjörður
Keflavík
Akranes
Borgarnes
Ísafjörður
Bolungarvík
Húsavík
Siglufjörður
Ólafsfjörður
Dalvík
Blönduós
Seyðisfjörður
Neskaupstaður
Eskifjörður
Grindavík
Selfoss
Stykkishólmur
Nordkapp
Hammerfest
Honningsvåg
Tromsø
Narvik
Harstad
Bodø
Mo i Rana
Mosjøen
Trondheim
Steinkjer
Levanger
Kristiansund
Molde
Ålesund
Åndalsnes
Dombås
Oppdal
Røros
Tynset
Støren
Kirkenes
Vardø
Vadsø
Alta
Lakselv
Karasjok
Kautokeino
Murmansk
Polyarnyy
Nikel'
Pechenga
Kola
Apatity
Kandalaksha
Monchegorsk
Olenegorsk
Kovdor
Kiruna
Gällivare
Luleå
Boden
Piteå
Skellefteå
Umeå
Örnsköldsvik
Kramfors
Härnösand
Sundsvall
Östersund
Sollefteå
Vilhelmina
Storuman
Lycksele
Jokkmokk
Haparanda
Tornio
Kemi
Rovaniemi
Oulu
Kemijärvi
Sodankylä
Ivalo
Inari
Utsjoki
Kajaani
Iisalmi
Kuopio
Joensuu
Jyväskylä
Kokkola
Vaasa
Seinäjoki
Varkaus
Savonlinna
Pieksämäki
Mikkeli
Outokumpu
Suonenjoki
Ylivieska
Raahe
Jakobstad
Kebnekaise 2111
Sarektjåkkå 2090
Halti 1328
Svartisen 1599
Snøhetta 2286
Sylarna 1710
Trollheimen 1667
Kvigtind 1703
Öræfajökull 2119
Snæfell 1833
Inarijärvi
Oulujärvi
Pielinen
Hailuoto
Hitra
Smøla
Vikna
Vega
Dønna
Torne
Kalix
Lule
Pite
Skellefte
Ume
Indals
Kemi
Oulu
Tana
Muonio
25W
20
15
10
5
25
30
35
70
65
62
7W

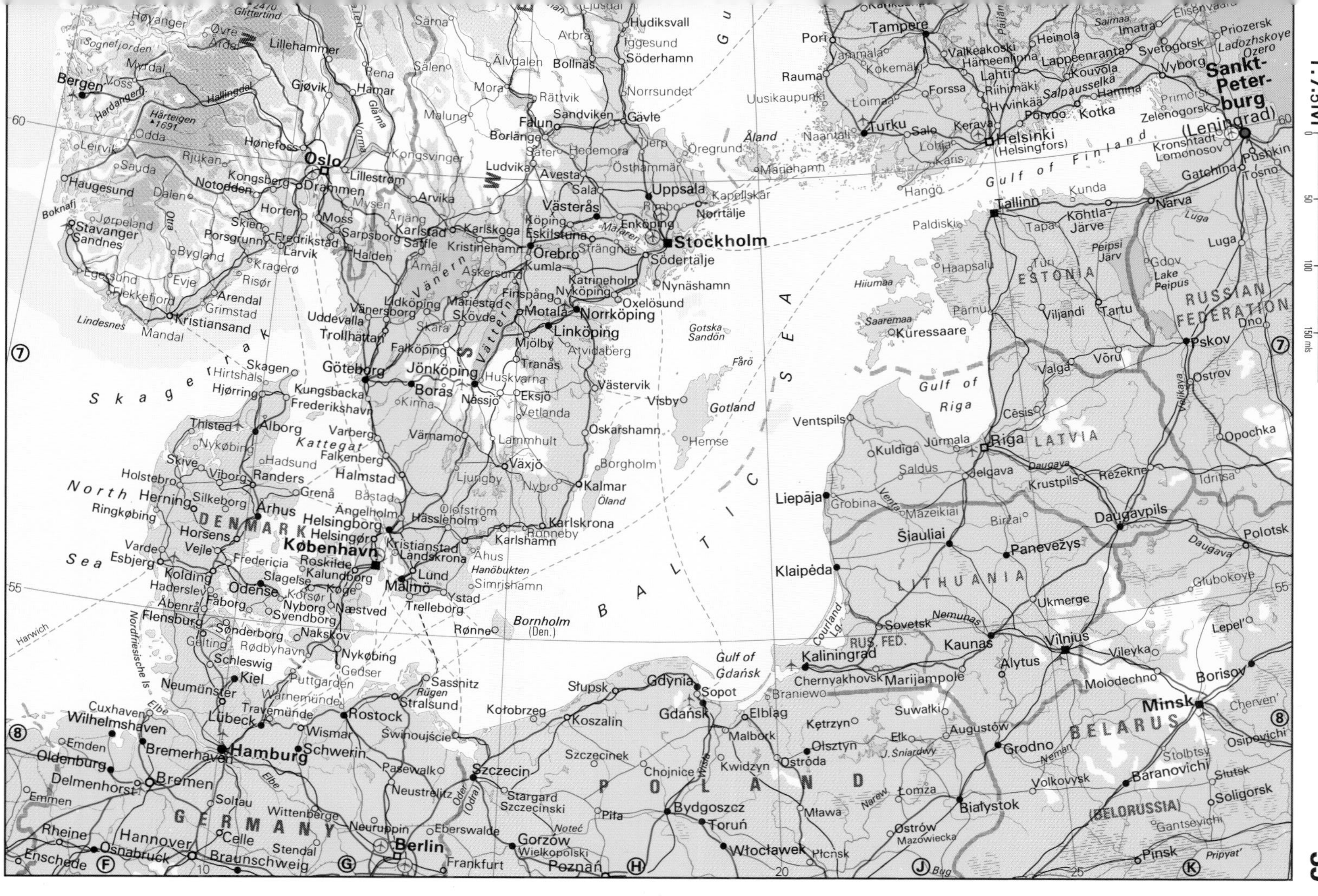
RUSSIAN FEDERATION
ESTONIA
LATVIA
LITHUANIA
BELARUS
(BELORUSSIA)
POLAND
GERMANY
DENMARK
Gulf of Finland
Gulf of Riga
Gulf of Gdańsk
BALTIC SEA
Skagerrak
Kattegat
North Sea
Sankt-Peterburg
(Leningrad)
Helsinki
(Helsingfors)
Tallinn
Riga
Vilnius
Minsk
Stockholm
Oslo
København
Berlin
Hamburg
Göteborg
Malmö
Gdańsk
Kaliningrad
Kaunas
Daugavpils
Pskov
Narva
Tartu
Tampere
Turku
Uppsala
Västerås
Örebro
Norrköping
Linköping
Jönköping
Borås
Bergen
Stavanger
Kristiansand
Ålborg
Århus
Odense
Kiel
Lübeck
Rostock
Szczecin
Bremen
Hannover
Gotland
Öland
Åland
Bornholm
(Den.)
Saaremaa
Hiiumaa
Lake Peipus
Vänern
Vättern
Mälaren
Rügen
Nordfriesische Is
RUS. FED.

1:5M

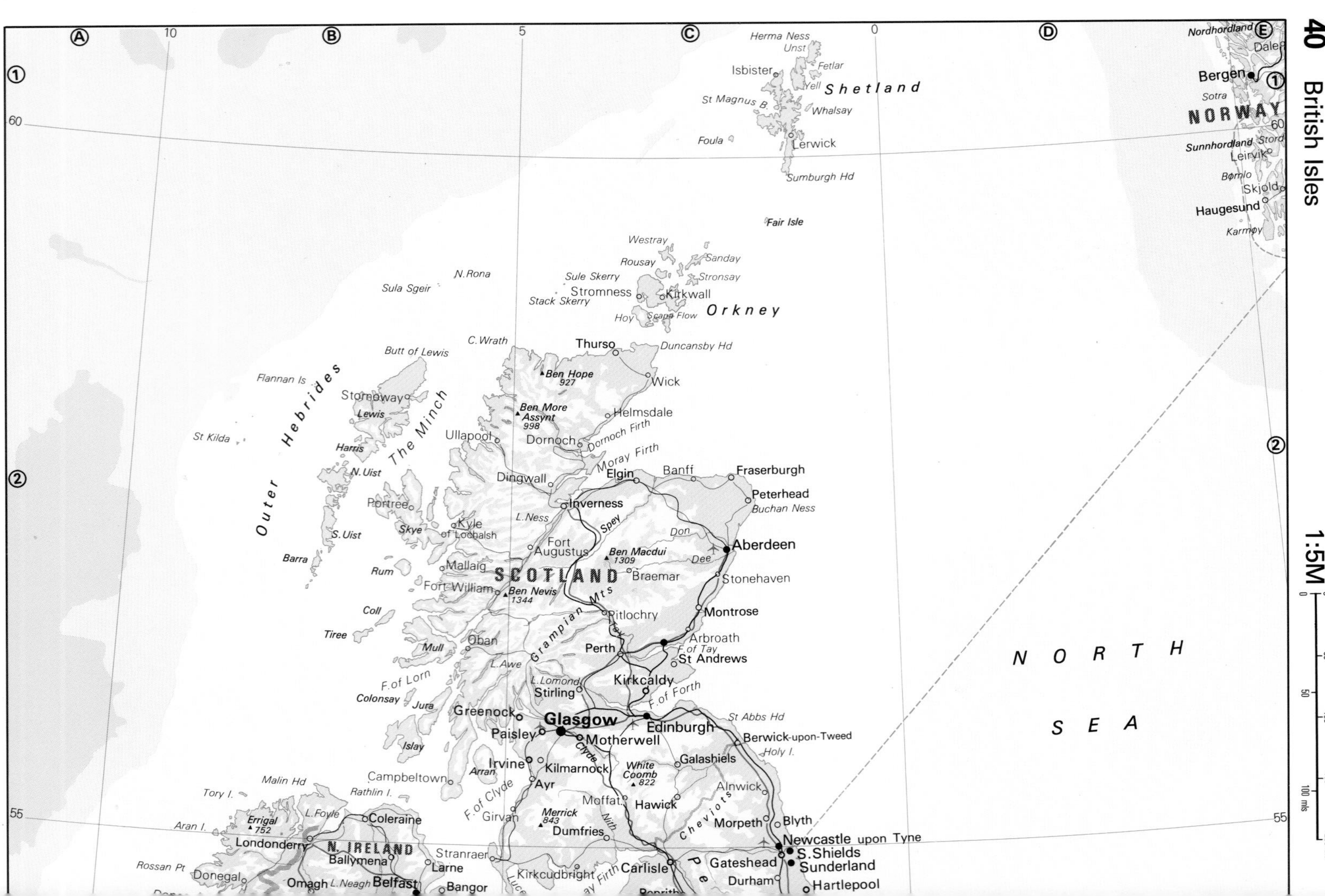

NORTH SEA

NORWAY

Bergen
Nordhordland
Dale
Sotra
Sunnhordland
Bømlo
Stord
Leirvik
Skjold
Haugesund
Karmøy

SHETLAND

Herma Ness
Unst
Fetlar
Yell
Whalsay
Isbister
St Magnus B.
Lerwick
Foula
Sumburgh Hd

Fair Isle

ORKNEY

Westray
Sanday
Rousay
Stronsay
Kirkwall
Hoy
Stromness
Scapa Flow
Sule Skerry
Stack Skerry
Duncansby Hd
N. Rona
C. Wrath
Wick
Thurso
Helmsdale
Ben Hope
927
Dornoch Firth
Moray Firth
Ben More
Assynt
998
Dingwall
Ullapool
Inverness
L. Ness
Fort
Augustus
Kyle
of Lochalsh
Mallaig
Fort William
Ben Nevis
1344

Sula Sgeir
Butt of Lewis
Stornoway
Lewis
Harris
N. Uist
The Minch
Flannan Is.
Outer Hebrides
S. Uist
Barra
St Kilda
Portree
Skye
Rum
Coll
Tiree
Mull
Jura
Colonsay
Islay

SCOTLAND
Grampian Mts
Elgin
Banff
Fraserburgh
Peterhead
Buchan Ness
Aberdeen
Stonehaven
Montrose
Ben Macdui
1309
Braemar
Dee
Don
Spey
Pitlochry
Perth
Arbroath
F. of Tay
St Andrews
Kirkcaldy
F. of Forth
Edinburgh
Stirling
L. Lomond
Clyde
Glasgow
Paisley
Motherwell
L. Awe
F. of Lorn
Oban
Greenock
Kilmarnock
Irvine
Ayr
Arran
Girvan
F. of Clyde
Campbeltown
Rathlin I.
Merrick
843
Dumfries
White
Coomb
822
Hawick
Moffat
Nith
Galashiels
Berwick-upon-Tweed
St Abbs Hd
Holy I.
Alnwick
Morpeth
Blyth
Newcastle upon Tyne
S. Shields
Sunderland
Gateshead
Hartlepool
Durham
Carlisle
Kirkcudbright Firth
Stranraer
Larne
Bangor
Luce
Solway Firth
Cheviot Hills
Pennines

N. IRELAND
Coleraine
Ballymena
Londonderry
L. Foyle
Malin Hd
Tory I.
Aran I.
Rossan Pt
Donegal
Erigal
752
Omagh
L. Neagh
Belfast

Banff
Duncansby Hd

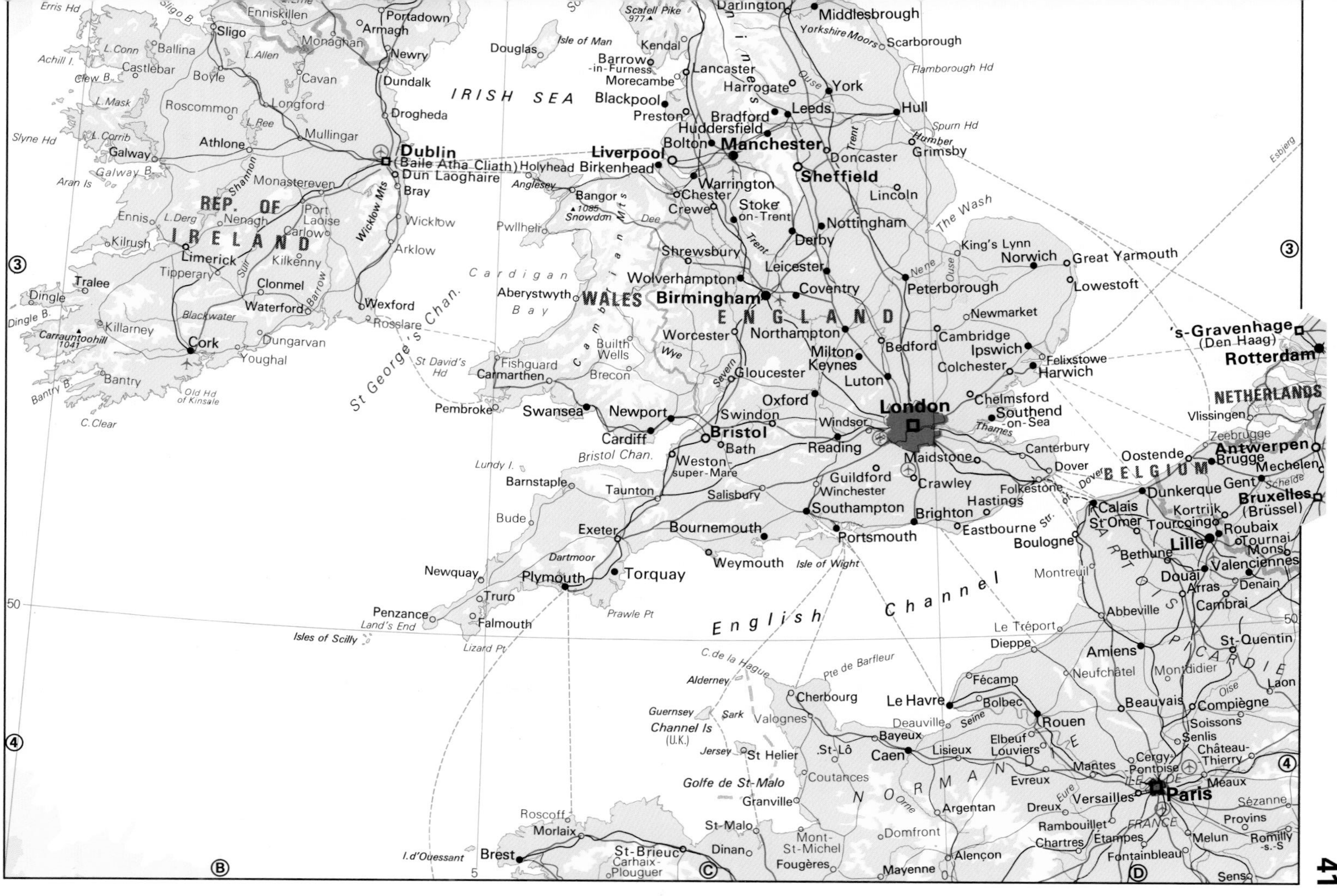
IRISH SEA
English Channel
REP. OF IRELAND
ENGLAND
WALES
BELGIUM
NETHERLANDS
NORMANDIE
PICARDIE
ARTOIS
ILE DE FRANCE
Cardigan Bay
Bristol Chan.
St George's Chan.
Golfe de St-Malo
Channel Is (U.K.)
Isles of Scilly
Isle of Man
Isle of Wight
Dublin (Baile Átha Cliath)
Dun Laoghaire
Bray
Wicklow
Arklow
Wexford
Rosslare
Drogheda
Dundalk
Newry
Armagh
Portadown
Monaghan
Cavan
Enniskillen
Sligo
Longford
Mullingar
Athlone
Roscommon
Boyle
Ballina
Castlebar
Galway
Ennis
Kilrush
Limerick
Nenagh
Tipperary
Clonmel
Kilkenny
Carlow
Port Laoise
Monasterevan
Waterford
Dungarvan
Youghal
Cork
Bantry
Killarney
Tralee
Dingle
Carrauntoohill 1041
Wicklow Mts
Liverpool
Birkenhead
Holyhead
Bangor
Snowdon 1085
Pwllheli
Aberystwyth
Fishguard
Carmarthen
Pembroke
Swansea
Cardiff
Newport
Brecon
Builth Wells
Douglas
Barrow-in-Furness
Morecambe
Blackpool
Preston
Kendal
Lancaster
Harrogate
Bradford
Huddersfield
Manchester
Bolton
Warrington
Chester
Crewe
Stoke-on-Trent
Shrewsbury
Wolverhampton
Birmingham
Worcester
Gloucester
Swindon
Bath
Bristol
Weston-super-Mare
Taunton
Barnstaple
Bude
Exeter
Torquay
Plymouth
Truro
Falmouth
Newquay
Penzance
Land's End
Lizard Pt
Dartmoor
Darlington
Middlesbrough
Scarborough
York
Leeds
Sheffield
Doncaster
Hull
Grimsby
Lincoln
Nottingham
Derby
Leicester
Coventry
Northampton
Milton Keynes
Luton
Bedford
Oxford
Reading
Windsor
Guildford
Winchester
Southampton
Portsmouth
Bournemouth
Weymouth
Salisbury
Brighton
Crawley
Hastings
Eastbourne
Maidstone
London
Peterborough
Cambridge
Newmarket
King's Lynn
Norwich
Great Yarmouth
Lowestoft
Ipswich
Felixstowe
Harwich
Colchester
Chelmsford
Southend-on-Sea
Canterbury
Dover
Folkestone
The Wash
's-Gravenhage (Den Haag)
Rotterdam
Vlissingen
Zeebrugge
Antwerpen
Brugge
Mechelen
Gent
Bruxelles (Brüssel)
Oostende
Dunkerque
Kortrijk
Roubaix
Tourcoing
Lille
Tournai
Mons
Valenciennes
Denain
Cambrai
Arras
Douai
Béthune
Calais
St Omer
Boulogne
Montreuil
Abbeville
Amiens
St-Quentin
Laon
Compiègne
Soissons
Beauvais
Senlis
Château-Thierry
Meaux
Paris
Cergy-Pontoise
Versailles
Rambouillet
Étampes
Fontainebleau
Melun
Provins
Sézanne
Romilly-s.-S
Sens
Chartres
Dreux
Évreux
Mantes
Louviers
Elbeuf
Rouen
Dieppe
Le Tréport
Neufchâtel
Fécamp
Bolbec
Le Havre
Deauville
Lisieux
Caen
Bayeux
Argentan
Alençon
Domfront
Mayenne
Fougères
Mont-St-Michel
Coutances
St-Lô
Cherbourg
Valognes
Granville
St-Malo
Dinan
St-Brieuc
Carhaix-Plouguer
Morlaix
Roscoff
Brest
I. d'Ouessant
Guernsey
Jersey
Sark
Alderney
St Helier
C. de la Hague

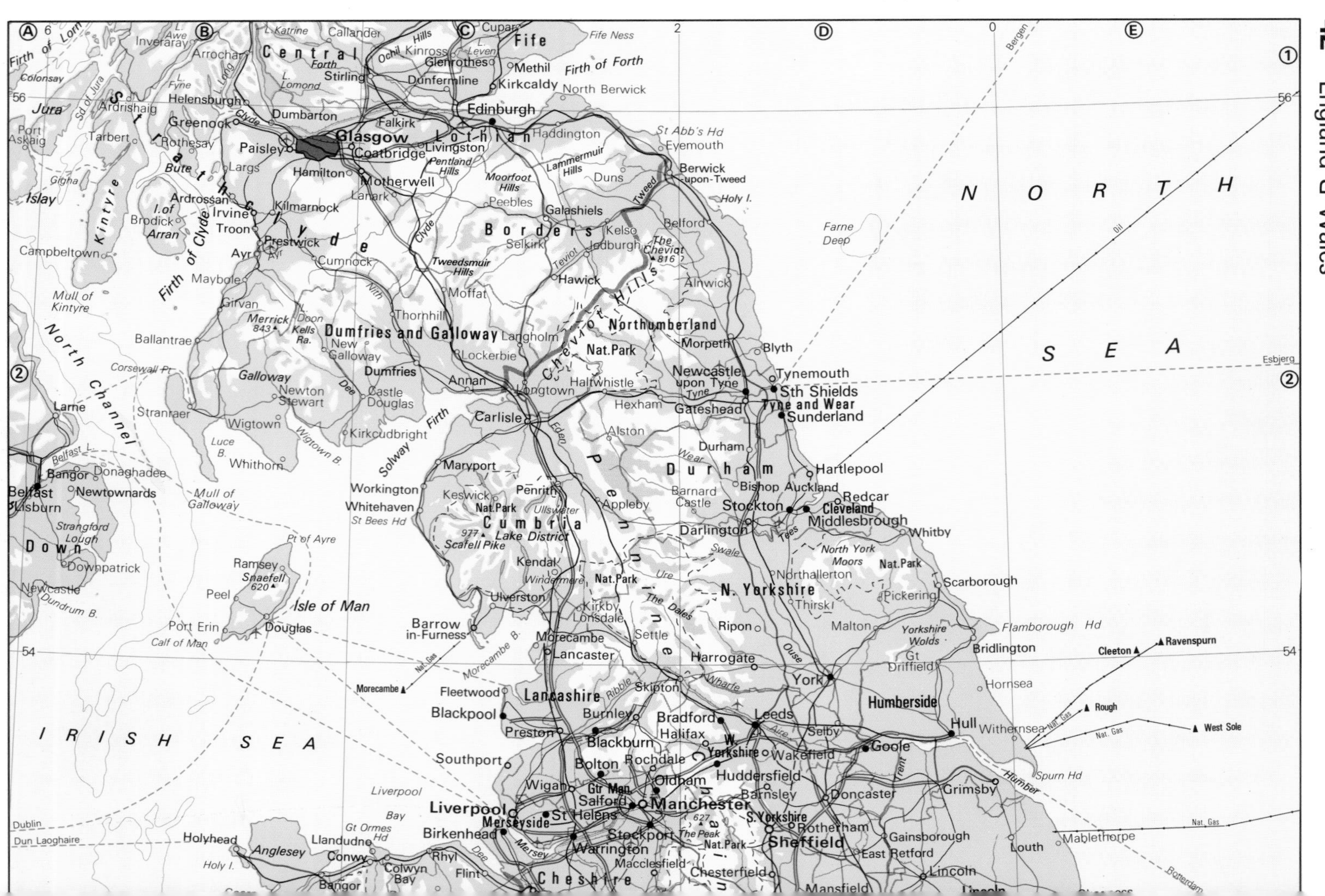
N O R T H   S E A
I R I S H   S E A
North Channel
Firth of Forth
Firth of Clyde
Solway Firth
Isle of Man
Anglesey
Kintyre
Jura
Islay
Arran
Fife
Central
Lothian
Borders
Strathclyde
Dumfries and Galloway
Northumberland
Tyne and Wear
Durham
Cleveland
Cumbria
N. Yorkshire
Humberside
Lancashire
W. Yorkshire
S. Yorkshire
Gtr Man
Merseyside
Cheshire
Down
Pennines
Cheviot Hills
Lake District
North York Moors
Yorkshire Wolds
The Dales
The Peak
Edinburgh
Glasgow
Newcastle upon Tyne
Sunderland
Middlesbrough
Carlisle
York
Leeds
Bradford
Hull
Sheffield
Manchester
Liverpool
Blackpool
Preston
Lancaster
Belfast
Douglas
Scarborough
Whitby
Bridlington
Hartlepool
Darlington
Durham
Gateshead
Hexham
Berwick upon-Tweed
Galashiels
Dumfries
Stranraer
Ayr
Kilmarnock
Paisley
Greenock
Dumbarton
Stirling
Falkirk
Kirkcaldy
Dunfermline
Workington
Whitehaven
Barrow in-Furness
Kendal
Penrith
Harrogate
Ripon
Huddersfield
Wakefield
Doncaster
Grimsby
Lincoln
Goole
Southport
Birkenhead
Wigan
Bolton
Blackburn
Burnley
Oldham
Rochdale
Stockport
Warrington
Chesterfield
Macclesfield
Holyhead
Bangor
Llandudno
Colwyn Bay
Rhyl
Flint
Scafell Pike 977
Snaefell 620
The Cheviot 816
Merrick 843
Ravenspurn
West Sole
Cleeton
Rough
Morecambe
Nat. Gas
Oil
Bergen
Esbjerg
Rotterdam
Dublin
Dun Laoghaire

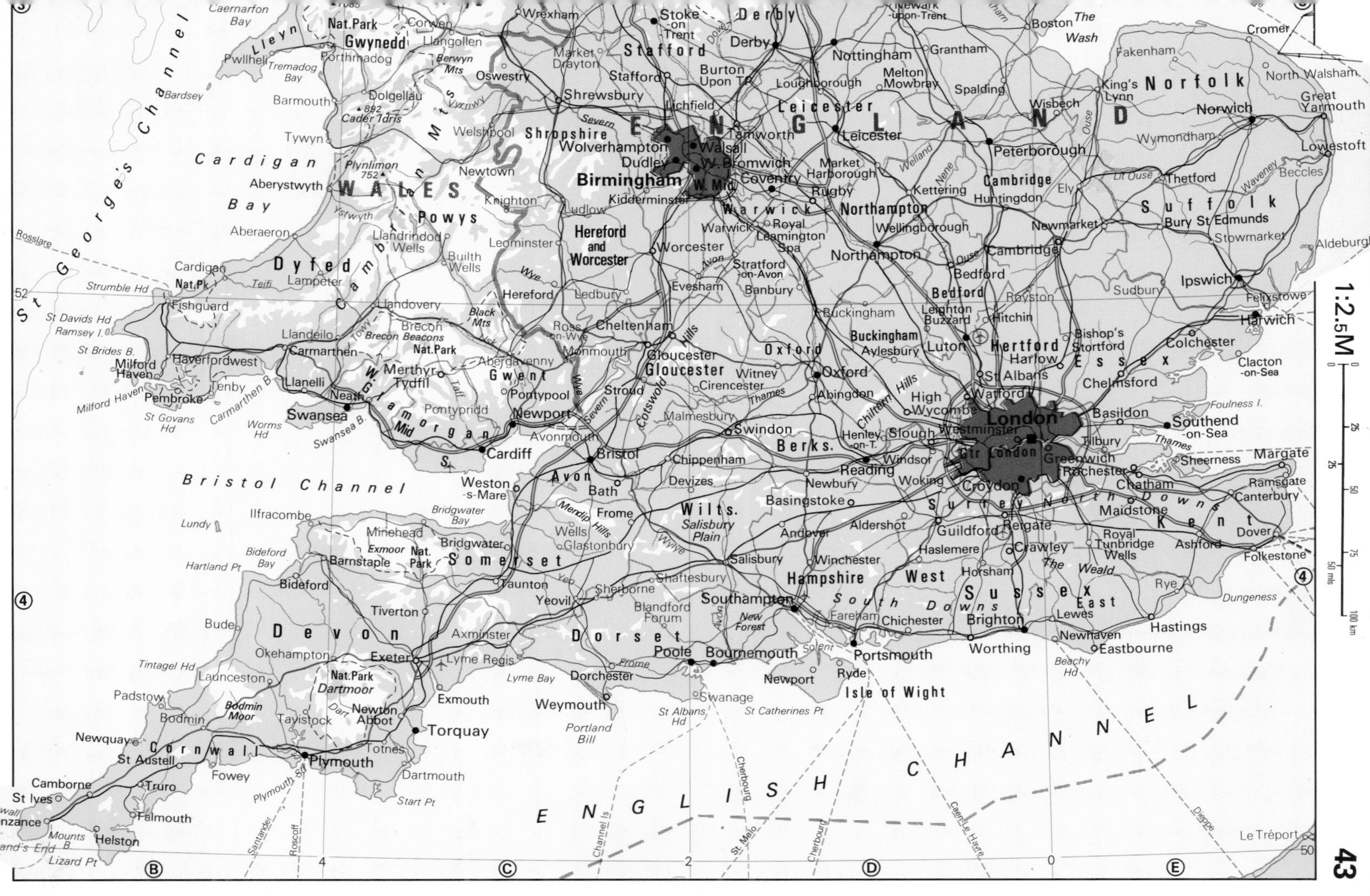

1:2.5M

1:2.5M

0 — 25 — 50 — 75 — 100 km
0 — 25 — 50 mls

Shetland (inset E)

Herma Ness
Unst
The Father
Fetlar
Yell
Isbister
Hillswick
St Magnus Bay
Brae
Whalsay
Bressay
Noss
Lerwick
Hanstholm-Bergen
Gruness
Scalloway
Papa Stour
Foula
Fitful Hd
Sumburgh Hd
Fair Isle
Aberdeen
Stromness

Orkney (inset C)

N. Ronaldsay
Sanday
Papa Westray
Westray
Eddy
Stronsay
Shapinsay
Rousay
Kirkwall
Birsay
Mainland
Stromness
Scapa Flow
Hoy
S. Ronaldsay
Duncansby Hd
Pentland Firth
Dunnet Hd
John o' Groats
Thurso

North Sea

N O R T H   S E A
Long Forties
Buchan Deep

Mainland

Peterhead
Buchan Ness
Fraserburgh
Kinnairds Hd
Rattray Head

C. Wrath
Durness
Kyle of Tongue
Ben Hope 927▲
Ben Kilbreck 961▲
Ben More Assynt 998▲
Lochinver
Enard Bay
Eddrachillis Bay
Ullapool
Ben Dearg 1081▲
L. Broom
L. Maree
Gairloch
Torridon
Rubha Hunish
Uig
Portree
Raasay
Sd of Raasay
L. Snizort
Isle of Skye
Cuillin Hills
Broadford
Canna
Rum
Eigg
Muck
Coll
Tiree
Tobermory
Ulva
Staffa
Iona
Mull
Colonsay
Jura
Islay
Port Askaig
Sd of Jura
Tarbert

Butt of Lewis
Lewis
Stornoway
Broad Bay
Loch Roag
Tarbert
Harris
Sd of Harris
North Uist
Lochmaddy
Benbecula
South Uist
Lochboisdale
Barra
Castlebay
Barra Hd
Flannan Is
Monach Is
Pabbay
Taransay
Scarp

Western Isles
Sea of the Hebrides
Little Minch
North Minch

C. Duncansby
S. Ronaldsay
Dunnet Hd
Pentland Firth
Thurso
Wick
Lybster
Helmsdale
Brora
Dornoch Firth
Golspie
Lairg
L. Shin
Oykel
Bonar Bridge
Tain
Dornoch
Alness
Cromarty Firth
Dingwall
Ben Wyvis 1045▲
Strathpeffer
Black Isle
Beauly
Inverness
Nairn
Forres
Elgin
Lossiemouth
Spey
Buckie
Keith
Huntly
Banff
Deveron
Inverurie
Ythan
Aberdeen
Girdle Ness

Grampian
Mountains
Cairngorms
Ben Macdui 1310▲
Grantown-on-Spey
Aviemore
Kingussie
Monadhliath Mts
L. Ness
Fort Augustus
Loch Laggan
Ben Nevis 1344▲
Fort William
Ballachulish
Lochy
Mallaig
Morar
Arisaig
Ardnamurchan Pt
Sunart
Morvern
Oban
Lorn
Firth of Lorn

Mar
Braemar
Lochnagar 1155▲
Ballater
Dee
Banchory
Stonehaven
A. Esk
Brechin
Montrose
Arbroath
Forfar
Sidlaw Hills
Dundee
Fife Ness
St Andrews
Firth of Forth
North Berwick
Tay
Cupar
Fife
Methil
Kirkcaldy
Glenrothes
Perth
Dunfermline
Edinburgh
Livingston
Haddington
Lammermuir Hills
St Abb's Hd
Eyemouth
Berwick

SCOTLAND
Highland
Tayside
Central
Grampian

Mountains of Tayside
Blair Atholl
Pitlochry
Aberfeldy
Blairgowrie
L. Tay
Ben Lawers 1214▲
Killin
L. Earn
Crieff
L. Rannoch
L. Ericht
Callander
Cranlarich
L. Katrine
L. Lomond
Stirling
Falkirk
Coatbridge
Motherwell
Pentland Hills
Glasgow
Paisley
Dumbarton
Greenock
Helensburgh
Arrochar
Inveraray
L. Fyne
Rothesay
Ardrishaig

Black Mount
Glen Coe
L. Awe
Etive
L. Linnhe
Ben Attow 1031▲
Glen Shiel
Kyle of Lochalsh
Glenelg
Sd of Sleat
L. Hourn
Glen Garry
Glen Moriston
Loch Ness
Aviemore
Spean Bridge
Ben Alder

Central

Long Forties

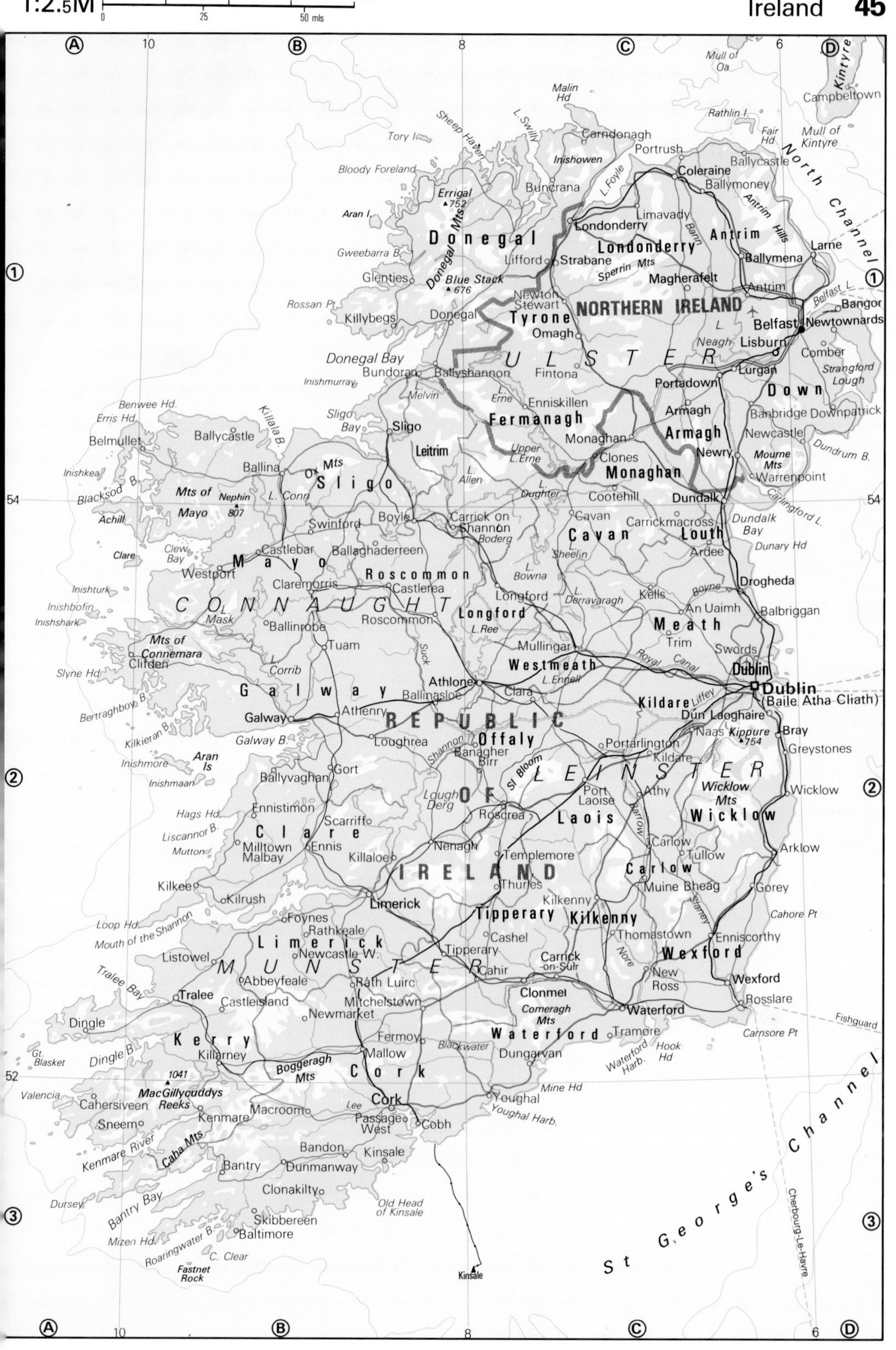
A
B
C
D
10
8
6
Mull of Oa
Kintyre
Campbeltown
Malin Hd
Rathlin I.
Fair Hd
Mull of Kintyre
Sheep Haven
L. Swilly
Carndonagh
Tory I.
Portrush
Inishowen
Ballycastle
North Channel
Bloody Foreland
Coleraine
Ballymoney
Buncrana
L. Foyle
Errigal ▲752
Aran I.
Limavady
Antrim Hills
Londonderry
Bann
Donegal
Antrim
Donegal Mts
Londonderry
Larne
Gweebarra B.
Lifford
Strabane
Sperrin Mts
Ballymena
Glenties
Blue Stack ▲676
Magherafelt
Antrim
Belfast L.
Newton Stewart
Bangor
Rossan Pt
NORTHERN IRELAND
Killybegs
Donegal
Tyrone
Belfast
Newtownards
Omagh
L. Neagh
Lisburn
Comber
Donegal Bay
ULSTER
Strangford Lough
Bundoran
Ballyshannon
Fintona
Lurgan
Inishmurray
Portadown
L. Melvin
Down
L. Erne
Enniskillen
Armagh
Banbridge
Downpatrick
Benwee Hd.
Erris Hd.
Killala B.
Sligo Bay
Fermanagh
Ballycastle
Sligo
Armagh
Newcastle
Belmullet
Leitrim
Monaghan
Newry
Mourne Mts
Dundrum B.
Ballina
Ox Mts
Upper L. Erne
Clones
Inishkea
L. Allen
Monaghan
Warrenpoint
Sligo
Blacksod B.
Mts of Mayo
Nephin ▲807
L. Conn
L. Oughter
Cootehill
Dundalk
Carlingford L.
Achill
Boyle
Carrick on Shannon
Cavan
Carrickmacross
Dundalk Bay
Swinford
Boderg
Louth
Clare
Clew Bay
Castlebar
Ballaghaderreen
Cavan
L. Sheelin
Ardee
Dunary Hd
Westport
Mayo
Roscommon
L. Bowna
Inishturk
Claremorris
Castlerea
Longford
Boyne
Drogheda
Inishbofin
CONNAUGHT
L. Derravaragh
Kells
Inishshark
L. Mask
Ballinrobe
Roscommon
Longford
An Uaimh
Balbriggan
L. Ree
Meath
Mts of Connemara
Tuam
Suck
Trim
Swords
Clifden
Mullingar
Royal Canal
Slyne Hd.
L. Corrib
Westmeath
Dublin
Athlone
L. Ennell
Dublin (Baile Atha Cliath)
Galway
Ballinasloe
Clara
Kildare
Liffey
Bertraghboy B.
REPUBLIC
Dún Laoghaire
Galway
Athenry
Naas
Kippure ▲754
Bray
Kilkieran B.
Galway B.
Loughrea
Shannon
Offaly
Portarlington
Greystones
Inishmore
Aran Is
Banagher
Birr
Kildare
Inishmaan
Gort
Sl Bloom
LEINSTER
Ballyvaghan
OF
Port Laoise
Athy
Wicklow Mts
Wicklow
Lough Derg
Hags Hd.
Ennistimon
Roscrea
Barrow
Wicklow
Scarriff
Laois
Liscannor B.
Clare
Milltown Malbay
Ennis
Nenagh
Carlow
Tullow
Arklow
Mutton
Killaloe
Templemore
IRELAND
Carlow
Kilkee
Thurles
Muine Bheag
Gorey
Kilrush
Limerick
Kilkenny
Slaney
Foynes
Tipperary
Kilkenny
Cahore Pt
Loop Hd.
Rathkeale
Mouth of the Shannon
Limerick
Cashel
Thomastown
Enniscorthy
Newcastle W.
Tipperary
Nore
Wexford
Listowel
MUNSTER
Carrick-on-Suir
Cahir
New Ross
Wexford
Tralee Bay
Abbeyfeale
Ráth Luirc
Tralee
Castleisland
Clonmel
Rosslare
Mitchelstown
Comeragh Mts
Waterford
Fishguard
Dingle
Newmarket
Fermoy
Waterford
Tramore
Carnsore Pt
Kerry
Blackwater
Waterford Harb.
Hook Hd
Gt. Blasket
Dingle B.
Killarney
Mallow
Dungarvan
Boggeragh Mts
Cork
52
▲1041
Mine Hd
Valencia
MacGillycuddys Reeks
Cork
Youghal
Cahersiveen
Macroom
Lee
Youghal Harb.
Kenmare
Passage West
Cobh
Sneem
Caha Mts
Bandon
Kinsale
Kenmare River
St George's Channel
Bantry
Dunmanway
Clonakilty
Dursey
Bantry Bay
Old Head of Kinsale
Cherbourg-Le-Havre
Skibbereen
Mizen Hd.
Baltimore
Roaringwater B.
C. Clear
Fastnet Rock
Kinsale
54
①
②
③

0 25 50 75 100 km
0 25 50 mls

NORTH SEA

WEST NETHERLANDS

BELGIUM

WESTFALEN

RHEINLAND

PFALZ

SAARLAND

LUXEMBOURG

ARDENNES

Rotterdam · Antwerpen (Anvers) · Bruxelles (Brussel) · Gent (Gand) · Brugge (Bruges) · Oostende (Ostend) · Lille · Calais · Dunkerque · Boulogne · Amiens · Reims · Paris · Versailles · Köln (Cologne) · Düsseldorf · Essen · Dortmund · Bonn · Aachen · Koblenz · Trier · Luxembourg · Metz · Nancy · Mannheim · Karlsruhe · Frankfurt am Main · Wiesbaden · Saarbrücken

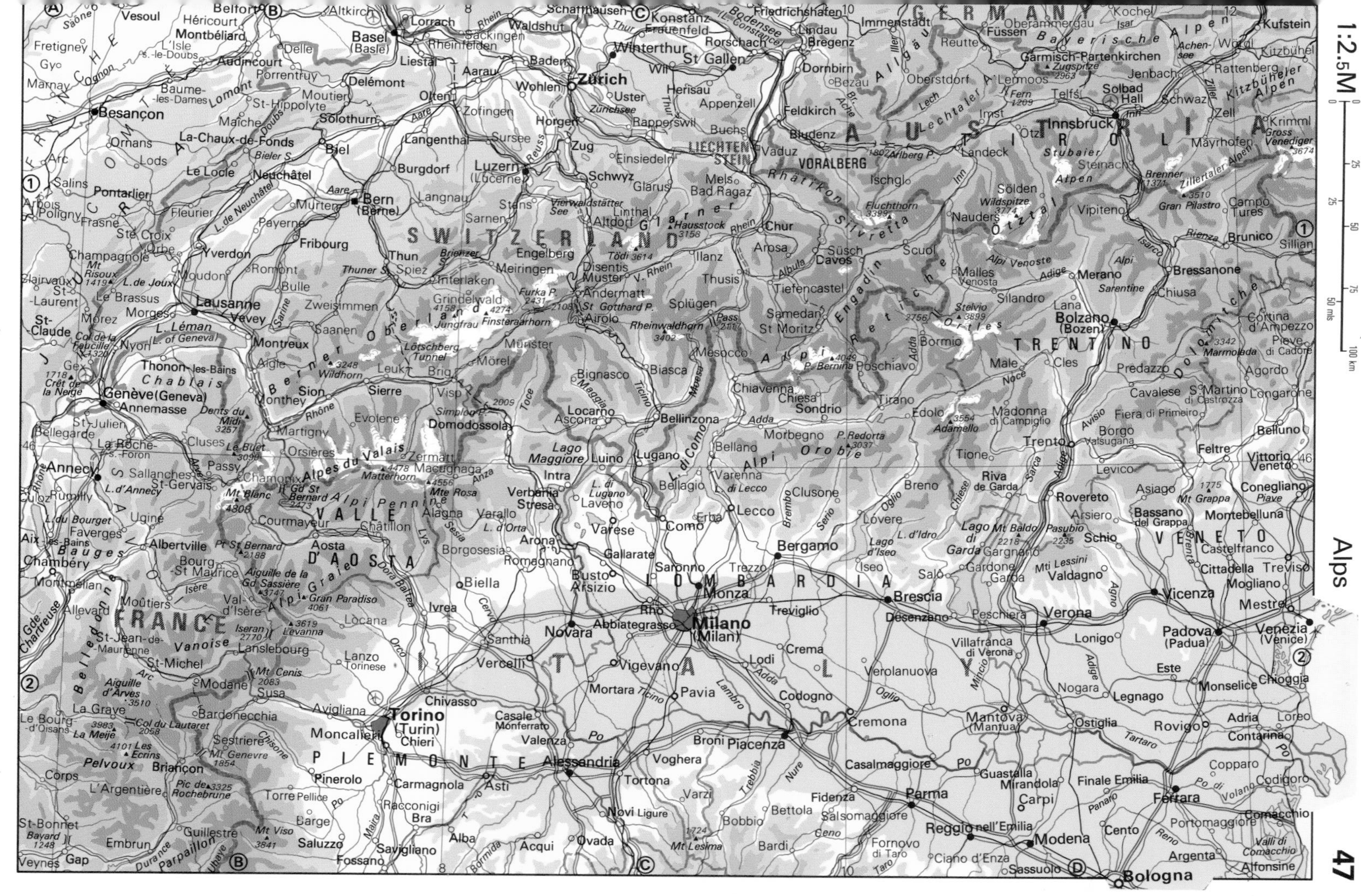
0 25 50 75 100 km
0 25 50 mls
GERMANY
AUSTRIA
SWITZERLAND
FRANCE
ITALY
LIECHTENSTEIN
TIROL
VORALBERG
TRENTINO
VENETO
LOMBARDIA
PIEMONTE
VALLE D'AOSTA
Zürich
Bern (Berne)
Luzern (Lucerne)
Lausanne
Genève (Geneva)
Basel (Basle)
Innsbruck
Bolzano (Bozen)
Milano (Milan)
Torino (Turin)
Venezia (Venice)
Padova (Padua)
Bologna
Verona
Brescia
Bergamo
Vicenza
Trento
Chur
Besançon
Annecy
Chambéry
Aosta
Novara
Piacenza
Parma
Modena
Cremona
Mantova (Mantua)
Ferrara

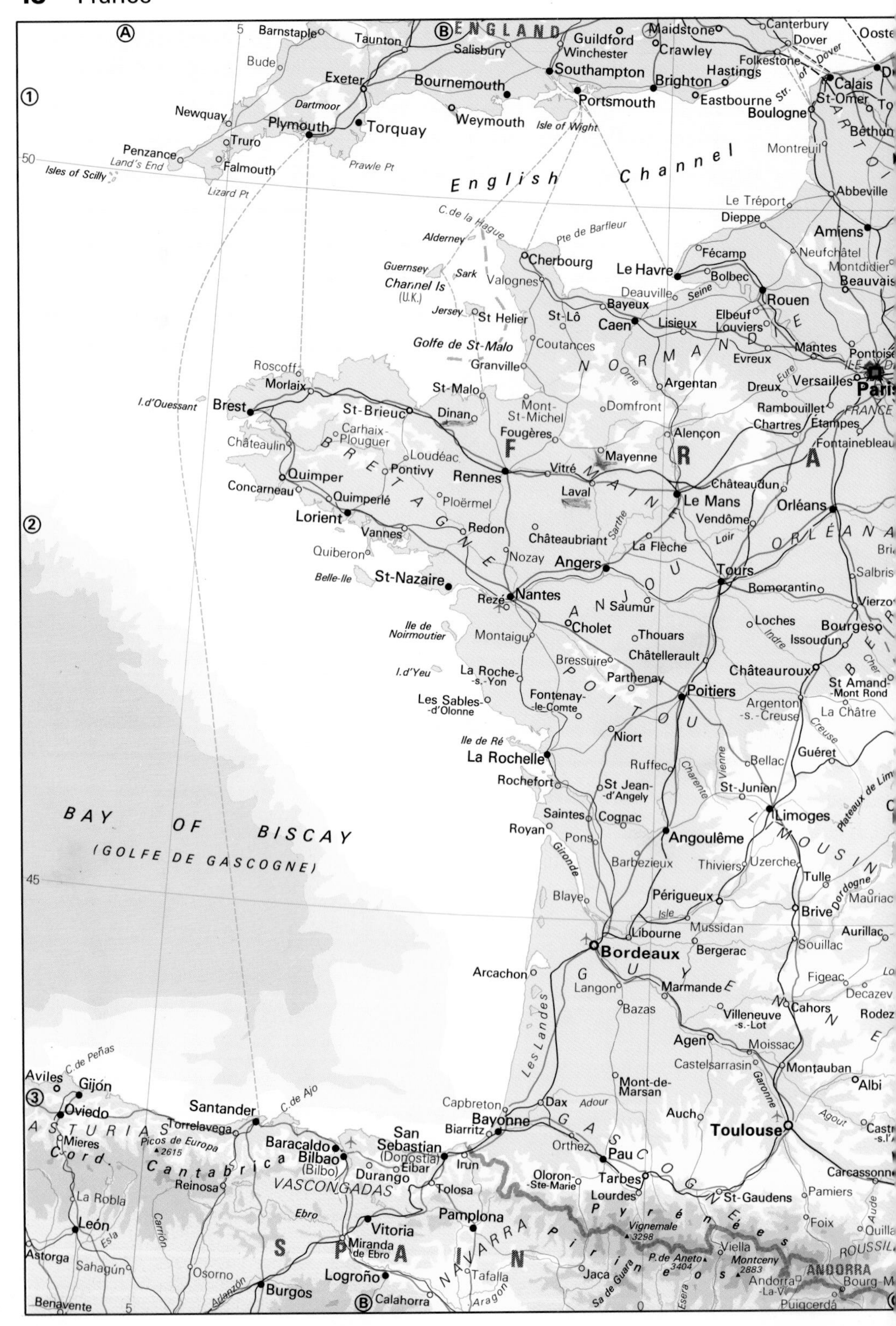

A

① B ENGLAND

5 Barnstaple
Taunton
Bude
Newquay
Exeter
Bournemouth
Plymouth Torquay
Penzance Truro
Dartmoor
Land's End
Falmouth
50 Isles of Scilly
Lizard Pt
Prawle Pt

Salisbury
Winchester Crawley
Southampton Brighton
Weymouth Portsmouth
Isle of Wight
Guildford
Maidstone
Canterbury
Dover
Folkestone
Hastings
Eastbourne
Ooste
Calais
St-Omer
Boulogne
Béthun
Montreuil

ENGLISH Channel

C. de la Hague
Alderney
Pte de Barfleur
Guernsey Sark
Channel Is (U.K.)
Jersey
St Helier

Cherbourg
Valognes
St-Lô
Coutances

Le Havre
Fécamp
Deauville Bolbec
Bayeux Seine
Caen Lisieux
Orne
Argentan
Domfront

Le Tréport
Dieppe
Amiens
Neufchâtel
Montdidier
Beauvais
Rouen
Elbeuf
Louviers
Evreux Mantes
Dreux Pontoise
Versailles Paris
FRANCE
Rambouillet Etampes
Chartres Fontainebleau

Golfe de St-Malo
Granville
Mont-St-Michel

NORMANDIE

Roscoff
Morlaix
I. d'Ouessant
Brest
Châteaulin
St-Brieuc
Carhaix-Plouguer
Dinan
Loudéac
Pontivy
Quimper
Concarneau
Quimperlé
Lorient
Vannes
Quiberon
Belle-Ile
St-Nazaire

BRETAGNE
St-Malo
Fougères
Vitré
Rennes
Ploërmel
Redon
Laval
Nozay
Châteaubriant
Angers
Rezé Nantes
Cholet
Montaigu

MAINE
Mayenne
Le Mans
Vendôme
La Flèche
Saumur
Thouars

Châteaudun
Orléans
ORLÉANAIS
Tours
Romorantin
Loches
Issoudun
Vierzo
Bourges
St Amand-Mont Rond
Châteauroux
La Châtre
Argenton-s.-Creuse
Salbris
Bri

Ile de Noirmoutier
I. d'Yeu
La Roche-s.-Yon
Les Sables-d'Olonne
Ile de Ré
La Rochelle
Rochefort
Royan

ANJOU
POITOU
Bressuire
Châtellerault
Parthenay
Fontenay-le-Comte
Niort
Poitiers
Ruffec

Saumur
Thouars

② BAY OF BISCAY
(GOLFE DE GASCOGNE)

45

LIMOUSIN
Bellac
Guéret
St-Junien
Limoges
Uzerche
Plateau de Lim
Tulle
Brive
Dordogne
Aurillac
Mauriac
Souillac
Figeac
Decazev
Cahors
Rodez
Albi
Castr
s.-l

Saintes
Cognac
Pons
Barbezieux
Blaye

Angoulême
Thiviers
Périgueux
Mussidan
Bergerac
Libourne

Arcachon
Bordeaux
Langon
Bazas

GUYENNE
Marmande
Agen
Castelsarrasin
Moissac
Villeneuve-s.-Lot
Montauban

Les Landes
GASCOGNE

Capbreton
Dax Adour
Bayonne
Biarritz
Mont-de-Marsan

Auch
Toulouse

③ Aviles
C. de Peñas
Gijón
Oviedo
Mieres
Cord.
La Robla
León
Astorga
Sahagún
Benavente
ASTURIAS
Torrelavega
Picos de Europa ▲2615
Reinosa
Santander
C. de Ajo
Cantabrica
Baracaldo
Bilbao (Bilbo)
Durango
Tolosa
Vitoria
Logroño
Burgos
VASCONGADAS
San Sebastian (Donostia)
Eibar
Irun
Orthez
Oloron-Ste-Marie
Pau
Tarbes
Lourdes
Jaca
Pamplona
Tafalla
Miranda de Ebro
Ebro
NAVARRA
Pirir
Pyrénées
Vignemale ▲3298
Gavarnie
P. de Aneto ▲3404
St-Gaudens
Pamiers
Foix
Montceny ▲2883
Aragón
Esera
Andorra-La-Vi
ANDORRA
Bourg-M
ROUSSILL
Carcassonne
Quilla
Viella
Puigcerdà

B Calahorra
Benavente 5

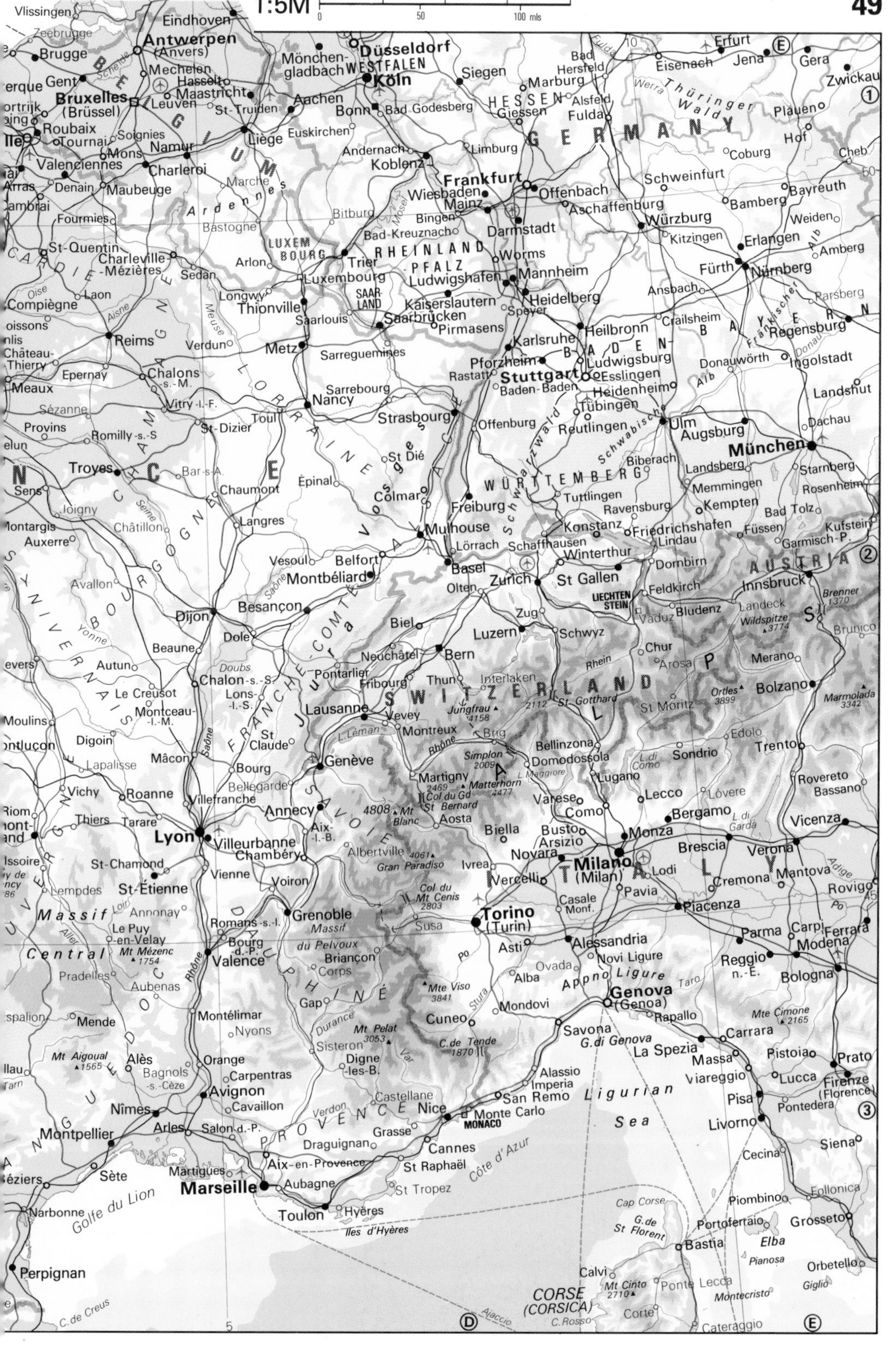

0 50 100 150 200 km

50 100 mls

Vlissingen
Zeebrugge
Brugge
Antwerpen
(Anvers)
Eindhoven
Mönchen-
gladbach WESTFALEN
Düsseldorf
Köln
Erfurt
Eisenach Jena Gera
Zwickau
Gent
erque
Mechelen
Hasselt
Maastricht
Leuven
Aachen
Bonn Bad Godesberg
Siegen
Marburg
Bad
Hersfeld
Fulda
Thüringer
Wald
Plauen
Hof
Cheb
Roubaix
Bruxelles
(Brüssel)
St-Truiden
Liège
Euskirchen
Bad Kreuznach
Limburg
Giessen
HESSEN
Coburg
Bamberg
Bayreuth
Weiden
Ittle
Tournai
Mons Namur
Soignies
Charleroi
Andernach
Koblenz
GERMANY
Schweinfurt
Würzburg
Amberg
Valenciennes
Denain Maubeuge
Marche
Ardennes
Bitburg
Frankfurt
Wiesbaden
Mainz
Offenbach
Aschaffenburg
Kitzingen
Erlangen
Fürth
Nürnberg
Rarsberg
Arras
Fourmies
St-Quentin
Charleville
-Mézières
Sedan
Arlon
LUXEM-
BOURG
Luxembourg
Trier
Bad Godesberg
Darmstadt
RHEINLAND
PFALZ
Worms
Mannheim
Heidelberg
Speyer
Ludwigsburg
Ansbach
Donauwörth
Ingolstadt
Regensburg
BAYERN
Donau
Compiègne
Laon
Oise
Château-
Thierry
Longwy
Thionville
SAAR
LAND
Saarlouis
Kaiserslautern
Saarbrücken
Pirmasens
Ludwigshafen
Karlsruhe
Pforzheim
Heilbronn
Crailsheim
Esslingen
Stuttgart
BADEN
Landshut
Dachau
Meaux
Epernay
Reims
Verdun
Metz
Sarreguemines
Rastatt
Baden-Baden
Tübingen
Reutlingen
Heidenheim
Ulm
Augsburg
München
Starnberg
Sézanne
Provins
Vitry-l-F.
Nancy
Sarrebourg
St-Dizier
Toul
Strasbourg
Offenburg
Schwäbische
Alb
Biberach
Landsberg
Memmingen
Rosenheim
elun
N
Troyes
Sens
Bar-s-A.
Chaumont
Epinal
St Dié
Colmar
Freiburg
Schwarzwald
Württemberg
Tuttlingen
Ravensburg
Friedrichshafen
Lindau
Kempten
Füssen
Garmisch-P.
Bad Tölz
Kufstein
Joigny
Montargis
Auxerre
Avallon
Langres
Vesoul
Mulhouse
Lörrach
Basel
Schaffhausen
Konstanz
Winterthur
Dornbirn
Feldkirch
AUSTRIA
Innsbruck
Brenner
1370
Nevers
Autun
Châtillon
Dijon
Besançon
Montbéliard
Belfort
Olten
Zürich
Zug
St Gallen
LIECHTEN
STEIN
Vaduz
Bludenz
Landeck
Wildspitze
3774
Brunico
Le Creusot
Moulins
Montceau
-l.-M.
Beaune
Dole
Biel
Luzern
Schwyz
Chur
Arosa
Merano
Ortles
3899
Marmolada
3342
Digoin
Lapalisse
Chalon-s.-S.
Lons
-l.-S.
Neuchâtel
Bern
Rhein
St Moritz
Bolzano
Mâcon
St
Claude
Pontarlier
Fribourg
SWITZERLAND
Thun
Interlaken
St-Gotthard
Edolo
Trento
ntlucon
Vichy
Roanne
Villefranche
Bourg
Bellegarde
Lausanne
Vevey
Montreux
Léman
Jungfrau
4158
2112
Simplon
2009
Brig
Bellinzona
Domodossola
L. di
Como
Sondrio
Rovereto
Bassano
Riom
mont-
and
Thiers
Tarare
Genève
Annecy
Martigny
Matterhorn
4477
L. Maggiore
Lugano
Lecco
Bergamo
L. di
Garda
Vicenza
St-Etienne
Lyon
Villeurbanne
Aix-
l.-B.
Chambéry
Mt
Blanc
4808
St Bernard
Aosta
Varese
Como
Monza
Brescia
Verona
Issoire
St-Chamand
Vienne
Voiron
Albertville
Gran Paradiso
4061
Ivrea
Biella
Bustp
Arsizio
Novara
Milano
(Milan)
Lodi
Cremona
Mantova
Rovigo
y de
ncy
86
Lempdes
Annonay
Romans-s.-l.
Grenoble
Massif
du Pelvoux
Col du
Mt Cenis
2803
Susa
Vercelli
ITALY
Pavia
Piacenza
Parma
Carpi
Ferrara
Modena
Massif
Central
Le Puy
-en-Velay
Mt Mézenc
1754
Bourg
Valence
Briançon
Corps
Torino
(Turin)
Asti
Casale
Mont.
Alessandria
Novi Ligure
Ligure
Reggio
n.-E.
Bologna
Pradelles
Aubenas
Gap
Montélimar
Nyons
Sisteron
Digne
-les-B.
Gap
Mt Pelat
3053
Po
Mte Viso
3841
Mondovi
Alba
Ovada
Savona
Genova
(Genoa)
Rapallo
Mte Cimone
2165
Mende
spalion
Alès
Bagnols
-s-Cèze
Orange
Carpentras
Cavaillon
Castellane
Verdon
Cuneo
C. de Tende
1870
Mondovi
G. di Genova
La Spezia
Savona
Carrara
Massa
Viareggio
Pistoiao
Lucca
Prato
Firenze
(Florence)
Nîmes
Avignon
Salon-d.-P.
Draguignan
Grasse
Cannes
Alassio
Imperia
San Remo
Nice
Monte Carlo
MONACO
PROVENCE
Ligurian
Sea
Pisa
Pontedera
Livorno
Siena
Montpellier
Arles
Aix-en-Provence
Aubagne
St Raphaël
St Tropez
Côte d'Azur
Cecina
éziers
Sète
Martigues
Marseille
Toulon
Hyères
Iles d'Hyères
Cap Corse
G. de
St Florent
Piombino
Portoferraio
Elba
Grosseto
Narbonne
Golfe du Lion
C. de Creus
Calvi
CORSE
(CORSICA)
Mte Cinto
2710
Ponte Leccia
Pianosa
Montecristo
Orbetello
Giglio
Perpignan
Ajaccio
C. Rosso
Corte
Cateraggio

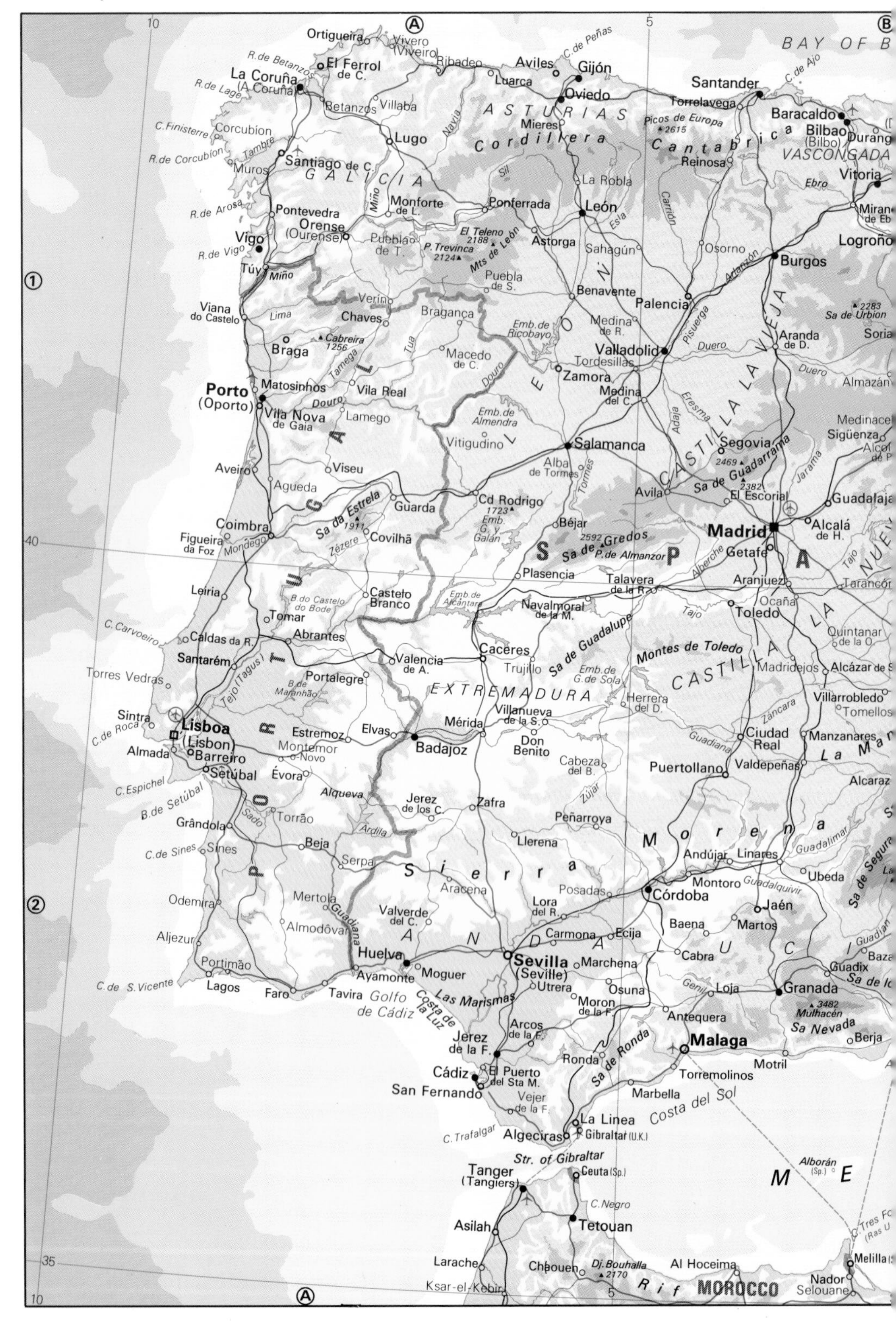
BAY OF B
Ortigueira
Vivero (Viveiro)
Ribadeo
Aviles
Gijón
C. de Peñas
R. de Betanzos
El Ferrol de C.
La Coruña (A Coruña)
R. de Lage
Luarca
Oviedo
Santander
C. de Ajo
Torrelavega
Baracaldo
Bilbao (Bilbo)
Durang
VASCONGADA
Betanzos
Villaba
ASTURIAS
Mieres
Picos de Europa 2615
C. Finisterre
Corcubión
Lugo
Cordillera Cantabrica
Reinosa
R. de Corcubion
Tambre
Santiago de C.
Muros
GALICIA
La Robla
Vitoria
Ebro
R. de Arosa
Pontevedra
Monforte de L.
Ponferrada
León
Miran de Eb
Orense (Ourense)
Vigo
R. de Vigo
Puebla de T.
El Teleno 2188
P. Trevinca 2124
Mts de León
Astorga
Sahagún
Osorno
Logroño
Túy
Miño
Burgos
Puebla de S.
Benavente
Palencia
Viana do Castelo
Lima
Verin
Chaves
Bragança
Medina de R.
2283 Sa de Urbion
Soria
Emb. de Ricobayo
Cabreira 1256
Braga
Macedo de C.
Valladolid
Aranda de D.
Tordesillas
Duero
Zamora
Almazán
Porto (Oporto)
Matosinhos
Vila Real
Medina del C.
Vila Nova de Gaia
Lamego
Emb. de Almendra
Medinacel
Sigüenza
Vitigudino
Salamanca
Segovia
2469
Sa de Guadarrama
Aveiro
Viseu
Alba de Tormes
Agueda
Avila
2382
El Escorial
Guadalaja
Sa da Estrela
Guarda
Cd Rodrigo 1723
Coimbra
1911
Covilhã
Emb. G. y Galán
Béjar
Madrid
Alcalá de H.
Figueira da Foz
Mondego
Zêzere
2592 Gredos
Sa de P. de Almanzor
Getafe
Plasencia
Talavera de la R.
Aranjuez
Tarancón
Leiria
B. do Castelo do Bode
Castelo Branco
Emb. de Alcántara
Navalmoral de la M.
Ocaña
Toledo
C. Carvoeiro
Tomar
Tajo
Quintanar de la O.
Caldas da R.
Abrantes
Montes de Toledo
Sa de Guadalupe
Santarém
Valencia de A.
Caceres
Madridejos
Alcázar de S
Torres Vedras
Tejo (Tagus)
Portalegre
B. de Maranhão
Trujillo
Emb. de G. de Sola
CASTILLA
EXTREMADURA
Herrera del D.
Villarrobledo
Tomellos
Sintra
C. de Roca
Lisboa (Lisbon)
Estremoz
Elvas
Mérida
Villanueva de la S.
Zancara
Ciudad Real
Manzanares
Almada
Barreiro
Montemor o-Novo
Badajoz
Don Benito
Guadiana
La Ma
Setúbal
Évora
Cabeza del B.
Puertollano
Valdepeñas
C. Espichel
B. de Setúbal
Alqueva
Jerez de los C.
Zafra
Zújar
Alcaraz
Grândola
Sado
Torrão
Peñarroya
Ardila
Llerena
Morena
C. de Sines
Sines
Beja
Andújar
Linares
Guadalimar
Serpa
Sierra
Ubeda
Sa de Segura
Aracena
Posadas
Montoro
Guadalquivir
Córdoba
Odemira
Mertola
Lora del R.
Jaén
Valverde del C.
Baena
Martos
Aljezur
Almodôvar
Guadiana
ANDALUCIA
Carmona
Ecija
Cabra
Baza
Portimão
Huelva
Sevilla (Seville)
Marchena
Guadix
Ayamonte
Moguer
Sa de la
C. de S. Vicente
Lagos
Faro
Tavira
Golfo de Cádiz
Costa de la Luz
Las Marismas
Utrera
Osuna
Genil
Loja
Granada
Moron de la F.
Antequera
3482 Mulhacén
Sa Nevada
Arcos de la F.
Jerez de la F.
Sa de Ronda
Malaga
Berja
Ronda
Cádiz
El Puerto del Sta M.
Torremolinos
Motril
San Fernando
Marbella
Vejer de la F.
Costa del Sol
C. Trafalgar
La Linea
Algeciras
Gibraltar (U.K.)
Str. of Gibraltar
Alborán (Sp.)
Tanger (Tangiers)
Ceuta (Sp.)
ME
C. Negro
Asilah
Tetouan
C. Tres Fo (Ras U
Larache
Chaouen
Dj. Bouhalla 2170
Al Hoceima
Melilla (S
Nador
Ksar-el-Kebir
Rif
MOROCCO
Selouane
10
5
35
40
A
B
1
2

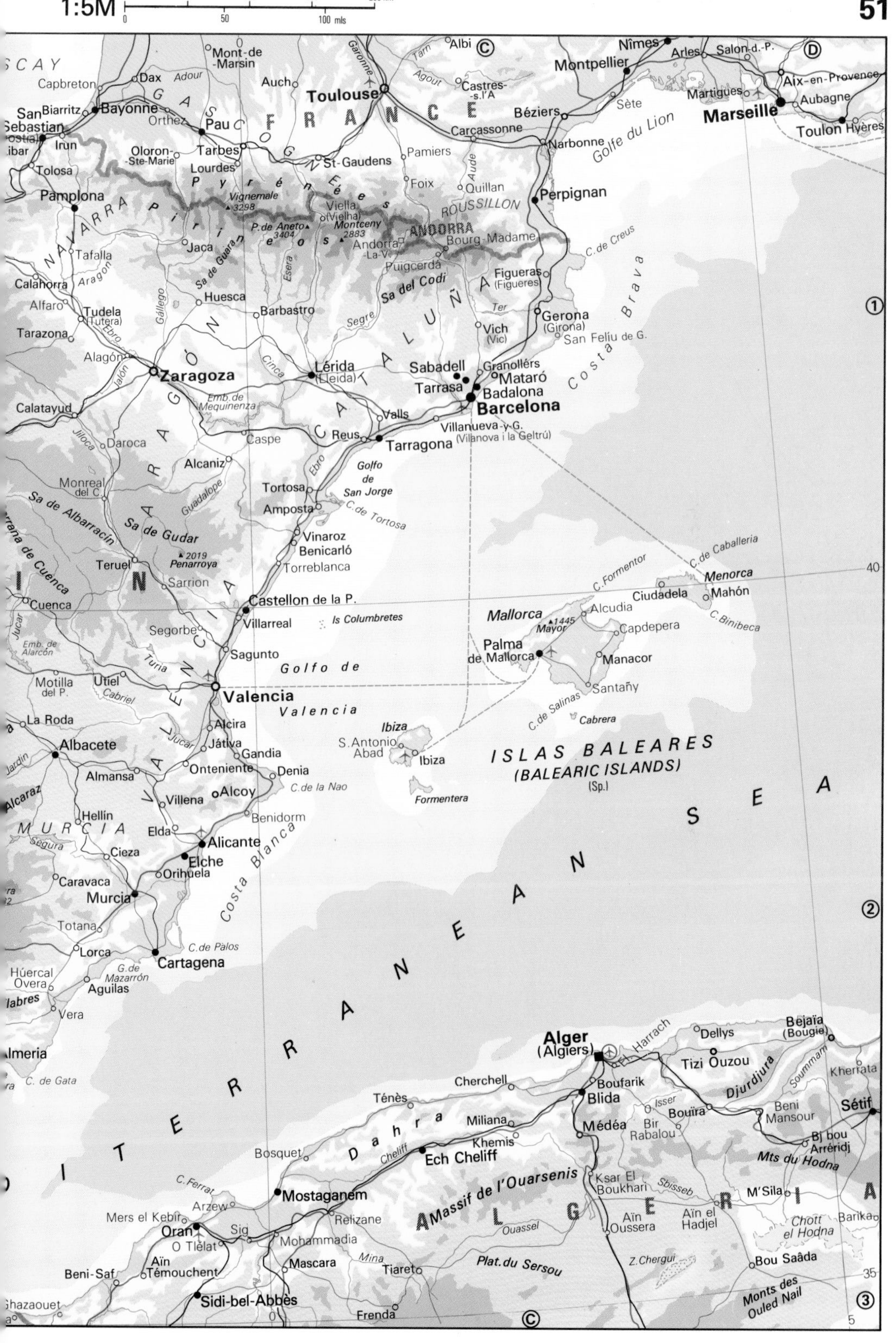

50   100   150   200 km
50   100 mils

BISCAY

Capbreton
San
Sebastian
Biarritz Bayonne
Irun
Tolosa
Pamplona

NAVARRA

Tafalla
Calahorra
Alfaro
Tudela
(Tutera)
Tarazona
Alagón

Zaragoza

Calatayud
Daroca
Jiloca

Monreal
del C.

Sa de Albarracín

Teruel

I   N

Sa de Gudar

Sierra de Cuenca

Cuenca

Emb. de
Alarcón

Motilla
del P.

La Roda

Albacete

Almansa

MURCIA

Hellín

Alcaraz

Elda

Caravaca

Cieza

Totana

Lorca

Húercar
Overa

Aguilas

Vera

Almeria

C. de Gata

Mont-de-
-Marsin
Dax
Adour

Orthez
Pau
Oloron-
Ste-Marie
Lourdes
Tarbes

Jaca
Huesca

ARAGÓN

Barbastro
Cinca

Lérida
(Lleida)

Caspe

Alcaniz

Guadalope

2019
Penarroya

Sarrion

Segorbe

VALENCIA

Villarreal

Sagunto

Valencia

Utiel
Cabriel

Alcira
Játiva
Gandia

Jucar

Onteniente
Denia

Villena
Alcoy

Benidorm

Alicante

Orihuela

Elche

Murcia

Segura

C. de Palos

G. de
Mazarrón

Cartagena

Auch

FRANCE

Toulouse

St-Gaudens

Pamiers

Foix

Quillan

ANDORRA

Vignemale
3298

P. de Aneto
3404

Andorra-
-La-V.

Monteny
2883

Puigcerdá

Bourg-Madame

Sa del Codi

Figueras
(Figueres)

Ter

Vich
(Vic)

Gerona
(Girona)

San Feliu de G.

CATALUÑA

Sabadell
Tarrasa

Granollérs
Mataró
Badalona

Barcelona

Valls
Reus

Villanueva-y-G.
(Vilanova i la Geltrú)

Tarragona

Ebro

Golfo
de
San Jorge

Tortosa
Amposta

C. de Tortosa

Vinaroz
Benicarló

Torreblanca

Castellon de la P.

Is Columbretes

Golfo de

Valencia

Ibiza

S. Antonio
Abad

Ibiza

Formentera

C. de la Nao

Costa Blanca

Albi

Castres-
-s. l'A.

Béziers

Carcassonne

Narbonne

ROUSSILLON

Perpignan

C. de Creus

Costa Brava

C. de Caballeria

C. Formentor

Menorca

Ciudadela

Mahón

C. Binibeca

Mallorca

1445
Mayor

Alcudia

Capdepera

Palma
de Mallorca

Manacor

Santañy

C. de Salinas

Cabrera

ISLAS BALEARES
(BALEARIC ISLANDS)
(Sp.)

Nîmes

Arles

Salon-d.-P.

Montpellier

Sète

Golfe du Lion

Martigues

Aix-en-Provence

Marseille

Aubagne

Toulon Hyères

40

M E D I T E R R A N E A N   S E A

Alger
(Algiers)

Harrach

Dellys

Béjaïa
(Bougie)

Tizi Ouzou

Djurdjura

Kherrata

Cherchell

Ténès

Boufarik
Blida

Isser

Bouira

Beni
Mansour

Sétif

Bosquet

Dahra

Miliana
Khemis

Médéa

Bir
Rabalou

Bj bou
Arréridj

C. Ferrat

Arzew

Mers el Kebir

Mostaganem

Relizane

Ech Cheliff

Cheliff

Massif de l'Ouarsenis

Ksar El
Boukhari

Sbisseb

Aïn el
Hadjel

M'Sila

Mts du Hodna

Chott
el Hodna

Barika

Oran

Sig

Mohammadia

Mina

ALGERIA

Ouassel

Aïn
Oussera

Ouassel

Plat. du Sersou

Bou Saâda

Beni-Saf

Aïn
Témouchent

O Tlélat

Mascara

Tiaretо

Z. Chergui

Monts des
Ouled Naïl

Ghazaouet

Sidi-bel-Abbes

Frenda

35

5

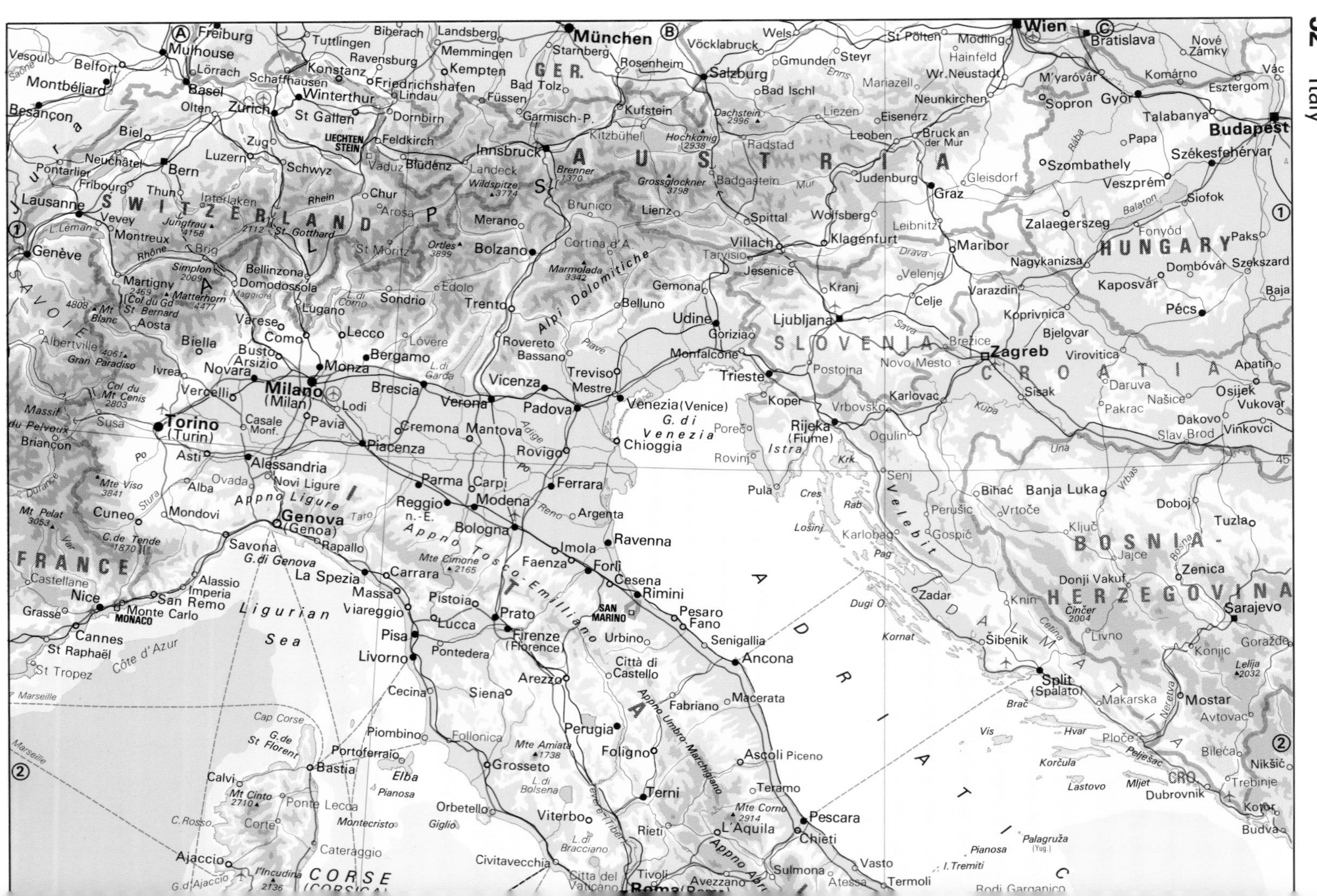
AUSTRIA
SWITZERLAND
GER.
HUNGARY
SLOVENIA
CROATIA
BOSNIA - HERZEGOVINA
FRANCE
ITALIA
SAN MARINO
MONACO
LIECHTENSTEIN
CORSE
ADRIATIC
Ligurian Sea
Wien
Budapest
Bratislava
München
Zürich
Bern
Genève
Lausanne
Basel
Innsbruck
Salzburg
Graz
Klagenfurt
Villach
Ljubljana
Zagreb
Sarajevo
Split
Rijeka (Fiume)
Trieste
Udine
Venezia (Venice)
Padova
Verona
Vicenza
Treviso
Trento
Bolzano
Milano (Milan)
Torino (Turin)
Genova (Genoa)
Bologna
Modena
Parma
Ferrara
Ravenna
Rimini
Firenze (Florence)
Pisa
Livorno
Lucca
Prato
Siena
Perugia
Ancona
Pescara
L'Aquila
Terni
Nice
Cannes
Monte Carlo
San Remo
Bastia
Ajaccio
Bergamo
Brescia
Como
Lugano
Novara
Alessandria
La Spezia
Reggio n.-E.
Piacenza
Cremona
Mantova
Rovigo
Chioggia
Arezzo
Grosseto
Viterbo
Civitavecchia
Zadar
Šibenik
Mostar
Dubrovnik
Pécs
Győr
Szombathely
Maribor
Dolomitiche
Appno Tosco-Emilliano
Appno Umbro-Marchigiano
Appno Ligure
Velebit
Dalmatia
Elba
Istra
G. di Venezia
G. di Genova

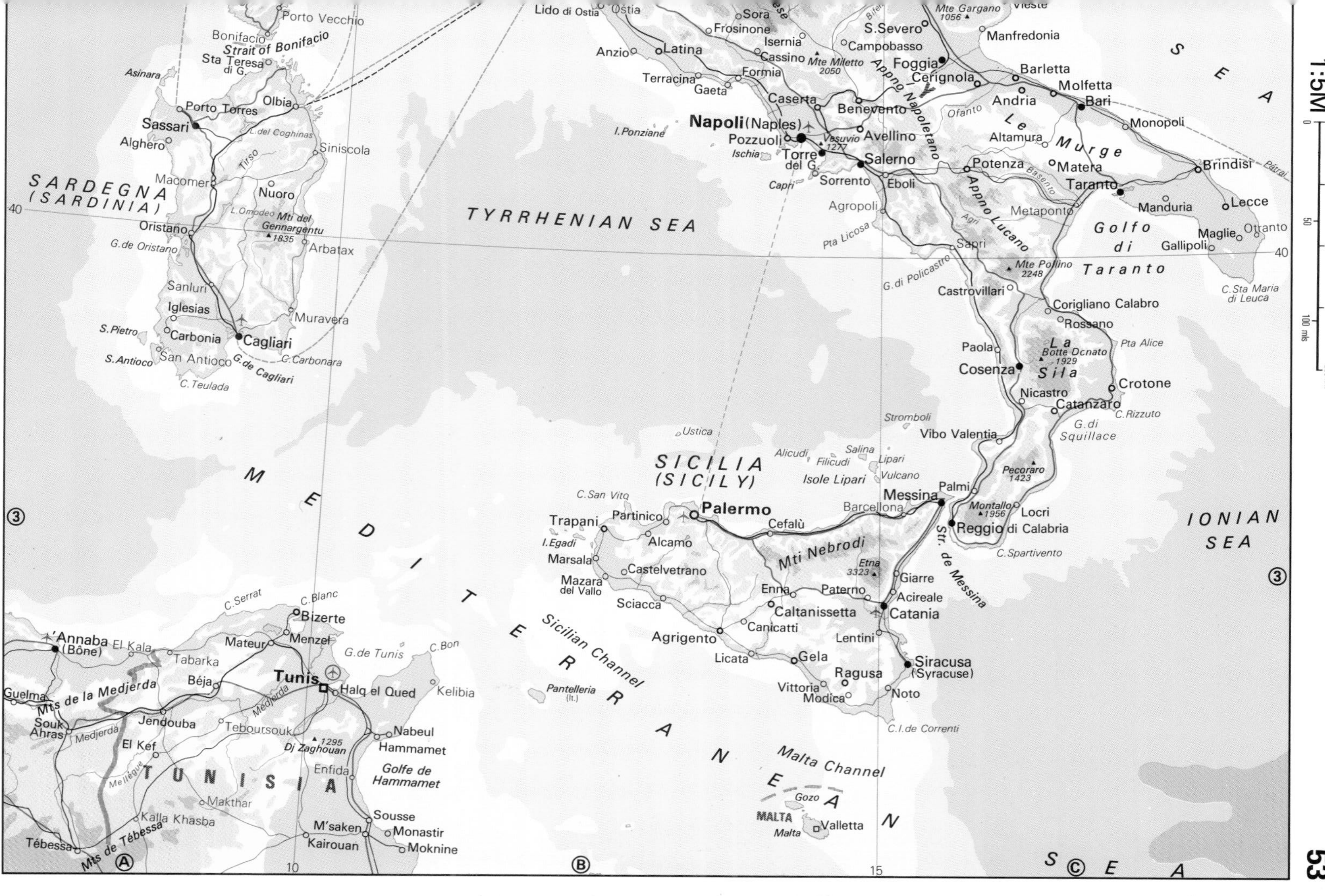

1:5M

50   100   150   200 km

50   100 mls

S   E   A

I.Ponziane

IONIAN SEA

TYRRHENIAN SEA

MEDITERRANEAN

Brindisi
Lecce
Monopoli
Maglie
Gallipoli
C.Sta.Maria
di Leuca
Oranto
Manduria
Bari
Molfetta
Barletta
Andria
Cerignola
Foggia
Manfredonia
Mte.Gargano
1056
Vieste
S.Severo
Campobasso
Mte.Miletto
2050
Benevento
Avellino
Salerno
Sorrento
Napoli(Naples)
Pozzuoli
Caserta
Torre del
Capri
Ischia
Isernia
Cassino
Sora
Frosinone
Formia
Gaeta
Terracina
Latina
Anzio
Lido di Ostia
Ostia

Golfo
di
Taranto
Taranto
Matera
Altamura
Potenza
Appno Lucano
Eboli
Agropoli
Pta Licosa
Metaponto
Castrovillari
Corigliano Calabro
Rossano
Mte.Pollino
2248
Mte.Pollino
Paola
Cosenza
Nicastro
Catanzaro
Batte Donato
1929
La
Sila
Crotone
Pta Alice
C.Rizzuto
G. di
Squillace
Pecoraro
1423
Montalto
1956
Locri
Reggio di Calabria
C.Spartivento
Palmi
Vibo Valentia
Str. de Messina
Stromboli

Salina
Lipari
Vulcano
Filicudi
Alicudi
Isole Lipari
Ustica
C.San Vito
Trapani
I.Egadi
Marsala
Mazara
del Vallo
Partinico
Alcamo
Castelvetrano
Sciacca
Palermo
Cefalù
Mti Nebrodi
Etna
3323
Paterno
Caltanissetta
Canicattì
Enna
Agrigento
Licata
Gela
Vittoria
Modica
Ragusa
Lentini
Catania
Acireale
Giarre
Barcellona
Messina
Siracusa
(Syracuse)
Noto
C.I.de Correnti
SICILIA
(SICILY)
Pantelleria
(It)
Sicilian Channel

Malta Channel
Gozo
Valletta
MALTA
Malta

PortoVecchio
Sta.Teresa
di G.
Strait of
Bonifacio
Bonifacio
Asinara
Porto Torres
Sassari
Alghero
Sininola
Olbia
C.del Coghinas
Tirso
Nuoro
Mti del
Gennargentu
1835
Oristano
G. de Oristano
Sanluri
Iglesias
Carbonia
S.Pietro
S.Antioco
San Antioco
C.Teulada
C.Carbonara
G. de Cagliari
Cagliari
Muravera
Arbatax
SARDEGNA
(SARDINIA)

TUNISIA
Annaba
(Bône)
Guelma
Tébessa
Mts de Tébessa
Souk
Ahras
Mts de la Medjerda
El Kala
Tabarka
Béja
Jendouba
El Kef
Kalaa Khasba
Makthar
Kairouan
M'saken
Moknine
Monastir
Sousse
Enfida
Dj Zaghouan
1295
Bizerte
C.Blanc
C.Serrat
Menzel
Mateur
Tunis
Halq el Qued
Nabeul
Hammamet
Golfe de
Hammamet
G. de Tunis
C.Bon
Kelibia

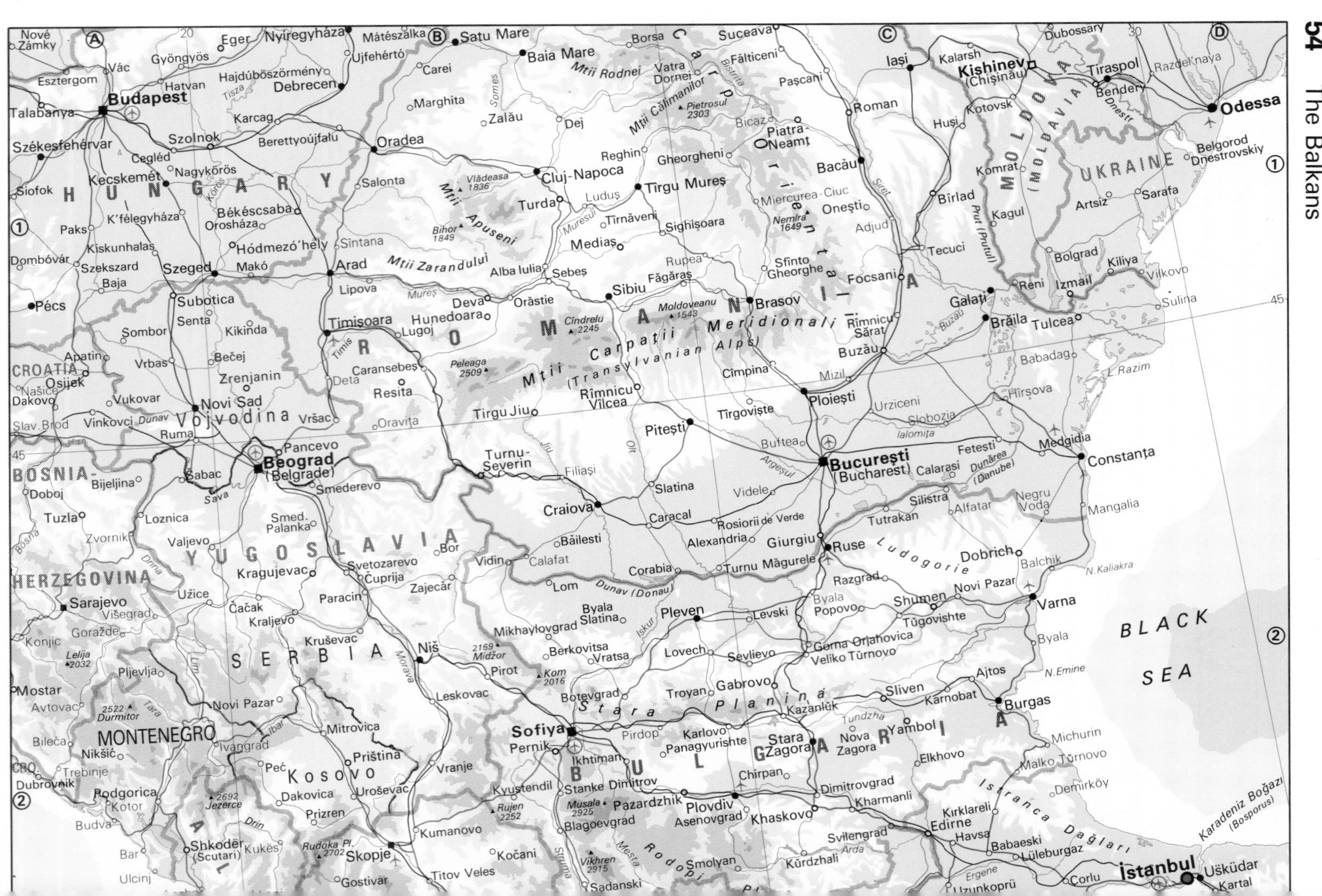

BLACK SEA
UKRAINE
MOLDAVIA
ROMANIA
BULGARIA
YUGOSLAVIA
HUNGARY
SERBIA
KOSOVO
MONTENEGRO
BOSNIA
HERZEGOVINA
CROATIA
Vojvodina
Odessa
Kishinev (Chişinău)
Tiraspol
Bendery
Iaşi
Galaţi
Brăila
Tulcea
Constanţa
Bucureşti (Bucharest)
Ploieşti
Braşov
Sibiu
Cluj-Napoca
Tîrgu Mureş
Timişoara
Arad
Oradea
Craiova
Piteşti
Bacău
Focşani
Buzău
Suceava
Baia Mare
Satu Mare
Varna
Burgas
Ruse
Pleven
Sofiya
Plovdiv
Stara Zagora
Istanbul
Edirne
Beograd (Belgrade)
Novi Sad
Niš
Skopje
Sarajevo
Budapest
Debrecen
Szeged
Kecskemét
Pécs
Dunav (Donau)
Carpaţii Meridionali (Transylvanian Alps)
Stara Planina
Rodopi
Ludogorie
Dobrich
Shumen
Tîrgu Jiu
Deva
Hunedoara
Rîmnicu Vîlcea
Slatina
Vidin
Lom
Kragujevac
Priština
Shkodër (Scutari)
Mostar
Tuzla
Osijek
Subotica
Karadeniz Boğazı (Bosporus)
Üsküdar
Kartal

| 0 | 50 | 100 | 150 | 200 km |

| 0 | 50 | 100 mls |

TURKEY

GREECE

MACEDONIA

ALBANIA

AEGEAN SEA

SPORADHES (DODECANESE)

Sea of Crete

Sea of Marmara

IONIAN SEA

IÓNIOI NÍSOI (Ionian Islands)

Mirtóön Sea

Thermaïkós Kólpos

Kikládhes (Cyclades)

Kríti

Bursa, Yalova, Gemlik, Mustafa-Kemalpaşa, Karacabey, İznik G, Tekirdağ, Tavşanlı, Simav, Denizli, Ak Dağ 2089, Akhisar, Turgutlu, Salihli, Alaşehir, Buldano, Odemiş, Nazilli, Cine, Muğla, Milas, Bodrum, Rodhos, Ródhos, Lindos, Marmaris

İzmir, Manisa, Menemen, Bornova, Çeşme, Söke, Aydın, Selçuk, Torbalı, Urla, Ürkmez

Kuşadası K., Sámos, Ikaría, Pátmos, Léros, Kálimnos, Kós, Kerme K., Simi, Símí, Alimniá, Khálki, Astipálaia, Anáfi, Kárpathos, Kásos

Balıkesir, Edremit, Burhaniye, Ayvalık, Bergama, Kırkağaç, Soma, Bandırma, Gönen, Biga, Çanakkale, Ezine, Edremit K., Mitlíni, Lésvos, Khíos, Psará, Ándros, Tínos, Síros, Páros, Náxos, Íos, Thíra

Gelibolu (Gallipoli), Keşan, Ipsala, Malkara, Tekirdağ, Uzunköprü, Saros Körfezi, Gökçeada, Bozcaada, Límnos, Áyios Evstrátios, Skíros, K. Kafirévs, Kéa, Kíthnos, Sérifos, Sífnos, Mílos

Alexandroúpolis, Komotiní, Xánthi, Kaválla, Thásos, Sámothráki, K. Kástron, Dráma, Sérrai, Nigríta, Kilkís, Thessaloníki (Saloníca), Khalkidhikí, K. Strimonikós, K. Síngitikós, K. Toronaíos, Áthos 2033, Políviros

Kavadárci, Prilep, Bitola, Prespansko Jez., Ohrid, Ohridsko Jez., Kičevo, Tiranë, Elbasan, Durrës, Kavajë, Lushnjë, Fier, Berat, Vlorë, Gjirokastër, Sarandë, Balsh, Vijosë, Tomorri 2480, Grammos 2503, Smólikas 2637, Kýjevo, Struga

Kozáni, Kastoría, Flórina, Édhessa, Véroia, Ptolemaïs, Kateríni, Kalabáka, Larísa, Tírnavos, Tríkala, Kardhítsa, Flórina, Ólimbos (Olympus) 2974, Aliákmon, Pilós, Ióannina, Metsovon, Tzoumérka 2429, Árta, Préveza, Kérkira (Corfu), Igoumenítsa, Amfilokhía, Agrínion 2355, Mesolóngion, Kalinos, Othrís 1726, Tríkala

Vólos, Skíathos, Skópelos, Alónnisos, Khalkís, Évvoia, Istiaía, Livanátais, Thívai, Thebes, Levádhia, Lamía, Domokós, Dhomokós, Tínfristos 2316, Gióna 2510, Naupaktos, Pátrai, Aíyion, Kórinthos, Sikionía, Kiáto

Athínai (Athens), Piraiévs, Akharnaí, Mégara, Eleusís, Salamís, Aíyina, Ídhra, Spétsai, Návplion, Argos, Tripolis, Sparti, Kalámai, Messíni, Pílos, Kipanissía, Filiatrá, Megalópolis, Amaliás, Pírgos, Kiparissiakós Kólpos, Zákinthos, Kefallinía, Zákinthos, Levkás

Parnon Ó. 1935, Taíyetos 2404, Ayíos Andréas, Mólaoi, Neápolis, Yíthion, Monemvasía, Kíthira, Akr. Maléa, Andíkithira, Lakonikós Kólpos, Messiniakós Kólpos, Akr. Taínaron, Argolikós K.

Iráklion, Réthimnon, Khaniá, Kastélli, Timbákion, Ídhi Óri 2456, Lévka Óri 2452, Akr. Spátha, Akr. Líthinon, Dhíkti Óri 2148, Ierápetra, Sitía, Akr. Sídheros, Mírabéllou K., Timbákion

Brindisi, Lecce, Maglie, Otranto, Gallipoli, C. Sta Maria di Leuca, **Strait of Otranto**

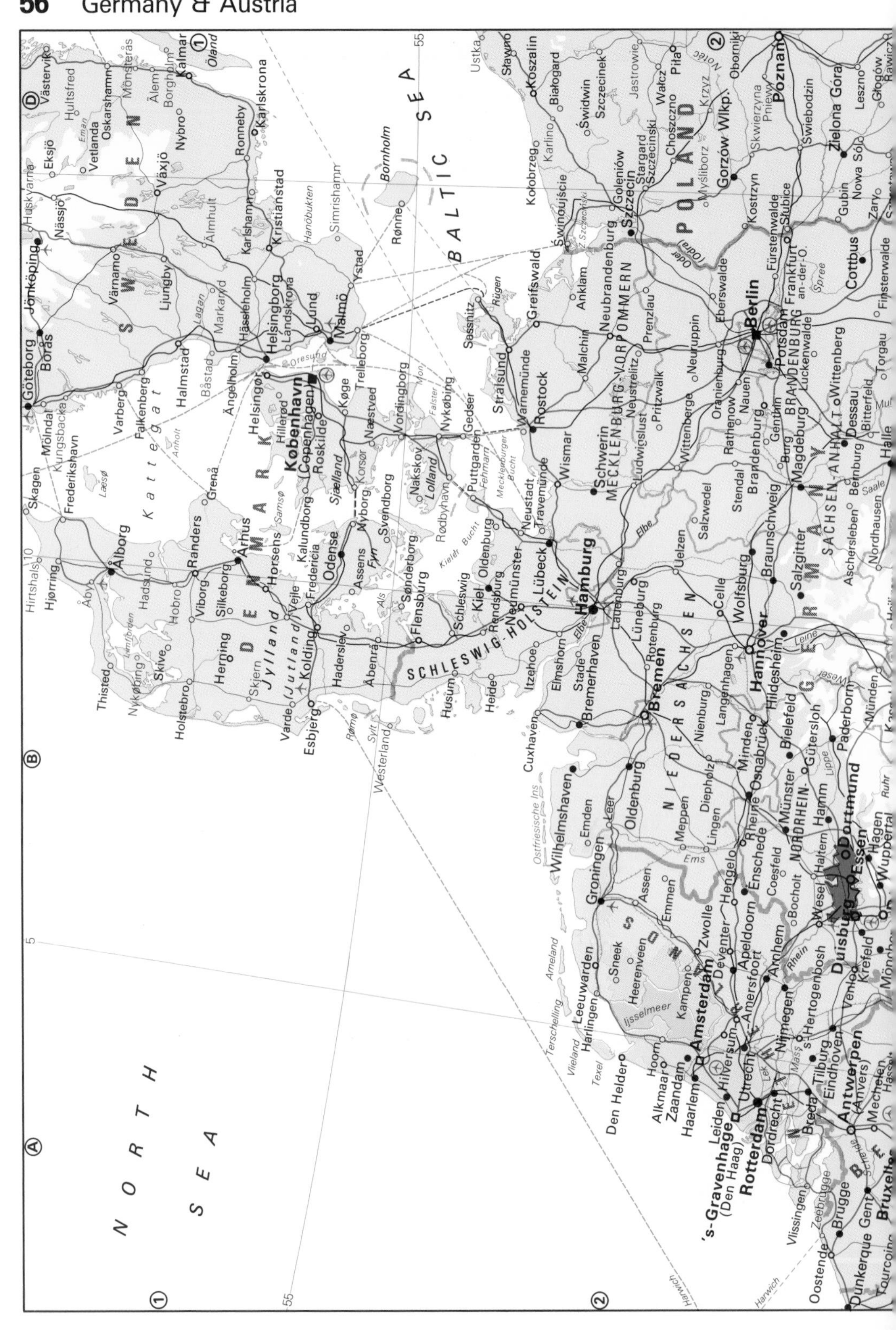
NORTH SEA
BALTIC SEA
Kattegat
SWEDEN
DENMARK
POLAND
GERMANY
SCHLESWIG-HOLSTEIN
MECKLENBURG-VORPOMMERN
NIEDERSACHSEN
BRANDENBURG
SACHSEN-ANHALT
NORDRHEIN-
Jylland (Jutland)
Sjælland
Fyn
Lolland
Falster
Bornholm
Rügen
Fehmarn
Öland
Oresund
Hanöbukten
Kieler Bucht
Mecklenburger Bucht
Ostfriesische Ins.
Ameland
Terschelling
Vlieland
Texel
Ijsselmeer
Göteborg
Borås
Jönköping
Malmö
Lund
Helsingborg
Halmstad
Kristianstad
Karlskrona
Kalmar
Växjö
København (Copenhagen)
Roskilde
Odense
Århus
Ålborg
Esbjerg
Kolding
Vejle
Flensburg
Kiel
Lübeck
Hamburg
Rostock
Stralsund
Greifswald
Szczecin
Berlin
Potsdam
Frankfurt an-der-O.
Cottbus
Poznań
Zielona Góra
Gorzów Wlkp.
Magdeburg
Dessau
Halle
Braunschweig
Wolfsburg
Hannover
Bremen
Bremerhaven
Cuxhaven
Wilhelmshaven
Oldenburg
Osnabrück
Bielefeld
Münster
Dortmund
Essen
Duisburg
Groningen
Leeuwarden
Amsterdam
Haarlem
Leiden
's-Gravenhage (Den Haag)
Rotterdam
Utrecht
Arnhem
Nijmegen
Eindhoven
Antwerpen (Anvers)
Brugge
Gent
Oostende
Dunkerque
Harwich

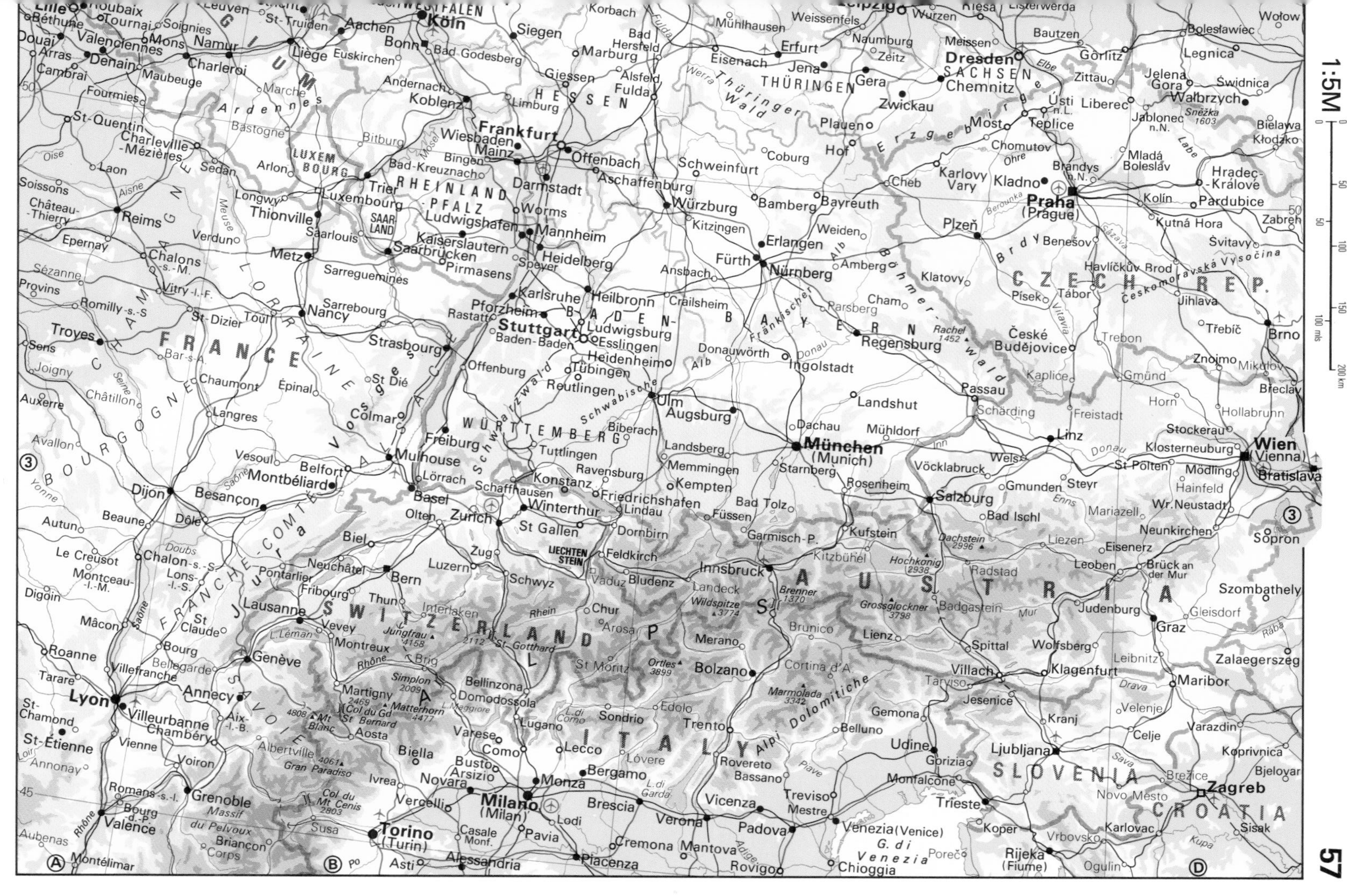

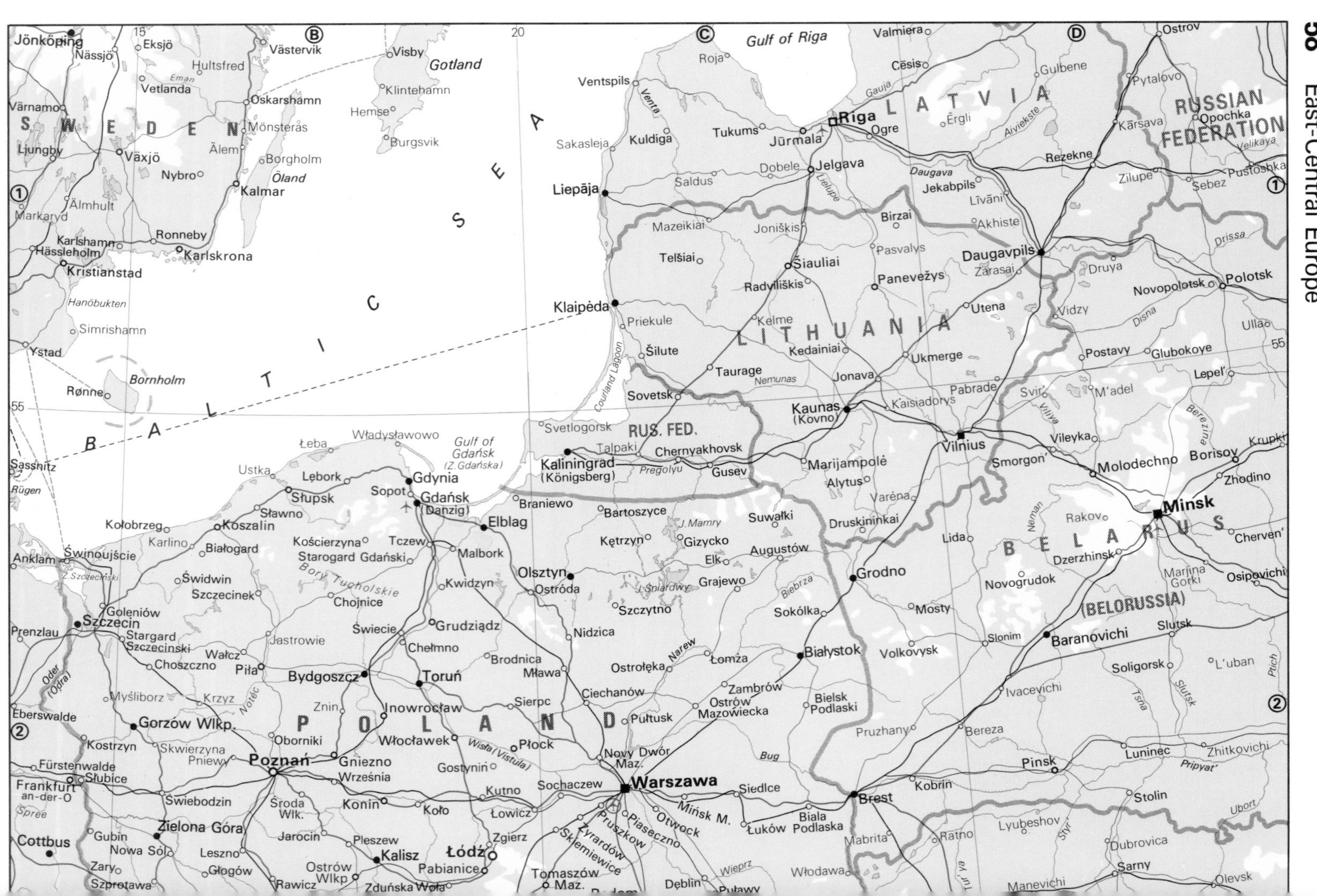
RUSSIAN FEDERATION
LATVIA
LITHUANIA
BELARUS
(BELORUSSIA)
POLAND
SWEDEN
BALTIC SEA
RUS. FED.
Gulf of Riga
Gulf of Gdańsk (Z. Gdańska)
Courland Lagoon
Gotland
Öland
Bornholm
Hanöbukten
Rügen
Riga
Minsk
Vilnius
Warszawa
Daugavpils
Kaunas (Kovno)
Kaliningrad (Königsberg)
Klaipėda
Liepāja
Ventspils
Jelgava
Jūrmala
Šiauliai
Panevėžys
Grodno
Brest
Białystok
Gdańsk (Danzig)
Gdynia
Sopot
Elbląg
Olsztyn
Toruń
Bydgoszcz
Poznań
Łódź
Szczecin
Kalisz
Gorzów Wlkp.
Zielona Góra
Pinsk
Baranovichi
Borisov
Polotsk
Novopolotsk
Molodechno
Slutsk
Kalmar
Karlskrona
Kristianstad
Växjö
Visby
Jönköping
Cottbus
Frankfurt an-der-O
Nemunas
Daugava
Berezina
Neman
Pripyat'
Bug
Narew
Wisła (Vistula)
Oder (Odra)
Noteć
Spree

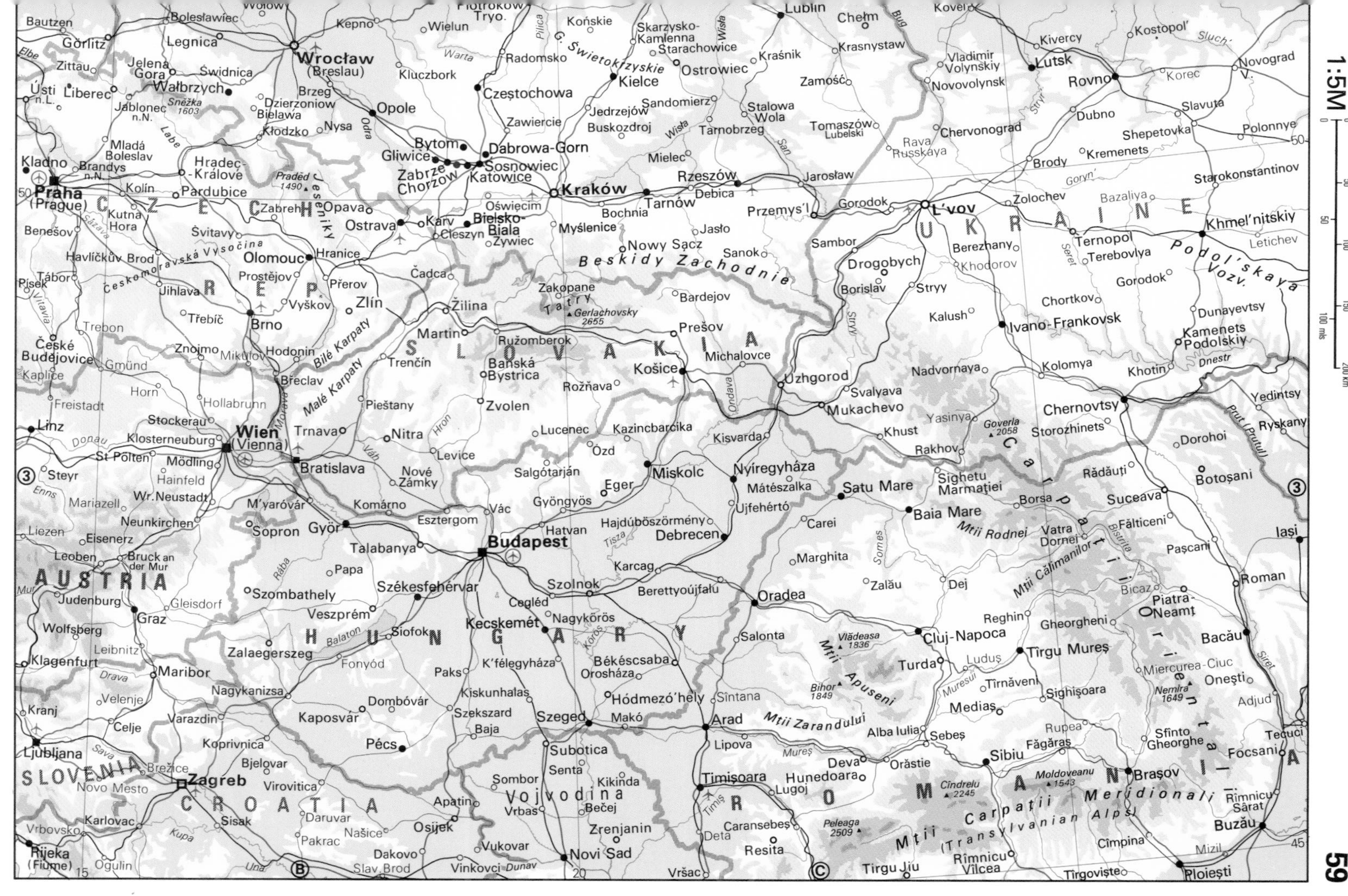
UKRAINE
POLAND
CZECH REPUBLIC
SLOVAKIA
HUNGARY
ROMANIA
AUSTRIA
SLOVENIA
CROATIA
Vojvodina
Carpaţii Meridionali (Transylvanian Alps)
Beskidy Zachodnie
Podol'skaya Vozv.
Mţii Apuseni
Mţii Rodnei
Mţii Zarandului
Tatry
Jeseníky
Malé Karpaty
Bílé Karpaty
Lutsk
Rovno
L'vov
Ternopol
Khmel'nitskiy
Ivano-Frankovsk
Chernovtsy
Uzhgorod
Mukachevo
Lublin
Kielce
Kraków
Katowice
Rzeszów
Tarnów
Częstochowa
Wrocław (Breslau)
Opole
Ostrava
Olomouc
Brno
Praha (Prague)
České Budějovice
Linz
Wien (Vienna)
Bratislava
Graz
Klagenfurt
Maribor
Ljubljana
Zagreb
Rijeka (Fiume)
Košice
Prešov
Miskolc
Debrecen
Nyíregyháza
Budapest
Győr
Székesfehérvár
Kecskemét
Szeged
Pécs
Subotica
Novi Sad
Osijek
Oradea
Arad
Timişoara
Cluj-Napoca
Satu Mare
Baia Mare
Tîrgu Mureş
Sibiu
Braşov
Bacău
Iaşi
Suceava
Buzău
Ploieşti
Danube
Dunav
Donau
Tisza
Balaton

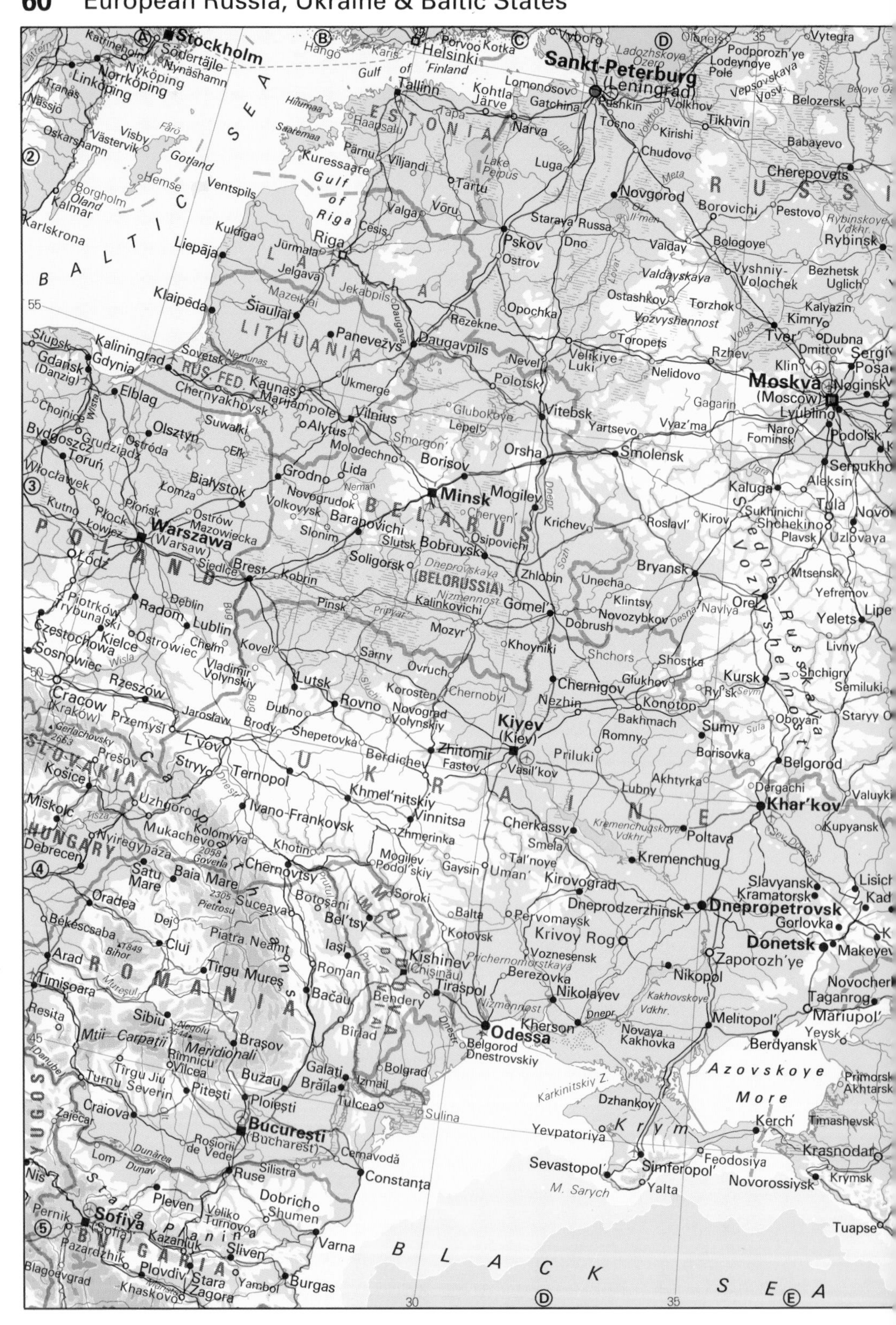
Stockholm
Södertälje
Nynäshamn
Nyköping
Norrköping
Linköping
Katrineholm
Tranås
Nässjö
Västervik
Oskarshamn
Visby
Fårö
Gotland
Hemse
Borgholm
Öland
Kalmar
Karlskrona
BALTIC SEA
Hangö
Karis
Porvoo
Kotka
Helsinki
Gulf of Finland
Vyborg
Sankt-Peterburg
(Leningrad)
Ladozhskoye Ozero
Olonets
Podporozh'ye
Lodeynoye Pole
Vytegra
Vepsovskaya Vosv.
Beloye Oz.
Belozersk
Tallinn
Kohtla Järve
Lomonosov
Gatchina
Pushkin
Volkhov
Tikhvin
Hiiumaa
Saaremaa
Haapsalu
Tapa
ESTONIA
Narva
Tosno
Kirishi
Babayevo
Pärnu
Viljandi
Kuressaare
Lake Peipus
Luga
Chudovo
Cherepovets
RUSSIA
Gulf of Riga
Tartu
Ventspils
Valga
Võru
Novgorod
Borovichi
Pestovo
Rybinskoye Vdkhr.
Rybinsk
Kuldīga
Cēsis
Riga
Jūrmala
Staraya Russa
Il'men
Pskov
Dno
Valday
Bologoye
Liepāja
Jelgava
Ostrov
Valdayskaya
Vyshniy-Volochek
Bezhetsk
Uglich
LATVIA
Mazeikiai
Jekabpils
Daugava
Ostashkov
Torzhok
Kalyazin
Kimry
Klaipėda
Šiauliai
Opochka
Vozvyshennost
Rezekne
Volga
Tver'
Dubna
Dmitrov
LITHUANIA
Panevežys
Daugavpils
Toropets
Rzhev
Słupsk
Kaliningrad
Sovetsk
Nemunas
Gdańsk
(Danzig)
Gdynia
RUS. FED.
Kaunas
Nevel
Velikiye Luki
Nelidovo
Klin
Moskva
(Moscow)
Noginsk
Elbląg
Chernyakhovsk
Marijampole
Ukmerge
Polotsk
Gagarin
Lyublino
Chojnice
Wisła
Suwałki
Vilnius
Alytus
Glubokoye
Vitebsk
Yartsevo
Vyaz'ma
Naro Fominsk
Podolsk
Bydgoszcz
Grudziądz
Olsztyn
Ostróda
Ełk
Lepel
Smorgon'
Molodechno
Orsha
Smolensk
Toruń
Borisov
Serpukhov
Włocławek
Białystok
Łomża
Grodno
Lida
Neman
Minsk
Mogilev
Kaluga
Aleksin
Kutno
Płock
Płońsk
Ostrów Mazowiecka
Novogrudok
Volkovysk
Baranovichi
Slonim
BELARUS
Cherven'
Krichev
Dnepr
Roslavl'
Kirov
Sukhinichi
Shchekino
Tula
Warszawa
(Warsaw)
Łowicz
POLAND
Łódź
Siedlce
Brest
Kobrin
Slutsk
Bobruysk
Osipovichi
Soligorsk
Dneprovskaya
(BELORUSSIA)
Nizmennost
Zhlobin
Sozh
Unecha
Bryansk
Plavsk
Uzlovaya
Mtsensk
Srednerusskaya Vozvyshennost
Piotrków Trybunalski
Radom
Dęblin
Lublin
Bug
Pinsk
Pripyat'
Kalinkovichi
Gomel'
Klintsy
Novozybkov
Desna
Navlya
Orel
Yefremov
Yelets
Lipetsk
Częstochowa
Kielce
Ostrowiec
Chełm
Kovel'
Mozyr'
Dobrush
Livny
Sosnowiec
Vladimir Volynskiy
Sarny
Ovruch
Khoyniki
Shchors
Shostka
Kursk
Shchigry
Rzeszów
Cracow
(Kraków)
Lutsk
Korosten'
Chernobyl
Chernigov
Glukhov
Ryl'sk
Seym
Semiluki
Gerlachovský
2663
Przemyśl
Jarosław
Dubno
Rovno
Novograd Volynskiy
Nezhin
Konotop
Starry Oskol
Oboyan'
Brody
Shepetovka
Kiyev
(Kiev)
Bakhmach
Sumy
Sula
SLOVAKIA
L'vov
Zhitomir
Romny
Prešov
Košice
Stryy
Dnestr
Ternopol
Berdichev
Fastov
Vasil'kov
Priluki
Borisovka
Belgorod
UKRAINE
Akhtyrka
Dergachi
Valuyki
Miskolc
Tisza
Uzhgorod
Ivano-Frankovsk
Khmel'nitskiy
Lubny
Khar'kov
HUNGARY
Mukachevo
Kolomyya
Vinnitsa
Cherkassy
Kremenchugskoye Vdkhr.
Poltava
Kupyansk
Debrecen
Nyíregyháza
Goverla
2058
Khotin
Zhmerinka
Smela
Sev. Donets
Satu Mare
Baia Mare
Chernovtsy
Mogilev Podol'skiy
Gaysin
Uman'
Tal'noye
Kremenchug
Lisichansk
Prut
MOLDOVA
Soroki
Kirovograd
Slavyansk
Kramatorsk
Kadiyevka
Oradea
2305
Pietrosu
Suceava
Botoşani
Bel'tsy
Balta
Pervomaysk
Dneprodzerzhinsk
Dnepropetrovsk
Gorlovka
Békéscsaba
Dej
Piatra Neamţ
Kotovsk
Krivoy Rog
1849
Bihor
Cluj
Iaşi
Kishinev
(Chişinău)
Voznesensk
Prichernomorskaya
Zaporozh'ye
Donetsk
Makeyevka
Arad
ROMANIA
Roman
Berezovka
Nikopol
Tîrgu Mureş
Bacău
Bendery
Tiraspol
Nikolayev
Kakhovskoye Vdkhr.
Novocherkassk
Timişoara
Mureşul
Nizmennost
Dnepr
Taganrog
Reşita
Sibiu
Negoiu
2544
Bîrlad
Odessa
Kherson
Melitopol'
Mariupol'
Mtii Carpaţii Meridionali
Braşov
Novaya Kakhovka
Belgorod Dnestrovskiy
Yeysk
Berdyansk
(Danube)
Rimnicu Vilcea
Tîrgu Jiu
Buzău
Galaţi
Brăila
Izmail
Bolgrad
Azovskoye More
Primorsko Akhtarsk
Turnu Severin
Piteşti
Ploieşti
Tulcea
Karkinitskiy Z.
Dzhankoy
YUGOSLAVIA
Zaječar
Craiova
Sulina
Krym
Kerch'
Timashevsk
Bucureşti
(Bucharest)
Roşiorii de Vede
Yevpatoriya
Krasnodar
Lom
Dunărea
Dunav
Cernavodă
Feodosiya
Sevastopol'
Simferopol'
Novorossiysk
Krymsk
Niš
Stara Planina
Ruse
Silistra
Constanţa
Pleven
M. Sarych
Yalta
Pernik
Sofiya
(Sofia)
Veliko Turnovo
Dobrich
Shumen
Tuapse
Kazanluk
BULGARIA
Sliven
Varna
BLACK SEA
Pazardzhik
Plovdiv
Stara Zagora
Yambol
Burgas
Blagoevgrad
Maritsa
Khaskovo
55
50
45
30
35

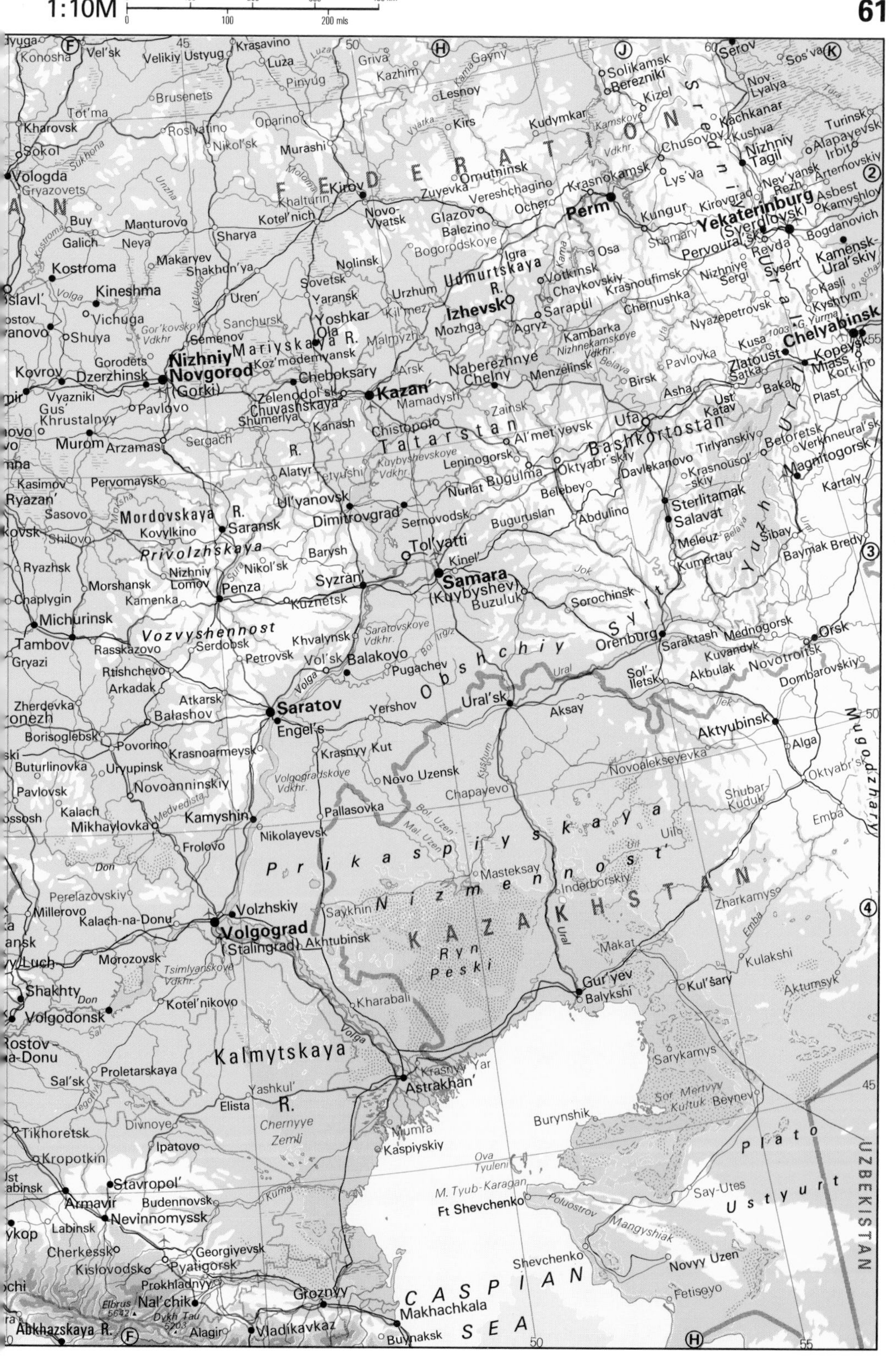
0 100 200 300 400 km
0 100 200 mls
FEDERATION
KAZAKHSTAN
UZBEKISTAN
CASPIAN SEA
Perm
Yekaterinburg (Sverdlovsk)
Chelyabinsk
Kazan'
Nizhniy Novgorod (Gorki)
Izhevsk
Kirov
Ufa
Samara (Kuybyshev)
Saratov
Volgograd (Stalingrad)
Astrakhan'
Orenburg
Ural'sk
Aktyubinsk
Gur'yev
Penza
Saransk
Tol'yatti
Ul'yanovsk
Cheboksary
Magnitogorsk
Orsk
Elista
Stavropol'
Groznyy
Makhachkala
Vladikavkaz
Nal'chik
Kostroma
Vologda
Tambov
Prikaspiyskaya Nizmennost'
Obshchiy Syrt
Tatarstan
Bashkortostan
Udmurtskaya R.
Mariyskaya R.
Mordovskaya R.
Chuvashskaya R.
Kalmytskaya R.
Privolzhskaya Vozvyshennost
Plato Ustyurt
Mugodzhary
Ryn Peski
Chernyye Zemli
Volga
Ural
Kama
Don
Abkhazskaya R.
Elbrus 5642
Dykh Tau 5203
Ft Shevchenko
Novyy Uzen
Mangyshlak
Kara-Bogaz-Gol

600 1200 1800 km
300 600 900 mils

INTERNATIONAL DATELINE

Kuril'skiye Ostrova

Bering Sea

Petropavlovsk-Kamchatskiy

Sakhalin

Sea of Okhotsk

HOKKAIDO

JAPAN

Sapporo

Nagoya Tokyo

Osaka

KYUSHU

SHIKOKU

Kita Kyūshū

Pusan

SOUTH KOREA

N. KOREA

Pyongyang

Vladivostok

Sea of Japan

Khabarovsk

M O N G O L I A

MONGOLIA

Ulaanbaatar

I N N E R   M O N G O L I A

Shenyang

Dalian

Beijing

Tianjin

Qingdao

Yellow Sea

Shanghai

Nanjing

Hangzhou

Wuhan

Zhengzhou

Xi'an

Taiyuan

Lanzhou

C H I N A

T I B E T

S I N K I A N G

Ürümqi

Kashmir

Lahore

Islamabad

AFGHANISTAN

Kābul

Herāt

Mashhad

TURKMENISTAN

Ashkhabad

Dushanbe

TAJ.

KYRGYZSTAN (KIRGHIZIA)

Bishkek

Alma Ata

Tashkent

UZBEKISTAN

KAZAKHSTAN

Karaganda

Aral Sea

Novosibirsk

Barnaul

Omsk

Krasnoyarsk

Yakutsk

R U S S I A N   F E D E R A T I O N

Lena

Yenisey

Ob'

Noril'sk

ARCTIC CIRCLE

Severnaya Zemlya

Novosibirskiye Ostrova

Novaya Zemlya

Zemlya Frantsa Iosifa

Svalbard (Nor.)

Barents Sea

A R C T I C   O C E A N

Murmansk

Arkhangel'sk

N O R W A Y

S W E D E N

FINLAND

Helsinki

Oslo

Stockholm

København

DENMARK

Edinburgh

UNITED KINGDOM

Dublin

IRELAND

London

Paris

NETH.

BEL.

LUX.

GERMANY

POLAND

Warszawa

CZECH R.

SLOVAKIA

AUSTRIA

HUNGARY

SLOV.

CRO.

B.-H.

YUGOS.

ROMANIA

București

BULGARIA

TURKEY

İstanbul

Ankara

Adana

CYPRUS

SYRIA

Dimashq

LEB.

Beirut

Jerusalem

ISR.

JOR.

Ammãn

IRAQ

Baghdād

Al Mawşil

Al Başrah

KUWAIT

SAUDI ARABIA

Ar Riyāḍ

BAHRAIN

The Gulf

QATAR

Kermãn

Eşfahān

IRAN

Tehrān

Tabrīz

Elburz

Bãkhtarãn

Baku

AZER.

ARM.

Yerevan

GEO.

Tbilisi

Caspian Sea

Astrakhan'

Volgograd

Rostov

Donetsk

Dnepropetrovsk

Kiyev

UKRAINE

Odessa

Kishinev

MOLD.

Black Sea

Khar'kov

Saratov

Samara

Ufa

Kazan'

Nizhniy Novgorod

Moskva

Minsk

BELARUS (BELORUSSIA)

RUS. FED.

LAT.

LITH.

Vilnius

Riga

EST.

Tallinn

Sankt-Peterburg (Leningrad)

Chelyabinsk

Yekaterinburg

Sergino

Vorkuta

Faerøerne (Den.)

1:20M

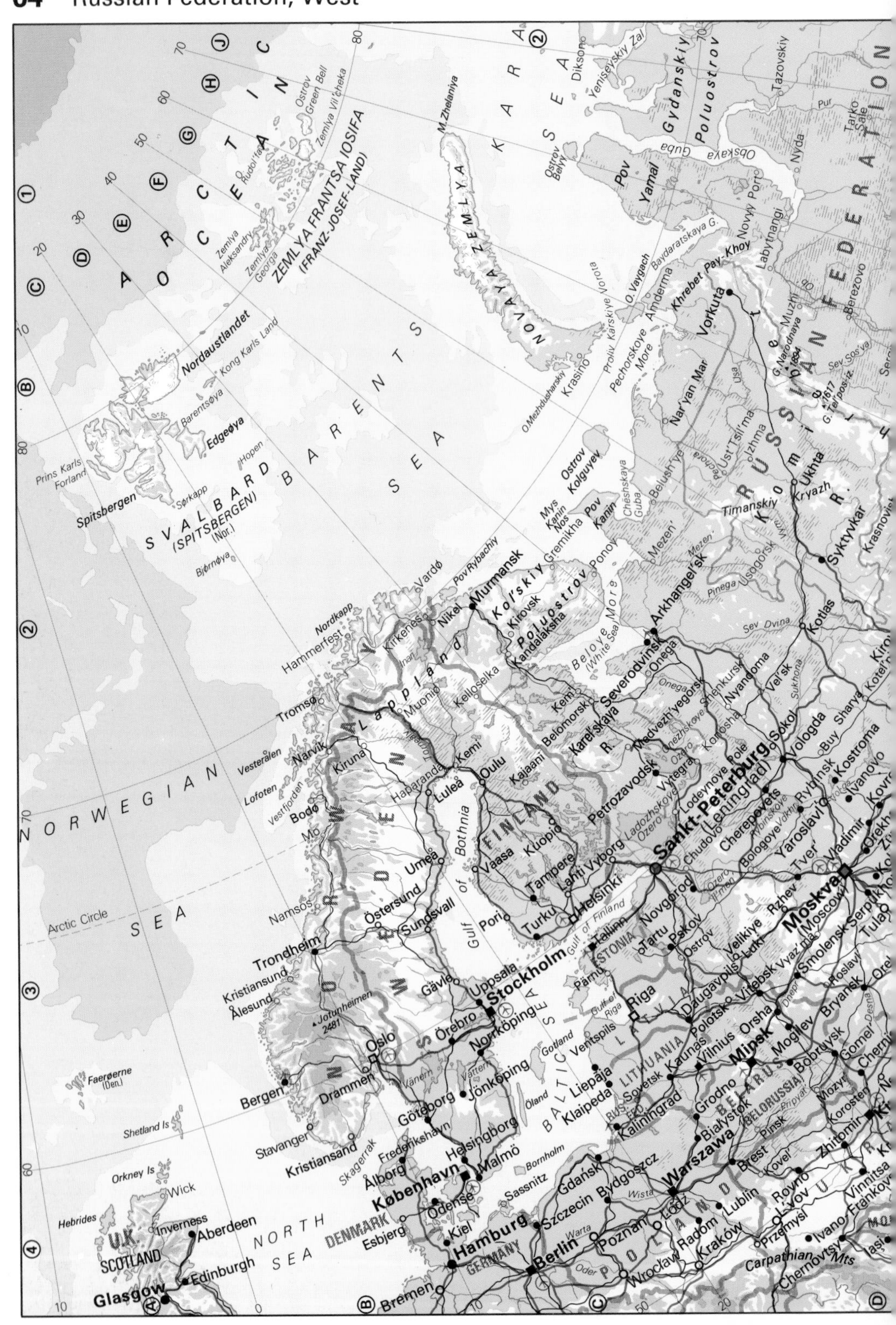
ARCTIC OCEAN
BARENTS SEA
NORWEGIAN SEA
NORTH SEA
KARA SEA
BALTIC SEA
SVALBARD (SPITSBERGEN) (Nor.)
ZEMLYA FRANTSA IOSIFA (FRANZ-JOSEF-LAND)
NOVAYA ZEMLYA
RUSSIAN FEDERATION
FINLAND
SWEDEN
NORWAY
DENMARK
ESTONIA
LATVIA
LITHUANIA
BELARUS (BELORUSSIA)
POLAND
GERMANY
UKRAINE
U.K.
SCOTLAND
Moskva (Moscow)
Sankt-Peterburg (Leningrad)
Stockholm
Helsinki
Oslo
København
Warszawa
Berlin
Hamburg
Riga
Tallinn
Minsk
Vilnius
Arkhangel'sk
Murmansk
Vorkuta
Syktyvkar
Arctic Circle
Lappland
Kol'skiy Poluostrov
Gulf of Bothnia
Gulf of Finland
Beloye More (White Sea)
Pechorskoye More
Poluostrov Yamal
Gydanskiy Poluostrov
Obskaya Guba
Ostrov Kolguyev
Spitsbergen
Nordaustlandet
Edgeøya
Faerøerne (Den.)
Shetland Is
Orkney Is
Hebrides
Glasgow
Edinburgh
Aberdeen
Bergen
Trondheim
Tromsø
Narvik
Kiruna
Luleå
Oulu
Tampere
Turku
Vaasa
Kuopio
Umeå
Göteborg
Malmö
Gdańsk
Kraków
Wrocław
Poznań
Łódź
Lublin
Brest
Gomel'
Smolensk
Tver'
Yaroslavl'
Vologda
Kotlas
Ukhta
Nar'yan Mar
Petrozavodsk
Novgorod
Pskov
Kaliningrad
Carpathian Mts

1:20M

| 0 | 200 | 400 | 600 | 800 km |
| 0 | 200 | 400 mls |

RUSSIAN FEDERATION
1 Chuvashkaya R.
2 Checheno-Ingushskaya R.
3 Severo-Osetinskaya R.
4 Kabardino-Balkarskaya R.
GEORGIA
5 Abkhazskaya R.
6 Adzharskaya R.
AZERBAIJAN
7 Nakhichevanskaya R.

SINKIANG

KAZAKHSTAN

UZBEKISTAN

TURKMENISTAN

KYRGYZSTAN

TAJIKISTAN

AFGHANISTAN

IRAN

IRAQ

GEORGIA

ARMENIA

AZERBAIJAN

BLACK SEA

CASPIAN SEA

Omsk
Novosibirsk
Barnaul
Biysk
Tomsk
Yekaterinburg
Chelyabinsk
Perm
Kazan
Samara
Saratov
Volgograd
Nizhniy Novgorod
Izhevsk
Orenburg
Aktyubinsk
Tashkent
Bishkek
Alma Ata
Semipalatinsk
Karaganda
Tselinograd
Balkhash
Kzyl Orda
Chimkent
Samarkand
Dushanbe
Ashkhabad
Chardzhou
Mashhad
Herat
Tehrān
Esfahan
Tabriz
Baku
Tbilisi
Yerevan
Makhachkala
Grozniy
Rostov-na-Donu
Donetsk
Dnepropetrovsk
Kharkov
Odessa
Astrakhan'
Gur'yev
Ufa
Magnitogorsk
Tyumen
Kurgan
Petropavlovsk
Kokchetav
Kustanay
Pavlodar
Ust'-Kamenogorsk
Zyryanovsk
Leninogorsk
Rubtsovsk

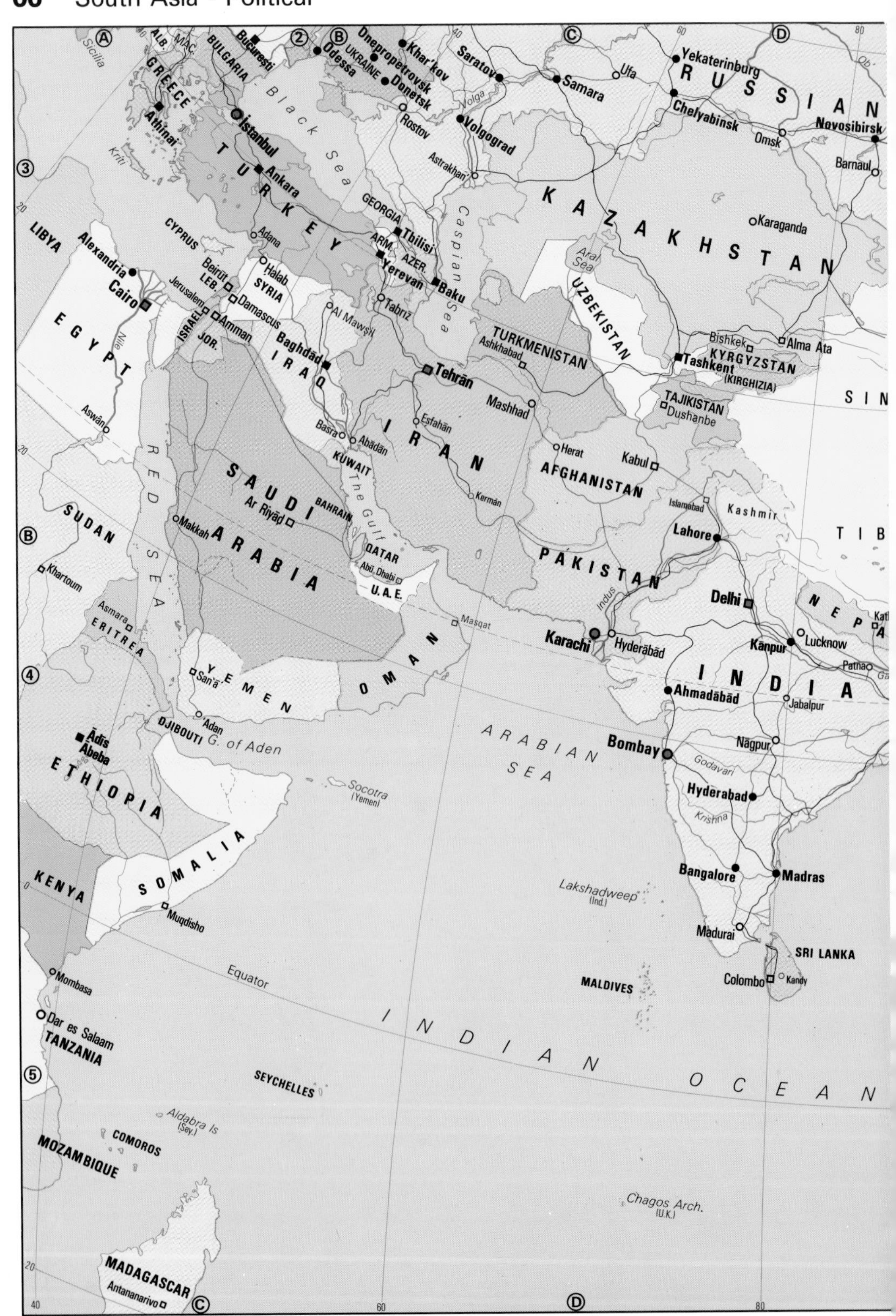

RUSSIAN
KAZAKHSTAN
TURKEY
IRAN
IRAQ
SAUDI ARABIA
EGYPT
SUDAN
ETHIOPIA
SOMALIA
KENYA
TANZANIA
MOZAMBIQUE
MADAGASCAR
YEMEN
OMAN
U.A.E.
QATAR
BAHRAIN
KUWAIT
SYRIA
JOR.
ISRAEL
LEB.
CYPRUS
LIBYA
GREECE
ALB.
MAC.
BULGARIA
UKRAINE
GEORGIA
ARM.
AZER.
TURKMENISTAN
UZBEKISTAN
KYRGYZSTAN
(KIRGHIZIA)
TAJIKISTAN
AFGHANISTAN
PAKISTAN
INDIA
NEPA
SRI LANKA
MALDIVES
SEYCHELLES
COMOROS
ERITREA
DJIBOUTI
Black Sea
Caspian Sea
Aral Sea
The Gulf
RED SEA
ARABIAN SEA
G. of Aden
INDIAN OCEAN
Equator
Bucureşti
Odessa
Dnepropetrovsk
Khar'kov
Donetsk
Rostov
Saratov
Samara
Ufa
Yekaterinburg
Chelyabinsk
Omsk
Novosibirsk
Barnaul
Volgograd
Volga
Astrakhan'
Karaganda
Athinai
Kriti
Sicilia
Istanbul
Ankara
Adana
Halab
Beirut
Damascus
Jerusalem
Amman
Alexandria
Cairo
Nile
Aswân
Tbilisi
Yerevan
Baku
Tabrīz
Al Mawşil
Baghdād
Basra
Abādān
Tehrān
Esfahān
Kermān
Mashhad
Ashkhabad
Herat
Kabul
Bishkek
Alma Ata
Tashkent
Dushanbe
Islamabad
Kashmir
Lahore
Ar Riyāḍ
Makkah
Abū Dhabi
Masqat
Khartoum
Asmara
San'ā
Adan
Ādīs Ābeba
Socotra
(Yemen)
Muqdisho
Mombasa
Dar es Salaam
Aldabra Is
(Sey.)
Antananarivo
Indus
Karachi
Hyderābād
Delhi
Lucknow
Kānpur
Patna
Ahmadābād
Jabalpur
Nāgpur
Bombay
Godavari
Hyderabad
Krishna
Bangalore
Madras
Madurai
Colombo
Kandy
Lakshadweep
(Ind.)
Chagos Arch.
(U.K.)
SIN
TIB

400   800   1200   1600 km
400   800 mils

E 100 **F** 120 **G** 140 **②** **H** 160

Yenisey

Krasnoyarsk   F E D E R A T I O N

Sakhalin

Irkutsk   Khabarovsk   Kuril'skiye Ostrova

Ulaanbaatar   Hokkaidō

M O N G O L I A   Qiqihar   Harbin   Changchun   Vladivostok   Sapporo

Sea of

I N N E R   M O N G O L I A   Shenyang   Japan   J A P A N

Ürümqi   N.KOREA   Tōkyō

Beijing   Dalian   Pyŏngyang   Nagoya

K I A N G   Tianjin   Sŏul   S.KOREA   Osaka

Taiyuan   Qingdao   Pusan   Shikoku

Lanzhou   Zhengzhou   Yellow   Kita-Kyūshū   Kyūshū

C H I N A   Xi'an   Sea

Hoang He

Lhasa   Nanjing   Shanghai

Kandu   Chengdu   Wuhan   Hangzhou

Thimphu   Chongqing   Changsha   Nanchang   Tropic of Cancer

BHUTAN   Chang Jiang   Fuzhou

BANGLA-   Brahmaputra   Guiyang   T'ai-pei   P A C I F I C

Dhāka   Kunming   TAIWAN   O C E A N

DESH   Chittagong   Mandalay   Guangzhou   Macau   Hong Kong

Calcutta   Hanoi   (Port.)   (U.K.)

B U R M A   Haiphong   Hainan   Luzon

(MYANMAR)   Chiang Mai   Vientiane   Da Nang   PHILIPPINES

Bay of   Manila

Bengal   Yangon   THAILAND   Mindanao

(Rangoon)

Moulmein   Bangkok   Davao

Andaman Is   CAMBODIA   Palawan   Sandakan

(Ind.)   Phnom   Ho Chi Minh   Manado

Penh   (Saigon)   S O U T H   Halmahera

Surat Thani   BRUNEI   Sabah   Irian

Nicobar Is   M A L A Y S I A   Sarawak   Sulawesi   Jaya

(Ind.)   George   Seram

Town   B O R N E O

Kuala   SINGAPORE

Lumpur

S U M A T E R A   Padang

Palembang   I N D O N E S I A   Flores   Timor

Jakarta   Surabaya   Sumba   Kupang   Darwin

J A W A

Christmas I   A U S T R A L I A

(Aust.)

Cocos Is

(Aust.)

E 100 **F** 120 **G**

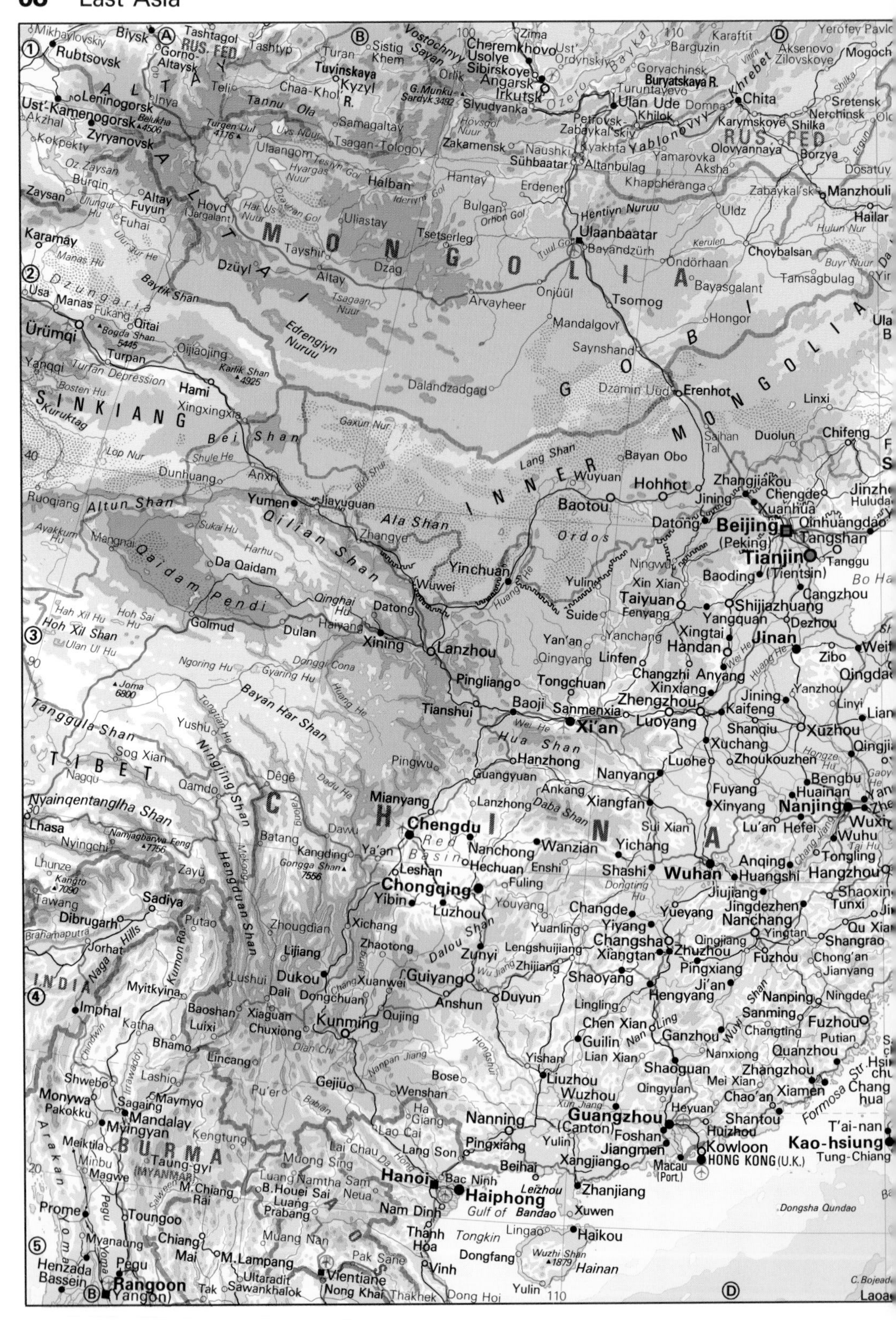

Biysk
Rubtsovsk
Tashtagol
RUS. FED.
Gorno-Altaysk
Tashtyp
Turan
Sistig Khem
Vostochnyy Sayan
Cheremkhovo
Zima
Usolye
Sibirskoye
Angarsk
Irkutsk
Ust'-Ordynskiy
Barguzin
Karaftit
Yerofey Pavlo
Aksenovo Zilovskoye
Mogoch
Goryachinsk
Buryatskaya R.
Turuntayevo
Ozero Baykal
Chita
Sretensk
Nerchinsk
Shilka
Karymskoye
Khilok
Ulan Ude
Yablonovyy Khrebet
Petrovsk-Zabaykal'skiy
Kyakhta
Olovyannaya
Borzya
RUS. FED.
Tuvinskaya R.
Kyzyl
Chaa-Khol
Teli
Tannu Ola
Leninogorsk
Ust'-Kamenogorsk
Belukha 4506
Zyryanovsk
Akzhal
Kokpekty
Turgen Uul 4116
Uvs Nuur
Samagaltay
Tsagan-Tologoy
Hovsgol Nuur
Zakamensk
Naushki
Sühbaatar
Altanbulag
Yamarovka
Aksha
Dosatuy
G. Munku-Sardyk 3492
Slyudyanka
Orlik
Ulaangom
Hyargas Nuur
Hälban
Hantay
Erdenet
Khapcheranga
Zabaykal'sk
Manzhouli
Hailar
Oz. Zaysan
Burqin
Zaysan
Ulungur Hu
Altay
Fuyun
Fuhai
Hovd (Jargalant)
Har Us Nuur
Uliastay
Bulgan
Orhon Gol
Hentiyn Nuruu
Uldz
Hulun Nur
Karamay
Manas Hu
Ulungur He
MONGOLIA
Tsetserleg
Tayshir
Dzag
Ulaanbaatar
Bayandzürh
Kerulen
Choybalsan
Buyr Nuur
Tuul Gol
Dzüyl
Altay
Öndörhaan
Bayasgalant
Tamsagbulag
Dzungaria
Baytik Shan
Usa
Manas
Fukang
Qitai
Ürümqi
Bogda Shan 5445
Tsagaan Nuur
Arvayheer
Onjüül
Tsomog
Hongor
Edrengiyn Nuruu
Mandalgovi
GOBI
Saynshand
Turpan
Qijiaojing
Yanqqi
Turfan Depression
Karlik Shan 4925
Hami
Xingxingxia
Dalandzadgad
Dzamin Üüd
Erenhot
Linxi
SINKIANG
Bosten Hu
Kuruktag
Bei Shan
Gaxun Nur
INNER MONGOLIA
Saihan Tal
Duolun
Chifeng
Lop Nur
Shule He
Lang Shan
Bayan Obo
Dunhuang
Anxi
Wuyuan
Hohhot
Zhangjiakou
Chengde
Ruoqiang
Altun Shan
Yumen
Jiayuguan
Baotou
Jining
Xuanhua
Ala Shan
Datong
Beijing (Peking)
Qinhuangdao
Tangshan
Ayakkum Hu
Sukai Hu
Qilian Shan
Zhangye
Ordos
Mangnai
Harhu
Qaidam Pendi
Da Qaidam
Yinchuan
Ningwu
Tianjin (Tientsin)
Tanggu
Huang He
Yulin
Baoding
Xin Xian
Bo Hai
Cangzhou
Wuwei
Qinghai Hu
Taiyuan
Fenyang
Shijiazhuang
Hah Xil Hu
Hoh Sai Hu
Datong
Suide
Yangquan
Dezhou
Golmud
Haiyang
Dulan
Xining
Xingtai
Jinan
Hoh Xil Shan
Ulan Ul Hu
Lanzhou
Yan'an
Yanchang
Handan
Zibo
Weif
Qingyang
Linfen
Wei He
Ngoring Hu
Gyaring Hu
Donggi Cona
Pingliang
Tongchuan
Changzhi
Anyang
Qingdao
Joma 6800
Bayan Har Shan
Xinxiang
Jining
Yanzhou
Tanggula Shan
Tianshui
Baoji
Sanmenxia
Zhengzhou
Kaifeng
Linyi
Xi'an
Luoyang
Yushu
Tongtian He
Hua Shan
Shanqiu
Xuzhou
TIBET
Sog Xian
Nagqu
Ningjing Shan
Pingwu
Hanzhong
Xuchang
Zhoukouzhen
Luohe
Nanyang
Bengbu
Huainan
Dêqê
Qamdo
Guangyuan
Ankang
Fuyang
Nyainqentanglha Shan
CHINA
Dadu He
Mianyang
Lanzhong
Daba Shan
Xiangfan
Xinyang
Nanjing
Lhasa
Nyingchi
Namjagbarwa Feng 7756
Hengduan Shan
Batang
Dawu
Chengdu
Red Basin
Sui Xian
Lu'an
Hefei
Wuhu
Wuxi
Kangding
Ya'an
Nanchong
Wanzian
Yichang
Tongling
Lhunze
Zayü
Gongga Shan 7556
Leshan
Hechuan
Enshi
Shashi
Wuhan
Anqing
Huangshi
Hangzhou
Kangto 7090
Tawang
Chongqing
Fuling
Dongting Hu
Jiujiang
Shaoxing
Sadiya
Yibin
Luzhou
Youyang
Changde
Jingdezhen
Tunxi
Dibrugarh
Putao
Mekong
Zhougdian
Xichang
Dalou Shan
Yiyang
Yueyang
Nanchang
Qu Xian
Brahamaputra
Jorhat
Naga Hills
Kumon Ra.
Zhaotong
Yuanling
Changsha
Qingjiang
Yingtan
Shangrao
Lijiang
Zunyi
Lengshuijiang
Xiangtan
Zhuzhou
Fuzhou
Chong'an
Jianyang
INDIA
Lushui
Dukou
Guiyang
Wu Jiang
Zhijiang
Shaoyang
Pingxiang
Ji'an
Myitkyina
Dali
Dongchuan
Xuanwei
Anshun
Duyun
Hengyang
Nanping
Ningde
Imphal
Baoshan
Xiaguan
Qujing
Lingling
Wuyi Shan
Sanming
Fuzhou
Katha
Luixi
Chuxiong
Kunming
Chen Xian
Nan Ling
Ganzhou
Changting
Putian
Chindwin
Bhamo
Dian Chi
Guilin
Lian Xian
Nanxiong
Quanzhou
Lincang
Nanpan Jiang
Hongshui
Yishan
Shaoguan
Zhangzhou
Shwebo
Irrawaddy
Lashio
Gejiu
Bose
Liuzhou
Qingyuan
Mei Xian
Xiamen
Hsinchu
Monywa
Sagaing
Maymyo
Pu'er
Wenshan
Wuzhou
Chao'an
Changhua
Pakokku
Mandalay
Myingyan
Kengtung
Ha Giang
Nanning
Xun Jiang
Guangzhou (Canton)
Heyuan
Shantou
Formosa Str.
Lao Cai
Yulin
Foshan
Huizhou
T'ai-nan
Meiktila
BURMA (MYANMAR)
Lai Chau
Lang Son
Pingxiang
Jiangmen
Kowloon
Kao-hsiung
Minbu
Taung-gyi
Muong Sing
Beihai
Xiangjiang
Macau (Port.)
HONG KONG (U.K.)
Tung-Chiang
Magwe
Arakan Yoma
Luang Namtha
Sam Neua
Hanoi
Bac Ninh
Leizhou
Zhanjiang
Salween
M. Chiang Rai
B. Houei Sai
Luang Prabang
LAOS
Haiphong
Gulf of Tongkin
Bandao
Xuwen
Dongsha Qundao
Prome
Pegu Yoma
Toungoo
Nam Dinh
Lingao
Haikou
Myanaung
Chiang Mai
Muang Nan
Thanh Hoa
Dongfang
Wuzhi Shan 1879
Hainan
Henzada
Pegu
M. Lampang
Pak Sane
Vinh
Bassein
Rangoon (Yangon)
Tak
Uttaradit
Sawankhalok
Vientiane
Nong Khai
Thakhek
Dong Hoi
Yulin
C. Bojeador
Laoag

1:20M

0   200   400   600   800 km

0   200   400 mls

SEA OF OKHOTSK

Mys Lopatka

Paramushir

Onekotan

Shiashkotan

Rasshua

Simushir

Kuril'skiye Ostrova (Kuril Islands)

(Rus.Fed. admin/claimed by Japan)

Vityaz Depth 10542

SAKHALIN

Skovorodino

Zeya

Ekimchan

Tugur

Tyrma

Ushumun

Peliny Osipenko

Moskal'vo

Okha

Nikolayevsk-na-Amure

Bogorodskoye

Opala

Dzhalinda

Svobodnyy

Shimanovsk

Norsk

Ust'-Umal'ta

Oz.Chukchagirskoye

DeKastri

Katangli

Tymovskoye

Aleksandrovsk-Sakhalinskiy

Belogorsk

Blagoveshchensk

Zavitinsk

Chekunda

Komsomol'sk na-Amure

Bolon'

Poliv

Tartarskiy

Pobedino

Poronaysk

Uglegorsk

Litovko

Obluch'ye

Bureya

Birobidzhan

Lehinskoye

Khabarovsk

Khor

Vanino

Sovetskaya Gavan'

'inskiy

Zaliv Terpeniya

Yuzhno-Sakhalinsk

Korsakov

Mys Aniva

Urup

(Rus.Fed.) Iturup

Fujin

Vyazemskiy

Bikin

Dal'nerechensk

Lesozavodsk

Nel'ma

Gornozavodsk

Svetlaya

Wakkanai

La Perouse Strait

Abashiri

Kunashir

Shikotan

Nemuro

Da'an

Songhua

Jixi

Turiy Rog

Plastun

Rudnaya Pristan'

Olga

Rumoi

Asahikawa

Asashi Dake 2290

Otaru

Sapporo

Muroran

HOKKAIDŌ

Kushiro

Erimo-misaki

Harbin

Changchun

Tongliao

Shuangliao

Jilin

Liaoyuan

Siping

Fushun

enyang

iaoyang

Benxi

Tonghua

Anshan

Dandong

Huich'ŏn

Samsu

Sŏho-ri

NORTH KOREA

Hamhŭng

Hŭngnam

Wŏnsan

SEA OF JAPAN

Uchiura-wan

Hakodate

Tsugaru-kaikyō

Aomori

Hirosaki

Noshiro

Akita

Hachinohe

Morioka

Ishinomaki

Sendai

Fukushima

HONSHŪ

Yamagata

Sado

Niigata

Nagaoka

Utsunomiya

Takaoka

Kanazawa

Mito

Tōkyō

Yokohama

Dalian

Lüshun

Korea Bay

P'yŏngyang

Haeju

Kaesŏng

Inch'ŏn

Sŏul (Seoul)

SOUTH KOREA

Ullŭng do

Tok-do

Ch'ungju

Ch'ŏngju

Sado

Fukui

Gifu

Fuji-San 3776

Shizuoka

YELLOW SEA

Taejŏn

Taegu

Chŏnju

Kunsan

Kwangju

Mokp'o

Masan

Pusan

Tsushima

Matsue

Tottori

Kyōto

Osaka

Sakai

Nagoya

Toyohashi

Kōbe

Wakayama

Miyake

Hiroshima

Kure

Matsuyama

Kōchi

Shikoku

Kii-suidō

Hachijō

Cheju haehyŏp

Cheju

Cheju do

Shimonoseki

Kita-Kyūshū

Fukuoka

Sasebo

Nagasaki

Kumamoto

Kyūshū

Miyazaki

Kagoshima

Ōsumi-kaikyō

Bungo-suidō

Myojin

Sumisu

Tori

Sofu Gan

Ramapo Deep 10374

Shanghai

Ningbo

Wenzhou

CHINA SEA

EAST

Wangpan Yang

Tokara Retto

Amami

Tokuno

Amami guntō

YAKU

Tanega

J A P A N

Nishino-shima

Muko-jima

Chichi-jima

Haha-jima

Ogasawara Guntō (Bonin Islands) (Jap.)

Okinawa

Naha gunto

Okinawa

Daitō Is

Kitaiō

Iwo Jima

Kazan Retto (Volcano Is) (Jap.)

Fleming Deep 8651

Chi-lung

T'ai-pei

Hsieh Shan 3884

Hua-lien

TAIWAN (FORMOSA) (China Nat. Rep.)

T'ai-tung

Sakishima guntō

Miyako

Ishigaki

Iriomote

R Y U K Y U

Tropic of Cancer

Senkaku Guntō

Farallon de Pajaros

Maug Is

Asuncion

Agrihan

Pagan

Alamagan

Guguan

Sarigan

Anatahan

Northern Marianas

M A R I A N A S

Luzon Strait

Babuyan Is

C.Engaño

Aparri

Batan Is

Parece Vela

P A C I F I C   O C E A N

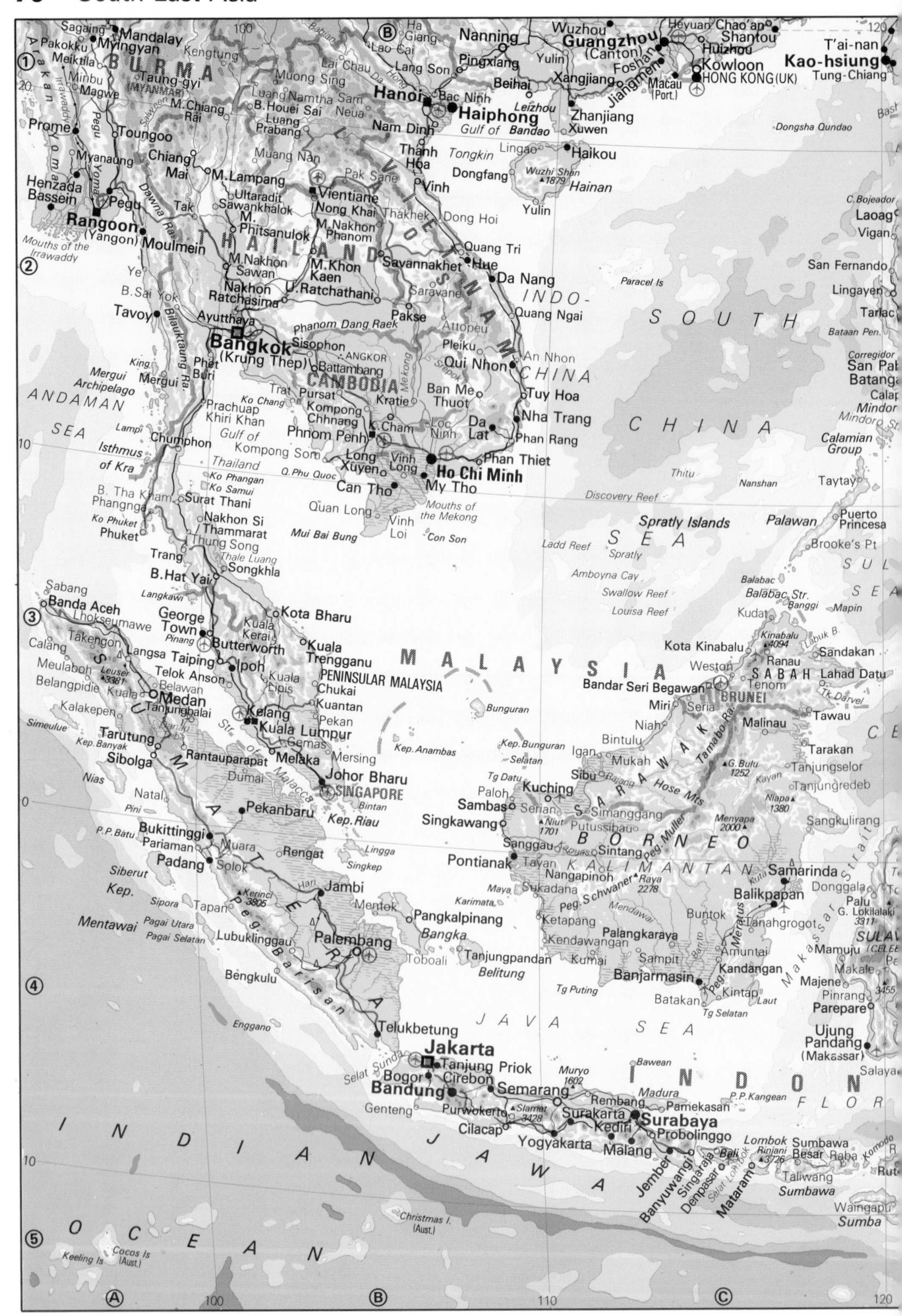

BURMA
(MYANMAR)
Sagaing
Mandalay
Pakokku
Myingyan
Meiktila
Minbu
Magwe
Taung-gyi
Kengtung
Prome
Pegu
Toungoo
Myanaung
Henzada
Bassein
Rangoon
(Yangon)
Moulmein
Mouths of the Irrawaddy
Ye
Tavoy
Mergui
Mergui Archipelago
ANDAMAN SEA
Chiang Mai
M.Chiang Rai
M.Lampang
Tak
Uttaradit
Sawankhalok
M. Phitsanulok
M.Nakhon Sawan
THAILAND
Nakhon Ratchasima
U.Ratchathani
Ayutthaya
Bangkok
(Krung Thep)
Phet Buri
Prachuap Khiri Khan
Chumphon
Isthmus of Kra
Gulf of Thailand
Ko Phangan
Ko Samui
Surat Thani
Phangnga
Ko Phuket
Phuket
Nakhon Si Thammarat
Thung Song
Trang
Thale Luang
Songkhla
B.Hat Yai
Langkawi
Vientiane
Nong Khai
M.Nakhon Phanom
M.Khon Kaen
Thakhek
Savannakhet
Saravane
Pakse
Attopeu
Luang Prabang
Luang Namtha
B.Houei Sai
Sam Neua
Muang Nan
Pak Sane
Phanom Dang Raek
Sisophon
ANGKOR
Battambang
CAMBODIA
Pursat
Trat
Ko Chang
Kompong Chhnang
Kratie
K.Cham
Phnom Penh
Gulf of Kompong Som
Q.Phu Quoc
Long Xuyen
Vinh Long
Can Tho
My Tho
Ho Chi Minh
Quan Long
Vinh Loi
Mouths of the Mekong
Con Son
Mui Bai Bung
VIETNAM
Hanoi
Haiphong
Bac Ninh
Nam Dinh
Thanh Hoa
Vinh
Dong Hoi
Quang Tri
Hue
Da Nang
Quang Ngai
Pleiku
Qui Nhon
An Nhon
Tuy Hoa
Ban Me Thuot
Nha Trang
Da Lat
Phan Rang
Phan Thiet
Loc Ninh
Lao Cai
Ha Giang
Lai Chau
Muong Sing
Lang Son
Nanning
Pingxiang
Beihai
Wuzhou
Yulin
Guangzhou
(Canton)
Foshan
Jiangmen
Heyuan
Chao'an
Shantou
Huizhou
Kowloon
HONG KONG (UK)
Macau
(Port.)
Xangjiang
Zhanjiang
Leizhou Bandao
Xuwen
Gulf of Tongkin
Lingao
Haikou
Dongfang
Wuzhi Shan 1879
Hainan
Yulin
T'ai-nan
Kao-hsiung
Tung-Chiang
Dongsha Qundao
Paracel Is
C.Bojeador
Laoag
Vigan
San Fernando
Lingayen
Tarlac
Bataan Pen.
Corregidor
Batanga
Mindoro
Calamian Group
Taytay
Puerto Princesa
Palawan
Brooke's Pt
Balabac
Balabac Str.
Banggi
Mapin
SULU SEA
SOUTH CHINA SEA
INDO-CHINA
Thitu
Nanshan
Discovery Reef
Spratly Islands
Ladd Reef
Spratly
Amboyna Cay
Swallow Reef
Louisa Reef
MALAYSIA
PENINSULAR MALAYSIA
Sabang
Banda Aceh
Lhokseumawe
Takengon
Calang
Meulaboh
Langsa
Leuser 3381
Belangpidie
Kuala
Belawan
Medan
Tanjungbalai
Kalakepen
Simeulue
Tarutung
Kep. Banyak
Sibolga
Rantauparapat
Nias
Natal
Pini
Dumai
Pekanbaru
P.P.Batu
Bukittinggi
Pariaman
Padang
Muara
Solok
Rengat
Siberut
Kep. Mentawai
Sipora
Pagai Utara
Pagai Selatan
Tapan
Kerinci 3805
Peg. Barisan
Jambi
Lubuklinggau
Palembang
Bengkulu
Enggano
Telukbetung
SUMATERA
George Town
Pinang
Butterworth
Taiping
Ipoh
Telok Anson
Kota Bharu
Kuala Kerai
Kuala Trengganu
Kuala Lipis
Chukai
Kuantan
Pekan
Kelang
Kuala Lumpur
Gemas
Melaka
Mersing
Str. of Malacca
Johor Bharu
SINGAPORE
Bintan
Kep. Riau
Lingga
Singkep
Mentok
Bangka
Pangkalpinang
Toboali
Tanjungpandan
Belitung
Bunguran
Kep. Anambas
Kep. Bunguran Selatan
Tg Datu
Paloh
Sambas
Singkawang
Kuching
Serian
Sibu
Mukah
Bintulu
Igan
SARAWAK
Niah
Miri
Seria
BRUNEI
Bandar Seri Begawan
Weston
Kota Kinabalu
Kudat
Kinabalu 4094
Ranau
Labuk B.
Sandakan
SABAH
Tenom
Lahad Datu
Tk. Darvel
Tawau
Tamabo Ra.
Malinau
Tarakan
Tanjungselor
Tanjungredeb
Hose Mts
G. Bulu 1252
Kayan
Niapa 1380
Menyapa 2000
Sangkulirang
Simanggang
Niut 1701
Putussibau
BORNEO
KALIMANTAN
Sanggau
Sintang
Peg. Muller
Pontianak
Tayan
Nangapinoh
Raya 2278
Peg. Schwaner
Maya
Sukadana
Karimata
Ketapang
Mendawai
Kendawangan
Palangkaraya
Sampit
Kumai
Tg Puting
Banjarmasin
Buntok
Peg. Meratus
Amuntai
Kandangan
Kintap
Batakan
Tg Selatan
Laut
Samarinda
Balikpapan
Tanahgrogot
Donggala
Palu
G. Lokilalaki 3311
SULAWESI
(CELEBES)
Mamuju
Makale
Majene
Pinrang
Parepare
Ujung Pandang
(Makassar)
Salaya
Makassar Strait
JAVA SEA
Jakarta
Tanjung Priok
Selat Sunda
Bogor
Bandung
Cirebon
Semarang
Muryo 1602
Genteng
Slamet 3428
Purwokerto
Cilacap
Rembang
Surakarta
Yogyakarta
Kediri
Surabaya
Madura
Bawean
Pamekasan
P.P.Kangean
Probolinggo
Malang
Jember
Banyuwangi
Bali
Singaraja
Denpasar
Selat Lombok
Lombok
Mataram
Rinjani 3726
Sumbawa Besar
Raba
Taliwang
Sumbawa
Komodo
Waingapu
Sumba
FLORES
INDONESIA
JAWA
INDIAN OCEAN
Christmas I.
(Aust.)
Cocos Is
(Aust.)
Keeling Is
A
B
C
1
2
3
4
5
100
110
120
10
20
0

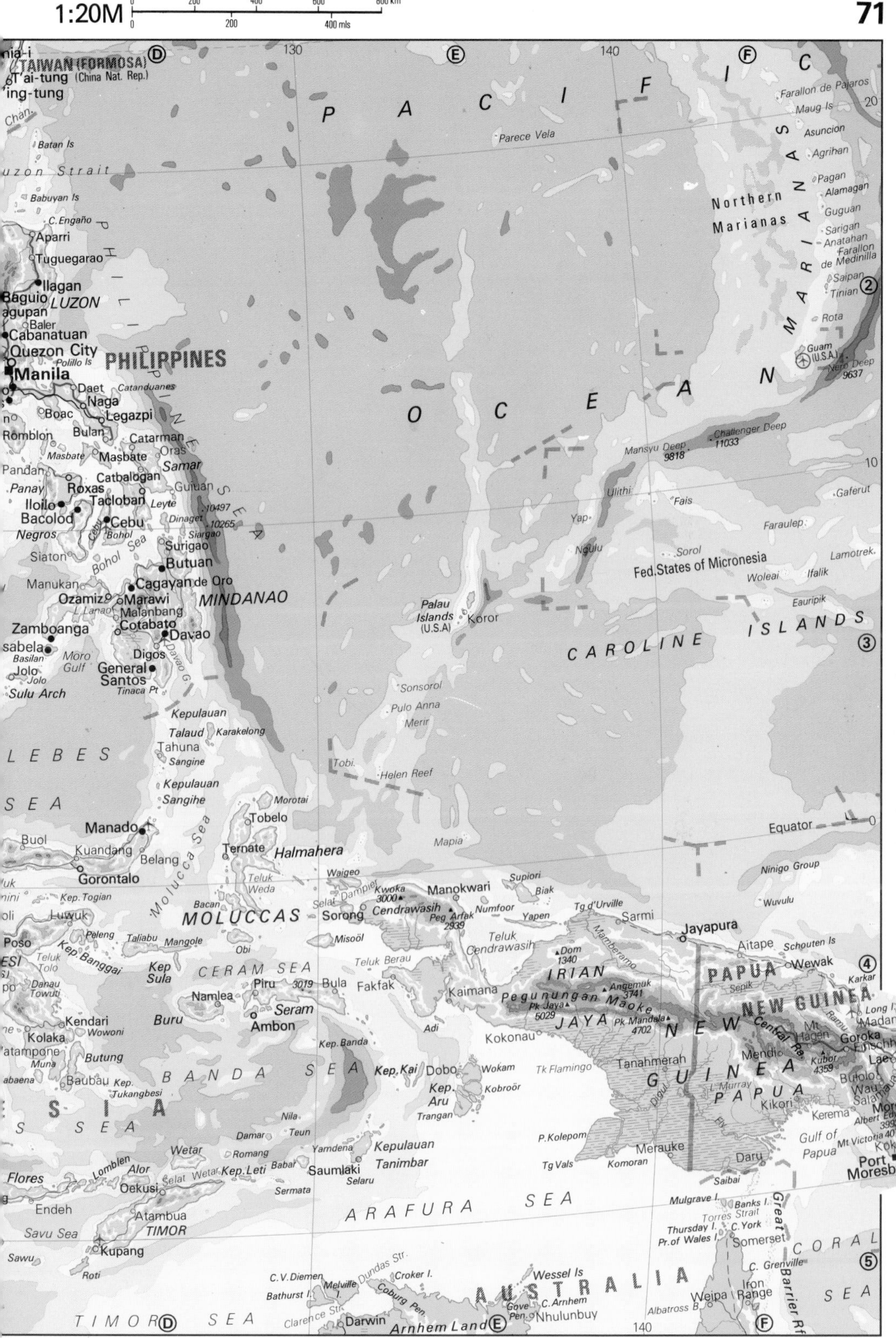

1:20M

200 400 600 800 km
200 400 mls

nia-i
TAIWAN (FORMOSA) (China Nat. Rep.)
T'ai-tung
ing-tung

P A C I F I C

Chan
Batan Is
uzon Strait
Babuyan Is
C. Engaño
Aparri
Tuguegarao
Ilagan
Baguio **LUZON**
agupan
Baler
Cabanatuan
Quezon City
Manila
no
Boac Daet Catanduanes
Naga **Legazpi**
Romblon Bulan
Masbate Catarman
PHILIPPINES
Pandan Masbate Oras
Panay **Samar**
Roxas Catbalogan
Iloilo Tacloban Leyte
Bacolod Guiuan
Negros Dinagat 10265
Siaton Cebu Siargao
Bohol Surigao
Manukan Butuan
Ozamiz Cagayan de Oro
Marawi **MINDANAO**
L.Lanao Malanbang
Zamboanga Cotabato
sabela Davao
Basilan Digos
Jolo **General Santos**
Sulu Arch Tinaca Pt.

Parece Vela

O C E A N

Mansyu Deep 9818
Challenger Deep 11033
Ulithi
Yap
Ngulu
Fais
Sorol
Fed.States of Micronesia
Faraulep
Gaferut
Woleai Ifalik Lamotrek
Eauripik

20
Northern Marianas
Farallon de Pajaros
Maug Is
Asuncion
Agrihan
Pagan
Alamagan
Guguan
Sarigan
Anatahan
Farallon de Medinilla
Saipan
Tinian
Rota
Guam (U.S.A)
Nero Deep 9637

10

C A R O L I N E   I S L A N D S

Palau Islands (U.S.A) Koror

Sonsorol
Pulo Anna
Merir

Kepulauan Talaud Karakelong
Tahuna
Sangine
Kepulauan Sangihe

Tobi
Helen Reef

Morotai
Tobelo
Ternate **Halmahera**

Mapia

Equator 0

Ninigo Group
Wuvulu

Manado
Kuandang Belang
Gorontalo

L E B E S
S E A

Buol

Waigeo
MOLUCCAS
Teluk Weda
Bacan Selat Dampier Kwoka 3000
Sorong Peg. Arfak 2939
Cendrawasih Manokwari
Numfoor
Yapen
Teluk Cendrawasih
Supiori
Biak
Tg d'Urville
Sarmi

Schouten Is
Aitape Wewak

PAPUA
Jayapura

Karkar

4

Luwuk
Kep. Togian
Poso
ESI
po
Peleng
Kep. Banggai
Teluk Tolo
Taliabu Mangole
Obi
Misoöl

MOLUCCA SEA

Kendari
Kolaka
atampone
Muna

Baubau Kep.
Tukangbesi

Namlea Piru 3079 Bula
Seram Berau
Fakfak

Kaimana

Dom 1340
IRIAN JAYA
Pegunungan Maoke
Pk.Jaya 5029
Angemuk 3741
Pk.Mandala 4702

NEW GUINEA
Central Ra.
Sepik
Mt Hagen
Mendi
Kubor 4359

Madang
Goroka
Wabag

Lae
Morob

B A N D A   S E A
CERAM SEA
SERAM
Ambon
Kep. Banda

Buru Butung
Wowoni

Adi
Kep. Kai Dobo
Kep. Aru
Trangan

Wokam
Kobroör

Tk Flamingo
Kokonau Tanahmerah

Kikori
Kerema

Wau
Salai 3933

GUINEA

Albert Edw 4075
Kokoda

Muna

Nila
Damar Teun

Yamdena
Saumlaki Selaru

Kepulauan Tanimbar

P.Kolepom
Merauke
Komoran

Mt Victoria 4073
Kokoda
PAPUA

Gulf of Papua
Daru

Port Moresby

Flores
Lomblen Alor
Oekusi Selat Wetar Kep. Leti Babar
Sermata

Wetar
Romang
Sawu
Endeh Atambua **TIMOR**
Kupang

Roti

A R A F U R A   S E A

Mulgrave I.
C. York
Saibai
Torres Strait
Thursday I. C. York
Pr.of Wales I. Somerset

Great Barrier Rf.

C O R A L
S E A

5

T I M O R   S E A

C.V.Diemen
Melville I. Croker I.
Bathurst I. Dundas Str.
Clarence Str. Coburg Pen
Darwin **Arnhem Land**

Wessel Is
Gove C.Arnhem
Pen. Nhulunbuy

A U S T R A L I A

Weipa
Iron Range
C. Grenville
Albatross B.

130 E 140 F C

130 140 E 140 F

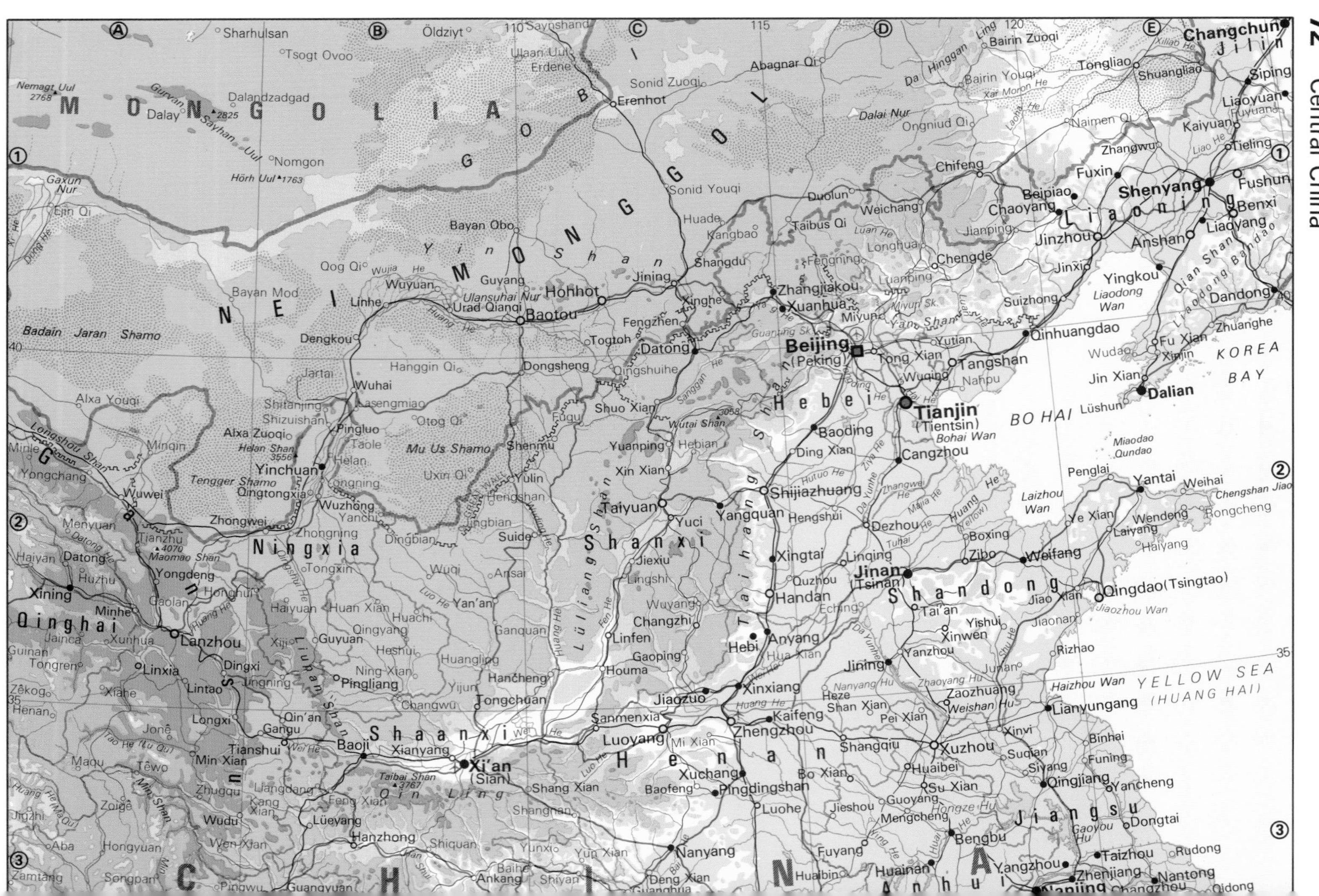
MONGOLIA
NEI MONGGOL
GOBI
Yin Shan
Changchun
Jilin
Siping
Liaoyuan
Tongliao
Shenyang
Fushun
Benxi
Liaoyang
Liaoning
Anshan
Dandong
Yingkou
Liaodong Wan
KOREA BAY
Dalian
Lüshun
Jinzhou
Fuxin
Chaoyang
Chifeng
Chengde
Qinhuangdao
BO HAI
Bohai Wan
Tianjin
(Tientsin)
Tangshan
Beijing
(Peking)
Zhangjiakou
Xuanhua
Hebei
Baoding
Shijiazhuang
Cangzhou
Dezhou
Jinan
(Tsinan)
Shandong
Yantai
Weihai
Qingdao(Tsingtao)
Weifang
Zibo
YELLOW SEA
(HUANG HAI)
Lianyungang
Xuzhou
Jiangsu
Bengbu
Huainan
Anhui
Yangzhou
Taizhou
Nantong
Henan
Zhengzhou
Kaifeng
Luoyang
Xinxiang
Anyang
Handan
Xingtai
Shanxi
Taiyuan
Yangquan
Datong
Hohhot
Baotou
Erenhot
Shaanxi
Xi'an
(Sian)
Baoji
Tianshui
Lanzhou
Qinghai
Xining
Ningxia
Yinchuan
Wuhai
Yan'an
Yulin
Nanyang
Pingdingshan
Xuchang
Hanzhong
Ankang
Mu Us Shamo
Tengger Shamo
Badain Jaran Shamo
Huang He
Qin Ling
Liupan Shan
Taihang Shan
Lüliang Shan
Da Hinggan Ling
CHINA

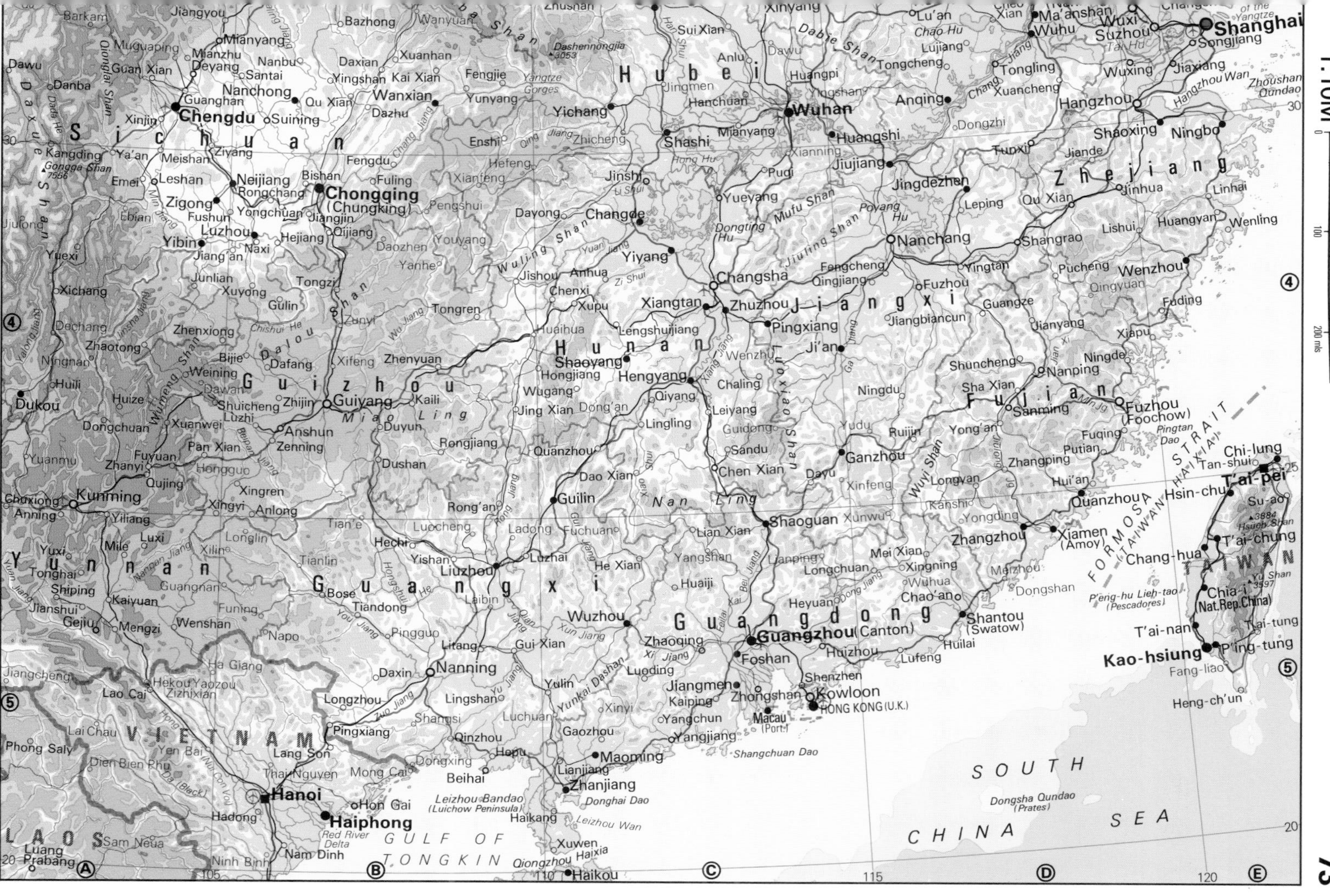
Sichuan
Hubei
Hunan
Jiangxi
Zhejiang
Fujian
Guizhou
Guangxi
Guangdong
Yunnan
TAIWAN
VIETNAM
LAOS
SOUTH CHINA SEA
GULF OF TONGKIN
FORMOSA STRAIT (TAIWAN HAIXIA)
Shanghai
Chengdu
Chongqing (Chungking)
Wuhan
Changsha
Nanchang
Hangzhou
Ningbo
Wenzhou
Fuzhou (Foochow)
Xiamen (Amoy)
Shantou (Swatow)
Guangzhou (Canton)
Kowloon
HONG KONG (U.K.)
Macau (Port.)
Nanning
Guilin
Guiyang
Kunming
Hanoi
Haiphong
Haikou
T'ai-pei
Kao-hsiung
Chia-i (Nat.Rep.China)
Dongsha Qundao (Prates)
Leizhou Bandao (Luichow Peninsula)
Nan Ling
Wuyi Shan
Daxue Shan

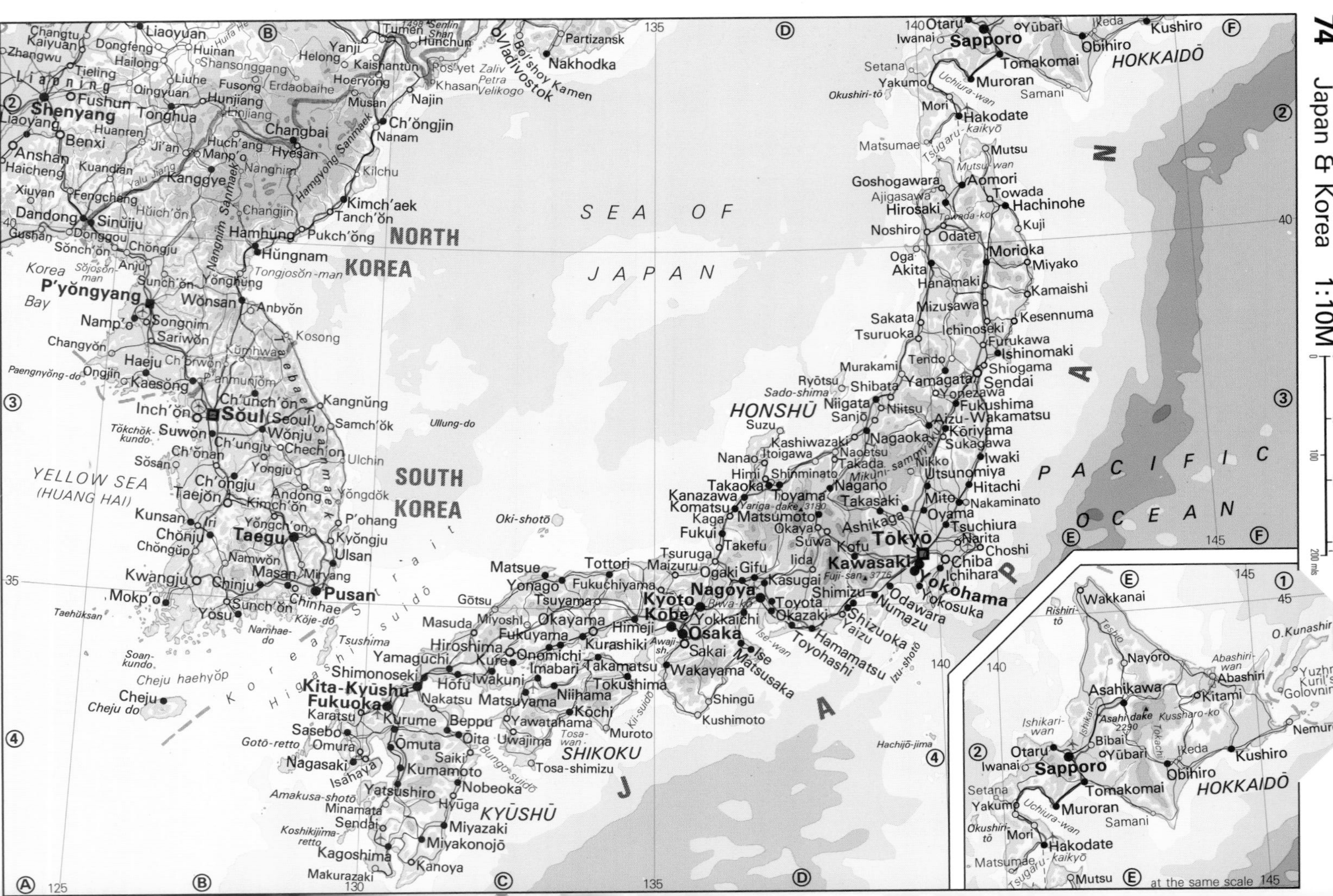

0 100 200 300 km
0 100 200 mls
SEA OF JAPAN
PACIFIC OCEAN
YELLOW SEA (HUANG HAI)
Korea Bay
NORTH KOREA
SOUTH KOREA
HONSHŪ
HOKKAIDŌ
SHIKOKU
KYŪSHŪ
Tōkyō
P'yŏngyang
Sŏul (Seoul)
Sapporo
Yokohama
Kawasaki
Nagoya
Kyoto
Osaka
Kobe
Kita-Kyūshū
Fukuoka
Hiroshima
Sendai
Pusan
Taegu
Inch'ŏn
Kwangju
Taejŏn
Shenyang
Vladivostok
Nakhodka
Niigata
Kanazawa
Hakodate
Aomori
Kagoshima
Nagasaki
Cheju
Hamhŭng
Ch'ŏngjin
Wŏnsan
Sinŭiju
Dandong
Fushun
Kushiro
Obihiro
Asahikawa
at the same scale

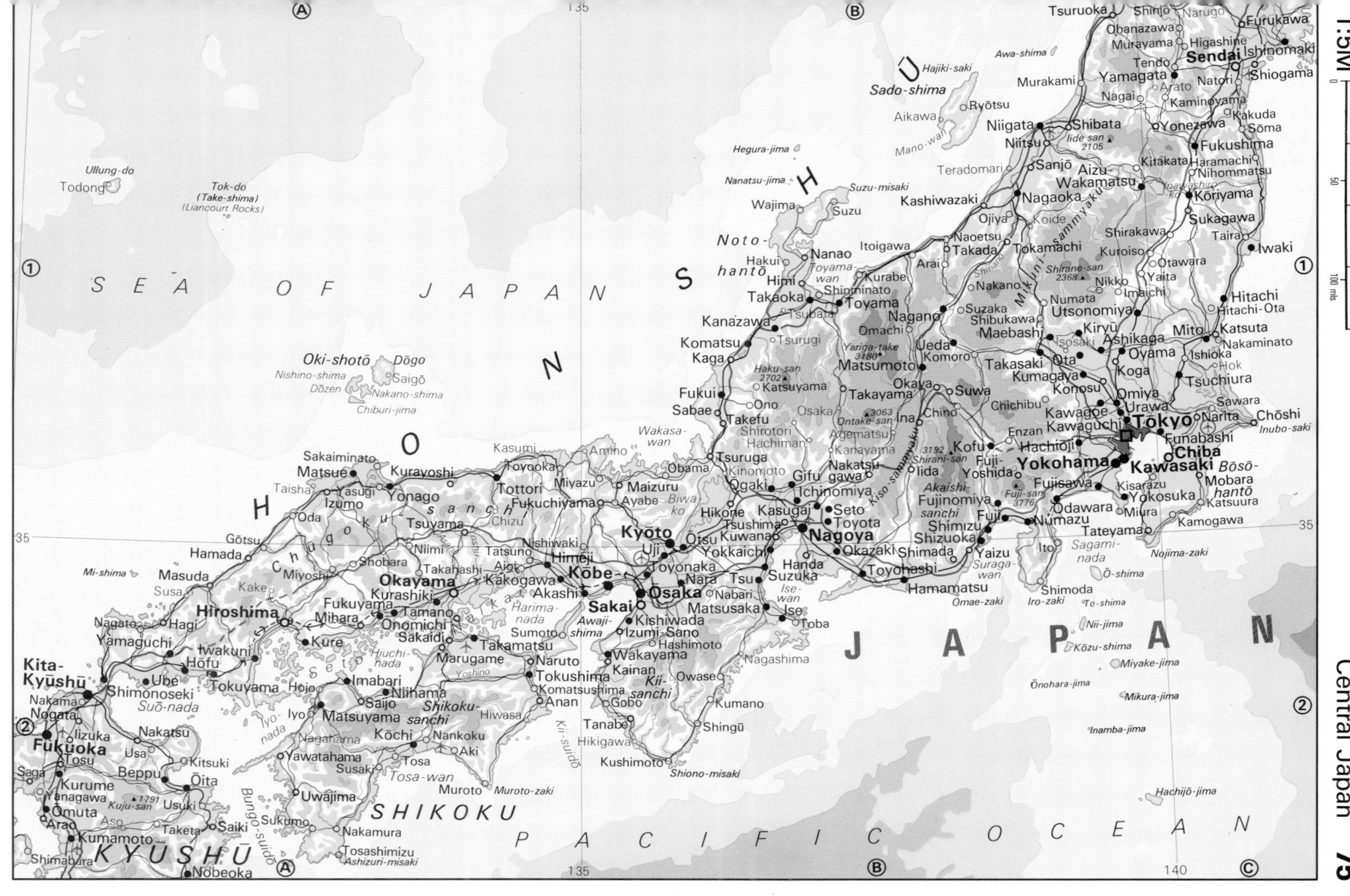

1:5M

0 50 100 150 200 km
0   50   100 mls

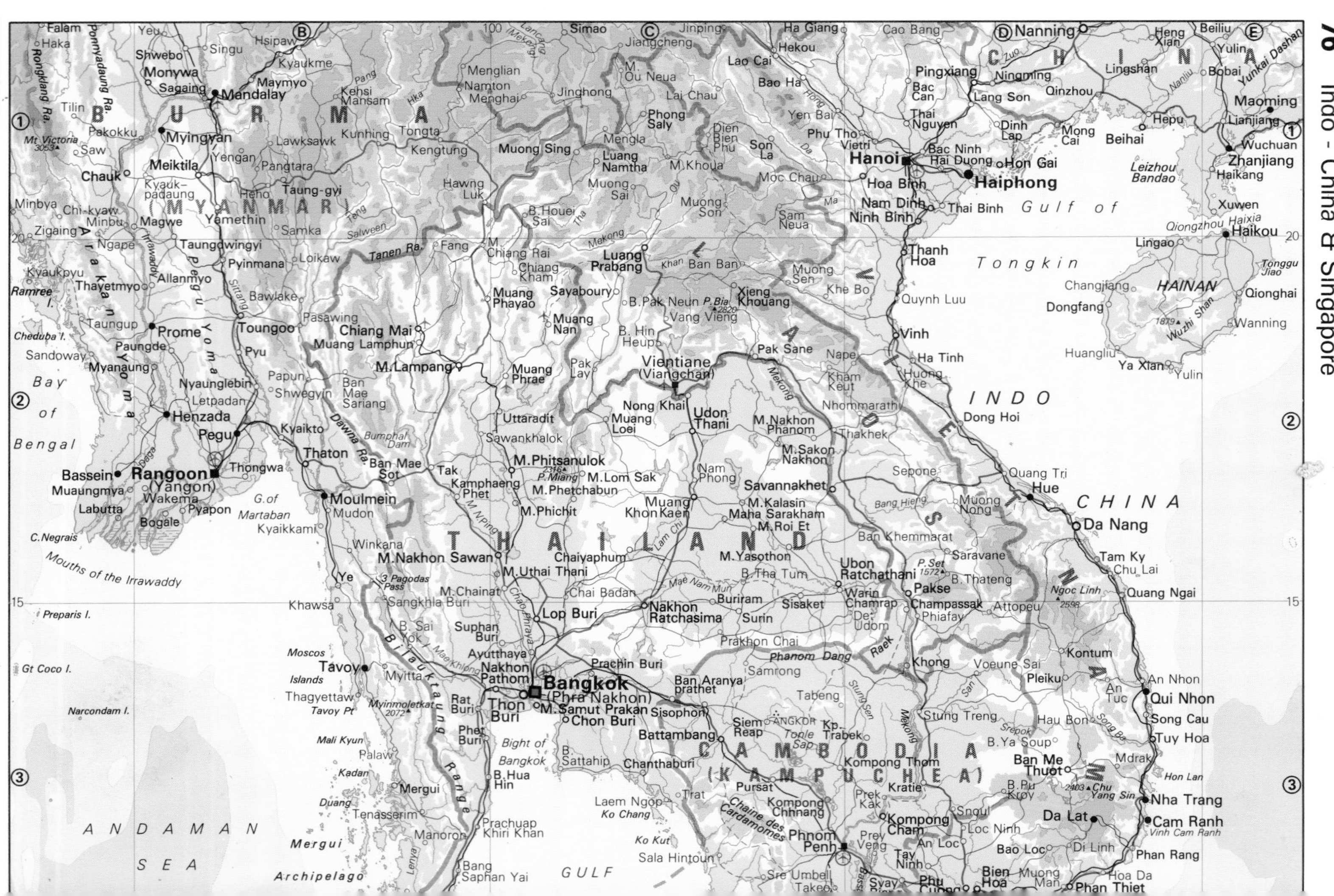
CHINA
BURMA
(MYANMAR)
LAOS
THAILAND
VIETNAM
CAMBODIA
(KAMPUCHEA)
INDO CHINA
Gulf of Tongkin
HAINAN
Bay of Bengal
ANDAMAN SEA
GULF
G. of Martaban
Bight of Bangkok
Mergui Archipelago
Mouths of the Irrawaddy
Hanoi
Haiphong
Nanning
Zhanjiang
Haikou
Beihai
Hue
Da Nang
Qui Nhon
Nha Trang
Cam Ranh
Da Lat
Phan Thiet
Vientiane (Viangchan)
Luang Prabang
Savannakhet
Pakse
Bangkok (Phra Nakhon)
Chiang Mai
Nakhon Ratchasima
Udon Thani
Ubon Ratchathani
Phnom Penh
Battambang
Kompong Cham
Rangoon (Yangon)
Mandalay
Moulmein
Bassein
Pegu
Prome
Toungoo
Taung-gyi
Tavoy
Mergui
Mekong
Irrawaddy
Salween
Chao Phraya
Tanen Ra.
Dawna Ra.
Bilauktaung Range
Arakan Yoma
Pegu Yoma
Chaine des Cardamomes
Phanom Dang
Ponnyadaung Ra.
Rongklang Ra.
Mt Victoria 3053
Preparis I.
Gt Coco I.
Narcondam I.
Cheduba I.
Ramree I.
C.Negrais
Moscos Islands
Ko Kut
Ko Chang

100   200   300   400 km
100   200 mls

10

④   5   ⑤   ⑥

SARAWAK
(Malaysia)
Niut
Serian
Saratok
Tg Sirik
Kuching
Sambas
Singkawang
BORNEO
Balaikarangan
Sanggau
Nangatayap
Ketapang
Kalimantan
Maya
Sukadana
Telukbatang
T.k Sukadana
Karimata

SOUTH
CHINA
SEA

Pontianak
Mempawah
Kertamulia

Subi
Binjai
Bunguran
Midai
Kep. Bunguran
Selatan
Kep. Badas
Tg Datu
Paloh

INDONESIA

Vung Tau
Phu Vinh
Mouths of
the Mekong
Long Xuyen
Vinh Long
Can Tho
Khanh Hung
Rach Gia
Quan Long
Nam Can
Vinh Loi
Kampot
O. Phu
Quoc
Con Son

Kep.
Anambas
Jenaja
Letong
Serasan

Kep. Tambelan

Belinyu

MY THO

Mui Bai Bung
Hon Khoai

Hon Panjang

Ko Way

Tioman

Kep. Riau
Bintan
Tanjungpinang

Kep. Lingga
Singtep

Bangka

Kuala Trengganu
Redang
Kuala
Dungun
Chukai
Kuantan
PENINSULAR
MALAYSIA
Pekan
Mersing
Keluang
Johor
Bharu
SINGAPORE
Bintan
Sawang
Burung
Tanjungpinang

Singtep
Tg
Jabung
Jambi

THAILAND

Ko Phangan
Ko Samui
Surat
Thani
Kapoe
Phangnga
Ban
Song
Ko
Lanta
Ban Kantang
Thale Luang
Trang

Nakhon
Si Thammarat
Ban Pak Phanang
Songkhla
Pattani
Narathiwat
Kota Bharu
Tumpat
Yala
Genik
Betong
Ban
Hat Yai
Satun

Kuala
Krai
Gua Musang
G. Tahan
2189
Kuala Lipis
Temerloh
Kuala Kubu
Bharu
Kuala
Lumpur
Seremban
Gemas
Segamat
Melaka
Muar
Batu
Pahat
Kukup
Bengkalis
Perawang

Chumphon
Isthmus
of Kra
Ranong
Kapoe

Kampar
Teluk
Anson
Pelabohan
Kelang
Kelang
Port Dickson
Tanjungbalai Kelang
Port Weld
Taiping
Ipoh
Butterworth
George
Town
Pinang
Port Weld
Labuhanbilik
Alor Setar
Laagkawi
Ban Khok Kloi
Ko Phuket
Phuket

M A L A Y S I A

Telok
Batu Puteh
Perak

Rupat
Dumai
Sebanga
Minas
Daludalu
Rentauparapat
Kisaran
Tebingtinggi
Pematangsiantar
Danau
Toba
Tarutung
Sibolga
Gunungsitoli
Telukdalam

Pekanbaru
Bangkinang
G. Kulabu
2124
G. Talakmau
2912
Bukittinggi
Payakumbuh
Pariaman
Padang
Solok
Muaratebo
Padangpanjang
Muara

Kerinci
3805
Peg.
Tigapuluh
722

Langsa
Seruwai
Kualasimpang
Belawan
Binjai
Medan
Kalakeng
Tapaktuan
Bakungan
Barus
Natal

Selat Mentawi
Selat Berhala

Sigli
Lhokseumawe
G. Geureudong
Takengon
Uwak
Alas
G. Leuser
3381
Belangpidie
Meulaboh
Calang

S

Sinabang
Simeulue

Tuangku
P.P. Banyak

Nias

Lahewa

Sigep
Pini
P.P. Batu
Pulautelo
Siberut

Sabang
Banda Aceh

NICOBAR
ISLANDS
(India)
Koihoa
Little Nicobar
Great
Nicobar
Henhoaha

Equator

THAILAND

95

Ⓐ   5   ⑤   0   ⑥

④   5

Ⓓ

Ⓒ

Ⓑ

0 100 200 300 400 km
0 100 200 mls

Celebes Sea

Flores Sea

SULAWESI (CELEBES)

MALAYSIA

SINGAPORE

BORNEO

KALIMANTAN

SARAWAK

SUMATERA

JAWA

INDONESIA

JAVA SEA

Makassar Strait

Bali Sea

Equator

Samarinda
Balikpapan
Samboja
Banjarmasin
Martapura
Pontianak
Singkawang
Sambas
Kuching
Palembang
Jambi
Pekanbaru
Bengkulu
Jakarta
Tanjung Priok
Bogor
Bandung
Sukabumi
Cirebon
Semarang
Surakarta
Yogyakarta
Magelang
Tegal
Pekalongan
Surabaya
Malang
Kediri
Madiun
Blitar
Probolinggo
Pasuruan
Denpasar
Mataram
Ujung Pandang (Makassar)
Pattallassang
Majene
Mamuju
Onang
Polewali
Palangkaraya
Sampit
Sukamara
Pangkalpinang
Bangka
Belitung
Kota Kinabalu
BRUNEI
SABAH
Bandar Seri Begawan

Kuala Lumpur
Seremban
Melaka
Johor Bahru
Batu Pahat
Tanjungpinang
Bintan

1:10M

0 100 200 300 400 km
0 100
0 200 mls

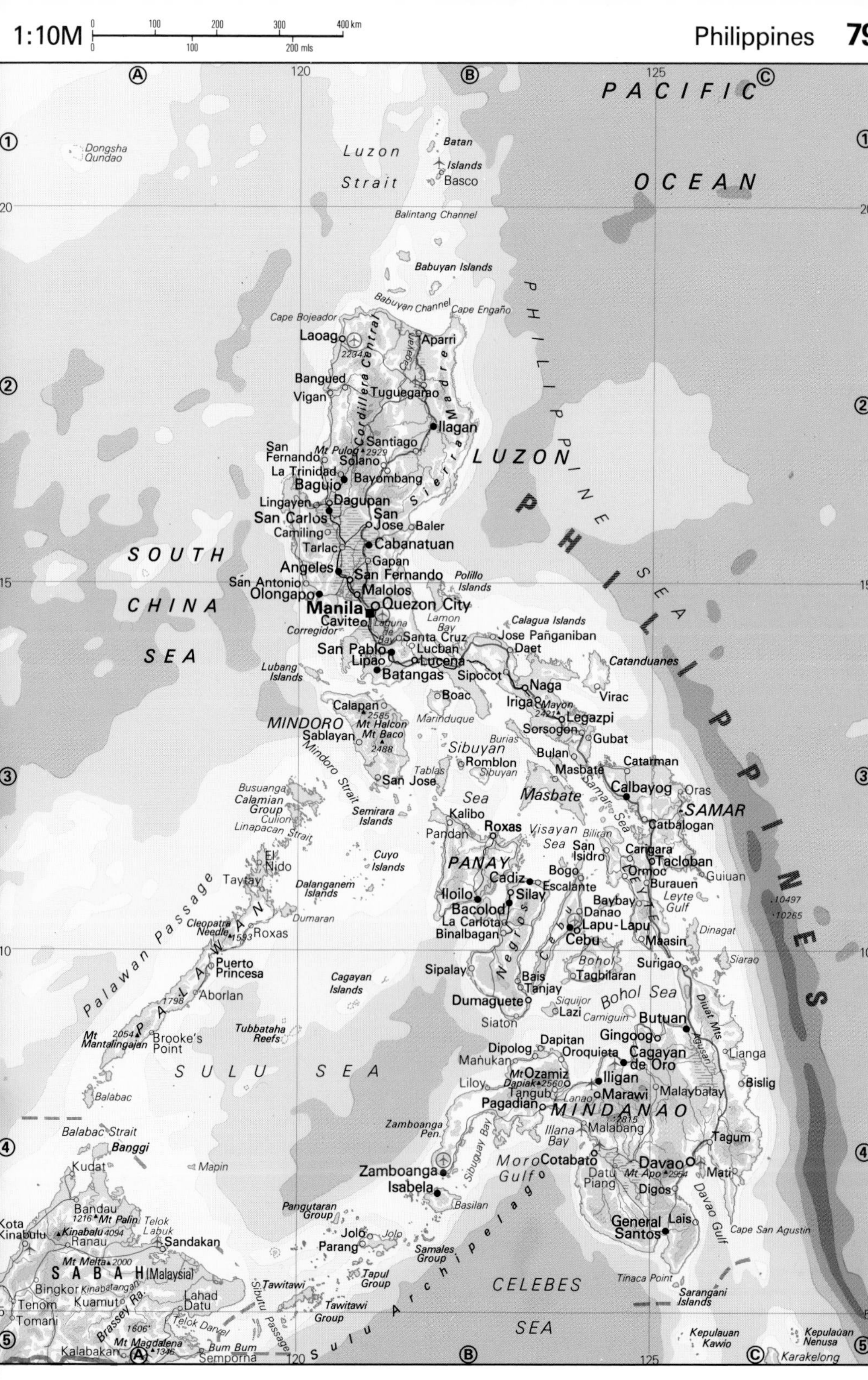

PACIFIC

① Dongsha
Qundao

OCEAN

Luzon
Strait

Batan
Islands
Basco

20

Balintang Channel

Babuyan Islands

②

Babuyan Channel
Cape Bojeador
Laoag
*2494
Aparri
Cape Engaño

Bangued
Vigan
Tuguegarao

P
H
I
L
I
P
P
I
N
E

Santiago
Ilagan

San
Fernando
Mt Pulog *2929
Solano
La Trinidad
Baguio
Bayombang

LUZON

Lingayen
Dagupan
San Carlos
San
Jose
Baler

Camiling
Tarlac
Cabanatuan

Angeles
Gapan
San Fernando
Polillo
Islands

San Antonio
Malolos
Quezon City
Olongapo
Manila
Cavite
Corregidor
Laguna
Lamon
Bay
Calauag Islands

Santa Cruz
Lucban
Jose Pañganiban
Daet

San Pablo
Lipao
Lucena
Sipocot

Lubang
Islands
Batangas
Boac
Naga
Iriga
Legazpi
Virac
Catanduanes

Calapan
*2585
Marinduque
Sorsogon
Gubat

MINDORO
Sablayan
Mt Halcon
Mt Baco
*2488

Burias
Bulan

Sibuyan
Romblon
Sibuyan
Masbate
Catarman

Busuanga
Calamian
Group
Culion
Linapacan Strait
Semirara
Islands

San Jose
Sea
Tablas
Masbate
Calbayog
Oras

SOUTH
CHINA
SEA

Kalibo
Roxas
Catbalogan

Cuyo
Islands
Pandan
SAMAR

El
Nido
Dalanganem
Islands
PANAY
Cadiz
San
Isidro
Catarman
Carigara
Tacloban
Ormoc
Burauen
Guiuan

Taytay
Dumaran
Iloilo
Silay
Bogo
Escalante
Baybay

Cleopatra
Needle
*1593
Bacolod
Danao
Leyte
Gulf
Dinagat

Roxas
La Carlota
Binalbagan
Lapu-Lapu
Cebu
Maasin

Puerto
Princesa
Aborlan
Cagayan
Islands
Sipalay
Bais
Tagbilaran
Surigao
Siarao

Mt
Mantalingajan
*1798
Brooke's
Point
Dumaguete
Tanjay
Siquijor
Lazi
Camiguin
Bohol Sea
Butuan

Tubbataha
Reefs
Siaton
Dipolog
Dapitan
Gingoog
Lianga

SULU
SEA
Oroquieta
Cagayan
de Oro

Balabac
Manukan
Mt Ozamiz
Iligan
Malaybalay
Bislig

Balabac Strait
Liloy
Tangub
Marawi
Banggi
Pagadian
MINDANAO

Kudat
Mapin
Zamboanga
Pen.
Lanao
Malabang
Tagum

Pangutaran
Group
Zamboanga
Illana
Bay
Cotabato
Davao
Mati

Kota
Kinabalu
Bandau
Mt Palin
Telok
Labuk
Isabela
Basilan
Datu
Piang
Digos

SABAH
(Malaysia)
Jolo
Jolo
Samales
Group
General
Santos
Lais
Cape San Agustin

Bingkor
Mt Melta 2000
Parang
Tapul
Group
CELEBES
Tinaca Point
Sarangani
Islands

Tenom
Mt Magdalena
Tawitawi
Group
SEA
Kepulauan
Kawio
Kepulauan
Nenusa

Tomani
Kuamut
Kalabakan
Bum Bum
Semporna
Karakelong

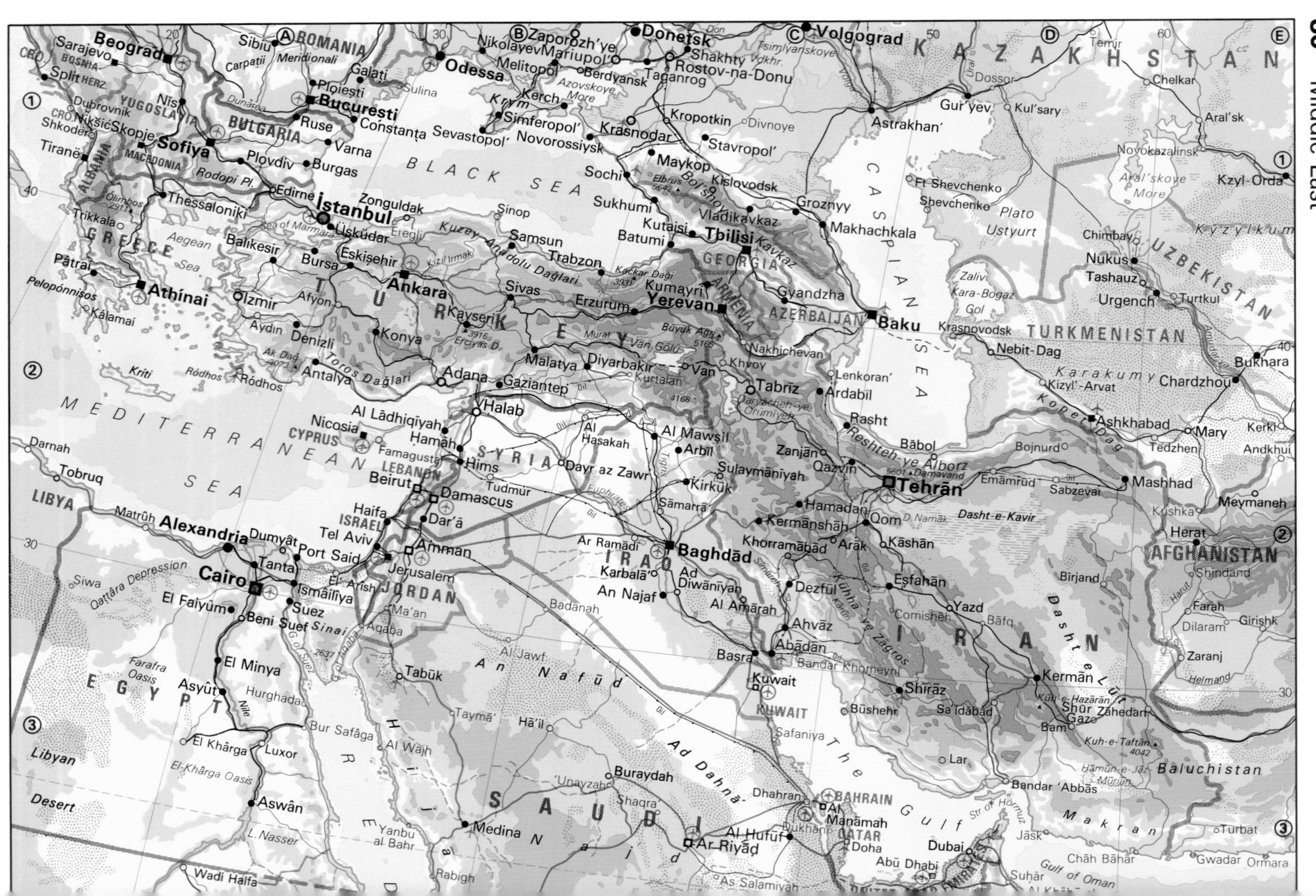
KAZAKHSTAN
UZBEKISTAN
TURKMENISTAN
AFGHANISTAN
IRAN
IRAQ
SAUDI ARABIA
SYRIA
TURKEY
JORDAN
ISRAEL
LEBANON
CYPRUS
KUWAIT
BAHRAIN
QATAR
GEORGIA
ARMENIA
AZERBAIJAN
ROMANIA
BULGARIA
YUGOSLAVIA
MACEDONIA
ALBANIA
BOSNIA-HERZ.
CRO.
GREECE
EGYPT
LIBYA
CASPIAN SEA
BLACK SEA
MEDITERRANEAN SEA
Aegean Sea
Sea of Marmara
Azovskoye More
Aral'skoye More
The Gulf
Gulf of Oman
Str. of Hormuz
G. of Suez
L. Nasser
Zaliv Kara-Bogaz Gol
Plato Ustyurt
Kyzylkum
Karakumy
Kopet Dag
Dasht-e-Kavir
Dasht-e Lūt
Reshteh-ye Alborz
Kūhhā-ye Zagros
Baluchistan
Makran
Kavkaz
Kuzey Anadolu Dağlari
Toros Dağlari
Ad Dahnā
An Nafūd
Najd
Hijaz
Sinai
Qattâra Depression
Libyan Desert
Pelopónnisos
Kríti
Ródhos
Volgograd
Astrakhan'
Gur'yev
Donetsk
Rostov-na-Donu
Odessa
Zaporozh'ye
Mariupol'
Simferopol'
Sevastopol'
Novorossiysk
Krasnodar
Stavropol'
Groznyy
Makhachkala
Tbilisi
Yerevan
Baku
Ashkhabad
Mashhad
Tehrān
Tabrīz
Bukhara
Nukus
Urgench
Chardzhou
Herat
Kermān
Shīrāz
Eşfahān
Yazd
Baghdād
Basra
Kuwait
Ar Riyāḑ
Dubai
Abū Dhabi
Al Manāmah
Doha
İstanbul
Ankara
İzmir
Bursa
Konya
Adana
Trabzon
Erzurum
Samsun
Sivas
Kayseri
Malatya
Diyarbakir
Gaziantep
Halab
Damascus
Beirut
Amman
Jerusalem
Tel Aviv
Haifa
Nicosia
Cairo
Alexandria
Port Said
Suez
Aswân
Luxor
Asyût
Medina
Tabūk
Buraydah
Beograd
Sofiya
Bucureşti
Athínai
Thessaloníki
Skopje
Tiranë
Sarajevo
Constanța
Varna
Burgas
Plovdiv
Edirne

200 400 600 800 km

200 400 mls

④ 10 ⑤ ⑥

Ⓔ

60

Ⓓ

50

Ⓒ

40

ARABIAN SEA

Carlsberg Ridge

Somali Basin

Tropic of Cancer

Al Hadd
Sūr
Nazwa
OMAN
Masīrah
Gulf of Masīrah
Ra's al Madrakah
Khalīj Maşīrah

Al Liwā'

R u b '   a l   K h ā l ī

Şalālah

Ras Fartak

Ra's al Madrakah

Socotra (Suqutra) [Yemen]
Hadiboh
Raas Caseyr
Raas Xaafuun

Sayhūt
Ash Shihr
Al Mukalla
H a d r a m a w t
Tarīm
Nişāb
Şan'ā'
Sa'dah
Al Hudaydah
Ta'izz
Al Mukhā
Jizan
Şabyā
Abhā
Al Qunfidhah
Al Luhayyah
T i h a m a h
Sabya

NORTH
SOUTH   YEMEN
A S I R

At Ţā'if
Al Līth
Makkah

Aden
(Adan)
(Aden)
Gulf of Aden
Bāb al Mandab
Asela
Djibouti
DJIBOUTI
Berbera
Hargeysa
Ceerigaabo
Ceeligaabo

Hobyo

Muqdisho
(Mogadishu)
Marka
Baraawe

S O M A L I A

Kismaayo

Equator

Juba (Giuba)

Shabēlie
Doolo
Dolo Odo
Negēlē
Wajīr
Tana
Movale

Port Sudan
Suakin
Mitsiwa
(Massawa)
Asmera
ERITREA
Gonder
Gebre Markos
Ras Dashan 4620
L. Tana
Dese
Dire Dawa
Nazret
Harēr
Jijiga
Ginir
Bāru 4307

Kassala
Atbara
Wad Medani
Singa
Asosa
Ādīs Ābeba
Dendī 3012
Jima
Gīdolē
Adaba

E T H I O P I A

Berber
Atbara
Ed Damer
Merowe
Dongola
Khartoum
Omdurman
Ed Dueim
El Obeid
Er Nahud
Singa
White Nile
Blue Nile
Nile

S U D A N

Malakal
Sudd
Rumbek
Juba
Nimule
Pakwach

L. Rudolf
Mt Kenya 5200
Nanyuki
Eldoret
Nakuru
Nairobi
Moshi
Kilimanjaro 5895
Mt Elgon 4321
Kitale
Kisumu
Lake Victoria
Mwanza
Bukoba
Musoma

K E N Y A

U G A N D A
Kampala
Jinja
Entebbe
Soroti
Tororo
Mbale
Mbarara
Kasese
Fort Portal

ZAIRE
Beni
Watsa
Bunia
L. Albert
L. Edward
Goma
Bukavu

RWANDA
Kigali
BURUNDI
Bujumbura
Gitega

TANZANIA

Nubian Desert

④ 10 ⑤ ⑥

KAZAKHSTAN
UZBEKISTAN
KYRGYZSTAN
TAJIKISTAN
AFGHANISTAN
PAKISTAN
INDIA
NEPAL
BHUTAN
BANGLADESH
MONGOLIA
INNER MONGOLIA
XINJIANG
QINGHAI
TIBET
KASHMIR

Aral'sk
Chelkar
Dzhezkazgan
Kzyl-Orda
Turkestan
Chimkent
Dzhambul
Tashkent
Bishkek
Alma-Ata
Taldy Kurgan
Ayaguz
Balkhash
Atasu
Nukus
Urgench
Bukhara
Samarkand
Karshi
Chardzhou
Mary
Tedzhen
Mashhad
Herat
Kabul
Kandahar
Quetta
Karachi
Hyderabad
Sukkur
Multan
Lahore
Islamabad
Rawalpindi
Peshawar
Srinagar
Amritsar
Delhi
Agra
Jaipur
Kanpur
Lucknow
Varanasi
Allahabad
Patna
Kathmandu
Thimphu
Dhaka
Lhasa
Xining
Lanzhou
Yumen
Hami
Turpan
Ürümqi
Kashi
Hotan
Aksu
Yining
Karamay
Golmud

Taklimakan Shamo
Tarim Pendi
Qaidam Pendi
Dzungaria
Turfan Depression
Kunlun Shan
Altun Shan
Qilian Shan
Tanggula Shan
Gangdise Shan
Karakoram
Himalaya
Hindu Kush
Pamir
Tien Shan
Mt Everest 8848
K2 (Godwin Austen) 8611
Nanga Parbat 8126
Kyzylkum
Betpak-Dala
Muyun Kum
Thar Desert
Balochistan
Indus
Ganga
Brahmaputra
Amudar'ya
Syrdar'ya
Ozero Balkhash
Oz. Issyk-Kul'
Lop Nor
Qinghai Hu

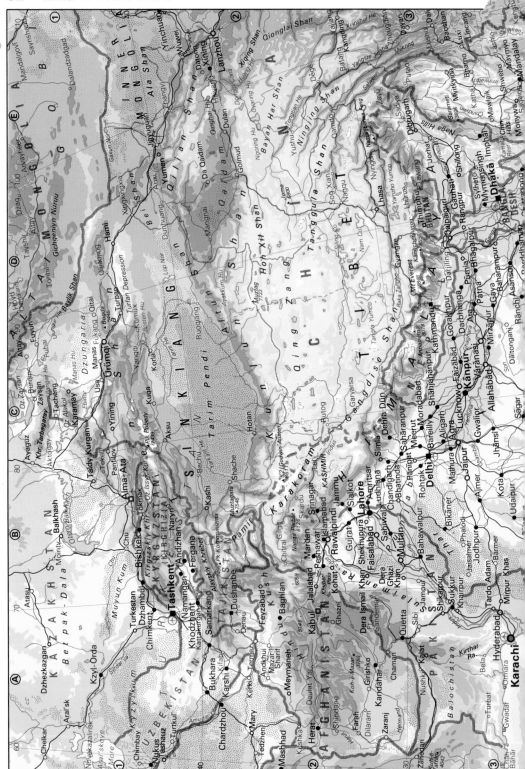

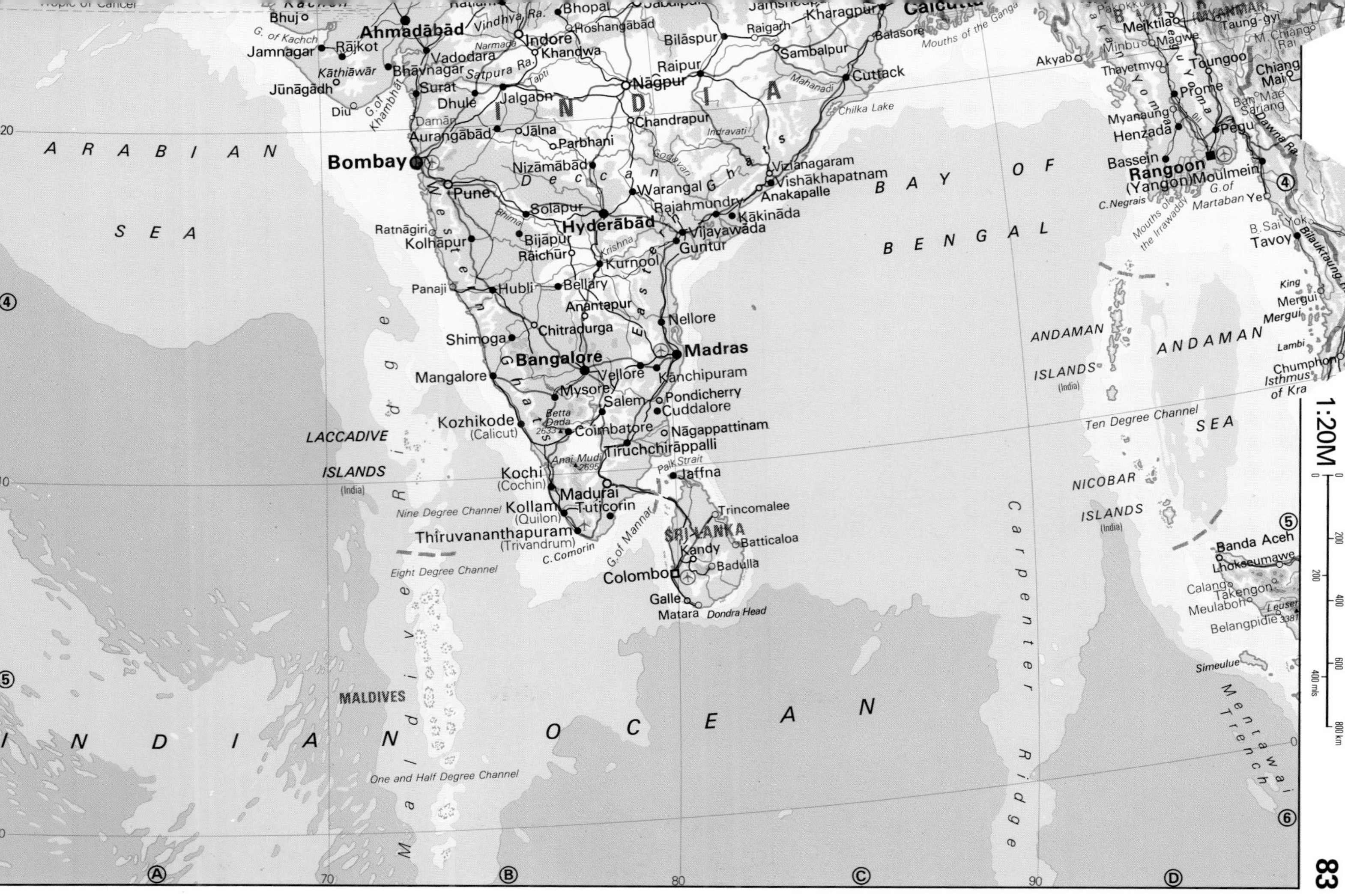

1:20M

200   400   600   800 km
200   400 mls

MENTAWAI Trench

INDIAN OCEAN

BAY OF BENGAL

ANDAMAN SEA

ARABIAN SEA

Carpenter Ridge

ANDAMAN ISLANDS (India)

NICOBAR ISLANDS (India)

LACCADIVE ISLANDS (India)

MALDIVES

SRI LANKA

Bombay
Ahmadābād
Calcutta
Madras
Bangalore
Hyderābād
Rangoon (Yangon)
Pune
Nāgpur
Colombo
Banda Aceh

Ten Degree Channel

Nine Degree Channel
Eight Degree Channel
One and Half Degree Channel

Gulf of Mannar
Palk Strait

C. Comorin

Tropic of Cancer

D
C
B
A

④ ⑤ ⑥
④ ⑤

20
10
90
80
70
0

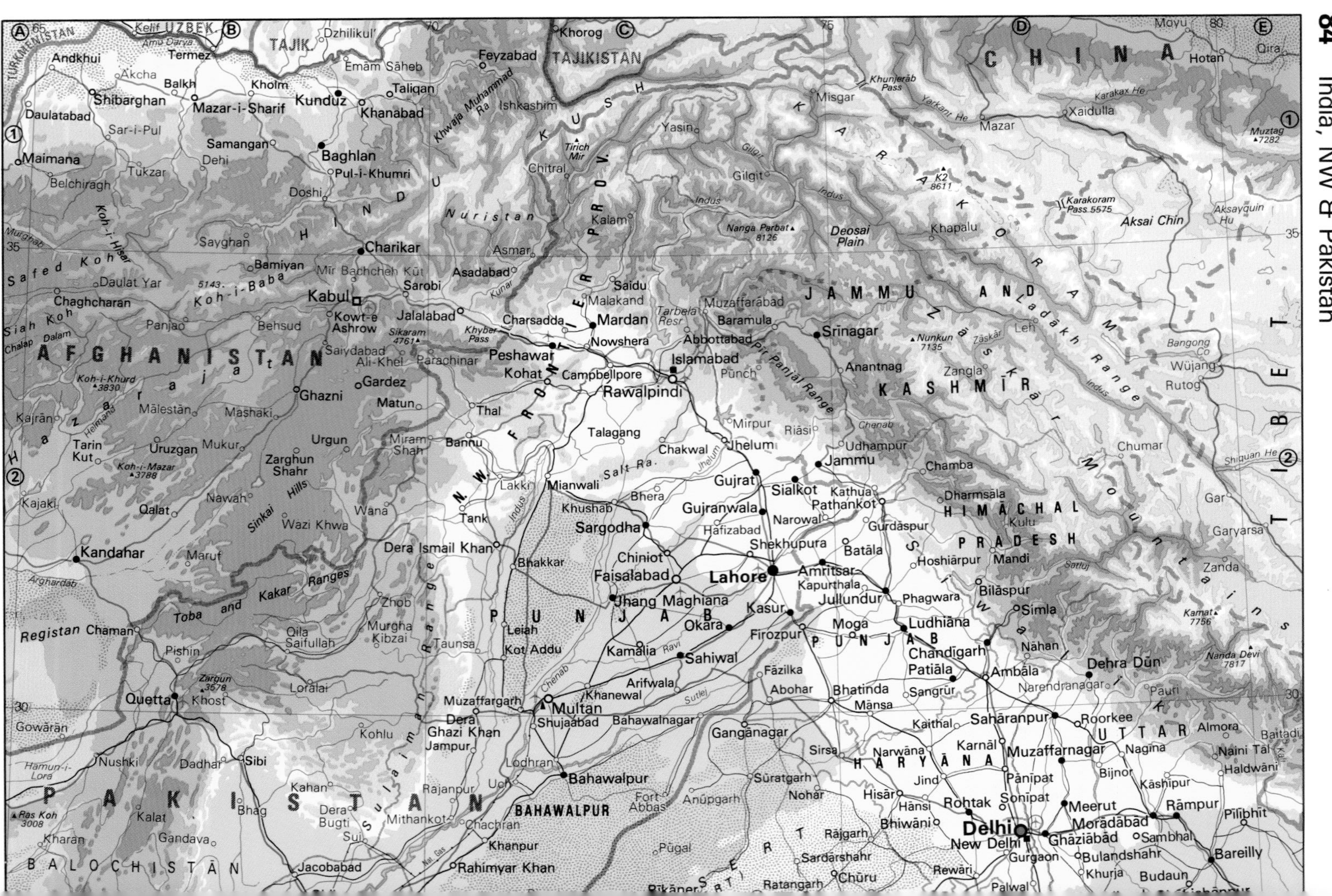

CHINA
TAJIKISTAN
TURKMENISTAN
UZBEK.
TAJIK.
AFGHANISTAN
PAKISTAN
TIBET
JAMMU AND KASHMĪR
HIMĀCHAL PRADESH
PUNJAB
HARYĀNA
UTTAR
BAHAWALPUR
BALOCHISTĀN
N.W. FRONTIER PROV.
HINDU KUSH
KARAKORAM
Ladākh Range
Pir Panjāl Range
Sulaiman Range
Toba and Kakar Ranges
Aksai Chin
Deosai Plain
Nuristan
Hotan
Kabul
Islamabad
Rawalpindi
Peshawar
Srinagar
Lahore
Amritsar
Faisalabad
Multan
Quetta
Kandahar
Ghazni
Jalalabad
Delhi
New Delhi
Meerut
Ludhiāna
Chandīgarh
Sialkot
Gujranwala
Sargodha
Bahawalpur
Dera Ismail Khan
Dera Ghazi Khan
Jacobabad
Sibi
Mazar-i-Sharif
Kunduz
Baghlan
Charikar
Shibarghan
Maimana
Andkhui
Termez
Khorog
Feyzabad
Gilgit
Chitral
Leh
Jammu
Simla
Dehra Dūn
Bareilly
Morādābād
Rāmpur
Sahāranpur
Muzaffarnagar
Rohtak
Hisār
Bhatinda
Firozpur
Kasur
Okara
Sahiwal
Jhang Maghiana
Gujrat
Jhelum
Mardan
Kohat
Bannu
K2 8611
Nanga Parbat 8126
Nanda Devi 7817
Tirich Mir
Indus
Chenab
Sutlej
Ravi

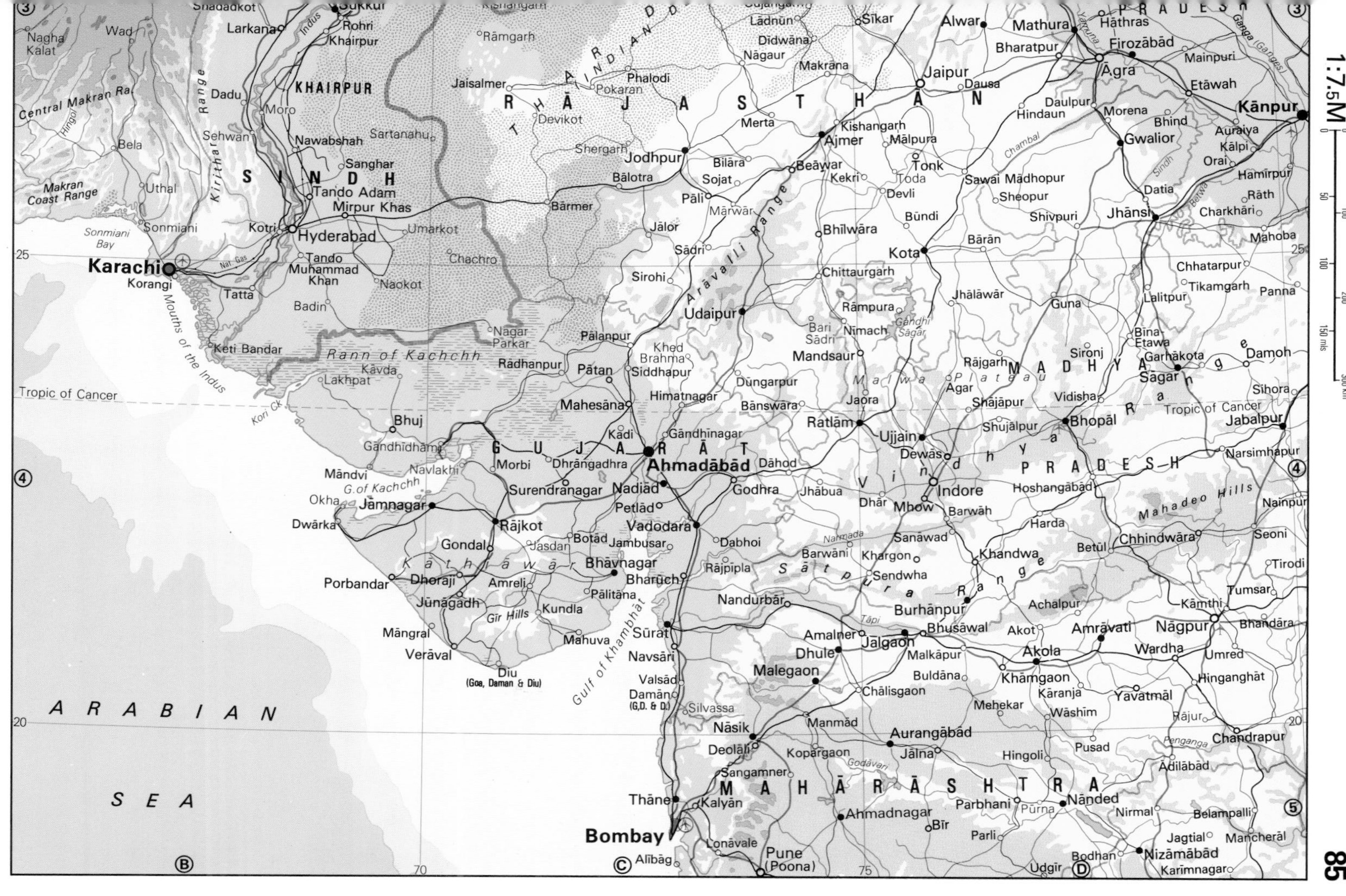

100
200
300 km

50
100
150 mls

ARABIAN

SEA

0   100   200   300 km
0   50   100   150 mls

Major labels

TIBET · CHINA · NEPAL · BHUTAN · BANGLADESH · INDIA · BURMA (MYANMAR)

ARUNACHAL Pradesh · ASSAM · NAGALAND · MANIPUR · MIZORAM · TRIPURA · MEGHALAYA · SIKKIM · BIHAR · WEST BENGAL · MADHYA PRADESH · ORISSA · UTTAR PRADESH

GREAT HIMALAYA · Mahabharat Range · Siwalik Hills · Ponnyadoung Ra. · Letha Range · Mizo Hills · Khasi · Jaintia Hills · Rajmahal Hills · Chota Nagpur · Ranchi Plateau · Maikala Range

Lhasa · Qüzü · Dagzê · Nang Xian · Nêdong · Yanzho · Yamco · Lhozhag · Tsona · Gyangzê · Xigazê · Lhazê · Tingri · Gamba · Dinggyê · Gyirong · Nyalam

BAY OF BENGAL

Mouths of the Ganga (Ganges)

Mt. Everest (Qomolangma Feng) 8848 · Makalu 8475 · Cho Oyu 8201 · Kangchenjunga 8586 · Dhaulagiri 8172 · Annapurna 8078 · Manaslu 8156 · Mt. Victoria 3053

Cities & towns

Tinsukia · Tezu · Dibrugarh · Sibsāgar · Jorhat · Golāghāt · Mariāni · Mokokchung · Kohima · Imphal · Ukhrul · Homalin · Mawlaik · Kalewa · Pakokku · Minbu · Magwe · Sittwe · Paletwa · Teknaf · Cox's Bazar · Chittagong · Rangamati · Lunglei · Saiha · Aizawl · Lungleh · Champhai · Falam · Haka · Lemro

 Itānagar · Bomdila · Bondila · Tashigang · Tawang · Dirang · Dewāngiri · Paro · Thimphu · Punakha · Tongsa · Bumthang · Chukha · Phuntsholing

NāgāLAND · Dimāpur · Diphu · Lumding · Hojāi · Nowgong · Gauhāti · Barpeta · Goālpāra · Dhubri · Tura · Shillong · Jowai · Cherrapunji · Silchar · Karimganj · Hailākāndi · Dullabchara

Sylhet · Sunāmganj · Mohanganj · Netrakona · Mymensingh · Habiganj · Brahmanbaria · Comilla · Chandpur · Noākhāli · Feni · Agartala · Narayanganj · Dhāka (Dacca) · Barra · Mādaripur · Barisal · Bāgerhāt · Khulna · Jessore · Patuākhāli · Majdi

Rangpur · Gaibanda · Bogra · Jamālpur · Sirājganj · Pabna · Kushtia · Faridpur · Rajbāri · Rajshāhi · Natore · Jessore · Sātkhira

Shiliguri · Jalpaiguri · Koch Bihār · Saidpur · Dinājpur · Bālurghāt · Ingrāj Bāzar · Baharampur · Krishnanagar · Bhatpāra · Halisahar · Bārāsat · Calcutta · Hāora · Haldia · Diamond Harbour · Port Canning · Contai · Kānthi

Darjiling (Darjeeling) · Kalimpong · Gangtok · Dhankuta · Biratnagar · Ilām · Okhaldunga · Taplejung · Namche Bāzar · Kathmandu · Patan · Bhadgaon · Bhaktapur · Pokhara · Gorkha · Butwāl · Tänsing · Mustang · Jumla · Dailekh · Dandeldhura · Silgarhi · Mahāmdra · Nepalganj · Dang

Purnia · Kishanganj · Katihār · Bhāgalpur · Munger · Bārauni · Begusarai · Nāwāda · Bihār · Patna · Ara · Buxar · Chhapra · Gorakhpur · Basti · Faizābād · Sultanpur · Jaunpur · Vārānasi · Mirzāpur · Allahābad · Banda · Fatehpur · Kānpur · Unnāo · Lucknow · Rāe Bareli · Gonda · Bahrāich · Sitāpur · Lakhimpur

Gaya · Sāsarām · Dehri · Daltenganj · Garwa · Hazāribāg · Giridih · Dhanbād · Dumka · Deoghar · Āsansol · Rānīganj · Barddhamān · Durgāpur · Bānkura · Jamshedpur · Rānchi · Lohardaga · Gumla · Rāmgarh · Chāibāsa · Keonjhargarh · Kharagpur · Medinīpur · Bishnupur · Tāmluk

Cuttack · Bhubaneswar · Khurda · Nayagarh · Talcher · Angul · Dhenkanāl · Kendrāpāra · Balasore · Bhadrakh · Barīpāda · Raurkela · Sundargarh · Raigarh · Jhārsuguda · Sambalpur · Bargarh · Bolāngir · Titlāgarh · Mahāsamund · Dhamtari · Kānker

Bilāspur · Champa · Korba · Raigarh · Ambikāpur · Baikunthpur · Shahdol · Umaria · Mandla · Kawardha · Durg · Bhilai · Raj Nandgaon · Dalli · Raipur · Mungeli · Kawardha · Satna · Maihar · Rewa · Sidhi · Bedhāri · Matendragarh

Rivers: Brahmaputra · Manas · Tsangpo · Ganges (Ganga) · Son · Mahānadi · Kosi · Gandak · Ghāghra · Yamuna · Tista · Meghna · Padma · Hooghly · Damodar

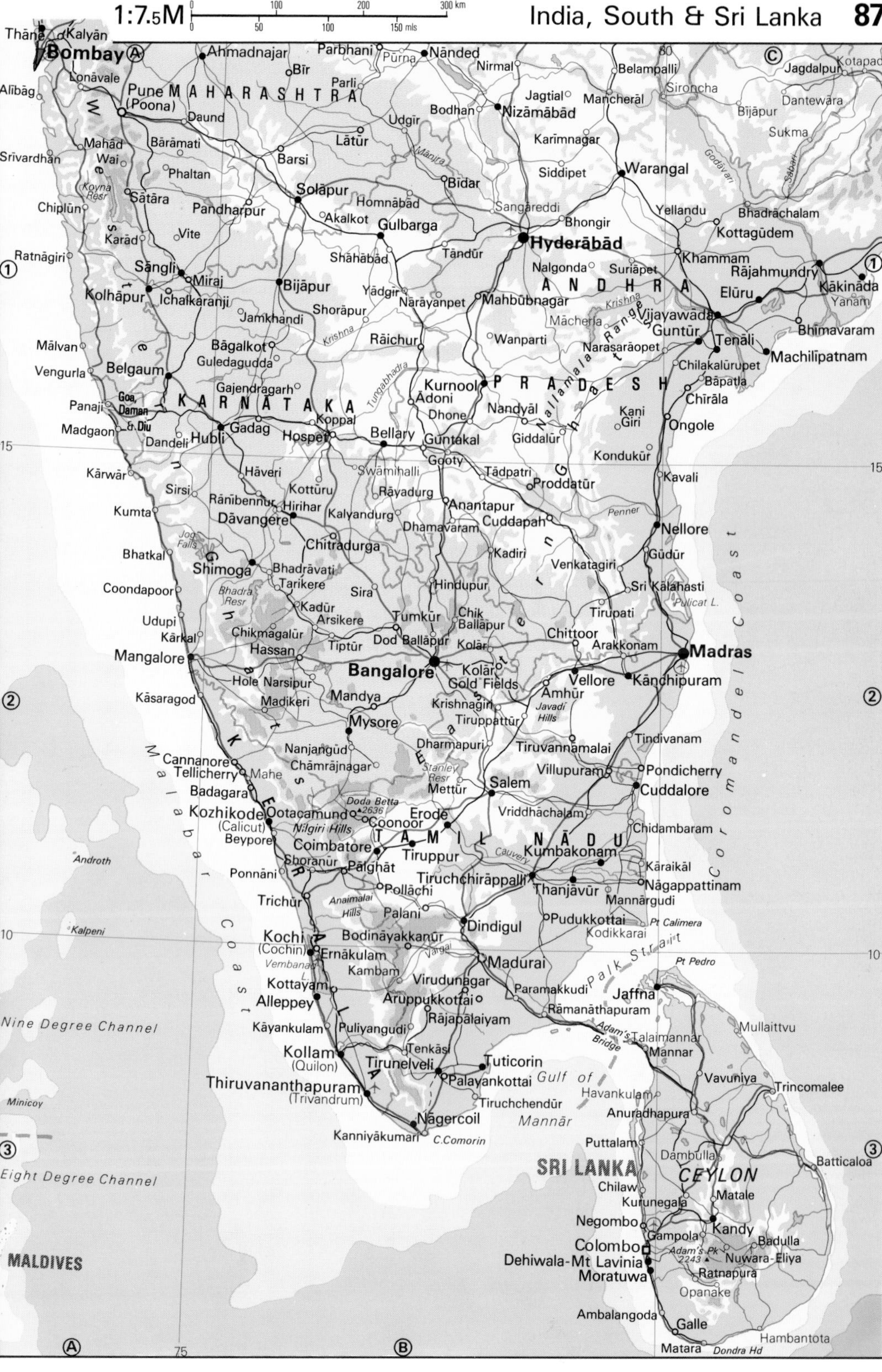
Thāna
Kalyān
Bombay
Lonāvale
Alībāg
Pune
(Poona)
MAHARASHTRA
Ahmadnajar
Bīr
Parbhani
Pūrna
Nānded
Parli
Daund
Mahād
Bārāmati
Srīvardhan
Wai
Phaltan
Koyna Resr
Sātāra
Chiplūn
Pandharpur
Barsi
Lātūr
Udgīr
Solāpur
Homnābād
Akalkot
Bīdar
Gulbarga
Vite
Karād
Ratnāgiri
Sāngli
Miraj
Kolhāpur
Ichalkaranji
Bijāpur
Jamkhandi
Shorāpur
Shāhābād
Yādgīr
Nārāyanpet
Rāichur
Krishna
Bāgalkot
Guledagudda
Mālvan
Vengurla
Belgaum
Gajendragarh
Panaji
Goa, Daman & Diu
Madgaon
KARNĀTAKA
Gadag
Hubli
Dandeli
Koppal
Hospet
Bellary
Kārwār
Hāveri
Sirsi
Kottūru
Rānibennur
Hirihar
Dāvangere
Kumta
Jog Falls
Chitradurga
Bhatkal
Shimoga
Bhadrāvati
Tarikere
Coondapoor
Bhadra Resr
Kadūr
Arsikere
Udupi
Kārkal
Chikmagalūr
Hassan
Tiptūr
Mangalore
Hole Narsipur
Kāsaragod
Madikeri
Mandya
Mysore
Nanjangūd
Chāmrājnagar
Cannanore
Tellicherry
Mahe
Badagara
Kozhikode
(Calicut)
Beypore
Ootacamund
Doda Betta 2636
Nilgiri Hills
Coonoor
Coimbatore
Shoranūr
Pālghāt
Ponnāni
Trichūr
Pollāchi
Anaimalai Hills
Palani
Kochi
(Cochin)
Ernākulam
Vembanad L.
Kottayam
Alleppey
Kāyankulam
Kollam
(Quilon)
Thiruvananthapuram
(Trivandrum)
Nāgercoil
Kanniyākumari
C.Comorin
Malabar Coast
Western Ghats
KERALA
Androth
Kalpeni
Nine Degree Channel
Minicoy
Eight Degree Channel
MALDIVES
Nirmal
Jagtial
Bodhan
Nizāmābād
Mancherāl
Belampalli
Sironcha
Karīmnagar
Siddipet
Warangal
Mānjra
Godāvari
Sabari
Jagdalpur
Kotapad
Dantewāra
Bījāpur
Sukma
Sangāreddi
Bhongir
Hyderābād
Tāndūr
Yellandu
Bhadrāchalam
Kottagūdem
Khammam
Nalgonda
Suriāpet
Rājahmundry
Kākināda
Yanam
ANDHRA
Mahbūbnagar
Māchērla
Nallamala Range
Eluru
Vijayawāda
Guntūr
Tenāli
Bhīmavaram
Machilīpatnam
Wanparti
Narasarāopet
Chilakalūrupet
Bāpatla
Chīrāla
PRADESH
Kurnool
Ādoni
Tungabhadra
Dhone
Nandyāl
Kani Giri
Ongole
Guntakal
Giddalūr
Gooty
Kondukūr
Swāmihalli
Tādpatri
Proddatūr
Kavali
Rāyadurg
Anantapur
Kalyandurg
Dhamavaram
Cuddapah
Penner
Nellore
Kadiri
Gūdūr
Venkatagiri
Sri Kālahasti
Pulicat L.
Hindupur
Sira
Tumkūr
Chik Ballāpur
Tirupati
Dod Ballāpur
Kolār
Chittoor
Arakkonam
Madras
Bangalore
Kolār Gold Fields
Vellore
Kānchipuram
Āmhūr
Krishnagiri
Javadi Hills
Tiruppattūr
Dharmapuri
Tiruvannamalai
Tindivanam
Stanley Resr
Mettūr
Salem
Villupuram
Pondicherry
Cuddalore
Eastern Ghats
Erode
Vriddhāchalam
Chidambaram
TAMIL NĀDU
Tiruppur
Cauvery
Kumbakonam
Kāraikāl
Tiruchchirāppalli
Thanjāvūr
Nāgappattinam
Mannārgudi
Dindigul
Pudukkottai
Pt Calimera
Kodikkarai
Bodināyakkanūr
Vaigai
Madurai
Kambam
Virudunagar
Paramakkudi
Aruppukkottai
Rāmanāthapuram
Rājapālaiyam
Puliyangudi
Tenkāsi
Tirunelveli
Tuticorin
Palayankottai
Tiruchchendūr
Gulf of Mannār
Palk Strait
Coromandel Coast
Pt Pedro
Jaffna
Adam's Bridge
Talaimannar
Mannar
Mullaittvu
Vavuniya
Trincomalee
Havankulam
Anuradhapura
Puttalam
Dambulla
SRI LANKA
CEYLON
Batticaloa
Chilaw
Kurunegala
Matale
Negombo
Kandy
Gampola
Colombo
Badulla
Adam's Pk 2243
Nuwara-Eliya
Dehiwala-Mt Lavinia
Moratuwa
Ratnapura
Opanake
Ambalangoda
Galle
Hambantota
Matara
Dondra Hd
15
10
75
80
A
B
C
1
2
3

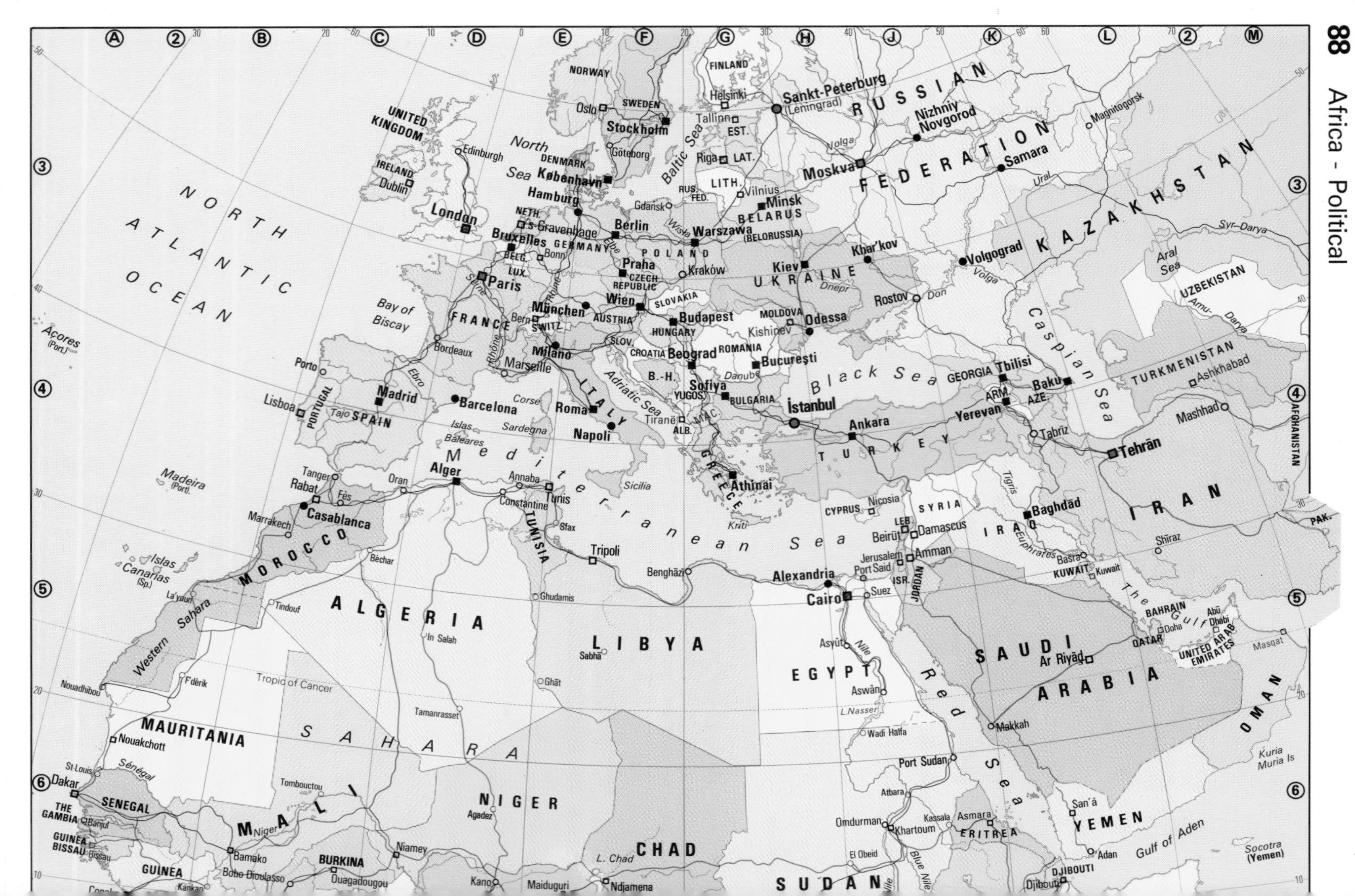
NORTH ATLANTIC OCEAN
Bay of Biscay
North Sea
Baltic Sea
Black Sea
Caspian Sea
Aral Sea
Mediterranean Sea
Adriatic Sea
Red Sea
Gulf of Aden
The Gulf
UNITED KINGDOM
IRELAND
NORWAY
SWEDEN
FINLAND
DENMARK
NETH.
BELG.
LUX.
GERMANY
POLAND
CZECH REPUBLIC
SLOVAKIA
AUSTRIA
SWITZ.
HUNGARY
SLOV.
CROATIA
B.-H.
YUGOS.
ALB.
MAC.
GREECE
BULGARIA
ROMANIA
MOLDOVA
UKRAINE
BELARUS (BELORUSSIA)
LITH.
LAT.
EST.
RUS. FED.
RUSSIAN FEDERATION
KAZAKHSTAN
UZBEKISTAN
TURKMENISTAN
AFGHANISTAN
PAK.
GEORGIA
ARM.
AZE.
TURKEY
CYPRUS
SYRIA
LEB.
ISR.
JORDAN
IRAQ
IRAN
KUWAIT
BAHRAIN
QATAR
UNITED ARAB EMIRATES
OMAN
SAUDI ARABIA
YEMEN
DJIBOUTI
ERITREA
SUDAN
EGYPT
LIBYA
TUNISIA
ALGERIA
MOROCCO
Western Sahara
MAURITANIA
MALI
NIGER
CHAD
SENEGAL
THE GAMBIA
GUINEA-BISSAU
GUINEA
BURKINA
FRANCE
SPAIN
PORTUGAL
ITALY
SAHARA
Tropic of Cancer
London
Dublin
Edinburgh
Oslo
Stockholm
Göteborg
Helsinki
Tallinn
Riga
Vilnius
Minsk
København
Hamburg
Berlin
Gdańsk
Warszawa
Kraków
Praha
Wien
München
Bonn
's-Gravenhage
Bruxelles
Paris
Bordeaux
Marseille
Bern
Milano
Roma
Napoli
Budapest
Beograd
Bucureşti
Sofiya
Tiranë
Athinai
Kishinev
Odessa
Kiev
Khar'kov
Rostov
Moskva
Sankt-Peterburg (Leningrad)
Nizhniy Novgorod
Samara
Volgograd
Magnitogorsk
Tbilisi
Baku
Yerevan
Tabriz
Tehrān
Mashhad
Ashkhabad
Shiraz
İstanbul
Ankara
Nicosia
Beirut
Damascus
Amman
Jerusalem
Baghdād
Basra
Kuwait
Doha
Abū Dhabi
Masqat
Ar Riyād
Makkah
San'ā
Adan
Djibouti
Asmara
Kassala
Khartoum
Omdurman
El Obeid
Atbara
Port Sudan
Wadi Halfa
Aswān
Asyūt
Cairo
Alexandria
Port Said
Suez
Benghāzi
Tripoli
Sabhā
Ghudamis
Ghāt
Tunis
Sfax
Constantine
Annaba
Alger
Oran
Béchar
In Salah
Tamanrasset
Agadez
Niamey
Kano
Maiduguri
Ndjamena
Ouagadougou
Bamako
Bobo Dioulasso
Tombouctou
Kankan
Dakar
St-Louis
Banjul
Bissau
Nouakchott
Nouadhibou
F'Derik
La'youn
Tindouf
Marrakech
Casablanca
Rabat
Fès
Tanger
Lisboa
Porto
Madrid
Barcelona
Corse
Sardegna
Sicilia
Kríti
Islas Baleares
Islas Canarias (Sp.)
Madeira (Port.)
Açores (Port.)
Socotra (Yemen)
Kuria Muria Is
Volga
Don
Dnepr
Danube
Wisła
Elbe
Rhine
Rhône
Seine
Ebro
Tajo
Ural
Syr-Darya
Amu-Darya
Tigris
Euphrates
Nile
Blue Nile
L. Nasser
L. Chad
Niger
Sénégal

400 800 1200 1600 km
400 800 mils

INDIAN OCEAN

Seychelles Arch.
Amirante Is.
Farquhar Is.
Tromelin (Fr.)
Réunion (Fr.)

SEYCHELLES

Aldabra Is.

MADAGASCAR

COMOROS
Mayotte (Fr.)

Mozambique Channel

Antananarivo
Antsiranana
Mahajanga
Toamasina
Toliara

SOMALIA
Muqdisho
Hargeysa

ETHIOPIA
Ādis Ābeba
Jīma

KENYA
Nairobi
Mombasa
L. Turkana
Golu

UGANDA
Kampala
Entebbe
Lake Victoria
Juba
Wau

RWANDA
Kigali
BURUNDI
Bujumbura

TANZANIA
Dodoma
Dar es Salaam
Zanzibar
Mwanza
Tabora
Mbeya
L. Edward
Lake Tanganyika
Kigoma

ZAIRE
Kisangani
Goma
Kindu
Kananga
Mbuji-Mayi
Kalemie
Mbandaka
Bandundu
Kinshasa
Matadi
Kananga
L. Albert

CENTRAL AFRICAN REPUBLIC
Bambari
Bangui

CAMEROON
Ngaoundéré
Yaoundé
Douala

NIGERIA
Abuja
Ibadan
Lagos
Ilorin
Onitsha
Port Harcourt
Kaduna

BENIN
Porto Novo

GABON
Libreville
Lambaréné

CONGO
Brazzaville

EQUAT. GUINEA
Malabo
Bata
Bioko

SÃO TOMÉ & PRINCIPE
Príncipe
São Tomé
Annobón (Eq.G.)

Gulf of Guinea

IVORY COAST
Yamoussoukro
Bouaké
Abidjan

GHANA
Kumasi
Accra
Tamale

TOGO
Lomé

LIBERIA
Monrovia
Buchanan

SIERRA LEONE
Freetown

MALAWI
Lilongwe
Lake Nyasa

MOZAMBIQUE
Nampula
Beira
Sofala
Tete
Maputo
Inhambane
Ruvuma
Zambezi

ZAMBIA
Lusaka
Ndola
Lubumbashi
Kabwe
Kasai

ZIMBABWE
Harare
Bulawayo
Gweru
Mutare
Gwen
Hwange

ANGOLA
Luanda
Lobito
Namibe
Benguela
Huambo
Bié
Malanje
Cubango
Kunene

NAMIBIA
Windhoek
Walvis Bay
Tsumeb
Keetmanshoop

BOTSWANA
Gaborone
Serowe

SOUTH AFRICA
Pretoria
Johannesburg
Kimberley
Bloemfontein
Durban
East London
Port Elizabeth
Cape Town
Orange

SWAZILAND
Mbabane

LESOTHO
Maseru

Tropic of Capricorn
Equator

SOUTH ATLANTIC OCEAN

St Helena (U.K.)
Ascension (U.K.)
Tristan da Cunha (U.K.)

Congo
Zaïre (Congo)
Limpopo

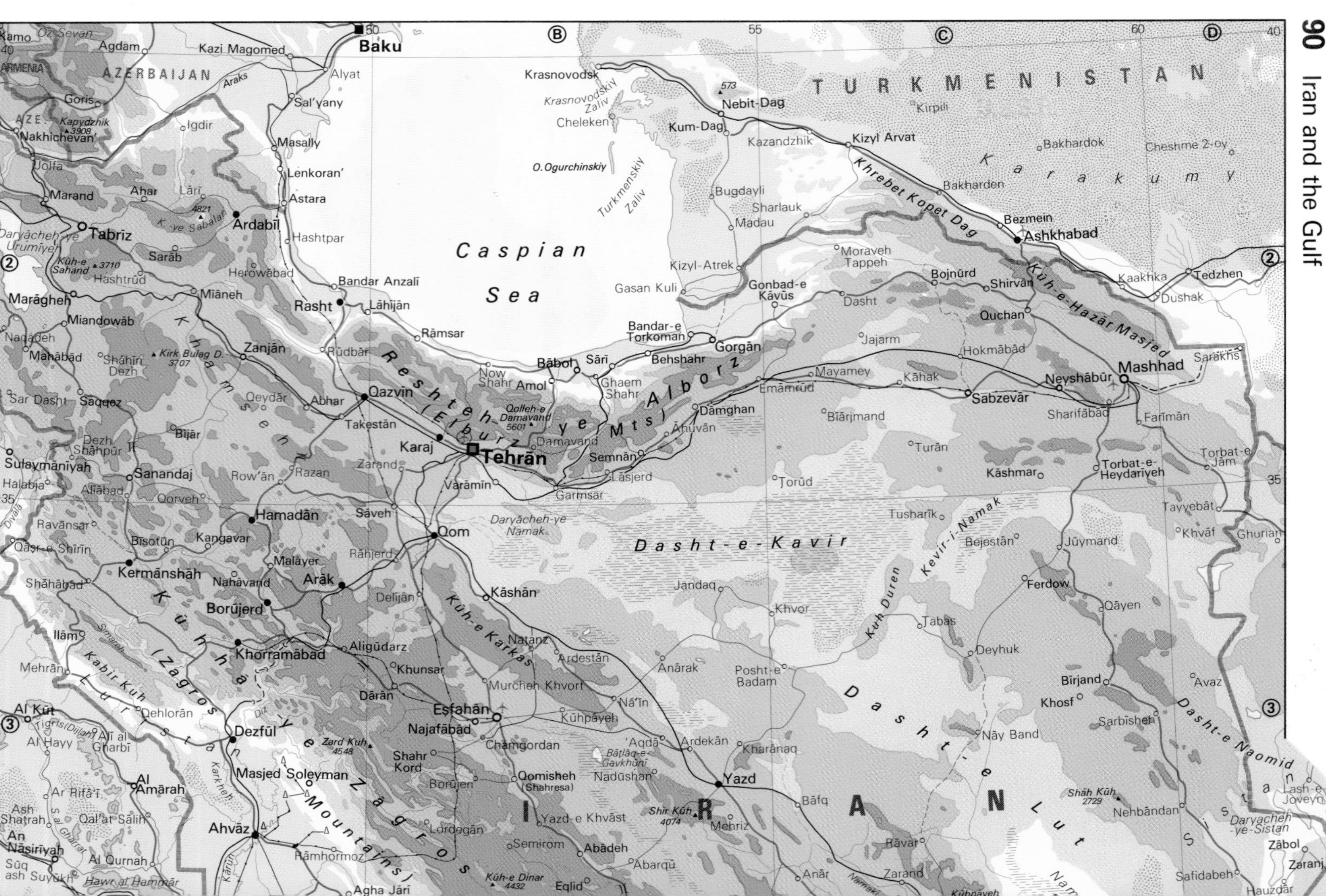
TURKMENISTAN
Karakumy
AZERBAIJAN
ARMENIA
IRAN
Caspian Sea
Turkmenskiy Zaliv
Krasnovodskiy Zaliv
O.Ogurchinskiy
Khrebet Kopet Dag
Kūh-e-Hazār Masjed
Reshteh-ye Alborz (Elburz Mts)
Dasht-e-Kavīr
Dasht-e Lut
Dasht-e Naomīd
Kūh-e Karkas
Kūhhā-ye Zagros (Zagros Mountains)
Kabir Kuh
Luristan
Kevīr-i-Namak
Kuh Duren
Daryācheh-ye Namak
Daryācheh-ye Orūmīyeh
Daryācheh-ye Sīstān
Qolleh-ye Damāvand 5601
Kūh-e Sahand 3710
Kapydzhik 3908
Kūh-e Dinar 4432
Zard Kūh 4548
Shīr Kūh 4074
Shāh Kūh 2729
Kirk Bulag D. 3707
Baku
Krasnovodsk
Nebit-Dag
Kum-Dag
Kizyl Arvat
Ashkhabad
Bezmein
Bakharden
Tedzhen
Dushak
Kaakhka
Sarakhs
Mashhad
Neyshābūr
Sabzevār
Quchan
Shīrvān
Bojnūrd
Gorgān
Gonbad-e Kāvūs
Bandar-e Torkoman
Behshahr
Sārī
Bābol
Amol
Tehrān
Karaj
Qazvīn
Rasht
Bandar Anzalī
Lāhījān
Rāmsar
Ardabīl
Astara
Lenkoran'
Tabrīz
Marand
Marāgheh
Mīāneh
Zanjān
Hamadān
Arāk
Qom
Kāshān
Esfahān
Najafābād
Shahr Kord
Yazd
Ardekān
Semnān
Dāmghan
Torbat-e Heydarīyeh
Torbat-e Jām
Kāshmar
Ferdow
Bīrjand
Qāyen
Tabas
Zābol
Zaranj
Kermānshāh
Sanandaj
Borūjerd
Khorramābād
Dezfūl
Ahvāz
Masjed Soleyman
Īlām
Al Kūt
Al Amārah
An Nāşirīyah
Sulaymānīyah
55
60
35
40
B
C
D
2
3

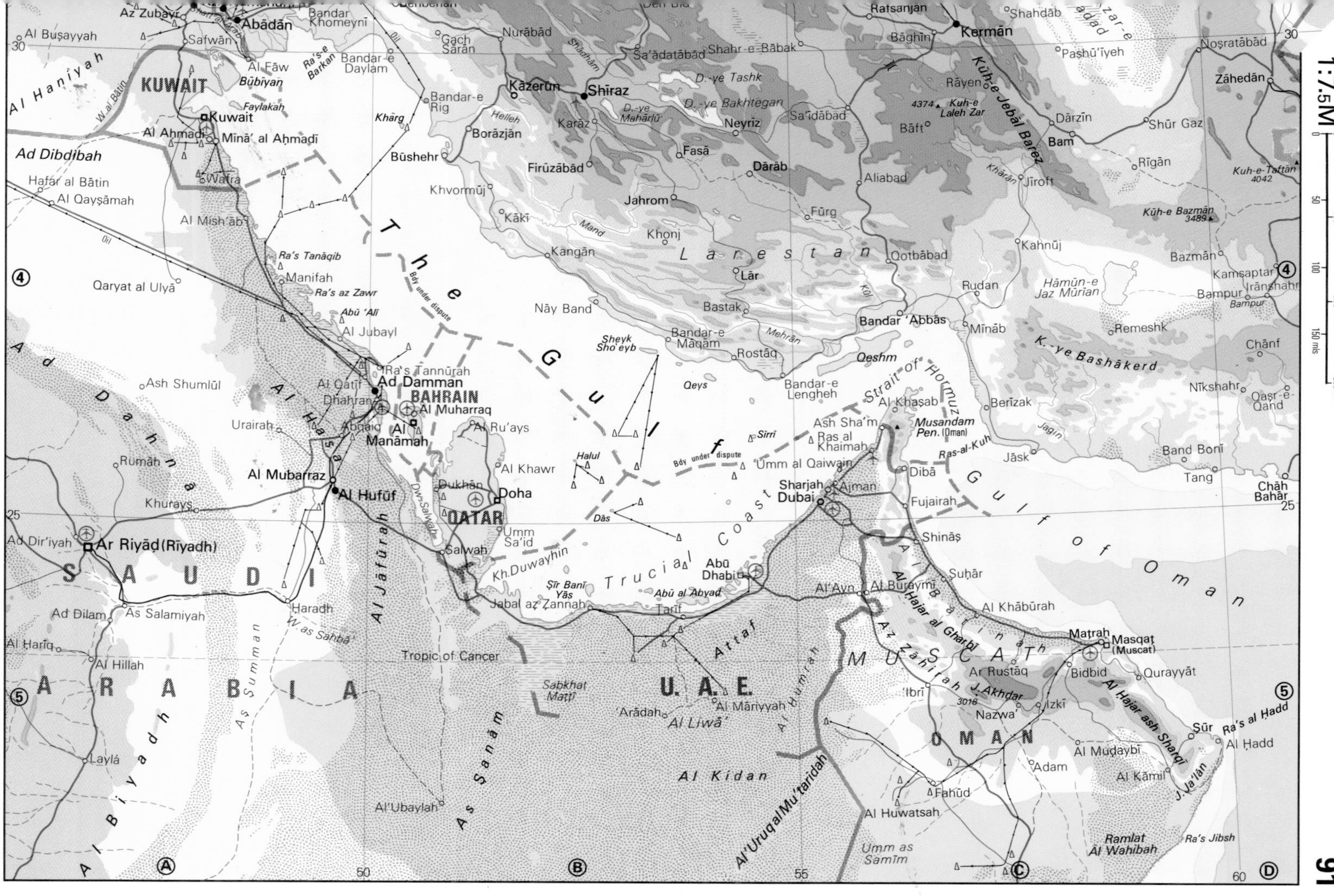
The Gulf
Gulf of Oman
Strait of Hormuz
Trucial Coast
Larestan
K.-ye Bashākerd
Kūh-e Jebāl Barez
Al Hajar al Gharbī
Al Hajar ash Sharqī
MUSCAT
OMAN
U.A.E.
QATAR
BAHRAIN
KUWAIT
SAUDI ARABIA
Al Jāfūrah
Al Hasa
Ad Dahnā
Ad Dibdibah
As Summan
As Sanām
Al Kidan
Al Liwā'
Al Biyadh
Al Haniyah
Az Zāhirah
Al Bātinah
Attaf
Al Humrah
Al 'Uruq al Mu'taridah
Ramlat Al Wahibah
Sabkhat Matti
Umm as Samīm
Kermān
Rafsanjān
Bam
Shīraz
Kāzerūn
Būshehr
Bandar 'Abbās
Qeshm
Musandam Pen. (Oman)
Dubai
Sharjah
Ajman
Umm al Qaiwain
Ras al Khaimah
Abū Dhabi
Doha
Dukhān
Al Manāmah
Al Muharraq
Ad Damman
Dhahran
Ra's Tannūrah
Al Jubayl
Al Hufūf
Al Mubarraz
Ar Riyād (Rīyadh)
Ad Dir'iyah
Kuwait
Al Ahmadi
Mīnā' al Ahmadī
Abādān
Bandar Khomeynī
Masqat (Muscat)
Matrah
Sūr
Ra's al Hadd
Ra's Jibsh
Tropic of Cancer
Bdy under dispute
Zāhedān
Chāh Bahār
Jāsk
Mīnāb
Fujairah
Dibā
Shināș
Suhār
Al Buraymī
Al 'Ayn
Ar Rustāq
Nazwa'
'Ibrī
Fahūd
Adam
Al Huwatsah
Haradh
Laylá
Al Hillah
Al Harīq
As Salamiyah
Khurays
Qaryat al Ulyā
Hafar al Bātin
Al Qayșāmah
Al Busayyah
Lār
Dārāb
Jahrom
Fasā
Neyrīz
Firūzābād
Borāzjān
Kangān
Nāy Band
Qotbābād
Aliabad
Jīroft

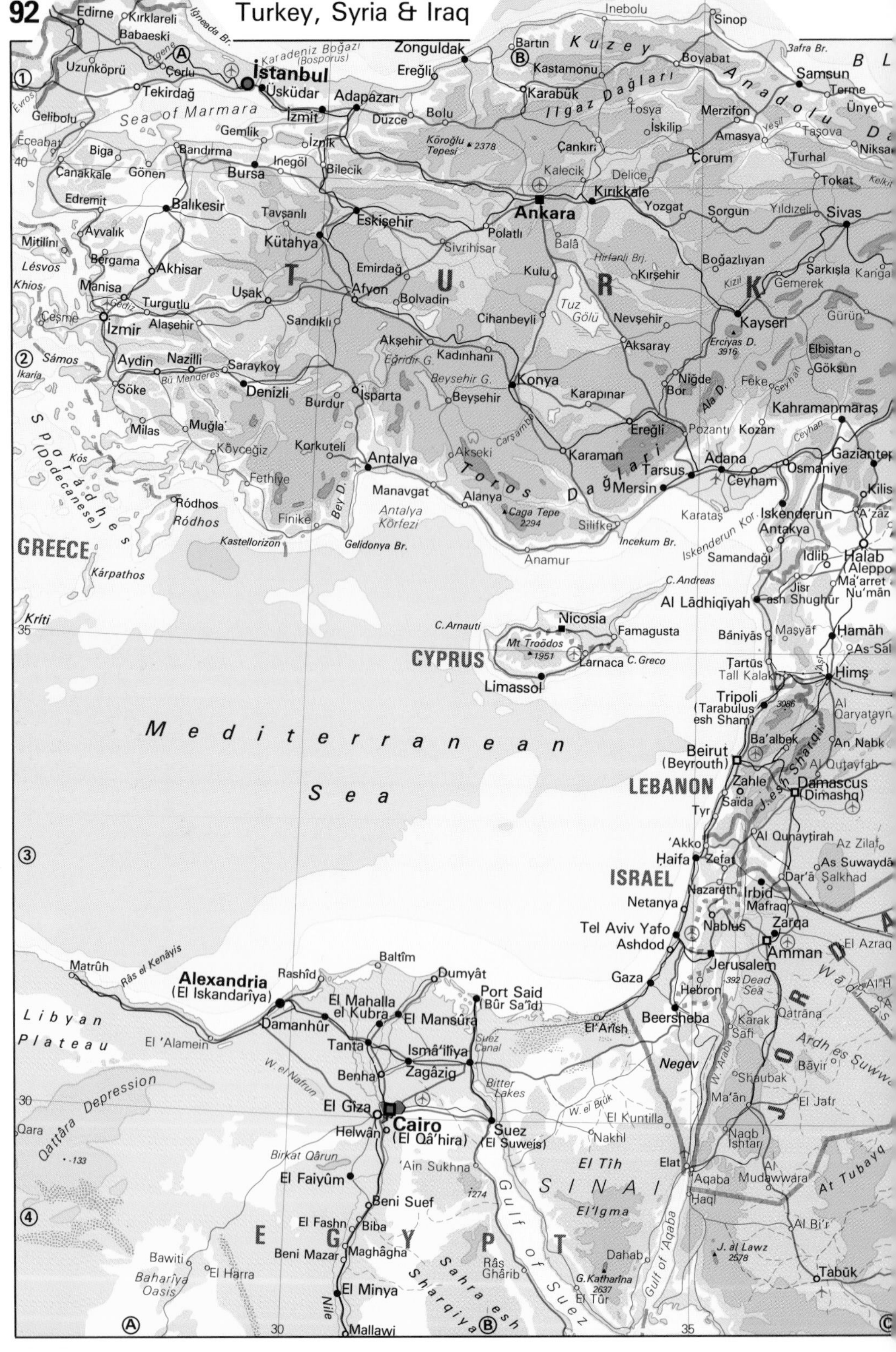
Edirne
Kırklareli
Babaeski
Uzunköprü
Çorlu
İstanbul
Üsküdar
Tekirdağ
Gelibolu
Sea of Marmara
Karadeniz Boğazı (Bosporus)
İzmit
Adapazarı
Zonguldak
Ereğli
Bartın
Kastamonu
Karabük
Inebolu
Sinop
Boyabat
Samsun
Kuzey Anadolu Dağları
Ilgaz Dağları
Düzce
Bolu
Köroğlu Tepesi 2378
Tosya
İskilip
Merzifon
Amasya
Çorum
Çankırı
Tokat
Turhal
Niksar
Ünye
Terme
Taşova
Eceabat
Gemlik
İznik
Biga
Bandırma
Çanakkale
Gönen
Bursa
İnegöl
Bilecik
Edremit
Balıkesir
Tavşanlı
Eskişehir
Ankara
Kalecik
Delice
Kırıkkale
Yozgat
Sorgun
Yıldızeli
Sivas
Mitilíni
Ayvalık
Kütahya
Sivrihisar
Polatlı
Balâ
Lésvos
Bergama
Akhisar
Emirdağ
Kulu
Hirfanlı Brj.
Kırşehir
Boğazlıyan
Şarkışla
Gemerek
Khios
Manisa
Uşak
Afyon
Bolvadin
TURKEY
Tuz Gölü
Nevşehir
Kayseri
Turgutlu
Çeşme
İzmir
Alaşehir
Sandıklı
Cihanbeyli
Gürün
Sámos
Ikaría
Aydın
Nazilli
Saraykoy
Büyük Menderes
Akşehir
Kadınhanı
Eğridir G.
Aksaray
Erciyas D. 3916
Elbistan
Göksun
Söke
Denizli
Burdur
Isparta
Beyşehir G.
Beyşehir
Konya
Karapınar
Niğde
Bor
Ala D.
Feke
Kahramanmaraş
Milas
Muğla
Köyceğiz
Korkuteli
Akseki
Ereğli
Pozantı
Kozan
Ceyhan
Gaziantep
Sporádhes (Dodecanese)
Kós
Fethiye
Antalya
Karaman
Toros Dağları
Tarsus
Adana
Osmaniye
Ceyham
Kilis
Ródhos
Manavgat
Alanya
Mersin
Antalya Körfezi
Caga Tepe 2294
Finike
Bey D.
Silifke
Karataş
İskenderun
A'zaz
GREECE
Kastellorizon
Gelidonya Br.
Incekum Br.
Anamur
İskenderun Kor.
Antakya
Samandağı
Idlib
Halab (Aleppo)
Kárpathos
C. Andreas
Jisr ash Shughur
Ma'arret Nu'mān
Al Lādhiqīyah
Kríti
Nicosia
Famagusta
C. Arnauti
Mt Troödos 1951
CYPRUS
Larnaca
C. Greco
Limassol
Bāniyās
Maşyāf
Ḩamāh
As-Sal
Ţarţūs
Tall Kalakh
Ḩimş
Tripoli (Tarabulus esh Sham)
Al Qaryatayn
Mediterranean Sea
Ba'albek
An Nabk
Beirut (Beyrouth)
Al Quţayfah
LEBANON
Zahle
Damascus (Dimashq)
Saïda
Tyr
Al Qunayţirah
Az Zilaf
'Akko
Ḩaifa
Zefat
As Suwaydā
ISRAEL
Dar'ā
Şalkhad
Nazareth
Irbid
Netanya
Mafraq
Tel Aviv Yafo
Nablus
Zarqa
Ashdod
Amman
El Azraq
Jerusalem
Gaza
-392 Dead Sea
Hebron
JORDAN
Baltîm
Matrûh
Râs el Kenâyis
Alexandria (El Iskandarîya)
Rashîd
Dumyât
Port Said (Bûr Sa'îd)
El Mahalla el Kubra
El Mansûra
Beersheba
Qatrāna
Karak
Safi
El 'Arîsh
Libyan Plateau
El 'Alamein
Damanhûr
Tanta
Ismâ'ilîya
Suez Canal
Negev
W. Araba
Ardh es Suwwan
Bāyir
W. el Natrun
Benha
Zagâzig
Bitter Lakes
Shaubak
Ma'ān
El Jafr
Qattâra Depression
El Gîza
Cairo (El Qâ'hira)
W. el Brûk
El Kuntilla
Helwân
Suez (El Suweis)
Nakhl
Naqb Ishtar
Birkat Qârun
'Ain Sukhna
El Tîh
Elat
Al Mudawwara
At Tubayq
El Faiyûm
SINAI
Aqaba
Haql
Beni Suef
El'Igma
Gulf of Suez
Gulf of 'Aqaba
El Fashn
Biba
EGYPT
Al Bi'r
Maghâgha
Beni Mazar
Bawiti
El Harra
Baharîya Oasis
Râs Ghârib
Sahra esh Sharqiya
Dahab
J. al Lawz 2578
El Minya
G. Katharîna 2637
El Tûr
Tabūk
Nile
Mallawi

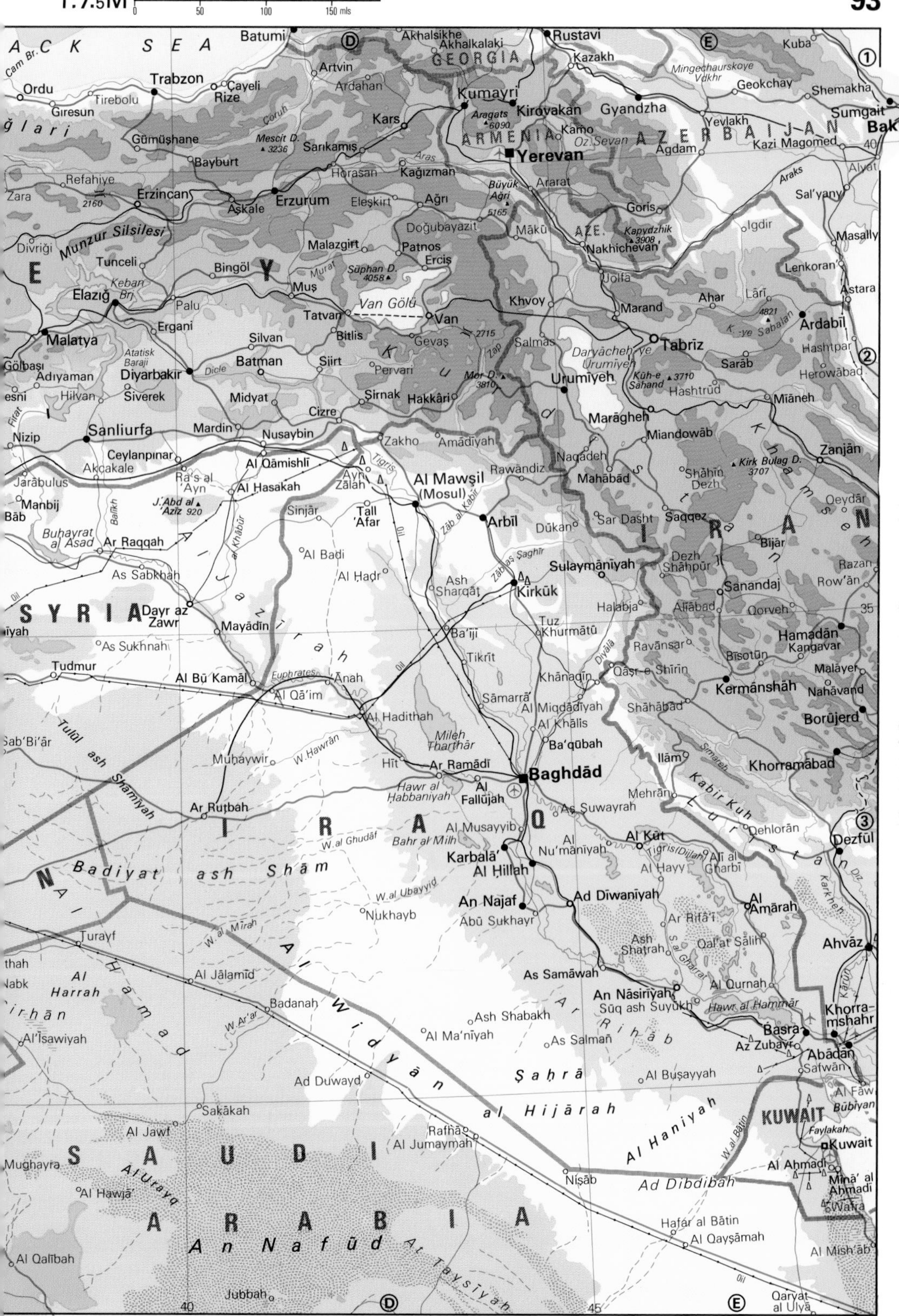
BLACK SEA
Batumi
Akhalsikhe
Akhalkalaki
GEORGIA
Rustavi
Kazakh
Kuba
Artvin
Ardahan
Trabzon
Çayeli
Rize
Ordu
Tirebolu
Giresun
Kumayri
Kirovakan
Gyandzha
Mingechaurskoye Vdkhr
Geokchay
Shemakha
Sumgait
Baku
Kars
Aragats 4090
ARMENIA
Kamo
Oz. Sevan
AZERBAIJAN
Yevlakh
Kazi Magomed
Agdam
Yerevan
Gümüşhane
Mescit D. 3236
Sarıkamış
Bayburt
Horasan
Kağızman
Aras
Refahiye
Zara
Erzincan
Aşkale
Erzurum
Eleşkirt
Ağrı
Büyük Ağrı 5165
Ararat
Goris
Araks
Sal'yany
Alyat
Munzur Silsilesi
Divriği
Doğubayazıt
Mākū
AZE.
Kapydzhik 3908
Nakhichevan
Igdir
Masally
Malazgirt
Patnos
Erciş
Süphan D. 4058
Tunceli
Bingöl
Murat
Muş
Jolfa
Lenkoran'
Keban Brj.
Elazığ
Palu
Van Gölü
Tatvan
Van
Khvoy
Marand
Ahar
Lārī
Astara
Malatya
Ergani
Bitlis
Gevaş
2715
Zap
Salmās
Daryācheh-ye Orūmīyeh
Tabrīz
4821
K.-ye Sabalan
Ardabīl
Hashtpar
Atatürk Barajı
Silvan
Batman
Siirt
Pervari
Sarāb
Herowābād
Gölbaşı
Adıyaman
Diyarbakır
Dicle
Mor D. 3810
Urumīyeh
Kūh-e Sahand 3710
Hashtrūd
Hilvan
Siverek
Midyat
Şırnak
Hakkâri
Mīāneh
Fırat
Cizre
Marāgheh
Miandowāb
Nizip
Sanliurfa
Mardin
Nusaybin
Zakho
Amādīyah
Zanjān
Ceylanpınar
Al Qāmishlī
Tigris
Naqadeh
Kirk Bulag D. 3707
Akçakale
Ra's al 'Ayn
Al Hasakah
'Ayn Zālah
Al Mawşil (Mosul)
Rawāndiz
Mahābād
Shāhīn Dezh
Qeydār
Jarābulus
J. 'Abd al 'Azīz 920
Sinjār
Tall 'Afar
Zāb al Kabīr
Arbīl
Sar Dasht
Saqqez
Manbij
Bāb
Buhayrat al Asad
Ar Raqqah
Balīkh
Al Badi
Dūkan
IRAN
Bījār
As Sabkhah
Al Jazīrah
Al Hadr
Ash Sharqāt
Zāb aş Şaghīr
Kirkūk
Sulaymānīyah
Dezh Shāhpūr
Razan
Row'ān
Sanandaj
SYRIA
Dayr az Zawr
Mayādīn
Halabja
Alīābād
Qorveh
35
Tuz Khurmātū
Hamadān
Kangavar
As Sukhnah
Ba'ījī
Ravānsar
Tikrīt
Bīsotūn
Diyālā
Malāyer
Tudmur
Al Bū Kamāl
Euphrates
'Ānah
Qaşr-e Shīrīn
Khānaqīn
Kermānshāh
Nahāvand
Al Qā'im
Sāmarrā'
Al Miqdādīyah
Shāhābād
Borūjerd
Al Hadithah
Al Khālis
Tulūl ash Shāmīyah
Sab'Bi'ār
Mileh Tharthār
Ba'qūbah
Muhaywir
W. Hawrān
Hīt
Ar Ramādī
Baghdād
Ilām
Simareh
Khorramābād
Hawr al Habbaniyah
Al Fallūjah
Mehrān
Kabir Kuh
Lorestan
Ar Rutbah
As Suwayrah
IRAQ
Al Musayyib
Dehlorān
Bahr al Milh
W. al Ghudāf
Al Kūt
Dezfūl
Badiyat ash Shām
Karbalā'
Al Hillah
Al Nu'mānīyah
Tigris (Dijlah)
Al Hayy
'Alī al Gharbī
W. al Ubayyid
An Najaf
Ad Dīwānīyah
Al 'Amārah
Nukhayb
Abū Sukhayr
Ar Rifā'ī
Karkheh
Ash Shatrah
Qal'at Sālih
Ahvāz
Turayf
W. al Mirah
Al Jalāmīd
As Samāwah
Al Harrah
An Nāsirīyah
Al Qurnah
Sūq ash Suyūkh
Hawr al Hammār
Khorramshahr
Karun
Badanah
Ash Shabakh
Al Hamad
W. Ar'ar
Al Widyān
Ar Rihāb
Basra
Al Ma'nīyah
As Salman
Az Zubayr
Abādān
Al 'Isawiyah
Safwān
Ad Duwayd
Şahrā
Al Busayyah
Al Fāw
Būbīyan
KUWAIT
Sakākah
al Hijārah
Al Haniyah
W. al Bātin
Faylakah
Kuwait
Al Jawf
Rafhā
Al Jumaymah
SAUDI ARABIA
Mughayra
Al Ahmadi
Nisāb
Ad Dibdibah
Mīnā' al Ahmadi
Al 'Urayq
Al Hawjā'
Wafra
Hafar al Bātin
Al Qaysūmah
An Nafūd
At Taysīyah
Al Mish'āb
Al Qalībah
Oil
Jubbah
Qaryat al Ulyā
40
45
D
E
1
2
3

0   25   50   75   100 km
0   25   50 mls

Paleokhorio   Larnaca   Larnaca Bay   34   C.Greco   B

Lefkara   C.Kiti

CYPRUS

Limassol   Akrotiri Bay   Zyyi

C.Gata

①   Tartus   Duraykish   Kafrūn Bashūr   Ah   Nāsirah   Tall Bīsah   ①

Arwad   Safītā   Qal'at al Hisn   Hims (Homs)
(KRAK-DES CHEVALIERS)

Hamīdīyah   Tall Kalakh   Al 'Oușayr

Kleia   Kebir   Qoubayat   Shinshār

El Mīna   El Hermel   Halba   Jūsīyah

Tripoli   Zgharta   Hisyah
(Tarābulus esh Shām)

Batroun   Amioune   Bcharre   Cornet es Saouda ▲3086   Laboue   Jabal Halimah ▲2464

Jubail   Kartaba   Deir el Ahmar   Dayr 'Atīyah
BYBLOS   Rhazīr

LEBANON   Ba'albek   An Nabk   ▲2659

Jounie   Bikfaya ▲2628   Yabrūd

Baie de St Georges

Beirut   Ba'abda   Zahle   Rayak   Al Ma'lūla   Jayrūd
(Beyrouth)

Aley   Az.   Qutayfah   Dūmayr

Damour   Zabdāni   1910   'Ayn al Fijah

Beit ed Dine   Machgharab   At Tall   Dūma 'Adhra

Saïda   Jezzine   Baradā   **Damascus**
(Sidon)   Rachaya   Qatana   (Dimāshq)

Hasbaya   J. ash Shaykh (Mt Hermon)   Al Kiswah

Litāni   Marjayoun   Al Hijānah   Dayr 'Alī

Tyr   Q. Shemona   Baniyas   Mas'adah   **SYRIA**
(Tyre, Sour)   Jouai'ya   CEASE FIRE LINES 1974   Ghabāghib   Burāq

Enn Nâqoūra   Al Qunaytirah   Mismīyah

Bennt   Yesud   As Sanamayn   Khabab

Nahariya   Jbail   Har Meron   Khushnīyah   Al Lajāh 863   Shaqqā

Ma'alot   1208   Nawā   Izra'   Shahbā
'Akko   Tarshīha   Zefat   Tiberias   ②
(Acre)   Rama   (Safad)   (Yam Kinneret)   Shaykh Miskīn   Jabal al 'Arab 1735

B. of Haifa   Q. Yam   Sea of Galilee)   Tasīl

Haifa   Shefar'am   Fiq   Dar'ā   Buşrā ash Shām
(Hefa)   Q.   Tiberias

Ata   528   Nazareth   Ma'agan   Irbid   Ramtha   Şalkhad

'Atlit   Mt   Afula   Deir Abu   Ḥusn   Tisīyah
Carmel   Sa'id

Zikhron Ya'aqov   MEGIDDO ARMAGEDDON   Beyt   Ajlūn   Mafraq   Sabhā
CAESAREA   Jenin   Shean   J. Umed Dara 1247   Es Samrā
Pardes Hanna   Qabatiya   Jarash
Hadera   Tubas   Er Rummān

Netanya   Tulkarm   Zarqa   Qa Kharina

ISRAEL   Sabastiya   Suweilih   **Zarqa**

Herzliyya   Kefar Sava   Nablus   Salt   Marka

Ramat Gan   Petah Tiqwa   Karama   **Amman**   Sahāb
Tel Aviv   Ba'al Hazor 1016   Wadi es Sir
Yafo (Jaffa)   Holon   Ramallah   Naur   Jiza

Rishon le Zion   Lod   Jericho   Qasr el Kharana   Jebel Mudeisisat 963
Rehovot   Ramla   (Arīha)   Dab'a
Latrun   **Jerusalem** (El Quds)   Mādabā   Khan ez Zabib
Ashdod   Beit Jala   (Yerushalayim)   Dhībān
Qiryat   Bethlehem   W. edh Ghadaf
Ashqelon   Gat   Bet Guvrin   (Bayt Lahm)   Heidan
LACHISH   Hebron   Mazra
Gaza   Sederot   Dura   (El Khalil)   En Gedi   Rabba   Qatrāna
Gaza Strip   derar   Yatta
Khan Yunis   Edh Dhahiriya   MEZADA   Qa'el Hafira
Rafah   Ofaqim   **Beersheba**   Karak
Zeelim   (Be'er Sheva)   El Lisān   T. el Meise   Manzil
Râs Burûn   Nevatim   Arad   1253   Mazar
Sabkhet el Bardawil   Be'er Sheva   Sedom   Safi   Qatrāna

③ El 'Arîsh   HALUZA   Dimona   MAMSHIT   1305   **JORDAN**   ③
Bîr Lahfân   Revivim   J. Ed Dabāb   Dhāhā   Qa'el Jinz
W. Arīsh   Yeroham   Oron   El Ghor   Tafila
Abu Aweigila   Qeziot   SHIVTA   Sede Boqer   Zin   1356   J. Qasred Deir   Hasā
NIZANA   AVEDAT   Hazeva   Rashādiya   Jurf ed Darāwish   Jebel Ithriyat
G.Maghâra 735   Mizpe   N e g e v   Dana   1641   J.el Atā'ita   1082
El Quseima   Ramon   Negarot   En Yahav   Shaubak
Bîr Gifgâfa   Har Ramon 1305   Nijil   Uneisa
EGYPT   Bîr Hasana   G.Libni 463   892 G.Halâl   Har Saggi 1006   Har Hakippa 467   1615   Jum Suwwāna   Ⓒ

A   34   36

M E D I T E R R A N E A N

S E A

Dead Sea (Bahrat Lut)

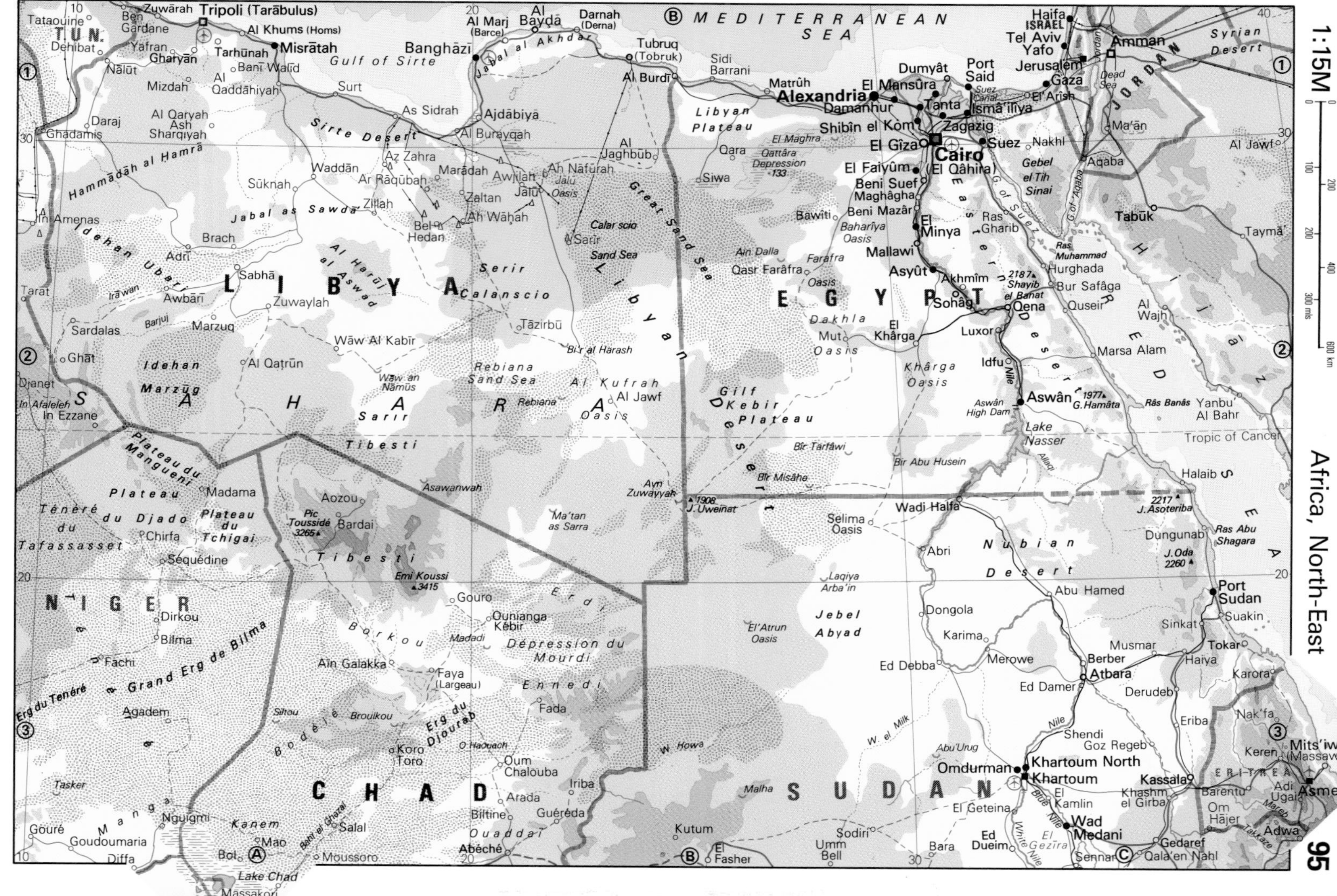
MEDITERRANEAN SEA
LIBYA
EGYPT
SUDAN
CHAD
NIGER
TUN.
ISRAEL
JORDAN
ERITREA
SAHARA
Syrian Desert
Libyan Desert
Eastern Desert
Nubian Desert
Sirte Desert
Great Sand Sea
Gulf of Sirte
Libyan Plateau
Gilf Kebir Plateau
Tibesti
Tropic of Cancer
Lake Nasser
Lake Chad
Tripoli (Tarābulus)
Misrātah
Banghāzī
Tubruq (Tobruk)
Al Burdī
Ajdābiyā
Sabhā
Ghadāmis
Ghāt
Alexandria
Cairo (El Qâhira)
El Gîza
Port Said
Suez
Ismâ'ilîya
Zagazig
Tanta
Damanhûr
El Mansûra
Dumyât
Matrûh
Siwa
El Faiyûm
Beni Suef
El Minya
Mallawi
Asyût
Sohâg
Qena
Luxor
Idfu
Aswân
Aswân High Dam
Hurghada
Bur Safâga
Quseir
Marsa Alam
El Khârga
Khârga Oasis
Dakhla Oasis
Qasr Farâfra
Tabūk
Aqaba
Amman
Jerusalem
Gaza
Tel Aviv Yafo
Haifa
Wadi Halfa
Selima Oasis
Abri
Dongola
Karima
Merowe
Abu Hamed
Berber
Atbara
Ed Damer
Ed Debba
Port Sudan
Suakin
Tokar
Kassala
Khartoum North
Khartoum
Omdurman
Wad Medani
Gedaref
Sennar
El Fasher
Kutum
Mits'iwa (Massawa)
Asmera
Keren
Aozou
Bardai
Pic Toussidé 3265
Emi Koussi 3415
Faya (Largeau)
Fada
Abéché
Biltine
Mao
Bol
Diffa
Bilma
Dirkou
Madama
Djanet
In Amenas
Al Kufrah Oasis
Al Jawf
J. Uweinat 1908

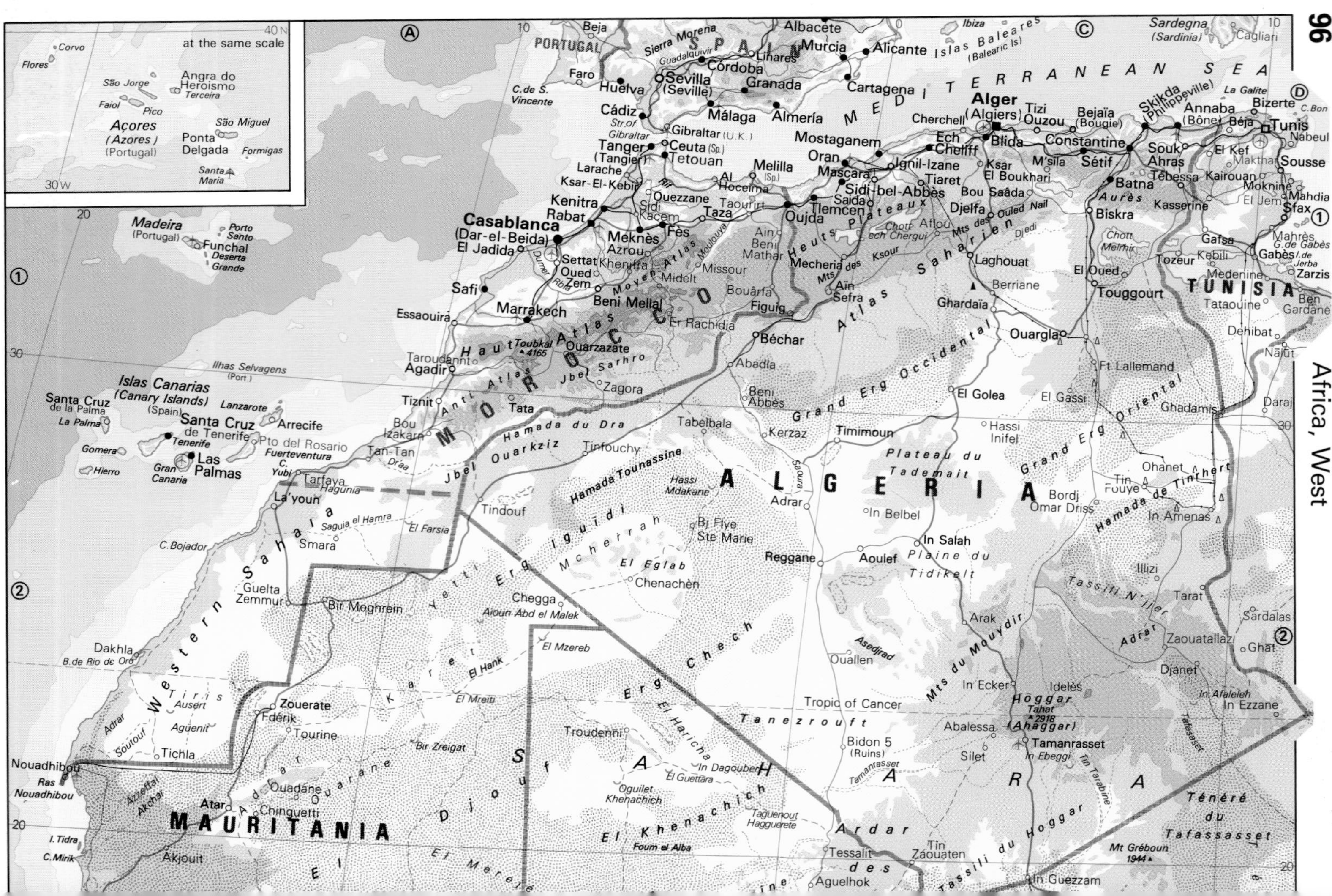
MEDITERRANEAN SEA
MOROCCO
ALGERIA
TUNISIA
MAURITANIA
SAHARA
Western Sahara
SPAIN
PORTUGAL
Madeira (Portugal)
Islas Canarias (Canary Islands) (Spain)
Açores (Azores) (Portugal)
at the same scale
Sardegna (Sardinia)
Islas Baleares (Balearic Is)
Alger (Algiers)
Tunis
Casablanca (Dar-el-Beida)
Rabat
Marrakech
Oran
Constantine
Tanger (Tangier)
Fès
Meknès
Agadir
Haut Atlas
Moyen Atlas
Anti Atlas
Grand Erg Occidental
Grand Erg Oriental
Hoggar (Ahaggar)
Tassili N'Ajjer
Tropic of Cancer
Tanezrouft
Erg Chech
El Djouf
Tindouf
Béchar
Ouargla
Ghardaïa
El Golea
In Salah
Tamanrasset
Adrar
Reggane
La'youn
Dakhla
Nouadhibou
Atar
Zouerate
Santa Cruz de Tenerife
Las Palmas
Funchal
Ponta Delgada

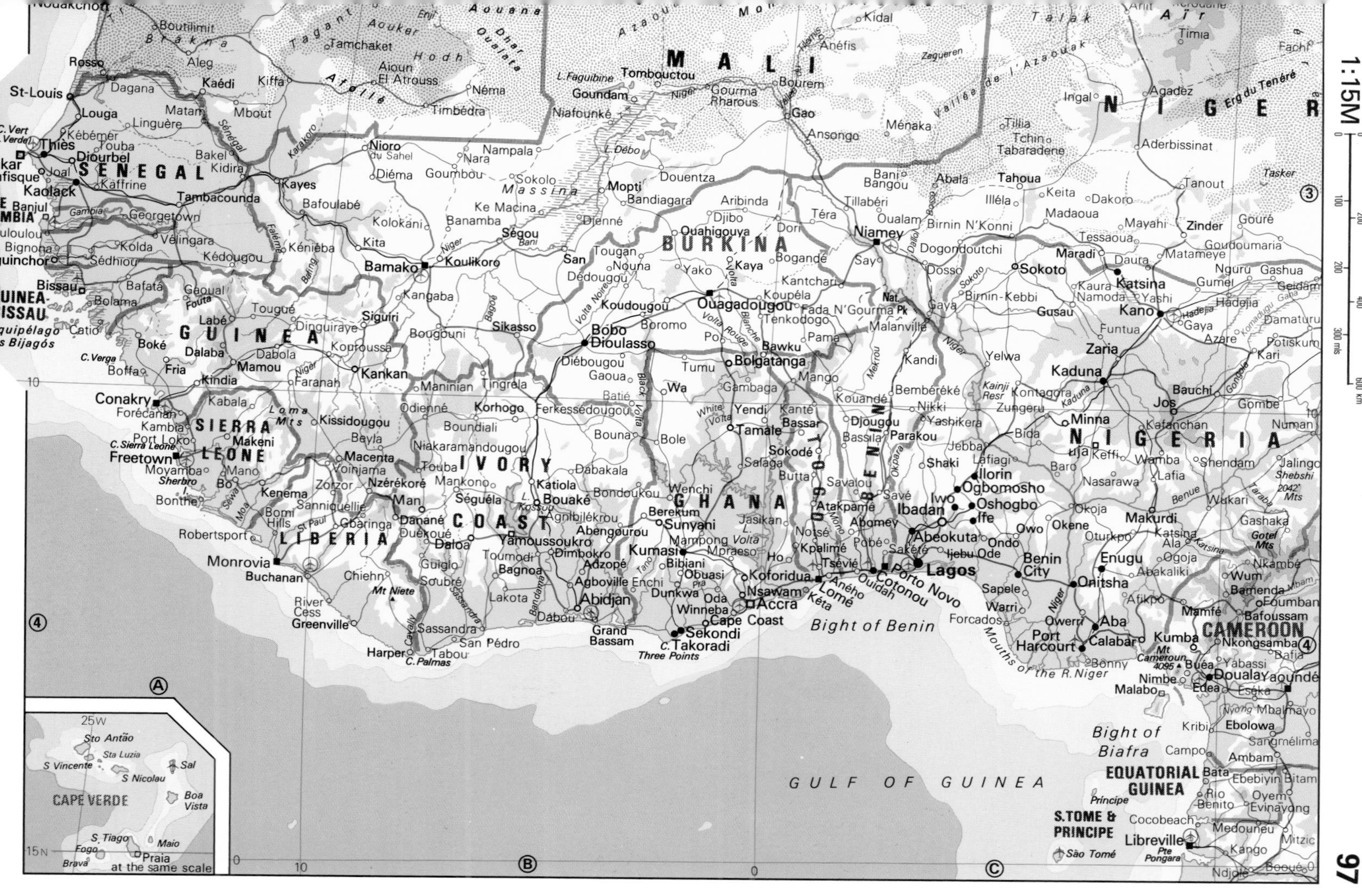

1:15M

200 400 600 km
100 200 300 mls

NIGER

Aïr

MALI

NIGERIA

CAMEROON

EQUATORIAL GUINEA

S.TOME & PRINCIPE

Libreville

GULF OF GUINEA

Bight of Biafra

Bight of Benin

Lagos

Ibadan

BENIN

TOGO

GHANA

Accra

IVORY COAST

Kumasi

Abidjan

BURKINA

Ouagadougou

Bobo Dioulasso

Bamako

SENEGAL

Dakar

THE GAMBIA

GUINEA BISSAU

GUINEA

Conakry

SIERRA LEONE

Freetown

LIBERIA

Monrovia

CAPE VERDE

Praia

25 W

15 N

at the same scale

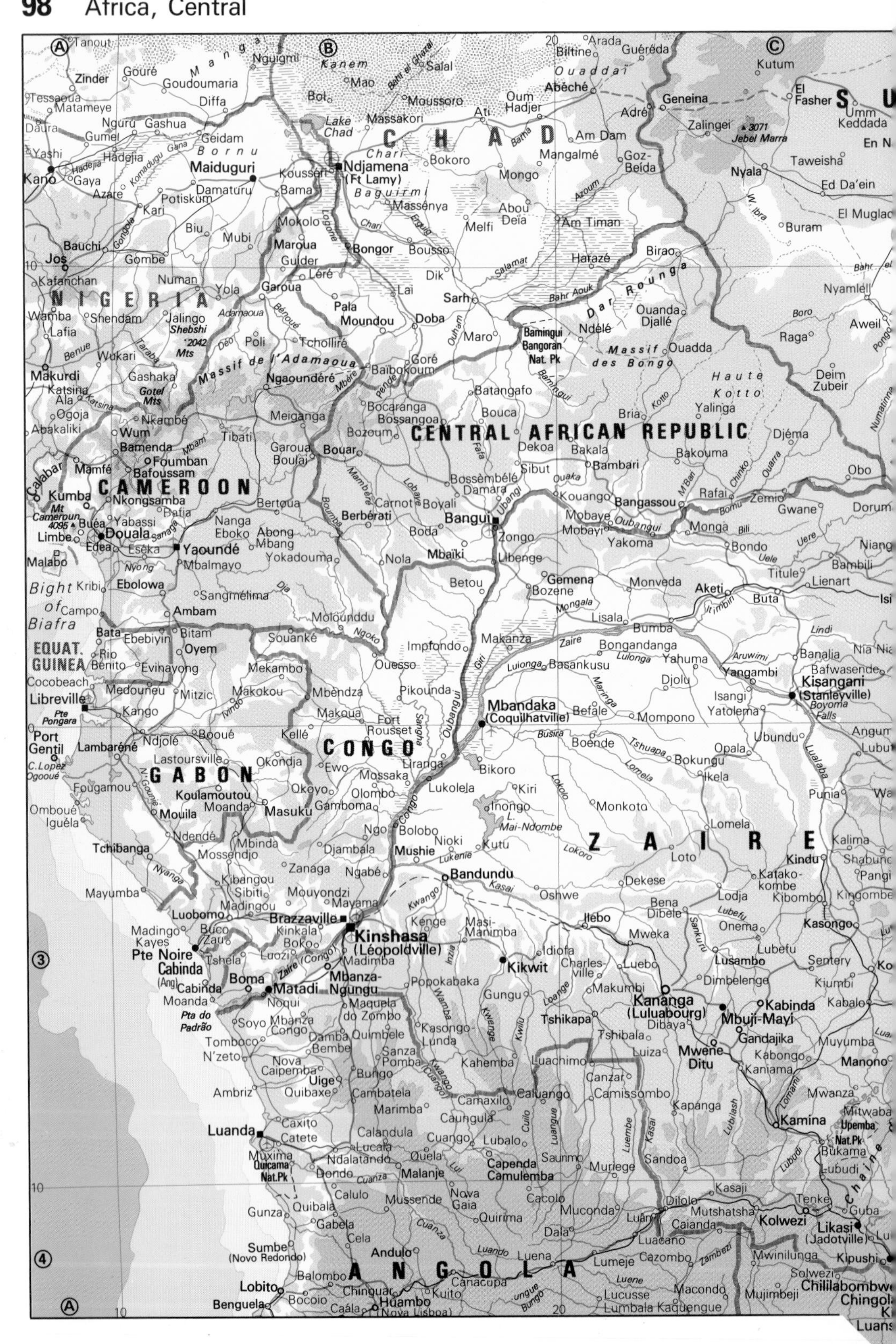

Tanout
Zinder
Gouré
Goudoumaria
Diffa
Nguigmi
Kanem
Mao
Salal
Bahr el Ghazal
Bol
Moussoro
Biltine
Arada
Guéréda
Ouaddaï
Abéché
Oum Hadjer
Kutum
El Fasher
Geneina
Adré
Ati
Lake Chad
Massakori
Tessaoua
Matameye
Daura
Nguru
Gashua
Gumel
Geidam
Bornu
Yashi
Hadejia
Kano
Gaya
Azare
Maiduguri
Damaturu
Potiskum
Kari
Bauchi
Jos
Kafanchan
Gombe
Biu
Mubi
Numan
Yola
Garoua
Maroua
Mokolo
Mora
Kousséri
Bama
Ndjamena
(Ft Lamy)
Chari
CHAD
Bokoro
Mongo
Baguirmi
Massénya
Batha
Am Dam
Mangalmé
Goz-Beïda
Zalingei
3071
Jebel Marra
Nyala
Taweisha
Ed Da'ein
El Muglad
Buram
Umm Keddada
En N
Abou Deïa
Am Timan
Melfi
Bongor
Bousso
Logone
Guider
Léré
Lai
Dik
Sarh
Haraze
Salamat
Birao
Bahr Aouk
Dar Rounga
Ouanda Djallé
Ndélé
Bamingui Bangoran Nat. Pk
Massif des Bongo
Ouadda
Haute Kotto
Yalinga
Nyamlell
Aweil
Raga
Deim Zubeir
Boro
NIGERIA
Wamba
Shendam
Jalingo
Shebshi Mts
2042
Lafia
Benue
Wukari
Taraba
Makurdi
Katsina Ala
Gashaka
Gotel Mts
Ogoja
Abakaliki
Poli
Tchollire
Pala
Moundou
Doba
Goré
Maro
Massif de l'Adamaoua
Adamaoua
Ngaoundéré
Baibokoum
Mbéré
Pendé
Batangafo
Bocaranga
Bossangoa
Meiganga
Bouca
Bria
Kotto
CENTRAL AFRICAN REPUBLIC
Djéma
Bakouma
Bambari
Dekoa
Bakala
Sibut
Nkambé
Wum
Bamenda
Tibati
Foumban
Bafoussam
Mamfé
Calabar
Kumba
CAMEROON
Nkongsamba
Mt Cameroun 4095
Buéa
Yabassi
Bafia
Douala
Limbe
Edea
Eséka
Sanaga
Yaoundé
Nanga Eboko
Abong Mbang
Bertoua
Garoua Boulaï
Bouar
Bozoum
Bossembélé
Damara
Ubangi
Bangui
Zongo
Carnot
Boyali
Berbérati
Boda
Mbaïki
Nola
Yokadouma
Mbalmayo
Nyong
Malabo
Bight of Biafra
Kribi
Ebolowa
Campo
Sangmélima
Ambam
Moloundou
Ngoko
Souanké
Bitam
Oyem
Bata
Ebebiyin
EQUAT. GUINEA
Rio Benito
Evinayong
Mekambo
Ouesso
Impfondo
Cocobeach
Libreville
Medouneu
Mitzic
Makokou
Ivindo
Mbéndza
Pikounda
Kango
Pte Pongara
Port Gentil
Lambaréné
Ndjolé
Booué
Kellé
Makoua
Fort Rousset
Sangha
Oubangui
CONGO
Lastoursville
Okondja
Ewo
Mossaka
Liranga
GABON
C. Lopez
Ogooué
Fougamou
Koulamoutou
Okoyo
Olombo
Omboué
Iguéla
Mouila
Moanda
Masuku
Gamboma
Ndendé
Mbinda
Mossendjo
Tchibanga
Nyanga
Mayumba
Kibangou
Sibiti
Madingou
Loubomo
Madingo-Kayes
Buco Zau
Pte Noire
Cabinda
(Ang) Cabinda
Tshela
Luozi
Zanaga
Djambala
Ngabé
Mouyondzi
Mayama
Brazzaville
Kinkala
Boko
Kinshasa
(Léopoldville)
Madimba
Zaire (Congo)
Boma
Matadi
Noqui
Moanda
Pta do Padrão
Soyo
Mbanza Congo
Mbanza-Ngungu
Maquela do Zombo
Damba
Quimbele
Bembe
Tomboco
N'zeto
Nova Caipemba
Uige
Ambriz
Quibaxe
Luanda
Caxito
Catete
Muxima
Quiçama Nat.Pk
Dondo
Ndalatando
Lucala
Calandula
Camabatela
Marimba
Bungo
Sanza Pomba
Kwango (Cuango)
Cuango
Caungula
Camaxilo
Caluango
Cuilo
Lubalo
Quela
Malanje
Capenda Camulemba
Cuanza
Calulo
Gunza
Quibala
Gabela
Mussende
Nova Gaia
Quirima
Cacolo
Sumbe
(Novo Redondo)
Cela
Andulo
Lobito
Benguela
Balombo
Bocoio
Chinguar
Huambo
(Nova Lisboa)
Caála
Kuito
Canacupa
ANGOLA
Luando
Luena
Bungo
Dala
Muconda
Saurimo
Muriege
Luau
Dilolo
Lumeje
Cazombo
Luacano
Luene
Lucusse
Lumbala Kaquengue
Macondo
Zambezi
Mwinilunga
Solwezi
Mujimbeji
Chililabombwe
Chingola
Kasaji
Mutshatsha
Kolwezi
Tenke
Likasi
(Jadotville)
Kipushi
Guba
Chaîne
Bukama
Lubudi
Upemba Nat.Pk
Kamina
Mitwaba
Mwanza
Kaniama
Lomami
Kabongo
Manono
Muyumba
Gandajika
Mbuji-Mayi
Kabinda
Kabalo
Mwene Ditu
Luiza
Kapanga
Lubilash
Camissombo
Canzar
Luachimo
Kahemba
Tshibala
Dibaya
Kananga
(Luluabourg)
Tshikapa
Makumbi
Luebo
Charlesville
Idiofa
Kikwit
Gungu
Kasongo-Lunda
Popokabaka
Wamba
Kwenge
Kwilu
Loange
Kasai
Inzia
Masi-Manimba
Kenge
Kwango
Bandundu
Mushie
Nioki
Kutu
Lukenie
Bolobo
Ngo
Lukolela
Bikoro
Inongo
L. Mai-Ndombe
Kiri
Lokolo
Monkoto
ZAIRE
Lokoro
Loto
Dekese
Oshwe
Ilebo
Mweka
Bena Dibele
Sankuru
Lodja
Lusambo
Dimbelenge
Lubefu
Onema
Kasongo
Sentery
Kiumbi
Kibombo
Katako-kombe
Kindu
Kalima
Lomela
Punia
Ikela
Bokungu
Opala
Ubundu
Lualaba
Tshuapa
Lomela
Boende
Busira
Mbandaka
(Coquilhatville)
Befale
Mompono
Basankusu
Lulonga
Maringa
Djolu
Isangi
Yatolema
Yangambi
Kisangani
(Stanleyville)
Boyoma Falls
Bafwasende
Banalia
Aruwimi
Yahuma
Bongandanga
Bumba
Lisala
Mongala
Makanza
Giri
Gemena
Bozene
Betou
Libenge
Mobaye
Mobayi
Oubangui
Yakoma
Monveda
Akéti
Itimbiri
Buta
Bondo
Uele
Titule
Bambili
Lienart
Monga
Bili
Uere
Bangassou
Kouango
Ouaka
M'Bari
Rafai
Chinko
Zemio
Mbomu
Gwane
Obo
Ouarra
Numatinna
Pongo
Dorum
Niangara
Nia Nia
Angumu
Lubutu
Walikale
Shabunda
Pangi
Kingombe
Kalole
Lulua
Bahr el

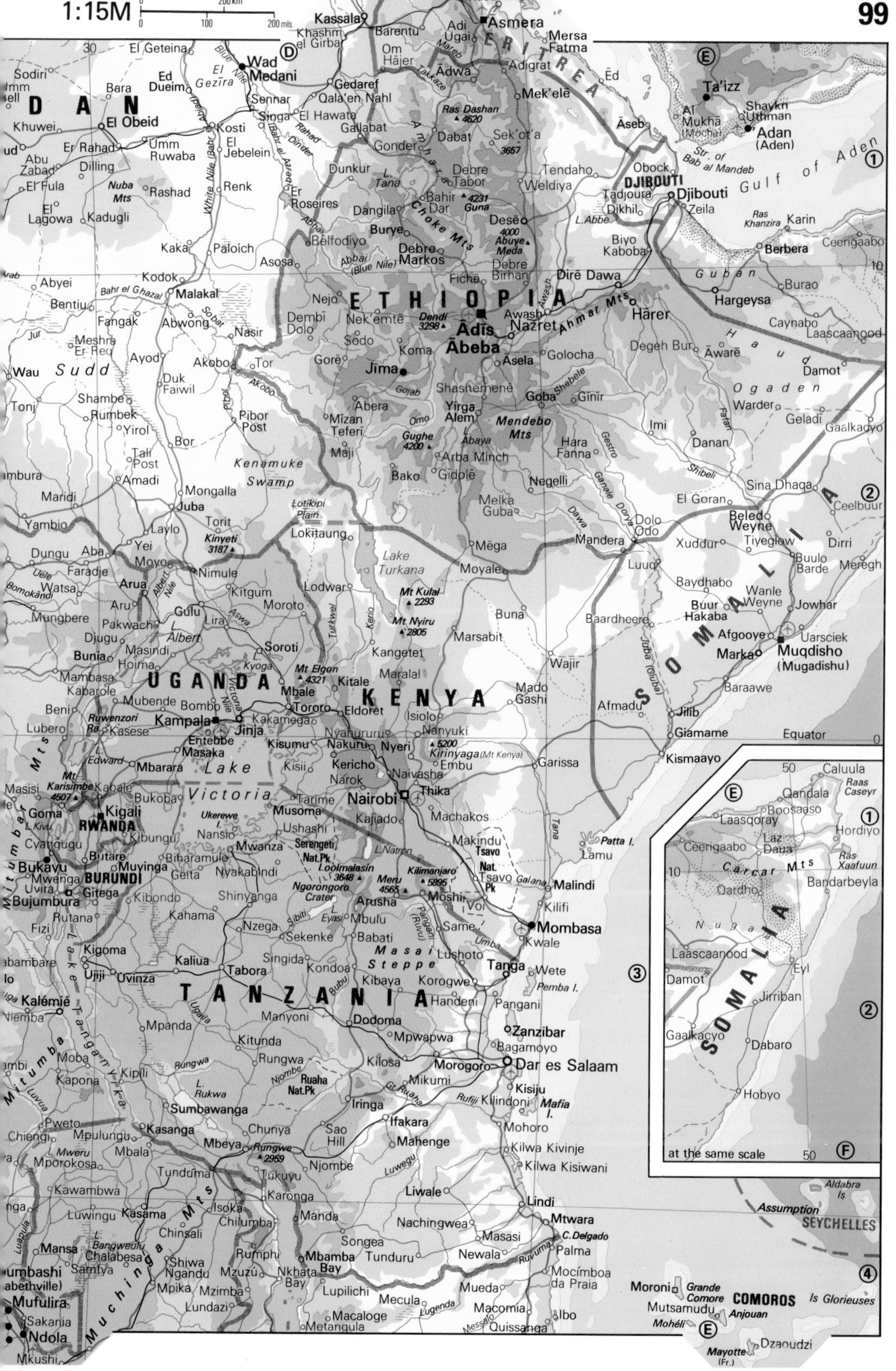
1:15M
200 km
100
200 mls
ETHIOPIA
KENYA
UGANDA
TANZANIA
SOMALIA
ERITREA
DJIBOUTI
RWANDA
BURUNDI
COMOROS
SEYCHELLES
Asmera
Ādīs Ābeba
Nairobi
Kampala
Dodoma
Dar es Salaam
Muqdisho (Mugadishu)
Djibouti
Mombasa
Gulf of Aden
Lake Victoria
Lake Turkana
Lake Tanganyika
at the same scale
Equator

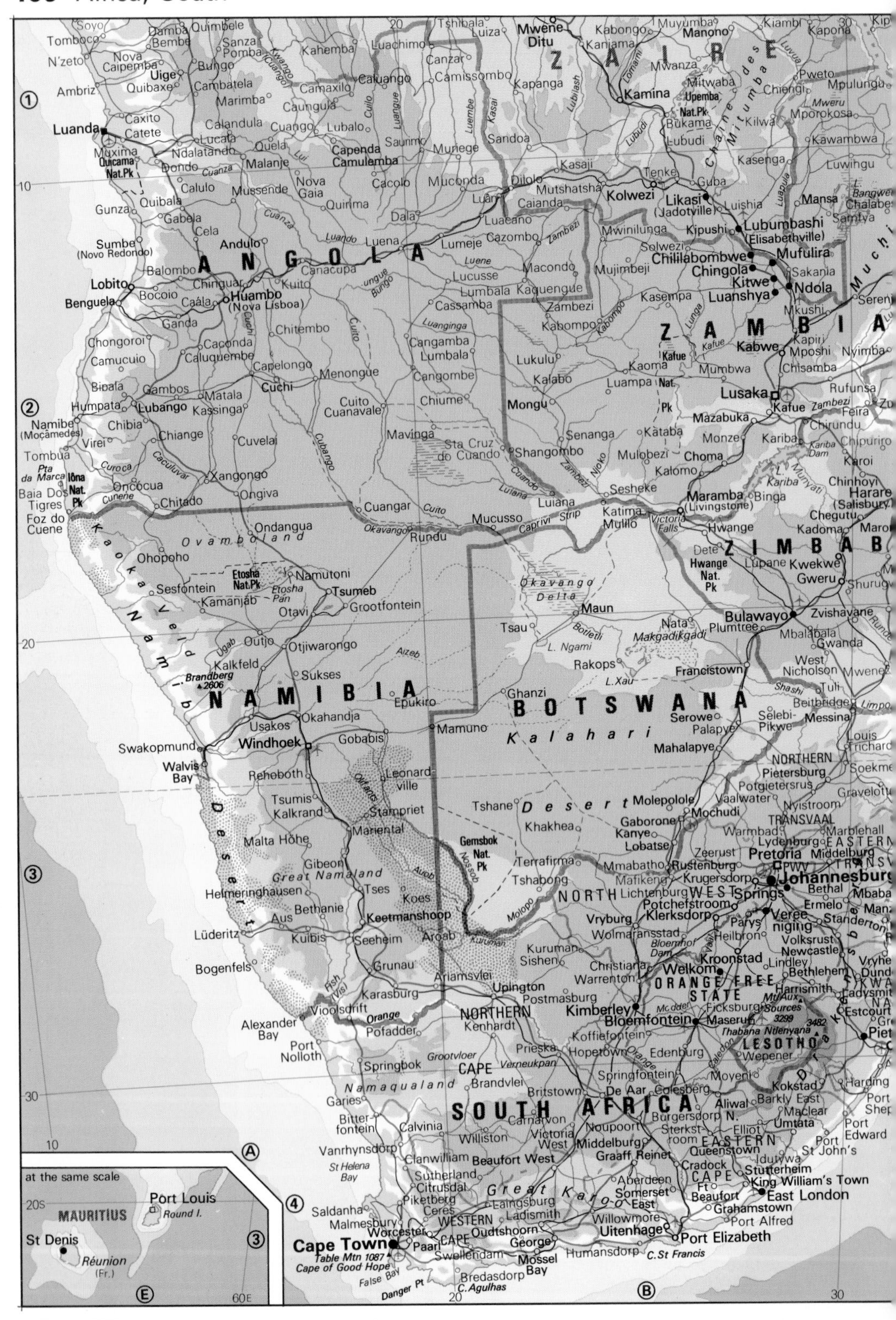
ANGOLA
ZAIRE
ZAMBIA
ZIMBABWE
NAMIBIA
BOTSWANA
SOUTH AFRICA
LESOTHO
Luanda
Ambriz
N'zeto
Tomboco
Soyo
Damba
Bembe
Quimbele
Nova Caipemba
Uige
Quibaxe
Bungo
Sanza Pomba
Cambatela
Kahemba
Luachimo
Tshibala
Luiza
Mwene Ditu
Kabongo
Kanjama
Muyumba
Manono
Kiambi
Kapona
Canzar
Camissombo
Camaxilo
Caluango
Kapanga
Kamina
Mitwaba
Upemba Nat.Pk
Bukama
Lubudi
Chiengi
Pweto
Mpulungu
Mweru
Mporokosa
Kilwa
Kawambwa
Caxito
Catete
Marimba
Caungula
Calandula
Cuango
Lubalo
Lucala
Ndalatando
Quela
Capenda Camulemba
Saurimo
Muriege
Sandoa
Muxima
Quicama Nat.Pk
Dondo
Malanje
Cuanza
Calulo
Mussende
Nova Gaia
Cacolo
Muconda
Dilolo
Kasaji
Mutshatsha
Tenke
Guba
Likasi (Jadotville)
Kolwezi
Kasenga
Luwingu
Mansa
Luishia
Lubumbashi (Elisabethville)
Chalabesa
Samfya
Bangweulu
Quibala
Gunza
Gabela
Quirima
Dala
Luau
Caianda
Luacano
Mwinilunga
Kipushi
Mufulira
Chililabombwe
Chingola
Kitwe
Ndola
Luanshya
Sakania
Cela
Sumbe (Novo Redondo)
Andulo
Luena
Lumeje
Cazombo
Zambezi
Solwezi
Mujimbeji
Macondo
Lucusse
Kaquengue
Lumbala
Kasempa
Balombo
Chinguar
Kuito
Canacupa
Lobito
Benguela
Bocoio
Caála
Huambo (Nova Lisboa)
Ganda
Cassamba
Chitembo
Kabompo
Mkushi
Kabwe
Kapiri Mposhi
Chisamba
Serenje
Nyimba
Chongoroi
Camucuio
Caconda
Caluquembe
Cangamba
Lumbala
Lukulu
Kaoma
Kafue
Mumbwa
Capelongo
Menongue
Cangombe
Kalabo
Luampa
Nat. Pk
Lusaka
Rufunsa
Bibala
Gambos
Matala
Cuchi
Humpata
Lubango
Kassinga
Cuito Cuanavale
Chiume
Mongu
Kafue
Feira
Namibe (Moçâmedes)
Chibia
Virei
Chiange
Cuvelai
Mavinga
Sta Cruz do Cuando
Shangombo
Senanga
Kataba
Mazabuka
Monze
Kariba
Chirundu
Chipuriro
Tombua
Pta da Marca
Iôna Nat. Pk
Baia Dos Tigres
Foz do Cuene
Oncocua
Xangongo
Chitado
Ongiva
Cuangar
Mucusso
Caprivi Strip
Mulobezi
Choma
Kalomo
Sesheke
Maramba (Livingstone)
Binga
Karoi
Chinhoyi
Harare (Salisbury)
Chegutu
Kadoma
Marondera
Katima Mulilo
Victoria Falls
Hwange
Dete
Hwange Nat. Pk
Lupane
Kwekwe
Gweru
Shurugwi
Ondangua
Ovamboland
Rundu
Okavango
Luiana
Ohopoho
Etosha Nat.Pk
Etosha Pan
Namutoni
Tsumeb
Grootfontein
Otavi
Sesfontein
Kamanjab
Kaokaveld
Okavango Delta
Maun
Tsau
Nata
Makgadikgadi
Plumtree
Bulawayo
Zvishavane
Mbalabala
Gwanda
Outjo
Otjiwarongo
Kalkfeld
Brandberg 2606
Sukses
Namib
L. Ngami
Rakops
L. Xau
Francistown
West Nicholson
Tuli
Mwenezi
Beitbridge
Limpopo
Messina
Shashi
Ghanzi
Epukiro
Okahandja
Usakos
Swakopmund
Walvis Bay
Windhoek
Gobabis
Mamuno
Kalahari
Serowe
Palapye
Selebi-Pikwe
Mahalapye
Louis Trichardt
Soekmekaar
NORTHERN
Pietersburg
Potgietersrus
Gravelotte
Rehoboth
Leonardville
Olifants
Tsumis
Kalkrand
Stampriet
Tshane
Desert
Molepolole
Mochudi
Vaalwater
Nylstroom
Gaborone
Kanye
Lobatse
Khakhea
TRANSVAAL
Warmbad
Lydenburg
Marblehall
EASTERN TRANSVAAL
Middelburg
Malta Höhe
Mariental
Gemsbok Nat. Pk
Nossob
Terrafirma
Mmabatho
Mafikeng
Zeerust
Rustenburg
Pretoria
Krugersdorp
Johannesburg
PWV
Gibeon
Great Namaland
Tshabong
NORTH WEST
Lichtenburg
Springs
Bethal
Mbabane
Helmeringhausen
Tses
Auob
Koes
Molopo
Potchefstroom
Klerksdorp
Ermelo
Vereeniging
Parys
Standerton
Bethanie
Aus
Keetmanshoop
Vryburg
Wolmaransstad
Heilbron
Volksrust
Newcastle
Lüderitz
Kuibis
Seeheim
Aroab
Kuruman
Bloemhof Dam
Kroonstad
Lindley
Vryheid
Sishen
Christiana
Welkom
Bethlehem
Dundee
Bogenfels
Grunau
Ariamsvlei
Warrenton
ORANGE FREE STATE
Harrismith
Ladysmith
Fish (Vis)
Karasburg
Upington
Postmasburg
Modder
Ficksburg
Mt Aux Sources 3299
Estcourt
Vioolsdrift
Orange
NORTHERN
Kimberley
Bloemfontein
Maseru
3482
Thabana Ntlenyana
Pietermaritzburg
Alexander Bay
Pofadder
Kenhardt
Koffiefontein
Drakensberg
Port Nolloth
Grootvloer
Prieska
Hopetown
Edenburg
Wepener
Verneukpan
Springbok
CAPE
Springfontein
Moyeni
Caledon
Namaqualand
Brandvlei
Britstown
De Aar
Colesberg
Kokstad
Harding
Garies
Aliwal N.
Barkly East
Port Shepstone
Bitterfontein
Calvinia
Carnarvon
Burgersdorp
Maclear
Umtata
Port Edward
Williston
Victoria West
Noupoort
Sterkstroom
Vanrhynsdorp
Middelburg
EASTERN CAPE
Queenstown
Idutywa
Port St John's
Clanwilliam
Beaufort West
Graaff Reinet
Cradock
Stutterheim
St Helena Bay
Sutherland
Citrusdal
Great Karoo
Aberdeen
Fort Beaufort
King William's Town
East London
Saldanha
Piketberg
Laingsburg
Somerset East
Grahamstown
Malmesbury
Ceres
WESTERN CAPE
Ladismith
Willowmore
Port Alfred
Worcester
Paarl
Oudtshoorn
Uitenhage
Port Elizabeth
Cape Town
Table Mtn 1087
Cape of Good Hope
False Bay
Danger Pt
Swellendam
George
Mossel Bay
Bredasdorp
C. Agulhas
Humansdorp
C. St Francis
at the same scale
MAURITIUS
Port Louis
Round I.
St Denis
Réunion (Fr.)
20S
60E
10
20
30
1
2
3
4
A
B
E

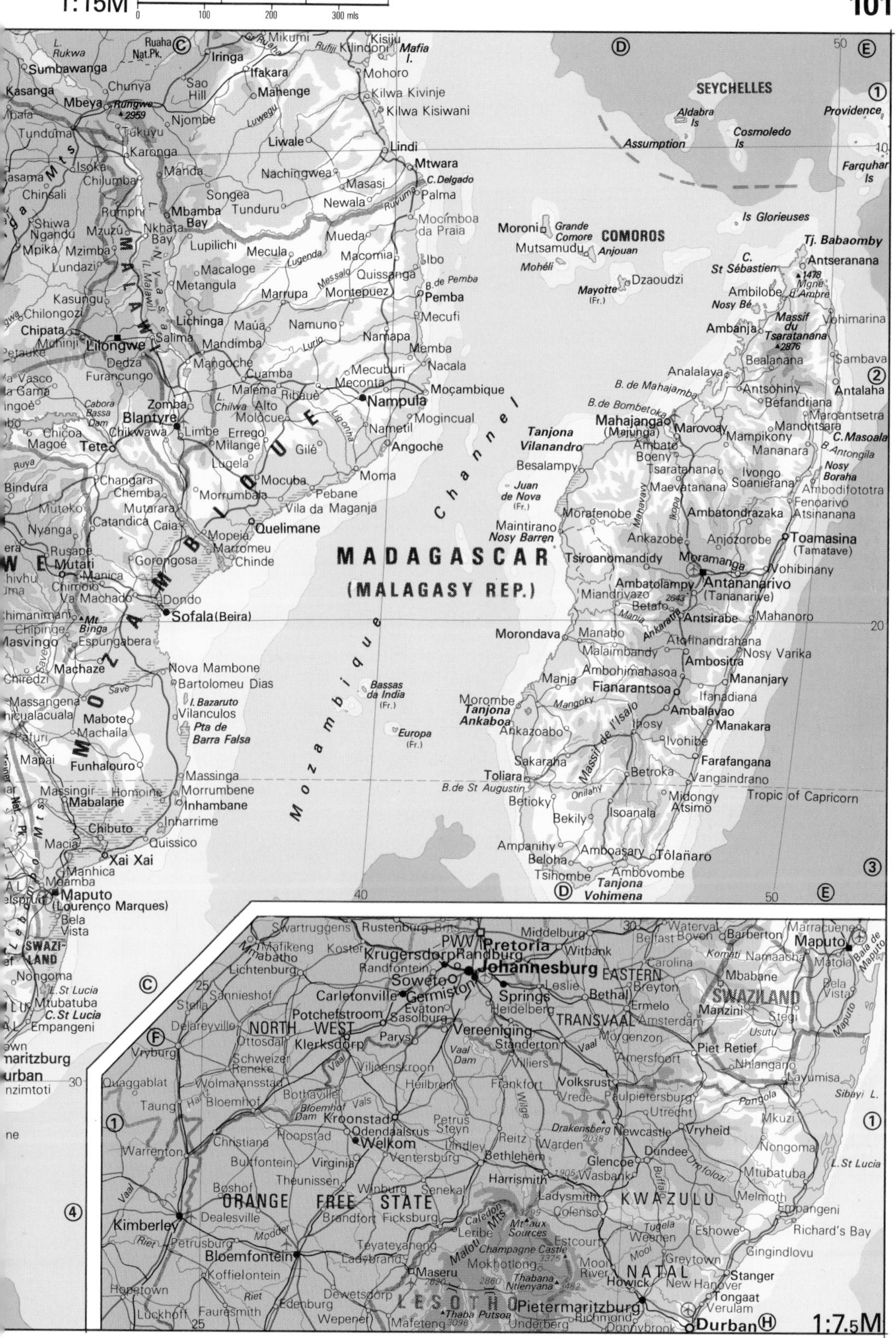
1:15M
0 200 400 600 km
0 100 200 300 mls
SEYCHELLES
Aldabra Is
Cosmoledo Is
Assumption
Providence
Farquhar Is
Is Glorieuses
COMOROS
Moroni
Grande Comore
Mutsamudu
Anjouan
Mohéli
Mayotte (Fr.)
Dzaoudzi
Tj. Babaomby
Antseranana
C. St Sébastien
Ambilobe
Nosy Bé
Ambanja
Massif du Tsaratanana
2876
Vohimarina
Sambava
Bealanana
Analalava
Antalaha
Antsohihy
Befandriana
Maroantsetra
Mandritsara
C. Masoala
B. Antongila
Nosy Boraha
B. de Mahajamba
B. de Bombetoka
Mahajanga (Majunga)
Marovoay
Mampikony
Mananara
Ambato Boeny
Tsaratanana
Ivongo Soanierana
Maevatanana
Ambodifototra
Fenoarivo Atsinanana
Ambatondrazaka
Tanjona Vilanandro
Besalampy
Juan de Nova (Fr.)
Morafenobe
Maintirano
Nosy Barren
Ankazobe
Anjozorobe
Toamasina (Tamatave)
Tsiroanomandidy
Moramanga
Vohibinany
Antananarivo (Tananarive)
Ambatolampy
Miandrivazo
Betafo
Antsirabe
Mahanoro
Morondava
Manabo
Ambositra
Nosy Varika
Malaimbandy
Fianarantsoa
Mananjary
Ifanadiana
Ambalavao
Manakara
Ihosy
Morombe
Tanjona Ankaboa
Ankazoabo
Massif de l'Isalo
Ivohibe
Farafangana
Vangaindrano
Sakaraha
Toliara
Betroka
B. de St Augustin
Betioky
Midongy Atsimo
Tropic of Capricorn
Bekily
Isoanala
Ampanihy
Beloha
Amboasary
Tôlañaro
Tsihombe
Ambovombe
Tanjona Vohimena
MADAGASCAR
(MALAGASY REP.)
Mozambique Channel
Bassas da India (Fr.)
Europa (Fr.)
MOZAMBIQUE
MALAWI
L. Nyasa (L. Malawi)
Mafia I.
Kisiju
Kilindoni
Mohoro
Kilwa Kivinje
Kilwa Kisiwani
Lindi
Mtwara
C. Delgado
Palma
Mocímboa da Praia
Ibo
B. de Pemba
Pemba
Mecufi
Memba
Nacala
Moçambique
Nampula
Mogincual
Angoche
Moma
Pebane
Vila da Maganja
Quelimane
Chinde
Sofala (Beira)
Dondo
Nova Mambone
Bartolomeu Dias
I. Bazaruto
Vilanculos
Pta de Barra Falsa
Massinga
Morrumbene
Inhambane
Inharrime
Quissico
Xai Xai
Chibuto
Manhica
Maputo (Lourenço Marques)
Bela Vista
SWAZILAND
Mbeya
Iringa
Sumbawanga
Ifakara
Mahenge
Njombe
Liwale
Nachingwea
Masasi
Newala
Songea
Tunduru
Mbamba Bay
Lupilichi
Mecula
Mueda
Macomia
Quissanga
Montepuez
Marrupa
Lichinga
Metangula
Maúa
Namuno
Namapa
Lilongwe
Salima
Mandimba
Dedza
Mangoche
Cuamba
Malema
Ribáuè
Mecuburi
Meconta
Zomba
Blantyre
Limbe
Chikwawa
Tete
Milange
Gilé
Lugela
Mocuba
Morrumbala
Mopeia
Marromeu
Caia
Gorongosa
Mutare
Manica
Chimoio
Vila Machado
Espungabera
Machaze
Mabote
Machaila
Funhalouro
Mabalane
Homoine
Karonga
Mzuzu
Nkhata Bay
Mzimba
Kasungu
Chipata
Mzimba
Nyanga
Rusape
Masvingo
Bindura
Chiredzi
Mapai
Macia
Namaacha
Empangeni
C. St Lucia
Mtubatuba
Nongoma
Pietermaritzburg
Durban
Amanzimtoti
1:7.5M
Pretoria
Johannesburg
Soweto
Krugersdorp
Randburg
Germiston
Springs
Middelburg
Witbank
Rustenburg
Mafikeng
Lichtenburg
Carletonville
Potchefstroom
Klerksdorp
Vereeniging
Sasolburg
Heidelberg
Standerton
Bethal
Ermelo
EASTERN TRANSVAAL
NORTH WEST
Barberton
Maputo
Mbabane
SWAZILAND
Manzini
Piet Retief
Vryburg
Schweizer Reneke
Wolmaransstad
Bothaville
Kroonstad
Welkom
Odendaalsrus
Virginia
Bethlehem
Harrismith
Frankfort
Vrede
Volksrust
Newcastle
Vryheid
Dundee
Glencoe
Ladysmith
ORANGE FREE STATE
KWAZULU
NATAL
Kimberley
Bloemfontein
Brandfort
Ficksburg
Maseru
LESOTHO
Mt aux Sources
Champagne Castle
Thabana Ntlenyana 3482
Thaba Putsoa
Drakensberg
Estcourt
Howick
Pietermaritzburg
Greytown
Stanger
Tongaat
Verulam
Durban
Richard's Bay
Eshowe
Melmoth
Gingindlovu
Mtubatuba
L. St Lucia
Sibayi L.
Mkuzi
Nhlangano
Lavumisa
Pongola
Utrecht
Paulpietersburg
Amersfoort
Morgenzon
Amsterdam
Warrenton
Christiana
Hoopstad
Bultfontein
Theunissen
Winburg
Senekal
Dealesville
Petrusburg
Koffiefontein
Hopetown
Luckhoff
Fauresmith
Edenburg
Dewetsdorp
Wepener
Mafeteng
Ladybrand
Teyateyaneng
Leribe
Mokhotlong
Underberg
Richmond
Donnybrook
New Hanover
Colenso
Weenen
Mooi River

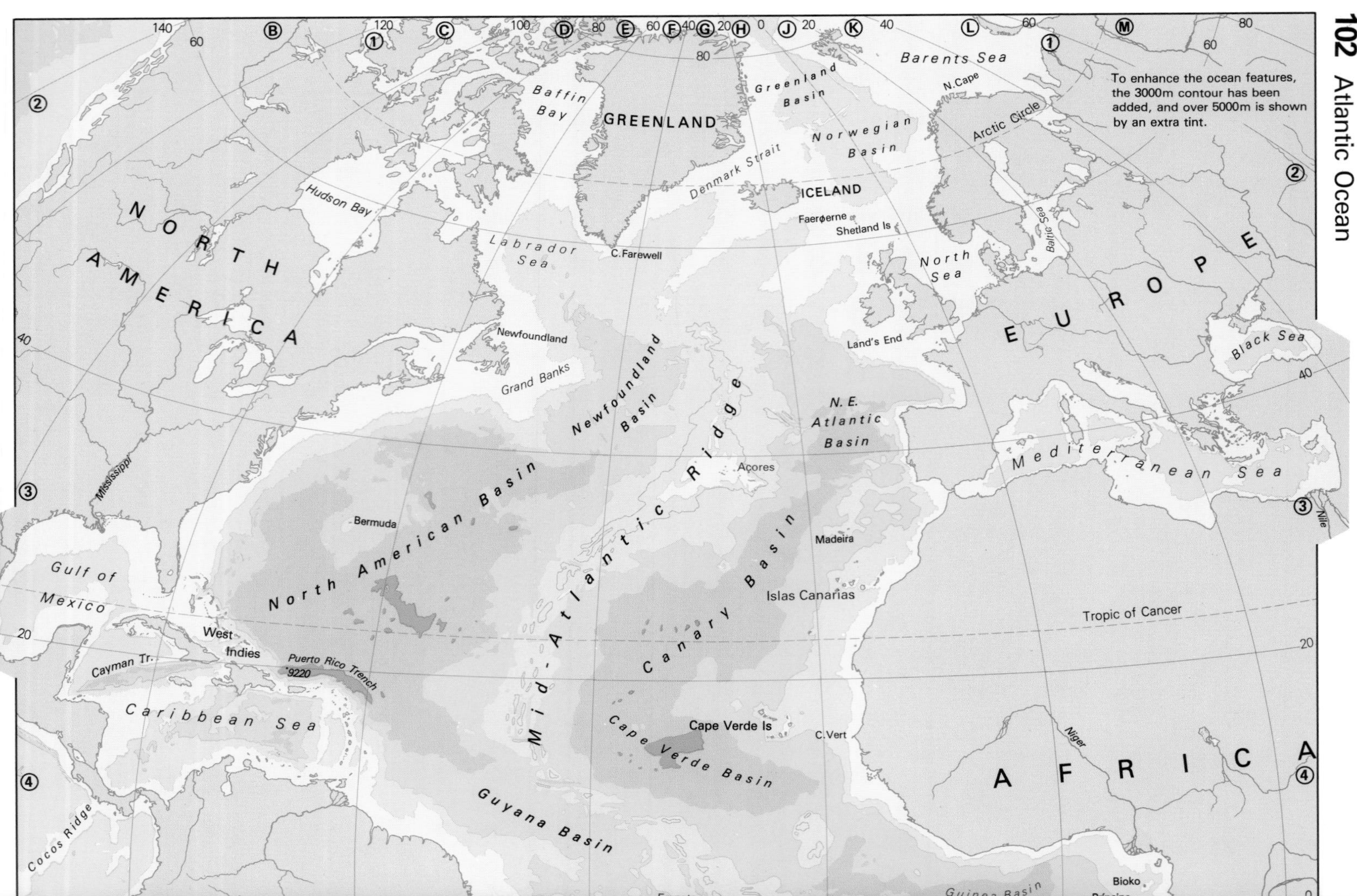

To enhance the ocean features, the 3000m contour has been added, and over 5000m is shown by an extra tint.

EUROPE

Black Sea

Mediterranean Sea

Nile

Tropic of Cancer

Niger

AFRICA

Bioko

Príncipe

Guinea Basin

Barents Sea

N.Cape

Arctic Circle

Baltic Sea

North Sea

Land's End

Faeroerne

Shetland Is

ICELAND

Norwegian Basin

Greenland Basin

N.E. Atlantic Basin

Madeira

Islas Canarias

Açores

C.Vert

Cape Verde Is

Cape Verde Basin

Denmark Strait

C.Farewell

GREENLAND

Baffin Bay

Labrador Sea

C.Farewell

Newfoundland

Grand Banks

Newfoundland Basin

Mid-Atlantic Ridge

Canary Basin

Guyana Basin

Hudson Bay

NORTH AMERICA

Bermuda

North American Basin

Puerto Rico Trench 9220

West Indies

Caribbean Sea

Cayman Tr.

Gulf of Mexico

Mississippi

Cocos Ridge

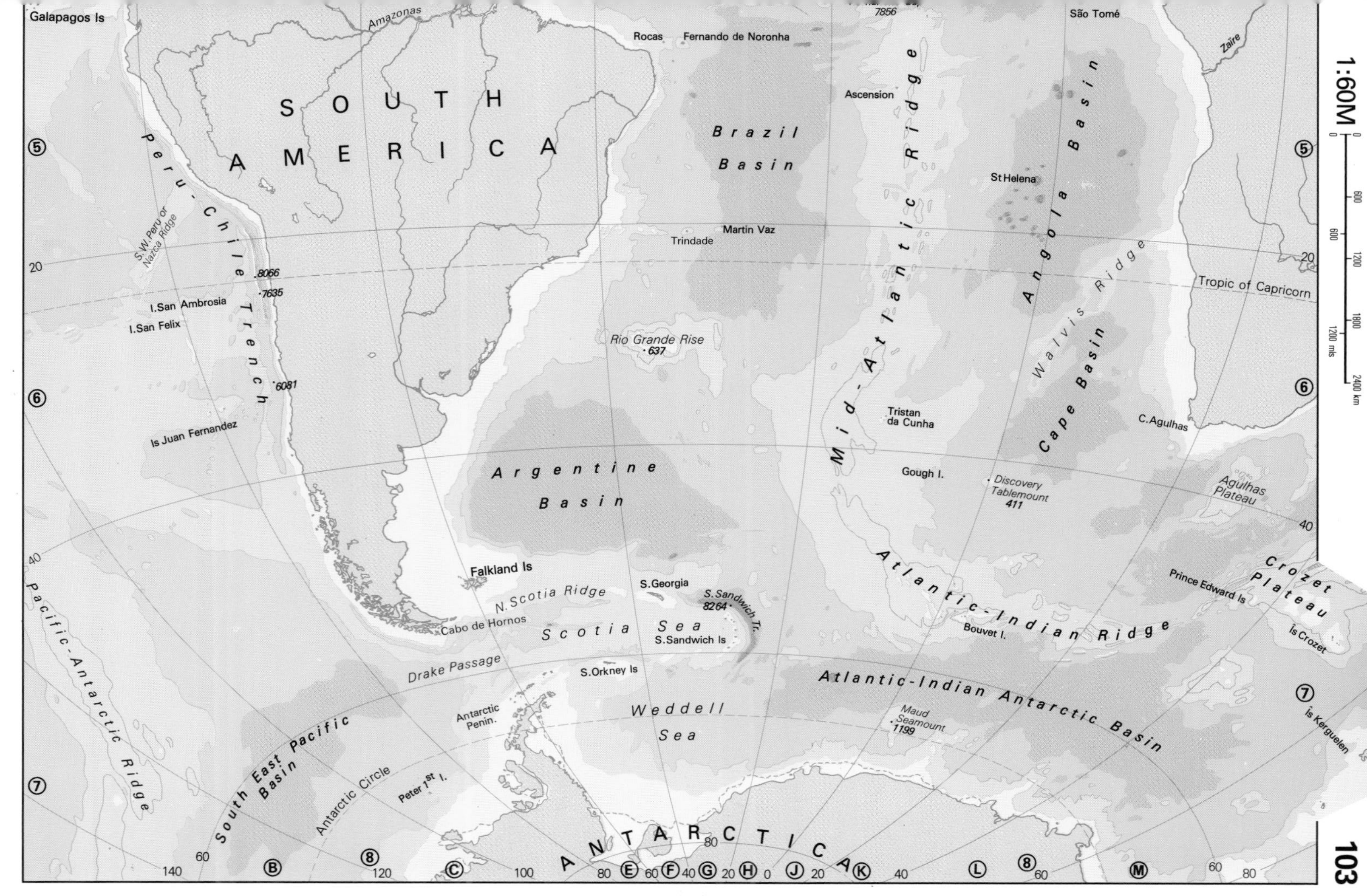

1:60M

0   600   1200   1800   2400 km
0   600   1200 mls

São Tomé

Zaïre

Tropic of Capricorn

Crozet Plateau

Is Crozet

Is Kerguelen

Agulhas Plateau

Prince Edward Is

C. Agulhas

Atlantic-Indian Ridge

Atlantic-Indian Antarctic Basin

Angola Basin

Walvis Ridge

Cape Basin

St Helena

Discovery Tablemount 411

Bouvet I.

Maud Seamount 1199

Mid-Atlantic Ridge

Ascension

Tristan da Cunha

Gough I.

Brazil Basin

Fernando de Noronha

Martin Vaz

Trindade

Rocas

7856

Rio Grande Rise 637

S. Georgia

S. Sandwich Tr. 8264

S. Sandwich Is

Scotia Sea

Weddell Sea

A N T A R C T I C A

Argentine Basin

N. Scotia Ridge

Falkland Is

S. Orkney Is

Antarctic Penin.

Peter I. Øy

Antarctic Circle

S O U T H   A M E R I C A

Cabo de Hornos

Drake Passage

South East Pacific Basin

Amazonas

8066
7635
6081

Peru-Chile Trench

I. San Ambrosia
I. San Felix

Is Juan Fernández

S.W. Peru or Nazca Ridge

Galápagos Is

Pacific-Antarctic Ridge

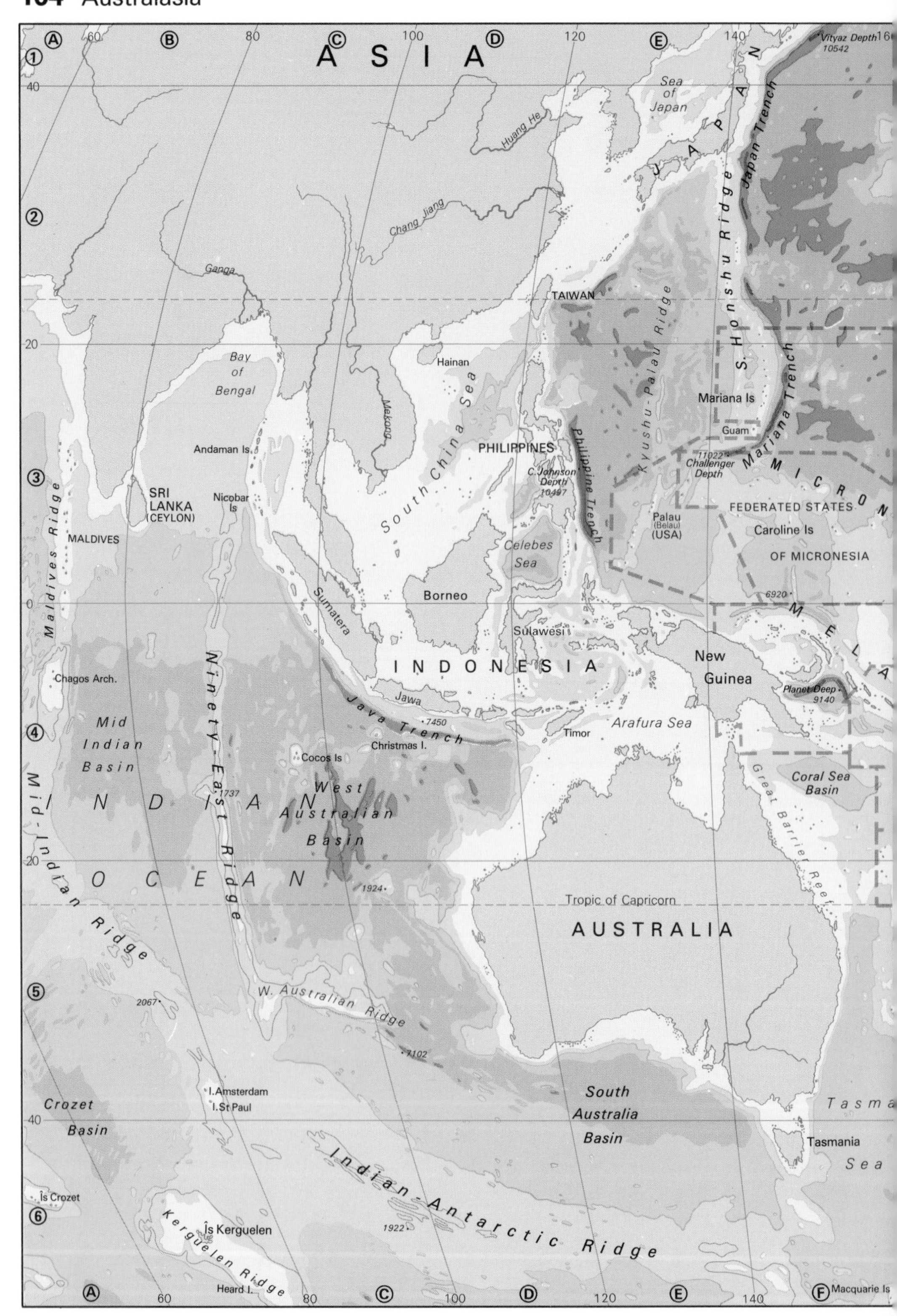
ASIA
Sea of Japan
JAPAN
Japan Trench
Vityaz Depth 10542
Huang He
Chang Jiang
Ganga
TAIWAN
S. Honshu Ridge
Kyushu-Palau Ridge
Bay of Bengal
Hainan
South China Sea
Mekong
Mariana Is
Guam
Mariana Trench
Andaman Is
PHILIPPINES
Philippine Trench
11022 Challenger Depth
C. Johnson Depth 10497
MICRONESIA
FEDERATED STATES OF MICRONESIA
Caroline Is
Palau (Belau) (USA)
SRI LANKA (CEYLON)
Nicobar Is
Maldives Ridge
MALDIVES
Celebes Sea
Borneo
6920
Sumatera
Sulawesi
MELANESIA
INDONESIA
New Guinea
Chagos Arch.
Jawa
Java Trench
7450
Planet Deep 9140
Mid Indian Basin
Christmas I.
Timor
Arafura Sea
Cocos Is
Ninety-East Ridge
1737
West Australian Basin
Coral Sea Basin
INDIAN OCEAN
Mid-Indian Ridge
Great Barrier Reef
1924
Tropic of Capricorn
AUSTRALIA
W. Australian Ridge
2067
7102
I. Amsterdam
I. St Paul
South Australia Basin
Tasman Sea
Crozet Basin
Tasmania
Indian-Antarctic Ridge
Îs Crozet
Îs Kerguelen
Kerguelen Ridge
1922
Heard I.
Macquarie Is

0 600 1200 1800 2400 km
0 600 1200 mls

G 180 H 160 J 140 K 120 L 100 ①

49

2926 ·

Mendocino Seascarp

N O R T H

A M E R I C A

②

Murray Seascarp

18 ·

104 · Midway Is

Tropic of Cancer

C. Falso

20

Hawaiian Islands

1477 ·

Mid-Pacific Mountains

Clarion Fracture Zone

Is Revilla Gigedo

③

Marshall Is

P A C I F I C

C

Line Is

Equator 0

NAURU

KIRIBATI

Phoenix Is

O C E A N

P

O

L

Y

TUVALU

Tokelau (N.Z.)

Îs Marquises

SOLOMON ISLANDS

6150 ·

American Samoa

N

④

French Polynesia

VANUATU

Wallis & (Fr.) Futuna

WRN. SAMOA

Cook Is. (N.Z.)

Samoa

Îs de la Société

Îs Tuamotu

E

S

FIJI

TONGA

Tahiti

East Pacific Ridge

Niue

Cook Is

Nouvelle Calédonie (Fr.)

Horizon Depth 10882

Îs Tubuai

Îs Gambier

20

I

Pitcairn (U.K.)

1344 · Sala y Gómez

Lord Howe Rise

Norfolk I. Ridge

S. Fiji Basin

Norfolk I.

10047

A

I. de Pascua

⑤

INTERNATIONAL DATE LINE

Tonga Trench

Kermadec Trench

N. Cape

South West Pacific Basin

40

NEW ZEALAND

Chatham Is

Pacific-Antarctic Ridge

New Zealand Plateau

732 ·

⑥

Auckland Is

Campbell I.

G 180 H 160 J 140 K 120 L 100 M

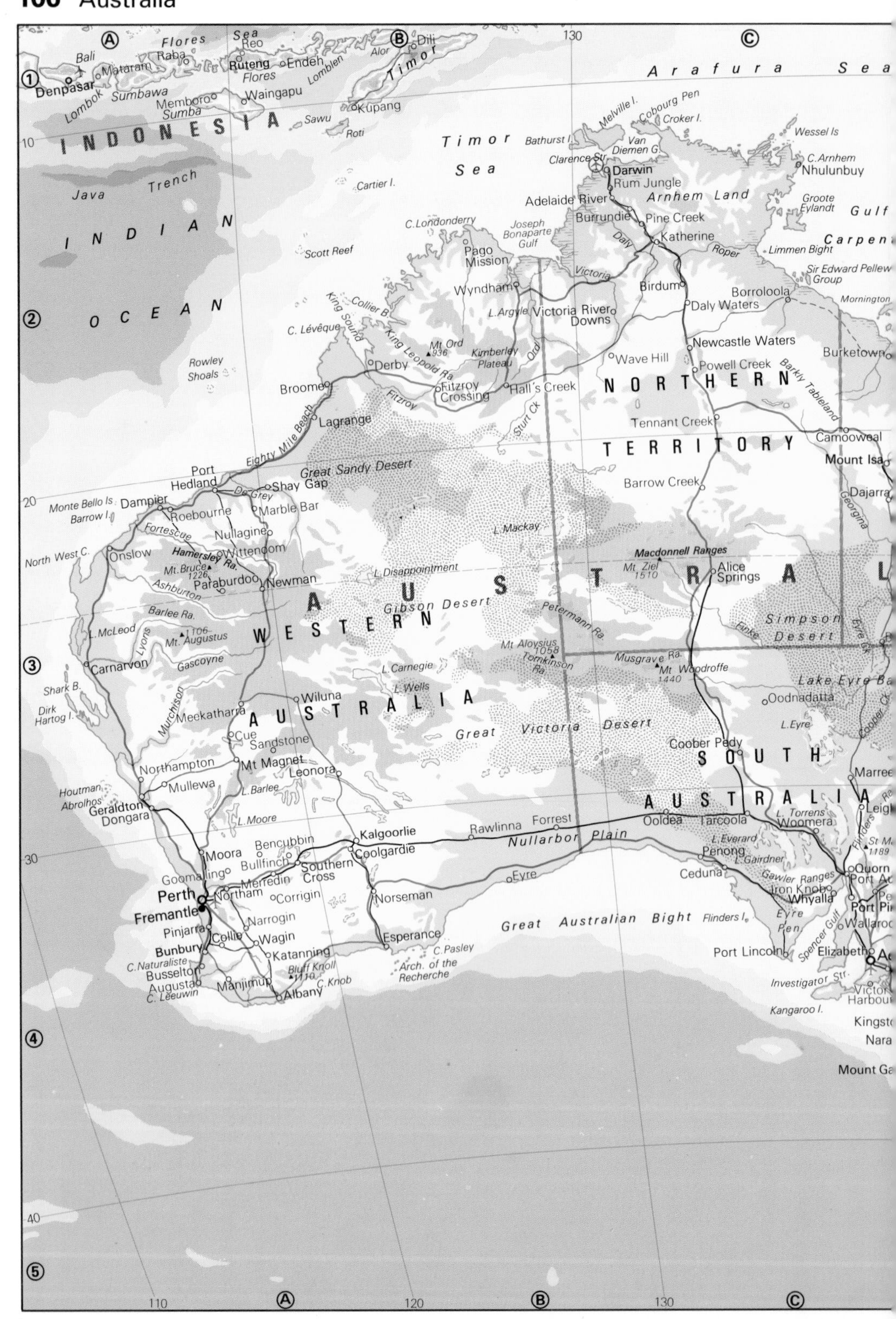
Arafura Sea
Timor Sea
INDONESIA
INDIAN OCEAN
Java Trench
Bali
Denpasar
Lombok
Mataram
Sumbawa
Flores Sea
Flores
Sumba
Waingapu
Timor
Dili
Kupang
Darwin
Katherine
Arnhem Land
Gulf of Carpentaria
NORTHERN TERRITORY
Alice Springs
Tennant Creek
Macdonnell Ranges
Simpson Desert
Great Sandy Desert
Gibson Desert
Great Victoria Desert
WESTERN AUSTRALIA
SOUTH AUSTRALIA
Broome
Derby
Port Hedland
Dampier
Carnarvon
Geraldton
Perth
Fremantle
Bunbury
Albany
Kalgoorlie
Coolgardie
Esperance
Nullarbor Plain
Great Australian Bight
Coober Pedy
Port Lincoln
Whyalla
Lake Eyre Basin
Mount Isa
Kangaroo I.
110
120
130
10
20
30
40
A
B
C
1
2
3
4
5

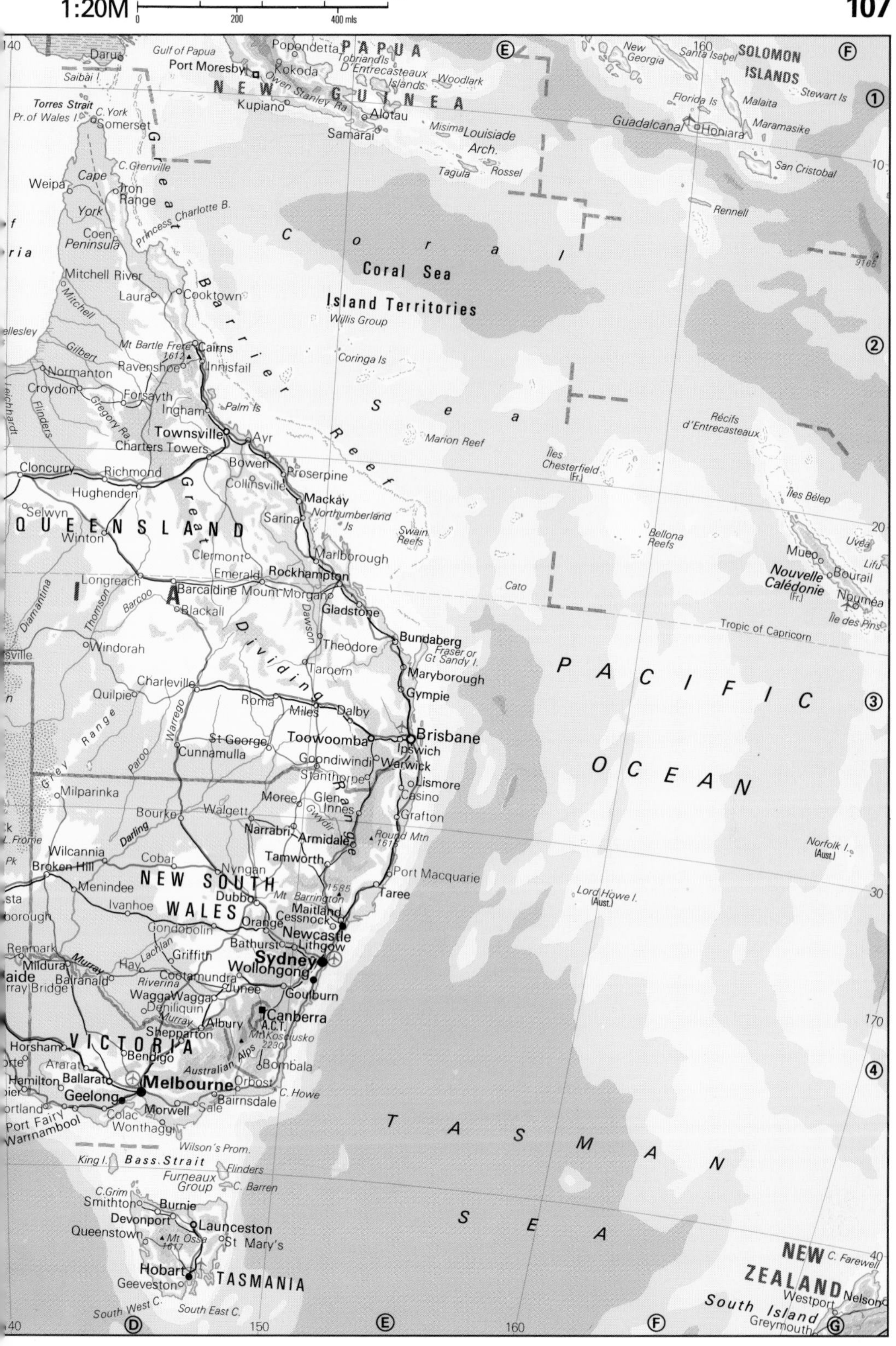

F

E

PAPUA

Gulf of Papua
Darú   Popondetta
Port Moresby   Kokoda
N E W   Kupiano
G U I N E A
Tobriand Is.
D'Entrecasteaux
Islands
Woodlark
Alotau
Samarai
Louisiade
Arch.
Misima
Tagula   Rossel

New
Georgia   Santa Isabel
SOLOMON
ISLANDS
Florida Is   Malaita   Stewart Is
Guadalcanal   Honiara   Maramasike
San Cristobal
Rennell

① 10

Torres Strait
Pr. of Wales I.
C. York
Somerset
Weipa
Cape   Iron
York   Range
Coen
Peninsula
Mitchell River
Laura
C. Grenville
Ravenshoe
Innisfail
Cooktown
Mt Bartle Frere   Cairns
1611▲
Normanton
Croydon   Forsayth
Gilbert
Ingham   Palm Is
Townsville
Charters Towers   Ayr
Cloncurry   Bowen   Proserpine
Richmond   Collinsville
Hughenden   Mackay
Sarina
Winton   Clermont   Northumberland
Is
Swain
Longreach   Emerald   Reefs
Barcaldine Mount Morgan
Blackall   Rockhampton
Gladstone
Theodore
Charleville   Taroom
Roma   Miles   Dalby
St George   Toowoomba
Cunnamulla   Ipswich
Goondiwindi   Warwick
Stanthorpe
Moree   Glen   Casino
Innes
Narrabri   Grafton
Armidale
Tamworth

C   o   r   a   l
Coral Sea
Island Territories
Willis Group
Coringa Is
S   e   a
Marion Reef

Îles
Chesterfield
(Fr.)

Récifs
d'Entrecasteaux

Îles Bélep

Muéo   Uvéa
Bourail   Lifu
Nouvelle
Calédonie   Nouméa
(Fr.)   Île des Pins

② 20

Tropic of Capricorn

P A C I F I C

O C E A N

③

Fraser or
Gt Sandy I.
Bundaberg
Maryborough
Gympie
Brisbane
Lismore

Cato

Q U E E N S L A N D
Selwyn
Windorah
Quilpie
Milparinka
Wilcannia
Broken Hill   Cobar
Menindee
Ivanhoe
NEW SOUTH
WALES
Dubbo

Bourke
Walgett
Nyngan

Port Macquarie
Taree

Norfolk I.
(Aust.)

Lord Howe I.
(Aust.)

30

170

④

TASMANIA

NEW
ZEALAND   C. Farewell
Westport   Nelson
South   Greymouth
Island

⑤ 40

D   150   **E**   160   **F**   **G**

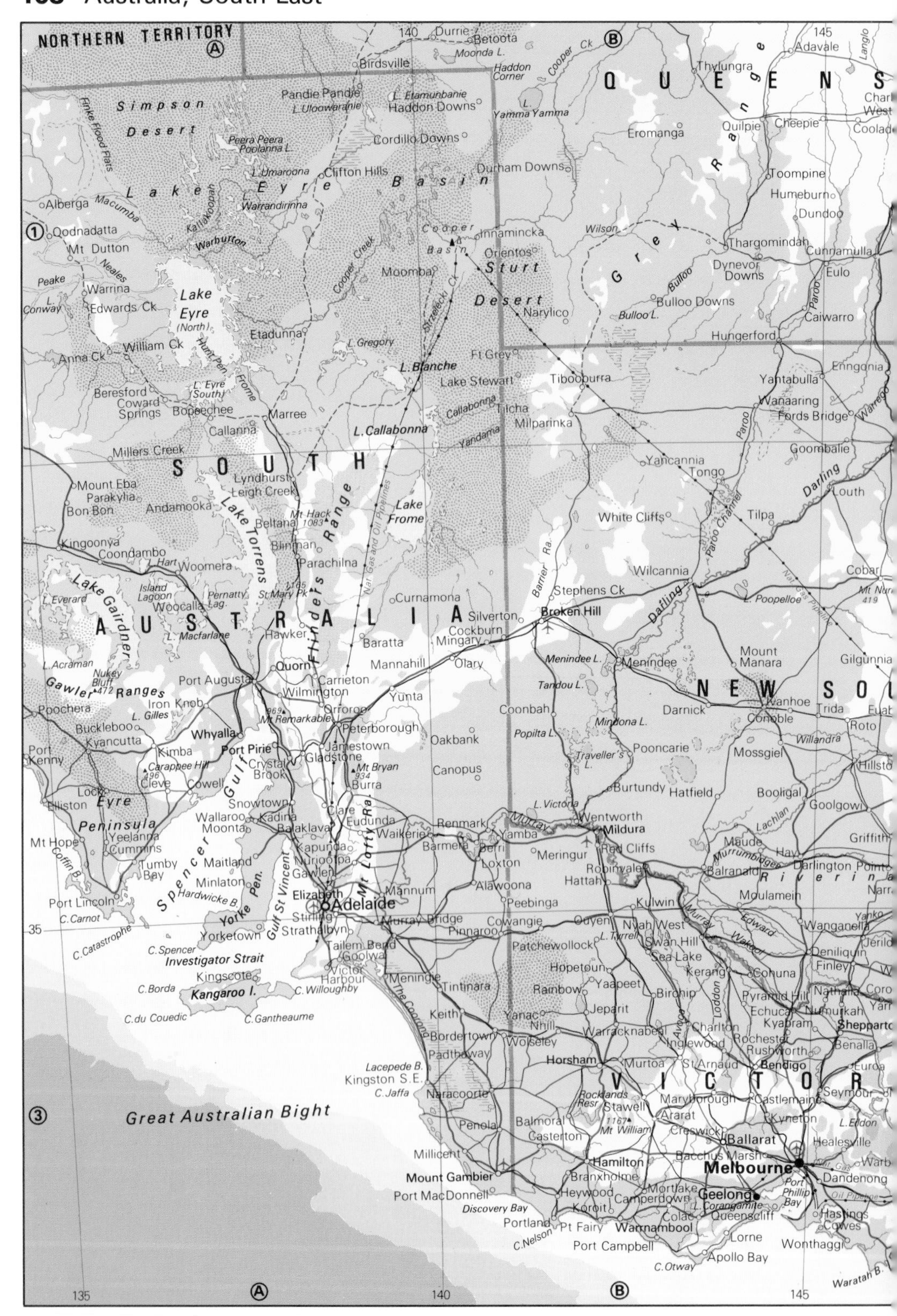
NORTHERN TERRITORY
QUEENSLAND
SOUTH AUSTRALIA
NEW SOUTH WALES
VICTORIA
Simpson Desert
Lake Eyre Basin
Sturt Desert
Grey Range
Lake Eyre (North)
Lake Eyre (South)
Lake Torrens
Lake Frome
Lake Gairdner
L. Blanche
L. Callabonna
Flinders Range
Mt Lofty Ra.
Gawler Ranges
Eyre Peninsula
Yorke Pen.
Spencer Gulf
Gulf St Vincent
Investigator Strait
Kangaroo I.
Great Australian Bight
Birdsville
Betoota
Haddon Downs
Cordillo Downs
Clifton Hills
Durham Downs
Innamincka
Moomba
Oodnadatta
Marree
Leigh Creek
Andamooka
Woomera
Port Augusta
Whyalla
Port Pirie
Port Lincoln
Peterborough
Adelaide
Elizabeth
Murray Bridge
Victor Harbour
Renmark
Berri
Loxton
Mount Gambier
Naracoorte
Kingston S.E.
Broken Hill
Wilcanna
White Cliffs
Menindee
Mildura
Wentworth
Ivanhoe
Hay
Griffith
Deniliquin
Echuca
Shepparton
Bendigo
Ballarat
Horsham
Hamilton
Warrnambool
Geelong
Melbourne
Dandenong
Portland
Port Campbell
Apollo Bay
Cunnamulla
Quilpie
Thargomindah
Eromanga
Charleville
Hungerford
Tibooburra
Bourke
Cobar
Murray
Darling
Great Dividing Range

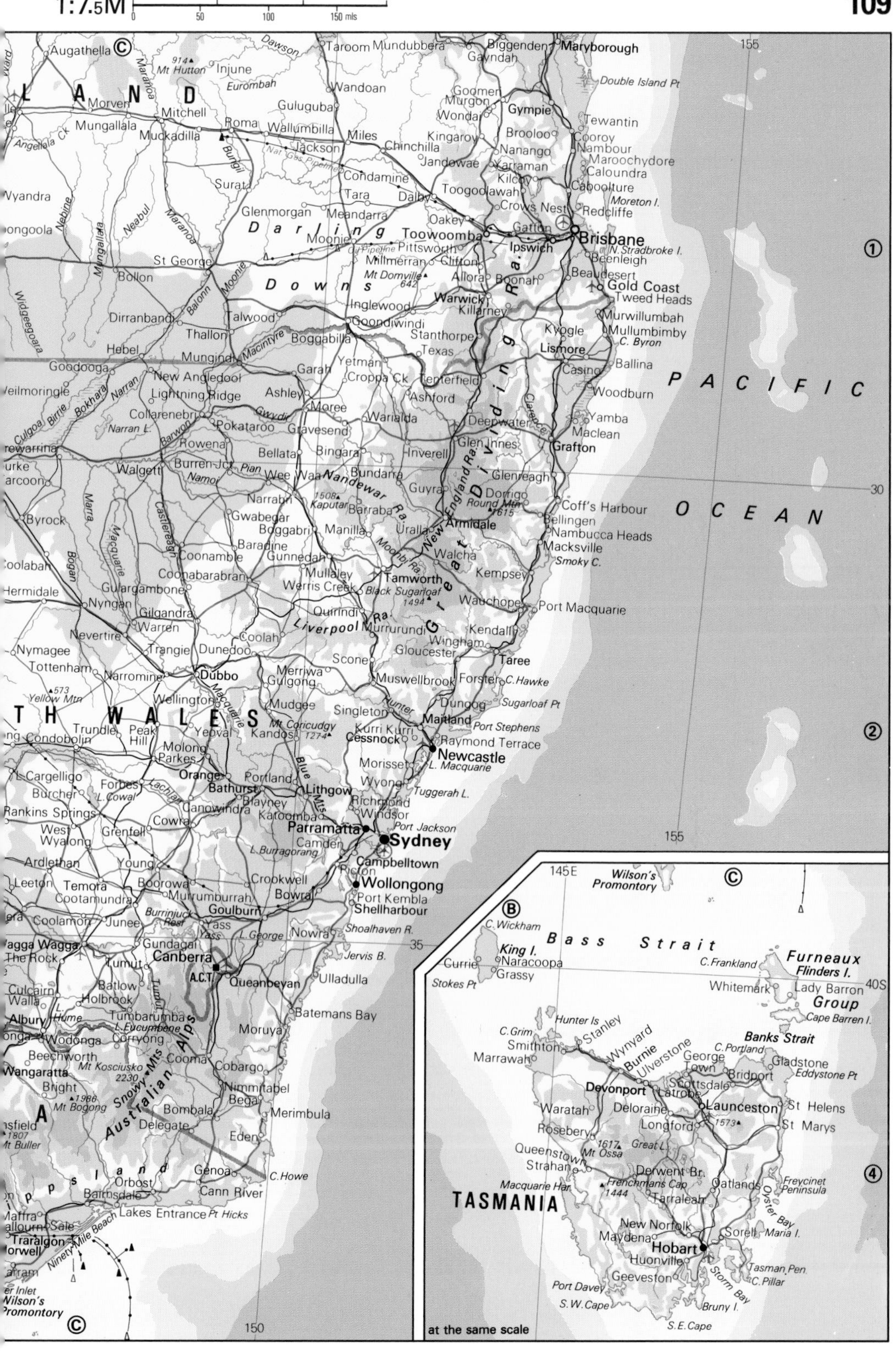

100 200 300 km
50 100 150 mls

Augathella C Dawson Taroom Mundubbera Biggenden Maryborough 155
Morven 914 Mt Hutton Injune Eurombah Gayndah Double Island Pt
L A N D Mitchell Gulugaba Wandoan Goomeri Murgon Gympie Tewantin
Mungallala Muckadilla Roma Wallumbilla Miles Chinchilla Kingaroy Nanango Brooloo Cooroy Nambour Maroochydore
Angellala Ck Jackson Condamine Jandowae Yarraman Kilcoy Caloundra
Vyandra Surat Tara Dalby Crows Nest Caboolture
St George Glenmorgan Meandarra Oakey Toowoomba Ipswich Brisbane N. Stradbroke I.
Bollon Dirranbandi Talwood Moonie Pittsworth Millmerran Clifton Gatton Beenleigh
Thallon Mungindi Goondiwindi Inglewood Warwick Killarney Boonah Gold Coast Tweed Heads
Hebel Boggabilla Stanthorpe Texas Kyogle Murwillumbah Mullumbimby
Goodooga New Angledool Yetman Croppa Ck Tenterfield Lismore C. Byron
Weilmoringle Lightning Ridge Ashley Moree Ashford Deepwater Casino Ballina
Collarenebri Pokataroo Gravesend Warialda Glen Innes Grafton Woodburn
Walgett Burren Jc Wee Waa Bingara Inverell Glenreagh Yamba Maclean
Byrock Rowena Narrabri Barraba Guyra Dorrigo Round Mtn Coff's Harbour
Gwabegar Boggabri Manilla Uralla Armidale Bellingen Nambucca Heads
Coonamble Baradine Gunnedah Walcha Macksville Smoky C.
Coonabarabran Mullaley Werris Creek Tamworth Kempsey
Nyngan Gilgandra Quirindi Wauchope Port Macquarie
Warren Coolah Murrurundi Wingham Kendall
Narromine Dunedoo Scone Gloucester Taree
Wellington Dubbo Merriwa Gulgong Muswellbrook Forster C. Hawke
Mudgee Singleton Dungog Sugarloaf Pt
Trundle Peak Hill Yeoval Kandos Kurri Kurri Maitland Port Stephens
Parkes Molong Orange Morisset Newcastle Raymond Terrace
Forbes Bathurst Lithgow Wyong L. Macquarie
Grenfell Cowra Blayney Katoomba Windsor
Young Canowindra Parramatta Port Jackson
Boorowa Crookwell Sydney Camden
Temora Murrumburrah Bowral Picton Wollongong
Junee Yass Goulburn Shellharbour
Wagga Wagga Gundagai Canberra Queanbeyan Nowra Shoalhaven R.
Tumut A.C.T. Ulladulla Jervis B.
Holbrook Cooma Batemans Bay
Albury Wodonga Mt Kosciusko 2230 Moruya
Beechworth Snowy Mts Nimmitabel Bega Merimbula
Bright Bombala Australian Alps Eden
Delegate Genoa C. Howe
Orbost Cann River
Bairnsdale Lakes Entrance Pt Hicks
Sale Ninety Mile Beach
Traralgon Wilson's Promontory

PACIFIC OCEAN 30 155

TASMANIA at the same scale
Bass Strait King I. Furneaux Flinders I. 40S
Naracoopa Grassy C. Frankland Whitemark Lady Barron Group
Stokes Pt Cape Barren I.
Hunter Is Stanley Banks Strait
C. Grim Smithton Wynyard George Town Bridport St Helens
Marrawah Burnie Ulverstone C. Portland Gladstone Eddystone Pt
Waratah Devonport Latrobe Scottsdale Launceston St Marys
Rosebery Deloraine Longford St Helens
Queenstown Strahan Mt Ossa 1617 Great L. Oatlands
Macquarie Har Frenchmans Cap 1444 Tarraleah Freycinet Peninsula
New Norfolk Sorell Maria I.
Maydena Hobart Tasman Pen. C. Pillar
Huonville Geeveston Bruny I.
Port Davey S.W. Cape S.E. Cape

150

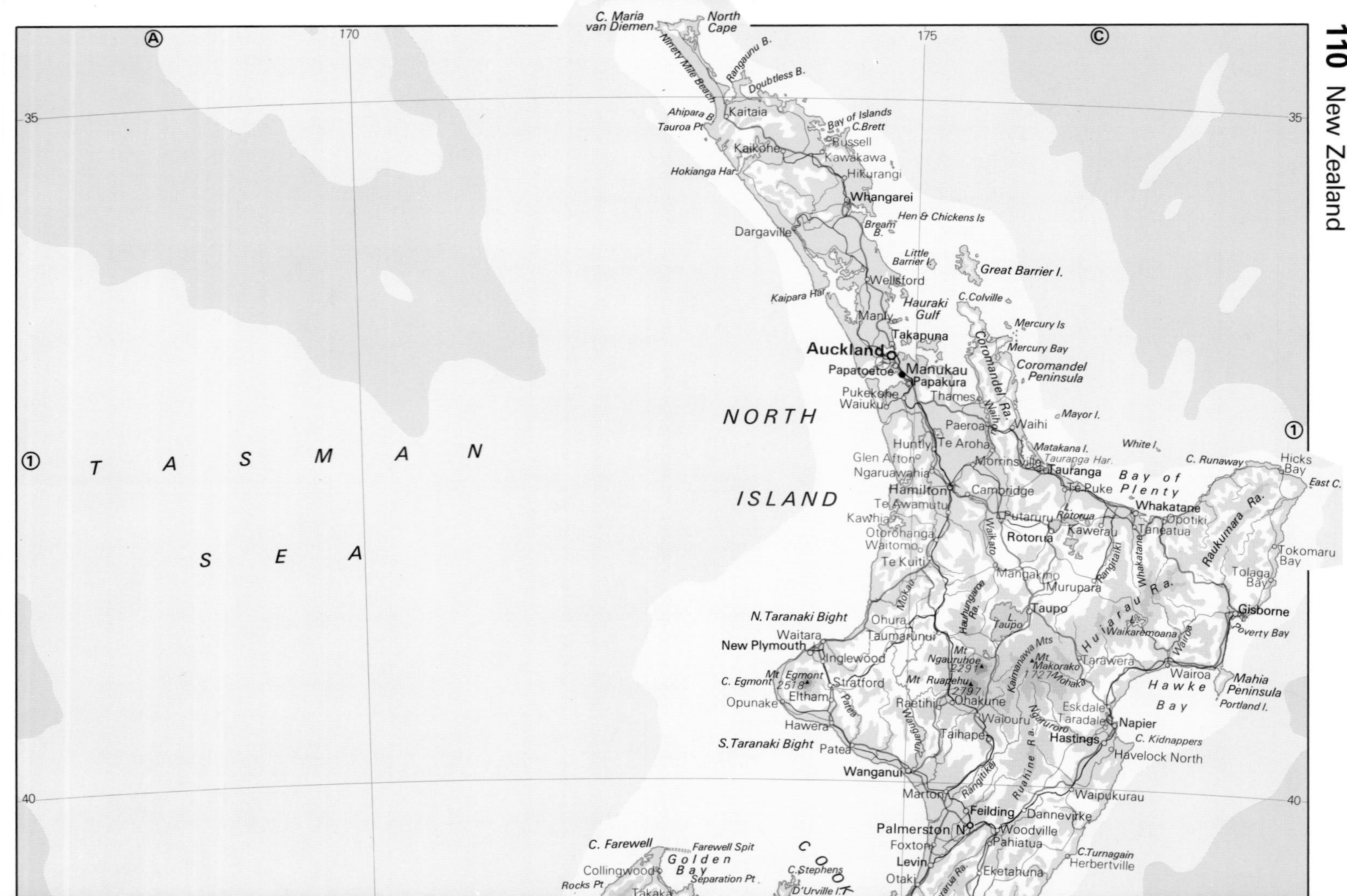

T A S M A N
S E A
NORTH
ISLAND
C. Maria van Diemen
North Cape
Ninety Mile Beach
Rangaunu B.
Doubtless B.
Kaitaia
Ahipara B.
Tauroa Pt.
Kaikohe
Hokianga Har.
Bay of Islands
C.Brett
Russell
Kawakawa
Hikurangi
Whangarei
Hen & Chickens Is
Bream B.
Dargaville
Little Barrier I.
Great Barrier I.
Wellsford
Kaipara Har.
Hauraki Gulf
C.Colville
Manly
Takapuna
Mercury Is
Mercury Bay
Coromandel Ra.
Coromandel Peninsula
Auckland
Papatoetoe
Manukau
Papakura
Pukekohe
Waiuku
Thames
Waihou
Mayor I.
Paeroa
Waihi
Huntly
Te Aroha
Matakana I.
White I.
Glen Afton
Morrinsville
Tauranga Har.
Tauranga
C. Runaway
Hicks Bay
East C.
Ngaruawahia
Hamilton
Cambridge
Te Puke
Bay of Plenty
Te Awamutu
Kawhia
Putaruru
L. Rotorua
Whakatane
Opotiki
Taneatua
Raukumara Ra.
Otorohanga
Waitomo
Waikato
Rotorua
Kawerau
Rangitaiki
Whakatane
Tokomaru Bay
Te Kuiti
Mangakino
Tolaga Bay
Murupara
Mokau
Taupo
Huiarau Ra.
Gisborne
N. Taranaki Bight
Hauhungaroa Ra.
L. Taupo
Waikaremoana
Poverty Bay
Ohura
Waitara
Taumarunui
Kaimanawa Mts
Wairoa
New Plymouth
Inglewood
Mt Ngauruhoe 2291
Mt Makorako 1727
Tarawera
Mohaka
Mahia Peninsula
C. Egmont
Mt Egmont 2518
Stratford
Mt Ruapehu 2797
Hawke Bay
Portland I.
Eltham
Opunake
Patea
Raetihi
Ohakune
Ngaruroro
Eskdale
Taradale
Napier
Hawera
Wanganui
Waiouru
S.Taranaki Bight
Patea
Taihape
Hastings
C. Kidnappers
Havelock North
Ruahine Ra.
Wanganui
Rangitikei
Marton
Waipukurau
Feilding
Dannevirke
Palmerston N.
Woodville
Pahiatua
Foxton
Levin
Otaki
Eketahuna
C.Turnagain
Herbertville
C. Farewell
Farewell Spit
Golden Bay
Collingwood
Separation Pt
Rocks Pt
Takaka
C.Stephens
D'Urville I.
COOK
35
40
170
175
A
C
1

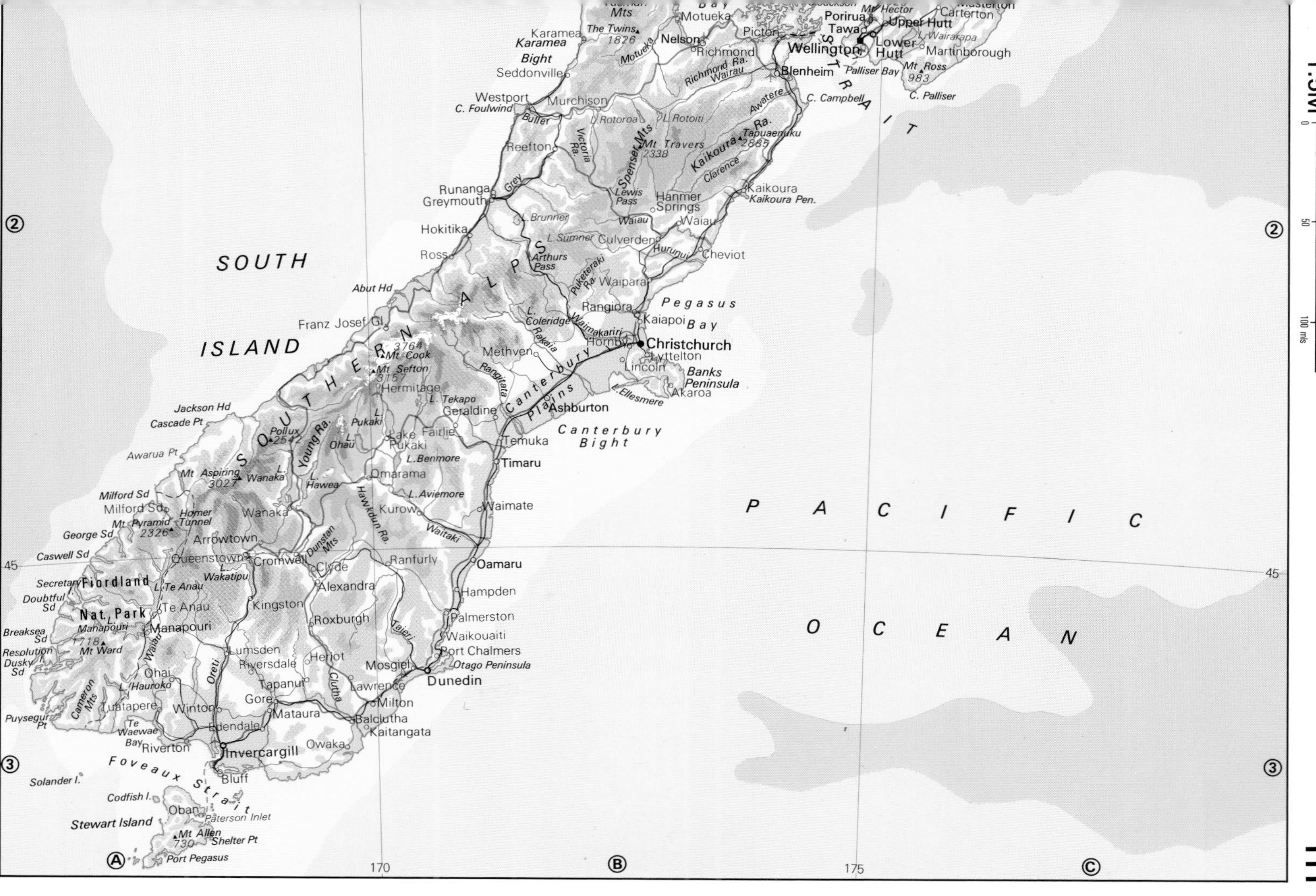

1:5M

0   50   100   150   200 km

0   50   100 mls

P A C I F I C

O C E A N

SOUTH

ISLAND

S O U T H E R N   A L P S

Wellington

Lower Hutt

Upper Hutt

Porirua

Tawa

Blenheim

Picton

Nelson

Motueka

Richmond

Kaikoura

Hanmer Springs

Cheviot

Christchurch

Lyttelton

Banks Peninsula

Akaroa

Rangiora

Kaiapoi

Ashburton

Geraldine

Temuka

Timaru

Waimate

Oamaru

Hampden

Palmerston

Port Chalmers

Otago Peninsula

Dunedin

Mosgiel

Milton

Balclutha

Kaitangata

Invercargill

Bluff

Gore

Mataura

Owaka

Riverton

Queenstown

Arrowtown

Cromwell

Clyde

Alexandra

Roxburgh

Kingston

Te Anau

Manapouri

Westport

Greymouth

Hokitika

Ross

Reefton

Seddonville

Karamea

Franz Josef

Fiordland Nat. Park

Foveaux Strait

Stewart Island

Pegasus Bay

Canterbury Bight

BANKS PENINSULA

Mt Cook

Mt Aspiring 3027

Mt Sefton

1:40M

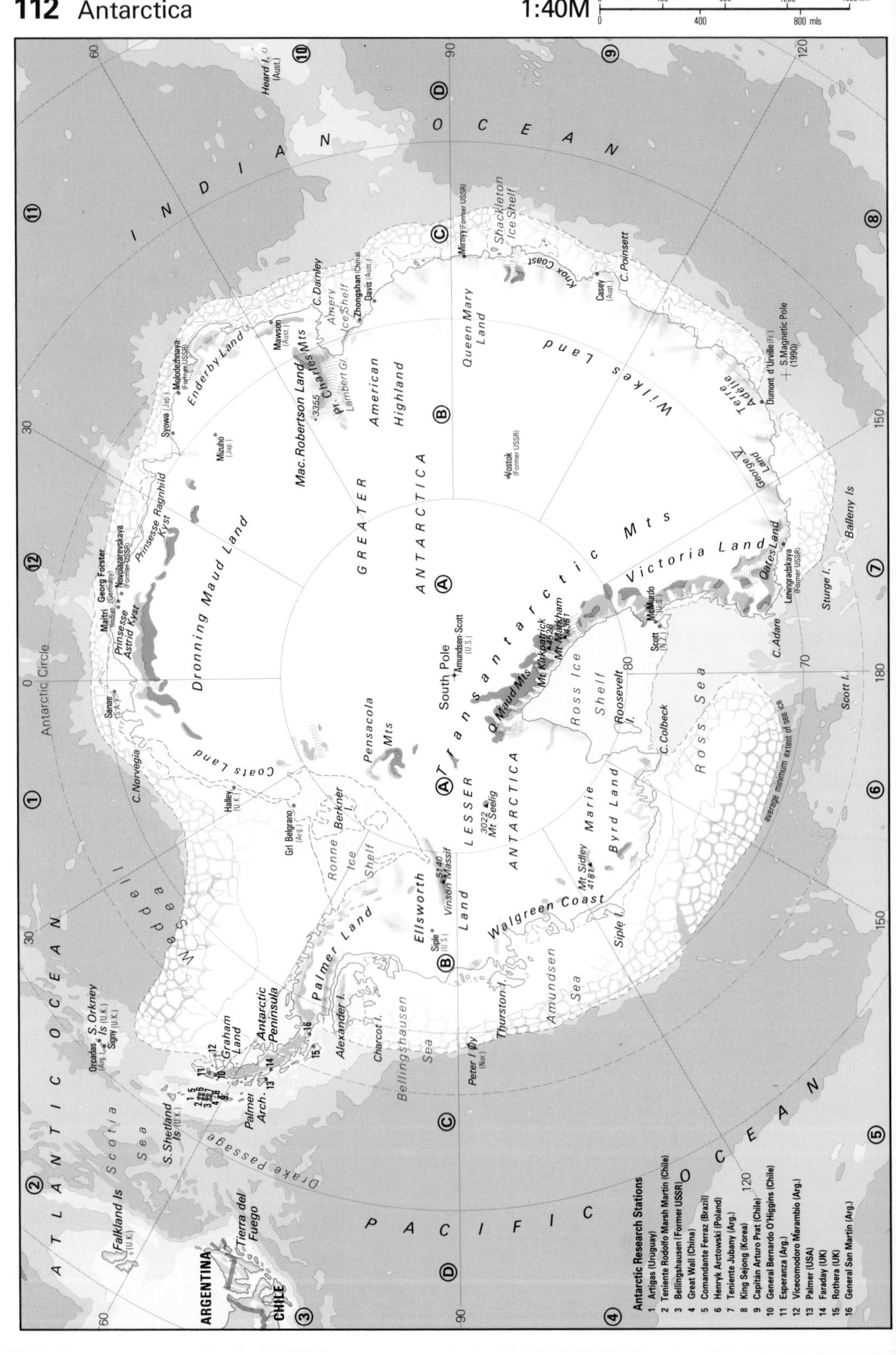

0
400
800
1200
1600 km
400
800 mls
INDIAN OCEAN
ATLANTIC OCEAN
PACIFIC OCEAN
Antarctic Circle
Heard I. (Aust.)
Scotia Sea
Drake Passage
Weddell Sea
Bellingshausen Sea
Amundsen Sea
Ross Sea
Falkland Is (U.K.)
Tierra del Fuego
ARGENTINA
CHILE
S. Orkney Is (U.K.)
Orcadas (Arg.)
Signy (U.K.)
S. Shetland Is (U.K.)
Palmer Arch.
Graham Land
Antarctic Peninsula
Alexander I.
Charcot I.
Peter I Øy (Nor.)
Thurston I.
Palmer Land
Ellsworth Land
Siple (U.S.)
Vinson Massif 5140
Ronne Ice Shelf
Berkner I.
Grl Belgrano (Arg.)
Halley (U.K.)
C. Norvegia
Coats Land
Sanae (S.A.)
Dronning Maud Land
Prinsesse Astrid Kyst
Maitri (India)
Georg Forster (Germany)
Novolazarevskaya (Former USSR)
Prinsesse Ragnhild Kyst
Syowa (Jap.)
Mizuho (Jap.)
Molodezhnaya (Former USSR)
Enderby Land
Mawson (Aust.)
Mac.Robertson Land
Prince Charles Mts
3355
Lambert Gl.
Amery Ice Shelf
C. Darnley
Zhongshan (China)
Davis (Aust.)
American Highland
Mirnyy (Former USSR)
Shackleton Ice Shelf
Queen Mary Land
Knox Coast
Casey (Aust.)
C. Poinsett
Wilkes Land
Dumont d'Urville (Fr.)
S. Magnetic Pole (1990)
Terre Adélie
George V Land
Vostok (Former USSR)
GREATER ANTARCTICA
LESSER ANTARCTICA
South Pole
Amundsen-Scott (U.S.)
Pensacola Mts
Mt Seelig 3022
Transantarctic Mts
Q. Maud Mts
Mt Kirkpatrick 4528
Mt Markham 4351
Victoria Land
Oates Land
Leningradskaya (Former USSR)
McMurdo (U.S.)
Scott (N.Z.)
C. Adare
Balleny Is
Sturge I.
Scott I.
Ross Ice Shelf
Roosevelt I.
C. Colbeck
Marie Byrd Land
Mt Sidley 4181
Walgreen Coast
Siple I.
average minimum extent of sea ice
Antarctic Research Stations
1 Artigas (Uruguay)
2 Teniente Rodolfo Marsh Martín (Chile)
3 Bellingshausen (Former USSR)
4 Great Wall (China)
5 Comandante Ferraz (Brazil)
6 Henryk Arctowski (Poland)
7 Teniente Jubany (Arg.)
8 King Sejong (Korea)
9 Capitán Arturo Prat (Chile)
10 General Bernardo O'Higgins (Chile)
11 Esperanza (Arg.)
12 Vicecomodoro Marambio (Arg.)
13 Palmer (USA)
14 Faraday (UK)
15 Rothera (UK)
16 General San Martín (Arg.)

Index

In the index, the first number refers to the page, and the following letter and number to the section of the map in which the index entry can be found. For example, 48C2 **Paris** means that Paris can be found on page 48 where column C and row 2 meet.

Abbreviations used in the index

Afghan	Afghanistan	Hung	Hungary	Pol	Poland	Arch	Archipelago
Alb	Albania	Ind	Indonesia	Port	Portugal	B	Bay
Alg	Algeria	Irish Rep	Ireland	Rom	Romania	C	Cape
Ant	Antarctica	Leb	Lebanon	Russian Fed	Russian Federation	Chan	Channel
Arg	Argentina	Lib	Liberia			Gl	Glacier
Aust	Australia	Liech	Liechtenstein	S Arabia	Saudi Arabia	I(s)	Island(s)
Bang	Bangladesh	Lux	Luxembourg	Scot	Scotland	Lg	Lagoon
Belg	Belgium	Madag	Madagascar	Sen	Senegal	L	Lake
Bol	Bolivia	Malay	Malaysia	S Africa	South Africa	Mt(s)	Mountain(s)
Bulg	Bulgaria	Maur	Mauritania	Switz	Switzerland	O	Ocean
Burk	Burkina	Mor	Morocco	Tanz	Tanzania	P	Pass
Camb	Cambodia	Mozam	Mozambique	Thai	Thailand	Pen	Peninsula
Can	Canada	Neth	Netherlands	Turk	Turkey	Plat	Plateau
CAR	Central African Republic	NZ	New Zealand	USA	United States of America	Pt	Point
Den	Denmark	Nic	Nicaragua			Res	Reservoir
Dom Rep	Dominican Republic	N Ire	Northern Ireland	Urug	Uruguay	R	River
El Sal	El Salvador	Nig	Nigeria	Ven	Venezuela	S	Sea
Eng	England	Nor	Norway	Viet	Vietnam	Sd	Sound
Eq Guinea	Equatorial Guinea	Pak	Pakistan	Yugos	Yugoslavia	Str	Strait
Eth	Ethiopia	PNG	Papua New Guinea	Zim	Zimbabwe	V	Valley
Fin	Finland	Par	Paraguay				
Germ	Germany	Phil	Philippines				

A

57B2 **Aachen** Germany
46C1 **Aalst** Belg
38K6 **Äänekoski** Fin
47C1 **Aarau** Switz
47B1 **Aare** *R* Switz
72A3 **Aba** China
97C4 **Aba** Nig
99D2 **Aba** Zaïre
91A3 **Abādān** Iran
90B3 **Abādeh** Iran
96B1 **Abadla** Alg
35B1 **Abaeté** Brazil
35B1 **Abaeté** *R* Brazil
31B2 **Abaetetuba** Brazil
72D1 **Abagnar Qi** China
97C4 **Abakaliki** Nig
63B2 **Abakan** Russian Fed
97C3 **Abala** Niger
96C2 **Abalessa** Alg
32C6 **Abancay** Peru
90B3 **Abarqū** Iran
74E2 **Abashiri** Japan
74E2 **Abashiri-wan** *B* Japan
71F4 **Abau** PNG
99D2 **Abaya** *L* Eth
99D1 **Abbai** *R* Eth
99E1 **Abbe** *L* Eth
48C1 **Abbeville** France
19B4 **Abbeville** Louisiana, USA
17B1 **Abbeville** S Carolina, USA
45B2 **Abbeyfeale** Irish Rep
47C2 **Abbiategrasso** Italy
20B1 **Abbotsford** Can
84C2 **Abbottabad** Pak
61H3 **Abdulino** Russian Fed
98C1 **Abéché** Chad
39F7 **Åbenrå** Den
97C4 **Abeokuta** Nig
99D2 **Abera** Eth
43B3 **Aberaeron** Wales
15C3 **Aberdeen** Maryland, USA
100B4 **Aberdeen** S Africa
44C3 **Aberdeen** Scot
8D2 **Aberdeen** S Dakota, USA
8A2 **Aberdeen** Washington, USA
4J3 **Aberdeen L** Can
44C3 **Aberfeldy** Scot
43C4 **Abergavenny** Wales
43B3 **Aberystwyth** Wales
81C4 **Abhā** S Arabia
90A2 **Abhar** Iran
97B4 **Abidjan** Ivory Coast
18A2 **Abilene** Kansas, USA
9D3 **Abilene** Texas, USA
43D4 **Abingdon** Eng
7B4 **Abitibi** *R* Can
7C5 **Abitibi,L** Can
61F5 **Abkhazskaya Respublika,** Georgia
84C2 **Abohar** India
97C4 **Abomey** Benin
98B2 **Abong Mbang** Cam
79A4 **Aborlan** Phil
98B1 **Abou Deïa** Chad
91A4 **Abqaiq** S Arabia
50A2 **Abrantes** Port
95C2 **Abri** Sudan
106A3 **Abrolhos** *Is* Aust
8B2 **Absaroka Range** *Mts* USA
91B5 **Abū al Abyad** *I* UAE
91A4 **Abū 'Ali** *I* S Arabia
91B5 **Abū Dhabi** UAE
95C3 **Abu Hamed** Sudan
97C4 **Abuja** Nig
33D5 **Abunā** Brazil
32D6 **Abunā** *R* Bol
93D3 **Abú Sukhayr** Iraq
111B2 **Abut Head** *C* NZ
95C3 **Abu 'Urug** *Well* Sudan
99D1 **Abuye Meda** *Mt* Eth
99C1 **Abu Zabad** Sudan
99D2 **Abwong** Sudan
56B1 **Åby** Den
94B3 **Aby 'Aweigîla** *Well* Egypt
99C2 **Abyei** Sudan
24B2 **Acambaro** Mexico
24B2 **Acaponeta** Mexico
24B3 **Acapulco** Mexico
31D2 **Acaraú** Brazil
32D2 **Acarigua** Ven
24C3 **Acatlán** Mexico
23B2 **Acatzingo** Mexico
97B4 **Accra** Ghana
85D4 **Achalpur** India
29B4 **Achao** Chile
47D1 **Achensee** *L* Austria
46E2 **Achern** Germany
41A3 **Achill** *I* Irish Rep
63B2 **Achinsk** Russian Fed
53C3 **Acireale** Italy
26C2 **Acklins** *I* Caribbean S
32C6 **Acobamba** Peru
29B2 **Aconcagua** *Mt* Chile
31D3 **Acopiara** Brazil
88B4 **Açores** *Is* Atlantic O
A Coruña = La Coruña
47C2 **Acqui** Italy
108A2 **Acraman,L** Aust
Acre = 'Akko
32C5 **Acre** State, Brazil
22C3 **Acton** USA
23B1 **Actopan** Mexico
19A3 **Ada** USA
50B1 **Adaja** *R* Spain
91C5 **Adam** Oman
35A2 **Adamantina** Brazil
98B2 **Adamaoua** Region, Nig/Cam
47D1 **Adamello** *Mt* Italy
16C1 **Adams** USA
87B3 **Adam's Bridge** India/Sri Lanka
13D2 **Adams L** Can
8A2 **Adams,Mt** USA
87C3 **Adam's Peak** *Mt* Sri Lanka
81C4 **'Adan** Yemen
92C2 **Adana** Turk
60D5 **Adapazari** Turk
112B7 **Adare,C** Ant
108B1 **Adavale** Aust
47C2 **Adda** *R* Italy
91A4 **Ad Dahna'** Region, S Arabia
96A2 **Ad Dakhla** Mor
81C4 **Ad Dālī'** Yemen
91B4 **Ad Damman** S Arabia
91A4 **Ad Dibdibah** Region, S Arabia
91A5 **Ad Dilam** S Arabia
91A5 **Ad Dir'iyah** S Arabia
93D3 **Ad Dīwanīyah** Iraq
93D3 **Ad Duwayd** S Arabia
106C4 **Adelaide** Aust
4J3 **Adelaide Pen** Can
22D3 **Adelanto** USA
Aden = 'Adan
81C4 **Aden,G of** Yemen/Somalia
97C3 **Aderbissinat** Niger
94C2 **Adhra** Syria
71E4 **Adi** *I* Indon
52B1 **Adige** *R* Italy
99D1 **Adigrat** Eth
85D5 **Adilābād** India
20B2 **Adin** USA
15D2 **Adirondack Mts** USA
99D2 **Ādīs Ābeba** Eth
95C3 **Adi Ugai** Eritrea
93C2 **Adıyaman** Turk
54C1 **Adjud** Rom
4E4 **Admiralty I** USA
6B2 **Admiralty Inlet** *B* Can
87B1 **Adoni** India
48B3 **Adour** *R* France
96A2 **Adrar** Region, Maur
96C2 **Adrar** *Mts* Alg
96A2 **Adrar Soutouf** Region, Mor
98C1 **Adré** Chad
95A2 **Adri** Libya
47E2 **Adria** Italy

Adrian

14B2 **Adrian** Michigan, USA	13E2 **Airdrie** Can	65J5 **Aktogay** Kazakhstan	95B1 **Al Burdī** Libya
52B2 **Adriatic S** S Europe	46B1 **Aire** France	61J4 **Aktumsyk** Kazakhstan	107D4 **Albury** Aust
99D1 **Adwa** Eth	42D3 **Aire** *R* Eng	65G4 **Aktyubinsk** Kazakhstan	93E3 **Al Buşayyah** Iraq
97B4 **Adzopé** Ivory Coast	46C2 **Aire** *R* France	38B1 **Akureyri** Iceland	50B1 **Alcalá de Henares** Spain
55B3 **Aegean** *S* Greece	6C3 **Airforce I** Can	**Akyab = Sittwe**	53B3 **Alcamo** Italy
80E2 **Afghanistan** Republic, Asia	47C1 **Airolo** Switz	65K5 **Akzhal** Kazakhstan	51B1 **Alcaniz** Spain
99E2 **Afgooye** Somalia	4E3 **Aishihik** Can	11B3 **Alabama** State, USA	31C2 **Alcântara** Brazil
97C4 **Afikpo** Nig	12G2 **Aishihik L** Can	11B3 **Alabama** *R* USA	50B2 **Alcaraz** Spain
38G6 **Afjord** Nor	46B2 **Aisne** Department, France	17A1 **Alabaster** USA	50B2 **Alcázar de San Juan** Spain
96C1 **Aflou** Alg	49C2 **Aisne** *R* France	92C2 **Ala Dağlari** *Mts* Turk	51B2 **Alcira** Spain
99E2 **Afmadu** Somalia	71F4 **Aitape** PNG	61F5 **Alagir** Russian Fed	35D1 **Alcobaça** Brazil
97A3 **Afollé** Region, Maur	58D1 **Aiviekste** *R* Latvia	47B2 **Alagna** Italy	50B1 **Alcolea de Pinar** Spain
94B2 **Afula** Israel	72B2 **Aixa Zuogi** China	31D3 **Alagoas** State, Brazil	51B2 **Alcoy** Spain
92B2 **Afyon** Turk	49D3 **Aix-en-Provence** France	31D4 **Alagoinhas** Brazil	51C2 **Alcudia** Spain
95A3 **Agadem** Niger	47A2 **Aix-les-Bains** France	51B1 **Alagón** Spain	89J8 **Aldabra** *Is* Indian O
97C3 **Agadez** Niger	86B2 **Aiyar Res** India	93E4 **Al Ahmadi** Kuwait	63E2 **Aldan** Russian Fed
96B1 **Agadir** Mor	55B3 **Aíyion** Greece	25D3 **Alajuela** Costa Rica	63E2 **Aldanskoye Nagor'ye** *Upland* Russian Fed
85D4 **Agar** India	55B3 **Aíyna** *I* Greece	12B2 **Alakanuk** USA	43E3 **Aldeburgh** Eng
86C2 **Agartala** India	86C2 **Aīzawl** India	38L5 **Alakurtti** Russian Fed	48B2 **Alderney** *I* UK
20B1 **Agassiz** Can	100A3 **Aizeb** *R* Namibia	93E3 **Al Amārah** Iraq	43D4 **Aldershot** Eng
97B4 **Agboville** Ivory Coast	74E3 **Aizu-Wakamatsu** Japan	21A2 **Alameda** USA	97A3 **Aleg** Maur
93E1 **Agdam** Azerbaijan	52A2 **Ajaccio** Corse	23B1 **Alamo** Mexico	30E4 **Alegrete** Brazil
75B1 **Agematsu** Japan	23B2 **Ajalpan** Mexico	9C3 **Alamogordo** USA	34C2 **Alejandro Roca** Arg
48C3 **Agen** France	95B1 **Ajdabiyā** Libya	9C3 **Alamosa** USA	30H6 **Alejandro Selkirk** *I* Chile
90A3 **Agha Jārī** Iran	74E2 **Ajigasawa** Japan	39H6 **Åland** *I* Fin	63G2 **Aleksandrovsk Sakhalinskiy** Russian Fed
96A2 **Aghwinit** *Well* Mor	94B2 **Ajlun** Jordan	92B2 **Alanya** Turk	65J4 **Alekseyevka** Kazakhstan
47D2 **Agno** *R* Italy	91C4 **Ajman** UAE	17B1 **Alapaha** *R* USA	60E3 **Aleksin** Russian Fed
47E1 **Agordo** Italy	85C3 **Ajmer** India	65H4 **Alapayevsk** Russian Fed	58B1 **Älem** Sweden
48C3 **Agout** *R* France	9B3 **Ajo** USA	92A2 **Alaşehir** Turk	35C2 **Além Paraíba** Brazil
85D3 **Agra** India	23A2 **Ajuchitan** Mexico	68C3 **Ala Shan** *Mts* China	49C2 **Alençon** France
93D2 **Ağri** Turk	55C3 **Ak** *R* Turk	4C3 **Alaska** State, USA	21C4 **Alenuihaha Chan** Hawaiian Is
53C2 **Agri** *R* Italy	75B1 **Akaishi-sanchi** *Mts* Japan	4D4 **Alaska,G of** USA	**Aleppo = Ḥalab**
53B3 **Agrigento** Italy	87B1 **Akalkot** India	12C3 **Alaska Pen** USA	6D1 **Alert** Can
55B3 **Agrínion** Greece	111B2 **Akaroa** NZ	4C3 **Alaska Range** *Mts* USA	49C3 **Alès** France
34A3 **Agrio** *R* Chile	75A2 **Akashi** Japan	52A2 **Alassio** Italy	52A2 **Alessandria** Italy
53B2 **Agropoli** Italy	61J3 **Akbulak** Russian Fed	12D1 **Alatna** *R* USA	64B3 **Ålesund** Nor
61H2 **Agryz** Russian Fed	93C2 **Akçakale** Turk	61G3 **Alatyr** Russian Fed	12C3 **Aleutian Range** *Mts* USA
6E3 **Agto** Greenland	96A2 **Akchar** *Watercourse* Maur	108B2 **Alawoona** Aust	4E4 **Alexander Arch** USA
27D3 **Aguadilla** Puerto Rico	55C3 **Akdağ** *Mt* Turk	91C5 **Al'Ayn** UAE	100A3 **Alexander Bay** S Africa
24B1 **Agua Prieta** Mexico	98C2 **Aketi** Zaïre	82B2 **Alayskiy Khrebet** *Mts* Tajikistan	17A1 **Alexander City** USA
24B2 **Aguascalientes** Mexico	93D1 **Akhalkalaki** Georgia	49D3 **Alba** Italy	112C3 **Alexander I** Ant
23A1 **Aguascalientes** State, Mexico	93D1 **Akhalsikhe** Georgia	92C2 **Al Bāb** Syria	111A3 **Alexandra** NZ
35C1 **Aguas Formosas** Brazil	55B3 **Akharnái** Greece	51B2 **Albacete** Spain	29G8 **Alexandra,C** South Georgia
50A1 **Agueda** Port	12D3 **Akhiok** USA	50A1 **Alba de Tormes** Spain	6C2 **Alexandra Fjord** Can
96C3 **Aguelhok** Mali	92A2 **Akhisar** Turk	93D2 **Al Badi** Iraq	95B1 **Alexandria** Egypt
50B2 **Aguilas** Spain	58D1 **Akhiste** Latvia	54B1 **Alba Iulia** Rom	11A3 **Alexandria** Louisiana, USA
23A2 **Aguililla** Mexico	95C2 **Akhmîm** Egypt	54A2 **Albania** Republic, Europe	10A2 **Alexandria** Minnesota, USA
100B4 **Agulhas,C** S Africa	61G4 **Akhtubinsk** Russian Fed	106A4 **Albany** Aust	10C3 **Alexandria** Virginia, USA
79C4 **Agusan** *R* Phil	60D4 **Akhtyrka** Ukraine	17B1 **Albany** Georgia, USA	55C2 **Alexandroúpolis** Greece
Ahaggar = Hoggar	75A2 **Aki** Japan	15D2 **Albany** New York, USA	13C2 **Alexis Creek** Can
93E2 **Ahar** Iran	7B4 **Akimiski I** Can	8A2 **Albany** Oregon, USA	94B2 **Aley** Leb
110B1 **Ahipara B** NZ	74E3 **Akita** Japan	7B4 **Albany** *R* Can	65K4 **Aleysk** Russian Fed
85C4 **Ahmadābād** India	96A3 **Akjoujt** Maur	34B2 **Albardón** Arg	93D3 **Al Fallūjah** Iraq
87A1 **Ahmadnagar** India	94B2 **'Akko** Israel	91C5 **Al Batinah** Region, Oman	51B1 **Alfaro** Spain
99E2 **Ahmar** *Mts* Eth	4E3 **Aklavik** USA	71F5 **Albatross B** Aust	54C2 **Alfatar** Bulg
46D1 **Ahr** *R* Germany	97B3 **Aklé Aouana** *Desert Region* Maur	95B1 **Al Baydā** Libya	93E3 **Al Fāw** Iraq
46D1 **Ahrgebirge** Region, Germany	99D2 **Akobo** Sudan	11C3 **Albemarle Sd** USA	35B2 **Alfenas** Brazil
23A1 **Ahuacatlán** Mexico	99D2 **Akobo** *R* Sudan	50B1 **Alberche** *R* Spain	55B3 **Alfiós** *R* Greece
23A1 **Ahualulco** Mexico	84B1 **Akoha** Afghan	108A1 **Alberga** Aust	47D2 **Alfonsine** Italy
39G7 **Åhus** Sweden	85D4 **Akola** India	46B1 **Albert** France	35C2 **Alfonzo Cláudio** Brazil
90B2 **Ahuvān** Iran	85D4 **Akot** India	5G4 **Alberta** Province, Can	35C2 **Alfredo Chaves** Brazil
90A3 **Ahvāz** Iran	6D3 **Akpatok I** Can	99D2 **Albert,L** Uganda/Zaïre	61J4 **Alga** Kazakhstan
26A4 **Aiajuela** Costa Rica	55B3 **Ákra Kafirévs** *C* Greece	10A2 **Albert Lea** USA	34B3 **Algarrobo del Águila** Arg
47B1 **Aigle** Switz	55B3 **Ákra Maléa** *C* Greece	99D2 **Albert Nile** *R* Uganda	50A2 **Algeciras** Spain
47B2 **Aiguille d'Arves** *Mt* France	38A2 **Akranes** Iceland	49D2 **Albertville** France	96C1 **Alger** Alg
47B2 **Aiguille de la Grand Sassière** *Mt* France	55C3 **Ákra Sídheros** *C* Greece	48C3 **Albi** France	96B2 **Algeria** Republic, Africa
75B1 **Aikawa** Japan	55B3 **Ákra Spátha** *C* Greece	18B1 **Albia** USA	53A2 **Alghero** Sardegna
17B1 **Aiken** USA	55B3 **Ákra Taínaron** *C* Greece	33G2 **Albina** Suriname	**Algiers = Alger**
73A5 **Ailao Shan** *Upland* China	10B2 **Akron** USA	14B2 **Albion** Michigan, USA	15C1 **Algonquin Park** Can
35C1 **Aimorés** Brazil	94A1 **Akrotiri B** Cyprus	15C2 **Albion** New York, USA	91C5 **Al Hadd** Oman
96B1 **Ain Beni Mathar** Mor	84D1 **Aksai Chin** *Mts* China	92C4 **Al Bi'r** S Arabia	93D3 **Al Hadīthah** Iraq
95B2 **Ain Dalla** *Well* Egypt	92B2 **Aksaray** Turk	91A5 **Al Biyādh** Region, S Arabia	92C3 **Al Hadīthah** S Arabia
51C2 **Aïn el Hadjel** Alg	61H3 **Aksay** Kazakhstan	50B2 **Alborán** */* Spain	93D2 **Al Haḍr** Iraq
95A3 **Aïn Galakka** Chad	84D1 **Aksayquin Hu** *L* China	39G7 **Ålborg** Den	
96B1 **Aïn Sefra** Alg	92B2 **Akşehir** Turk	93D3 **Al Bū Kamāl** Syria	
92B4 **'Ain Sukhna** Egypt	92B2 **Akseki** Turk	47C1 **Albula** *R* Switz	
75A2 **Aioi** Japan	63D2 **Aksenovo Zilovskoye** Russian Fed	9C3 **Albuquerque** USA	
96B2 **Aïoun Abd el Malek** *Well* Maur	68D1 **Aksha** Russian Fed	91C5 **Al Buraymi** Oman	
97B3 **Aïoun El Atrouss** Maur	82C1 **Aksu** China	95A1 **Al Burayqah** Libya	
30C2 **Aiquile** Bol	61H5 **Aktau** Kazakhstan		
97C3 **Aïr** *Desert Region* Niger			

Avesta

39H6 **Avesta** Sweden
52B2 **Avezzano** Italy
44C3 **Aviemore** Scot
111B2 **Aviemore,L** NZ
47B2 **Avigliana** Italy
49C3 **Avignon** France
50B1 **Avila** Spain
50A1 **Aviles** Spain
47D1 **Avisio** *R* Italy
108B3 **Avoca** *R* Aust
43C4 **Avon** County, Eng
43D4 **Avon** *R* Dorset, Eng
43D3 **Avon** *R* Warwick, Eng
43C4 **Avonmouth** Wales
17B2 **Avon Park** USA
46B2 **Avre** *R* France
54A2 **Avtovac** Bosnia-Herzegovina
94C2 **A'waj** *R* Syria
74D4 **Awaji-shima** *B* Japan
99E2 **Awarē** Eth
111A2 **Awarua Pt** NZ
99E2 **Awash** Eth
99E2 **Awash** *R* Eth
75B1 **Awa-shima** *I* Japan
111B2 **Awatere** *R* NZ
95A2 **Awbārī** Libya
98C2 **Aweil** Sudan
95B2 **Awjilah** Libya
96A2 **Awserd** *Well* Mor
6A2 **Axel Heiburg I** Can
43C4 **Axminster** Eng
75B1 **Ayabe** Japan
29E3 **Ayacucho** Arg
32C6 **Ayacucho** Peru
65K5 **Ayaguz** Kazakhstan
82C2 **Ayakkum Hu** *L* China
50A2 **Ayamonte** Spain
63F2 **Ayan** Russian Fed
32C6 **Ayauiri** Peru
92A2 **Aydin** Turk
55C3 **Áyios Evstrátios** *I* Greece
43D4 **Aylesbury** Eng
13D2 **Aylmer,Mt** Can
94C2 **'Ayn al Fijah** Syria
93D2 **Ayn Zālah** Iraq
95B2 **Ayn Zuwayyah** *Well* Libya
99D2 **Ayod** Sudan
107D2 **Ayr** Aust
42B2 **Ayr** Scot
42B2 **Ayr** *R* Scot
42B2 **Ayre,Pt of** Eng
54C2 **Aytos** Bulg
76C3 **Aytthaya** Thai
23A1 **Ayutla** Mexico
55C3 **Ayvacik** Turk
55C3 **Ayvalik** Turk
86A1 **Azamgarh** India
97B3 **Azaouad** *Desert Region* Mali
97D3 **Azare** Nig
92C2 **A'Zāz** Syria
Azbine = Aïr
65F5 **Azerbaijan** Republic, Russian Fed
32B4 **Azogues** Ecuador
Azores = Açores
98C1 **Azoum** *R* Chad
60E4 **Azov, Sea of** Russian Fed/Ukraine
Azovskoye More = Azov, Sea of
96B1 **Azrou** Mor
34D3 **Azucena** Arg
32A2 **Azuero,Pen de** Panama
29E3 **Azúl** Arg
94C2 **Az-Zabdānī** Syria
91C5 **Az Zāhirah** *Mts* Oman
95A2 **Az Zahra** Iraq
96A2 **Azzeffal** *R* Maur
93E3 **Az Zubayr** Iraq

B

94B2 **Ba'abda** Leb
92C3 **Ba'albek** Leb
94B3 **Ba'al Hazor** *Mt* Israel

99E2 **Baardheere** Somalia
54C2 **Babadag** Rom
92A1 **Babaeski** Turk
32B4 **Babahoyo** Ecuador
81C4 **Bāb al Mandab** *Str* Djibouti/Yemen
71D4 **Babar** *I* Indon
99D3 **Babati** Tanz
60E2 **Babayevo** Russian Fed
14B2 **Baberton** USA
13B1 **Babine** *R* Can
5F4 **Babine L** Can
90B2 **Bābol** Iran
79B2 **Babuyan Chan** Phil
79B2 **Babuyan Is** Phil
31C2 **Bacabal** Brazil
71D4 **Bacan** *I* Indon
60C4 **Bacău** Rom
76D1 **Bac Can** Viet
108B3 **Bacchus Marsh** Aust
82B2 **Bachu** China
4J3 **Back** *R* Can
12J2 **Backbone Ranges** *Mts* Can
76D1 **Bac Ninh** Viet
79B3 **Bacolod** Phil
79B3 **Baco,Mt** Phil
87B2 **Badagara** India
72A1 **Badain Jaran Shamo** *Desert* China
50A2 **Badajoz** Spain
51C1 **Badalona** Spain
93D3 **Badanah** S Arabia
46D2 **Bad Bergzabern** Germany
46D1 **Bad Ems** Germany
47C1 **Baden** Switz
57B3 **Baden-Baden** Germany
57B3 **Baden-Württemberg** State, Germany
57C3 **Badgastein** Austria
22C2 **Badger** USA
57B2 **Bad-Godesberg** Germany
57B2 **Bad Hersfeld** Germany
46D1 **Bad Honnef** Germany
85B4 **Badin** Pak
52B1 **Bad Ischl** Austria
93C3 **Badiyat ash Sham** *Desert Region* Jordan/Iraq
57B3 **Bad-Kreuznach** Germany
46D1 **Bad Nevenahr-Ahrweiler** Germany
47C1 **Bad Ragaz** Switz
57C3 **Bad Tolz** Germany
87C3 **Badulla** Sri Lanka
50B2 **Baena** Spain
97A3 **Bafatá** Guinea-Bissau
4H2 **Baffin** *Region* Can
6C2 **Baffin B** Greenland/Can
6C2 **Baffin I** Can
98B2 **Bafia** Cam
97A3 **Bafing** *R* Mali
97A3 **Bafoulabé** Mali
98B2 **Bafoussam** Cam
90C3 **Bāfq** Iran
60E5 **Bafra Burun** *Pt* Turk
91C4 **Bāft** Iran
98C2 **Bafwasende** Zaïre
86A1 **Bagaha** India
87B1 **Bāgalkot** India
99D3 **Bagamoyo** Tanz
29F2 **Bagé** Brazil
93D3 **Baghdād** Iraq
86B2 **Bagherhat** Bang
91C3 **Bāghīn** Iran
84B1 **Baghlan** Afghan
49C3 **Bagnols-sur-Cèze** France
97B3 **Bagoé** *R* Mali
Bagu = Pegu
79B2 **Baguio** Phil
86B1 **Bāhādurābād** India
11C4 **Bahamas,The** *Is* Caribbean S
86B2 **Baharampur** India
92A4 **Bahariya Oasis** Egypt

84C3 **Bahawalpur** Pak
84C3 **Bahawalpur** Province, Pak
85C3 **Bahawathagar** Pak
Bahia = Salvador
31C4 **Bahia** State, Brazil
29D3 **Bahía Blanca** Arg
29D3 **Bahía Blanca** *B* Arg
34A3 **Bahia Concepción** *B* Chile
35C2 **Bahia da Ilha Grande** *B* Brazil
24B2 **Bahia de Banderas** *B* Mexico
24C2 **Bahia de Campeche** *B* Mexico
25D3 **Bahia de la Ascension** *B* Mexico
24B3 **Bahia de Petacalco** *B* Mexico
96A2 **Bahia de Rio de Oro** *B* Mor
35C2 **Bahia de Sepetiba** *B* Brazil
29C6 **Bahía Grande** *B* Arg
9B4 **Bahia Kino** Mexico
24A2 **Bahia Magdalena** *B* Mexico
24A2 **Bahia Sebastia Vizcaino** *B* Mexico
99D1 **Bahar Dar** Eth
86A1 **Bahraich** India
80D3 **Bahrain** Sheikdom, Arabian Pen
93D3 **Bahr al Milh** *L* Iraq
98C2 **Bahr Aouk** *R* Chad/CAR
Bahrat Lut = Dead S
98C2 **Bahr el Arab** *Watercourse* Sudan
99D2 **Bahr el Ghazal** *R* Sudan
98B1 **Bahr el Ghazal** *Watercourse* Chad
101H1 **Baia de Maputo** *B* Mozam
31B2 **Baia de Marajó** *B* Brazil
101D2 **Baiá de Pemba** *B* Mozam
31C2 **Baia de São Marcos** *B* Brazil
50A2 **Baia de Setúbal** *B* Port
31D4 **Baia de Todos os Santos** *B* Brazil
100A2 **Baia dos Tigres** Angola
60B4 **Baia Mare** Rom
98B2 **Baïbokoum** Chad
69E2 **Baicheng** China
101E2 **Baie Antongila** *B* Madag
7D5 **Baie-Comeau** Can
101D2 **Baie de Bombetoka** *B* Madag
101D2 **Baie de Mahajamba** *B* Madag
101D3 **Baie de St Augustin** *B* Madag
94B2 **Baie de St Georges** *B* Leb
10D2 **Baie des Chaleurs** *B* Can
7C4 **Baie-du-Poste** Can
72B3 **Baihe** China
72C3 **Bai He** *R* China
93D3 **Ba'ījī** Iraq
86A2 **Baikunthpur** India
Baile Atha Cliath = Dublin
54B2 **Băilesti** Rom
46B1 **Bailleul** France
72A3 **Baima** China
17B1 **Bainbridge** USA
12B2 **Baird Inlet** USA
4B3 **Baird Mts** USA
72D1 **Bairin Youqi** China
72D1 **Bairin Zuoqi** China
107D4 **Bairnsdale** Aust
79B4 **Bais** Phil
54A1 **Baja** Hung
9B3 **Baja California** State, Mexico

24A1 **Baja California** *Pen* Mexico
61J2 **Bakal** Russian Fed
98C2 **Bakala** CAR
97A3 **Bakel** Sen
8C2 **Baker** Montana, USA
8B2 **Baker** Oregon, USA
6A3 **Baker Foreland** *Pt* Can
4J3 **Baker L** Can
4J3 **Baker Lake** Can
8A2 **Baker,Mt** USA
9B3 **Bakersfield** USA
90C2 **Bakharden** Turkmenistan
90C2 **Bakhardok** Turkmenistan
60D3 **Bakhmach** Ukraine
38C1 **Bakkaflói** *B* Iceland
99D2 **Bako** Eth
98C2 **Bakouma** CAR
65F5 **Baku** Azerbaijan
Baky = Baku
92B2 **Balā** Turk
79A4 **Balabac** *I* Phil
70C3 **Balabac** *Str* Malay
78C2 **Balaikarangan** Indon
108A2 **Balaklava** Aust
61G3 **Balakovo** Russian Fed
86A2 **Balāngir** India
61F3 **Balashov** Russian Fed
86B2 **Balasore** India
80A3 **Balāt** Egypt
52C1 **Balaton** *L* Hung
45C2 **Balbriggan** Irish Rep
29E3 **Balcarce** Arg
54C2 **Balchik** Bulg
111B3 **Balclutha** NZ
18B2 **Bald Knob** USA
17B1 **Baldwin** USA
9C3 **Baldy Peak** *Mt* USA
Balearic Is = Islas Baleares
78C2 **Baleh** *R* Malay
79B2 **Baler** Phil
61H2 **Balezino** Russian Fed
106A1 **Bali** *I* Indon
92A2 **Balikesir** Turk
93C2 **Balikh** *R* Syria
78D3 **Balikpapan** Indon
79B2 **Balintang Chan** Phil
78C4 **Bali S** Indon
35A1 **Baliza** Brazil
84B1 **Balkh** Afghan
65J5 **Balkhash** Kazakhstan
44B3 **Ballachulish** Scot
45B2 **Ballaghaderreen** Irish Rep
42B2 **Ballantrae** Scot
4G2 **Ballantyne Str** Can
87B2 **Ballapur** India
107D4 **Ballarat** Aust
44C3 **Ballater** Scot
112C7 **Balleny Is** Ant
86A1 **Ballia** India
109D1 **Ballina** Aust
41B3 **Ballina** Irish Rep
45B2 **Ballinasloe** Irish Rep
45B2 **Ballinrobe** Irish Rep
55A2 **Ballsh** Alb
45B1 **Ballycastle** Irish Rep
45C1 **Ballycastle** N Ire
45C1 **Ballymena** N Ire
45C1 **Ballymoney** N Ire
45B1 **Ballyshannon** Irish Rep
45B2 **Ballyvaghan** Irish Rep
108B3 **Balmoral** Aust
34C2 **Balnearia** Arg
84B3 **Balochistān** Region, Pak
100A2 **Balombo** Angola
109C1 **Balonn** *R* Aust
85C3 **Balotra** India
86A1 **Balrāmpur** India
107D4 **Balranald** Aust
31B3 **Balsas** Brazil
23B2 **Balsas** Mexico
24B3 **Balsas** *R* Mexico
60C4 **Balta** Ukraine
39H7 **Baltic S** N Europe

92B3 **Baltîm** Egypt
45B3 **Baltimore** Irish Rep
10C3 **Baltimore** USA
86B1 **Bālurghāt** India
61H4 **Balykshi** Kazakhstan
91C4 **Bam** Iran
98B1 **Bama** Nig
97B3 **Bamako** Mali
98C2 **Bambari** CAR
17B1 **Bamberg** USA
57C3 **Bamberg** Germany
98C2 **Bambili** Zaïre
35B2 **Bambui** Brazil
98B2 **Bamenda** Cam
13C3 **Bamfield** Can
98B2 **Bamingui** *R* CAR
98B2 **Bamingui Bangoran** *National Park* CAR
84B2 **Bamiyan** Afghan
91D4 **Bampur** Iran
91D4 **Bampur** *R* Iran
98C2 **Banalia** Zaïre
97B3 **Banamba** Mali
76C3 **Ban Aranyaprathet** Thai
76C2 **Ban Ban** Laos
77C4 **Ban Betong** Thai
45C1 **Banbridge** N Ire
43D3 **Banbury** Eng
44C3 **Banchory** Scot
25D3 **Banco Chinchorro** *Is* Mexico
15C1 **Bancroft** Can
86A1 **Bānda** India
70A3 **Banda Aceh** Indon
97B4 **Bandama** *R* Ivory Coast
91C4 **Bandar Abbās** Iran
90A2 **Bandar Anzali** Iran
99F2 **Bandarbeyla** Somalia
91B4 **Bandar-e Daylam** Iran
91B4 **Bandar-e Lengheh** Iran
91B4 **Bandar-e Māqām** Iran
91B4 **Bandar-e Rig** Iran
90B2 **Bandar-e Torkoman** Iran
91A3 **Bandar Khomeynī** Iran
78C2 **Bandar Seri Begawan** Brunei
71D4 **Banda S** Indon
91C4 **Band Boni** Iran
35C2 **Bandeira** *Mt* Brazil
97B3 **Bandiagara** Mali
60C5 **Bandirma** Turk
45B3 **Bandon** Irish Rep
98B3 **Bandundu** Zaïre
78B4 **Bandung** Indon
25E2 **Banes** Cuba
13D2 **Banff** Can
44C3 **Banff** Scot
5G4 **Banff** *R* Can
13D2 **Banff Nat Pk** Can
87B2 **Bangalore** India
98C2 **Bangassou** CAR
70C3 **Banggi** *I* Malay
95B1 **Banghāzī** Libya
76D2 **Bang Hieng** *R* Laos
78B3 **Bangka** *I* Indon
78A3 **Bangko** Indon
76C3 **Bangkok** Thai
82C3 **Bangladesh** Republic, Asia
84D2 **Bangong Co** *L* China
10D2 **Bangor** Maine, USA
45D1 **Bangor** N Ire
16B2 **Bangor** Pennsylvania, USA
42B3 **Bangor** Wales
78D3 **Bangsalsembera** Indon
76B3 **Bang Saphan Yai** Thai
79B2 **Bangued** Phil
98B2 **Bangui** CAR
100C2 **Bangweulu** *L* Zambia
77C4 **Ban Hat Yai** Thai
76C2 **Ban Hin Heup** Laos
76C1 **Ban Houei Sai** Laos
76B3 **Ban Hua Hin** Thai

97B3 **Bani** *R* Mali
97C3 **Bani Bangou** Niger
95A1 **Bani Walid** Libya
92C2 **Bāniyās** Syria
94B2 **Baniyas** Syria
52C2 **Banja Luka** Bosnia-Herzegovina
78C3 **Banjarmasin** Indon
97A3 **Banjul** The Gambia
77B4 **Ban Kantang** Thai
76D2 **Ban Khemmarat** Laos
77B4 **Ban Khok Kloi** Thai
71F5 **Banks I** Aust
5E4 **Banks I** British Columbia, Can
4F2 **Banks I** Northwest Territories, Can
20C1 **Banks L** USA
111B2 **Banks Pen** NZ
109C4 **Banks Str** Aust
86B2 **Bankura** India
76B2 **Ban Mae Sariang** Thai
76B2 **Ban Mae Sot** Thai
76D3 **Ban Me Thuot** Viet
45C1 **Bann** *R* N Ire
77B4 **Ban Na San** Thai
84C2 **Bannu** Pak
34A3 **Baños Maule** Chile
76C2 **Ban Pak Neun** Laos
77C4 **Ban Pak Phanang** Thai
76D3 **Ban Ru Kroy** Camb
76B3 **Ban Sai Yok** Thai
76C3 **Ban Sattahip** Thai
59B3 **Banská Bystrica** Slovakia
85C4 **Bānswāra** India
77B4 **Ban Tha Kham** Thai
76D2 **Ban Thateng** Laos
76C2 **Ban Tha Tum** Thai
41B3 **Bantry** Irish Rep
41A3 **Bantry** *B* Irish Rep
76D3 **Ban Ya Soup** Viet
78C4 **Banyuwangi** Indon
72C3 **Baofeng** China
76C1 **Bao Ha** Viet
72B3 **Baoji** China
76D3 **Bao Loc** Viet
68B4 **Baoshan** China
72C1 **Baotou** China
87C1 **Bāpatla** India
46B1 **Bapaume** France
93D3 **Ba'Qūbah** Iraq
32J7 **Baquerizo Morena** Ecuador
54A2 **Bar** Montenegro, Yugos
99D1 **Bara** Sudan
99E2 **Baraawe** Somalia
78D3 **Barabai** Indon
86A1 **Bāra Banki** India
65J4 **Barabinsk** Russian Fed
65J4 **Barabinskaya Step** *Steppe* Kazakhstan/Russian Fed
50B1 **Baracaldo** Spain
26C2 **Baracoa** Cuba
94C2 **Baradá** *R* Syria
109C2 **Baradine** Aust
87A1 **Bārāmati** India
84C2 **Baramula** Pak
85D3 **Bārān** India
79B3 **Barangas** Phil
4E4 **Baranof I** USA
60C3 **Baranovichi** Belorussia
108A2 **Baratta** Aust
86B1 **Barauni** India
31C6 **Barbacena** Brazil
27F4 **Barbados** *I* Caribbean S
51C1 **Barbastro** Spain
101H1 **Barberton** S Africa
48B2 **Barbezieux** France
32C2 **Barbòsa** Colombia
27E3 **Barbuda** *I* Caribbean S
107D3 **Barcaldine** Aust
Barce = Al Marj
53C3 **Barcellona** Italy
51C1 **Barcelona** Spain

33E1 **Barcelona** Ven
107D3 **Barcoo** *R* Aust
34B3 **Barda del Medio** Arg
95A2 **Bardai** Chad
29C3 **Bardas Blancas** Arg
86B2 **Barddhamān** India
59C3 **Bardejov** Slovakia
47C2 **Bardi** Italy
47B2 **Bardonecchia** Italy
43B3 **Bardsey** *I* Wales
84D3 **Bareilly** India
64D2 **Barentsøya** *I* Barents S
64E2 **Barents S** Russian Fed
95C3 **Barentu** Eritrea
86A2 **Bargarh** India
47B2 **Barge** Italy
63D2 **Barguzin** Russian Fed
63D2 **Barguzin** *R* Russian Fed
86B2 **Barhi** India
53C2 **Bari** Italy
51D2 **Barika** Alg
32C2 **Barinas** Ven
86B2 **Baripāda** India
85C4 **Bari Sādri** India
86C2 **Barisal** Bang
78C3 **Barito** *R* Indon
95A2 **Barjuj** *Watercourse* Libya
73A3 **Barkam** China
18C2 **Barkley,L** USA
13B3 **Barkley Sd** Can
100B4 **Barkly East** S Africa
106C2 **Barkly Tableland** *Mts* Aust
46C2 **Bar-le-Duc** France
106A3 **Barlee,L** Aust
106A3 **Barlee Range** *Mts* Aust
53C2 **Barletta** Italy
85C3 **Barmer** India
108B2 **Barmera** Aust
43B3 **Barmouth** Wales
42D2 **Barnard Castle** Eng
65K4 **Barnaul** Russian Fed
16B3 **Barnegat** USA
16B3 **Barnegat B** USA
6C2 **Barnes Icecap** Can
17B1 **Barnesville** Georgia, USA
14B3 **Barnesville** Ohio, USA
42D2 **Barnsley** Eng
43B4 **Barnstaple** Eng
97C4 **Baro** Nig
86C1 **Barpeta** India
32D1 **Barquisimeto** Ven
31C4 **Barra** Brazil
44A3 **Barra** *I* Scot
109D2 **Barraba** Aust
23A2 **Barra de Navidad** Mexico
35C2 **Barra de Piraí** Brazil
35A1 **Barragem de São Simão** *Res* Brazil
35A1 **Barra do Garças** Brazil
35B1 **Barragem Agua Vermelha** *Res* Brazil
35B1 **Barragem do Castelo do Bode** *Res* Port
50A2 **Barragem do Maranhão** *Res* Port
35A1 **Barragem Três Irmãos** *Res* Brazil
44A3 **Barra Head** *Pt* Scot
31C6 **Barra Mansa** Brazil
32B6 **Barranca** Peru
32C2 **Barrancabermeja** Colombia
33E2 **Barrancas** Ven
30E4 **Barranqueras** Arg
32C1 **Barranquilla** Colombia
44A3 **Barra,Sound of** *Chan* Scot
16C1 **Barre** USA
34B2 **Barreal** Arg
31C4 **Barreiras** Brazil
50A2 **Barreiro** Port

31D3 **Barreiros** Brazil
107D5 **Barren,C** Aust
12D3 **Barren Is** USA
31B6 **Barretos** Brazil
13E2 **Barrhead** Can
14C2 **Barrie** Can
13C2 **Barrière** Can
108B2 **Barrier Range** *Mts* Aust
107E4 **Barrington,Mt** Aust
27N2 **Barrouaillie** St Vincent and the Grenadines
4C2 **Barrow** USA
45C2 **Barrow** *R* Irish Rep
106C3 **Barrow Creek** Aust
106A3 **Barrow I** Aust
42C2 **Barrow-in-Furness** Eng
4C2 **Barrow,Pt** USA
6A2 **Barrow Str** Can
15C1 **Barry's Bay** Can
87B1 **Barsi** India
9B3 **Barstow** USA
49C2 **Bar-sur-Aube** France
33F2 **Bartica** Guyana
92B1 **Bartın** Turk
107D2 **Bartle Frere,Mt** Aust
9D3 **Bartlesville** USA
101C3 **Bartolomeu Dias** Mozam
58C2 **Bartoszyce** Pol
78C4 **Barung** *I* Indon
85D4 **Barwāh** India
85C4 **Barwāni** India
109C1 **Barwon** *R* Aust
61G3 **Barysh** Russian Fed
98B2 **Basankusu** Zaïre
34D2 **Basavilbas** Arg
79B1 **Basco** Phil
52A1 **Basel** Switz
53C2 **Basento** *R* Italy
13E2 **Bashaw** Can
79B1 **Bashi Chan** Phil
61H3 **Bashkortostan** Russian Fed
79B4 **Basilan** *I* Phil
43E4 **Basildon** Eng
43D4 **Basingstoke** Eng
8B2 **Basin Region** USA
93E3 **Basra** Iraq
46D2 **Bas-Rhin** Department, France
76D3 **Bassac** *R* Camb
13E2 **Bassano** Can
52B1 **Bassano** Italy
47D2 **Bassano del Grappa** Italy
97C4 **Bassari** Togo
101C3 **Bassas da India** *I* Mozam Chan
76A2 **Bassein** Burma
27E3 **Basse Terre** Guadeloupe
97C4 **Bassila** Benin
22C2 **Bass Lake** USA
107D4 **Bass Str** Aust
39G7 **Båstad** Sweden
91B4 **Bastak** Iran
86A1 **Basti** India
52A2 **Bastia** Corse
57B3 **Bastogne** Belg
19B3 **Bastrop** Louisiana, USA
19A3 **Bastrop** Texas, USA
98A3 **Bata** Eq Guinea
78C3 **Batakan** Indon
84D2 **Batala** India
68B3 **Batang** China
98B2 **Batangafo** CAR
79B1 **Batan Is** Phil
35B2 **Batatais** Brazil
15C2 **Batavia** USA
109D3 **Batemans Bay** Aust
17B1 **Batesburg** USA
18B2 **Batesville** Arkansas, USA
19C3 **Batesville** Mississippi, USA
43C4 **Bath** Eng
15C2 **Bath** New York, USA
98B1 **Batha** *R* Chad
107D4 **Bathurst** Aust
7D5 **Bathurst** Can

Block Island Sd

1C6 **Bering Str** USA/ Russian Fed
91C4 **Berizak** Iran
50B2 **Berja** Spain
8A3 **Berkeley** USA
112B2 **Berkner I** Ant
54B2 **Berkovitsa** Bulg
43D4 **Berkshire** County, Eng
16C1 **Berkshire Hills** USA
13D2 **Berland** R Can
56C2 **Berlin** Germany
56C2 **Berlin** State, Germany
15D2 **Berlin** New Hampshire, USA
30D3 **Bermejo** Bol
30D4 **Bermejo** R Arg
3M5 **Bermuda** I Atlantic O
52A1 **Bern** Switz
16B2 **Bernardsville** USA
34C3 **Bernasconi** Arg
56C2 **Bernburg** Germany
47B1 **Berner Oberland** Mts Switz
6B2 **Bernier B** Can
57C3 **Berounka** R Czech Republic
108B2 **Berri** Aust
96C1 **Berriane** Alg
48C2 **Berry** Region, France
22A1 **Berryessa,L** USA
11C4 **Berry Is** The Bahamas
98B2 **Bertoua** Cam
45B2 **Bertraghboy B** Irish Rep
15C2 **Berwick** USA
42C2 **Berwick-upon-Tweed** Eng
43C3 **Berwyn** Mts Wales
101D2 **Besalampy** Madag
49D2 **Besançon** France
59C3 **Beskidy Zachodnie** Mts Pol
93C2 **Besni** Turk
94B3 **Besor** R Israel
11B3 **Bessemer** USA
101D2 **Betafo** Madag
50A1 **Betanzos** Spain
94B3 **Bet Guvrin** Israel
101G1 **Bethal** S Africa
100A3 **Bethanie** Namibia
18B1 **Bethany** Missouri, USA
18A2 **Bethany** Oklahoma, USA
4B3 **Bethel** Alaska, USA
16C2 **Bethel** Connecticut, USA
14B2 **Bethel Park** USA
15C3 **Bethesda** USA
94B3 **Bethlehem** Israel
101G1 **Bethlehem** S Africa
15C2 **Bethlehem** USA
48C1 **Bethune** France
101D3 **Betioky** Madag
108B1 **Betoota** Aust
98B2 **Betou** Congo
82A1 **Betpak Dala** Steppe Kazakhstan
101D3 **Betroka** Madag
7D5 **Betsiamites** Can
86A1 **Bettiah** India
12D1 **Bettles** USA
47C2 **Béttola** Italy
85D4 **Betul** India
85D3 **Betwa** R India
46D1 **Betzdorf** Germany
12C3 **Beverley,L** USA
16D1 **Beverly** USA
21B3 **Beverly Hills** USA
97B4 **Beyla** Guinea
87B2 **Beypore** India
Beyrouth = Beirut
92B2 **Beyşehir** Turk
92B2 **Beyşehir Gölü** L Turk
94B2 **Beyt Shean** Israel
47C1 **Bezau** Austria
60E2 **Bezhetsk** Russian Fed
49C3 **Béziers** France
90C2 **Bezmein** Turkmenistan

63C2 **Beznosova** Russian Fed
86B1 **Bhadgaon** Nepal
87C1 **Bhadrachalam** India
86B2 **Bhadrakh** India
87B2 **Bhadra Res** India
87B2 **Bhadravati** India
84B3 **Bhag** Pak
86B1 **Bhagalpur** India
84C2 **Bhakkar** Pak
82D3 **Bhamo** Burma
85D4 **Bhandara** India
85D3 **Bharatpur** India
85C4 **Bharuch** India
86B2 **Bhatiapara Ghat** Bang
84C2 **Bhatinda** India
87A2 **Bhatkal** India
86B2 **Bhatpara** India
85C4 **Bhavnagar** India
84C2 **Bhera** Pak
86A1 **Bheri** R Nepal
86A2 **Bhilai** India
85C3 **Bhilwara** India
87C1 **Bhimavaram** India
85D3 **Bhind** India
84D3 **Bhiwani** India
87B1 **Bhongir** India
85D4 **Bhopal** India
86B2 **Bhubaneshwar** India
85B4 **Bhuj** India
85D4 **Bhusawal** India
82C3 **Bhutan** Kingdom, Asia
71E4 **Biak** I Indon
58C2 **Biala Podlaska** Pol
58B2 **Bialograd** Pol
58C2 **Bialystok** Pol
38A1 **Biargtangar** C Iceland
90C2 **Biarjmand** Iran
48B3 **Biarritz** France
47C1 **Biasca** Switz
92B4 **Biba** Egypt
74E2 **Bibai** Japan
100A2 **Bibala** Angola
57B3 **Biberach** Germany
97B4 **Bibiani** Ghana
54C1 **Bicaz** Rom
97C4 **Bida** Nig
87B1 **Bidar** India
91C5 **Bidbid** Oman
43B4 **Bideford** Eng
43B4 **Bideford B** Eng
96C2 **Bidon 5** Alg
58C2 **Biebrza** Pol
52A1 **Biel** Switz
59B2 **Bielawa** Pol
56B2 **Bielefeld** Germany
47B1 **Bieler See** L Switz
52A1 **Biella** Italy
58C2 **Bielsk Podlaski** Pol
76D3 **Bien Hoa** Viet
53B2 **Biferno** R Italy
92A1 **Biga** Turk
55C3 **Bigadiç** Turk
19C3 **Big Black** R USA
18A1 **Big Blue** R USA
17B2 **Big Cypress Swamp** USA
4D3 **Big Delta** USA
49D2 **Bigent** Germany
13F2 **Biggar** Can
5H4 **Biggar Kindersley** Can
109D1 **Biggenden** Aust
12G3 **Bigger,Mt** Can
8C2 **Bighorn** R USA
76C3 **Bight of Bangkok** B Thai
97C4 **Bight of Benin** B W Africa
97C4 **Bight of Biafra** B Cam
6C3 **Big I** Can
47C1 **Bignasco** Switz
97A3 **Bignona** Sen
21B2 **Big Pine** USA
17B2 **Big Pine Key** USA
22C3 **Big Pine Mt** USA
14A2 **Big Rapids** USA
5H4 **Big River** Can
9C3 **Big Spring** USA
7A4 **Big Trout L** Can

7B4 **Big Trout Lake** Can
52C2 **Bihać** Bosnia-Herzegovina
86B1 **Bihar** India
86B2 **Bihar** State, India
99D3 **Biharamulo** Tanz
60B4 **Bihor** Mt Rom
87B1 **Bijapur** India
87C1 **Bijapur** India
90A2 **Bijar** Iran
86A1 **Bijauri** Nepal
54A2 **Bijeljina** Bosnia-Herzegovina
73B4 **Bijie** China
84D3 **Bijnor** India
84C3 **Bijnot** Pak
84C3 **Bikaner** India
94B2 **Bikfaya** Leb
69F2 **Bikin** Russian Fed
98B3 **Bikoro** Zaïre
85C3 **Bilara** India
84D2 **Bilaspur** India
86A2 **Bilaspur** India
76B3 **Bilauktaung Range** Mts Thai
50B1 **Bilbao** Spain
Bilbo = Bilbao
59B3 **Bilé** R Czech Republic
54A2 **Bileća** Bosnia-Herzegovina
92B1 **Bilecik** Turk
98C2 **Bili** R Zaïre
79B3 **Biliran** I Phil
8C2 **Billings** USA
95A3 **Bilma** Niger
11B3 **Biloxi** USA
98C1 **Biltine** Chad
85D4 **Bina-Etawa** India
79B3 **Binalbagan** Phil
101C2 **Bindura** Zim
100B2 **Binga** Zim
101C2 **Binga** Mt Zim
109D1 **Bingara** Aust
57B3 **Bingen** Germany
10C2 **Binghamton** USA
78D1 **Bingkor** Malay
93D2 **Bingöl** Turk
72D3 **Binhai** China
78A2 **Bintan** I Indon
78A3 **Bintuhan** Indon
78C2 **Bintulu** Malay
29B3 **Bió Bió** R Chile
102J4 **Bioko** I Atlantic O
87B1 **Bir** India
95B2 **Bir Abu Husein** Well Egypt
95B2 **Bi'r al Harash** Well Libya
98C1 **Birao** CAR
86B1 **Biratnagar** Nepal
12E1 **Birch Creek** USA
108B3 **Birchip** Aust
5G4 **Birch Mts** Can
7A4 **Bird** Can
106C3 **Birdsville** Aust
106C2 **Birdum** Aust
86A1 **Birganj** Nepal
94A3 **Bir Gifgafa** Well Egypt
94A3 **Bir Hasana** Well Egypt
35A2 **Birigui** Brazil
90C3 **Birjand** Iran
92B4 **Birkat Qarun** L Egypt
46D2 **Birkenfeld** Germany
42C3 **Birkenhead** Eng
60C4 **Bîrlad** Rom
94A3 **Bir Lahfan** Well Egypt
43C3 **Birmingham** Eng
11B3 **Birmingham** USA
95B2 **Bir Misaha** Well Egypt
96A2 **Bir Moghrein** Maur
97C3 **Birnin Kebbi** Nig
97C3 **Birni N'Konni** Nig
69F2 **Birobidzhan** Russian Fed
45C2 **Birr** Irish Rep
51C2 **Bir Rabalou** Alg
109C1 **Birrie** R Aust
44C2 **Birsay** Scot
61J2 **Birsk** Russian Fed

95B2 **Bîr Tarfâwi** Well Egypt
63B2 **Biryusa** Russian Fed
39J7 **Biržai** Lithuania
96B2 **Bir Zreigat** Well Maur
48A2 **Biscay,B of** France/ Spain
17B2 **Biscayne B** USA
46D2 **Bischwiller** France
73B4 **Bishan** China
82B1 **Bishkek** Kirghizia
8B3 **Bishop** USA
42D2 **Bishop Auckland** Eng
43E4 **Bishop's Stortford** Eng
86A2 **Bishrampur** India
96C1 **Biskra** Alg
79C4 **Bislig** Phil
8C2 **Bismarck** USA
90A3 **Bisotûn** Iran
97A3 **Bissau** Guinea-Bissau
10A1 **Bissett** Can
5G4 **Bistcho L** Can
54C1 **Bistrita** R Rom
98B2 **Bitam** Gabon
57B3 **Bitburg** Germany
46D2 **Bitche** France
93D2 **Bitlis** Turk
55B2 **Bitola** Macedonia
56C2 **Bitterfeld** Germany
100A4 **Bitterfontein** S Africa
92B3 **Bitter Lakes** Egypt
8B2 **Bitteroot Range** Mts USA
74D3 **Biwa-ko** L Japan
99E1 **Biyo Kaboba** Eth
65K4 **Biysk** Russian Fed
96C1 **Bizerte** Tunisia
51C2 **Bj bou Arréridj** Alg
52C1 **Bjelovar** Croatia
96B2 **Bj Flye Ste Marie** Alg
64C2 **Bjørnøya** I Barents S
12F1 **Black** R USA
18B2 **Black** R USA
107D3 **Blackall** Aust
42C3 **Blackburn** Eng
4D3 **Blackburn,Mt** USA
13E2 **Black Diamond** Can
5H5 **Black Hills** USA
44B3 **Black Isle** Pen Scot
27R3 **Blackman's** Barbados
43C4 **Black Mts** Wales
43C3 **Blackpool** Eng
27H1 **Black River** Jamaica
8B2 **Black Rock Desert** USA
65E5 **Black S** Asia/Europe
45A1 **Blacksod B** Irish Rep
109D2 **Black Sugarloaf** Mt Aust
97B3 **Black Volta** R Ghana
41B3 **Blackwater** R Irish Rep
18A2 **Blackwell** USA
54B2 **Blagoevgrad** Bulg
63E2 **Blagoveshchensk** Russian Fed
20B1 **Blaine** USA
44C3 **Blair Atholl** Scot
44C3 **Blairgowrie** Scot
17B1 **Blakely** USA
108A1 **Blanche,L** Aust
34A2 **Blanco** R Arg
34B1 **Blanco** R Arg
8A2 **Blanco,C** USA
7E4 **Blanc Sablon** Can
43C4 **Blandford Forum** Eng
46A2 **Blangy-sur-Bresle** France
46B1 **Blankenberge** Belg
101C2 **Blantyre** Malawi
48B2 **Blaye** France
109C2 **Blayney** Aust
111B2 **Blenheim** NZ
96C1 **Blida** Alg
14B1 **Blind River** Can
108A2 **Blinman** Aust
78C4 **Blitar** Indon
15D2 **Block I** USA
16D2 **Block Island Sd** USA

Bloemfontein

Ref	Name
42D3	Bradford Eng
44E1	Brae Scot
44C3	Braemar Scot
50A1	Braga Port
34C3	Bragado Arg
50A1	Bragana Port
31B2	Bragança Brazil
35B2	Bragança Paulista Brazil
86C2	Brahman-Baria Bang
86B2	Brāhmani R India
86C1	Brahmaputra R India
7E5	Braie Verte Can
60C4	Brăila Rom
10A2	Brainerd USA
97A3	Brakna Region, Maur
5F4	Bralorne Can
14C2	Brampton Can
33E3	Branco R Brazil
100A3	Brandberg Mt Namibia
56C2	Brandenburg Germany
56C2	Brandenburg State, Germany
101G1	Brandfort S Africa
8D2	Brandon Can
100B4	Brandvlei S Africa
57C2	Brandys nad Lebem Czech Republic
58B2	Braniewo Pol
10B2	Brantford Can
108B3	Branxholme Aust
7D5	Bras D'Or L Can
35C1	Brasila de Minas Brazil
32D6	Brasiléia Brazil
31B5	Brasilia Brazil
54C1	Brasov Rom
78D1	Brassay Range Mts Malay
59B3	Bratislava Slovakia
63C2	Bratsk Russian Fed
15D2	Brattleboro USA
56C2	Braunschweig Germany
97A4	Brava I Cape Verde
9B3	Brawley USA
45C2	Bray Irish Rep
6C3	Bray I Can
13D2	Brazeau R Can
13D2	Brazeau,Mt Can
28D4	Brazil Republic, S America
103G5	Brazil Basin Atlantic O
9D3	Brazos R USA
98B3	Brazzaville Congo
57C3	Brdy Upland Czech Republic
111A3	Breaksea Sd NZ
110B1	Bream B NZ
78B4	Brebes Indon
44C3	Brechin Scot
46C1	Brecht Belg
59B3	Břeclav Czech Republic
43C4	Brecon Wales
43C4	Brecon Beacons Mts Wales
43B3	Brecon Beacons Nat Pk Wales
56A2	Breda Neth
100B4	Bredasdorp S Africa
38H6	Bredbyn Sweden
61J3	Bredy Russian Fed
15C2	Breezewood USA
47C1	Bregenz Austria
47C1	Bregenzer Ache R Austria
38A1	Breiðafjörður B Iceland
47C2	Brembo R Italy
17A1	Bremen USA
56B2	Bremen Germany
56B2	Bremerhaven Germany
20B1	Bremerton USA
19A3	Brenham USA
57C3	Brenner P Austria/Italy
47D2	Breno Italy
47D2	Brenta R Italy
22B2	Brentwood USA

Ref	Name
52B1	Brescia Italy
	Breslau = Wrocław
47D1	Bressanone Italy
44E1	Bressay I Scot
48B2	Bressuire France
58C2	Brest Belorussia
48B2	Brest France
48B2	Bretagne Region, France
46B2	Breteuil France
16B2	Breton Woods USA
110B1	Brett,C NZ
109C1	Brewarrina Aust
16C2	Brewster New York, USA
20C1	Brewster Washington, USA
101G1	Breyten S Africa
52C1	Brežice Slovenia
98C2	Bria CAR
49D3	Briancon France
49C2	Briare France
21B2	Bridgeport California, USA
15D2	Bridgeport Connecticut, USA
19A3	Bridgeport Texas, USA
22C1	Bridgeport Res USA
16B3	Bridgeton USA
27F4	Bridgetown Barbados
7D5	Bridgewater Can
16D2	Bridgewater USA
43C4	Bridgwater Eng
43C4	Bridgwater B Eng
42D2	Bridlington Eng
109C4	Bridport Aust
47B1	Brienzer See L Switz
46C2	Briey France
52A1	Brig Switz
8B2	Brigham City USA
109C3	Bright Aust
43D4	Brighton Eng
46E1	Brilon Germany
55A2	Brindisi Italy
19B3	Brinkley USA
107E3	Brisbane Aust
15D2	Bristol Connecticut, USA
43C4	Bristol Eng
15D2	Bristol Pennsylvania, USA
16D2	Bristol Rhode Island, USA
11B3	Bristol Tennessee, USA
12B3	Bristol B USA
43B4	Bristol Chan Eng/Wales
4D3	British Mts USA
5F4	British Columbia Province, Can
6B1	British Empire Range Mts Can
101G1	Brits S Africa
100B4	Britstown S Africa
48C2	Brive France
59B3	Brno Czech Republic
17B1	Broad R USA
7C4	Broadback R Can
44A2	Broad Bay Inlet Scot
44B3	Broadford Scot
5H4	Brochet Can
4G2	Brock I Can
15C2	Brockport USA
16D1	Brockton USA
15C2	Brockville Can
6B2	Brodeur Pen Can
42B2	Brodick Scot
58B2	Brodnica Pol
60C3	Brody Ukraine
19B3	Broken Bow Oklahoma, USA
19B3	Broken Bow L USA
107D4	Broken Hill Aust
47C2	Broni Italy
38G5	Brønnøysund Nor
16C2	Bronx Borough, New York, USA
79A4	Brooke's Point Phil
18B2	Brookfield Missouri, USA
11A3	Brookhaven USA

Ref	Name
20B2	Brookings Oregon, USA
8D2	Brookings South Dakota, USA
16D1	Brookline USA
16C2	Brooklyn Borough, New York, USA
5G4	Brooks Can
12C3	Brooks,L USA
12A1	Brooks Mt USA
4C3	Brooks Range Mts USA
17B2	Brooksville USA
109D1	Brooloo Aust
106B2	Broome Aust
44C2	Brora Scot
20B2	Brothers USA
95A3	Broulkou Chad
13E3	Browning USA
9D4	Brownsville USA
9D3	Brownwood USA
46B1	Bruay-en-Artois France
106A3	Bruce,Mt Aust
14B1	Bruce Pen Can
59B3	Brück an der Mur Austria
	Bruges = Brugge
46B1	Brugge Belg
46D1	Brühl Germany
78C2	Brunei Sultanate, S E Asia
52B1	Brunico Italy
111B2	Brunner,L NZ
11B3	Brunswick Georgia, USA
18B2	Brunswick Mississippi, USA
29B6	Brunswick,Pen de Chile
109C4	Bruny I Aust
61F1	Brusenets Russian Fed
26A3	Brus Laguna Honduras
	Brüssel = Bruxelles
56A2	Bruxelles Belg
9D3	Bryan USA
108A2	Bryan,Mt Aust
60D3	Bryansk Russian Fed
19B3	Bryant USA
59B2	Brzeg Pol
93E4	Būbiyan I Kuwait/Iraq
99D3	Bubu R Tanz
32C2	Bucaramanga Colombia
44D3	Buchan Oilfield N Sea
97A4	Buchanan Lib
44D3	Buchan Deep N Sea
6C2	Buchan G Can
40C2	Buchan Ness Pen Scot
7E5	Buchans Can
34C2	Buchardo Arg
	Bucharest = Bucureşti
47C1	Buchs Switz
43D3	Buckingham Eng
12B1	Buckland USA
12B1	Buckland R USA
108A2	Buckleboo Aust
98B3	Buco Zau Congo
54C2	Bucureşti Rom
59B3	Budapest Hung
84D3	Budaun India
43B4	Bude Eng
19B3	Bude USA
61F5	Budennovsk Russian Fed
54A2	Budva Montenegro, Yugos
98A2	Buéa Cam
22B3	Buellton USA
34B2	Buena Esperanza Arg
32B3	Buenaventura Colombia
23A2	Buenavista Mexico
29E2	Buenos Aires Arg
29D3	Buenos Aires State, Arg
18B2	Buffalo Mississipi, USA

Ref	Name
10C2	Buffalo New York, USA
8C2	Buffalo South Dakota, USA
19A3	Buffalo Texas, USA
8C2	Buffalo Wyoming, USA
101H1	Buffalo R S Africa
13E2	Buffalo L Alberta, Can
5G3	Buffalo L Northwest Territories, Can
5H4	Buffalo Narrows Can
17B1	Buford USA
54C2	Buftea Rom
59C2	Bug R Pol/Ukraine
32B3	Buga Colombia
90B2	Bugdayli Turkmenistan
61H3	Bugulma Russian Fed
61H3	Buguruslan Russian Fed
93C2	Buhayrat al Asad Res Syria
41C3	Builth Wells Wales
34A2	Buin Chile
99C3	Bujumbura Burundi
98C3	Bukama Zaïre
99C3	Bukavu Zaïre
80E2	Bukhara Uzbekistan
78C2	Bukit Batubrok Mt Indon
70B4	Bukittinggi Indon
99D3	Bukoba Tanz
78D3	Buku Gandadiwata Mt Indon
71E4	Bula Indon
79B3	Bulan Phil
84D3	Bulandshahr India
100B3	Bulawayo Zim
55C3	Buldan Turk
85D4	Buldāna India
68C2	Bulgan Mongolia
54B2	Bulgaria Republic, Europe
47B1	Bulle Switz
111B2	Buller R NZ
109C3	Buller,Mt Aust
106A4	Bullfinch Aust
108B1	Bulloo R Aust
108B1	Bulloo Downs Aust
108B1	Bulloo L Aust
18B2	Bull Shoals Res USA
34A3	Bulnes Chile
71F4	Bulolo PNG
101G1	Bultfontein S Africa
98C2	Bumba Zaïre
76B2	Bumphal Dam Thai
99D2	Buna Kenya
106A4	Bunbury Aust
45C1	Buncrana Irish Rep
107E3	Bundaberg Aust
109D2	Bundarra Aust
85D3	Bündi India
45B1	Bundoran Irish Rep
109C1	Bungil R Aust
98B3	Bungo Angola
75A2	Bungo-suidō Str Japan
70B3	Bunguran I Ind
99D2	Bunia Zaïre
18B2	Bunker USA
19B3	Bunkie USA
17B2	Bunnell USA
78C3	Buntok Indon
71D3	Buol Indon
94C2	Burāg Syria
98C1	Buram Sudan
99E2	Burao Somalia
79B3	Burauen Phil
80C3	Buraydah S Arabia
21B3	Burbank USA
109C2	Burcher Aust
92B2	Burdur Turk
63F3	Bureinskiy Khrebet Mts Russian Fed
56C2	Burg Germany
54C2	Burgas Bulg
17C1	Burgaw USA
47B1	Burgdorf Switz
100B4	Burgersdorp S Africa
50B1	Burgos Spain
58B1	Burgsvik Sweden

Burhaniye

55C3 **Burhaniye** Turk
85D4 **Burhänpur** India
79B3 **Burias** / Phil
76C2 **Buriram** Thai
35B1 **Buritis** Brazil
13B2 **Burke Chan** Can
106C2 **Burketown** Aust
97B3 **Burkina** Republic, Africa
15C1 **Burks Falls** Can
8B2 **Burley** USA
10A2 **Burlington** Iowa, USA
16B2 **Burlington** New Jersey, USA
10C2 **Burlington** Vermont, USA
20B1 **Burlington** Washington, USA
83D3 **Burma** Republic, Asia
20B2 **Burney** USA
16A2 **Burnham** USA
107D5 **Burnie** Aust
42C3 **Burnley** Eng
20C2 **Burns** USA
5F4 **Burns Lake** Can
82C1 **Burqin** China
108A2 **Burra** Aust
109D2 **Burragorang,L** Aust
44C2 **Burray** / Scot
109C2 **Burren Junction** Aust
109C2 **Burrinjuck Res** Aust
60C5 **Bursa** Turk
80B3 **Bur Safâga** Egypt
Bûr Sa'îd = Port Said
14B2 **Burton** USA
43D3 **Burton upon Trent** Eng
38J6 **Burtrask** Sweden
108B2 **Burtundy** Aust
71D4 **Buru** Indon
99C3 **Burundi** Republic, Africa
78A2 **Burung** Indon
63D2 **Buryatskaya Respublika,** Russian Fed
99D1 **Burye** Eth
61H4 **Burynshik** Kazakhstan
43E3 **Bury St Edmunds** Eng
91B4 **Büshehr** Iran
98B3 **Busira** R Zaïre
58C2 **Buskozdroj** Pol
94C2 **Busrä ash Shäm** Syria
106A4 **Busselton** Aust
49D2 **Busto** Italy
52A1 **Busto Arsizio** Italy
79A3 **Busuanga** / Phil
98C2 **Buta** Zaire
34B3 **Buta Ranquil** Arg
99C3 **Butare** Rwanda
42B2 **Bute** / Scot
69E2 **Butha Qi** China
14C2 **Butler** USA
8B2 **Butte** USA
77C4 **Butterworth** Malay
40B2 **Butt of Lewis** C Scot
6D3 **Button Is** Can
79C4 **Butuan** Phil
71D4 **Butung** / Indon
61F3 **Buturlinovka** Russian Fed
86A1 **Butwal** Nepal
99E2 **Buulo Barde** Somalia
99E2 **Buur Hakaba** Somalia
61F2 **Buy** Russian Fed
72B1 **Buyant Ovvo** Mongolia
61G5 **Buynaksk** Russian Fed
63D3 **Buyr Nuur** L Mongolia
93D2 **Büyük Ağri** Mt Turk
92A2 **Büyük Menderes** R Turk
54C1 **Buzău** Rom
54C1 **Buzau** R Rom
61H3 **Buzuluk** Russian Fed

16D2 **Buzzards B** USA
54C2 **Byala** Bulg
54B2 **Byala Slatina** Bulg
4H2 **Byam Martin** Chan Can
4H2 **Byam Martin I** Can
Byblos = Jubail
94B1 **Byblos** Hist Site, Leb
58B2 **Bydgoszcz** Pol
39F7 **Bygland** Nor
6C2 **Bylot I** Can
109C2 **Byrock** Aust
22B2 **Byron** USA
109D1 **Byron,C** Aust
59B2 **Bytom** Pol

C

30E4 **Caacupé** Par
100A2 **Caála** Angola
13B2 **Caamano Sd** Can
30E4 **Caazapá** Par
79B2 **Cabanatuan** Phil
31E3 **Cabedelo** Brazil
50A2 **Cabeza del Buey** Spain
34C3 **Cabildo** Arg
34A2 **Cabildo** Chile
32C1 **Cabimas** Ven
98B3 **Cabinda** Angola
98B3 **Cabinda** Province, Angola
27C3 **Cabo Beata** Dom Rep
51C2 **Cabo Binibeca** C Spain
53A3 **Cabo Carbonara** C Sardegna
34A3 **Cabo Carranza** C Chile
50A2 **Cabo Carvoeiro** C Port
9B3 **Cabo Colnett** C Mexico
32B2 **Cabo Corrientes** C Colombia
24B2 **Cabo Corrientes** C Mexico
26B3 **Cabo Cruz** C Cuba
50B1 **Cabo de Ajo** C Spain
51C1 **Cabo de Caballeria** C Spain
51C1 **Cabo de Creus** C Spain
50B2 **Cabo de Gata** C Spain
29C7 **Cabo de Hornos** C Chile
51C2 **Cabo de la Nao** C Spain
50A1 **Cabo de Peñas** C Spain
50A2 **Cabo de Roca** C Port
51C2 **Cabo de Salinas** C Spain
35C2 **Cabo de São Tomé** C Brazil
50A2 **Cabo de São Vicente** C Port
50A2 **Cabo de Sines** C Port
51C1 **Cabo de Tortosa** C Spain
29C4 **Cabo Dos Bahias** C Arg
50A2 **Cabo Espichel** C Port
9B4 **Cabo Falso** C Mexico
51B2 **Cabo Ferrat** C Alg
50A1 **Cabo Finisterre** C Spain
51C1 **Cabo Formentor** C Spain
35C2 **Cabo Frio** Brazil
35C2 **Cabo Frio** C Brazil
26A4 **Cabo Gracias à Dios** Honduras
31B2 **Cabo Maguarinho** C Brazil
50A2 **Cabo Negro** C Mor
109D1 **Caboolture** Aust
33G3 **Cabo Orange** C Brazil
21B3 **Cabo Punta Banda** C Mexico
101C2 **Cabora Bassa Dam** Mozam

24A1 **Caborca** Mexico
24C2 **Cabo Rojo** C Mexico
23B1 **Cabos** Mexico
29C6 **Cabo San Diego** C Arg
32A4 **Cabo San Lorenzo** C Ecuador
53A3 **Cabo Teulada** C Sardegna
50A2 **Cabo Trafalgar** C Spain
50B2 **Cabo Tres Forcas** C Mor
29C5 **Cabo Tres Puntas** C Arg
7D5 **Cabot Str** Can
50B2 **Cabra** Spain
50A1 **Cabreira** Mt Port
51C2 **Cabrera** / Spain
34A3 **Cabrero** Chile
51B2 **Cabriel** R Spain
23B2 **Cacahuamilpa** Mexico
54B2 **Čačak** Serbia, Yugos
23B2 **C A Carillo** Mexico
30E2 **Cáceres** Brazil
50A2 **Caceres** Spain
18B2 **Cache** R USA
13C2 **Cache Creek** Can
30C4 **Cachi** Arg
33G5 **Cachimbo** Brazil
31D4 **Cachoeira** Brazil
35A1 **Cachoeira Alta** Brazil
31D3 **Cachoeira de Paulo Alfonso** Waterfall Brazil
29F2 **Cachoeira do Sul** Brazil
31C6 **Cachoeiro de Itapemirim** Brazil
22C3 **Cachuma,L** USA
100A2 **Cacolo** Angola
100A2 **Caconda** Angola
35A1 **Caçu** Brazil
100A2 **Çaculuvar** R Angola
59B3 **Čadca** Slovakia
43C3 **Cader Idris** Mts Wales
10B2 **Cadillac** USA
79B3 **Cadiz** Phil
50A2 **Cadiz** Spain
48B2 **Caen** France
42B3 **Caernarfon** Wales
43B3 **Caernarfon B** Wales
94B2 **Caesarea** Hist Site Israel
31C4 **Caetité** Brazil
30C4 **Cafayate** Arg
92B2 **Çaga Tepe** Turk
79B2 **Cagayan** R Phil
79B4 **Cagayan de Oro** Phil
79B4 **Cagayan Is** Phil
53A3 **Cagliari** Sardegna
27D3 **Caguas** Puerto Rico
45B3 **Caha Mts** Irish Rep
45A3 **Cahersiveen** Irish Rep
45C2 **Cahir** Irish Rep
45C2 **Cahone Pt** Irish Rep
48C3 **Cahors** France
101C2 **Caia** Mozam
100B2 **Caianda** Angola
35A1 **Caiapó** R Brazil
35A1 **Caiapônia** Brazil
31D3 **Caicó** Brazil
26C2 **Caicos Is** Caribbean S
11C4 **Caicos Pass** The Bahamas
12C2 **Cairn Mt** USA
44C3 **Cairngorms** Mts Scot
107D2 **Cairns** Aust
92B3 **Cairo** Egypt
11B3 **Cairo** USA
108B1 **Caiwarro** Aust
32B5 **Cajabamba** Peru
32B5 **Cajamarca** Peru
27D5 **Cajabozo** Ven
54B2 **Calafat** Rom
29B6 **Calafate** Arg
79B3 **Calagua Is** Phil
51B1 **Calahorra** Spain
48C1 **Calais** France

30C3 **Calama** Chile
32C3 **Calamar** Colombia
79A3 **Calamian Group** Is Phil
98B3 **Calandula** Angola
70A3 **Calang** Indon
95B2 **Calanscio Sand Sea** Libya
79B3 **Calapan** Phil
54C2 **Calarasi** Rom
51B1 **Calatayud** Spain
22B2 **Calaveras Res** USA
79B3 **Calbayog** Phil
19B4 **Calcasieu L** USA
86B2 **Calcutta** India
50A2 **Caldas da Rainha** Port
31B5 **Caldas Novas** Brazil
30B4 **Caldera** Chile
8B2 **Caldwell** USA
29C5 **Caleta Olivia** Arg
9B3 **Calexico** USA
5G4 **Calgary** Can
17B1 **Calhoun** USA
17B1 **Calhoun Falls** USA
32B3 **Cali** Colombia
87B2 **Calicut** India
8B3 **Caliente** Nevada, USA
8A3 **California** State, USA
22C3 **California Aqueduct** USA
87B2 **Calimera,Pt** India
34B2 **Calingasta** Arg
22A1 **Calistoga** USA
108B1 **Callabonna** R Aust
108A1 **Callabonna,L** Aust
15C1 **Callander** Can
44B3 **Callander** Scot
108A1 **Callanna** Aust
32B6 **Callao** Peru
13E1 **Calling L** Can
23B1 **Calnali** Mexico
17B2 **Caloosahatchee** R USA
109D1 **Caloundra** Aust
23B2 **Calpulalpan** Mexico
53B3 **Caltanissetta** Italy
98B3 **Caluango** Angola
100A2 **Calulo** Angola
100A2 **Caluquembe** Angola
99F1 **Caluula** Somalia
13B2 **Calvert I** Can
52A2 **Calvi** Corse
23A1 **Calvillo** Mexico
100A4 **Calvinia** S Africa
25E2 **Camagüey** Cuba
25E2 **Camagüey,Arch de** Is Cuba
30B2 **Camaná** Peru
30C3 **Camargo** Bol
22C3 **Camarillo** USA
29C4 **Camarones** Arg
20B1 **Camas** USA
98B3 **Camaxilo** Angola
98B3 **Cambatela** Angola
76C3 **Cambodia** Republic, S E Asia
43B4 **Camborne** Eng
49C1 **Cambrai** France
43C3 **Cambrian Mts** Wales
14B2 **Cambridge** Can
43D3 **Cambridge** County, Eng
43E3 **Cambridge** Eng
27H1 **Cambridge** Jamaica
15C3 **Cambridge** Maryland, USA
15D2 **Cambridge** Massachussets, USA
110C1 **Cambridge** NZ
14B2 **Cambridge** Ohio, USA
4H3 **Cambridge Bay** Can
60E5 **Cam Burun** Pt Turk
11A3 **Camden** Arkansas, USA
109D2 **Camden** Aust
15D3 **Camden** New Jersey, USA
17B1 **Camden** South Carolina, USA
18B2 **Cameron** Missouri, USA

19A3 **Cameron** Texas, USA
4H2 **Cameron I** Can
111A3 **Cameron Mts** NZ
98A2 **Cameroon** Federal Republic, Africa
98A2 **Cameroun** *Mt* Cam
31B2 **Cametá** Brazil
79B4 **Camiguin** *I* Phil
79B2 **Camiling** Phil
17B1 **Camilla** USA
22B1 **Camino** USA
30D3 **Camiri** Bol
31C2 **Camocim** Brazil
98C3 **Camissombo** Angola
106C2 **Camooweal** Aust
34D2 **Campana** Arg
29A5 **Campana** *I* Chile
13B2 **Campania I** Can
111B2 **Campbell,C** NZ
13B2 **Campbell I** Can
105G6 **Campbell I** NZ
4E3 **Campbell,Mt** Can
84C2 **Campbellpore** Pak
5F5 **Campbell River** Can
7D5 **Campbellton** Can
109D2 **Campbelltown** Aust
42B2 **Campbeltown** Scot
25C3 **Campeche** Mexico
108B3 **Camperdown** Aust
31D3 **Campina Grande** Brazil
31B6 **Campinas** Brazil
35B1 **Campina Verde** Brazil
98A2 **Campo** Cam
53B2 **Campobasso** Italy
35B2 **Campo Belo** Brazil
35B1 **Campo Florido** Brazil
30D4 **Campo Gallo** Arg
30F3 **Campo Grande** Brazil
31C2 **Campo Maior** Brazil
30F3 **Campo Mourão** Brazil
35C2 **Campos** Brazil
35B1 **Campos Altos** Brazil
47D1 **Campo Tures** Italy
76D3 **Cam Ranh** Viet
5G4 **Camrose** Can
100A2 **Camucuio** Angola
27K1 **Canaan** Tobago
16C1 **Canaan** USA
100A2 **Canacupa** Angola
2F3 **Canada** Dominion, N America
29D2 **Cañada de Gomez** Arg
9C3 **Canadian** *R* USA
60C5 **Canakkale** Turk
34B3 **Canalejas** Arg
13D2 **Canal Flats** Can
24A1 **Cananea** Mexico
102G3 **Canary Basin** Atlantic O
Canary Is = Islas Canarias
23A2 **Canas** Mexico
24B2 **Canatlán** Mexico
11B4 **Canaveral,C** USA
31D5 **Canavieiras** Brazil
107D4 **Canberra** Aust
20B2 **Canby** California, USA
55C3 **Çandarli Körfezi** *B* Turk
16C2 **Candlewood,L** USA
29E2 **Canelones** Urug
18A2 **Caney** USA
100A2 **Cangamba** Angola
100B2 **Cangombe** Angola
72D2 **Cangzhou** China
7D4 **Caniapiscau** *R* Can
53B3 **Canicatti** Italy
31D2 **Canindé** Brazil
92B1 **Çankırı** Turk
13D2 **Canmore** Can
44A3 **Canna** *I* Scot
87B2 **Cannanore** India
49D3 **Cannes** France
109C3 **Cann River** Aust
30F4 **Canoãs** Brazil
13F1 **Canoe L** Can
9C3 **Canon City** USA
108B2 **Canopus** Aust

5H4 **Canora** Can
109C2 **Canowindra** Aust
45C2 **Cansore Pt** Irish Rep
43E4 **Canterbury** Eng
111B2 **Canterbury Bight** *B* NZ
111B2 **Canterbury Plains** NZ
77D4 **Can Tho** Viet
Canton = Guangzhou
19C3 **Canton** Mississippi, USA
18B1 **Canton** Missouri, USA
10B2 **Canton** Ohio, USA
12E2 **Cantwell** USA
20C2 **Canyon City** USA
12J2 **Canyon Range** *Mts* Can
20B2 **Canyonville** USA
98C3 **Canzar** Angola
76D1 **Cao Bang** Viet
31B2 **Capanema** Brazil
35B2 **Capão Bonito** Brazil
48B3 **Capbreton** France
24B2 **Cap Corrientes** *C* Mexico
52A2 **Cap Corse** *C* Corse
48B2 **Cap de la Hague** *C* France
15D1 **Cap-de-la-Madeleine** Can
6C3 **Cap de Nouvelle-France** *C* Can
51C2 **Capdepera** Spain
23A2 **Cap de Tancitiario** *C* Mexico
109C4 **Cape Barren I** Aust
103J6 **Cape Basin** Atlantic O
7E5 **Cape Breton I** Can
97B4 **Cape Coast** Ghana
15D2 **Cape Cod B** USA
6C3 **Cape Dorset** Can
17C1 **Cape Fear** *R* USA
18C2 **Cape Girardeau** USA
6B3 **Cape Henrietta Maria** Can
Cape Horn = Cabo de Hornos
104E3 **Cape Johnston Depth** Pacific O
35C1 **Capelinha** Brazil
4B3 **Cape Lisburne** USA
100A2 **Capelongo** Angola
15D3 **Cape May** USA
5F5 **Cape Mendocino** USA
98B3 **Capenda Camulemba** Angola
4F2 **Cape Perry** Can
7A4 **Cape Tatnam** Can
100A4 **Cape Town** S Africa
102G4 **Cape Verde** *Is* Atlantic O
102G4 **Cape Verde Basin** Atlantic O
12F3 **Cape Yakataga** USA
107D2 **Cape York Pen** Aust
46A1 **Cap Gris Nez** *C* France
26C3 **Cap-Haïtien** Haiti
31B2 **Capim** *R* Brazil
112C2 **Capitán Arturo Prat** *Base* Ant
27P2 **Cap Moule à Chique** *C* St Lucia
53C3 **Capo Isola de Correnti** *C* Italy
53C3 **Capo Rizzuto** *C* Italy
55A3 **Capo Santa Maria di Leuca** *C* Italy
53B3 **Capo San Vito** Italy
53C3 **Capo Spartivento** *C* Italy
27P2 **Cap Pt** St Lucia
53B2 **Capri** *I* Italy
100B2 **Caprivi Strip** Region, Namibia
52A2 **Cap Rosso** *C* Corse
102H4 **Cap Vert** *C* Sen
32C4 **Caquetá** *R* Colombia
54B2 **Caracal** Rom

33E3 **Caracaraí** Brazil
32D1 **Caracas** Ven
35B2 **Caraguatatuba** Brazil
29B3 **Carahue** Chile
35C1 **Caraí** Brazil
35C2 **Carandaí** Brazil
31C6 **Carangola** Brazil
54B1 **Caransebeş** Rom
108A2 **Carappee Hill** *Mt* Aust
26A3 **Caratasca** Honduras
35C1 **Caratinga** Brazil
51B2 **Caravaca** Spain
35D1 **Caravelas** Brazil
18C2 **Carbondale** Illinois, USA
53A3 **Carbonia** Sardegna
7E5 **Carborear** Can
5G4 **Carcaion** Can
99E1 **Carcar Mts** Somalia
48C3 **Carcassonne** France
4E3 **Carcross** Can
23B2 **Cardel** Mexico
25D2 **Cardenas** Cuba
23B1 **Cárdenas** Mexico
43C4 **Cardiff** Wales
43B3 **Cardigan** Wales
43B3 **Cardigan B** Wales
13E2 **Cardston** Can
54B1 **Carei** Rom
33F4 **Careiro** Brazil
34A2 **Carén** Chile
14B2 **Carey** USA
48B2 **Carhaix-Plouguer** France
29D3 **Carhué** Arg
31C6 **Cariacica** Brazil
5J4 **Caribou** Can
5G4 **Caribou Mts** Alberta, Can
5F4 **Caribou Mts** British Columbia, Can
79B3 **Carigara** Phil
46C2 **Carignan** France
33E1 **Caripito** Ven
15C1 **Carleton Place** Can
101G1 **Carletonville** S Africa
18C2 **Carlinville** USA
42C2 **Carlisle** Eng
15C2 **Carlisle** USA
34C3 **Carlos** Arg
35C1 **Carlos Chagas** Brazil
45C2 **Carlow** County, Irish Rep
45C2 **Carlow** Irish Rep
21B3 **Carlsbad** California, USA
9C3 **Carlsbad** New Mexico, USA
5H5 **Carlyle** Can
12G2 **Carmacks** Can
47B2 **Carmagnola** Italy
43B4 **Carmarthen** Wales
43B4 **Carmarthen B** Wales
22B2 **Carmel** California, USA
16C2 **Carmel** New York, USA
94B2 **Carmel,Mt** Israel
34D2 **Carmelo** Urug
22B2 **Carmel Valley** USA
9B4 **Carmen** *I* Mexico
29D4 **Carmen de Patagones** Arg
18C2 **Carmi** USA
21A2 **Carmichael** USA
35B1 **Carmo do Paranaíba** Brazil
50A2 **Carmona** Spain
106A3 **Carnarvon** Aust
100B4 **Carnarvon** S Africa
35D1 **Carncacá** Brazil
45C1 **Carndonagh** Irish Rep
106B3 **Carnegi,L** Aust
98B2 **Carnot** CAR
108A2 **Carnot,C** Aust
17B2 **Carol City** USA
31B3 **Carolina** Brazil
101H1 **Carolina** S Africa
17C1 **Carolina Beach** USA
104F3 **Caroline Is** Pacific O
60B4 **Carpathians** *Mts* E Europe

59D3 **Carpatii Orientali** *Mts* Rom
106C2 **Carpentaria,G of** Aust
83C5 **Carpenter Ridge** Indian O
49D3 **Carpentras** France
52B2 **Carpi** Italy
22C3 **Carpinteria** USA
17B2 **Carrabelle** USA
52B2 **Carrara** Italy
41B3 **Carrauntoohill** *Mt* Irish Rep
45C2 **Carrickmacross** Irish Rep
45B2 **Carrick on Shannon** Irish Rep
45C2 **Carrick-on-Suir** Irish Rep
108A2 **Carrieton** Aust
8D2 **Carrington** USA
50B1 **Carrión** *R* Spain
10A2 **Carroll** USA
17A1 **Carrollton** Georgia, USA
14A3 **Carrollton** Kentucky, USA
18B2 **Carrollton** Missouri, USA
18C2 **Carruthersville** USA
60E5 **Carsamba** Turk
92B2 **Carsamba** *R* Turk
8B3 **Carson City** USA
14B2 **Carsonville** USA
26B4 **Cartagena** Colombia
51B2 **Cartagena** Spain
32B3 **Cartago** Colombia
25D4 **Cartago** Costa Rica
111C2 **Carterton** NZ
18B2 **Carthage** Missouri, USA
15C2 **Carthage** New York, USA
19B3 **Carthage** Texas, USA
106B2 **Cartier I** Timor S
7E4 **Cartwright** Can
31D3 **Caruaru** Brazil
33E1 **Carúpano** Ven
46B1 **Carvin** France
34A2 **Casablanca** Chile
96B1 **Casablanca** Mor
35B2 **Casa Branca** Brazil
9B3 **Casa Grande** USA
52A1 **Casale Monferrato** Italy
47D2 **Casalmaggiore** Italy
34C3 **Casares** Arg
13C3 **Cascade Mts** Can/ USA
111A2 **Cascade Pt** NZ
8A2 **Cascade Range** *Mts* USA
30F3 **Cascavel** Brazil
53B2 **Caserta** Italy
112C9 **Casey** *Base* Ant
45C2 **Cashel** Irish Rep
34C2 **Casilda** Arg
107E3 **Casino** Aust
32B5 **Casma** Peru
51B1 **Caspe** Spain
8C2 **Casper** USA
61G4 **Caspian Depression** *Region* Kazakhstan
65G6 **Caspian S** Asia/ Europe
14C3 **Cass** USA
100B2 **Cassamba** Angola
46B1 **Cassel** France
12J3 **Cassiar** Can
4E3 **Cassiar Mts** Can
35A1 **Cassilândia** Brazil
53B2 **Cassino** Italy
22C3 **Castaic** USA
34B2 **Castaño** *R* Arg
47D2 **Castelfranco** Italy
49D3 **Castellane** France
34D3 **Castelli** Arg
51B2 **Castellon de la Plana** Spain
31C3 **Castelo** Brazil
50A2 **Castelo Branco** Port
48C3 **Castelsarrasin** France
53B3 **Castelvetrano** Italy
108B3 **Casterton** Aust

50B2	**Castilla La Nueva** Region, Spain
50B1	**Castilla La Vieja** Region, Spain
41B3	**Castlebar** Irish Rep
44A3	**Castlebay** Scot
42C2	**Castle Douglas** Scot
20C1	**Castlegar** Can
45B2	**Castleisland** Irish Rep
108B3	**Castlemain** Aust
45B2	**Castlerea** Irish Rep
109C2	**Castlereagh** Aust
48C3	**Castres-sur-l'Agout** France
27E4	**Castries** St Lucia
29B4	**Castro** Arg
30F3	**Castro** Brazil
31D4	**Castro Alves** Brazil
53C3	**Castrovillari** Italy
22B2	**Castroville** USA
111A2	**Caswell Sd** NZ
25E2	**Cat** I The Bahamas
79B3	**Catabalogan** Phil
32A5	**Catacaos** Peru
35C2	**Cataguases** Brazil
19B3	**Catahoula L** USA
35B1	**Catalão** Brazil
51C1	**Cataluña** Region, Spain
30C4	**Catamarca** Arg
30C4	**Catamarca** State, Arg
101C2	**Catandica** Mozam
79B3	**Catanduanes** I Phil
31B6	**Catanduva** Brazil
53C3	**Catania** Italy
53C3	**Catanzaro** Italy
79B3	**Catarman** Phil
108A2	**Catastrophe,C** Aust
26C5	**Catatumbo** R Ven
16A2	**Catawissa** USA
23B2	**Catemaco** Mexico
49D3	**Cater** Corse
52A2	**Cateraggio** Corse
98B3	**Catete** Angola
97A3	**Catio** Guinea-Bissau
7A4	**Cat Lake** Can
13D3	**Catlegar** Can
107E3	**Cato** I Aust
25D2	**Catoche,C** Mexico
16A3	**Catoctin Mt** USA
15C3	**Catonsville** USA
34C3	**Catrilo** Arg
15D2	**Catskill** USA
15D2	**Catskill Mts** USA
32C2	**Cauca** R Colombia
31D2	**Caucaia** Brazil
32B2	**Caucasia** Colombia
65F5	**Caucasus** Mts Georgia
46B1	**Caudry** France
98B3	**Caungula** Angola
29B3	**Cauquenes** Chile
87B2	**Cauvery** R India
49D3	**Cavaillon** France
47D1	**Cavalese** Italy
97B4	**Cavally** R Lib
45C2	**Cavan** County, Irish Rep
45C2	**Cavan** Irish Rep
79B3	**Cavite** Phil
31C2	**Caxias** Brazil
32C4	**Caxias** Brazil
30F4	**Caxias do Sul** Brazil
98B3	**Caxito** Angola
17B1	**Cayce** USA
93D1	**Çayeli** Turk
33G3	**Cayenne** French Guiana
46A1	**Cayeux-sur-Mer** France
25E3	**Cayman Brac** I Caribbean S
26A3	**Cayman Is** Caribbean S
26A3	**Cayman Trench** Caribbean S
99E2	**Caynabo** Somalia
25E2	**Cayo Romana** I Cuba
25D3	**Cayos Miskitos** Is Nic
26A2	**Cay Sal** I Caribbean S
100B2	**Cazombo** Angola
	Ceará = Fortaleza
31C3	**Ceara** State, Brazil
79B3	**Cebu** Phil
79B3	**Cebu** I Phil
16B3	**Cecilton** USA
52B2	**Cecina** Italy
8B3	**Cedar City** USA
19A3	**Cedar Creek Res** USA
5J4	**Cedar L** Can
10A2	**Cedar Rapids** USA
17A1	**Cedartown** USA
24A2	**Cedros** I Mexico
106C4	**Ceduna** Aust
99E2	**Ceelbuur** Somalia
99E1	**Ceerigaabo** Somalia
53B3	**Cefalù** Italy
59B3	**Cegléd** Hung
100A2	**Cela** Angola
24B2	**Celaya** Mexico
	Celebes = Sulawesi
70C3	**Celebes S** S E Asia
14B2	**Celina** USA
52C1	**Celje** Slovenia
56C2	**Celle** Germany
71E4	**Cendrawasih** Pen Indon
47C2	**Ceno** R Italy
19B3	**Center** USA
16C2	**Center Moriches** USA
17A1	**Center Point** USA
47D2	**Cento** Italy
44B3	**Central** Region, Scot
98B2	**Central African Republic** Africa
16D2	**Central Falls** USA
18C2	**Centralia** Illinois, USA
8A2	**Centralia** Washington, USA
20B2	**Central Point** USA
71F4	**Central Range** Mts PNG
16A3	**Centreville** Maryland, USA
78C4	**Cepu** Indon
	Ceram = Seram
71D4	**Ceram Sea** Indon
34C3	**Cereales** Arg
31B5	**Ceres** Brazil
100A4	**Ceres** S Africa
22B2	**Ceres** USA
48C2	**Cergy-Pontoise** France
53C2	**Cerignola** Italy
60C5	**Cernavodă** Rom
9C4	**Cerralvo** I Mexico
23A1	**Cerritos** Mexico
34B2	**Cerro Aconcagua** Mt Arg
23B1	**Cerro Azul** Mexico
34A3	**Cerro Campanario** Mt Chile
34C2	**Cerro Champaqui** Mt Arg
23A2	**Cerro Cuachaia** Mt Mexico
23B1	**Cerro de Astillero** Mexico
34B2	**Cerro de Olivares** Mt Arg
32B6	**Cerro de Pasco** Peru
27D3	**Cerro de Punta** Mt Puerto Rico
23A2	**Cerro El Cantado** Mt Mexico
34B3	**Cerro El Nevado** Mt Arg
23A2	**Cerro Grande** Mts Mexico
34A2	**Cerro Juncal** Mt Arg/ Chile
23A1	**Cerro la Ardilla** Mts Mexico
34B1	**Cerro las Tortolas** Mt Chile
23A2	**Cerro Laurel** Mt Mexico
34A2	**Cerro Mercedario** Mt Arg
34A3	**Cerro Mora** Mt Chile
27C4	**Cerron** Mt Ven
34B3	**Cerro Payún** Mt Arg
23B2	**Cerro Penón del Rosario** Mt Mexico
34B2	**Cerro Sosneado** Mt Arg
23A2	**Cerro Teotepec** Mt Mexico
34B2	**Cerro Tupungato** Mt Arg
23B2	**Cerro Yucuyacau** Mt Mexico
47C2	**Cervo** R Italy
52B2	**Cesena** Italy
60B2	**Cēsis** Latvia
57C3	**České Budejovice** Czech Republic
59B3	**Českomoravská Vysocina** Mts Czech Republic
55C3	**Cesme** Turk
107E4	**Cessnock** Aust
52C2	**Cetina** R Croatia
96B1	**Ceuta** N W Africa
92C2	**Ceyhan** Turk
92C2	**Ceyhan** R Turk
93C2	**Ceylanpınar** Turk
	Ceylon = Sri Lanka
63B2	**Chaa-Khol** Russian Fed
48C2	**Chaâteaudun** France
47B1	**Chablais** Region, France
34C2	**Chacabuco** Arg
32B5	**Chachapoyas** Peru
34B3	**Chacharramendi** Arg
84C3	**Chachran** Pak
30D4	**Chaco** State, Arg
98B1	**Chad** Republic, Africa
98B1	**Chad** L C Africa
34B3	**Chadileuvu** R Arg
8C2	**Chadron** USA
18C2	**Chaffee** USA
85A3	**Chagai** Pak
63F2	**Chagda** Russian Fed
84B2	**Chaghcharan** Afghan
104B4	**Chagos Arch** Indian O
27L1	**Chaguanas** Trinidad
91D4	**Chāh Bahār** Iran
76C2	**Chai Badan** Thai
76C3	**Chaine des Cardamomes** Mts Camb
98C4	**Chaine des Mitumba** Mts Zaire
76C2	**Chaiyaphum** Thai
34D2	**Chajari** Arg
84C2	**Chakwal** Pak
30B2	**Chala** Peru
100C2	**Chalabesa** Zambia
84A2	**Chalap Dalam** Mts Afghan
73C4	**Chaling** China
85C4	**Chālisgaon** India
12F1	**Chalkyitsik** USA
46C2	**Challerange** France
46C2	**Châlons sur Marne** France
49C2	**Chalon sur Saône** France
57C3	**Cham** Germany
84B2	**Chaman** Pak
84D2	**Chamba** India
85D3	**Chambal** R India
15C3	**Chambersburg** USA
49D2	**Chambéry** France
46B2	**Chambly** France
85A3	**Chambor Kalat** Pak
90B3	**Chamgordan** Iran
34B2	**Chamical** Arg
47B2	**Chamonix** France
86A2	**Champa** India
49C2	**Champagne** Region, France
101G1	**Champagne Castle** Mt Lesotho
47A1	**Champagnole** France
10B2	**Champaign** USA
76D3	**Champassak** Laos
10C2	**Champlain,L** USA
87B2	**Chāmrājnagar** India
30B4	**Chañaral** Chile
34A3	**Chanco** Chile
4D3	**Chandalar** USA
4D3	**Chandalar** R USA
84D2	**Chandīgarh** India
86C2	**Chandpur** Bang
85D5	**Chandrapur** India
91D4	**Chänf** Iran
101C2	**Changara** Mozam
74B2	**Changbai** China
69E2	**Changchun** China
73C4	**Changde** China
68E4	**Chang-hua** Taiwan
76D2	**Changjiang** China
73D3	**Chang Jiang** R China
74B2	**Changjin** N Korea
73C4	**Changsha** China
72E3	**Changshu** China
74A2	**Changtu** China
72B2	**Changwu** China
74B3	**Changyŏn** N Korea
72C2	**Changzhi** China
73E3	**Changzhou** China
48B2	**Channel Is** Europe
9B3	**Channel Is** USA
7E5	**Channel Port-aux-Basques** Can
76C3	**Chanthaburi** Thai
46B2	**Chantilly** France
18A2	**Chanute** USA
73D5	**Chaoàn** China
73D5	**Chao'an** China
73D3	**Chao Hu** L China
76C3	**Chao Phraya** R Thai
72E1	**Chaoyang** China
31C4	**Chapada Diamantina** Mts Brazil
31C2	**Chapadinha** Brazil
23A1	**Chapala** Mexico
23A1	**Chapala,Lac de** L Mexico
61H3	**Chapayevo** Kazakhstan
30F4	**Chapecó** Brazil
27H1	**Chapeltown** Jamaica
7B5	**Chapleau** Can
61E3	**Chaplygin** Russian Fed
112C3	**Charcot I** Ant
80E2	**Chardzhou** Turkmenistan
48C2	**Charente** R France
98B1	**Chari** R Chad
98B1	**Chari Baguirmi** Region, Chad
84B1	**Charikar** Afghan
18B1	**Chariton** R USA
33F2	**Charity** Guyana
85D3	**Charkhāri** India
46C1	**Charleroi** Belg
18C2	**Charleston** Illinois, USA
18C2	**Charleston** Missouri, USA
11C3	**Charleston** S Carolina, USA
10B3	**Charleston** W Virginia, USA
98C3	**Charlesville** Zaïre
107D3	**Charleville** Aust
49C2	**Charleville-Mézières** France
14A1	**Charlevoix** USA
14B2	**Charlotte** Michigan, USA
11B3	**Charlotte** N Carolina, USA
17B2	**Charlotte Harbor** B USA
10C3	**Charlottesville** USA
7D5	**Charlottetown** Can
27K1	**Charlotteville** Tobago
108B3	**Charlton** Aust
10C1	**Charlton I** Can
84C2	**Charsadda** Pak
107D3	**Charters Towers** Aust
48C2	**Chartres** France
29E3	**Chascomús** Arg
13D2	**Chase** Can
48B2	**Châteaubriant** France
48C2	**Châteaudun** France
48B2	**Châteaulin** France
48C2	**Châteauroux** France

46D2 **Château-Salins** France
49C2 **Château-Thierry** France
46C1 **Châtelet** Belg
48C2 **Châtellerault** France
43E4 **Chatham** Eng
7D5 **Chatham** New Brunswick, Can
16C1 **Chatham** New York, USA
14B2 **Chatham** Ontario, Can
13A2 **Chatham Sd** Can
12H3 **Chatham Str** USA
49C2 **Châtillon** France
47B2 **Châtillon** Italy
16B3 **Chatsworth** USA
17B1 **Chattahoochee** USA
17A1 **Chattahoochee** *R* USA
11B3 **Chattanooga** USA
76A1 **Chauk** Burma
49D2 **Chaumont** France
46B2 **Chauny** France
77D3 **Chau Phu** Viet
50A1 **Chaves** Port
61H2 **Chaykovskiy** Russian Fed
50B2 **Chazaouet** Alg
34C2 **Chazón** Arg
32C2 **Chcontá** Colombia
57C2 **Cheb** Czech Republic
65F4 **Cheboksary** Russian Fed
10B2 **Cheboygan** USA
74B3 **Chech'on** S Korea
85C3 **Chechro** Pak
18A2 **Checotah** USA
76A2 **Cheduba** *I* Burma
108B1 **Cheepie** Aust
96B2 **Chegga** Maur
100C2 **Chegutu** Zim
20B1 **Chehalis** USA
74B4 **Cheju** S Korea
74B4 **Cheju do** *I* S Korea
74B4 **Cheju-haehyŏp** *Str* S Korea
63F2 **Chekunda** Russian Fed
20B1 **Chelan,L** USA
90B2 **Cheleken** Turkmenistan
34B3 **Chelforo** Arg
80D1 **Chelkar** Kazakhstan
59C2 **Chelm** Pol
58B2 **Chelmno** Pol
43E4 **Chelmsford** Eng
43C4 **Cheltenham** Eng
65H4 **Chelyabinsk** Russian Fed
101C2 **Chemba** Mozam
57C2 **Chemnitz** Germany
84D2 **Chenab** *R* India/Pak
96B2 **Chenachane** Alg
20C1 **Cheney** USA
18A2 **Cheney Res** USA
72D1 **Chengda** China
73A3 **Chengdu** China
72E2 **Chengshan Jiao** *Pt* China
73C4 **Chenxi** China
73C4 **Chen Xian** China
73D3 **Cheo Xian** China
32B5 **Chepén** Peru
34B2 **Chepes** Arg
48C2 **Cher** *R* France
23A2 **Cheran** Mexico
17C1 **Cheraw** USA
48B2 **Cherbourg** France
96C1 **Cherchell** Alg
63C2 **Cheremkhovo** Russian Fed
60E2 **Cherepovets** Russian Fed
60D4 **Cherkassy** Ukraine
61F5 **Cherkessk** Russian Fed
60D3 **Chernigov** Ukraine
60D2 **Chernobyl** Ukraine
60C4 **Chernovtsy** Ukraine
61J2 **Chernushka** Russian Fed
60B3 **Chernyakhovsk** Russian Fed
61G4 **Chernyye Zemli** Region, Russian Fed
18A2 **Cherokees,L o'the** USA
34A3 **Cherquenco** Chile
86C1 **Cherrapunji** India
60C3 **Cherven'** Belorussia
59C2 **Chervonograd** Ukraine
10C3 **Chesapeake** *B* USA
42C3 **Cheshire** County, Eng
16C1 **Cheshire** USA
64F3 **Chëshskaya Guba** *B* Russian Fed
21A1 **Chester** California, USA
42C3 **Chester** Eng
18C2 **Chester** Illinois, USA
16C1 **Chester** Massachusets, USA
15C3 **Chester** Pennsylvania, USA
17B1 **Chester** S Carolina, USA
16A3 **Chester** *R* USA
42D3 **Chesterfield** Eng
6A3 **Chesterfield Inlet** Can
16A3 **Chestertown** USA
25D3 **Chetumal** Mexico
13C1 **Chetwynd** Can
12A2 **Chevak** USA
111B2 **Cheviot** NZ
40C2 **Cheviots** *Hills* Eng/Scot
13D3 **Chewelah** USA
8C2 **Cheyenne** USA
86A1 **Chhapra** India
86C1 **Chhātak** Bang
85D4 **Chhatarpur** India
85D4 **Chhindwāra** India
86B1 **Chhuka** Bhutan
73E5 **Chia'i** Taiwan
100A2 **Chiange** Angola
76C2 **Chiang Kham** Thai
76B2 **Chiang Mai** Thai
47C1 **Chiavenna** Italy
74E3 **Chiba** Japan
86B2 **Chībāsa** India
100A2 **Chibia** Angola
7C4 **Chibougamou** Can
75A1 **Chiburi-jima** *I* Japan
101C3 **Chibuto** Mozam
10B2 **Chicago** USA
14A2 **Chicago Heights** USA
12G3 **Chichagof I** USA
43D4 **Chichester** Eng
75B1 **Chichibu** Japan
69G4 **Chichi-jima** *I* Japan
11B3 **Chickamauga L** USA
19C3 **Chickasawhay** *R* USA
9D3 **Chickasha** USA
12F2 **Chicken** USA
32A5 **Chiclayo** Peru
8A3 **Chico** USA
29C4 **Chico** *R* Arg
101C2 **Chicoa** Mozam
15D2 **Chicopee** USA
7C5 **Chicoutimi** Can
101C3 **Chicualacuala** Mozam
87B2 **Chidambaram** India
6D3 **Chidley,C** Can
17B2 **Chiefland** USA
99C3 **Chiengi** Zambia
47B2 **Chieri** Italy
46C2 **Chiers** *R* France
47C1 **Chiesa** Italy
47D2 **Chiese** *R* Italy
52B2 **Chieti** Italy
72D1 **Chifeng** China
12C3 **Chiginigak,Mt** USA
4C3 **Chigmit Mts** USA
23B2 **Chignahuapán** Mexico
12C3 **Chignik** USA
24B2 **Chihuahua** Mexico
87B2 **Chik Ballāpur** India
87B2 **Chikmagalūr** India
12C2 **Chikuminuk L** USA
101C2 **Chikwawa** Malawi
76A1 **Chi-kyaw** Burma
87C1 **Chilakalūrupet** India
23B2 **Chilapa** Mexico
87B3 **Chilaw** Sri Lanka
28B6 **Chile** Republic
34B2 **Chilecito** Mendoza, Arg
100B2 **Chililabombwe** Zambia
86B2 **Chilka** *L* India
13C2 **Chilko** *R* Can
5F4 **Chilko L** Can
13C2 **Chilkotin** *R* Can
34A3 **Chillán** Chile
34D3 **Chillar** Arg
18B2 **Chillicothe** Missouri, USA
14B3 **Chillicothe** Ohio, USA
13C3 **Chilliwack** Can
86B1 **Chilmari** India
101C2 **Chilongozi** Zambia
20B2 **Chiloquin** USA
24C3 **Chilpancingo** Mexico
43D4 **Chiltern Hills** *Upland* Eng
14A2 **Chilton** USA
101C2 **Chilumba** Malawi
69E4 **Chi-lung** Taiwan
101C2 **Chilwa** *L* Malawi
100C2 **Chimanimani** Zim
46C1 **Chimay** Belg
65G5 **Chimbay** Uzbekistan
32B4 **Chimborazo** *Mt* Ecuador
32B5 **Chimbote** Peru
65H5 **Chimkent** Kazakhstan
101C2 **Chimoio** Mozam
67E3 **China** Republic, Asia
China National Republic = Taiwan
25D3 **Chinandega** Nic
32B6 **Chincha Alta** Peru
109D1 **Chinchilla** Aust
101C2 **Chinde** Mozam
86C2 **Chindwin** *R* Burma
100B2 **Chingola** Zambia
100A2 **Chinguar** Angola
96A2 **Chinguetti** Maur
74B3 **Chinhae** S Korea
100C2 **Chinhoyi** Zim
12D3 **Chiniak,C** USA
84C2 **Chiniot** Pak
74B3 **Chinju** S Korea
98C2 **Chinko** *R* CAR
75B1 **Chino** Japan
101C2 **Chinsali** Zambia
52B1 **Chioggia** Italy
101C2 **Chipata** Zambia
101C3 **Chipinge** Zim
87A1 **Chiplūn** India
43C4 **Chippenham** Eng
10A2 **Chippewa Falls** USA
32A4 **Chira** *R* Peru
87C1 **Chīrāla** India
101C3 **Chiredzi** Zim
95A2 **Chirfa** Niger
32A2 **Chiriqui** *Mt* Panama
54C2 **Chirpan** Bulg
32A2 **Chirrípo Grande** *Mt* Costa Rica
100B2 **Chirundu** Zim
100B2 **Chisamba** Zambia
7C4 **Chisasibi** Can
73B4 **Chishui He** *R* China
Chişinău = Kishinev
47B2 **Chisone** *R* Italy
61H2 **Chistopol** Russian Fed
68D1 **Chita** Russian Fed
100A2 **Chitado** Angola
100A2 **Chitembo** Angola
12F2 **Chitina** USA
12F2 **Chitina** *R* USA
87B2 **Chitradurga** India
84C1 **Chitral** Pak
32A2 **Chitré** Panama
86C2 **Chittagong** Bang
85C4 **Chittaurgarh** India
87B2 **Chittoor** India
100B2 **Chiume** Angola
47D1 **Chiusa** Italy
47B2 **Chivasso** Italy
100C2 **Chivhu** Zim
29D2 **Chivilcoy** Arg
100C2 **Chivu** Zim
75A1 **Chizu** Japan
29C3 **Choele Choel** Arg
34C3 **Choique** Arg
24B2 **Choix** Mexico
58B2 **Chojnice** Pol
99D1 **Choke** *Mts* Eth
48B2 **Cholet** France
23B2 **Cholula** Mexico
100B2 **Choma** Zambia
86B1 **Chomo Yummo** *Mt* China/India
57C2 **Chomutov** Czech Republic
63C1 **Chona** *R* Russian Fed
74B3 **Ch'ŏnan** S Korea
76C3 **Chon Buri** Thai
32A4 **Chone** Ecuador
74B2 **Ch'ŏngjin** N Korea
74B3 **Chongju** N Korea
74B3 **Ch'ŏngju** S Korea
100A2 **Chongoroi** Angola
73B4 **Chongqing** China
74B3 **Chŏngŭp** S Korea
74B3 **Chŏnju** S Korea
86B1 **Chooyu** *Mt* China/Nepal
59D3 **Chortkov** Ukraine
74B3 **Ch'ŏrwŏn** N Korea
59B2 **Chorzow** Pol
74E3 **Choshi** Japan
34A3 **Chos-Malal** Arg
58B2 **Choszczno** Pol
86A2 **Chotanāgpur** Region, India
96C1 **Chott Melrhir** Alg
22B2 **Chowchilla** USA
63D3 **Choybalsan** Mongolia
6A3 **Chrantrey Inlet** *B* Can
111B2 **Christchurch** NZ
101G1 **Christiana** S Africa
6D2 **Christian,C** Can
12H3 **Christian Sd** USA
6E3 **Christianshab** Greenland
104D4 **Christmas I** Indian O
65J5 **Chu** Kazakhstan
65J5 **Chu** *R* Kazakhstan
29C4 **Chubut** State, Arg
29C4 **Chubut** *R* Arg
60D2 **Chudovo** Russian Fed
Chudskoye Ozero = Peipus, Lake
4D3 **Chugach Mts** USA
12E2 **Chugiak** USA
75A1 **Chūgoku-sanchi** *Mts* Japan
29F2 **Chuí** Brazil
29B3 **Chuillán** Chile
77C5 **Chukai** Malay
76D2 **Chu Lai** Viet
21B3 **Chula Vista** USA
12E2 **Chulitna** USA
63E2 **Chulman** Russian Fed
32A5 **Chulucanas** Peru
30C2 **Chulumani** Bol
65K4 **Chulym** Russian Fed
63A2 **Chulym** *R* Russian Fed
63B2 **Chuma** *R* Russian Fed
84D2 **Chumar** India
63F2 **Chumikan** Russian Fed
77B3 **Chumphon** Thai
74B3 **Ch'unch'ŏn** S Korea
86B2 **Chunchura** India
74B3 **Ch'ungju** S Korea
Chungking = Chongqing
99D3 **Chunya** Tanz
63C1 **Chunya** *R* Russian Fed
27L1 **Chupara Pt** Trinidad
30C3 **Chuquicamata** Chile
52A1 **Chur** Switz

Churāchāndpur

47C2 **Crema** Italy
52B1 **Cremona** Italy
46B2 **Crépy-en-Valois** France
52B2 **Cres** *I* Yugos
20B2 **Crescent City** USA
34C2 **Crespo** Arg
13D3 **Creston** Can
18B1 **Creston** USA
17A1 **Crestview** USA
108B3 **Creswick** Aust
47A1 **Crêt de la Neige** *Mt* France
Crete = Kríti
18A1 **Crete** USA
55B3 **Crete,S of** Greece
48C2 **Creuse** *R* France
43C3 **Crewe** Eng
44B3 **Crianlarich** Scot
30G4 **Criciuma** Brazil
44C3 **Crieff** Scot
12G3 **Crillon,Mt** USA
35B1 **Cristalina** Brazil
52C1 **Croatia** Republic, Europe
78D1 **Crocker Range** *Mts* Malay
19A3 **Crockett** USA
106C2 **Croker I** Aust
44C3 **Cromarty** Scot
43E3 **Cromer** Eng
111A3 **Cromwell** NZ
11C4 **Crooked** *I* The Bahamas
13C2 **Crooked** *R* Can
8D2 **Crookston** USA
109C2 **Crookwell** Aust
109D1 **Croppa Creek** Aust
11A3 **Crossett** USA
12G3 **Cross Sd** USA
53C3 **Crotone** Italy
19B3 **Crowley** USA
27K1 **Crown Pt** Tobago
109D1 **Crows Nest** Aust
107D2 **Croydon** Aust
43D4 **Croydon** Eng
104B5 **Crozet Basin** Indian O
4F2 **Crozier Chan** Can
30F4 **Cruz Alta** Brazil
25E3 **Cruz,C** Cuba
29D2 **Cruz del Eje** Arg
35C2 **Cruzeiro** Brazil
32C5 **Cruzeiro do Sul** Brazil
13C1 **Crysdale,Mt** Can
108A2 **Crystal Brook** Aust
18B2 **Crystal City** Missouri, USA
14A1 **Crystal Falls** USA
101C2 **Cuamba** Mozam
100B2 **Cuando** *R* Angola
100A2 **Cuangar** Angola
Cuango,R = Kwango,R
34C2 **Cuarto** *R* Arg
24B2 **Cuauhtémoc** Mexico
23B2 **Cuautla** Mexico
25D2 **Cuba** Republic, Caribbean S
100A2 **Cubango** *R* Angola
100A2 **Cuchi** Angola
100A2 **Cuchi** *R* Angola
34C3 **Cuchillo Có** Arg
32D3 **Cucui** Brazil
32C2 **Cúcuta** Colombia
87B2 **Cuddalore** India
87B2 **Cuddapah** India
106A3 **Cue** Aust
32B4 **Cuenca** Ecuador
51B1 **Cuenca** Spain
24C3 **Cuernavaca** Mexico
19A4 **Cuero** USA
30E2 **Cuiabá** Brazil
30E2 **Cuiabá** *R* Brazil
23B2 **Cuicatlan** Mexico
35C1 **Cuieté** *R* Brazil
44A3 **Cuillin Hills** *Mts* Scot
98B3 **Cuilo** *R* Angola
100A2 **Cuito** *R* Angola
100A2 **Cuito Cunavale** Angola
23A2 **Cuitzeo** Mexico
77D3 **Cu Lao Hon** *I* Viet
109C3 **Culcairn** Aust
109C1 **Culgoa** *R* Aust
24B2 **Culiacán** Mexico
79A3 **Culion** *I* Phil
17A1 **Cullman** USA
47A2 **Culoz** France
15C3 **Culpeper** USA
32J7 **Culpepper** *I* Ecuador
17B2 **Culter Ridge** USA
111B2 **Culverden** NZ
33E1 **Cumaná** Ven
10C3 **Cumberland** Maryland, USA
11B3 **Cumberland** *R* USA
6D3 **Cumberland Pen** Can
6D3 **Cumbernauld Sd** Can
42C2 **Cumbria** Eng
21A2 **Cummings** USA
108A2 **Cummins** Aust
42B2 **Cumnock** Scot
34A3 **Cunco** Chile
100A2 **Cunene** *R* Angola/Namibia
52A2 **Cuneo** Italy
107D3 **Cunnamulla** Aust
44C3 **Çupar** Scot
54B2 **Čuprija** Serbia, Yugos
27D4 **Curaçao** *I* Caribbean S
34A3 **Curacautin** Chile
34B3 **Curaco** *R* Arg
34A3 **Curanilahue** Chile
34A3 **Curepto** Chile
29B2 **Curicó** Chile
30G4 **Curitiba** Brazil
108A2 **Curnamona** Aust
100A2 **Curoca** *R* Angola
31C5 **Curvelo** Brazil
18A2 **Cushing** USA
13D2 **Cutbank** *R* Can
17B1 **Cuthbert** USA
34B3 **Cutral-Có** Arg
86B2 **Cuttack** India
100A2 **Cuvelai** Angola
56B2 **Cuxhaven** Germany
14B2 **Cuyahoga Falls** USA
79B3 **Cuyo Is** Phil
32C6 **Cuzco** Peru
99C3 **Cyangugu** Zaïre
Cyclades = Kikládhes
13F3 **Cypress Hills** *Mts* Can
92B3 **Cyprus** Republic, Medit S
6D3 **Cyrus Field B** Can
59B3 **Czech Republic** Republic, Europe
59B2 **Częstochowa** Pol

D

76C1 **Da** *R* Viet
69E2 **Da'an** China
94C3 **Dab'a** Jordan
27C4 **Dabajuro** Ven
99E2 **Dabaro** Somalia
73B3 **Daba Shan** *Mts* China
99D1 **Dabat** Eth
85C4 **Dabhoi** India
73C3 **Dabie Shan** *Mts* China
97A3 **Dabola** Guinea
97B4 **Dabou** Ivory Coast
59B2 **Dabrowa Gorn** Pol
57C3 **Dachau** Germany
52B1 **Dachstein** *Mt* Austria
73A3 **Dada He** *R* China
17B2 **Dade City** USA
84B3 **Dadhar** Pak
85B3 **Dadu** Pak
68C3 **Dadu He** *R* China
79B3 **Daet** Phil
73B4 **Dafang** China
76B2 **Daga** *R* Burma
99E2 **Dagabur** Eth
97A3 **Dagana** Sen
65F5 **Dagestanskaya Respublic,** Russian Fed
79B2 **Dagupan** Phil
92B4 **Dahab** Egypt
63E3 **Da Hinggan Ling** *Mts* China
17B1 **Dahlonega** USA
85C4 **Dāhod** India
86A1 **Dailekh** Nepal
34C3 **Daireaux** Arg
69F4 **Daitō** *Is* Pacific O
106C3 **Dajarra** Aust
97A3 **Dakar** Sen
95B2 **Dakhla Oasis** Egypt
97C3 **Dakoro** Niger
54B2 **Dakovica** Serbia, Yugos
54A1 **Dakovo** Croatia
100B2 **Dala** Angola
97A3 **Dalaba** Guinea
72D1 **Dalai Nur** *L* China
68C2 **Dalandzadgad** Mongolia
79B3 **Dalanganem Is** Phil
76D3 **Da Lat** Viet
72A1 **Dalay** Mongolia
107E3 **Dalby** Aust
39F7 **Dalen** Nor
42C2 **Dales,The** *Upland* Eng
17A1 **Daleville** USA
9C3 **Dalhart** USA
4E2 **Dalhousie,C** Can
72E2 **Dalian** China
9D3 **Dallas** USA
20B1 **Dalles,The** USA
5E4 **Dall I** USA
86A2 **Dalli Rajhara** India
97C3 **Dallol** *R* Niger
97C3 **Dallol Bosso** *R* Niger
52C2 **Dalmatia** *Region* Bosnia-Herzegovina
69F2 **Dal'nerechensk** Russian Fed
97B4 **Daloa** Ivory Coast
73B4 **Dalou Shan** *Mts* China
86A2 **Dāltenganj** India
17B1 **Dalton** Georgia, USA
16C1 **Dalton** Massachusetts, USA
106C2 **Daly** *R* Aust
21A2 **Daly City** USA
106C2 **Daly Waters** Aust
79B4 **Damaguete** Phil
85C4 **Damān** India
92B3 **Damanhûr** Egypt
71D4 **Damar** *I* Indon
98B2 **Damara** CAR
92C3 **Damascus** Syria
16A3 **Damascus** USA
97D3 **Damaturu** Nig
90B2 **Damavand** Iran
98B3 **Damba** Angola
87C3 **Dambulla** Sri Lanka
90B2 **Damghan** Iran
85D4 **Damoh** India
99E2 **Damot** Eth
94B2 **Damour** Leb
106A3 **Dampier** Aust
94B3 **Danā** Jordan
22C2 **Dana,Mt** USA
97B4 **Danané** Lib
76D2 **Da Nang** Viet
79B3 **Danao** Phil
70A3 **Danau Tobu** *L* Indon
71D4 **Danau Tuwuti** *L* Indon
73A3 **Danbu** China
15D2 **Danbury** USA
86A1 **Dandeldhura** Nepal
87A1 **Dandeli** India
108C3 **Dandenong** Aust
74A2 **Dandong** China
100A4 **Danger Pt** S Africa
99D1 **Dangila** Eth
6D1 **Danguard Jenson Land** *Region* Can
7E4 **Daniels Harbour** Can
6G3 **Dannebrogs Øy** *I* Greenland
110C2 **Dannevirke** NZ
87C1 **Dantewāra** India
Danube = Donau
10B2 **Danville** Illinois, USA
11B3 **Danville** Kentucky, USA
16A2 **Danville** Pennsylvania, USA
11C3 **Danville** Virginia, USA
Danzig = Gdańsk
73C4 **Dao Xian** China
73B4 **Daozhen** China
79B4 **Dapiak,Mt** Phil
79B4 **Dapitan** Phil
68B3 **Da Qaidam** China
69E2 **Daqing** China
94C2 **Dar'a** Syria
91B4 **Dārāb** Iran
95A1 **Daraj** Libya
90B3 **Dārān** Iran
92C3 **Dar'ā Salkhad** Syria
86B1 **Darbhanga** India
22C1 **Dardanelle** USA
18B2 **Dardanelle,L** USA
Dar-el-Beida = Casablanca
99D3 **Dar es Salaam** Tanz
110B1 **Dargaville** NZ
17B1 **Darien** USA
Darjeeling = Dārjiling
86B1 **Dārjiling** India
107D4 **Darling** *R* Aust
109C1 **Darling Downs** Aust
6C1 **Darling Pen** Can
108B2 **Darlington** Aust
42D2 **Darlington** Eng
17C1 **Darlington** USA
57B3 **Darmstadt** Germany
95B1 **Darnah** Libya
108B2 **Darnick** Aust
4F3 **Darnley B** Can
112C10 **Darnley,C** Ant
51B1 **Daroca** Spain
98C2 **Dar Rounga** Region, CAR
43C4 **Dart** *R* Eng
41C3 **Dartmoor** *Moorland* Eng
43C4 **Dartmoor Nat Pk** Eng
7D5 **Dartmouth** Can
43C4 **Dartmouth** Eng
107D1 **Daru** PNG
52C1 **Daruvar** Croatia
106C2 **Darwin** Aust
91B4 **Daryacheh-ye Bakhtegan** *L* Iran
91B4 **Daryacheh-ye Mahārlū** *L* Iran
90B3 **Daryācheh-ye Namak** *Salt Flat* Iran
90D3 **Daryacheh-ye-Sistan** *Salt L* Iran/Afghan
91B4 **Daryacheh-ye Tashk** *L* Iran
80C2 **Daryācheh-ye Orūmīyeh** *L* Iran
91C4 **Dārzīn** Iran
91B4 **Das** *I* UAE
73C3 **Dashennonglia** *Mt* China
90C2 **Dasht** Iran
90B3 **Dasht-e-Kavir** *Salt Desert* Iran
90C3 **Dasht-e Lut** *Salt Desert* Iran
90D3 **Dasht-e Naomid** *Desert Region* Iran
85D3 **Datia** India
72A2 **Datong** China
72C1 **Datong** China
72A2 **Datong He** *R* China
79B4 **Datu Piang** Phil
39K7 **Daugava** *R* Latvia
60C2 **Daugavpils** Latvia
6D1 **Dauguard Jensen Land** Greenland
84A1 **Daulatabad** Afghan
85D3 **Daulpur** India
46D1 **Daun** Germany
87A1 **Daund** India
5H4 **Dauphin** Can
16A2 **Dauphin** USA
49D2 **Dauphiné** Region, France
97C3 **Daura** Nig
85D3 **Dausa** India
87B2 **Dāvangere** India
79C4 **Davao** Phil
79C4 **Davao G** Phil
22A2 **Davenport** California, USA

10A2 **Davenport** Iowa, USA
32A2 **David** Panama
4D3 **Davidson Mts** USA
21A2 **Davis** USA
112C10 **Davis** *Base* Ant
7D4 **Davis Inlet** Can
6E3 **Davis Str** Greenland/Can
61J3 **Davlekanovo** Russian Fed
47C1 **Davos** Switz
99E2 **Dawa** *R* Eth
73A4 **Dawan** China
84B2 **Dawat Yar** Afghan
Dawei = Tavoy
91B4 **Dawhat Salwah** *B* Qatar/S Arabia
76B2 **Dawna Range** *Mts* Burma
4E3 **Dawson** Can
17B1 **Dawson** Georgia, USA
107D3 **Dawson** *R* Aust
5F4 **Dawson Creek** Can
13D2 **Dawson,Mt** Can
12G2 **Dawson Range** *Mts* Can
73A3 **Dawu** China
73C3 **Dawu** China
48B3 **Dax** France
73B3 **Daxian** China
73B5 **Daxin** China
73A3 **Daxue Shan** *Mts* China
73C4 **Dayong** China
94C2 **Dayr'Ali** Syria
94C1 **Dayr'Atiyah** Syria
93D2 **Dayr az Zawr** Syria
10B3 **Dayton** Ohio, USA
19B4 **Dayton** Texas, USA
20C1 **Dayton** Washington, USA
11B4 **Daytona Beach** USA
73C4 **Dayu** China
78D3 **Dayu** Indon
72D2 **Da Yunhe** *R* China
20C2 **Dayville** USA
73B3 **Dazhu** China
100B4 **De Aar** S Africa
26C2 **Deadman's Cay** The Bahamas
92C3 **Dead S** Israel/Jordan
46A1 **Deal** Eng
101G1 **Dealesville** S Africa
13B2 **Dean** *R* Can
13B2 **Dean Chan** Can
34C2 **Deán Funes** Arg
14B2 **Dearborn** USA
4F3 **Dease Arm** *B* Can
4E4 **Dease Lake** Can
9B3 **Death V** USA
48C2 **Deauville** France
97B4 **Debakala** Ivory Coast
12B2 **Debauch Mt** USA
27L1 **Débé** Trinidad
59C2 **Debica** Pol
58C2 **Deblin** Pol
97B3 **Débo,L** Mali
59C3 **Debrecen** Hung
99D2 **Debre Birhan** Eth
99D1 **Debre Markos** Eth
99D1 **Debre Tabor** Eth
11B3 **Decatur** Alabama, USA
17B1 **Decatur** Georgia, USA
10B3 **Decatur** Illinois, USA
14B2 **Decatur** Indiana, USA
48C3 **Decazeville** France
73A4 **Dechang** China
97B3 **Dédougou** Burkina
101C2 **Dedza** Malawi
42B2 **Dee** *R* Dumfries and Galloway, Scot
42C3 **Dee** *R* Eng/Wales
44C3 **Dee** *R* Grampian, Scot
15C1 **Deep River** Can
16C2 **Deep River** USA
109D1 **Deepwater** Aust
7E5 **Deer Lake** Can
8B2 **Deer Lodge** USA

34D3 **Defferrari** Arg
17A1 **De Funiak Springs** USA
68B3 **Dêgê** China
99E1 **Degeh Bur** Eth
106A3 **De Grey** *R* Aust
91B3 **Deh Bid** Iran
84B1 **Dehi** Afghan
96D1 **Dehibat** Tunisia
87B3 **Dehiwala-Mt Lavinia** Sri Lanka
90A3 **Dehlorān** Iran
84D2 **Dehra Dūn** India
86A2 **Dehri** India
98C2 **Deim Zubeir** Sudan
94B2 **Deir Abu Sa'id** Jordan
94C1 **Deir el Ahmar** Leb
60B4 **Dej** Rom
19B3 **De Kalb** Texas, USA
63G2 **De Kastri** Russian Fed
98C3 **Dekese** Zaire
98B2 **Dekoa** CAR
106B1 **Dekusi** Indon
9B3 **Delano** USA
10C3 **Delaware** State, USA
14B2 **Delaware** USA
15C2 **Delaware** *R* USA
10C3 **Delaware B** USA
109C3 **Delegate** Aust
47B1 **Delemont** Switz
101D2 **Delgado** *C* Mozam
84D3 **Delhi** India
15D2 **Delhi** New York, USA
92B1 **Delice** Turk
24B2 **Delicias** Mexico
90B3 **Delijān** Iran
47B1 **Delle** France
22D4 **Del Mar** USA
39F8 **Delmenhorst** Germany
4B3 **De Long** *Mts* USA
109C4 **Deloraine** Aust
5H5 **Deloraine** Can
17B2 **Delray Beach** USA
9C4 **Del Rio** USA
8B3 **Delta** USA
12E2 **Delta** *R* USA
12E2 **Delta Junction** USA
99D2 **Dembī Dolo** Eth
46C1 **Demer** *R* Belg
9C3 **Deming** USA
54C2 **Demirköy** Turk
49C1 **Denain** France
82A2 **Denau** Uzbekistan
42C3 **Denbigh** Wales
12B2 **Denbigh,C** USA
78B3 **Dendang** Indon
46C1 **Dendermond** Belg
99D2 **Dendi** *Mt* Eth
46B1 **Dèndre** *R* Belg
72B1 **Dengkou** China
72C3 **Deng Xian** China
Den Haag = 's-Gravenhage
27H1 **Denham,Mt** Jamaica
56A2 **Den Helder** Neth
51C2 **Denia** Spain
107D4 **Deniliquin** Aust
20C2 **Denio** USA
9D3 **Denison** Texas, USA
12D3 **Denison,Mt** USA
92A2 **Denizli** Turk
39F7 **Denmark** Kingdom, Europe
1C1 **Denmark Str** Greenland/Iceland
27P2 **Dennery** St Lucia
78D4 **Denpasar** Indon
16B3 **Denton** Maryland, USA
9D3 **Denton** Texas, USA
107E1 **D'Entrecasteaux Is** PNG
47B1 **Dents du Midi** *Mt* Switz
8C3 **Denver** USA
98B2 **Déo** *R* Cam
86B2 **Deoghar** India
85C5 **Deolāli** India
84D1 **Deosai Plain** India

95B3 **Dépression du Mourdi** Chad
19B3 **De Queen** USA
84C3 **Dera** Pak
84B3 **Dera Bugti** Pak
84C2 **Dera Ismail Khan** Pak
106B2 **Derby** Aust
16C2 **Derby** Connecticut, USA
43D3 **Derby** County, Eng
43D3 **Derby** Eng
18A2 **Derby** Kansas, USA
60E3 **Dergachi** Ukraine
19B3 **De Ridder** USA
Derna = Darnah
95C3 **Derudeb** Sudan
109C4 **Derwent Bridge** Aust
34B2 **Desaguadero** Arg
34B2 **Desaguadero** *R* Arg
30C2 **Désaguadero** *R* Bol
21B3 **Descanso** Mexico
20B2 **Deschutes** *R* USA
99D1 **Desē** Eth
29C5 **Deseado** Arg
29C5 **Deseado** *R* Arg
47D2 **Desenzano** Italy
96A1 **Deserta Grande** *I* Medeira
30C4 **Desierto de Atacama** *Desert* Chile
18B2 **Desloge** USA
10A2 **Des Moines** Iowa, USA
60D3 **Desna** *R* Russian Fed
29B6 **Desolacion** *I* Chile
14A2 **Des Plaines** USA
56C2 **Dessau** Germany
12G2 **Destruction Bay** Can
46A1 **Desvres** France
54B1 **Deta** Rom
100B2 **Dete** Zim
10B2 **Detroit** USA
76D3 **Det Udom** Thai
54B1 **Deva** Rom
56B2 **Deventer** Neth
44C3 **Deveron** *R* Scot
85C3 **Devikot** India
22C2 **Devil Postpile Nat Mon** USA
22C1 **Devils Gate** *P* USA
Devil's Island = Isla du Diable
8D2 **Devils Lake** USA
12H3 **Devils Paw** *Mt* Can
43D4 **Devizes** Eng
85D3 **Devli** India
55B2 **Devoll** *R* Alb
43B4 **Devon** County, Eng
6A2 **Devon I** Can
107D5 **Devonport** Aust
86C1 **Dewangiri** Bhutan
85D4 **Dewās** India
101G1 **Dewetsdorp** S Africa
11B3 **Dewey Res** USA
19B3 **De Witt** USA
18C2 **Dexter** Missouri, USA
73A3 **Deyang** China
90C3 **Deyhuk** Iran
90A3 **Dezfūl** Iran
72D2 **Dezhou** China
90A2 **Dezh Shāhpūr** Iran
91B4 **Dhahran** S Arabia
86C2 **Dhākā** Bang
87B2 **Dhamavaram** India
86A2 **Dhamtari** India
86B2 **Dhanbād** India
86A1 **Dhangarhi** Nepal
86B1 **Dhankuta** Nepal
85D4 **Dhār** India
87B2 **Dharmapuri** India
84D2 **Dharmshala** India
97B3 **Dhar Oualata** *Desert Region* Maur
86A1 **Dhaulagiri** *Mt* Nepal
86B2 **Dhenkānāi** India
94B3 **Dhibah** Jordan
55C3 **Dhikti Óri** *Mt* Greece
55C3 **Dhodhekánisos** *Is* Greece
55B3 **Dhomokós** Greece
87B1 **Dhone** India

85C4 **Dhoraji** India
85C4 **Dhrāngadhra** India
86B1 **Dhuburi** India
85C4 **Dhule** India
22B2 **Diablo,Mt** USA
21A2 **Diablo Range** *Mts* USA
34C2 **Diamante** Arg
34B2 **Diamante** *R* Arg
31C5 **Diamantina** Brazil
107D3 **Diamantina** *R* Aust
86B2 **Diamond Harbours** India
22B1 **Diamond Springs** USA
91C4 **Dibā** UAE
98C3 **Dibaya** Zaïre
86C1 **Dibrugarh** India
8C2 **Dickinson** USA
15C2 **Dickson City** USA
93D2 **Dicle** *R* Turk
13E2 **Didsbury** Can
85C3 **Dīdwāna** India
97B3 **Diébougou** Burkina
46D2 **Diekirch** Lux
97B3 **Diéma** Mali
76C1 **Dien Bien Phu** Viet
56B2 **Diepholz** Germany
48C2 **Dieppe** France
46C1 **Diest** Belg
46D2 **Dieuze** France
7D5 **Digby** Can
49D3 **Digne-les-Bains** France
49C2 **Digoin** France
79C4 **Digos** Phil
71E4 **Digul** *R* Indon
86C1 **Dihang** *R* India
Dijlah = Tigris
49C2 **Dijon** France
98B2 **Dik** Chad
99E1 **Dikhil** Djibouti
46B1 **Diksmuide** Belg
18I0 **Dikson** Russian Fed
82A2 **Dilaram** Afghan
106B1 **Dili** Indon
76D3 **Di Linh** Viet
46E1 **Dillenburg** Germany
99C1 **Dilling** Sudan
12C3 **Dillingham** USA
8B2 **Dillon** USA
16A2 **Dillsburg** USA
100B2 **Dilolo** Zaïre
Dimashq = Damascus
98C3 **Dimbelenge** Zaïre
97B4 **Dimbokro** Ivory Coast
54C2 **Dimitrovgrad** Bulg
61G3 **Dimitrovgrad** Russian Fed
94B3 **Dimona** Israel
86C1 **Dimpāpur** India
79C3 **Dinagat** *I* Phil
86B1 **Dinajpur** India
48B2 **Dinan** France
46C1 **Dinant** Belg
92B2 **Dinar** Turk
99D1 **Dinder** *R* Sudan
87B2 **Dindigul** India
72B2 **Dingbian** China
86B1 **Dinggyê** China
41A3 **Dingle** Irish Rep
41A3 **Dingle** *B* Irish Rep
97A3 **Dinguiraye** Guinea
44B3 **Dingwall** Scot
72A2 **Dingxi** China
72D2 **Ding Xian** China
76D1 **Dinh Lap** Viet
22C2 **Dinuba** USA
97A3 **Diouloulou** Sen
86C1 **Diphu** India
99E2 **Dirē Dawa** Eth
106A3 **Dirk Hartog** *I* Aust
95A3 **Dirkou** Niger
109C1 **Dirranbandi** Aust
99E2 **Dirri** Somalia
29G8 **Disappointment,C** South Georgia
20B1 **Disappointment,C** USA
106B3 **Disappointment,L** Aust
108B3 **Discovery B** Aust

Discovery Tablemount

42D2 **Durham** Eng
11C3 **Durham** N Carolina, USA
16D1 **Durham** New Hampshire, USA
108B1 **Durham Downs** Aust
54A2 **Durmitor** *Mt* Montenegro, Yugos
44B2 **Durness** Scot
55A2 **Durrës** Alb
108B1 **Durrie** Aust
45A3 **Dursey** *I* Irish Rep
55C3 **Dursunbey** Turk
110B2 **D'Urville I** NZ
90D2 **Dushak** Turkmenistan
73B4 **Dushan** China
82A2 **Dushanbe** Tajikistan
111A3 **Dusky Sd** NZ
56B2 **Düsseldorf** Germany
73B4 **Duyun** China
92B1 **Düzce** Turk
60C2 **Dvina** *R* Latvia
85B4 **Dwärka** India
6D3 **Dyer,C** Can
11B3 **Dyersburg** USA
43B3 **Dyfed** County, Wales
61F5 **Dykh Tau** *Mt* Russian Fed
108B1 **Dynevor Downs** Aust
68B2 **Dzag** Mongolia
63C3 **Dzamin Üüd** Mongolia
101D2 **Dzaoudzi** Mayotte
68C2 **Dzarnïn Üüd** Mongolia
68B2 **Dzavhan Gol** *R* Mongolia
80E1 **Dzehezkazgan** Kazakhstan
61F2 **Dzerzhinsk** Russian Fed
63E2 **Dzhalinda** Russian Fed
65J5 **Dzhambul** Kazakhstan
60D4 **Dzhankoy** Ukraine
Dzharkent = Panfilov
65H4 **Dzhezkazgan** Kazakhstan
84B1 **Dzhilikul'** Tajikistan
65J5 **Dzhungarskiy Alatau** *Mts* Kazakhstan
59B2 **Dzierzoniow** Pol
63B3 **Dzüyl** Mongolia
82C1 **Dzungaria** Basin, China

E

7B4 **Eabamet L** Can
12F2 **Eagle** Alaska, USA
20B2 **Eagle L** California, USA
19A3 **Eagle Mountain L** USA
9C4 **Eagle Pass** USA
4E3 **Eagle Plain** Can
12E2 **Eagle River** USA
21B2 **Earlimart** USA
17B1 **Easley** USA
15C2 **East Aurora** USA
43E4 **Eastbourne** Eng
14A2 **East Chicago** USA
69E3 **East China Sea** China/Japan
100B4 **Eastern Cape** Province, S Africa
83B4 **Eastern Ghats** *Mts* India
100B3 **Eastern Transvaal** Province, S Africa
29E6 **East Falkland** *I* Falkland Is
12E1 **East Fork** *R* USA
21B2 **Eastgate** USA
16C1 **Easthampton** USA
16C2 **East Hampton** USA
14A2 **East Lake** USA
14B2 **East Liverpool** USA
100B4 **East London** S Africa
7C4 **Eastmain** Can
7C4 **Eastmain** *R* Can
17B1 **Eastman** USA
15C3 **Easton** Maryland, USA
15C2 **Easton** Pennsylvania, USA
16B2 **East Orange** USA
105L4 **East Pacific Ridge** Pacific O
17B1 **East Point** USA
42D3 **East Retford** Eng
11A3 **East St Louis** USA
1B7 **East Siberian S** Russian Fed
43E4 **East Sussex** County, Eng
17B1 **Eatonton** USA
10A2 **Eau Claire** USA
71F3 **Eauripik** *I* Pacific O
23B1 **Ebano** Mexico
98B2 **Ebebiyin** Eq Guinea
56C2 **Eberswalde** Germ
73A4 **Ebian** China
65K5 **Ebinur** *L* China
53C2 **Eboli** Italy
98B2 **Ebolowa** Cam
51B1 **Ebro** *R* Spain
92A1 **Eceabat** Turk
96C1 **Ech Cheliff** Alg
72D2 **Eching** China
20C1 **Echo** USA
4G3 **Echo Bay** Can
46D2 **Echternach** Lux
108B3 **Echuca** Aust
50A2 **Ecija** Spain
6B2 **Eclipse Sd** Can
32B4 **Ecuador** Republic, S America
99E1 **Ed** Eritrea
44C2 **Eday** *I* Scot
98C1 **Ed Da'ein** Sudan
95C3 **Ed Damer** Sudan
95C3 **Ed Debba** Sudan
44B2 **Eddrachillis** *B* Scot
99D1 **Ed Dueim** Sudan
109C4 **Eddystone Pt** Aust
98A2 **Edea** Cam
109C3 **Eden** Aust
42C2 **Eden** *R* Eng
101G1 **Edenburg** S Africa
111A3 **Edendale** NZ
46E2 **Edenkoben** Germany
46E1 **Eder** *R* Germany
6D3 **Edgell I** Can
64D2 **Edgeøya** *I* Barents S
16A3 **Edgewood** USA
94B3 **Edh Dhahiriya** Israel
55B2 **Edhessa** Greece
44C3 **Edinburgh** Scot
60C5 **Edirne** Turk
17B1 **Edisto** *R* USA
13D2 **Edith Cavell,Mt** Can
20B1 **Edmonds** USA
5G4 **Edmonton** Can
7D5 **Edmundston** Can
19A4 **Edna** USA
12H3 **Edna Bay** USA
52B1 **Edolo** Italy
94B3 **Edom** Region, Jordan
92A2 **Edremit** Turk
55C3 **Edremit Körfezi** *B* Turk
68B2 **Edrengiyn Nuruu** *Mts* Mongolia
5G4 **Edson** Can
34C3 **Eduardo Castex** Arg
12J2 **Eduni,Mt** Can
108B3 **Edward** *R* Aust
99C3 **Edward,L** Uganda/Zaïre
108A1 **Edwards Creek** Aust
9C3 **Edwards Plat** USA
18C2 **Edwardsville** USA
12H3 **Edziza,Mt** Can
12B2 **Eek** USA
46B1 **Eeklo** Belg
10B3 **Effingham** USA
6E3 **Egedesminde** Greenland
12C3 **Egegik** USA
59C3 **Eger** Hung
39F7 **Egersund** Nor
16B3 **Egg Harbor City** USA
4G2 **Eglinton I** Can
110B1 **Egmont,C** NZ
110B1 **Egmont,Mt** NZ
92B2 **Eğridir Gölü** *L* Turk
95B2 **Egypt** Republic, Africa
50B1 **Eibar** Spain
49C2 **Eibeuf** France
46D1 **Eifel** Region, Germ
44A3 **Eigg** *I* Scot
83B5 **Eight Degree Chan** Indian O
106B2 **Eighty Mile Beach** Aust
108C3 **Eildon,L** Aust
56B2 **Eindhoven** Neth
47C1 **Einsiedeln** Switz
94B3 **Ein Yahav** Israel
57C2 **Eisenach** Germany
57C3 **Eisenerz** Austria
46D1 **Eitorf** Germany
72A1 **Ejin qi** China
23B2 **Ejutla** Mexico
110C2 **Eketahuna** NZ
65J4 **Ekibastuz** Kazakhstan
63F2 **Ekimchan** Russian Fed
92B3 **Ek Mahalla el Kubra** Egypt
39H7 **Eksjo** Sweden
10B1 **Ekwen** *R* Can
92A3 **El'Alamein** Egypt
92B3 **El'Arîsh** Egypt
92B4 **Elat** Israel
95B3 **El'Atrun Oasis** Sudan
93C2 **Elazig** Turk
92C3 **El Azraq** Jordan
52B2 **Elba** *I* Italy
95C2 **El Balyana** Egypt
32C2 **El Banco** Colombia
55B2 **Elbasan** Alb
27D5 **El Baúl** Ven
57C2 **Elbe** *R* Germany
94C1 **El Bega'a** *R* Leb
14A2 **Elberta** USA
8C3 **Elbert,Mt** USA
17B1 **Elberton** USA
92C2 **Elbistan** Turk
58B2 **Elblag** Pol
29B4 **El Bolson** Arg
61F5 **Elbrus** *Mt* Russian Fed
Elburz Mts = Reshteh-ye Alborz
21B3 **El Cajon** USA
19A4 **El Campo** USA
51B2 **Elche** Spain
51B2 **Elda** Spain
32B3 **El Diviso** Colombia
96B2 **El Djouf** *Desert Region* Maur
18B2 **Eldon** USA
11A3 **El Dorado** Arkansas, USA
35B2 **Eldorado** Brazil
9D3 **El Dorado** Kansas, USA
24B2 **El Dorado** Mexico
33E2 **El Dorado** Ven
99D2 **Eldoret** Kenya
22C1 **Eleanor,L** USA
96B2 **El Eglab** Region, Alg
50B1 **El Escorial** Spain
93D2 **Eleşkirt** Turk
11C4 **Eleuthera** *I* The Bahamas
92B4 **El Faiyûm** Egypt
96B2 **El Farsia** *Well* Mor
98C1 **El Fasher** Sudan
92B4 **El Fashn** Egypt
50A1 **El Ferrol del Caudillo** Spain
99C1 **El Fula** Sudan
96C1 **El Gassi** Alg
99D1 **El Geteina** Sudan
99D1 **El Gezîra** Region, Sudan
94B3 **El Ghor** *V* Israel/Jordan
10B2 **Elgin** Illinois, USA
44C3 **Elgin** Scot
92B3 **El Gîza** Egypt
96C1 **El Golea** Alg
99D2 **Elgon,Mt** Uganda/Kenya
99E2 **El Goran** Eth
23A2 **El Grullo** Mexico
96B2 **El Guettara** *Well* Mali
96B2 **El Haricha** *Desert Region* Mali
92A4 **El Harra** Egypt
51C2 **El Harrach** Alg
99D1 **El Hawata** Sudan
23B1 **El Higo** Mexico
34A3 **El Huecu** Arg
92B4 **El'Igma** *Desert Region* Egypt
12B2 **Elim** USA
4H2 **Elira,C** Can
Elisabethville = Lubumbashi
39K6 **Elisenvaara** Fin
El Iskandarîya = Alexandria
61F4 **Elista** Russian Fed
106C4 **Elizabeth** Aust
15D2 **Elizabeth** USA
11C3 **Elizabeth City** USA
17C1 **Elizabethtown** N Carolina, USA
16A2 **Elizabethtown** Pennsylvania, USA
96B1 **El Jadida** Mor
92C3 **El Jafr** Jordan
99D1 **El Jebelein** Sudan
96D1 **El Jem** Tunisia
58C2 **Elk** Pol
16B3 **Elk** *R* Maryland, USA
14B3 **Elk** *R* W Virginia, USA
95C3 **El Kamlin** Sudan
22B1 **Elk Grove** USA
El Khalil = Hebron
80B3 **El Khârga** Egypt
80B3 **El-Khârga Oasis** Egypt
14A2 **Elkhart** USA
96B2 **El Khenachich** *Desert Region* Mali
54C2 **Elkhovo** Bulg
14C3 **Elkins** USA
8B2 **Elko** USA
16B3 **Elkton** USA
92B3 **El Kuntilla** Egypt
99C1 **El Lagowa** Sudan
4H2 **Ellef Ringnes I** Can
8A2 **Ellensburg** USA
16B2 **Ellenville** USA
6B2 **Ellesmere I** Can
111B2 **Ellesmere,L** NZ
16A3 **Ellicott City** USA
100B4 **Elliot** S Africa
7B5 **Elliot Lake** Can
94B3 **El Lisan** *Pen* Jordan
112B3 **Ellsworth Land** *Region* Ant
95B1 **El Maghra** *L* Egypt
92B3 **El Mansûra** Egypt
16B3 **Elmer** USA
96B3 **El Merelé** *Desert Region* Maur
34B2 **El Milagro** Arg
94B1 **El Mîna** Leb
92B4 **El Minya** Egypt
22B1 **Elmira** California, USA
10C2 **Elmira** New York, USA
96B2 **El Mreitl** *Well* Maur
56B2 **Elmshorn** Germany
98C1 **El Muglad** Sudan
96B2 **El Mzereb** *Well* Mali
79A3 **El Nido** Phil
99D1 **El Obeid** Sudan
23A2 **El Oro** Mexico
96C1 **El Oued** Alg
9C3 **El Paso** USA
21A2 **El Porta** USA
22C2 **El Portal** USA
50A2 **El Puerto del Sta Maria** Spain
El Qâhira = Cairo
El Quds = Jerusalem
94B3 **El Quseima** Egypt
9D3 **El Reno** USA
4E3 **Elsa** Can
25D3 **El Salvador** Republic, Cent America
22D4 **Elsinore L** USA
34B3 **El Sosneade** Arg

Elsterwerde

5G4 **Fort Mackay** Can
5G5 **Fort Macleod** Can
5G4 **Fort McMurray** Can
4E3 **Fort McPherson** Can
18B2 **Fort Madison** USA
8C2 **Fort Morgan** USA
11B4 **Fort Myers** USA
5F4 **Fort Nelson** Can
4F3 **Fort Norman** Can
17A1 **Fort Payne** USA
8C2 **Fort Peck Res** USA
11B4 **Fort Pierce** USA
4G3 **Fort Providence** Can
5G3 **Fort Resolution** Can
98B3 **Fort Rousset** Congo
5F4 **Fort St James** Can
13C1 **Fort St John** Can
13E2 **Fort Saskatchewan** Can
18B2 **Fort Scott** USA
4E3 **Fort Selkirk** Can
7B4 **Fort Severn** Can
61H5 **Fort Shevchenko** Kazakhstan
4F3 **Fort Simpson** Can
5G3 **Fort Smith** Can
4G3 **Fort Smith** Region, Can
11A3 **Fort Smith** USA
9C3 **Fort Stockton** USA
20B2 **Fortuna** California, USA
5G4 **Fort Vermillion** Can
17A1 **Fort Walton Beach** USA
10B2 **Fort Wayne** USA
44B3 **Fort William** Scot
9D3 **Fort Worth** USA
12F2 **Fortymile** *R* USA
12E1 **Fort Yukon** USA
73C5 **Foshan** China
47B2 **Fossano** Italy
12G3 **Foster,Mt** USA
98B3 **Fougamou** Gabon
48B2 **Fougères** France
44D1 **Foula** *I* Scot
43E4 **Foulness I** Eng
111B2 **Foulwind,C** NZ
98B2 **Foumban** Cam
49C1 **Fourmies** France
55C3 **Foúrnoi** *I* Greece
97A3 **Fouta Djallon** *Mts* Guinea
111B3 **Foveaux** *Str* NZ
43B4 **Fowey** Eng
13D2 **Fox Creek** Can
6B3 **Foxe Basin** *G* Can
6B3 **Foxe Chan** Can
6C3 **Foxe Pen** Can
110C2 **Foxton** NZ
13F2 **Fox Valley** Can
45B2 **Foynes** Irish Rep
100A2 **Foz do Cuene** Angola
30F4 **Foz do Iquaçu** Brazil
16A2 **Frackville** USA
34B2 **Fraga** Arg
16D1 **Framingham** USA
31B6 **Franca** Brazil
49C2 **France** Republic, Europe
10A2 **Frances** Can
12J2 **Frances** *R* Can
49D2 **Franche Comté** Region, France
100B3 **Francistown** Botswana
13B2 **Francois L** Can
14A2 **Frankfort** Indiana, USA
11B3 **Frankfort** Kentucky, USA
101G1 **Frankfort** S Africa
57B2 **Frankfurt** Germany
46E1 **Frankfurt am Main** Germany
56C2 **Frankfurt-an-der-Oder** Germany
57C3 **Fränkischer Alb** *Upland* Germany
14A3 **Franklin** Indiana, USA
19B4 **Franklin** Louisiana, USA
16D1 **Franklin** Massachusetts, USA
16B2 **Franklin** New Jersey, USA
14C2 **Franklin** Pennsylvania, USA
4F2 **Franklin B** Can
20C1 **Franklin D Roosevelt** *L* USA
4F3 **Franklin Mts** Can
4J2 **Franklin Str** Can
111B2 **Franz Josef Glacier** NZ
Franz-Joseph-Land = Zemlya Frantsa Iosifa
5F5 **Fraser** *R* Can
44C3 **Fraserburgh** Scot
107E3 **Fraser I** Aust
13B2 **Fraser L** Can
47B1 **Frasne** France
47C1 **Frauenfield** Switz
34D2 **Fray Bentos** Urug
40C2 **Frazerburgh** Scot
16B3 **Frederica** USA
56B1 **Fredericia** Den
15C3 **Frederick** Maryland, USA
15C3 **Fredericksburg** Virginia, USA
12H3 **Frederick Sd** USA
18B2 **Fredericktown** USA
7D5 **Fredericton** Can
6E3 **Frederikshab** Greenland
39G7 **Frederikshavn** Den
15C2 **Fredonia** USA
39G7 **Fredrikstad** Nor
16B2 **Freehold** USA
26B1 **Freeport** The Bahamas
19A4 **Freeport** Texas, USA
97A4 **Freetown** Sierra Leone
57B3 **Freiburg** Germany
57C3 **Freistadt** Austria
106A4 **Fremantle** Aust
22B2 **Fremont** California, USA
18A1 **Fremont** Nebraska, USA
14B2 **Fremont** Ohio, USA
33G3 **French Guiana** Dependency, S America
109C4 **Frenchmans Cap** *Mt* Aust
105J4 **French Polynesia** *Is* Pacific O
24B2 **Fresnillo** Mexico
8B3 **Fresno** USA
22C2 **Fresno** *R* USA
47A1 **Fretigney** France
46B1 **Frévent** France
109C4 **Freycinet Pen** Aust
97A3 **Fria** Guinea
22C2 **Friant** USA
22C2 **Friant Dam** USA
52A1 **Fribourg** Switz
57B3 **Friedrichshafen** Germany
6D3 **Frobisher B** Can
6D3 **Frobisher Bay** Can
5H4 **Frobisher L** Can
61F4 **Frolovo** Russian Fed
43C4 **Frome** Eng
108A1 **Frome** *R* Aust
43C4 **Frome** *R* Eng
106C4 **Frome,L** Aust
25C3 **Frontera** Mexico
15C3 **Front Royal** USA
53B2 **Frosinone** Italy
73C5 **Fuchuan** China
73E4 **Fuding** China
24B2 **Fuerte** *R* Mexico
30E3 **Fuerte Olimpo** Par
96A2 **Fuerteventura** *I* Canary Is
72C2 **Fugu** China
68A2 **Fuhai** China
91C4 **Fujairah** UAE
75B1 **Fuji** Japan
73D4 **Fujian** Province, China
69F2 **Fujin** China
75B1 **Fujinomiya** Japan
74D3 **Fuji-san** *Mt* Japan
75B1 **Fujisawa** Japan
75B1 **Fuji-Yoshida** Japan
63A3 **Fukang** China
74C3 **Fukuchiyima** Japan
74D3 **Fukui** Japan
74C4 **Fukuoka** Japan
74E3 **Fukushima** Japan
74C4 **Fukuyama** Japan
57B2 **Fulda** Germany
57B2 **Fulda** *R* Germany
73B4 **Fuling** China
27L1 **Fullarton** Trinidad
22D4 **Fullerton** USA
18C2 **Fulton** Kentucky, USA
15C2 **Fulton** New York, USA
46C1 **Fumay** France
75C1 **Funabashi** Japan
96A1 **Funchal** Medeira
35C1 **Fundão** Brazil
7D5 **Fundy,B of** Can
101C3 **Funhalouro** Mozam
72D3 **Funing** China
73B5 **Funing** China
97C3 **Funtua** Nig
73D4 **Fuqing** China
101C2 **Furancungo** Mozam
91C4 **Fürg** Iran
47C1 **Furka** *P* Switz
107D5 **Furneaux Group** *Is* Aust
56C2 **Fürstenwalde** Germany
57C3 **Fürth** Germany
74D3 **Furukawa** Japan
6B3 **Fury and Hecla St** Can
74A2 **Fushun** Liaoning, China
73A4 **Fushun** Sichuan, China
74B2 **Fusong** China
57C3 **Füssen** Germany
72E2 **Fu Xian** China
72E1 **Fuxin** China
72D3 **Fuyang** China
72E1 **Fuyuan** Liaoning, China
73A4 **Fuyuan** Yunnan, China
68A2 **Fuyun** China
73D4 **Fuzhou** China
56C1 **Fyn** *I* Den

G

99E2 **Gaalkacyo** Somalia
21B2 **Gabbs** USA
100A2 **Gabela** Angola
96D1 **Gabe's** Tunisia
22B2 **Gabilan Range** *Mts* USA
98B3 **Gabon** Republic, Africa
100B3 **Gaborone** Botswana
54C2 **Gabrovo** Bulg
91B3 **Gach Sārān** Iran
17A1 **Gadsden** Alabama, USA
10A1 **Gads L** Can
53B2 **Gaeta** Italy
71F3 **Gaferut** *I* Pacific O
96C1 **Gafsa** Tunisia
60D2 **Gagarin** Russian Fed
97B4 **Gagnoa** Ivory Coast
7D4 **Gagnon** Can
61F5 **Gagra** Georgia
86B1 **Gaibanda** India
29C4 **Gaimán** Arg
17B2 **Gainesville** Florida, USA
17B1 **Gainesville** Georgia, USA
19A3 **Gainesville** Texas, USA
42D3 **Gainsborough** Eng
108A2 **Gairdner,L** Aust
44B3 **Gairloch** Scot
16A3 **Gaithersburg** USA
87B1 **Gajendragarh** India
73D4 **Ga Jiang** *R* China
99D3 **Galana** *R* Kenya
103D5 **Galapagos Is** Pacific O
42C2 **Galashiels** Scot
54C1 **Galaţi** Rom
4C3 **Galena** Alaska, USA
18B2 **Galena** Kansas, USA
27L1 **Galeota Pt** Trinidad
27L1 **Galera Pt** Trinidad
10A2 **Galesburg** USA
15C2 **Galeton** USA
61F2 **Galich** Russian Fed
50A1 **Galicia** Region, Spain
Galilee,S of = Tiberias,L
27J1 **Galina Pt** Jamaica
99D1 **Gallabat** Sudan
47C2 **Gallarate** Italy
87C3 **Galle** Sri Lanka
51B1 **Gállego** *R* Spain
Gallipoli = Gelibolu
55A2 **Gallipoli** Italy
38J5 **Gällivare** Sweden
42B2 **Galloway** District
42B2 **Galloway,Mull of** *C* Scot
8C3 **Gallup** USA
22B1 **Galt** USA
96A2 **Galtat Zemmour** Mor
25C2 **Galveston** USA
11A4 **Galveston B** USA
34C2 **Galvez** Arg
49D3 **Galvi** Corse
45B2 **Galway** County, Irish Rep
41B3 **Galway** Irish Rep
41B3 **Galway** *B* Irish Rep
86B1 **Gamba** China
97B3 **Gambaga** Ghana
4A3 **Gambell** USA
97A3 **Gambia** *R* The Gambia/Sen
97A3 **Gambia,The** Republic, Africa
98B3 **Gamboma** Congo
100A2 **Gambos** Angola
87C3 **Gampola** Sri Lanka
99E2 **Ganale Dorya** *R* Eth
15C2 **Gananoque** Can
Gand = Gent
100A2 **Ganda** Angola
98C3 **Gandajika** Zaïre
84B3 **Gandava** Pak
7E5 **Gander** Can
85C4 **Gāndhīdhām** India
85C4 **Gāndhīnagar** India
85D4 **Gāndhi Sāgar** *L* India
51B2 **Gandia** Spain
86B2 **Ganga** *R* India
85C3 **Ganganar** India
86C2 **Gangaw** Burma
72A2 **Gangca** China
82C2 **Gangdise Shan** *Mts* China
Ganges = Ganga
86B1 **Gangtok** India
72B3 **Gangu** China
8C2 **Gannett Peak** *Mt* USA
72B2 **Ganquan** China
108A3 **Gantheaume** *C* Aust
39K8 **Gantsevichi** Belorussia
73D4 **Ganzhou** China
97C3 **Gao** Mali
72A2 **Gaolan** China
72C2 **Gaoping** China
97B3 **Gaoua** Burkina
97A3 **Gaoual** Guinea
72D3 **Gaoyou Hu** *L* China
73C5 **Gaozhou** China
49D3 **Gap** France
79B2 **Gapan** Phil
84D2 **Gar** China
109C1 **Garah** Aust
31D3 **Garanhuns** Brazil
21A1 **Garberville** USA
35B2 **Garça** Brazil
35A2 **Garcias** Brazil
47D2 **Garda** Italy
9C3 **Garden City** USA
14A1 **Garden Pen** USA
34D3 **Gardey** Arg
84B2 **Gardez** Afghan

106B4	**Great Australian Bight** G Aust
16B3	**Great B** New Jersey, USA
25E2	**Great Bahama Bank** The Bahamas
110C1	**Great Barrier I** NZ
107D2	**Great Barrier Reef** Is Aust
16C1	**Great Barrington** USA
4F3	**Great Bear L** Can
9D2	**Great Bend** USA
107D3	**Great Dividing Range** Mts Aust
42D2	**Great Driffield** Eng
16B3	**Great Egg Harbor** B USA
112B10	**Greater Antarctic Region**, Ant
26B2	**Greater Antilles** Is Caribbean S
43D4	**Greater London Metropolitan County**, Eng
43C3	**Greater Manchester County**, Eng
25E2	**Great Exuma** I The Bahamas
8B2	**Great Falls** USA
44B3	**Great Glen** V Scot
86B1	**Great Himalayan Range** Mts Asia
11C4	**Great Inagua** I The Bahamas
100B4	**Great Karroo** Mts S Africa
109C4	**Great L** Aust
100A3	**Great Namaland Region**, Namibia
42C3	**Great Ormes Head** C Wales
11C4	**Great Ragged** I The Bahamas
99D3	**Great Ruaha** R Tanz
15D2	**Great Sacandaga L** USA
8B2	**Great Salt L** USA
95B2	**Great Sand Sea** Libya/Egypt
106B3	**Great Sandy Desert** Aust
8A2	**Great Sandy Desert** USA
	Great Sandy I = Fraser I
4G3	**Great Slave L** Can
16C2	**Great South B** USA
106B3	**Great Victoria Desert** Aust
112C2	**Great Wall** Base Ant
72B2	**Great Wall** China
43E3	**Great Yarmouth** Eng
94B1	**Greco,C** Cyprus
55B3	**Greece Republic**, Europe
15C2	**Greece** USA
8C2	**Greeley** USA
6B1	**Greely Fjord** Can
14A1	**Green B** USA
14A2	**Green Bay** USA
14A3	**Greencastle** Indiana, USA
16C1	**Greenfield** Massachusetts, USA
14A2	**Greenfield** Wisconsin, USA
13F2	**Green Lake** Can
6F2	**Greenland Dependency**, N Atlantic O
102H1	**Greenland Basin** Greenland S
1B1	**Greenland S** Greenland
42B2	**Greenock** Scot
16C2	**Greenport** USA
16B3	**Greensboro** Maryland, USA
11C3	**Greensboro** N Carolina, USA
15C2	**Greensburg** Pennsylvania, USA
44B3	**Greenstone** Pt Scot

18C2	**Greenup** USA
17A1	**Greenville** Alabama, USA
97B4	**Greenville** Lib
19B3	**Greenville** Mississippi, USA
16D1	**Greenville** N Hampshire, USA
14B2	**Greenville** Ohio, USA
17B1	**Greenville** S Carolina, USA
19A3	**Greenville** Texas, USA
43E4	**Greenwich** Eng
16C2	**Greenwich** USA
16B3	**Greenwood** Delaware, USA
19B3	**Greenwood** Mississippi, USA
17B1	**Greenwood** S Carolina, USA
18B2	**Greers Ferry L** USA
108A1	**Gregory,L** Aust
107D2	**Gregory Range** Mts Aust
56C2	**Greifswald** Germany
64F3	**Gremikha** Russian Fed
56C1	**Grenå** Den
19C3	**Grenada** USA
27E4	**Grenada** I Caribbean S
109C2	**Grenfell** Aust
49D2	**Grenoble** France
27M2	**Grenville** Grenada
107D2	**Grenville,C** Aust
20B1	**Gresham** USA
78C4	**Gresik** Jawa, Indon
78A3	**Gresik** Sumatera, Indon
19B4	**Gretna** USA
111B2	**Grey** R NZ
12G2	**Grey Hunter Pk** Mt Can
7E4	**Grey Is** Can
16C1	**Greylock,Mt** USA
111B2	**Greymouth** NZ
107D3	**Grey Range** Mts Aust
45C2	**Greystones** Irish Rep
101H1	**Greytown** S Africa
101F1	**Griekwastad** S Africa
17B1	**Griffin** USA
108C2	**Griffith** Aust
107D5	**Grim,C** Aust
15C2	**Grimsby** Can
42D3	**Grimsby** Eng
38B1	**Grimsey** I Iceland
13D1	**Grimshaw** Can
39F7	**Grimstad** Nor
47C1	**Grindelwald** Switz
6A2	**Grinnell Pen** Can
6B2	**Grise Fjord** Can
61H1	**Griva** Russian Fed
39J7	**Grobina** Latvia
58C2	**Grodno** Belorussia
86A1	**Gromati** R India
56B2	**Groningen** Neth
106C2	**Groote Eylandt** I Aust
100A2	**Grootfontein** Namibia
100B3	**Grootvloer** Salt L S Africa
27P2	**Gros Islet** St Lucia
46E1	**Grosser Feldberg** Mt Germany
52B2	**Grosseto** Italy
46E2	**Gross-Gerau** Germany
57C3	**Grossglockner** Mt Austria
47E1	**Gross Venediger** Mt Austria
12C3	**Grosvenor,L** USA
22B2	**Groveland** USA
21A2	**Grover City** USA
15D2	**Groveton** USA
61G5	**Groznyy** Russian Fed
58B2	**Grudziadz** Pol
100A3	**Grünau** Namibia
44E2	**Grutness** Scot
61F3	**Gryazi** Russian Fed

61E2	**Gryazovets** Russian Fed
29G8	**Grytviken** South Georgia
45A2	**Gt Blasket** I Irish Rep
35C2	**Guaçuí** Brazil
23A1	**Guadalajara** Mexico
50B1	**Guadalajara** Spain
107E1	**Guadalcanal** I Solomon Is
50B2	**Guadalimar** R Spain
51B1	**Guadalope** R Spain
50B2	**Guadalqivir** R Spain
24B2	**Guadalupe** Mexico
3G6	**Guadalupe** I Mexico
27E3	**Guadeloupe** I Caribbean S
50B2	**Guadian** R Spain
50A2	**Guadiana** R Port
50B2	**Guadix** Spain
32D6	**Guajará Mirim** Brazil
32C1	**Guajira,Pen de** Colombia
32B4	**Gualaceo** Ecuador
34D2	**Gualeguay** Arg
34D2	**Gualeguaychú** Arg
71F2	**Guam** I Pacific O
34C3	**Guamini** Arg
77C5	**Gua Musang** Malay
23A1	**Guanajuato** Mexico
23A1	**Guanajuato** State, Mexico
32D2	**Guanare** Ven
25D2	**Guane** Cuba
73C5	**Guangdong** Province, China
73A3	**Guanghan** China
72C3	**Guanghua** China
73A4	**Guangmao Shan** Mt China
73B5	**Guangnan** China
72B3	**Guangyuan** China
73D4	**Guangze** China
67F3	**Guangzhou** China
35C1	**Guanhães** Brazil
32D3	**Guania** R Colombia
27E5	**Guanipa** R Ven
26B2	**Guantánamo** Cuba
72D1	**Guanting Shuiku** Res China
73B5	**Guanxi** Province, China
73A3	**Guan Xian** China
32B2	**Guapa** Colombia
33E6	**Guaporé** R Brazil/Bol
30C2	**Guaquí** Bol
32B4	**Guaranda** Ecuador
30F4	**Guarapuava** Brazil
35B2	**Guaratinguetá** Brazil
50A1	**Guarda** Port
35B1	**Guarda Mor** Brazil
9C4	**Guasave** Mexico
47D2	**Guastalla** Italy
25C3	**Guatemala** Guatemala
25C3	**Guatemala Republic**, Cent America
34C3	**Guatraché** Arg
32C3	**Guavrare** R Colombia
35B2	**Guaxupé** Brazil
27L1	**Guayaguayare** Trinidad
32A4	**Guayaquil** Ecuador
24A2	**Guaymas** Mexico
34D2	**Guayquiraro** R Arg
100B2	**Guba** Zaïre
99E2	**Guban** Region Somalia
79B3	**Gubat** Phil
56C2	**Gubin** Pol
87B2	**Güdür** India
14B2	**Guelpho** Can
26A2	**Guenabacoa** Cuba
98C1	**Guéréda** Chad
48C2	**Guéret** France
48B2	**Guernsey** I UK
23A2	**Guerrero** State, Mexico
99D2	**Gughe** Mt Eth
63E2	**Gugigu** China
71F2	**Guguan** I Pacific O
109C2	**Guiargambone** Aust

73C4	**Guidong** China
97B4	**Guiglo** Ivory Coast
73C5	**Gui Jiang** R China
43D4	**Guildford** Eng
73C4	**Guilin** China
47B2	**Guillestre** France
72A2	**Guinan** China
97A3	**Guinea Republic**, Africa
102H4	**Guinea Basin** Atlantic O
97A3	**Guinea-Bissau Republic**, Africa
97C4	**Guinea,G of** W Africa
26A2	**Güines** Cuba
97B3	**Guir** Well Mali
84C2	**Guiranwala** Pak
33E1	**Güiria** Ven
46B2	**Guise** France
79C3	**Guiuan** Phil
73B5	**Gui Xian** China
73B4	**Guiyang** China
73B4	**Guizhou** Province, China
85C4	**Gujarāt** State, India
84C2	**Gujrat** Pak
87B1	**Gulbarga** India
58D1	**Gulbene** Latvia
87B1	**Guledagudda** India
80D3	**Gulf,The** S W Asia
109C2	**Gulgong** Aust
73B4	**Gulin** China
12E2	**Gulkana** USA
12E2	**Gulkana** R USA
13E2	**Gull L** Can
13F2	**Gull Lake** Can
55C3	**Güllük Körfezi** B Turk
99D2	**Gulu** Uganda
109C1	**Guluguba** Aust
97C3	**Gumel** Nig
46D1	**Gummersbach** Germany
86A2	**Gumpla** India
93C1	**Gümüşhane** Turk
85D4	**Guna** India
99D1	**Guna** Mt Eth
109C3	**Gundagai** Aust
98B3	**Gungu** Zaïre
6H3	**Gunnbjørn Fjeld** Mt Greenland
109D2	**Gunnedah** Aust
87B1	**Guntakal** India
17A1	**Guntersville** USA
17A1	**Guntersville L** USA
87C1	**Guntür** India
77C5	**Gunung Batu Putch** Mt Malay
78D3	**Gunung Besar** Mt Indon
78D2	**Gunung Bulu** Mt Indon
78A3	**Gunung Gedang** Mt Indon
78C2	**Gunung Lawit** Mt Malay
78C4	**Gunung Lawu** Mt Indon
78D2	**Gunung Menyapa** Mt Indon
78D2	**Gunung Niapa** Mt Indon
78A3	**Gunung Patah** Mt Indon
78C4	**Gunung Raung** Mt Indon
78A3	**Gunung Resag** Mt Indon
78D3	**Gunung Sarempaka** Mt Indon
78C4	**Gunung Sumbing** Mt Indon
77C5	**Gunung Tahan** Mt Malay
78A2	**Gunung Talakmau** Mt Indon
100A2	**Gunza** Angola
72D3	**Guoyang** China
84D2	**Gurdāspur** India
84D3	**Gurgaon** India
86A1	**Gurkha** Nepal
92C2	**Gürün** Turk
31B2	**Gurupi** R Brazil

110C1 **Havelock North** NZ
43B4 **Haverfordwest**
    Wales
16D1 **Haverhill** USA
87B2 **Hāveri** India
16C2 **Haverstraw** USA
59B3 **Havlíčkův Brod**
    Czech Republic
8C2 **Havre** USA
16A3 **Havre de Grace** USA
7D4 **Havre-St-Pierre** Can
54C2 **Havsa** Turk
21C4 **Hawaii** I / Hawaiian Is
21C4 **Hawaii Volcanoes**
    Nat Pk Hawaiian Is
111A2 **Hawea,L** NZ
110B1 **Hawera** NZ
42C2 **Hawick** Scot
111A2 **Hawkdun Range** Mts
    NZ
110C1 **Hawke B** NZ
109D2 **Hawke,C** Aust
108A2 **Hawker** Aust
76B1 **Hawng Luk** Burma
93D3 **Hawr al Habbaniyah**
    L Iraq
93E3 **Hawr al Hammár** L
    Iraq
21B2 **Hawthorne** USA
108B2 **Hay** Aust
5G3 **Hay** R Can
46D2 **Hayange** France
4B3 **Haycock** USA
7A4 **Hayes** R Can
6D2 **Hayes Halvø** Region
    Greenland
12E2 **Hayes,Mt** USA
5G3 **Hay River** Can
18A2 **Haysville** USA
22A2 **Hayward** California,
    USA
86B2 **Hazāribāg** India
46B1 **Hazebrouck** France
19B3 **Hazelhurst** USA
4G2 **Hazel Str** Can
5F4 **Hazelton** Can
13B1 **Hazelton Mts** Can
6C1 **Hazen L** Can
94B3 **Hazeva** Israel
16B2 **Hazleton** USA
22A1 **Healdsburg** USA
108C3 **Healesville** Aust
12E2 **Healy** USA
104B6 **Heard I** Indian O
19A3 **Hearne** Can
10B2 **Hearst** Can
72D2 **Hebei** Province,
    China
109C1 **Hebel** Aust
72C2 **Hebi** China
72C2 **Hebian** China
7D4 **Hebron** Can
94B3 **Hebron** Israel
18A1 **Hebron** Nebraska,
    USA
5E4 **Hecate** Str Can
12H3 **Heceta I** USA
73B5 **Hechi** China
4G2 **Hecla and Griper B**
    Can
111C2 **Hector,Mt** NZ
38G6 **Hede** Sweden
39H6 **Hedemora** Sweden
20C1 **He Devil Mt** USA
56B2 **Heerenveen** Neth
46C1 **Heerlen** Neth
    Hefa = Haifa
73D3 **Hefei** China
73B4 **Hefeng** China
69F2 **Hegang** China
75B1 **Hegura-jima** I Japan
94B3 **Heidan** R Jordan
56B2 **Heide** Germany
101G1 **Heidelberg**
    Transvaal, S Africa
57B3 **Heidelberg** Germany
63E2 **Heihe** China
101G1 **Heilbron** S Africa
57B3 **Heilbronn** Germany
56C2 **Heiligenstadt**
    Germany
38K6 **Heinola** Fin
73B4 **Hejiang** China
6J3 **Hekla** Mt Iceland

76C1 **Hekou** Viet
73A5 **Hekou Yaozou**
    Zizhixian China
72B2 **Helan** China
72B2 **Helan Shan** Mt
    China
19B3 **Helena** Arkansas,
    USA
8B2 **Helena** Montana,
    USA
22D3 **Helendale** USA
71E3 **Helen Reef** I
    Pacific O
44B3 **Helensburgh** Scot
91B4 **Helleh** R Iran
51B2 **Hellin** Spain
20C1 **Hells Canyon** R USA
46D1 **Hellweg** Region,
    Germany
22B2 **Helm** USA
80E2 **Helmand** R Afghan
100A3 **Helmeringhausen**
    Namibia
46C1 **Helmond** Neth
44C2 **Helmsdale** Scot
74B2 **Helong** China
39G7 **Helsingborg** Sweden
    Helsingfors = Helsinki
56C1 **Helsingør** Den
38J6 **Helsinki** Fin
43B4 **Helston** Eng
92B4 **Helwân** Egypt
19A3 **Hempstead** USA
72A3 **Henan** China
72C3 **Henan** Province,
    China
110B1 **Hen and Chicken Is**
    NZ
14A3 **Henderson** Kentucky,
    USA
9B3 **Henderson** Nevada,
    USA
19B3 **Henderson** Texas,
    USA
73E5 **Heng-ch'un** Taiwan
68B4 **Hengduan Shan** Mts
    China
56B2 **Hengelo** Neth
72B2 **Hengshan** China
72D2 **Hengshui** China
76D1 **Heng Xian** China
73C4 **Hengyang** China
77A4 **Henhoaha** Nicobar Is
43D4 **Henley-on-Thames**
    Eng
16B3 **Henlopen,C** USA
7B4 **Henrietta Maria,C**
    Can
18A2 **Henryetta** USA
112C2 **Henryk Arctowski**
    Base Ant
6D3 **Henry Kater Pen** Can
68C2 **Hentiyn Nuruu** Mts
    Mongolia
76B2 **Henzada** Burma
73B5 **Hepu** China
80E2 **Herat** Afghan
5H4 **Herbert** Can
110C2 **Herbertville** NZ
46E1 **Herborn** Germany
26A4 **Heredia** Costa Rica
43C3 **Hereford** Eng
43C3 **Hereford & Worcester**
    County, Eng
46C1 **Herentals** Belg
47B1 **Héricourt** France
18A2 **Herington** USA
111A3 **Heriot** NZ
47C1 **Herisau** Switz
15D2 **Herkimer** USA
44E1 **Herma Ness** Pen
    Scot
109C2 **Hermidale** Aust
111B2 **Hermitage** NZ
    Hermon,Mt = Jebel
    ash Shaykh
24A2 **Hermosillo** Mexico
16A2 **Herndon**
    Pennsylvania, USA
22C2 **Herndon** California,
    USA
46D1 **Herne** Germany
56B1 **Herning** Den

90A2 **Herowābad** Iran
50A2 **Herrera del Duque**
    Spain
16A2 **Hershey** USA
43D4 **Hertford** County, Eng
94B2 **Herzliyya** Israel
46C1 **Hesbaye** Region,
    Belg
46B1 **Hesdin** France
72B2 **Heshui** China
22D3 **Hesperia** USA
12H2 **Hess** R Can
57B2 **Hessen** State,
    Germany
22C2 **Hetch Hetchy Res**
    USA
42C2 **Hexham** Eng
73C5 **He Xian** China
73C5 **Heyuan** China
108B3 **Heywood** Aust
72D2 **Heze** China
17B2 **Hialeah** USA
10A2 **Hibbing** USA
110C1 **Hicks Bay** NZ
109C3 **Hicks,Pt** Aust
23B1 **Hidalgo** State,
    Mexico
24B2 **Hidalgo del Parral**
    Mexico
35B1 **Hidrolândia** Brazil
96A2 **Hierro** I Canary Is
75C1 **Higashine** Japan
74B4 **Higashi-suidō** Str
    Japan
20B2 **High Desert** USA
19B4 **High Island** USA
44B3 **Highland** Region,
    Scot
22D3 **Highland** USA
22C1 **Highland Peak** Mt
    USA
16B2 **Highlands Falls** USA
11B3 **High Point** USA
13D1 **High Prairie** Can
5G4 **High River** Can
17B2 **High Springs** USA
16B2 **Hightstown** USA
43D4 **High Wycombe** Eng
39J7 **Hiiumaa** I / Estonia
80B3 **Hijaz** Region,
    S Arabia
75B2 **Hikigawa** Japan
75B1 **Hikone** Japan
110B1 **Hikurangi** NZ
9C4 **Hildago** Mexico
9C4 **Hildago del Parral**
    Mexico
56B2 **Hildesheim** Germany
27R3 **Hillaby,Mt** Barbados
56C1 **Hillerød** Den
14B3 **Hillsboro** Ohio, USA
20B1 **Hillsboro** Oregon,
    USA
19A3 **Hillsboro** Texas, USA
108C2 **Hillston** Aust
44E1 **Hillswick** Scot
21C4 **Hilo** Hawaiian Is
93C2 **Hilvan** Turk
56B2 **Hilversum** Neth
84D2 **Himachal Pradesh**
    State, India
82B3 **Himalaya** Mts Asia
85C4 **Himatnagar** India
74C4 **Himeji** Japan
74D3 **Himi** Japan
92C3 **Hims** Syria
12E2 **Hinchinbrook**
    Entrance USA
12E2 **Hinchinbrook I** USA
85D3 **Hindaun** India
84B1 **Hindu Kush** Mts
    Afghan
87B2 **Hindupur** India
13D1 **Hines Creek** Can
85D4 **Hinganghāt** India
69E2 **Hinggan Ling** Upland
    China
85B3 **Hingol** R Pak
85D5 **Hingoli** India
38H5 **Hinnøya** I Nor
16C1 **Hinsdale** USA
13D2 **Hinton** Can
34B2 **Hipolito Itrogoyen**
    Arg

86A2 **Hirakud Res** India
92B2 **Hirfanli Baraji** Res
    Turk
87B2 **Hirihar** India
74E2 **Hirosaki** Japan
74C4 **Hiroshima** Japan
46C2 **Hirson** France
54C2 **Hirşova** Rom
56B1 **Hirtshals** Den
84D3 **Hisār** India
26C3 **Hispaniola** I
    Caribbean S
94C1 **Hisyah** Syria
93D3 **Hīt** Iraq
74E3 **Hitachi** Japan
75C1 **Hitachi-Ota** Japan
43D4 **Hitchin** Eng
38F6 **Hitra** I Nor
75A2 **Hiuchi-nada** B Japan
75A2 **Hiwasa** Japan
56B1 **Hjørring** Den
76B1 **Hka** R Burma
97C4 **Ho** Ghana
76D1 **Hoa Binh** Viet
76D3 **Hoa Da** Viet
109C4 **Hobart** Aust
9C3 **Hobbs** USA
56B1 **Hobro** Den
13C2 **Hobson L** Can
99E2 **Hobyo** Somalia
76D3 **Ho Chi Minh** Viet
57C3 **Hochkonig** Mt
    Austria
54B1 **Hódmező'hely** Hung
59B3 **Hodonin**
    Czech Republic
74B2 **Hoeryong** N Korea
57C2 **Hof** Germany
38B2 **Hofsjökull** Mts
    Iceland
74C4 **Hōfu** Japan
96C2 **Hoggar** Upland Alg
46D1 **Hohe Acht** Mt
    Germany
72C1 **Hohhot** China
6J3 **Höhn** Iceland
68B3 **Hoh Sai Hu** L China
82C2 **Hoh Xil Shan** Mts
    China
99D2 **Hoima** Uganda
86C1 **Hojāi** India
75A2 **Hojo** Japan
110B1 **Hokianga Harbour** B
    NZ
111B2 **Hokitika** NZ
74E2 **Hokkaidō** Japan
90C2 **Hokmābād** Iran
109C3 **Holbrook** Aust
9B3 **Holbrook** USA
19A2 **Holdenville** USA
87B2 **Hole Narsipur** India
27R3 **Holetown** Barbados
26B2 **Holguín** Cuba
111B2 **Holitika** NZ
12C2 **Holitna** R USA
59B3 **Hollabrunn** Austria
14A2 **Holland** USA
22B2 **Hollister** USA
19C3 **Holly Springs** USA
22C3 **Hollywood**
    California, USA
17B2 **Hollywood** Florida,
    USA
4G2 **Holman Island** Can
38J6 **Holmsund** Sweden
94B2 **Holon** Israel
56B1 **Holstebro** Den
6E3 **Holsteinborg**
    Greenland
14B2 **Holt** USA
18A2 **Holton** USA
12C2 **Holy Cross** USA
42B3 **Holyhead** Wales
42D2 **Holy I** Eng
43B3 **Holy I** Wales
16C1 **Holyoke**
    Massachusetts, USA
86C2 **Homalin** Burma
6D3 **Home B** Can
12D3 **Homer** Alaska, USA
19B3 **Homer** Louisiana,
    USA
111A2 **Homer Tunnel** NZ
17B1 **Homerville** USA

17B2 **Homestead** USA
17A1 **Homewood** USA
87B1 **Homnābād** India
101C3 **Homoine** Mozam
25D3 **Hondo** *R* Mexico
25D3 **Honduras** Republic, Cent America
25D3 **Honduras,G of** Honduras
39G6 **Hønefoss** Nor
15C2 **Honesdale** USA
21A1 **Honey L** USA
76C1 **Hong** *R* Viet
76D1 **Hon Gai** Viet
73A4 **Hongguo** China
73C4 **Hong Hu** *L* China
72B2 **Honghui** China
73C4 **Hongjiang** China
73C5 **Hong Kong** Colony, S E Asia
68D2 **Hongor** Mongolia
73B5 **Hongshui He** *R* China
72A3 **Hongyuan** China
72D3 **Hongze Hu** *L* China
107E1 **Honiara** Solomon Is
77C4 **Hon Khoai** *I* Camb
76D3 **Hon Lan** *I* Viet
38K4 **Honnigsvåg** Nor
21C4 **Honolulu** Hawaiian Is
77C4 **Hon Panjang** *I* Viet
74D3 **Honshu** *I* Japan
20B1 **Hood,Mt** USA
20B1 **Hood River** USA
45C2 **Hook Head** *C* Irish Rep
12G3 **Hoonah** USA
12A2 **Hooper Bay** USA
101G1 **Hoopstad** S Africa
56A2 **Hoorn** Neth
9B3 **Hoover Dam** USA
12E2 **Hope** Alaska, USA
19B3 **Hope** Arkansas, USA
13C3 **Hope** Can
7D4 **Hopedale** Can
64D2 **Hopen** *I* Barents S
6D3 **Hopes Advance,C** Can
108B3 **Hopetoun** Aust
100B3 **Hopetown** S Africa
18C2 **Hopkinsville** USA
20B1 **Hoquiam** USA
93D1 **Horasan** Turk
99F1 **Hordiyo** Somalia
47C1 **Horgen** Switz
105H5 **Horizon Depth** Pacific O
91C4 **Hormuz,Str of** Oman/Iran
59B3 **Horn** Austria
6H3 **Horn** *C* Iceland
38H5 **Hornavan** *L* Sweden
19B3 **Hornbeck** USA
20B2 **Hornbrook** USA
111B2 **Hornby** NZ
7B5 **Hornepayne** Can
4F3 **Horn Mts** Can
42D3 **Hornsea** Eng
72B1 **Horn Uul** *Mt* Mongolia
30E3 **Horqueta** Par
15C2 **Horseheads** USA
56C1 **Horsens** Den
20B1 **Horseshoe Bay** Can
108B3 **Horsham** Aust
43D4 **Horsham** Eng
39G7 **Horten** Nor
4F3 **Horton** *R* Can
78C2 **Hose Mts** Malay
85D4 **Hoshangābād** India
84D2 **Hoshiārpur** India
87B1 **Hospet** India
29C7 **Hoste** *I* Chile
82B2 **Hotan** China
19B3 **Hot Springs** Arkansas, USA
8C2 **Hot Springs** S. Dakota, USA
4G3 **Hottah** Can
46A2 **Houdan** France
72C2 **Houma** China
19B4 **Houma** USA
16C2 **Housatonic** *R* USA
13B2 **Houston** Can
19C3 **Houston** Mississippi, USA
19A4 **Houston** Texas, USA
106A3 **Houtman** *Is* Aust
68B2 **Hovd** Mongolia
68C1 **Hövsgol Nuur** *L* Mongolia
14A2 **Howard City** USA
12C1 **Howard P** USA
109C3 **Howe,C** Aust
101H1 **Howick** S Africa
44C2 **Hoy** *I* Scot
39F6 **Høyanger** Nor
59B2 **Hradeç-Králové** Czech Republic
59B3 **Hranice** Czech Republic
59B3 **Hron** *R* Slovakia
73E5 **Hsin-chu** Taiwan
73E5 **Hsüeh Shan** *Mt* Taiwan
72B2 **Huachi** China
32B6 **Huacho** Peru
72C1 **Huade** China
72D3 **Huaibei** China
72D3 **Huaibin** China
72D3 **Huai He** *R* China
73C4 **Huaihua** China
73C5 **Huaiji** China
72D3 **Huainan** China
69E4 **Hua-lien** Taiwan
32B5 **Huallaga** *R* Peru
32B5 **Huallanca** Peru
32B5 **Huamachuco** Peru
100A2 **Huambo** Angola
30C2 **Huanay** Bol
32B5 **Huancabamba** Peru
32B6 **Huancavelica** Peru
32B6 **Huancayo** Peru
73D3 **Huangchuan** China
Huang Hai = Yellow S
72D2 **Huang He** *R* China
72B2 **Huangling** China
76D2 **Huangliu** China
73C3 **Huangpi** China
73D4 **Huangshan** China
73D3 **Huangshi** China
34C3 **Huanguelén** Arg
73E4 **Huangyan** China
74B2 **Huanren** China
32B5 **Huānuco** Peru
30C2 **Huanuni** Bol
72B2 **Huan Xian** China
32B5 **Huaráz** Peru
32B6 **Huarmey** Peru
32B5 **Huascarán** *Mt* Peru
30B4 **Huasco** Chile
23B2 **Huatusco** Mexico
23B1 **Huauchinango** Mexico
23B2 **Huautla** Mexico
72C2 **Hua Xian** China
24B2 **Huayapan** *R* Mexico
73C3 **Hubei** Province, China
87B1 **Hubli** India
34C3 **Hucal** Arg
74B2 **Huch'ang** N Korea
42D3 **Huddersfield** Eng
39H6 **Hudiksvall** Sweden
17B2 **Hudson** Florida, USA
14B2 **Hudson** Michigan, USA
16C1 **Hudson** New York, USA
16C1 **Hudson** *R* USA
7B4 **Hudson B** Can
5H4 **Hudson Bay** Can
13C1 **Hudson's Hope** Can
6C3 **Hudson Str** Can
76D2 **Hue** Viet
23B1 **Huejutla** Mexico
50A2 **Huelva** Spain
23A2 **Hueramo** Mexico
51B2 **Húercal Overa** Spain
51B1 **Huesca** Spain
23B2 **Huexotla** *Hist Site* Mexico
107D3 **Hughenden** Aust
12D1 **Hughes** USA
86B2 **Hugli** *R* India
19A3 **Hugo** USA
73D4 **Hui'an** China
110C1 **Huiarau Range** *Mts* NZ
74B2 **Huich'ŏn** N Korea
74B2 **Huifa He** *R* China
32B3 **Huila** *Mt* Colombia
73D5 **Huilai** China
73A4 **Huili** China
74B2 **Huinan** China
34C2 **Huinca Renancó** Arg
25C3 **Huixtla** Mexico
73A4 **Huize** China
73C5 **Huizhou** China
23B2 **Hujuápan de Léon** Mexico
69F2 **Hulin** China
15C1 **Hull** Can
42D3 **Hull** Eng
58B1 **Hultsfred** Sweden
63D3 **Hulun Nur** *L* China
69E1 **Huma** China
33E5 **Humaita** Brazil
100B4 **Humansdorp** S Africa
42D3 **Humber** *R* Eng
42D3 **Humberside** County, Eng
5H4 **Humboldt** Can
20C2 **Humboldt** *R* USA
20B2 **Humboldt B** USA
6D2 **Humboldt Gletscher** *Gl* Greenland
21B2 **Humboldt L** USA
108C1 **Humeburn** Aust
109C3 **Hume,L** Aust
100A2 **Humpata** Angola
22C2 **Humphreys** USA
38A1 **Húnaflóri** *B* Iceland
73C4 **Hunan** Province, China
74C2 **Hunchun** China
13C2 **Hundred Mile House** Can
54B1 **Hunedoara** Rom
59B3 **Hungary** Republic, Europe
108B1 **Hungerford** Aust
74B3 **Hŭngnam** N Korea
74B2 **Hunjiang** China
46D2 **Hunsrück** Mts, Germany
109D2 **Hunter** *R* Aust
13B2 **Hunter I** Can
109C4 **Hunter Is** Aust
12D2 **Hunter,Mt** USA
14A3 **Huntingburg** USA
43D3 **Huntingdon** Eng
14A2 **Huntingdon** Indiana, USA
14B3 **Huntington** W Virginia, USA
22C4 **Huntington Beach** USA
22C2 **Huntington L** USA
110C1 **Huntly** NZ
44C3 **Huntly** Scot
12J2 **Hunt,Mt** Can
108A1 **Hunt Pen** Aust
17A1 **Huntsville** Alabama, USA
15C1 **Huntsville** Can
19A3 **Huntsville** Texas, USA
76D2 **Huong Khe** Viet
71F4 **Huon Peninsula** *Pen* PNG
109C4 **Huonville** Anst
14B1 **Hurd,C** Can
80B3 **Hurghada** Egypt
8D2 **Huron** S. Dakota, USA
14B1 **Huron,L** Can/USA
34A2 **Hurtado** Chile
111B2 **Hurunui** *R* NZ
38B1 **Husavik** Iceland
54C1 **Huşi** Rom
39G7 **Huskvarna** Sweden
12C1 **Huslia** USA
94B2 **Husn** Jordan
56B2 **Husum** Germany
109C1 **Hutton,Mt** Aust
72D2 **Hutuo He** *R* China
46C1 **Huy** Belg
72A2 **Huzhu** China
52C2 **Hvar** *I* Croatia
100B2 **Hwange** Zim
100B2 **Hwange Nat Pk** Zim
15D2 **Hyannis** USA
68B2 **Hyaryas Nuur** *L* Mongolia
5E4 **Hydaburg** Can
16C2 **Hyde Park** USA
87B1 **Hyderābād** India
85B3 **Hyderabad** Pak
49D3 **Hyères** France
12J2 **Hyland** *R* Can
8B2 **Hyndman Peak** *Mt* USA
38K6 **Hyrynsalmi** Fin
13D1 **Hythe** Can
74C4 **Hyūga** Japan
39J6 **Hyvikää** Fin

I

31C4 **Iaçu** Brazil
54C2 **Ialomiţa** *R* Rom
54C1 **Iaşi** Rom
97C4 **Ibadan** Nig
32B3 **Ibagué** Colombia
54B2 **Ibar** *R* Montenegro/Serbia, Yugos
32B3 **Ibarra** Ecuador
35B1 **Ibiá** Brazil
30E4 **Ibicui** *R* Brazil
34D2 **Ibicuy** Arg
51C2 **Ibiza** Spain
51C2 **Ibiza** *I* Spain
101D2 **Ibo** Mozam
31C4 **Ibotirama** Brazil
91C5 **'Ibrī** Oman
32B6 **Ica** Peru
32D4 **Icá** *R* Brazil
32D3 **Icana** Brazil
38A1 **Iceland** Republic, N Atlantic O
13C2 **Ice Mt** Can
87A1 **Ichalkaranji** India
74E3 **Ichihara** Japan
75B1 **Ichinomiya** Japan
74E3 **Ichinoseki** Japan
12F3 **Icy B** USA
4B2 **Icy C** USA
19B3 **Idabell** USA
8B2 **Idaho Falls** USA
20B2 **Idanha** USA
46D2 **Idar Oberstein** Germany
95A2 **Idehan Marzūg** *Desert* Libya
95A2 **Idehan Ubari** *Desert* Libya
96C2 **Idelés** Alg
68B2 **Iderlym Gol** *R* Mongolia
95C2 **Idfu** Egypt
55B3 **Idhi Oros** *Mt* Greece
55B3 **Idhra** *I* Greece
98B3 **Idiofa** Zaïre
12C2 **Iditarod** *R* USA
92C2 **Idlib** Syria
39K7 **Idritsa** Russian Fed
100B4 **Idutywa** S Africa
55C3 **Ierápetra** Greece
46B1 **Ieper** Belg
63D2 **Iet Oktyobr'ya** Russian Fed
99D3 **Ifakara** Tanz
71F3 **Ifalik** *I* Pacific O
101D3 **Ifanadiana** Madag
97C4 **Ife** Nig
97C3 **Iférouane** Niger
78C2 **Igan** Malay
35B2 **Igaranava** Brazil
93E2 **Igdir** Iran
39H6 **Iggesund** Sweden
34B2 **Iglesia** Arg
53A3 **Iglesias** Sardegna
6B3 **Igloolik** Can
10A2 **Ignace** Can
55B3 **Igoumenítsa** Greece
61H2 **Igra** Russian Fed
23B2 **Iguala** Mexico
35B2 **Iguape** Brazil
35B2 **Iguatama** Brazil
31D3 **Iguatu** Brazil
98A3 **Iguéla** Gabon
101D3 **Ihosy** Madag
74D3 **Iida** Japan
75B1 **Iide-san** *Mt* Japan
38K6 **Iisalmi** Fin

75A2 **Iizuka** Japan
97C4 **Ijebu Ode** Nig
56B2 **Ijsselmeer** *S* Neth
55C3 **Ikaría** *I* Greece
74E2 **Ikeda** Japan
98C3 **Ikela** Zaïre
54B2 **Ikhtiman** Bulg
12D3 **Ikolik,C** USA
101D2 **Ikopa** *R* Madag
79B2 **Ilagan** Phil
90A3 **Ilām** Iran
47C1 **Ilanz** Switz
13F1 **Île à la Crosse** Can
13F1 **Île à la Crosse,L** Can
89G8 **Ilebo** Zaïre
96D1 **Île de Jerba** *I* Tunisia
48B2 **Ile de Noirmoutier** *I* France
48B2 **Ile de Ré** *I* France
107F3 **Île des Pins** *I* Nouvelle Calédonie
48A2 **Ile d'Ouessant** *I* France
48B2 **Ile d'Yeu** *I* France
61J3 **Ilek** *R* Russian Fed
107F2 **Îles Bélèp** Nouvelle Calédonie
107E2 **Îles Chesterfield** Nouvelle Calédonie
49D3 **Iles d'Hyères** *Is* France
43B4 **Ilfracombe** Eng
92B1 **Ilgaz Dağları** *Mts* Turk
101C3 **Ilha Bazaruto** *I* Mozam
33G3 **Ilha De Maracá** *I* Brazil
33G4 **Ilha de Marajó** *I* Brazil
35B2 **Ilha de São Sebastião** *I* Brazil
33G6 **Ilha do Bananal** *Region* Brazil
35C2 **Ilha Grande** *I* Brazil
35B2 **Ilha Santo Amaro** *I* Brazil
96A1 **Ilhas Selvegens** *I* Atlantic O
35A2 **Ilha Solteira Dam** Brazil
31D4 **Ilhéus** Brazil
12C3 **Iliamna L** USA
12D2 **Iliamna V** USA
79B4 **Iligan** Phil
63C2 **Ilim** *R* Russian Fed
63C2 **Ilim** Russian Fed
63G3 **Il'inskiy** Russian Fed
55B3 **Iliodhrómia** *I* Greece
79B4 **Illana B** Phil
34A2 **Illapel** Chile
34A2 **Illapel** *R* Chile
97C3 **Illéla** Niger
47D1 **Iller** *R* Germany
4C4 **Illiamna L** USA
10A2 **Illinois** State, USA
18B2 **Illinois** *R* USA
96C2 **Illizi** Alg
30B2 **Ilo** Peru
79B3 **Iloilo** Phil
38L6 **Ilomantsi** Fin
97C4 **Ilorin** Nig
75A2 **Imabari** Japan
75B1 **Imalchi** Japan
60C1 **Imatra** Fin
30G4 **Imbituba** Brazil
99E2 **Imi** Eth
20C2 **Imlay** USA
47D1 **Immenstadt** Germany
52B2 **Imola** Italy
31B3 **Imperatriz** Brazil
52A2 **Imperia** Italy
98B2 **Impfondo** Congo
86C2 **Imphāl** India
47D1 **Imst** Austria
12B1 **Imuruk L** USA
75B1 **Ina** Japan
96C2 **In Afahleleh** *Well* Alg
75B2 **Inamba-jima** *I* Japan
96C2 **In Amenas** Alg
38K5 **Inari** Fin
38K5 **Inarijärvi** *L* Fin
75C1 **Inawashiro-ko** *L* Japan
96C2 **In Belbel** Alg
60E5 **Ince Burun** *Pt* Turk
92B2 **Incekum Burun** *Pt* Turk
74B3 **Inch'ŏn** S Korea
96B2 **In Dagouber** *Well* Mali
35B1 **Indaia** *R* Brazil
38H6 **Indals** *R* Sweden
21B2 **Independence** California, USA
18A2 **Independence** Kansas, USA
18B2 **Independence** Missouri, USA
78A3 **Inderagiri** *R* Indon
61H4 **Inderborskly** Kazakhstan
83B3 **India** Federal Republic, Asia
14A2 **Indiana** State, USA
15C2 **Indiana** USA
104C6 **Indian-Antarctic Ridge** Indian O
14A3 **Indianapolis** USA
Indian Desert = Thar Desert
7E4 **Indian Harbour** Can
104B4 **Indian O**
18B1 **Indianola** Iowa, USA
19B3 **Indianola** Mississippi, USA
35B1 **Indianópolis** Brazil
76D2 **Indo China** Region, S E Asia
70C4 **Indonesia** Republic, S E Asia
85D4 **Indore** India
78B4 **Indramayu** Indon
48C2 **Indre** *R* France
85B3 **Indus** *R* Pak
60D5 **Inebdu** Turk
96C2 **In Ebeggi** *Well* Alg
96C2 **In Ecker** Alg
92A1 **Inegöl** Turk
96D2 **In Ezzane** Alg
97C3 **Ingal** Niger
14B2 **Ingersoll** Can
107D2 **Ingham** Aust
6D2 **Inglefield Land** *Region* Can
110B1 **Inglewood** NZ
109D1 **Inglewood** Queensland, Aust
22C4 **Inglewood** USA
108B3 **Inglewood** Victoria, Aust
38B2 **Ingólfshöfði** *I* Iceland
57C3 **Ingolstadt** Germany
86B2 **Ingrāj Bāzār** India
96C3 **In-Guezzam** *Well* Alg
101C3 **Inhambane** Mozam
101C3 **Inharrime** Mozam
35B1 **Inhumas** Brazil
32D3 **Inirida** *R* Colombia
45A2 **Inishbofin** *I* Irish Rep
45A1 **Inishkea** *I* Irish Rep
45B2 **Inishmaan** *I* Irish Rep
45B2 **Inishmore** *I* Irish Rep
45B1 **Inishmurray** *I* Irish Rep
45C1 **Inishowen** District, Irish Rep
45A2 **Inishshark** *I* Irish Rep
45A2 **Inishturk** *I* Irish Rep
109C1 **Injune** Aust
12H3 **Inklin** Can
12H3 **Inklin** *R* Can
12C1 **Inland L** USA
47D1 **Inn** *R* Austria
108B1 **Innamincka** Aust
68C2 **Inner Mongolia** Autonomous Region, China
107D2 **Innisfail** Aust
12C2 **Innoko** *R* USA
57C3 **Innsbruck** Austria
98B3 **Inongo** Zaïre
58B2 **Inowrocław** Pol
96C2 **In Salah** Alg
47B1 **Interlaken** Switz
24C3 **Intexpec** Mexico
47C2 **Intra** Italy
78D3 **Intu** Indon
75C1 **Inubo-saki** *C* Japan
7C4 **Inukjuak** Can
4E3 **Inuvik** Can
4F3 **Inuvik** *Region* Can
44B3 **Inveraray** Scot
111A3 **Invercargill** NZ
109D1 **Inverell** Aust
13D2 **Invermere** Can
44B3 **Inverness** Scot
44C3 **Inverurie** Scot
108A3 **Investigator Str** Aust
68A1 **Inya** Russian Fed
21B2 **Inyokern** USA
98B3 **Inzia** *R* Zaïre
55B3 **Ioánnina** Greece
18A2 **Iola** USA
44A3 **Iona** *I* Scot
100A2 **Iôna Nat Pk** Angola
20C1 **Ione** USA
Ionian Is = Ioníoi Nísoi
55A3 **Ionian S** Italy/Greece
55B3 **Ioníoi Nísoi** *Is* Greece
55C3 **Íos** *I* Greece
10A2 **Iowa** *R* USA
10A2 **Iowa City** USA
35B1 **Ipameri** Brazil
35C1 **Ipanema** Brazil
61F4 **Ipatovo** Russian Fed
32B3 **Ipiales** Colombia
77C5 **Ipoh** Malay
30F2 **Iporá** Brazil
55C2 **Ipsala** Turk
109D1 **Ipswich** Aust
43E3 **Ipswich** Eng
16D1 **Ipswich** USA
30B3 **Iquique** Chile
32C4 **Iquitos** Peru
55C3 **Iráklion** Greece
80D2 **Iran** Republic, S W Asia
91D4 **Irānshahr** Iran
23A1 **Irapuato** Mexico
93D3 **Iraq** Republic, S W Asia
95A2 **Irā Wan** *Watercourse* Libya
94B2 **Irbid** Jordan
61K2 **Irbit** Russian Fed
36C3 **Ireland** Republic, NW Europe
33F3 **Ireng** *R* Guyana
74B3 **Iri** S Korea
71E4 **Irian Jaya** Province, Indon
95B3 **Iriba** Chad
79B3 **Iriga** Phil
99D3 **Iringa** Tanz
69E4 **Iriomote** *I* Japan
33G5 **Iriri** *R* Brazil
42B3 **Irish S** Eng/Irish Rep
12D1 **Irkillik** *R* USA
63C2 **Irkutsk** Russian Fed
65J4 **Irlysh** *R* Kazakhstan
108A2 **Iron Knob** Aust
14A1 **Iron Mountain** USA
107D2 **Iron Range** Aust
14A1 **Iron River** USA
14B3 **Irontown** USA
10A2 **Ironwood** USA
10B2 **Iroquois Falls** Can
75B2 **Iro-zaki** *C* Japan
76A2 **Irrawaddy,Mouths of the** Burma
65H4 **Irtysh** *R* Russian Fed
51B1 **Irun** Spain
42B2 **Irvine** Scot
19A3 **Irving** USA
79B4 **Isabela** Phil
32J7 **Isabela** *I* Ecuador
4H2 **Isachsen** Can
4H2 **Isachsen,C** Can
6H3 **Ísafjörður** Iceland
74C4 **Isahaya** Japan
98C2 **Isangi** Zaïre
47D1 **Isar** *R* Germany
47D1 **Isarco** *R* Italy
44E1 **Isbister** Scot
47D1 **Ischgl** Austria
53B2 **Ischia** *I* Italy
75B2 **Ise** Japan
47D2 **Iseo** Italy
46D1 **Iserlohn** Germany
53B2 **Isernia** Italy
75B2 **Ise-wan** *B* Japan
69E4 **Ishigaki** *I* Japan
74E2 **Ishikari** *R* Japan
74E2 **Ishikari-wan** *B* Japan
65H4 **Ishim** Russian Fed
65H4 **Ishim** *R* Kazakhstan
74E3 **Ishinomaki** Japan
75C1 **Ishioka** Japan
84C1 **Ishkashim** Afghan
14A1 **Ishpeming** USA
65J4 **Isil'kul** Russian Fed
99D2 **Isiolo** Kenya
98C2 **Isiro** Zaïre
92C2 **Iskenderun** Turk
92C2 **Iskenferun Körfezi** *B* Turk
92B1 **İskilip** Turk
65K4 **Iskitim** Russian Fed
54B2 **Iskur** *R* Bulg
12H3 **Iskut** *R* Can/USA
23B2 **Isla** Mexico
34C3 **Isla Bermejo** *I* Arg
27E4 **Isla Blanquilla** Ven
32A2 **Isla Coiba** *I* Panama
9B4 **Isla de Cedros** *I* Mexico
29B4 **Isla de Chiloé** *I* Chile
25D2 **Isla de Cozumel** *I* Mexico
26C3 **Isla de la Gonâve** Cuba
26A2 **Isla de la Juventud** *I* Cuba
34D2 **Isla de las Lechiguanas** *I* Arg
3K8 **Isla del Coco** *I* Costa Rica
25D3 **Isla del Maiz** *I* Caribbean S
23B1 **Isla de Lobos** *I* Mexico
29D6 **Isla de los Estados** *I* Arg
28E2 **Isla de Marajó** *I* Brazil
105L5 **Isla de Pascua** *I* Pacific O
26A4 **Isla de Providencia** *I* Caribbean S
26A4 **Isla de San Andres** *I* Caribbean S
30G4 **Isla de Santa Catarina** *I* Brazil
33G2 **Isla du Diable** *I* French Guiana
31E2 **Isla Fernando de Noronha** *I* Brazil
29C6 **Isla Grande de Tierra del Fuego** *I* Arg/Chile
27D4 **Isla la Tortuga** *I* Ven
84C2 **Islamabad** Pak
24A2 **Isla Magdalena** *I* Mexico
27E4 **Isla Margarita** Ven
34A3 **Isla Mocha** Chile
17B2 **Islamorada** USA
10A1 **Island L** Can
108A2 **Island Lg** Aust
110B1 **Islands,B of** NZ
32A4 **Isla Puná** *I* Ecuador
103D6 **Isla San Ambrosia** *I* Pacific O
103D6 **Isla San Felix** *I* Pacific O
24A2 **Isla Santa Margarita** *I* Mexico
34A3 **Isla Santa Maria** *I* Chile
51C2 **Islas Baleares** *Is* Spain
96A2 **Islas Canarias** *Is* Atlantic O
51C2 **Islas Columbretes** *Is* Spain
25D3 **Islas de la Bahia** *Is* Honduras
26A4 **Islas del Maíz** *Is* Caribbean S
33E1 **Islas de Margarita** *Is* Ven

Islas Diego Ramírez

29C7 **Islas Diego Ramírez** *Is* Chile
32J7 **Islas Galapagos** *Is* Pacific O
30H6 **Islas Juan Fernández** Chile
32D1 **Islas los Roques** *Is* Ven
Islas Malvinas = Falkland Is
105L3 **Islas Revilla Gigedo** *Is* Pacific O
29C7 **Islas Wollaston** *Is* Chile
97A3 **Isla Tidra** *I* Maur
29B5 **Isla Wellington** *I* Chile
48C2 **Isle** *R* France
104B5 **Isle Amsterdam** *I* Indian O
43D4 **Isle of Wight** *I* Eng
10B2 **Isle Royale** *I* USA
104B5 **Isle St Paul** *I* Indian O
104A6 **Isles Crozet** *I* Indian O
105J4 **Isles de la Société** Pacific O
105K5 **Isles Gambier** *Is* Pacific O
101D2 **Isles Glorieuses** *Is* Madag
104B6 **Isles Kerguelen** *Is* Indian O
105K4 **Isles Marquises** *Is* Pacific O
105J4 **Isles Tuamotu** *Is* Pacific O
105J5 **Isles Tubai** *Is* Pacific O
22B1 **Isleton** USA
92B3 **Ismâ'iliya** Egypt
101D3 **Isoanala** Madag
101C2 **Isoka** Zambia
53B3 **Isola Egadi** *I* Italy
52B2 **Isola Ponziane** *I* Italy
53B3 **Isole Lipari** *I* Italy
52C2 **Isoles Tremiti** *Is* Italy
75B1 **Isosaki** Japan
92B2 **Isparta** Turk
94B2 **Israel** Republic, S W Asia
51C2 **Isser** *R* Alg
48C2 **Issoire** France
49C2 **Issoudun** France
92A1 **Istanbul** Turk
55B3 **Istiáia** Greece
25C3 **Istmo de Tehuantepec** *Isthmus* Mexico
17B2 **Istokpoga,L** USA
52B1 **Istra** *Pen* Croatia
35B1 **Itaberai** Brazil
35C1 **Itabira** Brazil
35C2 **Itabirito** Brazil
31D4 **Itabuna** Brazil
33F4 **Itacoatiara** Brazil
32B2 **Itagui** Colombia
33F4 **Itaituba** Brazil
30G4 **Itajaí** Brazil
35B2 **Itajuba** Brazil
52B2 **Italy** Repubic, Europe
35D1 **Itamaraju** Brazil
35C1 **Itamarandiba** Brazil
35C1 **Itambacuri** Brazil
35C1 **Itambé** *Mt* Brazil
86C1 **Itanagar** India
35B2 **Itanhaém** Brazil
35C1 **Itanhém** Brazil
35C1 **Itanhém** *R* Brazil
35B2 **Itapecerica** Brazil
35C2 **Itaperuna** Brazil
31C5 **Itapetinga** Brazil
35B2 **Itapetininga** Brazil
35B2 **Itapeva** Brazil
31D2 **Itapipoca** Brazil
35B1 **Itapuranga** Brazil
30E4 **Itaqui** Brazil
35C1 **Itarantim** Brazil
35B2 **Itararé** Brazil
35B2 **Itararé** *R* Brazil
35C2 **Itaúna** Brazil
33E6 **Iténez** *R* Brazil/Bol

15C2 **Ithaca** USA
98C2 **Itimbiri** *R* Zaïre
35C1 **Itinga** Brazil
6E3 **Itivdleg** Greenland
75B2 **Ito** Japan
74D3 **Itoigawa** Japan
33E6 **Itonomas** *R* Bol
35B2 **Itu** Brazil
35B1 **Itumbiara** Brazil
35A1 **Iturama** Brazil
30C3 **Iturbe** Arg
35B1 **Iturutaba** Brazil
56B2 **Itzehoe** Germany
58D2 **Ivacevichi** Belorussia
35A2 **Ivai** *R* Brazil
38K5 **Ivalo** Fin
54A2 **Ivangrad** Montenegro, Yugos
108B2 **Ivanhoe** Aust
59C3 **Ivano-Frankovsk** Ukraine
61F2 **Ivanovo** Russian Fed
65H3 **Ivdel'** Russian Fed
98B2 **Ivindo** *R* Gabon
101D3 **Ivohibe** Madag
101D2 **Ivongo Soanierana** Madag
97B4 **Ivory Coast** Republic, Africa
52A1 **Ivrea** Italy
6C3 **Ivujivik** Can
74E3 **Iwaki** Japan
74C4 **Iwakuni** Japan
74E2 **Iwanai** Japan
97C4 **Iwo** Nig
69G4 **Iwo Jima** *I* Japan
23B1 **Ixmiquilpa** Mexico
23A2 **Ixtapa** Mexico
23A1 **Ixtlan** Mexico
75A2 **Iyo** Japan
75A2 **Iyo-nada** *B* Japan
65G4 **Izhevsk** Russian Fed
64G3 **Izhma** Russian Fed
91C5 **Izki** Oman
60C4 **Izmail** Ukraine
92A2 **Izmir** Turk
55C3 **Izmir Körfezi** *B* Turk
92A1 **Izmit** Turk
92A1 **Iznik** Turk
55C2 **Iznik Golü** *L* Turk
94C2 **Izra'** Syria
23B2 **Izúcar de Matamoros** Mexico
75B2 **Izumi-sano** Japan
75A1 **Izumo** Japan
74D4 **Izu-shotō** *Is* Japan

J

95B1 **Jabal al Akhdar** *Mts* Libya
94C2 **Jabal al 'Arab** Syria
95A2 **Jabal as Sawdā** *Mts* Libya
91B5 **Jabal az Zannah** UAE
94C1 **Jabal Halimah** *Mt* Leb/Syria
83B3 **Jabalpur** India
59B2 **Jablonec nad Nisou** Czech Republic
31D3 **Jaboatão** Brazil
35B2 **Jaboticabal** Brazil
51B1 **Jaca** Spain
23B1 **Jacala** Mexico
33F5 **Jacareacanga** Brazil
35B2 **Jacarei** Brazil
30F3 **Jacarezinho** Brazil
29C2 **Jáchal** Arg
35C1 **Jacinto** Brazil
13F2 **Jackfish L** Can
109C1 **Jackson** Aust
22B1 **Jackson** California, USA
14B2 **Jackson** Michigan, USA
19B3 **Jackson** Mississippi, USA
18C2 **Jackson** Missouri, USA
14B3 **Jackson** Ohio, USA
11B3 **Jackson** Tennessee, USA
111B2 **Jackson,C** NZ
111A2 **Jackson Head** *Pt* NZ

19B3 **Jacksonville** Arkansas, USA
17B1 **Jacksonville** Florida, USA
18B2 **Jacksonville** Illinois, USA
17C1 **Jacksonville** N Carolina, USA
19A3 **Jacksonville** Texas, USA
17B1 **Jacksonville Beach** USA
26C3 **Jacmel** Haiti
84B3 **Jacobabad** Pak
31C4 **Jacobina** Brazil
23A2 **Jacona** Mexico
Jadotville = Likasi
32B5 **Jaén** Peru
50B2 **Jaén** Spain
Jaffa = Tel Aviv Yafo
108A3 **Jaffa,C** Aust
87B3 **Jaffna** Sri Lanka
86B2 **Jagannathganj Ghat** Bang
87C1 **Jagdalpur** India
91C4 **Jagin** *R* Iran
87B1 **Jagtial** India
29F2 **Jaguarão** *R* Brazil
35B2 **Jaguarialva** Brazil
91B4 **Jahrom** Iran
85D5 **Jaina** India
72A2 **Jainca** China
85D3 **Jaipur** India
85C3 **Jaisalmer** India
90C2 **Jajarm** Iran
52C2 **Jajce** Bosnia-Herzegovina
78B4 **Jakarta** Indon
6E3 **Jakobshavn** Greenland
38J6 **Jakobstad** Fin
23B2 **Jalaca** Mexico
84B2 **Jalai-Kut** Afghan
84D2 **Jalandhar** India
23B2 **Jalapa** Mexico
35A2 **Jales** Brazil
86B1 **Jaleswar** Nepal
85D4 **Jalgaon** India
97D4 **Jalingo** Nig
51B1 **Jalón** *R* Spain
85C3 **Jālor** India
23A1 **Jalostotitlan** Mexico
86B1 **Jalpāiguri** India
23B1 **Jalpan** Mexico
95B2 **Jālū Oasis** Libya
32A4 **Jama** Ecuador
26B3 **Jamaica** *I* Caribbean S
26B3 **Jamaica Chan** Caribbean S
86B2 **Jamalpur** Bang
78A3 **Jambi** Indon
85C4 **Jambussar** India
7B4 **James B** Can
5J5 **Jameston** USA
108A2 **Jamestown** Aust
8D2 **Jamestown** N. Dakota, USA
15C2 **Jamestown** New York, USA
16D2 **Jamestown** Rhode Island, USA
23B2 **Jamiltepec** Mexico
87B1 **Jamkhandi** India
84C2 **Jammu** India
84D2 **Jammu and Kashmir** State, India
85B4 **Jamnagar** India
84C3 **Jampur** Pak
38K6 **Jämsä** Fin
86B2 **Jamshedpur** India
86B1 **Janakpur** Nepal
35C1 **Janaúba** Brazil
90B3 **Jandaq** Iran
109D1 **Jandowae** Aust
1B1 **Jan Mayen** *I* Norwegian S
35C1 **Januária** Brazil
85D4 **Jaora** India
51 **Japan** Empire, E Asia
74C3 **Japan,S of** S E Asia
104F2 **Japan Trench** Pacific O

32D4 **Japurá** *R* Brazil
93C2 **Jarābulus** Syria
35B1 **Jaraguá** Brazil
50B1 **Jarama** *R* Spain
94B2 **Jarash** Jordan
30E3 **Jardim** Brazil
51B2 **Jardin** *R* Spain
26B2 **Jardines de la Reina** *Is* Cuba
Jargalant = Hovd
33G3 **Jari** *R* Brazil
86C1 **Jaria Jhānjail** Bang
46C2 **Jarny** France
58B2 **Jarocin** Pol
59C2 **Jaroslaw** Pol
38G6 **Järpen** Sweden
72B2 **Jartai** China
85C4 **Jasdan** India
97C4 **Jasikan** Ghana
91C4 **Jāsk** Iran
59C3 **Jaslo** Pol
29D6 **Jason Is** Falkland Is
18B2 **Jasper** Arkansas, USA
13D2 **Jasper** Can
17B1 **Jasper** Florida, USA
14A3 **Jasper** Indiana, USA
19B3 **Jasper** Texas, USA
13D2 **Jasper Nat Pk** Can
58B2 **Jastrowie** Pol
35A1 **Jatai** Brazil
51B2 **Játiva** Spain
35B2 **Jau** Brazil
32B6 **Jauja** Peru
86A1 **Jaunpur** India
Java = Jawa
87B2 **Javadi Hills** India
Javari = Yavari
70B4 **Java S** Indon
106A2 **Java Trench** Indon
78A4 **Jawa** *I* Indon
71F4 **Jayapura** Indon
94C2 **Jayrūd** Syria
96B2 **Jbel Ouarkziz** *Mts* Mor
96B1 **Jbel Sarhro** *Mt* Mor
19B4 **Jeanerette** USA
97C4 **Jebba** Nig
93D2 **Jebel 'Abd al 'Azīz** *Mt* Syria
95B3 **Jebel Abyad** Sudan
91C5 **Jebel Akhdar** *Mt* Oman
92C4 **Jebel al Lawz** *Mt* S Arabia
94B2 **Jebel ash Shaykh** *Mt* Syria
95C2 **Jebel Asoteriba** *Mt* Sudan
94B3 **Jebel Ed Dabab** *Mt* Jordan
94B3 **Jebel el Ata'ita** *Mt* Jordan
92C3 **Jebel esh Sharqi** *Mts* Leb/Syria
94C3 **Jebel Ithriyat** *Mt* Jordan
91C5 **Jebel Ja'lan** *Mt* Oman
94B2 **Jebel Liban** *Mts* Leb
94C2 **Jebel Ma'lūlā** *Mt* Syria
98C1 **Jebel Marra** Sudan
94C3 **Jebel Mudeisisat** *Mt* Jordan
95C2 **Jebel Oda** *Mt* Sudan
94B3 **Jebel Qasr ed Deir** *Mt* Jordan
94B2 **Jebel Um ed Daraj** *Mt* Jordan
95B2 **Jebel Uweinat** *Mt* Sudan
42C2 **Jedburgh** Scot
Jedda = Jiddah
59C2 **Jedrzejów** Pol
19B3 **Jefferson** Texas, USA
11A3 **Jefferson City** USA
8B3 **Jefferson,Mt** USA
14A3 **Jeffersonville** USA
60C2 **Jekabpils** Latvia
59B2 **Jelena Gora** Pol
60B2 **Jelgava** Latvia

100B3 **Kalahari Desert** Botswana
38J6 **Kalajoki** Fin
63D2 **Kalakan** Russian Fed
70A3 **Kalakepen** Indon
84C1 **Kalam** Pak
55B3 **Kalámai** Greece
10B2 **Kalamazoo** USA
84B3 **Kalat** Pak
92B1 **Kalecik** Turk
78D3 **Kalembau** *I* Indon
99C3 **Kalémié** Zaïre
38L5 **Kalevala** Russian Fed
86C2 **Kalewa** Burma
12D2 **Kalgin I** USA
106B4 **Kalgoorlie** Aust
78B4 **Kalianda** Indon
79B3 **Kalibo** Phil
98C3 **Kalima** Zaïre
78C3 **Kalimantan** Province, Indon
55C3 **Kálimnos** *I* Greece
86B1 **Kālimpang** India
60B3 **Kaliningrad** Russian Fed
60C3 **Kalinkovichi** Belorussia
8B2 **Kalispell** USA
58B2 **Kalisz** Pol
99D3 **Kaliua** Tanz
38J5 **Kalix** *R* Sweden
100A3 **Kalkfeld** Namibia
100A3 **Kalkrand** Namibia
108A1 **Kallakoopah** *R* Aust
38K6 **Kallávesi** *L* Fin
55C3 **Kallonis Kólpos** *B* Greece
39H7 **Kalmar** Sweden
61G4 **Kalmytskaya Respublika,** Russian Fed
100B2 **Kalomo** Zambia
18B1 **Kalona** USA
13B2 **Kalone Peak** *Mt* Can
87A2 **Kalpeni** *I* India
85D3 **Kālpi** India
53A3 **Kalsat Khasba** Tunisia
12B2 **Kalskag** USA
12C2 **Kaltag** USA
60E3 **Kaluga** Russian Fed
39G7 **Kalundborg** Den
59C3 **Kalush** Ukraine
87B2 **Kalyandurg** India
60E2 **Kalyazin** Russian Fed
61H1 **Kama** *R* Russian Fed
74E3 **Kamaishi** Japan
84C2 **Kamalia** Pak
110C1 **Kamanawa Mts** NZ
100A2 **Kamanjab** Namibia
84D2 **Kamat** *Mt* India
87B3 **Kamban** India
61H2 **Kambarka** Russian Fed
97A4 **Kambia** Sierra Leone
59D3 **Kamenets Podolskiy** Ukraine
61F3 **Kamenka** Russian Fed
65K4 **Kamen-na-Obi** Russian Fed
61K2 **Kamensk-Ural'skiy** Russian Fed
5H3 **Kamilukuak L** Can
98C3 **Kamina** Zaïre
7A3 **Kaminak L** Can
75C1 **Kaminoyama** Japan
5F4 **Kamloops** Can
93E1 **Kamo** Armenia
75C1 **Kamogawa** Japan
99D2 **Kampala** Uganda
77C5 **Kampar** Malay
78A2 **Kampar** *R* Indon
56B2 **Kampen** Neth
76B2 **Kamphaeng Phet** Thai
77C3 **Kampot** Camb
91D4 **Kamsaptar** Iran
61J2 **Kamskoye Vodokhranilishche** *Res* Russian Fed
85D4 **Kāmthi** India
61G3 **Kamyshin** Russian Fed
61K2 **Kamyshlov** Russian Fed
7C4 **Kanaaupscow** *R* Can
98C3 **Kananga** Zaïre
61G2 **Kanash** Russian Fed
75B1 **Kanayama** Japan
74D3 **Kanazawa** Japan
4C3 **Kanbisha** USA
87B2 **Kānchipuram** India
84B2 **Kandahar** Afghan
64E3 **Kandalaksha** Russian Fed
38L5 **Kandalakshskaya Guba** *B* Russian Fed
97C3 **Kandi** Benin
109C2 **Kandos** Aust
87C3 **Kandy** Sri Lanka
15C2 **Kane** USA
6C1 **Kane Basin** *B* Can
98B1 **Kanem** *Desert Region* Chad
97B3 **Kangaba** Mali
92C2 **Kangal** Turk
6E3 **Kangâmiut** Greenland
91B4 **Kangān** Iran
77C4 **Kangar** Malay
106C4 **Kangaroo I** Aust
6E3 **Kangâtsiaq** Greenland
90A3 **Kangavar** Iran
72C1 **Kangbao** China
82C3 **Kangchenjunga** *Mt* Nepal
73A4 **Kangding** China
6G3 **Kangerdlugssuaq** *B* Greenland
6G3 **Kangerdlugssvatsaiq** *B* Greenland
99D2 **Kangetet** Kenya
74B2 **Kanggye** N Korea
7D4 **Kangiqsualujjuaq** Can
6C3 **Kangiqsujuaq** Can
7C3 **Kangirsuk** Can
74B3 **Kangnŭng** S Korea
98B2 **Kango** Gabon
68B4 **Kanĝto** *Mt* China
72B3 **Kang Xian** China
77D4 **Kanh Hung** Viet
98C3 **Kaniama** Zaïre
87B1 **Kani Giri** India
39J6 **Kankaanpää** Fin
14A2 **Kankakee** USA
14A2 **Kankakee** *R* USA
97B3 **Kankan** Guinea
86A2 **Kānker** India
87B3 **Kanniyākuman** India
97C3 **Kano** Nig
74C4 **Kanoya** Japan
86A1 **Kānpur** India
9D3 **Kansas** State, USA
18A2 **Kansas** *R* USA
10A3 **Kansas City** USA
73D5 **Kanshi** China
63B2 **Kansk** Russian Fed
97C3 **Kantchari** Burkina
86B2 **Kanthi** India
12D2 **Kantishna** USA
12D2 **Kantishna** *R* USA
100B3 **Kanye** Botswana
68D4 **Kao-hsiung** Taiwan
100A2 **Kaoka Veld** *Plain* Namibia
97A3 **Kaolack** Sen
100B2 **Kaoma** Zambia
21C4 **Kapaau** Hawaiian Is
98C3 **Kapanga** Zaïre
6F3 **Kap Cort Adelaer** *C* Greenland
6H3 **Kap Dalton** *C* Greenland
39H7 **Kapellskär** Sweden
6F3 **Kap Farvel** *C* Greenland
6G3 **Kap Gustav Holm** *C* Greenland
100B2 **Kapiri** Zambia
78C2 **Kapit** Malay
19B3 **Kaplan** USA
57C3 **Kaplice** Czech Republic
77B4 **Kapoe** Thai
99C3 **Kapona** Zaïre
52C1 **Kaposvár** Hung
6C2 **Kap Parry** *C* Can
6H3 **Kap Ravn** *C* Greenland
78B3 **Kapuas** *R* Indon
108A2 **Kapunda** Aust
84D2 **Kapurthala** India
7B5 **Kapuskasing** Can
109D2 **Kaputar** *Mt* Aust
93E2 **Kapydzhik** *Mt* Armenia
6D2 **Kap York** *C* Greenland
92B1 **Karabük** Turk
55C2 **Karacabey** Turk
85B4 **Karachi** Pak
87A1 **Karād** India
60E5 **Kara Daglari** *Mt* Turk
54C5 **Karadeniz Boğazi** *Sd* Turk
68D1 **Karaftit** Russian Fed
65J5 **Karaganda** Kazakhstan
65J5 **Karagayly** Kazakhstan
87B2 **Kāraikāl** India
90B2 **Karaj** Iran
92C3 **Karak** Jordan
65G5 **Kara Kalpakskaya Respublika,** Uzbekistan
84D1 **Karakax He** *R* China
71D3 **Karakelong** *I* Indon
84D1 **Karakoram** *Mts* India
84D1 **Karakoram** *P* India/China
97A3 **Karakoro** *R* Maur/Sen
65G6 **Karakumy** *Desert* Russian Fed
94B3 **Karama** Jordan
92B2 **Karaman** Turk
65K5 **Karamay** China
111B2 **Karamea** NZ
111B2 **Karamea Bight** *B* NZ
85D4 **Kāranja** India
92B2 **Karapınar** Turk
64H2 **Kara S** Russian Fed
100A3 **Karasburg** Namibia
38K5 **Karasjok** Nor
65J4 **Karasuk** Russian Fed
92C2 **Karataş** Turk
65H5 **Kara Tau** *Mts* Kazakhstan
76B3 **Karathuri** Burma
74B4 **Karatsu** Japan
91B4 **Karāz** Iran
93D3 **Karbalā'** Iraq
59C3 **Karcag** Hung
55B3 **Kardhítsa** Greece
64E3 **Karel'skaya Respublika,** Russian Fed
38J5 **Karesvando** Sweden
96B2 **Karet** *Desert Region* Maur
65K4 **Kargasok** Russian Fed
97D3 **Kari** Nig
100B2 **Kariba** Zim
100B2 **Kariba** *L* Zim/Zambia
100B2 **Kariba Dam** Zim/Zambia
95C3 **Karima** Sudan
78B3 **Karimata** *I* Indon
86C2 **Karimganj** Bang
87B1 **Karīmnagar** India
99E1 **Karin** Somalia
39J6 **Karis** Fin
99C3 **Karishimbe** *Mt* Zaïre
55B3 **Káristos** Greece
87A2 **Kārkal** India
71F4 **Karkar** *I* PNG
90A3 **Karkheh** *R* Iran
60D4 **Karkinitskiy Zaliv** *B* Ukraine
63B3 **Karlik Shan** *Mt* China
58B2 **Karlino** Pol
52C2 **Karlobag** Croatia
52C1 **Karlovac** Croatia
54B2 **Karlovo** Bulg
57C2 **Karlovy Vary** Czech Republic
39G7 **Karlshamn** Sweden
39G7 **Karlskoga** Sweden
39H7 **Karlskrona** Sweden
57B3 **Karlsruhe** Germany
39G7 **Karlstad** Sweden
12D3 **Karluk** USA
86C2 **Karnafuli Res** Bang
84D3 **Karnal** India
87A1 **Karnataka** State, India
54C2 **Karnobat** Bulg
100B2 **Karoi** Zim
99D3 **Karonga** Malawi
95C3 **Karora** Sudan
78D3 **Karossa** Indon
55C3 **Kárpathos** *I* Greece
6E2 **Karrats Fjord** Greenland
93D1 **Kars** Turk
65H4 **Karsakpay** Kazakhstan
58D1 **Kārsava** Latvia
80E2 **Karshi** Uzbekistan
38J6 **Karstula** Fin
94B1 **Kartaba** Leb
54C2 **Kartal** Turk
61K3 **Kartaly** Russian Fed
90A3 **Kārūn** *R* Iran
86A1 **Karwa** India
87A2 **Kārwār** India
68D1 **Karymskoye** Russian Fed
98B3 **Kasai** *R* Zaïre
100B2 **Kasaji** Zaïre
101C2 **Kasama** Zambia
99D3 **Kasanga** Tanz
87A2 **Kāsaragod** India
5H3 **Kasba L** Can
100B2 **Kasempa** Zambia
100B2 **Kasenga** Zaïre
99D2 **Kasese** Uganda
90B3 **Kāshān** Iran
12C2 **Kashegelok** USA
82B2 **Kashi** China
84D3 **Kāshipur** India
74D3 **Kashiwazaki** Japan
90C2 **Kashmar** Iran
66D3 **Kashmir** State, India
61F3 **Kasimov** Russian Fed
18C2 **Kaskaskia** *R* USA
38J6 **Kaskinen** Fin
61K2 **Kasli** Russian Fed
5G5 **Kaslo** Can
98C3 **Kasonga** Zaïre
98B3 **Kasongo-Lunda** Zaïre
55C3 **Kásos** *I* Greece
Kaspiyskiy = Lagan'
95C3 **Kassala** Sudan
56B2 **Kassel** Germany
96C1 **Kasserine** Tunisia
100A2 **Kassinga** Angola
92B1 **Kastamonou** Turk
55B3 **Kastélli** Greece
92A2 **Kastellorizon** *I* Greece
55B2 **Kastoría** Greece
55C3 **Kástron** Greece
74D3 **Kasugai** Japan
75A1 **Kasumi** Japan
101C2 **Kasungu** Malawi
84C2 **Kasur** Pak
100B2 **Kataba** Zambia
98C3 **Katako-kombe** Zaïre
4D3 **Katalla** USA
63G2 **Katangli** Russian Fed
106A4 **Katanning** Aust
55B2 **Kateríni** Greece
5E4 **Kates Needle** *Mt* Can/USA
82D3 **Katha** Burma
106C2 **Katherine** Aust
85C4 **Kāthiāwār** *Pen* India
86B1 **Kathmandu** Nepal
84D2 **Kathua** India
86B1 **Katihār** India
100B2 **Katima Mulilo** Namibia
4C4 **Katmai,Mt** USA
12D3 **Katmai Nat Mon** USA
86A2 **Katni** India
109D2 **Katoomba** Aust
59B2 **Katowice** Pol
39H7 **Katrineholm** Sweden

97C3 **Katsina** Nig
97C4 **Katsina Ala** Nig
75C1 **Katsuta** Japan
75C1 **Katsuura** Japan
75B1 **Katsuy** Japan
65H6 **Kattakurgan** Uzbekistan
39G7 **Kattegat** *Str* Den/ Sweden
21C4 **Kauai** *I* Hawaiian Is
21C4 **Kauai Chan** Hawaiian Is
21C4 **Kaulakahi Chan** Hawaiian Is
21C4 **Kaunakaki** Hawaiian Is
60B3 **Kaunas** Lithuania
97C3 **Kaura Namoda** Nig
38J5 **Kautokeino** Nor
55B2 **Kavadarci** Macedonia
55A2 **Kavajë** Alb
87B2 **Kavali** India
55B2 **Kavála** Greece
85B4 **Kāvda** India
75B1 **Kawagoe** Japan
75B1 **Kawaguchi** Japan
110B1 **Kawakawa** NZ
99C3 **Kawambwa** Zambia
86A2 **Kawardha** India
15C2 **Kawartha Lakes** Can
74D3 **Kawasaki** Japan
110C1 **Kawerau** NZ
110B1 **Kawhia** NZ
97B3 **Kaya** Burkina
12F3 **Kayak I** USA
78D2 **Kayan** *R* Indon
87B3 **Kāyankulam** India
97A3 **Kayes** Mali
92C2 **Kayseri** Turk
1B8 **Kazach'ye** Russian Fed
93E1 **Kazakh** Azerbaijan
65G5 **Kazakhstan** Republic, Asia
61G2 **Kazan'** Russian Fed
54C2 **Kazanlŭk** Bulg
69G4 **Kazan Retto** *Is* Japan
91B4 **Kāzerūn** Iran
61H1 **Kazhim** Russian Fed
93E1 **Kazi Magomed** Azerbaijan
59C3 **Kazincbarcika** Hung
55B3 **Kéa** *I* Greece
21C4 **Kealaikahiki Chan** Hawaiian Is
8D2 **Kearney** USA
93C2 **Keban Baraji** *Res* Turk
97A3 **Kébémer** Sen
96C1 **Kebili** Tunisia
94C1 **Kebīr** *R* Leb/Syria
38H5 **Kebrekaise** *Mt* Sweden
59B3 **Kecskemét** Hung
58C1 **Kedainiai** Lithuania
97A3 **Kédougou** Sen
12J2 **Keele** *R* Can
12H2 **Keele Pk** *Mt* Can
21B2 **Keeler** USA
15D2 **Keene** New Hampshire, USA
100A3 **Keetmanshoop** Namibia
18C1 **Keewanee** USA
6A3 **Keewatin** *Region* Can
55B3 **Kefallinía** *I* Greece
94B2 **Kefar Sava** Israel
97C4 **Keffi** Nig
38A2 **Keflavik** Iceland
5G4 **Keg River** Can
76B1 **Kehsi Mansam** Burma
108B3 **Keith** Aust
44C3 **Keith** Scot
4F3 **Keith Arm** *B* Can
6D3 **Kekertuk** Can
85D3 **Kekri** India
77C5 **Kelang** Malay
77C4 **Kelantan** *R* Malay
84B1 **Kelif** Turkmenistan
92C1 **Kelkit** *R* Turk
98B3 **Kellé** Congo
4F2 **Kellet,C** Can
20C1 **Kellogg** USA
64D3 **Kelloselka** Fin
45C2 **Kells** Irish Rep
42B2 **Kells Range** *Hills* Scot
58C1 **Kelme** Lithuania
5G5 **Kelowna** Can
5F4 **Kelsey Bay** Can
42C2 **Kelso** Scot
20B1 **Kelso** USA
64E3 **Kem'** Russian Fed
38L6 **Kem'** *R* Russian Fed
97B3 **Ke Macina** Mali
13B2 **Kemano** Can
65K4 **Kemerovo** Russian Fed
38J5 **Kemi** Fin
38K5 **Kemi** *R* Fin
38K5 **Kemijärvi** Fin
46C1 **Kempen** Region, Belg
26B2 **Kemps Bay** The Bahamas
109D2 **Kempsey** Aust
57C3 **Kempten** Germany
12D2 **Kenai** USA
12D3 **Kenai Mts** USA
12D2 **Kenai Pen** USA
99D2 **Kenamuke Swamp** Sudan
42C2 **Kendal** Eng
109D2 **Kendall** Aust
71D4 **Kendari** Indon
78C3 **Kendawangan** Indon
86B2 **Kendrāpāra** India
20C1 **Kendrick** USA
97A4 **Kenema** Sierra Leone
98B3 **Kenge** Zaïre
76B1 **Kengtung** Burma
100B3 **Kenhardt** S Africa
97A3 **Kéniéba** Mali
96B1 **Kenitra** Mor
45B3 **Kenmare** Irish Rep
45B3 **Kenmare** *R* Irish Rep
19B4 **Kenner** USA
18C2 **Kennett** USA
16B3 **Kennett Square** USA
20C1 **Kennewick** USA
5F4 **Kenny Dam** Can
7A5 **Kenora** Can
10B2 **Kenosha** USA
43E4 **Kent** County, Eng
20B1 **Kent** Washington, USA
14A2 **Kentland** USA
14B2 **Kenton** USA
4H3 **Kent Pen** Can
11B3 **Kentucky** State, USA
11B3 **Kentucky L** USA
19B3 **Kentwood** Louisiana, USA
14A2 **Kentwood** Michigan, USA
99D2 **Kenya** Republic, Africa
Kenya,Mt = Kirinyaga
18B1 **Keokuk** USA
86A2 **Keonchi** India
86B2 **Keonjhargarh** India
71E4 **Kepaluan Tanimbar** *Arch* Indon
6H3 **Keplavik** Iceland
59B2 **Kepno** Pol
78B2 **Kepulauan Anambas** *Arch* Indon
71E4 **Kepulauan Aru** *Arch* Indon
78B2 **Kepulauan Badas** *Is* Indon
71E4 **Kepulauan Banda** *Arch* Indon
71D4 **Kepulauan Banggai** *I* Indon
78B2 **Kepulauan Bunguran Seletan** *Arch* Indon
71E4 **Kepulauan Kai** *Arch* Indon
71D4 **Kepulauan Leti** *I* Indon
78A3 **Kepulauan Lingga** *Is* Indon
70A4 **Kepulauan Mentawi** *Arch* Indon
78A2 **Kepulauan Riau** *Arch* Indon
78D4 **Kepulauan Sabalana** *Arch* Indon
71D3 **Kepulauan Sangihe** *Arch* Indon
71D4 **Kepulauan Sula** *I* Indon
71D3 **Kepulauan Talaud** *Arch* Indon
78B2 **Kepulauan Tambelan** *Is* Indon
71E4 **Kepulauan Tanimbar** *I* Indon
71D4 **Kepulauan Togian** *I* Indon
71D4 **Kepulauan Tukambesi** *Is* Indon
87B2 **Kerala** State, India
108B3 **Kerang** Aust
39K6 **Kerava** Fin
60E4 **Kerch'** Ukraine
71F4 **Kerema** PNG
20C1 **Keremeps** Can
95C3 **Keren** Eritrea
104B6 **Kerguelen Ridge** Indian O
99D3 **Kericho** Kenya
70B4 **Kerinci** *Mt* Indon
99D2 **Kerio** *R* Kenya
80E2 **Kerki** Turkmenistan
55A3 **Kérkira** Greece
55A3 **Kérkira** *I* Greece
91C3 **Kerman** Iran
22B2 **Kerman** USA
90A3 **Kermānshāh** Iran
21B2 **Kern** *R* USA
13F2 **Kerrobert** Can
45B2 **Kerry** County, Irish Rep
17B1 **Kershaw** USA
78B3 **Kertamulia** Indon
63D3 **Kerulen** *R* Mongolia
96B2 **Kerzaz** Alg
55C2 **Keşan** Turk
74E3 **Kesennuma** Japan
38L5 **Kesten 'ga** Russian Fed
42C2 **Keswick** Eng
65K4 **Ket** *R* Russian Fed
97C4 **Kéta** Ghana
78C3 **Ketapang** Indon
5E4 **Ketchikan** USA
97C3 **Ketia** Niger
85B4 **Keti Bandar** Pak
58C2 **Kętrzyn** Pol
43D3 **Kettering** Eng
14B3 **Kettering** USA
20C1 **Kettle** *R* Can
20C1 **Kettle River Range** *Mts* USA
7C3 **Kettlestone B** Can
90C3 **Kevir-i Namak** *Salt Flat* Iran
14A2 **Kewaunee** USA
14B1 **Key Harbour** Can
17B2 **Key Largo** USA
11B4 **Key West** USA
63C2 **Kezhma** Russian Fed
54A1 **K'félegháza** Hung
12B2 **Kgun L** USA
94C2 **Khabab** Syria
62H3 **Khabarovsk** Russian Fed
85B3 **Khairpur** Pak
85B3 **Khairpur** Region, Pak
100B3 **Khakhea** Botswana
55C3 **Khálki** *I* Greece
55B2 **Khalkidhíki** *Pen* Greece
55B3 **Khalkís** Greece
61G2 **Khalturin** Russian Fed
85C4 **Khambhāt,G of** India
85D4 **Khāmgaon** India
76C2 **Kham Keut** Laos
87C1 **Khammam** India
90A2 **Khamseh** *Mts* Iran
76C2 **Khan** *R* Laos
84B1 **Khanabad** Afghan
93E3 **Khānaqīn** Iraq
85D4 **Khandwa** India
84C2 **Khanewal** Pak
94C3 **Khan ez Zabib** Jordan
77D4 **Khanh Hung** Viet
55B3 **Khaniá** Greece
84C3 **Khanpur** Pak
65H3 **Khanty-Mansiysk** Russian Fed
94B3 **Khan Yunis** Egypt
84D1 **Khapalu** India
68C2 **Khapcheranga** Russian Fed
61G4 **Kharabali** Russian Fed
86B2 **Kharagpur** India
91C4 **Khārān** Iran
84B3 **Kharan** Pak
90B3 **Kharānaq** Iran
91B4 **Khārg** *Is* Iran
95C2 **Khârga Oasis** Egypt
85D4 **Khargon** India
60E4 **Khar'kov** Ukraine
54C2 **Kharmanli** Bulg
61F2 **Kharovsk** Russian Fed
95C3 **Khartoum** Sudan
95C3 **Khartoum North** Sudan
74C2 **Khasan** Russian Fed
95C3 **Khashm el Girba** Sudan
86C1 **Khasi-Jaīntīa Hills** India
54C2 **Khaskovo** Bulg
1B9 **Khatanga** Russian Fed
76B3 **Khawsa** Burma
76C2 **Khe Bo** Viet
85C4 **Khed Brahma** India
51C2 **Khemis** Alg
96B1 **Khenifra** Mor
51D2 **Kherrata** Alg
60D4 **Kherson** Ukraine
63D2 **Khilok** Russian Fed
55C3 **Khíos** Greece
55C3 **Khíos** *I* Greece
60C4 **Khmel'nitskiy** Ukraine
59C3 **Khodorov** Ukraine
84B1 **Kholm** Afghan
76D3 **Khong** Laos
91B4 **Khonj** Iran
69F2 **Khor** Russian Fed
91A3 **Khoramshahr** Iran
91B5 **Khōr Duwayhin** *B* UAE
84C1 **Khorog** Tajikistan
90A3 **Khorramābad** Iran
90C3 **Khosf** Iran
84B2 **Khost** Pak
60C4 **Khotin** Ukraine
12C2 **Khotol** *Mt* USA
60C3 **Khoyniki** Belorussia
63F2 **Khrebet Dzhugdzhur** *Mts* Russian Fed
90C2 **Khrebet Kopet Dag** *Mts* Turkmenistan
64H3 **Khrebet Pay-khoy** *Mts* Russian Fed
82C1 **Khrebet Tarbagatay** *Mts* Kazakhstan
63E2 **Khrebet Tukuringra** *Mts* Russian Fed
82A1 **Khudzhand** Tajikistan
86B2 **Khulna** Bang
84D1 **Khunjerab** *P* China/ India
90B3 **Khunsar** Iran
91A4 **Khurays** S Arabia
86B2 **Khurda** India
84D3 **Khurja** India
84C2 **Khushab** Pak
94B2 **Khushnīyah** Syria
59C3 **Khust** Ukraine
99C1 **Khuwei** Sudan
85B3 **Khuzdar** Pak
90D3 **Khvāf** Iran
61G3 **Khvalynsk** Russian Fed
90C3 **Khvor** Iran
91B4 **Khvormūj** Iran
93D2 **Khvoy** Iran
84C1 **Khwaja Muhammad** *Mts* Afghan
84C2 **Khyber P** Afghan/Pak

Kupyansk

Leighton Buzzard

Lubuklinggau

78A3 **Lubuklinggau** Indon
100B2 **Lubumbashi** Zaïre
98C3 **Lubutu** Zaïre
79B3 **Lucban** Phil
52B2 **Lucca** Italy
42B2 **Luce** *B* Scot
19C3 **Lucedale** USA
79B3 **Lucena** Phil
59B3 **Lucenec** Slovakia
  Lucerne = Luzern
73C5 **Luchuan** China
56C2 **Luckenwalde**
  Germany
101F1 **Luckhoff** S Africa
86A1 **Lucknow** India
100B2 **Lucusse** Angola
46D1 **Lüdenscheid**
  Germany
100A3 **Lüderitz** Namibia
84D2 **Ludhiana** India
14A2 **Ludington** USA
43C3 **Ludlow** Eng
54C2 **Ludogorie** *Upland*
  Bulg
17B1 **Ludowici** USA
54B1 **Luduş** Rom
39H6 **Ludvika** Sweden
57B3 **Ludwigsburg**
  Germany
57B3 **Ludwigshafen**
  Germany
56C2 **Ludwigslust**
  Germany
98C3 **Luebo** Zaïre
98C3 **Luema** *R* Zaïre
98C3 **Luembe** *R* Angola
100A2 **Luena** Angola
100B2 **Luene** *R* Angola
72B3 **Lüeyang** China
73D5 **Lufeng** China
11A3 **Lufkin** USA
60C2 **Luga** Russian Fed
60C2 **Luga** *R* Russian Fed
52A1 **Lugano** Switz
60E4 **Lugansk** Ukraine
101C2 **Lugela** Mozam
101C2 **Lugenda** *R* Mozam
50A1 **Lugo** Spain
54B1 **Lugoj** Rom
72A3 **Luhuo** China
98B3 **Lui** *R* Angola
100B2 **Luiana** Angola
100B2 **Luiana** *R* Angola
  Luichow Peninsula =
  Leizhou Bandao
47C2 **Luino** Italy
98B2 **Luionga** *R* Zaïre
72B2 **Luipan Shan** *Upland*
  China
100B2 **Luishia** Zaïre
68B4 **Luixi** China
98C3 **Luiza** Zaïre
34B2 **Luján** Arg
34C2 **Luján** Arg
73D3 **Lujiang** China
98B3 **Lukenie** *R* Zaïre
64E4 **Luki** Russian Fed
98B3 **Lukolela** Zaïre
58C2 **Luków** Pol
98C3 **Lukuga** *R* Zaïre
100B2 **Lukulu** Zambia
38J5 **Lule** *R* Sweden
38J5 **Luleå** Sweden
54C2 **Lüleburgaz** Turk
72C2 **Lüliang Shan** *Mts*
  China
19A4 **Luling** USA
98C2 **Lulonga** *R* Zaïre
  Luluabourg =
  Kananga
100B2 **Lumbala Kaquengue**
  Angola
11C3 **Lumberton** USA
78D1 **Lumbis** Indon
86C1 **Lumding** India
100B2 **Lumeje** Angola
111A3 **Lumsden** NZ
39G7 **Lund** Sweden
101C2 **Lundazi** Zambia
43B4 **Lundy** *I* Eng
56C2 **Lüneburg** Germany
46D2 **Lunéville** France
100B2 **Lunga** *R* Zambia
86C2 **Lunglei** India

100A2 **Lungue Bungo** *R*
  Angola
58D2 **Luninec** Belorussia
98B3 **Luobomo** Congo
73B5 **Luocheng** China
73C5 **Luoding** China
72C3 **Luohe** China
72C3 **Luo He** *R* Henan,
  China
72B2 **Luo He** *R* Shaanxi,
  China
73C4 **Luoxiao Shan** *Hills*
  China
72C3 **Luoyang** China
98B3 **Luozi** Zaïre
100B2 **Lupane** Zim
101C2 **Lupilichi** Mozam
  Lu Qu = Tao He
30E4 **Luque** Par
45C1 **Lurgan** N Ire
101C2 **Lurio** *R* Mozam
90A3 **Luristan** *Region,* Iran
100B2 **Lusaka** Zambia
98C3 **Lusambo** Zaïre
55A2 **Lushnjë** Alb
99D3 **Lushoto** Tanz
68B4 **Lushui** China
72E2 **Lüshun** China
43D4 **Luton** Eng
60C3 **Lutsk** Ukraine
99E2 **Luuq** Somalia
99C3 **Luvua** *R* Zaïre
99D3 **Luwegu** *R* Tanz
100C2 **Luwingu** Zambia
71D4 **Luwuk** Indon
46D2 **Luxembourg** Grand
  Duchy, N W Europe
49D2 **Luxembourg** Lux
73A5 **Luxi** China
95C2 **Luxor** Egypt
61G1 **Luza** Russian Fed
61G1 **Luza** *R* Russian Fed
52A1 **Luzern** Switz
73B5 **Luzhai** China
73B4 **Luzhi** China
73B4 **Luzhou** China
35B1 **Luziânia** Brazil
79B2 **Luzon** *I* Phil
79B1 **Luzon Str** Phil
59C3 **L'vov** Ukraine
44C2 **Lybster** Scot
38H6 **Lycksele** Sweden
100B3 **Lydenburg** S Africa
8B3 **Lyell,Mt** USA
16A2 **Lykens** USA
43C4 **Lyme B** Eng
43C4 **Lyme Regis** Eng
11C3 **Lynchburg** USA
108A2 **Lyndhurst** Aust
15D2 **Lynn** USA
12G3 **Lynn Canal** *Sd* USA
17A1 **Lynn Haven** USA
5H4 **Lynn Lake** Can
5H3 **Lynx L** Can
49C2 **Lyon** France
12G3 **Lyon Canal** *Sd* USA
17B1 **Lyons** Georgia, USA
106A3 **Lyons** *R* Aust
47B2 **Lys** *R* Italy
61J2 **Lys'va** Russian Fed
111B2 **Lyttelton** NZ
13C2 **Lytton** Can
22A1 **Lytton** USA
58D2 **Lyubeshov** Ukraine
60E2 **Lyublino** Russian Fed

M

76C1 **Ma** *R* Viet
94B2 **Ma'agan** Jordan
94B2 **Ma'alot Tarshiha**
  Israel
92C3 **Ma'an** Jordan
73D3 **Ma'anshan** China
92C2 **Ma'arrat an Nu'mān**
  Syria
46C1 **Maas** *R* Neth
46C1 **Maaseik** Belg
79B3 **Maasin** Phil
57B2 **Maastricht** Neth
101C3 **Mabalane** Mozam
33F2 **Mabaruma** Guyana
42E3 **Mablethorpe** Eng
101C3 **Mabote** Mozam
58C2 **Mabrita** Belorussia

58D2 **M'adel** Belorussia
35C2 **Macaé** Brazil
9D3 **McAlester** USA
9D4 **McAllen** USA
101C2 **Macaloge** Mozam
33G3 **Macapá** Brazil
35C1 **Macaraní** Brazil
32B4 **Macas** Ecuador
31D3 **Macaú** Brazil
73C5 **Macau** Dependency,
  China
98C2 **M'Bari** *R* CAR
13C2 **McBride** Can
12F2 **McCarthy** USA
13A2 **McCauley I** Can
42C3 **Macclesfield** Eng
6B1 **McClintock B** Can
4H2 **McClintock Chan**
  Can
16A2 **McClure** USA
22B2 **McClure,L** USA
4G2 **McClure Str** Can
19B3 **McComb** USA
8C2 **McCook** USA
6C2 **Macculloch,C** Can
13C1 **McCusker,Mt** Can
4F4 **McDame** Can
20C2 **McDermitt** USA
13E2 **Macdonald** *R* Can
106C3 **Macdonnell Ranges**
  Mts Aust
50A1 **Macedo de Cavaleiros**
  Port
55B2 **Macedonia** Republic,
  Europe
31D3 **Maceió** Brazil
97B4 **Macenta** Guinea
52B2 **Macerata** Italy
108A2 **Macfarlane,L** Aust
19B3 **McGehee** USA
45B3 **MacGillycuddys**
  Reeks *Mts* Irish Rep
4C3 **McGrath** USA
35B2 **Machado** Brazil
101C3 **Machaila** Mozam
99D3 **Machakos** Kenya
32B4 **Machala** Ecuador
101C3 **Machaze** Mozam
87B1 **Mācherla** India
94B2 **Machgharab** Leb
87C1 **Machilipatnam** India
32C1 **Machiques** Ven
32C6 **Machu-Picchu** *Hist*
  Site Peru
101C3 **Macia** Mozam
109C1 **McIntyre** *R* Aust
107D3 **Mackay** Aust
106B3 **Mackay,L** Aust
14C2 **McKeesport** USA
13C1 **Mackenzie** Can
4F3 **Mackenzie** *R* Can
4E3 **Mackenzie B** Can
4G2 **Mackenzie King I** Can
4E3 **Mackenzie Mts** Can
14B1 **Mackinac,Str of** USA
14B1 **Mackinaw City** USA
12D2 **McKinley,Mt** USA
19A3 **McKinney** USA
6C2 **Mackinson Inlet** *B*
  Can
109E2 **Macksville** Aust
20B2 **Mclaoughlin,Mt** USA
109D1 **Maclean** Aust
100B4 **Maclear** S Africa
5G4 **McLennan** Can
13D2 **McLeod** *R* Can
4G3 **McLeod B** Can
106A3 **McLeod,L** Aust
13C1 **McLeod Lake** Can
4E3 **Macmillan** *R* Can
12H2 **Macmillan P** Can
20B1 **McMinnville** Oregon,
  USA
112B7 **McMurdo** *Base* Ant
13D2 **McNaughton L** Can
18B1 **Macomb** USA
53A2 **Macomer** Sardegna
101C2 **Macomia** Mozam
49C2 **Mâcon** France
11B3 **Macon** Georgia, USA
18B2 **Macon** Missouri,
  USA
100B2 **Macondo** Angola
18A2 **McPherson** USA

104F6 **Macquarie** *Is* Aust
109C2 **Macquarie** *R* Aust
109C4 **Macquarie Harbour** *B*
  Aust
109D2 **Macquarie,L** Aust
17B1 **McRae** USA
112B11 **Mac. Robertson Land**
  Region, Ant
45B3 **Macroom** Irish Rep
96C1 **M'Sila** Alg
4G3 **McTavish Arm** *B*
  Can
108A1 **Macumba** *R* Aust
47C2 **Macunaga** Italy
4F3 **McVicar Arm** *B* Can
59B3 **M'yaróvár** Hung
94B3 **Mādabā** Jordan
95A3 **Madadi** *Well* Chad
89J10 **Madagascar** *I*
  Indian O
95A2 **Madama** Niger
71F4 **Madang** PNG
97C3 **Madaoua** Niger
86C2 **Madaripur** Bang
90B2 **Madau** Turkmenistan
15C1 **Madawaska** *R* Can
96A1 **Madeira** *I* Atlantic O
33E5 **Madeira** *R* Brazil
7D5 **Madeleine, Ïsle de la**
  Can
24B2 **Madera** Mexico
21A2 **Madera** USA
87A1 **Madgaon** India
86B1 **Madhubani** India
86A2 **Madhya Pradesh**
  State, India
87B2 **Madikeri** India
98B3 **Madimba** Zaïre
98B3 **Madingo Kayes**
  Congo
98B3 **Madingou** Congo
10B3 **Madison** Indiana,
  USA
10B2 **Madison** Wisconsin,
  USA
18C2 **Madisonville**
  Kentucky, USA
19A3 **Madisonville** Texas,
  USA
78C4 **Madiun** Indon
99D2 **Mado Gashi** Kenya
47D1 **Madonna Di**
  Campiglio Italy
87C2 **Madras** India
20B2 **Madras** USA
29A6 **Madre de Dios** *I*
  Chile
32D6 **Madre de Dios** *R* Bol
50B1 **Madrid** Spain
50B2 **Madridejos** Spain
78C4 **Madura** *I* Indon
87B3 **Madurai** India
75B1 **Maebashi** Japan
76B3 **Mae Khlong** *R* Thai
77B4 **Mae Nam Lunang** *R*
  Thai
76C2 **Mae Nam Mun** *R*
  Thai
76B2 **Mae Nam Ping** *R*
  Thai
101D2 **Maevatanana** Madag
101G1 **Mafeteng** Lesotho
109C3 **Maffra** Aust
99D3 **Mafia** *I* Tanz
101G1 **Mafikeng** S Africa
30G4 **Mafra** Brazil
92C3 **Mafraq** Jordan
32C2 **Magangué** Colombia
34D3 **Magdalena** Arg
24A1 **Magdalena** Mexico
26C4 **Magdalena**
  Colombia
78D1 **Magdalena,Mt** Malay
56C2 **Magdeburg** Germany
31C6 **Magé** Brazil
78C4 **Magelang** Indon
47C1 **Maggia** *R* Switz
92B4 **Maghāgha** Egypt
45C1 **Magherafelt** N Ire
55A2 **Maglie** Italy
61J3 **Magnitogorsk**
  Russian Fed
19B3 **Magnolia** USA
101C2 **Magoé** Mozam

15D1 **Magog** Can
23B1 **Magosal** Mexico
13E2 **Magrath** Can
7A3 **Maguse River** Can
76B1 **Magwe** Burma
90A2 **Mahābād** Iran
86B1 **Mahabharat Range**
　　Mts Nepal
87A1 **Mahād** India
85D4 **Mahadeo Hills** India
101D2 **Mahajanga** Madag
100B3 **Mahalapye** Botswana
86A2 **Mahānadi** *R* India
101D2 **Mahanoro** Madag
16A2 **Mahanoy City** USA
87A1 **Maharashtra** State,
　　India
86A2 **Māhāsamund** India
76C2 **Maha Sarakham** Thai
101D2 **Mahavavy** *R* Madag
87B1 **Mahbūbnagar** India
96D1 **Mahdia** Tunisia
87B2 **Mahe** India
85D4 **Mahekar** India
101D2 **Mahéli** *I* Comoros
86A2 **Mahendragarh** India
99D3 **Mahenge** Tanz
85C4 **Mahesāna** India
110C1 **Mahia Pen** NZ
85D3 **Mahoba** India
51C2 **Mahón** Spain
12J1 **Mahony L** Can
96D1 **Mahrés** Tunisia
85C4 **Mahuva** India
32C1 **Maicao** Colombia
47B1 **Maîche** France
43E4 **Maidstone** Eng
98B1 **Maiduguri** Nig
86A2 **Maihar** India
86C2 **Maijdi** Bang
76B3 **Mail Kyun** *I* Burma
84A1 **Maimana** Afghan
14B1 **Main Chan** Can
98B3 **Mai-Ndombe** *L* Zaïre
10D2 **Maine** State, USA
48B2 **Maine** *Region*
　　France
44C2 **Mainland** *I* Scot
85D3 **Mainpuri** India
46A2 **Maintenon** France
101D2 **Maintirano** Madag
57B2 **Mainz** Germany
97A4 **Maio** *I* Cape Verde
29C2 **Maipó** *Mt* Arg/Chile
34D3 **Maipú** Arg
32D1 **Maiquetía** Ven
47B2 **Maira** *R* Italy
86C1 **Mairābāri** India
86C2 **Maiskhal I** Bang
107E4 **Maitland** New South
　　Wales, Aust
108A2 **Maitland** S Australia,
　　Aust
112C12 **Maitri** *Base* Ant
74D3 **Maizuru** Japan
70C4 **Majene** Indon
30B2 **Majes** *R* Peru
99D2 **Maji** Eth
72D2 **Majia He** *R* China
　　Majunga =
　　Mahajanga
70C4 **Makale** Indon
86B1 **Makalu** *Mt* China/
　　Nepal
98B2 **Makanza** Zaïre
52C2 **Makarska** Croatia
61F2 **Makaryev**
　　Russian Fed
　　Makassar = Ujung
　　Pandang
78D3 **Makassar Str** Indon
61H4 **Makat** Kazakhstan
97A4 **Makeni** Sierra Leone
60E4 **Makeyevka** Ukraine
100B3 **Makgadikgadi** *Salt*
　　Pan Botswana
61G5 **Makhachkala**
　　Russian Fed
99D3 **Makindu** Kenya
88H5 **Makkah** S Arabia
7E4 **Makkovik** Can
59C3 **Makó** Hung
98B2 **Makokou** Gabon
110C1 **Makorako,Mt** NZ

98B2 **Makoua** Congo
85C3 **Makrāna** India
85A3 **Makran Coast Range**
　　Mts Pak
96C1 **Makthar** Tunisia
93D2 **Mākū** Iran
98C3 **Makumbi** Zaïre
74C4 **Makurazaki** Japan
97C4 **Makurdi** Nig
79B4 **Malabang** Phil
87A2 **Malabar Coast** India
89E7 **Malabo** Bioko
77C5 **Malacca,Str of**
　　S E Asia
32C2 **Málaga** Colombia
50B2 **Malaga** Spain
101D3 **Malaimbandy**
　　Madag
107F1 **Malaita** *I*
　　Solomon Is
99D2 **Malakal** Sudan
84C2 **Malakand** Pak
78C4 **Malang** Indon
98B3 **Malange** Angola
97C3 **Malanville** Benin
39H7 **Mälaren** *L* Sweden
34B3 **Malargüe** Arg
12F3 **Malaspina Gl** USA
93C2 **Malatya** Turk
101C2 **Malawi** Republic,
　　Africa
　　Malawi,L = Nyasa,L
79C4 **Malaybalay** Phil
90A3 **Malāyer** Iran
70B3 **Malaysia** Federation,
　　S E Asia
93D2 **Malazgirt** Turk
58B2 **Malbork** Pol
56C2 **Malchin** Germany
18C2 **Malden** USA
83B5 **Maldives Is** Indian O
104B4 **Maldives Ridge**
　　Indian O
29F2 **Maldonado** Urug
47D1 **Male** Italy
85C4 **Malegaon** India
59B3 **Malé Karpaty** *Upland*
　　Slovakia
101C2 **Malema** Mozam
84B2 **Mālestān** Afghan
38H5 **Malgomaj** *L* Sweden
95B3 **Malha** *Well* Sudan
20C2 **Malheur L** USA
97B3 **Mali** Republic, Africa
78D1 **Malinau** Indon
99E3 **Malindi** Kenya
　　Malines = Mechelen
40B2 **Malin Head** *Pt*
　　Irish Rep
86A2 **Malkala Range** *Mts*
　　India
85D4 **Malkāpur** India
55C2 **Malkara** Turk
54C2 **Malko Tŭrnovo** Bulg
44B3 **Mallaig** Scot
95C2 **Mallawi** Egypt
47D1 **Málles Venosta** Italy
51C2 **Mallorca** *I* Spain
45B2 **Mallow** Irish Rep
38G6 **Malm** Nor
38J5 **Malmberget** Sweden
46D1 **Malmédy** Germany
43C4 **Malmesbury** Eng
100A4 **Malmesbury** S Africa
39G7 **Malmö** Sweden
61G2 **Malmyzh**
　　Russian Fed
79B3 **Malolos** Phil
15D2 **Malone** USA
101G1 **Maloti Mts** Lesotho
38F6 **Måløy** Nor
28A2 **Malpelo** *I* Colombia
34A2 **Malpo** *R* Chile
85D3 **Mālpura** India
8C2 **Malta** Montana, USA
53B3 **Malta** *Chan* Malta/
　　Italy
53B3 **Malta** *I* Medit S
100A3 **Maltahöhe** Namibia
42D2 **Malton** Eng
39G6 **Malung** Sweden
87A1 **Mālvan** India
19B3 **Malvern** USA
85D4 **Malwa Plat** India

61G4 **Malyy Uzen'** *R*
　　Kazakhstan
63D2 **Mama** Russian Fed
61H2 **Mamadysh**
　　Russian Fed
99C2 **Mambasa** Zaïre
71E4 **Mamberamo** *R*
　　Indon
98B2 **Mambéré** *R* CAR
98A2 **Mamfé** Cam
33D6 **Mamoré** *R* Bol
97A3 **Mamou** Guinea
101D2 **Mampikony** Madag
97B4 **Mampong** Ghana
94B3 **Mamshit** *Hist Site*
　　Israel
100B3 **Mamuno** Botswana
97B4 **Man** Ivory Coast
21C4 **Mana** Hawaiian Is
101D3 **Manabo** Madag
33E4 **Manacapuru** Brazil
51C2 **Manacor** Spain
71D3 **Manado** Indon
25D3 **Managua** Nic
101D3 **Manakara** Madag
101D2 **Mananara** Madag
101D3 **Mananjary** Madag
111A3 **Manapouri** NZ
111A3 **Manapouri,L** NZ
86C1 **Manas** Bhutan
82C1 **Manas** China
65K5 **Manas Hu** *L* China
86A1 **Manaslu** *Mt* Nepal
16B2 **Manasquan** USA
33F4 **Manaus** Brazil
92B2 **Manavgat** Turk
93C2 **Manbij** Syria
42B2 **Man,Calf of** *I* Eng
87B1 **Mancheral** India
15D2 **Manchester**
　　Connecticut, USA
42C3 **Manchester** Eng
10C2 **Manchester** New
　　Hampshire, USA
16A2 **Manchester**
　　Pennsylvania, USA
69E2 **Manchuria** *Hist*
　　Region, China
91B4 **Mand** *R* Iran
101C2 **Manda** Tanz
35A2 **Mandaguari** Brazil
39F7 **Mandal** Nor
76B1 **Mandalay** Burma
68C2 **Mandalgovĭ**
　　Mongolia
8C2 **Mandan** USA
14A2 **Mandelona** USA
99E2 **Mandera** Eth
26B3 **Mandeville** Jamaica
101C2 **Mandimba** Mozam
86A2 **Mandla** India
101D2 **Mandritsara** Madag
85D4 **Mandsaur** India
53C2 **Manduria** Italy
85B4 **Māndvi** India
87B2 **Mandya** India
58D2 **Manevichi** Ukraine
42D3 **Manfield** Eng
53C2 **Manfredonia** Italy
98B1 **Manga** *Desert*
　　Region Niger
110C1 **Mangakino** NZ
54C2 **Mangalia** Rom
98B1 **Mangalmé** Chad
87A2 **Mangalore** India
78B3 **Manggar** Indon
68B3 **Mangnia** China
101C2 **Mangoche** Malawi
101D3 **Mangoky** *R* Madag
71D4 **Mangole** *I* Indon
85B4 **Māngral** India
63E2 **Mangui** China
8D3 **Manhattan** USA
31C6 **Manhuacu** Brazil
101D2 **Mania** *R* Madag
101C2 **Manica** Mozam
7D5 **Manicouagan** *R* Can
91A4 **Manifah** S Arabia
79B3 **Manila** Phil
109D2 **Manilla** Aust
97B3 **Maninian** Ivory Coast
86C2 **Manipur** State, India
86C2 **Manipur** *R* Burma
92A2 **Manisa** Turk

41C3 **Man,Isle of** Irish S
14A2 **Manistee** USA
14A2 **Manistee** *R* USA
14A1 **Manistique** USA
5H4 **Manitoba** Province,
　　Can
5J4 **Manitoba,L** Can
13F2 **Manito L** Can
14A1 **Manitou Is** USA
7B5 **Manitoulin** *I* Can
14A2 **Manitowoc** USA
15C1 **Maniwaki** Can
32B2 **Manizales** Colombia
101D3 **Manja** Madag
106A4 **Manjimup** Aust
87B1 **Mānjra** *R* India
10A2 **Mankato** USA
97B4 **Mankono** Ivory Coast
12D2 **Manley Hot Springs**
　　USA
110B1 **Manly** NZ
85C4 **Manmād** India
78A3 **Manna** Indon
108A2 **Mannahill** Aust
87B3 **Mannar** Sri Lanka
87B3 **Mannār,G of** India
87B2 **Mannārgudi** India
57B3 **Mannheim** Germany
13D1 **Manning** Can
17B1 **Manning** USA
108A2 **Mannum** Aust
97A4 **Mano** Sierra Leone
71E4 **Manokwari** Indon
98C3 **Manono** Zaïre
76B3 **Manoron** Burma
75B1 **Mano-wan** *B* Japan
74B2 **Manp'o** N Korea
84D3 **Mänsa** India
100B2 **Mansa** Zambia
6B3 **Mansel I** Can
19B2 **Mansfield** Arkansas,
　　USA
108C3 **Mansfield** Aust
19B3 **Mansfield** Louisiana,
　　USA
16D1 **Mansfield**
　　Massachusetts, USA
10B2 **Mansfield** Ohio, USA
15C2 **Mansfield**
　　Pennsylvania, USA
71E2 **Mansyu Deep**
　　Pacific O
32A4 **Manta** Ecuador
79A4 **Mantalingajan,Mt**
　　Phil
32B6 **Mantaro** *R* Peru
22B2 **Manteca** USA
48C2 **Mantes** France
52B1 **Mantova** Italy
38J6 **Mantta** Fin
61F2 **Manturovo**
　　Russian Fed
35A2 **Manuel Ribas** Brazil
79B4 **Manukan** Phil
110B1 **Manukau** NZ
71F4 **Manus** *I* Pacific O
50B2 **Manzanares** Spain
25E2 **Manzanillo** Cuba
24B3 **Manzanillo** Mexico
63D3 **Manzhouli** China
94C3 **Manzil** Jordan
101C3 **Manzini** Swaziland
98B1 **Mao** Chad
72A2 **Maomao Shan** *Mt*
　　China
73C5 **Maoming** China
101C3 **Mapai** Mozam
71E3 **Mapia** *Is* Pacific O
79A4 **Mapin** *I* Phil
5H5 **Maple Creek** Can
101H1 **Maputo** Mozam
101H1 **Maputo** *R* Mozam
　　Ma Qu = Huange He
72A3 **Maqu** China
86B1 **Maquan He** *R* China
98B3 **Maquela do Zombo**
　　Angola
29C4 **Maquinchao** Arg
31B3 **Marabá** Brazil
32C1 **Maracaibo** Ven
32D1 **Maracay** Ven
95A2 **Marādah** Libya
97C3 **Maradi** Niger
90A2 **Marāgheh** Iran

Midongy Atsimo

101D2 **Mayotte** / Indian O
27H2 **May Pen** Jamaica
16B3 **May Point,C** USA
47D1 **Mayrhofen** Austria
16B3 **Mays Landing** USA
14B3 **Maysville** USA
98B3 **Mayumba** Gabon
100B2 **Mazabuka** Zambia
84D1 **Mazar** China
94B3 **Mazăr** Jordan
53B3 **Mazara del Vallo** Italy
84B1 **Mazar-i-Sharif** Afghan
24B2 **Mazatlán** Mexico
60B2 **Mazeikiai** Lithuania
94B3 **Mazra** Jordan
101C3 **Mbabane** Swaziland
98B2 **Mbaïki** CAR
99D3 **Mbala** Zambia
100B3 **Mbalabala** Zim
99D2 **Mbale** Uganda
98B2 **Mbalmayo** Cam
98B2 **Mbam** *R* Cam
101C2 **Mbamba Bay** Tanz
98B2 **Mbandaka** Zaïre
98B3 **Mbanza Congo** Angola
98B3 **Mbanza-Ngungu** Zaïre
99D3 **Mbarara** Uganda
98B2 **Mbènza** Congo
98B2 **Mbéré** *R* Cam
99D3 **Mbeya** Tanz
98B3 **Mbinda** Congo
97A3 **Mbout** Maur
98C3 **Mbuji-Mayi** Zaïre
99D3 **Mbulu** Tanz
96B2 **Mcherrah** Region, Alg
101C2 **Mchinji** Malawi
76D3 **Mdrak** Viet
9B3 **Mead,L** USA
5H4 **Meadow Lake** Can
14B2 **Meadville** USA
7E4 **Mealy Mts** Can
109C1 **Meandarra** Aust
5G4 **Meander River** Can
45C2 **Meath** County, Irish Rep
49C2 **Meaux** France
16C1 **Mechanicville** USA
56A2 **Mechelen** Belg
96B1 **Mecheria** Alg
56C2 **Mecklenburg-Vorpommern** *State* Germany
56C2 **Mecklenburger Bucht** *B* Germany
101C2 **Meconta** Mozam
101C2 **Mecuburi** Mozam
101D2 **Mecufi** Mozam
101C2 **Mecula** Mozam
70A3 **Medan** Indon
34C3 **Medanos** Arg
34D2 **Médanos** Arg
13E2 **Medecine Hat** Can
32B2 **Medellin** Colombia
96D1 **Medenine** Tunisia
8A2 **Medford** USA
54C2 **Medgidia** Rom
34B2 **Media Agua** Arg
54B1 **Mediaş** Rom
20C1 **Medical Lake** USA
5G5 **Medicine Hat** Can
35C1 **Medina** Brazil
80B3 **Medina** S Arabia
50B1 **Medinaceli** Spain
50B1 **Medina del Campo** Spain
50A1 **Medina de Rio Seco** Spain
86B2 **Medinipur** India
88E4 **Mediterranean S** Europe
13F2 **Medley** Can
61J3 **Mednogorsk** Russian Fed
86D1 **Mêdog** China
98B2 **Medouneu** Gabon
61F3 **Medvedista** *R* Russian Fed
64E3 **Medvezh'yegorsk** Russian Fed

106A3 **Meekatharra** Aust
84D3 **Meerut** India
99D2 **Mēga** Eth
55B3 **Megalópolis** Greece
55B3 **Mégara** Greece
86C1 **Meghālaya** State, India
86C2 **Meghna** *R* Bang
94B2 **Megiddo** *Hist Site* Israel
91B4 **Mehran** *R* Iran
90B3 **Mehriz** Iran
35B1 **Meia Ponte** *R* Brazil
98B2 **Meiganga** Cam
76B1 **Meiktila** Burma
47C1 **Meiringen** Switz
73A4 **Meishan** China
57C2 **Meissen** Germany
73D5 **Mei Xian** China
73D5 **Meizhou** China
30B3 **Mejillones** Chile
98B2 **Mekambo** Gabon
99D1 **Mek'elē** Eth
96B1 **Meknès** Mor
76D3 **Mekong** *R* Camb
97C3 **Mekrou** *R* Benin
77C5 **Melaka** Malay
104F4 **Melanesia** *Region* Pacific O
78C3 **Melawi** *R* Indon
107D4 **Melbourne** Aust
11B4 **Melbourne** USA
9C4 **Melchor Muzquiz** Mexico
61J3 **Meleuz** Russian Fed
98B1 **Melfi** Chad
5H4 **Melfort** Can
96B1 **Melilla** N W Africa
29B4 **Melimoyu** *Mt* Chile
34C2 **Melincué** Arg
34A2 **Melipilla** Chile
60E4 **Melitopol'** Ukraine
6D2 **Meliville Bugt** *B* Greenland
99D2 **Melka Guba** Eth
101H1 **Melmoth** S Africa
34C2 **Melo** Arg
29F2 **Melo** Urug
22B2 **Melones Res** USA
12D1 **Melozitna** *R* USA
47C1 **Mels** Switz
43D3 **Melton Mowbry** Eng
49C2 **Melun** France
5H4 **Melville** Can
27Q2 **Melville,C** Dominica
4F3 **Melville Hills** *Mts* Can
106C2 **Melville I** Aust
4G2 **Melville I** Can
7E4 **Melville,L** Can
6B3 **Melville Pen** Can
45B1 **Melvin,L** Irish Rep
101D2 **Memba** Mozam
106A1 **Memboro** Indon
57C3 **Memmingen** Germany
78B2 **Mempawan** Indon
11B3 **Memphis** Tennessee, USA
19B3 **Mena** USA
43B3 **Menai Str** Wales
97C3 **Ménaka** Mali
14A2 **Menasha** USA
78C3 **Mendawai** *R* Indon
49C3 **Mende** France
99D2 **Mendebo** *Mts* Eth
43C4 **Mendip Hills** *Upland* Eng
20B2 **Mendocino,C** USA
105J2 **Mendocino Seascarp** Pacific O
22B2 **Mendota** California, USA
29C2 **Mendoza** Arg
29C3 **Mendoza** State, Arg
55C3 **Menemen** Turk
46B1 **Menen** Belg
72D3 **Mengcheng** China
78B3 **Menggala** Indon
76B1 **Menghai** China
73A5 **Mengla** China
76B1 **Menglian** China
73A5 **Mengzi** China
107D4 **Menindee** Aust

108B2 **Menindee L** Aust
108A3 **Meningie** Aust
14A1 **Menominee** USA
14A2 **Menomonee Falls** USA
100A2 **Menongue** Angola
51C1 **Menorca** / Spain
12F2 **Mentasta Mts** USA
78B3 **Mentok** Indon
14B2 **Mentor** USA
46B2 **Ménu** France
72A2 **Menyuan** China
61H2 **Menzelinsk** Russian Fed
56B2 **Meppen** Germany
78D2 **Merah** Indon
18B2 **Meramec** *R* USA
52B1 **Merano** Italy
71F4 **Merauke** Indon
8A3 **Merced** USA
22B2 **Merced** *R* USA
29B2 **Mercedario** *Mt* Chile
29C2 **Mercedes** Arg
29E2 **Mercedes** Buenos Aires, Arg
30E4 **Mercedes** Corrientes, Arg
29E2 **Mercedes** Urug
110C1 **Mercury B** NZ
110C1 **Mercury Is** NZ
4F2 **Mercy B** Can
6D3 **Mercy,C** Can
99E2 **Meregh** Somalia
76B3 **Mergui** Burma
76B3 **Mergui Arch** Burma
25D2 **Mérida** Mexico
50A2 **Mérida** Spain
32C2 **Mérida** Ven
11B3 **Meridian** USA
109C3 **Merimbula** Aust
108B2 **Meringur** Aust
95C3 **Merowe** Sudan
106A4 **Merredin** Aust
42B2 **Merrick** *Mt* Scot
14A2 **Merrillville** USA
13C2 **Merritt** Can
17B2 **Merritt Island** USA
109D2 **Merriwa** Aust
99E1 **Mersa Fatma** Eritrea
51B2 **Mers el Kebir** Alg
42C3 **Mersey** *R* Eng
42C3 **Merseyside** Metropolitan County, Eng
92B2 **Mersin** Turk
77C5 **Mersing** Malay
85C3 **Merta** India
43C4 **Merthyr Tydfil** Wales
50A2 **Mertola** Port
99D3 **Meru** *Mt* Tanz
60E5 **Merzifon** Turk
46D2 **Merzig** Germany
9B3 **Mesa** USA
46E1 **Meschede** Germany
93D1 **Mescit Dağ** *Mt* Turk
12C3 **Meshik** USA
99C2 **Meshra Er Req** Sudan
47C1 **Mesocco** Switz
55B3 **Mesolóngion** Greece
19A3 **Mesquite** Texas, USA
101C2 **Messalo** *R* Mozam
53C3 **Messina** Italy
100B3 **Messina** S Africa
55B3 **Messini** Greece
55B3 **Messiniakós Kólpos** *G* Greece
54B2 **Mesta** *R* Bulg
52B1 **Mestre** Italy
32C3 **Meta** *R* Colombia
60D2 **Meta** *R* Russian Fed
32D2 **Meta** *R* Ven
6C3 **Meta Incognito Pen** Can
19B4 **Metairie** USA
20C1 **Metaline Falls** USA
30D4 **Metán** Arg
101C2 **Metangula** Mozam
53C2 **Metaponto** Italy
44C3 **Methil** Scot
16D1 **Methuen** USA
111B2 **Methven** NZ
12H3 **Metlakatla** USA

18C2 **Metropolis** USA
87B2 **Mettŭr** India
49D2 **Metz** France
70A3 **Meulaboh** Indon
46A2 **Meulan** France
46C2 **Meuse** Department, France
49D2 **Meuse** *R* France
19A3 **Mexia** USA
24A1 **Mexicali** Mexico
24B2 **Mexico** Federal Republic, Cent America
24C3 **México** Mexico
23A2 **México** State, Mexico
18B2 **Mexico** USA
24C2 **Mexico,G of** Cent America
94B3 **Mezada** *Hist Site* Israel
23B2 **Mezcala** Mexico
64F3 **Mezen'** Russian Fed
64G2 **Mezhdusharskiy, Ostrov** / Russian Fed
85D4 **Mhow** India
23B2 **Miahuatlán** Mexico
11B4 **Miami** Florida, USA
18B2 **Miami** Oklahoma, USA
11B4 **Miami Beach** USA
90A2 **Miandowāb** Iran
101D2 **Miandrivazo** Madag
90A2 **Miāneh** Iran
84C2 **Mianwali** Pak
73A3 **Mianyang** China
73C3 **Mianyang** China
73A3 **Mianzhu** China
72E2 **Miaodao Qundao** *Arch* China
73B4 **Miao Ling** *Upland* China
61K3 **Miass** Russian Fed
59C3 **Michalovce** Slovakia
27D3 **Miches** Dom Rep
10B2 **Michigan** State, USA
14A2 **Michigan City** USA
10B2 **Michigan,L** USA
7B5 **Michipicoten I** Can
23A2 **Michoacan** State, Mexico
54C2 **Michurin** Bulg
61F3 **Michurinsk** Russian Fed
104F3 **Micronesia** *Region* Pacific O
78B2 **Midai** / Indon
102F4 **Mid Atlantic Ridge** Atlantic O
46B1 **Middelburg** Neth
20B2 **Middle Alkali L** USA
16D2 **Middleboro** USA
100B4 **Middleburg** Cape Province, S Africa
16A2 **Middleburg** Pennsylvania, USA
101G1 **Middleburg** Transvaal, S Africa
16B1 **Middleburgh** USA
15D2 **Middlebury** USA
11B3 **Middlesboro** USA
42D2 **Middlesbrough** Eng
16C2 **Middletown** Connecticut, USA
16B3 **Middletown** Delaware, USA
15D2 **Middletown** New York, USA
14B3 **Middletown** Ohio, USA
16A2 **Middletown** Pennsylvania, USA
96B1 **Midelt** Mor
43C4 **Mid Glamorgan** County, Wales
104B4 **Mid Indian Basin** Indian O
104B4 **Mid Indian Ridge** Indian O
7C5 **Midland** Can
14B2 **Midland** Michigan, USA
9C3 **Midland** Texas, USA
101D3 **Midongy Atsimo** Madag

105G2 **Mid Pacific Mts** Pacific O
20C2 **Midvale** USA
105H2 **Midway Is** Pacific O
18A2 **Midwest City** USA
93D2 **Midyat** Turk
54B2 **Midžor** *Mt* Serbia, Yugos
59B2 **Mielec** Pol
54C1 **Miercurea-Ciuc** Rom
50A1 **Mieres** Spain
16A2 **Mifflintown** USA
75A2 **Mihara** Japan
72D1 **Mijun Shuiku** *Res* China
54B2 **Mikhaylovgrad** Bulg
61F3 **Mikhaylovka** Russian Fed
65J4 **Mikhaylovskiy** Russian Fed
38K6 **Mikkeli** Fin
55C3 **Míkonos** *I* Greece
59B3 **Mikulov** Czech Republic
99D3 **Mikumi** Tanz
74D3 **Mikuni-sammyaku** *Mts* Japan
75B2 **Mikura-jima** *I* Japan
32B4 **Milagro** Ecuador
Milan = Milano
51C2 **Milana** Alg
101C2 **Milange** Mozam
52A1 **Milano** Italy
92A2 **Milas** Turk
107D4 **Mildura** Aust
73A5 **Mile** China
93D3 **Mileh Tharthār** *L* Iraq
107E3 **Miles** Aust
8C2 **Miles City** USA
16C2 **Milford** Connecticut, USA
15C3 **Milford** Delaware, USA
15D2 **Milford** Massachusetts, USA
18A1 **Milford** Nebraska, USA
16B2 **Milford** Pennsylvania, USA
43B4 **Milford Haven** Wales
43B4 **Milford Haven** *Sd* Wales
18A2 **Milford L** USA
111A2 **Milford Sd** NZ
13E2 **Milk River** Can
49C3 **Millau** France
16C2 **Millbrook** USA
17B1 **Milledgeville** USA
12F2 **Miller,Mt** USA
61F4 **Millerovo** Russian Fed
16A2 **Millersburg** USA
108A1 **Millers Creek** Aust
16C1 **Millers Falls** USA
16C2 **Millerton** USA
22C2 **Millerton L** USA
108B3 **Millicent** Aust
109D1 **Millmerran** Aust
45B2 **Milltown Malbay** Irish Rep
22A2 **Mill Valley** USA
15D3 **Millville** USA
6H2 **Milne Land** *I* Greenland
21C4 **Milolii** Hawaiian Is
55B3 **Mílos** *I* Greece
107D3 **Milparinka** Aust
16A2 **Milroy** USA
111A3 **Milton** NZ
16A2 **Milton** Pennsylvania, USA
10B2 **Milwaukee** USA
51C2 **Mina** *R* Alg
93E4 **Mīnā' al Ahmadī** Kuwait
91C4 **Mīnāb** Iran
74C4 **Minamata** Japan
78A2 **Minas** Indon
29E2 **Minas** Urug
31B5 **Minas Gerais** State, Brazil
35C1 **Minas Novas** Brazil
25C3 **Minatitlan** Mexico
76A1 **Minbu** Burma
76A1 **Minbya** Burma
34A2 **Mincha** Chile
44A3 **Minch,Little** *Sd* Scot
44A2 **Minch,North** *Sd* Scot
40B2 **Minch,The** *Sd* Scot
12D2 **Minchumina,L** USA
47D2 **Mincio** *R* Italy
79B4 **Mindanao** *I* Phil
19B3 **Minden** Louisiana, USA
56B2 **Minden** Germany
108B2 **Mindona L** Aust
79B3 **Mindoro** *I* Phil
79B3 **Mindoro Str** Phil
45C3 **Mine Hd** *C* Irish Rep
43C4 **Minehead** Eng
30F2 **Mineiros** Brazil
19A3 **Mineola** USA
23B1 **Mineral de Monte** Mexico
16A2 **Minersville** USA
108B2 **Mingary** Aust
72A2 **Minhe** China
87A3 **Minicoy** *I* India
73D4 **Min Jiang** *R* Fujian, China
73A4 **Min Jiang** *R* Sichuan, China
22C2 **Minkler** USA
108A2 **Minlaton** Aust
72A2 **Minle** China
97C4 **Minna** Nig
10A2 **Minneapolis** USA
5J4 **Minnedosa** Can
10A2 **Minnesota** State, USA
50A1 **Miño** *R* Spain
8C2 **Minot** USA
72A2 **Minqin** China
72A3 **Min Shan** *Upland* China
60C3 **Minsk** Belorussia
58C2 **Mińsk Mazowiecki** Pol
12E2 **Minto** USA
4G2 **Minto Inlet** *B* Can
7C4 **Minto,L** Can
63B2 **Minusinsk** Russian Fed
72A3 **Min Xian** China
7E5 **Miquelon** Can
22D3 **Mirage L** USA
87A1 **Miraj** India
29E3 **Miramar** Arg
84B2 **Miram Shah** Pak
50B1 **Miranda de Ebro** Spain
47D2 **Mirandola** Italy
84B2 **Mir Bachchen Kūt** Afghan
78D1 **Miri** Malay
96A3 **Mirik,C** Maur
63A1 **Mirnoye** Russian Fed
63D1 **Mirnyy** Russian Fed
112C9 **Mirnyy** *Base* Ant
84C2 **Mirpur** Pak
85B3 **Mirpur Khas** Pak
55B3 **Mirtoan S** Greece
74B3 **Miryang** S Korea
86A1 **Mirzāpur** India
23B2 **Misantla** Mexico
84C1 **Misgar** Pak
14A2 **Mishawaka** USA
12B1 **Misheguk Mt** USA
75A2 **Mi-shima** *I* Japan
107E2 **Misima** *I* Solomon Is
30F4 **Misiones** State, Arg
59C3 **Miskolc** Hung
94C2 **Mismīyah** Syria
71E4 **Misoöl** *I* Indon
95A1 **Misrātah** Libya
7B5 **Missinaibi** *R* Can
20B1 **Mission City** Can
15C2 **Mississauga** Can
11A3 **Mississippi** State, USA
11A3 **Mississippi** *R* USA
19C3 **Mississippi Delta** USA
8B2 **Missoula** USA
96B1 **Missour** Mor
11A3 **Missouri** State, USA
10A2 **Missouri** *R* USA
10C1 **Mistassini,L** Can
30B2 **Misti** *Mt* Peru
109C1 **Mitchell** Aust
8D2 **Mitchell** USA
107D2 **Mitchell** *R* Aust
11B3 **Mitchell,Mt** USA
45B2 **Mitchelstown** Irish Rep
84C3 **Mithankot** Pak
55C3 **Mitilíni** Greece
23B2 **Mitla** Mexico
54B2 **Mitrovica** Serbia, Yugos
95C3 **Mits'iwa** Eritrea
32C3 **Mitu** Colombia
99C3 **Mitumbar** *Mts* Zaïre
98C3 **Mitwaba** Zaïre
98B2 **Mitzic** Gabon
75B1 **Miura** Japan
72C3 **Mi Xian** China
69F3 **Miyake** *I* Japan
75B2 **Miyake-jima** *I* Japan
69E4 **Miyako** *I* Japan
74C4 **Miyakonojō** Japan
74C4 **Miyazaki** Japan
75B1 **Miyazu** Japan
74C4 **Miyoshi** Japan
72D1 **Miyun** China
99D2 **Mīzan Teferi** Eth
95A1 **Mizdah** Libya
45B3 **Mizen Hd** *C* Irish Rep
54C1 **Mizil** Rom
86C2 **Mizo Hills** India
86C2 **Mizoram** Union Territory, India
94B3 **Mizpe Ramon** Israel
112B11 **Mizuho** *Base* Ant
74E3 **Mizusawa** Japan
39H7 **Mjolby** Sweden
100B2 **Mkushi** Zambia
101H1 **Mkuzi** S Africa
57C2 **Mladá Boleslav** Czech Republic
58C2 **Mława** Pol
52C2 **Mljet** *I* Croatia
100B3 **Mmabatho** S Africa
84D2 **Mnadi** India
97A4 **Moa** *R* Sierra Leone
94B3 **Moab** Region, Jordan
9C3 **Moab** USA
98B3 **Moanda** Congo
98B3 **Moanda** Gabon
99C3 **Moba** Zaïre
75C1 **Mobara** Japan
98C2 **Mobaye** CAR
98C2 **Mobayi** Zaïre
10A3 **Moberly** USA
11B3 **Mobile** USA
11B3 **Mobile B** USA
8C2 **Mobridge** USA
101D2 **Moçambique** Mozam
76C1 **Moc Chau** Viet
100B3 **Mochudi** Botswana
101D2 **Mocimboa da Praia** Mozam
32B3 **Mocoa** Colombia
35B2 **Mococa** Brazil
34D2 **Mocoreta** *R* Arg
23B1 **Moctezuma** *R* Mexico
101C2 **Mocuba** Mozam
47B2 **Modane** France
101G1 **Modder** *R* S Africa
52B2 **Modena** Italy
46D2 **Moder** *R* France
8A3 **Modesto** USA
22B2 **Modesto Res** USA
53B3 **Modica** Italy
59B3 **Mödling** Austria
107D4 **Moe** Aust
47C1 **Moesa** *R* Switz
42C2 **Moffat** Scot
84D2 **Moga** India
35B2 **Mogi das Cruzes** Brazil
60C3 **Mogilev** Belorussia
60C4 **Mogilev Podolskiy** Ukraine
35B2 **Mogi-Mirim** Brazil
101D2 **Mogincual** Mozam
47E2 **Mogliano** Italy
34B2 **Mogna** Arg
68D1 **Mogocha** Russian Fed
65K4 **Mogochin** Russian Fed
50A2 **Moguer** Spain
110C1 **Mohaka** *R* NZ
86C2 **Mohanganj** Bang
15D2 **Mohawk** *R* USA
99D3 **Mohoro** Tanz
65J5 **Mointy** Kazakhstan
38G5 **Mo i Rana** Nor
48C3 **Moissac** France
21B2 **Mojave** USA
22D3 **Mojave** *R* USA
9B3 **Mojave Desert** USA
78C4 **Mojokerto** Indon
86B1 **Mokama** India
110B1 **Mokau** *R* NZ
22B1 **Mokelumne Aqueduct** USA
22B1 **Mokelumne Hill** USA
22B1 **Mokelumne North Fork** *R* USA
101G1 **Mokhotlong** Lesotho
96D1 **Moknine** Tunisia
86C1 **Mokokchūng** India
98B1 **Mokolo** Cam
74B4 **Mokp'o** S Korea
61F3 **Moksha** *R* Russian Fed
23B1 **Molango** Mexico
55B3 **Moláoi** Greece
Moldavia = Moldova
38F6 **Molde** Nor
60C4 **Moldova** Republic, Europe
Moldoveanu *Mt* Rom
100B3 **Molepolole** Botswana
53C2 **Molfetta** Italy
34A3 **Molina** Chile
30B2 **Mollendo** Peru
60C3 **Molodechno** Belorussia
112C11 **Molodezhnaya** *Base* Ant
21C4 **Molokai** *I* Hawaiian Is
61G2 **Moloma** *R* Russian Fed
109C2 **Molong** Aust
100B3 **Molopo** *R* Botswana
98B2 **Molounddu** Cam
8D1 **Molson L** Can
71D4 **Molucca** *S* Indon
71D4 **Moluccas** *Is* Indon
101C2 **Moma** Mozam
31C3 **Mombaca** Brazil
99D3 **Mombasa** Kenya
98C2 **Mompono** Zaïre
56C2 **Mon** *I* Den
44A3 **Monach** *Is* Scot
49D3 **Monaco** Principality, Europe
44B3 **Monadhliath** *Mts* Scot
45C1 **Monaghan** County, Irish Rep
45C1 **Monaghan** Irish Rep
27D3 **Mona Pass** Caribbean S
13B2 **Monarch Mt** Can
5G4 **Monashee Mts** Can
41B3 **Monastereven** Irish Rep
47B2 **Moncalieri** Italy
31B2 **Monção** Brazil
38L5 **Monchegorsk** Russian Fed
56B2 **Mönchen-gladbach** Germany
24B2 **Monclova** Mexico
7D5 **Moncton** Can
9C4 **Monctova** Mexico
50A1 **Mondego** *R* Port
52A2 **Mondovi** Italy
27H1 **Moneague** Jamaica
14C2 **Monessen** USA
18B2 **Monett** USA
52B1 **Monfalcone** Italy

50A1 **Monforte de Lemos** Spain
98C2 **Monga** Zaïre
98C2 **Mongala** *R* Zaïre
99D2 **Mongalla** Sudan
76D1 **Mong Cai** Viet
98B1 **Mongo** Chad
68B2 **Mongolia** Republic, Asia
100B2 **Mongu** Zambia
21B2 **Monitor Range** *Mts* USA
98C3 **Monkoto** Zaïre
43C4 **Monmouth** Eng
18B1 **Monmouth** USA
13C2 **Monmouth,Mt** Can
97C4 **Mono** *R* Togo
21B2 **Mono L** USA
53C2 **Monopoli** Italy
51B1 **Monreal del Campo** Spain
19B3 **Monroe** Louisiana, USA
14B2 **Monroe** Michigan, USA
20B1 **Monroe** Washington, USA
18B2 **Monroe City** USA
97A4 **Monrovia** Lib
20D3 **Monrovia** USA
56A2 **Mons** Belg
47D2 **Monselice** Italy
16C1 **Monson** USA
58B1 **Mönsterås** Sweden
101D2 **Montagne d'Ambre** *Mt* Madag
96C1 **Montagnes des Ouled Nail** *Mts* Alg
12E3 **Montague I** USA
49C3 **Mont Aigoual** *Mt* France
48B2 **Montaigu** France
53C3 **Montallo** *Mt* Italy
8B2 **Montana** State, USA
50A1 **Montañas de León** *Mts* Spain
49C2 **Montargis** France
48C3 **Montauban** France
15D2 **Montauk** USA
15D2 **Montauk Pt** USA
49D2 **Montbéliard** France
52A1 **Mont Blanc** *Mt* France/Italy
49C2 **Montceau les Mines** France
51C1 **Montceny** *Mt* Spain
49D3 **Mont Cinto** *Mt* Corse
46C2 **Montcornet** France
48B3 **Mont-de-Marsan** France
48C2 **Montdidier** France
30D2 **Monteagudo** Bol
33G4 **Monte Alegre** Brazil
52B2 **Monte Amiata** *Mt* Italy
47D2 **Monte Baldo** *Mt* Italy
15C1 **Montebello** Can
106A3 **Monte Bello Is** Aust
47E2 **Montebelluna** Italy
49D3 **Monte Carlo** Monaco
35B1 **Monte Carmelo** Brazil
34D2 **Monte Caseros** Arg
52B2 **Monte Cimone** *Mt* Italy
52A2 **Monte Cinto** *Mt* Corse
34B2 **Monte Coman** Arg
52B2 **Monte Corno** *Mt* Italy
27C3 **Montecristi** Dom Rep
52B2 **Montecristo** *I* Italy
23A1 **Monte Escobedo** Mexico
53C2 **Monte Gargano** *Mt* Italy
26B3 **Montego Bay** Jamaica
47D2 **Monte Grappa** *Mt* Italy
47C2 **Monte Lesima** *Mt* Italy

49C3 **Montélimar** France
53B2 **Monte Miletto** *Mt* Italy
50A2 **Montemo-o-Novo** Port
24C2 **Montemorelos** Mexico
26B5 **Montená** Colombia
54A2 **Montenegro** Republic, Yugos
35D1 **Monte Pascoal** *Mt* Brazil
34A2 **Monte Patria** Chile
53C3 **Monte Pollino** *Mt* Italy
101C2 **Montepuez** Mozam
8A3 **Monterey** California, USA
15C3 **Monterey** Virginia, USA
8A3 **Monterey B** USA
32B2 **Montería** Colombia
30D2 **Montero** Bol
47B2 **Monte Rosa** *Mt* Italy/Switz
24B2 **Monterrey** Mexico
31C5 **Montes Claros** Brazil
50B2 **Montes de Toledo** *Mts* Spain
29E2 **Montevideo** Urug
52A2 **Monte Viso** *Mt* Italy
27P2 **Mont Gimie** *Mt* St Lucia
11B3 **Montgomery** Alabama, USA
96C2 **Mont Gréboun** Niger
46C2 **Montherme** France
47B1 **Monthey** Switz
19B3 **Monticello** Arkansas, USA
16B2 **Monticello** New York, USA
9C3 **Monticello** Utah, USA
53A2 **Monti del Gennargentu** *Mt* Sardegna
47D2 **Monti Lessini** *Mts* Italy
53B3 **Monti Nebrodi** *Mts* Italy
7C5 **Mont-Laurier** Can
48C2 **Montluçon** France
7C5 **Montmagny** Can
46C2 **Montmédy** France
49C3 **Mont Mézenc** *Mt* France
46B2 **Montmirail** France
50B2 **Montoro** Spain
49D3 **Mont Pelat** *Mt* France
14B2 **Montpelier** Ohio, USA
10C2 **Montpelier** Vermont, USA
49C3 **Montpellier** France
7C5 **Montréal** Can
48C1 **Montreuil** France
52A1 **Montreux** Switz
47B1 **Mont Risoux** *Mt* France
8C3 **Montrose** Colorado, USA
40C2 **Montrose** Scot
48B2 **Mont-St-Michel** France
96B1 **Monts des Ksour** *Mts* Alg
51C3 **Monts des Ouled Neil** *Mts* Alg
51C2 **Monts du Hodna** *Mts* Alg
27E3 **Montserrat** *I* Caribbean S
10C1 **Monts Otish** *Mts* Can
12B1 **Monument Mt** USA
9B3 **Monument V** USA
98C2 **Monveda** Zaïre
76B1 **Monywa** Burma
52A1 **Monza** Italy
100B2 **Monze** Zambia
101H1 **Mooi** *R* S Africa
101G1 **Mooi River** S Africa

108B1 **Moomba** Aust
109D2 **Moonbi Range** *Mts* Aust
108B1 **Moonda L** Aust
109D1 **Moonie** Aust
109C1 **Moonie** *R* Aust
108A2 **Moonta** Aust
106A4 **Moora** Aust
106A3 **Moore,L** Aust
42C2 **Moorfoot Hills** Scot
8D2 **Moorhead** USA
22C3 **Moorpark** USA
7B4 **Moose** *R* Can
5H4 **Moose Jaw** Can
5H4 **Moosomin** Can
7B4 **Moosonee** Can
16D2 **Moosup** USA
101C2 **Mopeia** Mozam
97B3 **Mopti** Mali
30B2 **Moquegua** Peru
39G6 **Mora** Sweden
31D3 **Morada** Brazil
84D3 **Morādābād** India
35B1 **Morada Nova de Minas** *L* Brazil
101D2 **Morafenobe** Madag
101D2 **Moramanga** Madag
27J2 **Morant Bay** Jamaica
27J2 **Morant Pt** Jamaica
87B3 **Moratuwa** Sri Lanka
59B3 **Morava** *R* Austria/Slovakia
54B2 **Morava** *R* Serbia, Yugos
90C2 **Moraveh Tappeh** Iran
40C2 **Moray Firth** *Estuary* Scot
47C1 **Morbegno** Italy
85C4 **Morbi** India
93D2 **Mor Dağ** *Mt* Turk
5J5 **Morden** Can
61F3 **Mordovskaya Respublika,** Russian Fed
42C2 **Morecambe** Eng
42C2 **Morecambe B** Eng
107D3 **Moree** Aust
14B3 **Morehead** USA
47C1 **Mörel** Switz
24B3 **Morelia** Mexico
23B2 **Morelos** State, Mexico
85D3 **Morena** India
5E4 **Moresby I** Can
109D1 **Moreton I** Aust
46B2 **Moreuil** France
47B1 **Morez** France
19B4 **Morgan City** USA
22B2 **Morgan Hill** USA
14C3 **Morgantown** USA
101G1 **Morgenzon** S Africa
47B1 **Morges** Switz
46D2 **Morhange** France
74E2 **Mori** Japan
27K1 **Moriatio** Tobago
13B2 **Morice L** Can
13E2 **Morinville** Can
74E3 **Morioka** Japan
109D2 **Morisset** Aust
63D1 **Morkoka** *R* Russian Fed
48B2 **Morlaix** France
27Q2 **Morne Diablotin** *Mt* Dominica
106C2 **Mornington** *I* Aust
85B3 **Moro** Pak
96B2 **Morocco** Kingdom, Africa
79B4 **Moro G** Phil
99D3 **Morogoro** Tanz
23A1 **Moroleon** Mexico
101D3 **Morombe** Madag
26B2 **Morón** Cuba
101D3 **Morondava** Madag
50A2 **Moron de la Frontera** Spain
101D2 **Moroni** Comoros
71D3 **Morotai** *I* Indon
99D2 **Moroto** Uganda
61F4 **Morozovsk** Russian Fed
42D2 **Morpeth** Eng
19B2 **Morrilton** USA
35B1 **Morrinhos** Brazil

110C1 **Morrinsville** NZ
16B2 **Morristown** New Jersey, USA
15C2 **Morristown** New York, USA
16B2 **Morrisville** Pennsylvania, USA
21A2 **Morro Bay** USA
23A2 **Morro de Papanoa** Mexico
23A2 **Morro de Petatlán** Mexico
101C2 **Morrumbala** Mozam
101C3 **Morrumbene** Mozam
61F3 **Morshansk** Russian Fed
47C2 **Mortara** Italy
34C2 **Morteros** Arg
33G6 **Mortes** *R* Mato Grosso, Brazil
35C2 **Mortes** *R* Minas Gerais, Brazil
108B3 **Mortlake** Aust
27L1 **Moruga** Trinidad
109D3 **Moruya** Aust
109C1 **Morven** Aust
44B3 **Morvern** *Pen* Scot
109C3 **Morwell** Aust
76B3 **Moscos Is** Burma
Moscow = Moskva
20C1 **Moscow** Idaho, USA
56B2 **Mosel** *R* Germany
46D2 **Moselle** Department, France
46D2 **Moselle** *R* France
20C1 **Moses Lake** USA
111B3 **Mosgiel** NZ
99D3 **Moshi** Tanz
38G5 **Mosjøen** Nor
63G2 **Moskal'vo** Russian Fed
64E4 **Moskva** Russian Fed
35C1 **Mosquito** *R* Brazil
39G7 **Moss** Nor
98B3 **Mossaka** Congo
100B4 **Mossel Bay** S Africa
98B3 **Mossendjo** Congo
108B2 **Mossgiel** Aust
31D3 **Mossoró** Brazil
57C2 **Most** Czech Republic
96C1 **Mostaganem** Alg
54A2 **Mostar** Bosnia-Herzegovina
58C2 **Mosty** Belorussia
Mosul = Al Mawşil
39H7 **Motala** Sweden
42C2 **Motherwell** Scot
86A1 **Motihāri** India
51B2 **Motilla del Palancar** Spain
50B2 **Motril** Spain
111B2 **Motueka** NZ
111B2 **Motueka** *R* NZ
47B1 **Moudon** Switz
98B3 **Mouila** Gabon
108B2 **Moulamein** Aust
4G2 **Mould Bay** Can
49C2 **Moulins** France
76B2 **Moulmein** Burma
96B1 **Moulouya** *R* Mor
17B1 **Moultrie** USA
17C1 **Moultrie,L** USA
18C2 **Mound City** Illinois, USA
18A1 **Mound City** Missouri, USA
98B2 **Moundou** Chad
14B3 **Moundsville** USA
12J1 **Mountain** *R* Can
17A1 **Mountain Brook** USA
18B2 **Mountain Grove** USA
18B2 **Mountain Home** Arkansas, USA
22A2 **Mountain View** USA
12B2 **Mountain Village** USA
16A3 **Mount Airy** Maryland, USA
16A2 **Mount Carmel** USA
108A1 **Mount Dutton** Aust
108A2 **Mount Eba** Aust
108B3 **Mount Gambier** Aust
16B3 **Mount Holly** USA

19B3	**Nacogdoches** USA
76A3	**Nacondam** / Indian O
24B1	**Nacozari** Mexico
85C4	**Nadiād** India
50B2	**Nador** Mor
90B3	**Nadūshan** Iran
59C3	**Nadvornaya** Ukraine
56C1	**Naestved** Den
95B2	**Nāfūrah** Libya
75A2	**Nagahama** Japan
82D3	**Naga Hills** Burma
75B1	**Nagai** Japan
86C1	**Nāgāland** State, India
74D3	**Nagano** Japan
74D3	**Nagaoka** Japan
86C1	**Nagaon** India
87B2	**Nāgappattinam** India
85C4	**Nagar Parkar** Pak
74B4	**Nagasaki** Japan
75B2	**Nagashima** Japan
75A2	**Nagato** Japan
85C3	**Nāgaur** India
87B3	**Nāgercoil** India
85B3	**Nagha Kalat** Pak
84D3	**Nagina** India
74D3	**Nagoya** Japan
85D4	**Nāgpur** India
82D2	**Nagqu** China
59B3	**Nagykanizsa** Hung
59B3	**Nagykörös** Hung
69E4	**Naha** Japan
8A2	**Nahaimo** Can
84D2	**Nāhan** India
4F3	**Nahanni Butte** Can
94B2	**Nahariya** Israel
90A3	**Nahāvand** Iran
46D2	**Nahe** R Germany
72D2	**Nahpu** China
72E1	**Naimen Qi** China
7D4	**Nain** Can
90B3	**Nā'īn** Iran
84D3	**Naini Tai** India
44C3	**Nairn** Scot
99D3	**Nairobi** Kenya
90B3	**Najafābād** Iran
74C2	**Najin** N Korea
75A2	**Nakama** Japan
74E3	**Nakaminato** Japan
75A2	**Nakamura** Japan
75B1	**Nakano** Japan
75A1	**Nakano-shima** / Japan
74C4	**Nakatsu** Japan
75B1	**Nakatsu-gawa** Japan
95C3	**Nak' fa** Eritrea
93E2	**Nakhichevan** Azerbaijan
92B4	**Nakhl** Egypt
74C2	**Nakhodka** Russian Fed
76C3	**Nakhon Pathom** Thai
76C3	**Nakhon Ratchasima** Thai
77C4	**Nakhon Si Thammarat** Thai
12H3	**Nakina** Can
7B4	**Nakina** Ontario, Can
12C3	**Naknek** USA
12C3	**Naknek L** USA
4C4	**Nakrek** USA
39G8	**Nakskov** Den
99D3	**Nakuru** Kenya
13D2	**Nakusp** Can
61F5	**Nal'chik** Russian Fed
87B1	**Nalgonda** India
87B1	**Nallamala Range** Mts India
95A1	**Nālūt** Libya
101H1	**Namaacha** Mozam
65G6	**Namak** L Iran
90C3	**Namakzar-e Shadad** Salt Flat Iran
65J5	**Namangan** Uzbekistan
101C2	**Namapa** Mozam
100A4	**Namaqualand** Region, S Africa
109D1	**Nambour** Aust
109D2	**Nambucca Heads** Aust

77D4	**Nam Can** Viet
82D2	**Nam Co** L China
76D1	**Nam Dinh** Viet
101C2	**Nametil** Mozam
74B4	**Namhae-do** / S Korea
100A2	**Namib Desert** Namibia
100A2	**Namibe** Angola
100A3	**Namibia Republic,** Africa
82D3	**Namjagbarwa Feng** Mt China
71D4	**Namlea** Indon
109C2	**Namoi** R Aust
13D1	**Nampa** Can
20C2	**Nampa** USA
97B3	**Nampala** Mali
76C2	**Nam Phong** Thai
74B3	**Namp'o** N Korea
101C2	**Nampula** Mozam
38G6	**Namsos** Nor
76B1	**Namton** Burma
86D2	**Namtu** Burma
13B2	**Namu** Can
101C2	**Namuno** Mozam
46C1	**Namur** Belg
100A2	**Namutoni** Namibia
74B3	**Namwŏn** S Korea
13C3	**Nanaimo** Can
74B2	**Nanam** N Korea
109D1	**Nanango** Aust
74D3	**Nanao** Japan
75B1	**Nanatsu-jima** / Japan
73B3	**Nanbu** China
73D4	**Nanchang** China
73B3	**Nanchong** China
49D2	**Nancy** France
87B1	**Nānded** India
109D2	**Nandewar Range** Mts Aust
85C4	**Nandurbar** India
87B1	**Nandyāl** India
98B2	**Nanga Eboko** Cam
84C1	**Nanga Parbat** Mt Pak
78C3	**Nangapinoh** Indon
78C3	**Nangatayap** Indon
74B2	**Nangnim Sanmaek** Mts N Korea
86C1	**Nang Xian** China
67F3	**Nangzhou** China
87B2	**Nanjangüd** India
72D3	**Nanjing** China
	Nanking = Nanjing
75A2	**Nankoku** Japan
73C4	**Nan Ling** Region, China
76D1	**Nanliu** R China
73B5	**Nanning** China
6F3	**Nanortalik** Greenland
73A5	**Nanpan Jiang** R China
86A1	**Nānpāra** India
73D4	**Nanping** China
6A1	**Nansen Sd** Can
99D3	**Nansio** Tanz
48B2	**Nantes** France
13E2	**Nanton** Can
72E3	**Nantong** China
10C2	**Nantucket** / USA
35C1	**Nanuque** Brazil
72C3	**Nanyang** China
72D2	**Nanyang Hu** L China
99D2	**Nanyuki** Kenya
74D3	**Naoetsu** Japan
85B4	**Naokot** Pak
22A1	**Napa** USA
12B2	**Napaiskak** USA
15C2	**Napanee** Can
65K4	**Napas** Russian Fed
6E3	**Napassoq** Greenland
76D2	**Nape** Laos
110C1	**Napier** NZ
	Naples = Napoli
17B2	**Naples** Florida, USA
19B3	**Naples** Texas, USA
73B5	**Napo** China
32C4	**Napo** R Peru/ Ecuador
53B2	**Napoli** Italy
90A2	**Naqadeh** Iran

92C4	**Naqb Ishtar** Jordan
75B2	**Nara** Japan
97B3	**Nara** Mali
107D4	**Naracoorte** Aust
23B1	**Naranjos** Mexico
87C1	**Narasarāopet** India
77C4	**Narathiwat** Thai
86C2	**Narayanganj** Bang
87B1	**Nārāyenpet** India
49C3	**Narbonne** France
84D2	**Narendranagar** India
6C2	**Nares Str** Can
58C2	**Narew** R Pol
75C1	**Narita** Japan
85C4	**Narmada** R India
84D3	**Nārnaul** India
60E2	**Naro Fominsk** Russian Fed
99D3	**Narok** Kenya
84C2	**Narowal** Pak
107D4	**Narrabri** Aust
109C1	**Narran** L Aust
109C1	**Narran** R Aust
109C2	**Narrandera** Aust
106A4	**Narrogin** Aust
109C2	**Narromine** Aust
85D4	**Narsimhapur** India
87C1	**Narsipatnam** India
6F3	**Narssalik** Greenland
6F3	**Narssaq** Greenland
6F3	**Narssarssuaq** Greenland
75C1	**Narugo** Japan
75A2	**Naruto** Japan
60C2	**Narva** Russian Fed
38H5	**Narvik** Nor
84D3	**Narwāna** India
64G3	**Nar'yan Mar** Russian Fed
108B1	**Narylico** Aust
65J5	**Naryn** Kirghizia
97C4	**Nasarawa** Nig
103D5	**Nasca Ridge** Pacific O
16D1	**Nashua** USA
19B3	**Nashville** Arkansas, USA
11B3	**Nashville** Tennessee, USA
54A1	**Našice** Croatia
85D4	**Nāsik** India
99D2	**Nasir** Sudan
13B1	**Nass** R Can
26B1	**Nassau** The Bahamas
16C1	**Nassau** USA
95C2	**Nasser,L** Egypt
39G7	**Nässjö** Sweden
7C4	**Nastapoka Is** Can
100B3	**Nata** Botswana
31D3	**Natal** Brazil
70A3	**Natal** Indon
90B3	**Natanz** Iran
7D4	**Natashquan** Can
7D4	**Natashquan** R Can
19B3	**Natchez** USA
19B3	**Natchitoches** USA
108C3	**Nathalia** Aust
6H2	**Nathorsts Land** Region Greenland
13C1	**Nation** R Can
21B3	**National City** USA
75C1	**Natori** Japan
99D3	**Natron** L Tanz
106A4	**Naturaliste,C** Aust
47D1	**Nauders** Austria
56C2	**Nauen** Germany
16C2	**Naugatuck** USA
57C2	**Naumburg** Germany
94B3	**Naur** Jordan
105G4	**Nauru** / Pacific O
63C2	**Naushki** Russian Fed
23B1	**Nautla** Mexico
9C3	**Navajo Res** USA
50A2	**Navalmoral de la Mata** Spain
29C7	**Navarino** / Chile
51B1	**Navarra** Province, Spain
34D3	**Navarro** Arg
19A3	**Navasota** USA
19A3	**Navasota** R USA
50A1	**Navia** R Spain
34A2	**Navidad** Chile

85C4	**Navlakhi** India
60D3	**Navlya** Russian Fed
24B2	**Navojoa** Mexico
55B3	**Návpaktos** Greece
55B3	**Návplion** Greece
85C4	**Navsāri** India
94C2	**Nawá** Syria
86B2	**Nawāda** India
84B2	**Nawah** Afghan
85B3	**Nawrabshah** Pak
73B4	**Naxi** China
55C3	**Náxos** / Greece
23A1	**Nayar** Mexico
90C3	**Nay Band** Iran
91B4	**Nāy Band** Iran
74E2	**Nayoro** Japan
94B2	**Nazareth** Israel
48B2	**Nazay** France
32C6	**Nazca** Peru
92A2	**Nazilli** Turk
63B2	**Nazimovo** Russian Fed
13C2	**Nazko** R Can
99D2	**Nazret** Eth
91C5	**Nazwa** Oman
65J4	**Nazyvayevsk** Russian Fed
98B3	**Ndalatando** Angola
98C2	**Ndélé** CAR
98B3	**Ndendé** Gabon
98B1	**Ndjamena** Chad
98B3	**Ndjolé** Gabon
100B2	**Ndola** Zambia
109C1	**Neabul** Aust
108A1	**Neales** R Aust
55B3	**Neápolis** Greece
43C4	**Neath** Wales
109C1	**Nebine** R Aust
65G6	**Nebit Dag** Turkmenistan
8C2	**Nebraska** State, USA
18A1	**Nebraska City** USA
13C2	**Nechako** R Can
19A3	**Neches** R USA
34D3	**Necochea** Arg
86C1	**Nêdong** China
9B3	**Needles** USA
14A2	**Neenah** USA
5J4	**Neepawa** Can
46C1	**Neerpelt** Belg
63C2	**Neftelensk** Russian Fed
99D2	**Negelē** Eth
94B3	**Negev** Desert Israel
60B4	**Negolu** Mt Rom
87B3	**Negombo** Sri Lanka
76A2	**Negrais,C** Burma
32A4	**Negritos** Peru
33E4	**Negro** R Amazonas, Brazil
29C4	**Negro** R Arg
34D2	**Negro** R Urug
79B4	**Negros** / Phil
54C2	**Negru Voda** Rom
90D3	**Nehbandan** Iran
73B4	**Neijiang** China
72B1	**Nei Monggol** Autonomous Region, China
32B3	**Neiva** Colombia
99D2	**Nejo** Eth
99D2	**Nek'emtē** Eth
60D2	**Nelidovo** Russian Fed
87B2	**Nellore** India
69F2	**Nel'ma** Russian Fed
13D3	**Nelson** Can
111B2	**Nelson** NZ
7A4	**Nelson** R Can
108B3	**Nelson,C** Aust
12B2	**Nelson I** USA
97B3	**Néma** Maur
72A1	**Nemagt Uul** Mt Mongolia
58C1	**Neman** R Lithuania
54C1	**Nemira** Mt Rom
74F2	**Nemuro** Japan
63E3	**Nen** R China
41B3	**Nenagh** Irish Rep
12E2	**Nenana** USA
12E2	**Nenana** R USA
43D3	**Nene** R Eng
69E2	**Nenjiang** China
18A2	**Neodesha** USA

Padstow

43B4 **Padstow** Eng
108B3 **Padthaway** Aust
Padua = Padova
14A3 **Paducah** Kentucky, USA
11B3 **Paducah** USA
38L5 **Padunskoye More** L Russian Fed
74A3 **Paengnyŏng-do** I S Korea
110C1 **Paeroa** NZ
100C3 **Pafuri** Mozam
52B2 **Pag** I Croatia
79B4 **Pagadian** Phil
70B4 **Pagai Selatan** I Indon
70B4 **Pagai Utara** I Indon
71F2 **Pagan** I Pacific O
78D3 **Pagatan** Indon
55C3 **Pagondhas** Greece
110C2 **Pahiatua** NZ
21C4 **Pahoa** Hawaiian Is
17B2 **Pahokee** USA
39K6 **Päijänna** L Fin
21C4 **Pailola Chan** Hawaiian Is
14B2 **Painesville** USA
9B3 **Painted Desert** USA
42B2 **Paisley** Scot
32A5 **Paita** Peru
38J5 **Pajala** Sweden
80E3 **Pakistan** Republic, Asia
76C2 **Pak Lay** Laos
86D2 **Pakokku** Burma
13E2 **Pakowki L** Can
52C1 **Pakrac** Croatia
54A1 **Paks** Hung
76C2 **Pak Sane** Laos
76D2 **Pakse** Laos
99D2 **Pakwach** Uganda
98B2 **Pala** Chad
52C2 **Palagruža** I Croatia
46B2 **Palaiseau** France
Palakhat = Palghat
78C3 **Palangkaraya** Indon
87B2 **Palani** India
85C4 **Palanpur** India
100B3 **Palapye** Botswana
17B2 **Palatka** USA
71E3 **Palau Is** Pacific O
76B3 **Palaw** Burma
79A4 **Palawan** I Phil
79A4 **Palawan Pass** Phil
87B3 **Palayankottai** India
39J7 **Paldiski** Estonia
78A3 **Palembang** Indon
50B1 **Palencia** Spain
94A1 **Paleokhorio** Cyprus
53B3 **Palermo** Italy
19A3 **Palestine** USA
86C2 **Paletwa** Burma
87B2 **Pālghāt** India
85C3 **Pāli** India
85C4 **Pālitāna** India
87B3 **Palk Str** India/ Sri Lanka
61G3 **Pallasovka** Russian Fed
38J5 **Pallastunturi** Mt Fin
111B2 **Palliser B** NZ
111C2 **Palliser,C** NZ
101D2 **Palma** Mozam
51C2 **Palma de Mallorca** Spain
31D3 **Palmares** Brazil
26A5 **Palmar Sur** Costa Rica
97B4 **Palmas,C** Lib
26B2 **Palma Soriano** Cuba
17B2 **Palm Bay** USA
17B2 **Palm Beach** USA
22C3 **Palmdale** USA
31D3 **Palmeira dos Indos** Brazil
12E2 **Palmer** USA
112C3 **Palmer** Base Ant
112C3 **Palmer Arch** Ant
112B3 **Palmer Land** Region Ant
111B3 **Palmerston** NZ
110C2 **Palmerston North** NZ
16B2 **Palmerton** USA
17B2 **Palmetto** USA

53C3 **Palmi** Italy
32B3 **Palmira** Colombia
107D2 **Palm Is** Aust
21B3 **Palm Springs** USA
18B2 **Palmyra** Missouri, USA
16A2 **Palmyra** Pennsylvania, USA
86B2 **Palmyras Pt** India
22A2 **Palo Alto** USA
78B2 **Paloh** Indon
99D1 **Paloich** Sudan
21B3 **Palomar Mt** USA
70D4 **Palopo** Indon
70C4 **Palu** Indon
93C2 **Palu** Turk
84D3 **Palwal** India
97C3 **Pama** Burkina
78C4 **Pamekasan** Indon
78B4 **Pameungpeuk** Indon
48C3 **Pamiers** France
82B2 **Pamir** Mts China
65J6 **Pamir** R Russian Fed
11C3 **Pamlico Sd** USA
9C3 **Pampa** USA
34B2 **Pampa de la Salinas** Salt pan Arg
34B3 **Pampa de la Varita** Plain Arg
32C2 **Pamplona** Colombia
50B1 **Pamplona** Spain
18C2 **Pana** USA
54B2 **Panagyurishte** Bulg
87A1 **Panaji** India
32B2 **Panamá** Panama
32A2 **Panama** Republic, Cent America
26B5 **Panama Canal** Panama
17A1 **Panama City** USA
21B2 **Panamint Range** Mts USA
21B2 **Panamint V** USA
47D2 **Panaro** R Italy
79B3 **Panay** I Phil
54B2 **Pancevo** Serbia, Yugos
79B3 **Pandan** Phil
87B1 **Pandharpur** India
108A1 **Pandie Pandie** Aust
58C1 **Panevėžys** Lithuania
65K5 **Panfilov** Kazakhstan
76B1 **Pang** R Burma
99D3 **Pangani** Tanz
99D3 **Pangani** R Tanz
98C3 **Pangi** Zaïre
78B3 **Pangkalpinang** Indon
6D3 **Pangnirtung** Can
76B1 **Pangtara** Burma
79B4 **Pangutaran Group** Is Phil
84D3 **Panipat** India
84B2 **Panjao** Afghan
74B3 **P'anmunjŏm** N Korea
86A2 **Panna** India
35A2 **Panorama** Brazil
53B3 **Pantelleria** I Medit S
23B1 **Pantepec** Mexico
23B1 **Panuco** Mexico
23B1 **Pánuco** R Mexico
73A4 **Pan Xian** China
53C3 **Paola** Italy
18B2 **Paola** USA
14A3 **Paoli** USA
59B3 **Pápa** Hung
110B1 **Papakura** NZ
23B2 **Papaloapan** R Mexico
23B1 **Papantla** Mexico
44E1 **Papa Stour** I Scot
110B1 **Papatoetoe** NZ
44C2 **Papa Westray** I Scot
107D1 **Papua,G of** PNG
107D1 **Papua New Guinea** Republic, S E Asia
34A2 **Papudo** Chile
76B2 **Papun** Burma
33G4 **Para** State, Brazil
31B2 **Pará** R Brazil
106A3 **Paraburdoo** Aust
32B6 **Paracas,Pen de** Peru
35B1 **Paracatu** Brazil
35B1 **Paracatu** R Brazil

108A2 **Parachilna** Aust
84C2 **Parachinar** Pak
54B2 **Paracin** Serbia, Yugos
35C1 **Pará de Minas** Brazil
21A2 **Paradise** California, USA
18B2 **Paragould** USA
33E6 **Paraguá** R Bol
33E2 **Paragua** R Ven
30E2 **Paraguai** R Brazil
30E4 **Paraguari** Par
30E3 **Paraguay** Republic, S America
30E3 **Paraguay** R Par
31D3 **Paraiba** State, Brazil
35B2 **Paraiba** R Brazil
35C2 **Paraíba do Sul** R Brazil
97C4 **Parakou** Benin
108A2 **Parakylia** Aust
87B3 **Paramakkudi** India
33F2 **Paramaribo** Surinam
69H1 **Paramushir** I Russian Fed
30F3 **Paraná** State, Brazil
34C2 **Paraná** Urug
29E2 **Paraná** R Arg
31B4 **Paraná** R Brazil
35A2 **Paraná** R Brazil
30G4 **Paranaguá** Brazil
35A1 **Paranaiba** Brazil
35A1 **Paranaiba** R Brazil
35A2 **Paranapanema** R Brazil
35A2 **Paranavai** Brazil
79B4 **Parang** Phil
35C1 **Paraope** R Brazil
110B2 **Paraparaumu** NZ
87B1 **Parbhani** India
94B2 **Pardes Hanna** Israel
34D3 **Pardo** Arg
35D1 **Pardo** R Bahia, Brazil
35A2 **Pardo** R Mato Grosso do Sul, Brazil
35B1 **Pardo** R Minas Gerais, Brazil
35B2 **Pardo** R Sao Paulo, Brazil
59B2 **Pardubice** Czech Republic
69F4 **Parece Vela** Reef Pacific O
10C2 **Parent** Can
70C4 **Parepare** Indon
34C3 **Parera** Arg
70B4 **Pariaman** Indon
33E1 **Paria,Pen de** Ven
48C2 **Paris** France
14B3 **Paris** Kentucky, USA
19A3 **Paris** Texas, USA
14B3 **Parkersburg** USA
109C2 **Parkes** Aust
16B3 **Parkesburg** USA
14A2 **Park Forest** USA
20B1 **Parksville** Can
87B1 **Parli** India
47D2 **Parma** Italy
14B2 **Parma** USA
31C2 **Parnaiba** Brazil
31C2 **Parnaiba** R Brazil
55B3 **Párnon Óros** Mts Greece
60B2 **Pärnu** Estonia
86B1 **Paro** Bhutan
108B1 **Paroo** R Aust
108B2 **Paroo Channel** R Aust
55C3 **Páros** I Greece
47B2 **Parpaillon** Mts France
34A3 **Parral** Chile
109D2 **Parramatta** Aust
9C4 **Parras** Mexico
6B3 **Parry B** Can
4G2 **Parry Is** Can
7C5 **Parry Sd** Can
14B1 **Parry Sound** Can
57C3 **Parsberg** Germany
5F4 **Parsnip** R Can
18A2 **Parsons** Kansas, USA
14C3 **Parsons** West Virginia, USA
48B2 **Parthenay** France

53B3 **Partinico** Italy
74C2 **Partizansk** Russian Fed
33G4 **Paru** R Brazil
101G1 **Parys** S Africa
19A4 **Pasadena** Texas, USA
22C3 **Pasadena** California, USA
78D3 **Pasangkayu** Indon
76B2 **Pasawing** Burma
19C3 **Pascagoula** USA
54C1 **Paşcani** Rom
20C1 **Pasco** USA
46B1 **Pas-de-Calais** Department, France
39G8 **Pasewalk** Germany
91C4 **Pashū'īyeh** Iran
106B4 **Pasley,C** Aust
29E2 **Paso de los Toros** Urug
29B4 **Paso Limay** Arg
21A2 **Paso Robles** USA
45B3 **Passage West** Irish Rep
16B2 **Passaic** USA
57C3 **Passau** Germany
30E4 **Passo de los Libres** Arg
47D1 **Passo di Stelvio** Mt Italy
30F4 **Passo Fundo** Brazil
35B2 **Passos** Brazil
47B2 **Passy** France
32B4 **Pastaza** R Peru
34C3 **Pasteur** Arg
5H4 **Pas,The** Can
32B3 **Pasto** Colombia
12B2 **Pastol B** USA
47D2 **Pasubio** Mt Italy
78C4 **Pasuruan** Indon
58C1 **Pasvalys** Lithuania
85C4 **Pātan** India
86B1 **Patan** Nepal
108B3 **Patchewollock** Aust
110B1 **Patea** NZ
111B2 **Patea** R NZ
53B3 **Paterno** Italy
16B2 **Paterson** USA
111A3 **Paterson Inlet** B NZ
84D2 **Pathankot** India
Pathein = Bassein
84D2 **Patiāla** India
32B6 **Pativilca** Peru
55C3 **Pátmos** I Greece
86B1 **Patna** India
93D2 **Patnos** Turk
63D2 **Patomskoye** Nagor'ye Upland Russian Fed
31D3 **Patos** Brazil
35B1 **Patos de Minas** Brazil
34B2 **Patquia** Arg
55B3 **Pátrai** Greece
35B1 **Patrocinio** Brazil
99E3 **Patta** I Kenya
78D4 **Pattallasang** Indon
77C4 **Pattani** Thai
22B2 **Patterson** California, USA
19B4 **Patterson** Louisiana, USA
12H2 **Patterson,Mt** Can
22C2 **Patterson Mt** USA
13B1 **Pattullo,Mt** Can
31D3 **Patu** Brazil
86C2 **Patuakhali** Bang
25D3 **Patuca** R Honduras
23A2 **Patzcuaro** Mexico
48B3 **Pau** France
4F3 **Paulatuk** Can
31C3 **Paulistana** Brazil
101H1 **Paulpietersburg** S Africa
19A3 **Pauls Valley** USA
76B2 **Paungde** Burma
84D2 **Pauri** India
38H5 **Pauske** Nor
35C1 **Pavão** Brazil
47C2 **Pavia** Italy
65J4 **Pavlodar** Kazakhstan
61J2 **Pavlovka** Russian Fed

52B1 **Poreč** Croatia
35A2 **Porecatu** Brazil
39J6 **Pori** Fin
111B2 **Porirua** NZ
38H5 **Porjus** Sweden
69G2 **Poronaysk** Russian Fed
47B1 **Porrentruy** Switz
38K4 **Porsangen** *Inlet* Nor
39F7 **Porsgrunn** Nor
45C1 **Portadown** N Ire
8D2 **Portage la Prairie** Can
13C3 **Port Alberni** Can
50A2 **Portalegre** Port
9C3 **Portales** USA
100B4 **Port Alfred** S Africa
13B2 **Port Alice** Can
19B3 **Port Allen** USA
20B1 **Port Angeles** USA
26B3 **Port Antonio** Jamaica
45C2 **Portarlington** Irish Rep
19B4 **Port Arthur** USA
108A2 **Port Augusta** Aust
26C3 **Port-au-Prince** Haiti
14B2 **Port Austin** USA
108B3 **Port Campbell** Aust
86B2 **Port Canning** India
7D5 **Port Cartier** Can
111B3 **Port Chalmers** NZ
17B2 **Port Charlotte** USA
16C2 **Port Chester** USA
15C2 **Port Colborne** Can
15C2 **Port Credit** Can
109C4 **Port Davey** Aust
26C3 **Port-de-Paix** Haiti
77C5 **Port Dickson** Malay
100C4 **Port Edward** S Africa
35C1 **Porteirinha** Brazil
14B2 **Port Elgin** Can
100B4 **Port Elizabeth** S Africa
27N2 **Porter Pt** St Vincent and the Grenadines
21B2 **Porterville** USA
107D4 **Port Fairy** Aust
98A3 **Port Gentil** Gabon
19B3 **Port Gibson** USA
12D3 **Port Graham** USA
20B1 **Port Hammond** Can
89E7 **Port Harcourt** Nig
13B2 **Port Hardy** Can
7D5 **Port Hawkesbury** Can
106A3 **Port Hedland** Aust
Port Heiden = Meshik
43B3 **Porthmadog** Wales
7E4 **Port Hope Simpson** Can
22C3 **Port Hueneme** USA
14B2 **Port Huron** USA
50A2 **Portimão** Port
109D2 **Port Jackson** *B* Aust
16C2 **Port Jefferson** USA
16B2 **Port Jervis** USA
109D2 **Port Kembla** Aust
14B2 **Portland** Indiana, USA
10C2 **Portland** Maine, USA
109C2 **Portland** New South Wales, Aust
20B1 **Portland** Oregon, USA
108B3 **Portland** Victoria, Aust
27H2 **Portland Bight** *B* Jamaica
43C4 **Portland Bill** *Pt* Eng
109C4 **Portland,C** Aust
13A1 **Portland Canal** Can/ USA
110C1 **Portland I** NZ
27H2 **Portland Pt** Jamaica
45C2 **Port Laoise** Irish Rep
108A2 **Port Lincoln** Aust
97A4 **Port Loko** Sierra Leone
101E3 **Port Louis** Mauritius
108B3 **Port MacDonnell** Aust
13B2 **Port McNeill** Can

109D2 **Port Macquarie** Aust
12B3 **Port Moller** USA
107D1 **Port Moresby** PNG
100A3 **Port Nolloth** S Africa
16B3 **Port Norris** USA
89E7 **Port Novo** Benin
50A1 **Porto** Port
30F5 **Pôrto Alegre** Brazil
33F6 **Pôrto Artur** Brazil
30F3 **Pôrto E Cunha** Brazil
52B2 **Portoferraio** Italy
27E4 **Port of Spain** Trinidad
47D2 **Portomaggiore** Italy
97C4 **Porto Novo** Benin
20B1 **Port Orchard** USA
20B2 **Port Orford** USA
96A1 **Porto Santo** *I* Medeira
31D5 **Pôrto Seguro** Brazil
53A2 **Porto Torres** Sardegna
53A2 **Porto Vecchio** Corse
33E5 **Pôrto Velho** Brazil
111A3 **Port Pegasus** *B* NZ
108B3 **Port Phillip B** Aust
108A2 **Port Pirie** Aust
44A3 **Portree** Scot
20B1 **Port Renfrew** Can
27J2 **Port Royal** Jamaica
17B1 **Port Royal Sd** USA
45C1 **Portrush** N Ire
92B3 **Port Said** Egypt
17A2 **Port St Joe** USA
100B4 **Port St Johns** S Africa
7E4 **Port Saunders** Can
100C4 **Port Shepstone** S Africa
13A2 **Port Simpson** Can
27Q2 **Portsmouth** Dominica
43D4 **Portsmouth** Eng
14B3 **Portsmouth** Ohio, USA
11C3 **Portsmouth** Virginia, USA
109D2 **Port Stephens** *B* Aust
95C3 **Port Sudan** Sudan
19C3 **Port Sulphur** USA
38K5 **Porttipahdan Tekojärvi** *Res* Fin
50A2 **Portugal** Republic, Europe
14A2 **Port Washington** USA
77C5 **Port Weld** Malay
32D6 **Porvenir** Bol
39K6 **Porvoo** Fin
30E4 **Posadas** Arg
50A2 **Posadas** Spain
47D1 **Poschiavo** Switz
6B2 **Posheim Pen** Can
90C3 **Posht-e Badam** Iran
71D4 **Poso** Indon
58D1 **Postavy** Belorussia
14B2 **Post Clinton** USA
100B3 **Postmasburg** S Africa
52B1 **Postojna** Slovenia
74C2 **Pos'yet** Russian Fed
101G1 **Potchetstroom** S Africa
19B2 **Poteau** USA
53C2 **Potenza** Italy
100B3 **Potgietersrus** S Africa
97D3 **Potiskum** Nig
20C1 **Potlatch** USA
15C3 **Potomac** *R* USA
30C2 **Potosi** Bol
30C4 **Potrerillos** Chile
56C2 **Potsdam** Germany
16B2 **Pottstown** USA
16A2 **Pottsville** USA
16C2 **Poughkeepsie** USA
35B2 **Pouso Alegre** Brazil
110C1 **Poverty B** NZ
61F3 **Povorino** Russian Fed
7C4 **Povungnituk** Can
8C2 **Powder** *R* USA
106C2 **Powell Creek** Aust

9B3 **Powell,L** USA
13C3 **Powell River** Can
8C2 **Power** *R* USA
43C3 **Powys** County, Wales
73D4 **Poyang Hu** *L* China
92B2 **Pozantı** Turk
23B1 **Poza Rica** Mexico
58B2 **Poznań** Pol
30E3 **Pozo Colorado** Par
53B2 **Pozzuoli** Italy
97B4 **Pra** *R* Ghana
76C3 **Prachin Buri** Thai
76B3 **Prachuap Khiri Khan** Thai
59B2 **Praděd** *Mt* Czech Republic
49C3 **Pradelles** France
35D1 **Prado** Brazil
Prague = Praha
57C2 **Praha** Czech Republic
97A4 **Praia** Cape Verde
33E5 **Prainha** Brazil
18B2 **Prairie Village** USA
76C3 **Prakhon Chai** Thai
35B1 **Prata** Brazil
35B1 **Prata** *R* Brazil
Prates = Dongsha Qundao
49E3 **Prato** Italy
16B1 **Prattsville** USA
17A1 **Prattville** USA
48B1 **Prawle Pt** Eng
78D4 **Praya** Indon
47D1 **Predazzo** Italy
63B2 **Predivinsk** Russian Fed
58C2 **Pregolyu** *R* Russian Fed
76D3 **Prek Kak** Camb
56C2 **Prenzlau** Germany
76A3 **Preparis** *I* Burma
76A2 **Preparis North Chan** Burma
59B3 **Přerov** Czech Republic
23A2 **Presa del Infiernillo** Mexico
9B3 **Prescott** Arizona, USA
19B3 **Prescott** Arkansas, USA
15C2 **Prescott** Can
30D4 **Presidencia Roque Sáenz Peña** Arg
35A2 **Presidente Epitácio** Brazil
112C2 **Presidente Frei** *Base* Ant
23B2 **Presidente Migúel Aleman** *L* Mexico
35A2 **Presidente Prudente** Brazil
35A2 **Presidente Venceslau** Brazil
59C3 **Prešov** Slovakia
55B2 **Prespansko Jezero** *L* Macedonia, Yugos
10D2 **Presque Isle** USA
42C3 **Preston** Eng
8B2 **Preston** Idaho, USA
18B2 **Preston** Missouri, USA
42B2 **Prestwick** Scot
31B6 **Prêto** Brazil
35B1 **Prêto** *R* Brazil
101G1 **Pretoria** S Africa
55B3 **Préveza** Greece
76D3 **Prey Veng** Camb
8B3 **Price** USA
13B2 **Price I** Can
60D4 **Prichernomorskaya Nizmennost'** *Lowland* Ukraine
27M2 **Prickly Pt** Grenada
58C1 **Priekule** Lithuania
100B3 **Prieska** S Africa
20C1 **Priest L** USA
20C1 **Priest River** USA
55B2 **Prilep** Macedonia, Yugos
60D3 **Priluki** Ukraine
34C2 **Primero** *R* Arg

39K6 **Primorsk** Russian Fed
60E4 **Primorsko-Akhtarsk** Russian Fed
13F2 **Primrose L** Can
5H4 **Prince Albert** Can
4F2 **Prince Albert,C** Can
4G2 **Prince Albert Pen** Can
4G2 **Prince Albert Sd** Can
6C3 **Prince Charles I** Can
112B10 **Prince Charles Mts** Ant
7D5 **Prince Edward I** Can
13C2 **Prince George** Can
4H2 **Prince Gustaf Adolp** *S* Can
5E4 **Prince of Wales** *I* USA
71F5 **Prince of Wales I** Aust
4H2 **Prince of Wales I** Can
4G2 **Prince of Wales Str** Can
4F2 **Prince Patrick I** Can
6A2 **Prince Regent Inlet** *Str* Can
13A2 **Prince Rupert** Can
107D2 **Princess Charlotte B** Aust
13B2 **Princess Royal I** Can
27L1 **Princes Town** Trinidad
13C3 **Princeton** Can
18C2 **Princeton** Kentucky, USA
18B1 **Princeton** Missouri, USA
16B2 **Princeton** New Jersey, USA
4D3 **Prince William** USA
12E2 **Prince William Sd** USA
97C4 **Principe** *I* W Africa
20B2 **Prineville** USA
12E1 **Pringle,Mt** USA
6F3 **Prins Christian Sund** *Sd* Greenland
112B12 **Prinsesse Astrid Kyst** Region, Ant
112B12 **Prinsesse Ragnhild Kyst** Region, Ant
64B2 **Prins Karls Forland** *I* Barents S
25D3 **Prinzapolca** Nic
58D2 **Pripet** *R* Belorussia
Pripyat' = Pripet
54B2 **Priština** Serbia, Yugos
56C2 **Pritzwalk** Germany
61F3 **Privolzhskaya Vozvyshennost'** *Upland* Russian Fed
54B2 **Prizren** Serbia, Yugos
78C4 **Probolinggo** Indon
5G5 **Procatello** USA
87B2 **Proddatür** India
25D2 **Progreso** Mexico
20B2 **Project City** USA
61F5 **Prokhladnyy** Russian Fed
65K4 **Prokop'yevsk** Russian Fed
61F4 **Proletarskaya** Russian Fed
64G2 **Proliv Karskiye Vorota** *Str* Russian Fed
83D4 **Prome** Burma
31D4 **Propriá** Brazil
20B2 **Prospect** Oregon, USA
107D3 **Prosperine** Aust
59B3 **Prostějov** Czech Republic
6E2 **Prøven** Greenland
49D3 **Provence** Region, France
16D2 **Providence** USA
15D2 **Provincetown** USA
49C2 **Provins** France
8B2 **Provo** USA

Provost

13E2 **Provost** Can
4D2 **Prudhoe Bay** USA
6D2 **Prudhoe Land**
Greenland
58C2 **Pruszkow** Pol
60C4 **Prut** R Romania/
Moldavia
60C4 **Prutul** R Romania
58C2 **Pruzhany** Belorussia
18A2 **Pryor** USA
59C3 **Przemys'l** Pol
55C3 **Psará** I Greece
60C2 **Pskov** Russian Fed
58D2 **Ptich** R Belorussia
55B2 **Ptolemaïs** Greece
32C5 **Pucallpa** Peru
73D4 **Pucheng** China
34A3 **Pucón** Chile
38K5 **Pudasjärvi** Fin
87B2 **Pudukkottai** India
23B2 **Puebla** Mexico
23B2 **Puebla** State, Mexico
50A1 **Puebla de Sanabria**
Spain
50A1 **Puebla de Trives**
Spain
9C2 **Pueblo** USA
34B3 **Puelches** Arg
34B3 **Puelén** Arg
23A2 **Puenta Ixbapa**
Mexico
34B2 **Puente del Inca** Arg
32A5 **Puerta Aguja** Peru
30B2 **Puerta Coles** Peru
34B2 **Puerta de los Llanos**
Arg
31D3 **Puerta do Calcanhar**
Pt Brazil
32C1 **Puerta Gallinas**
Colombia
23B2 **Puerta Maldonado** Pt
Mexico
32A2 **Puerta Mariato**
Panama
29C5 **Puerta Médanosa** Pt
Arg
23A2 **Puerta Mongrove**
Mexico
25E4 **Puerta San Blas** Pt
Panama
23A2 **Puerta San Telmo**
Mexico
29B5 **Puerto Aisén** Chile
25D4 **Puerto Armuelles**
Panama
33F6 **Puerto Artur** Brazil
32B3 **Puerto Asis**
Colombia
32D2 **Puerto Ayacucho**
Ven
25D3 **Puerto Barrios**
Guatemala
32C2 **Puerto Berrio**
Colombia
32D1 **Puerto Cabello** Ven
25D3 **Puerto Cabezas** Nic
32D2 **Puerto Carreño**
Colombia
25D4 **Puerto Cortes** Costa
Rica
25D3 **Puerto Cortés**
Honduras
96A2 **Puerto del Rosario**
Canary Is
30F3 **Puerto E Cunha**
Brazil
32C1 **Puerto Fijo** Ven
31B3 **Puerto Franco** Brazil
32D6 **Puerto Heath** Bol
25D2 **Puerto Juarez**
Mexico
33E1 **Puerto la Cruz** Ven
50B2 **Puertollano** Spain
27C4 **Puerto Lopez**
Colombia
29D4 **Puerto Madryn** Arg
32D6 **Puerto Maldonado**
Peru
23B2 **Puerto Marquéz**
Mexico
29B4 **Puerto Montt** Chile
30E3 **Puerto Murtinho**
Brazil
29B6 **Puerto Natales** Chile

24A1 **Puerto Peñasco**
Mexico
29D4 **Puerto Pirámides**
Arg
27C3 **Puerto Plata** Dom
Rep
79A4 **Puerto Princesa** Phil
32B3 **Puerto Rico**
Colombia
27D3 **Puerto Rico** I
Caribbean S
27D3 **Puerto Rico Trench**
Caribbean S
23A2 **Puerto San Juan de
Lima** Mexico
33G4 **Puerto Santanga**
Brazil
30E2 **Puerto Suárez** Bol
24B2 **Puerto Vallarta**
Mexico
29B4 **Puerto Varas** Chile
30D2 **Puerto Villarroel** Bol
61G3 **Pugachev**
Russian Fed
84C3 **Pugal** India
51C1 **Puigcerdá** Spain
111B2 **Pukaki,L** L NZ
74B2 **Pukch'öng** N Korea
110B1 **Pukekobe** NZ
111B2 **Puketeraki Range**
Mts NZ
52B2 **Pula** Croatia
15C2 **Pulaski** New York,
USA
71E4 **Pulau Kolepom** I
Indon
70A4 **Pulau Pulau Batu** Is
Indon
58C2 **Pulawy** Pol
87C2 **Pulicat,L** India
84B1 **Pul-i-Khumri** Afghan
87B3 **Puliyangudi** India
20C1 **Pullman** USA
71E3 **Pulo Anna Merir** I
Pacific O
79B2 **Pulog,Mt** Phil
38L5 **Pulozero** Russian Fed
58C2 **Pultusk** Pol
30C4 **Puna de Atacama**
Arg
86B1 **Punakha** Bhutan
84C2 **Punch** Pak
87A1 **Pune** India
23A2 **Punéper** Mexico
98C3 **Punia** Zaïre
34A2 **Punitaqui** Chile
84C2 **Punjab** Province, Pak
84D2 **Punjab** State, India
30B2 **Puno** Peru
24A2 **Punta Abreojos** Pt
Mexico
53C3 **Punta Alice** Pt Italy
34C3 **Punta Alta** Arg
29B6 **Punta Arenas** Chile
24A2 **Punta Baja** Pt
Mexico
34A2 **Punta Curaumilla** Pt
Chile
100A2 **Punta da Marca** Pt
Angola
101C3 **Punta de Barra Falsa**
Pt Mozam
29F2 **Punta del Este** Urug
24A2 **Punta Eugenia** Pt
Mexico
25D3 **Punta Gorda** Belize
17B2 **Punta Gorda** USA
34A3 **Punta Lavapié** Pt
Chile
34A2 **Punta Lengua de
Vaca** Pt Chile
53B2 **Punta Licosa** Pt Italy
34A1 **Punta Poroto** Pt
Chile
9B4 **Punta San Antonia** Pt
Mexico
34A2 **Punta Topocalma**
Chile
73C4 **Puqi** China
64J3 **Pur** R Russian Fed
19A2 **Purcell** USA
12C1 **Purcell Mt** USA
13D2 **Purcell Mts** Can
34A3 **Purén** Chile

86B2 **Puri** India
87B1 **Pūrna** India
86B1 **Pūrnia** India
76C3 **Pursat** Camb
23A1 **Puruandro** Mexico
33E4 **Purus** R Brazil
19C3 **Purvis** USA
78B4 **Purwokerto** Indon
78C4 **Purworejo** Indon
85D5 **Pusad** India
74B3 **Pusan** S Korea
60D2 **Pushkin** Russian Fed
58D1 **Pustoshka**
Russian Fed
82D3 **Puta** Burma
34A2 **Putaendo** Chile
110C1 **Putaruru** NZ
73D4 **Putian** China
16D2 **Putnam** USA
87B3 **Puttalam** Sri Lanka
56C2 **Puttgarden** Germany
32B4 **Putumayo** R
Ecuador
78C2 **Putussibau** Indon
38K6 **Puulavesl** L Fin
20B1 **Puyallup** USA
49C2 **Puy de Sancy** Mt
France
111A3 **Puysegur Pt** NZ
99C3 **Pweto** Zaïre
43B3 **Pwllheli** Wales
76B2 **Pyapon** Burma
61F5 **Pyatigorsk**
Russian Fed
Pyè = Prome
74B3 **P'yŏngyang** N Korea
108B3 **Pyramid Hill** Aust
21B1 **Pyramid L** USA
111A2 **Pyramid,Mt** NZ
48B3 **Pyrénées** Mts France
58D1 **Pytalovo** Russian Fed
76B2 **Pyu** Burma

Q

94B2 **Qabatiya** Israel
94C3 **Qā'el Hafira** Mud
Flats Jordan
94C3 **Qa'el Jinz** Mud Flats
Jordan
68B3 **Qaidam Pendi** Salt
Flat China
94C2 **Qa Khanna** Salt
Marsh Jordan
99D1 **Qala'en Nahl** Sudan
84B2 **Qalat** Afghan
94C1 **Qal'at al Hisn** Syria
81C3 **Qal'at Bishah**
S Arabia
93E3 **Qal'at Sālih** Iraq
68B3 **Qamdo** China
99E1 **Qandala** Somalia
99E2 **Qardho** Somalia
95B2 **Qara** Egypt
90A3 **Qare Shirin** Iran
91A4 **Qaryat al Ulyā**
S Arabia
94C3 **Qasr el Kharana**
Jordan
91D4 **Qasr-e-Qand** Iran
95B2 **Qasr Farafra** Egypt
94C2 **Qatana** Syria
91B4 **Qatar** Emirate,
Arabian Pen
94C3 **Qatrāna** Jordan
95B2 **Qattâra Depression**
Egypt
90C3 **Qāyen** Iran
90A2 **Qazvin** Iran
95C2 **Qena** Egypt
90A2 **Qeydār** Iran
91B4 **Qeys** I Iran
94B3 **Qeziot** Israel
73B5 **Qian Jiang** R China
72E1 **Qian Shan** Upland
72E3 **Qidong** China
73B4 **Qijiang** China
84B2 **Qila Saifullah** Pak
72A2 **Qilian** China
68B3 **Qilian Shan** China
72B3 **Qin'an** China
72E2 **Qingdao** China
72A2 **Qinghai** Province,
China

68B3 **Qinghai Hu** L China
72D3 **Qingjiang** Jiangsu,
China
73D4 **Qingjiang** Jiangxi,
China
72B3 **Qing Jiang** R China
72C2 **Qingshuihe** China
72B2 **Qingshui He** R China
72B2 **Qingtonxia** China
72B2 **Qingyang** China
74B2 **Qingyuan** Liaoning,
China
73D4 **Qingyuan** Zhejiang,
China
82C2 **Qing Zang** Upland
China
72D2 **Qinhuangdao** China
72B3 **Qin Ling** Mts China
73B5 **Qinzhou** China
76E2 **Qionghai** China
73A3 **Qionglai Shan**
Upland China
76D1 **Qiongzhou Haixia** Str
China
69E2 **Qiqihar** China
94B2 **Qiryat Ata** Israel
94B3 **Qiryat Gat** Israel
94B2 **Qiryat Shemona**
Israel
94B2 **Qiryat Yam** Israel
94B2 **Qishon** R Israel
63A3 **Qitai** China
73C4 **Qiyang** China
72B1 **Qog Qi** China
90B2 **Qolleh-ye Damavand**
Mt Iran
90B3 **Qom** Iran
90B3 **Qomisheh** Iran
**Qomolangma Feng =
Everest,Mt**
94C1 **Qornet es Saouda** Mt
Leb
6E3 **Qôrnoq** Greenland
90A2 **Qorveh** Iran
91C4 **Qotābad** Iran
16C1 **Quabbin Res** USA
16B2 **Quakertown** USA
77C3 **Quam Phu Quoc** I
Viet
76D2 **Quang Ngai** Viet
76D2 **Quang Tri** Viet
77D4 **Quan Long** Viet
73D5 **Quanzhou** Fujian,
China
73C4 **Quanzhou** Guangxi,
China
5H4 **Qu' Appelle** R Can
91C5 **Quarayyāt** Oman
13B2 **Quatsino Sd** Can
90C2 **Quchan** Iran
109C3 **Queanbeyan** Aust
15D1 **Québec** Can
7C4 **Quebec** Province,
Can
35B1 **Quebra-Anzol** R
Brazil
34D2 **Quebracho** Urug
30F4 **Quedas do Iguaçu**
Brazil/Arg
16A3 **Queen Anne** USA
13B2 **Queen Bess,Mt** Can
5E4 **Queen Charlotte** Is
Can
13B2 **Queen Charlotte Sd**
Can
13B2 **Queen Charlotte Str**
Can
4H1 **Queen Elizabeth Is**
Can
112B9 **Queen Mary Land**
Region, Ant
4H3 **Queen Maud G** Can
112A **Queen Maud Mts** Ant
16C2 **Queens** Borough,
New York, USA
108B3 **Queenscliff** Aust
107D3 **Queensland** State,
Aust
109C4 **Queenstown** Aust
111A3 **Queenstown** NZ
100B4 **Queenstown** S Africa
16A3 **Queenstown** USA
98B3 **Quela** Angola
101C2 **Quelimane** Mozam

34C3 **Quemuquemú** Arg
13C2 **Quensel L** Can
34D3 **Quequén** Arg
34D3 **Quequén** *R* Arg
23A1 **Querétaro** Mexico
23A1 **Queretaro** *State* Mexico
13C2 **Quesnel** Can
84B2 **Quetta** Pak
25C3 **Quezaltenango** Guatemala
79B3 **Quezon City** Phil
100A2 **Quibala** Angola
98B3 **Quibaxe** Angola
32B2 **Quibdó** Colombia
48B2 **Quiberon** France
98B3 **Quicama Nat Pk** Angola
73A4 **Quijing** China
34A2 **Quilima** Chile
34C2 **Quilino** Arg
32C6 **Quillabamba** Peru
30C2 **Quillacollo** Bol
48C3 **Quillan** France
5H4 **Quill L** Can
5H4 **Quill Lakes** Can
34A2 **Quillota** Chile
87B3 **Quilon** India
108B1 **Quilpie** Aust
34A2 **Quilpué** Chile
98B3 **Quimbele** Angola
48B2 **Quimper** France
48B2 **Quimperlé** France
21A2 **Quincy** California, USA
10A3 **Quincy** Illinois, USA
16D1 **Quincy** Massachusetts, USA
34B2 **Quines** Arg
12B3 **Quinhagak** USA
76D3 **Qui Nhon** Viet
50B2 **Quintanar de la Orden** Spain
34A2 **Quintero** Chile
34C2 **Quinto** *R* Arg
34A3 **Quirihue** Chile
100A2 **Quirima** Angola
109D2 **Quirindi** Aust
101D2 **Quissanga** Mozam
101C3 **Quissico** Mozam
32B4 **Quito** Ecuador
31D2 **Quixadá** Brazil
108A2 **Quorn** Aust
4G3 **Qurlurtuuk** Can
95C2 **Quseir** Egypt
6E3 **Qutdligssat** Greenland
Quthing = Moyeni
73B3 **Qu Xian** Sichuan, China
73D4 **Qu Xian** Zhejiang, China
76D2 **Quynh Luu** Viet
72C2 **Quzhou** China
86C1 **Qüzü** China

R

38J6 **Raahe** Fin
44A3 **Raasay** *I* Scot
44A3 **Raasay,Sound of** *Chan* Scot
99F1 **Raas Caseyr** *C* Somalia
52B2 **Rab** *I* Croatia
78D4 **Raba** Indon
59B3 **Rába** *R* Hung
96B1 **Rabat** Mor
94B3 **Rabba** Jordan
80B3 **Rabigh** S Arabia
47B2 **Racconigi** Italy
7E5 **Race,C** Can
94B2 **Rachaya** Leb
57C3 **Rachel** *Mt* Germany
76D3 **Rach Gia** Viet
14A2 **Racine** USA
59D3 **Rădăuţi** Rom
85C4 **Radhanpur** India
27L1 **Radix,Pt** Trinidad
58C2 **Radom** Pol
59B2 **Radomsko** Pol
58C1 **Radviliškis** Lithuania
4G3 **Rae** Can
86A1 **Rāe Bareli** India
6B3 **Rae Isthmus** Can
4G3 **Rae L** Can
110C1 **Raetihi** NZ
34C2 **Rafaela** Arg
94B3 **Rafah** Egypt
98C2 **Rafai** CAR
93D3 **Rafhā Al Jumaymah** S Arabia
91C3 **Rafsanjān** Iran
98C2 **Raga** Sudan
27R3 **Ragged Pt** Barbados
53B3 **Ragusa** Italy
99D1 **Rahad** *R* Sudan
84C3 **Rahimyar Khan** Pak
90B3 **Rāhjerd** Iran
34D2 **Raíces** Arg
87B1 **Rāichur** India
86A2 **Raigarh** India
108B3 **Rainbow** Aust
17A1 **Rainbow City** USA
20B1 **Rainier** USA
20B1 **Rainier,Mt** USA
10A2 **Rainy L** Can
12D2 **Rainy P** USA
10A2 **Rainy River** Can
86A2 **Raipur** India
87C1 **Rājahmundry** India
78C2 **Rajang** *R* Malay
84C3 **Rajanpur** Pak
87B3 **Rājapālaiyam** India
85C3 **Rājasthan** State, India
84D3 **Rājgarh** India
85D4 **Rājgarh** State, India
85C4 **Rājkot** India
86B2 **Rājmahāl Hills** India
86A2 **Raj Nāndgaon** India
85C4 **Rājpīpla** India
86B2 **Rajshahi** Bang
85D4 **Rajur** India
111B2 **Rakaia** *R* NZ
78B4 **Rakata** *I* Indon
82C3 **Raka Zangbo** *R* China
59C3 **Rakhov** Ukraine
100B3 **Rakops** Botswana
58D2 **Rakov** Belorussia
11C3 **Raleigh** USA
7A5 **Ralny L** Can
94B2 **Rama** Israel
94B3 **Ramallah** Israel
87B3 **Rāmanāthapuram** India
69G3 **Ramapo Deep** Pacific O
94B2 **Ramat Gan** Israel
46A2 **Rambouillet** France
86B2 **Rāmgarh** Bihar, India
85C3 **Rāmgarh** Rajosthan, India
90A3 **Rāmhormoz** Iran
94B3 **Ramla** Israel
91C5 **Ramlat Al Wahibah** Region, Oman
21B3 **Ramona** USA
84D3 **Rāmpur** India
85D4 **Rāmpura** India
90B2 **Rāmsar** Iran
42B2 **Ramsey** Eng
16B2 **Ramsey** USA
43B4 **Ramsey I** Wales
43E4 **Ramsgate** Eng
94C2 **Ramtha** Jordan
71F4 **Ramu** *R* PNG
34A2 **Rancagua** Chile
86B2 **Rānchi** India
86A2 **Rānchi Plat** India
101G1 **Randburg** S Africa
39G7 **Randers** Den
101G1 **Randfontein** S Africa
15D2 **Randolph** Vermont, USA
111B3 **Ranfurly** NZ
86C2 **Rangamati** Bang
111B2 **Rangiora** NZ
110C1 **Rangitaiki** *R* NZ
111B2 **Rangitate** *R* NZ
110C1 **Rangitikei** *R* NZ
Rangoon = Yangon
86B1 **Rangpur** India
87B2 **Rānībennur** India
8A2 **Ranier,Mt** *Mt* USA
86B2 **Rānīganj** India
109C2 **Rankins Springs** Aust
6A3 **Ranklin Inlet** Can
85B4 **Rann of Kachchh** *Flood Area* India
77B4 **Ranong** Thai
70A3 **Rantauparapat** Indon
18C1 **Rantoul** USA
49D3 **Rapallo** Italy
34A2 **Rapel** *R* Chile
6D3 **Raper,C** Can
8C2 **Rapid City** USA
14A1 **Rapid River** USA
15C3 **Rappahannock** *R* USA
47C1 **Rapperswil** Switz
16B2 **Raritan B** USA
95C2 **Ras Abu Shagara** *C* Sudan
93D2 **Ra's al 'Ayn** Syria
91C5 **Ra's al Hadd** *C* Oman
91C4 **Ras al Kaimah** UAE
91C4 **Ras-al-Kuh** *C* Iran
81D4 **Ra's al Madrakah** *C* Oman
91A4 **Ra's az Zawr** *C* S Arabia
95C2 **Rās Bânas** *C* Egypt
94A3 **Ras Burûn** *C* Egypt
99D1 **Ras Dashan** *Mt* Eth
90A3 **Ra's-e-Barkan** *Pt* Iran
92A3 **Râs el Kenâyis** *Pt* Egypt
81D4 **Ra's Fartak** *C* Yemen
95C2 **Râs Ghârib** Egypt
99D1 **Rashad** Sudan
94B3 **Rashādīya** Jordan
92B3 **Rashîd** Egypt
90A2 **Rasht** Iran
91C5 **Ra's Jibish** *C* Oman
99E1 **Ras Khanzira** *C* Somalia
84B3 **Ras Koh** *Mt* Pak
95C2 **Râs Muhammad** *C* Egypt
96A2 **Ras Nouadhibou** *C* Maur
69H2 **Rasshua** *I* Russian Fed
61F3 **Rasskazovo** Russian Fed
91A4 **Ra's Tanāqib** *C* S Arabia
91B4 **Ra's Tannūrah** S Arabia
57B3 **Rastatt** Germany
Ras Uarc = Cabo Tres Forcas
99F1 **Ras Xaafuun** *C* Somalia
84C3 **Ratangarh** India
76B3 **Rat Buri** Thai
85D3 **Rath** India
56C2 **Rathenow** Germany
45B2 **Rathkeale** Irish Rep
45C1 **Rathlin** *I* N Ire
45B2 **Ráth Luirc** Irish Rep
85D4 **Ratlām** India
87A1 **Ratnāgiri** India
87C3 **Ratnapura** Sri Lanka
58C2 **Ratno** Ukraine
47D1 **Rattenberg** Austria
39H6 **Rättvik** Sweden
12H3 **Ratz,Mt** Can
34D3 **Rauch** Arg
110C1 **Raukumara Range** *Mts* NZ
35C2 **Raul Soares** Brazil
39J6 **Rauma** Fin
86A2 **Raurkela** India
90A3 **Ravānsar** Iran
90C3 **Rāvar** Iran
59C2 **Rava Russkaya** Ukraine
16C1 **Ravena** USA
52B2 **Ravenna** Italy
57B3 **Ravensburg** Germany
107D2 **Ravenshoe** Aust
42E2 **Ravenspurn** *Oilfield* N Sea
84C2 **Ravi** *R* Pak
84C2 **Rawalpindi** Pak
93D2 **Rawāndiz** Iraq
58B2 **Rawicz** Pol
106B4 **Rawlinna** Aust
8C2 **Rawlins** USA
29C4 **Rawson** Arg
78C3 **Raya** *Mt* Indon
87B2 **Rāyadurg** India
94C2 **Rayak** Leb
7E5 **Ray,C** Can
91C4 **Rāyen** Iran
22C2 **Raymond** California, USA
20B1 **Raymond** Washington, USA
109D2 **Raymond Terrace** Aust
12D1 **Ray Mts** USA
23B1 **Rayon** Mexico
90A2 **Razan** Iran
54C2 **Razgrad** Bulg
54C2 **Razim** *L* Rom
43D4 **Reading** Eng
16B2 **Reading** USA
4G3 **Read Island** Can
16C1 **Readsboro** USA
34B2 **Real de Padre** Arg
34C3 **Realicó** Arg
95B2 **Rebiana** *Well* Libya
95B2 **Rebiana Sand Sea** Libya
38L6 **Reboly** Russian Fed
106B4 **Recherche,Arch of the** *Is* Aust
31E3 **Recife** Brazil
107F2 **Récifs D'Entrecasteaux** Nouvelle Calédonie
46D1 **Recklinghausen** Germany
30E4 **Reconquista** Arg
19B3 **Red** *R* USA
77C4 **Redang** *I* Malay
16B2 **Red Bank** New Jersey, USA
21A1 **Red Bluff** USA
42D2 **Redcar** Eng
13E2 **Redcliff** Can
109D1 **Redcliffe** Aust
108B2 **Red Cliffs** Aust
13E2 **Red Deer** Can
13E2 **Red Deer** *R* Can
20B2 **Redding** USA
10A2 **Red L** USA
7A4 **Red Lake** Can
22D3 **Redlands** USA
16A3 **Red Lion** USA
20B2 **Redmond** USA
18A1 **Red Oak** USA
48B2 **Redon** France
22C4 **Redondo Beach** USA
12D2 **Redoubt V** USA
73B5 **Red River Delta** Vietnam
80B3 **Red Sea** Africa/ Arabian Pen
13E2 **Redwater** Can
22A2 **Redwood City** USA
14A2 **Reed City** USA
22C2 **Reedley** USA
20B2 **Reedsport** USA
111B2 **Reefton** NZ
93C2 **Refahiye** Turk
35D1 **Regência** Brazil
57C3 **Regensburg** Germany
96C2 **Reggane** Alg
53C3 **Reggio di Calabria** Italy
47D2 **Reggio Nell'Emilia** Italy
54B1 **Reghin** Rom
5H4 **Regina** Can
100A3 **Rehoboth** Namibia
15C3 **Rehoboth Beach** USA
94B3 **Rehovot** Israel
32D1 **Reicito** Ven
43D4 **Reigate** Eng
46C2 **Reims** France
5H4 **Reindeer** *R* Can
50B1 **Reinosa** Spain
16A3 **Reisterstown** USA
101G1 **Reitz** S Africa
4H3 **Reliance** Can
108A2 **Remarkable,Mt** Aust
78C4 **Rembang** Indon
91C4 **Remeshk** Iran

Remscheid

46D1 **Remscheid** Germany
18C2 **Rend,L** USA
56B2 **Rendsburg** Germany
15C1 **Renfrew** Can
78A3 **Rengat** Indon
34A2 **Rengo** Chile
59D3 **Reni** Ukraine
99D1 **Renk** Sudan
6H2 **Renland** *Pen*
Greenland
108B2 **Renmark** Aust
107F2 **Rennell** *I* Solomon Is
48B2 **Rennes** France
21B2 **Reno** USA
47D2 **Reno** *R* Italy
15C2 **Renovo** USA
16C1 **Rensselaer** USA
20B1 **Renton** USA
70D4 **Reo** Indon
35B2 **Reprêsa de Furnas**
Dam Brazil
30E3 **Reprêsa Ilha Grande**
Dam Brazil
30E3 **Reprêsa Itaipu** *Dam*
Brazil
35A2 **Reprêsa Porto**
Primavera *Dam*
Brazil
35B1 **Reprêsa Três Marias**
Dam Brazil
20C1 **Republic** USA
41B3 **Republic of Ireland**
NW Europe
6B3 **Repulse Bay** Can
15C1 **Réservoir Baskatong**
Res Can
10C1 **Réservoir de la**
Grande 2 *Res* Can
10C1 **Réservoir de la**
Grande 3 *Res* Can
7C4 **Réservoir de la**
Grande 4 *Res* Can
7C5 **Réservoir Cabonga**
Res Can
7D4 **Réservoir**
Caniapiscau *Res* Can
7C5 **Réservoir Gouin** *Res*
Can
10D1 **Réservoir**
Manicouagan *Res*
Can
90B2 **Reshteh-ye Alborz**
Mts Iran
72A2 **Reshui** China
30E4 **Resistencia** Arg
54B1 **Resita** Rom
6A2 **Resolute** Can
111A3 **Resolution I** NZ
6D3 **Resolution Island**
Can
101H1 **Ressano Garcia**
Mozam
34B2 **Retamito** Arg
46C2 **Rethel** France
55B3 **Réthimnon** Greece
89K10 **Reunion** *I* Indian O
51C1 **Reus** Spain
47C1 **Reuss** *R* Switz
47D1 **Reutte** Austria
61K3 **Revda** Russian Fed
13D2 **Revelstoke** Can
24A3 **Revillagigedo** *Is*
Mexico
12H3 **Revillagigedo I** USA
61N4 **Revin** France
94B3 **Revivim** Israel
86A2 **Rewa** India
84D3 **Rewari** India
8B2 **Rexburg** USA
38A2 **Reykjavik** Iceland
24C2 **Reynosa** Mexico
48B2 **Rezé** France
58D1 **Rezekne** Latvia
61K2 **Rezh** Russian Fed
47C1 **Rhätikon** *Mts*
Austria/Switz
94B1 **Rhazir** Republic, Leb
56B2 **Rhein** *R* W Europe
56B2 **Rheine** Germany
47B1 **Rheinfielden** Switz
49D2 **Rheinland Pfalz**
Region, Germany
47C1 **Rheinwaldhorn** *Mt*
Switz

Rhine = **Rhein**
16C2 **Rhinebeck** USA
10B2 **Rhinelander** USA
47C2 **Rho** Italy
15D2 **Rhode Island** State,
USA
16D2 **Rhode Island Sd** USA
Rhodes = **Ródhos**
49C3 **Rhône** *R* France
43C3 **Rhyl** Wales
31D4 **Riachão do Jacuipe**
Brazil
50A1 **Ria de Arosa** *B*
Spain
50A1 **Ria de Betanzos** *B*
Spain
50A1 **Ria de Corcubion** *B*
Spain
50A1 **Ria de Lage** *B* Spain
50A1 **Ria de Sta Marta** *B*
Spain
50A1 **Ria de Vigo** *B* Spain
84C2 **Riäsi** Pak
50A1 **Ribadeo** Spain
35A2 **Ribas do Rio Pardo**
Brazil
101C2 **Ribauè** Mozam
42C3 **Ribble** *R* Eng
35B2 **Ribeira** Brazil
35B2 **Ribeirão Prêto** Brazil
32D6 **Riberalta** Bol
15C2 **Rice L** Can
10A2 **Rice Lake** USA
101H1 **Richard's Bay**
S Africa
19A3 **Richardson** USA
12G1 **Richardson Mts** Can
8B3 **Richfield** USA
20C1 **Richland** USA
22A2 **Richmond** California,
USA
101H1 **Richmond** Natal,
S Africa
109D2 **Richmond** New
South Wales, Aust
111B2 **Richmond** NZ
107D3 **Richmond**
Queensland, Aust
10C3 **Richmond** Virginia,
USA
111B2 **Richmond Range** *Mts*
NZ
15C2 **Rideau,L** Can
17B1 **Ridgeland** USA
15C2 **Ridgway** USA
27D4 **Riecito** Ven
47D1 **Rienza** *R* Italy
57C2 **Riesa** Germany
29B6 **Riesco** *I* Chile
101F1 **Riet** *R* S Africa
52B2 **Rieti** Italy
50B2 **Rif** *Mts* Mor
58C1 **Riga** Latvia
60B2 **Riga,G of** Estonia/
Latvia
91C4 **Rigän** Iran
20C1 **Riggins** USA
7E4 **Rigolet** Can
39J6 **Riihimaki** Fin
52B1 **Rijeka** Croatia
13E2 **Rimbey** Can
39H7 **Rimbo** Sweden
52B2 **Rimini** Italy
54C1 **Rimnicu Sărat** Rom
54B1 **Rimnicu Vilcea** Rom
10D2 **Rimouski** Can
23A1 **Rincón de Romos**
Mexico
39F7 **Ringkøbing** Den
98A2 **Rio Benito** Eq Guinea
32D5 **Rio Branco** Brazil
24B1 **Rio Bravo del Norte**
R Mexico/USA
32C1 **Riochacha** Colombia
35B2 **Rio Claro** Brazil
27L1 **Rio Claro** Trinidad
34C3 **Rio Colorado** Arg
34C2 **Rio Cuarto** Arg
31D4 **Rio de Jacuipe** Brazil
35C2 **Rio de Janeiro** Brazil
35C2 **Rio de Janeiro** State,
Brazil
29E3 **Rio de la Plata** *Est*
Arg/Urug

29C6 **Rio Gallegos** Arg
29C6 **Rio Grande** Arg
30F5 **Rio Grande** Brazil
26A4 **Rio Grande** Nic
25D3 **Rio Grande** *R* Nic
24B2 **Rio Grande** *R*
Mexico/USA
23A1 **Rio Grande de**
Santiago Mexico
31D3 **Rio Grande do Norte**
State, Brazil
30F4 **Rio Grande do Sul**
State, Brazil
103G6 **Rio Grande Rise**
Atlantic O
26C4 **Riohacha** Colombia
49C2 **Riom** France
32B4 **Riombamba** Ecuador
30C2 **Rio Mulatos** Bol
29C3 **Rio Negro** State, Arg
30F4 **Rio Pardo** Brazil
34C2 **Rio Tercero** Arg
33E6 **Rio Theodore**
Roosevelt *R* Brazil
29B6 **Rio Turbio** Arg
35A1 **Rio Verde** Brazil
23A1 **Rio Verde** Mexico
14B3 **Ripley** Ohio, USA
14B3 **Ripley** West Virginia,
USA
42D2 **Ripon** Eng
22B2 **Ripon** USA
94B3 **Rishon le Zion** Israel
16A3 **Rising Sun** USA
39F7 **Risør** Nor
6E2 **Ritenberk** Greenland
22C2 **Ritter,Mt** USA
20C1 **Ritzville** USA
34B2 **Rivadavia** Arg
34A1 **Rivadavia** Chile
34C3 **Rivadavia Gonzalez**
Moreno Arg
47D2 **Riva de Garda** Italy
34C3 **Rivera** Arg
29E2 **Rivera** Urug
22B2 **Riverbank** USA
97B4 **River Cess** Lib
16C2 **Riverhead** USA
108B3 **Riverina** Aust
111A3 **Riversdale** NZ
22D4 **Riverside** USA
13B2 **Rivers Inlet** Can
111A3 **Riverton** NZ
8C2 **Riverton** USA
17B2 **Riviera Beach** USA
7C4 **Rivière aux Feuilles** *R*
Can
7D4 **Rivière de la Baleine**
R Can
7D4 **Rivière du Petit**
Mècatina *R* Can
46C2 **Rivigny-sur-Ornain**
France
93D1 **Rize** Turk
72D2 **Rizhao** China
Rizhskiy Zaliv =
Riga,G of
39F7 **Rjukan** Nor
6B2 **Roanes Pen** Can
49C2 **Roanne** France
17A1 **Roanoke** Alabama,
USA
11C3 **Roanoke** Virginia,
USA
11C3 **Roanoke** *R* USA
45B3 **Roaringwater B**
Irish Rep
38J6 **Robertsforz** Sweden
19B2 **Robert S Kerr Res**
USA
97A4 **Robertsport** Lib
7C5 **Roberval** Can
30H6 **Robinson Crusoe** *I*
Chile
108B2 **Robinvale** Aust
13D2 **Robson,Mt** Can
24A3 **Roca Partida** *I*
Mexico
103G5 **Rocas** *I* Atlantic O
31E2 **Rocas** *I* Brazil
29F2 **Rocha** Urug
42C3 **Rochdale** Eng
48B2 **Rochefort** France
5G3 **Rocher River** Can

108B3 **Rochester** Aust
7C5 **Rochester** Can
43E4 **Rochester** Eng
10A2 **Rochester**
Minnesota, USA
15D2 **Rochester** New
Hampshire, USA
10C2 **Rochester** New York,
USA
10B2 **Rockford** USA
11B3 **Rock Hill** USA
10A2 **Rock Island** USA
108B3 **Rocklands Res** Aust
17B2 **Rockledge** USA
8C2 **Rock Springs**
Wyoming, USA
110B2 **Rocks Pt** NZ
109C3 **Rock,The** Aust
16C2 **Rockville**
Connecticut, USA
14A3 **Rockville** Indiana,
USA
16A3 **Rockville** Maryland,
USA
14B1 **Rocky Island L** Can
13E2 **Rocky Mountain**
House Can
8B1 **Rocky Mts** Can/USA
12B2 **Rocky Pt** USA
56C2 **Rødbyhavn** Den
34B2 **Rodeo** Arg
49C3 **Rodez** France
55C3 **Ródhos** Greece
55C3 **Ródhos** *I* Greece
52C2 **Rodi Garganico** Italy
54B2 **Rodopi Planina** *Mts*
Bulg
106A3 **Roebourne** Aust
46C1 **Roermond** Neth
46B1 **Roeselare** Belg
6B3 **Roes Welcome Sd**
Can
18B2 **Rogers** USA
14B1 **Rogers City** USA
20B2 **Rogue** *R* USA
85B3 **Rohn** Pak
84D3 **Rohtak** India
58C1 **Roja** Latvia
35A2 **Rolândia** Brazil
18B2 **Rolla** USA
109C1 **Roma** Aust
52B2 **Roma** Italy
47C2 **Romagnano** Italy
17C1 **Romain,C** USA
54C1 **Roman** Rom
103H5 **Romanche Gap**
Atlantic O
71D4 **Romang** *I* Indon
60B4 **Romania** Republic,
E Europe
17B2 **Romano,C** USA
49D2 **Romans sur Isère**
France
79B3 **Romblon** Phil
17A1 **Rome** Georgia, USA
15C2 **Rome** New York,
USA
49C2 **Romilly-sur-Seine**
France
15C3 **Romney** USA
60D3 **Romny** Ukraine
56B1 **Rømø** *I* Den
47B1 **Romont** Switz
48C2 **Romorantin** France
50A2 **Ronda** Spain
33E6 **Rondônia** Brazil
24F6 **Rondônia** State,
Brazil
30F2 **Rondonópolis** Brazil
73B4 **Rong'an** China
73B4 **Rongchang** China
72E2 **Rongcheng** China
73B4 **Rongjiang** China
73B4 **Rong Jiang** *R* China
76A1 **Rongklang Range**
Mts Burma
39G7 **Rønne** Den
39H7 **Ronneby** Sweden
112B2 **Ronne Ice Shelf** Ant
46B1 **Ronse** Belg
46A1 **Ronthieu** Region,
France
9C3 **Roof Butte** *Mt* USA

84D3	**Roorkee** India
46C1	**Roosendaal** Neth
112B6	**Roosevelt I** Ant
106C2	**Roper** R Aust
33E3	**Roraima** State, Brazil
33E2	**Roraime** Mt Ven
38G6	**Røros** Nor
47C1	**Rorschach** Switz
38G6	**Rørvik** Nor
27Q2	**Rosalie** Dominica
22C3	**Rosamond L** USA
34C2	**Rosario** Arg
31C2	**Rosário** Brazil
34D2	**Rosario del Tala** Arg
48B2	**Roscoff** France
45B2	**Roscommon** County, Irish Rep
41B3	**Roscommon** Irish Rep
45C2	**Roscrea** Irish Rep
27E3	**Roseau** Dominica
109C4	**Rosebery** Aust
20B2	**Roseburg** USA
19A4	**Rosenberg** USA
57C3	**Rosenheim** Germany
13F2	**Rosetown** Can
54B2	**Roşiori de Vede** Rom
39G7	**Roskilde** Den
60D3	**Roslavl'** Russian Fed
61E2	**Roslyatino** Russian Fed
111B2	**Ross** NZ
12H2	**Ross** R Can
40B3	**Rossan** Pt Irish Rep
53C3	**Rossano** Italy
19C3	**Ross Barnet Res** USA
15C1	**Rosseau L** L Can
107E2	**Rossel I** Solomon Is
112A	**Ross Ice Shelf** Ant
20B1	**Ross L** USA
13D3	**Rossland** Can
45C2	**Rosslare** Irish Rep
111C2	**Ross,Mt** NZ
97A3	**Rosso** Maur
43C4	**Ross-on-Wye** Eng
60E4	**Rossosh** Russian Fed
4E3	**Ross River** Can
112B6	**Ross S** Ant
91B4	**Rostaq** Iran
56C2	**Rostock** Germany
	Rostov = Rostov-na-Donu
61E4	**Rostov-na-Donu** Russian Fed
17B1	**Roswell** Georgia, USA
9C3	**Roswell** New Mexico, USA
71F2	**Rota** Pacific O
56B2	**Rotenburg** Niedersachsen, Germany
46E1	**Rothaar-Geb** Region Germany
112C3	**Rothera** Base Ant
42D3	**Rotherham** Eng
42B2	**Rothesay** Scot
71D5	**Roti** I Indon
108C2	**Roto** Aust
111B2	**Rotoiti,L** NZ
111B2	**Rotoroa,L** NZ
110C1	**Rotorua** NZ
110C1	**Rotorua,L** NZ
56A2	**Rotterdam** Neth
46B1	**Roubaix** France
48C2	**Rouen** France
42E3	**Rough** Oilfield N Sea
	Roulers = Roeselare
101E3	**Round I** Mauritius
109D2	**Round Mt** Aust
8C2	**Roundup** USA
44C2	**Rousay** I Scot
48C3	**Roussillon** Region, France
10C2	**Rouyn** Can
38K5	**Rovaniemi** Fin
47D2	**Rovereto** Italy
47D2	**Rovigo** Italy
52B1	**Rovinj** Croatia
59D2	**Rovno** Ukraine
90A2	**Row'ān** Iran
109C1	**Rowena** Aust
6C3	**Rowley I** Can
106A2	**Rowley Shoals** Aust
79A3	**Roxas** Palawan, Phil
79B3	**Roxas** Panay, Phil
111A3	**Roxburgh** NZ
45C2	**Royal Canal** Irish Rep
43D3	**Royal Leamington Spa** Eng
14B2	**Royal Oak** USA
43E4	**Royal Tunbridge Wells** Eng
48B2	**Royan** France
46B2	**Roye** France
43D3	**Royston** Eng
59C3	**Rožňava** Slovakia
46B2	**Rozoy** France
61F3	**Rtishchevo** Russian Fed
99D3	**Ruaha Nat Pk** Tanz
110C1	**Ruahine Range** Mts NZ
110C1	**Ruapehu,Mt** NZ
65D3	**Rub al Khāli** Desert S Arabia
44A3	**Rubha Hunish** Scot
35A2	**Rubinéia** Brazil
65K4	**Rubtsovsk** Russian Fed
12C2	**Ruby** USA
91C4	**Rudan** Iran
90A2	**Rūdbār** Iran
69F2	**Rudnaya Pristan'** Russian Fed
54B2	**Rudoka Planina** Mt Macedonia
72E3	**Rudong** China
14B1	**Rudyard** USA
46A1	**Rue** France
48C2	**Ruffec** France
99D3	**Rufiji** R Tanz
34C2	**Rufino** Arg
97A3	**Rufisque** Sen
100B2	**Rufunsa** Zambia
43D3	**Rugby** Eng
39G8	**Rügen** I Germany
56B2	**Ruhr** R Germany
73D4	**Ruijin** China
54B2	**Rujen** Mt Bulg/Macedonia
99D3	**Rukwa** L Tanz
44A3	**Rum** I Scot
54A1	**Ruma** Serbia, Yugos
91A4	**Rumāh** S Arabia
98C2	**Rumbek** Sudan
26C2	**Rum Cay** I Caribbean S
47A2	**Rumilly** France
106C2	**Rum Jungle** Aust
101C2	**Rumphi** Malawi
111B2	**Runanga** NZ
110C1	**Runaway,C** NZ
100C3	**Rundi** R Zim
100A2	**Rundu** Namibia
99D3	**Rungwa** Tanz
99D3	**Rungwa** R Tanz
99D3	**Rungwe** Mt Tanz
82C2	**Ruoqiang** China
68C2	**Ruo Shui** R China
54C1	**Rupea** Rom
7C4	**Rupert** R Can
46D1	**Rur** R Germany
32D6	**Rurrenabaque** Bol
101C2	**Rusape** Zim
54C2	**Ruse** Bulg
18B1	**Rushville** Illinois, USA
108B3	**Rushworth** Aust
19A3	**Rusk** USA
17B2	**Ruskin** USA
110B1	**Russell** NZ
18B2	**Russellville** Arkansas, USA
18C2	**Russellville** Kentucky, USA
21A2	**Russian** R USA
62C3	**Russian Fed** Asia/Europe
93E1	**Rustavi** Georgia
101G1	**Rustenburg** S Africa
19B3	**Ruston** USA
99C3	**Rutana** Burundi
46E1	**Rüthen** Germany
23B2	**Rutla** Mexico
15D2	**Rutland** USA
84D2	**Rutog** China
	Ruvu = Pangani
101D2	**Ruvuma** R Tanz/Mozam
99D2	**Ruwenzori Range** Mts Uganda/Zaire
101C2	**Ruya** R Zim
59B3	**Ružomberok** Slovakia
99C3	**Rwanda** Republic, Africa
60E3	**Ryazan'** Russian Fed
61F3	**Ryazhsk** Russian Fed
60E2	**Rybinsk** Russian Fed
60E2	**Rybinskoye Vodokhranilishche** Res Russian Fed
13D1	**Rycroft** Can
43D4	**Ryde** Eng
43E4	**Rye** Eng
20C2	**Rye Patch Res** USA
60D3	**Ryl'sk** Russian Fed
61G4	**Ryn Peski** Desert Kazakhstan
74D3	**Ryōtsu** Japan
59D3	**Ryskany** Moldavia
69E4	**Ryūkyū Retto** Arch Japan
59C2	**Rzeszów** Pol
60D2	**Rzhev** Russian Fed

S

91B3	**Sa'ādatābād** Iran
56C2	**Saale** R Germany
47B1	**Saanen** Switz
46D2	**Saar** R Germany
46D2	**Saarbrücken** Germany
46D2	**Saarburg** Germany
39J7	**Saaremaa** I Estonia
46D2	**Saarland** State, Germany
46D2	**Saarlouis** Germany
34C3	**Saavedra** Arg
54A2	**Šabac** Serbia, Yugos
51C1	**Sabadell** Spain
75B1	**Sabae** Japan
78D1	**Sabah** State, Malay
26C4	**Sabanalarga** Colombia
70A3	**Sabang** Indon
87C1	**Sabari** R India
94B2	**Sabastiya** Israel
30C2	**Sabaya** Bol
93C3	**Sab'Bi'ār** Syria
94C2	**Sabhā** Jordan
95A2	**Sabhā** Libya
24B2	**Sabinas** Mexico
24B2	**Sabinas Hidalgo** Mexico
19A3	**Sabine** R USA
19B4	**Sabine L** USA
91B5	**Sabkhat Matti** Salt Marsh UAE
94A3	**Sabkhet El Bardawil** Lg Egypt
79B3	**Sablayan** Phil
7D5	**Sable,C** Can
17B2	**Sable,C** USA
7D5	**Sable I** Can
90C2	**Sabzevār** Iran
20C1	**Sacajawea Peak** USA
10A1	**Sachigo** R Can
57C2	**Sachsen** State, Germany
56C2	**Sachsen-Anhalt** State, Germany
4F2	**Sachs Harbour** Can
47B1	**Säckingen** Germany
22B1	**Sacramento** USA
22B1	**Sacramento** R USA
21A1	**Sacramento** V USA
9C3	**Sacramento Mts** USA
81C4	**Sa'dah** Yemen
54B2	**Sadanski** Bulg
82D3	**Sadiya** India
50A2	**Sado** R Port
74D3	**Sado-shima** I Japan
85C3	**Sādri** India
	Safad = Zefat
84A2	**Safed Koh** Mts Afghan
39G7	**Saffle** Sweden
92C3	**Safi** Jordan
96B1	**Safi** Mor
90D3	**Safidabeh** Iran
94C1	**Şafītā** Syria
93E3	**Şafwān** Iraq
75A2	**Saga** Japan
76B1	**Sagaing** Burma
75B2	**Sagami-nada** B Japan
85D4	**Sāgar** India
16C2	**Sag Harbor** USA
14B2	**Saginaw** USA
14B2	**Saginaw B** USA
26B2	**Sagua de Tánamo** Cuba
26B2	**Sagua la Grande** Cuba
7C5	**Saguenay** R Can
51B2	**Sagunto** Spain
94C3	**Sahāb** Jordan
50A1	**Sahagún** Spain
96C2	**Sahara** Desert N Africa
84D3	**Saharanpur** India
84C2	**Sahiwal** Pak
93D3	**Sahrā al Hijārah** Desert Region Iraq
23A1	**Sahuayo** Mexico
107D1	**Saibai I** Aust
96C1	**Saïda** Alg
94B2	**Saïda** Leb
91C4	**Sa'īdabad** Iran
51B2	**Saïdia** Mor
86B1	**Saidpur** India
84C2	**Saidu** Pak
75A1	**Saigō** Japan
	Saigon = Ho Chi Minh
86C2	**Saiha** India
68D2	**Saihan Tal** China
75A2	**Saijo** Japan
74C4	**Saiki** Japan
42C2	**St Abb's Head** Pt Scot
43D4	**St Albans** Eng
15D2	**St Albans** Vermont, USA
14B3	**St Albans** West Virginia, USA
43C4	**St Albans Head** C Eng
13E2	**St Albert** Can
46B1	**St Amand-les-Eaux** France
48C2	**St Amand-Mont Rond** France
17A2	**St Andrew B** USA
44C3	**St Andrews** Scot
17B1	**St Andrew Sd** USA
27H1	**St Ann's Bay** Jamaica
7E4	**St Anthony** Can
108B3	**St Arnaud** Aust
17B2	**St Augustine** USA
43B4	**St Austell** Eng
46D2	**St-Avold** France
42C2	**St Bees Head** Pt Eng
47B2	**St-Bonnet** France
43B4	**St Brides B** Wales
48B2	**St-Brieuc** France
15C2	**St Catharines** Can
27M2	**St Catherine,Mt** Grenada
17B1	**St Catherines I** USA
43D4	**St Catherines Pt** Eng
49C2	**St Chamond** France
18B2	**St Charles** Missouri, USA
14B2	**St Clair** USA
14B2	**St Clair,L** Can/USA
14B2	**St Clair Shores** USA
49D2	**St Claud** France
10A2	**St Cloud** USA
47B1	**Ste Croix** Switz
27E3	**St Croix** I Caribbean S
43B4	**St Davids Head** Pt Wales
46B2	**St Denis** France
101E3	**St Denis** Réunion
46C2	**St Dizier** France
12F2	**St Elias,Mt** USA
12G2	**St Elias Mts** Can
48B2	**Saintes** France
49C2	**St Étienne** France
18B2	**St Francis** R USA
100B4	**St Francis,C** S Africa

St Gallen

29B4 **San Carlos de Bariloche** Arg
69E4 **San-chung** Taiwan
61G2 **Sanchursk** Russian Fed
34A3 **San Clemente** Chile
22D4 **San Clemente** USA
21B3 **San Clemente I** USA
34C2 **San Cristóbal** Arg
25C3 **San Cristóbal** Mexico
32C2 **San Cristóbal** Ven
32J7 **San Cristóbal** *I* Ecuador
107F2 **San Cristobal** *I* Solomon Is
25E2 **Sancti Spíritus** Cuba
78C3 **Sandai** Indon
70C3 **Sandakan** Malay
44C2 **Sanday** *I* Scot
9C3 **Sanderson** USA
13F1 **Sandfly L** Can
21B3 **San Diego** USA
92B2 **Sandikli** Turk
86A1 **Sandīla** India
39F7 **Sandnes** Nor
38G5 **Sandnessjøen** Nor
98C3 **Sandoa** Zaïre
59C2 **Sandomierz** Pol
38D3 **Sandoy** Føroyar
20C1 **Sandpoint** USA
49D2 **Sandrio** Italy
18A2 **Sand Springs** USA
106A3 **Sandstone** Aust
73C4 **Sandu** China
14B2 **Sandusky** USA
39H6 **Sandviken** Sweden
7A4 **Sandy L** Can
34C2 **San Elcano** Arg
9B3 **San Felipe** Baja Cal, Mexico
34A2 **San Felipe** Chile
23A1 **San Felipe** Guanajuato, Mexico
27D4 **San Felipe** Ven
51C1 **San Feliu de Guixols** Spain
28A5 **San Felix** *I* Pacific O
34A2 **San Fernando** Chile
79B2 **San Fernando** Phil
79B2 **San Fernando** Phil
50A2 **San Fernando** Spain
27E4 **San Fernando** Trinidad
22C3 **San Fernando** USA
32D2 **San Fernando** Ven
17B2 **Sanford** Florida, USA
12F2 **Sanford,Mt** USA
34C2 **San Francisco** Arg
27C3 **San Francisco** Dom Rep
22A2 **San Francisco** USA
22A2 **San Francisco B** USA
24B2 **San Francisco del Oro** Mexico
23A1 **San Francisco del Rincon** Mexico
22D3 **San Gabriel Mts** USA
85C5 **Sangamner** India
18C2 **Sangamon** *R* USA
71F2 **Sangan** *I* Pacific O
87B1 **Sangāreddi** India
78D4 **Sangeang** *I* Indon
22C2 **Sanger** USA
72C2 **Sanggan He** *R* China
78C2 **Sanggau** Indon
98B2 **Sangha** *R* Congo
85B3 **Sanghar** Pak
76B2 **Sangkhla Buri** Thai
78D2 **Sangkulirang** Indon
87A1 **Sāngli** India
98B2 **Sangmélima** Cam
9B3 **San Gorgonio Mt** USA
9C3 **Sangre de Cristo** *Mts* USA
34C2 **San Gregorio** Arg
22A2 **San Gregorio** USA
84D2 **Sangrūr** India
30E4 **San Ignacio** Arg
79B3 **San Isidro** Phil
32B2 **San Jacinto** Colombia
21B3 **San Jacinto Peak** *Mt* USA
34A3 **San Javier** Chile
34D2 **San Javier** Sante Fe, Arg
74D3 **Sanjō** *I* Japan
31C6 **San João del Rei** Brazil
22B2 **San Joaquin** *R* USA
22B2 **San Joaquin Valley** USA
32A1 **San José** Costa Rica
25C3 **San José** Guatemala
79B2 **San Jose** Luzon, Phil
79B3 **San Jose** Mindoro, Phil
22B2 **San Jose** USA
9B4 **San José** *I* Mexico
30D2 **San José de Chiquitos** Bol
34D2 **San José de Feliciano** Arg
34B2 **San José de Jachal** Arg
34C2 **San José de la Dormida** Arg
31B6 **San José do Rio Prêto** Brazil
24B2 **San José del Cabo** Mexico
34B2 **San Juan** Arg
27D3 **San Juan** Puerto Rico
34B2 **San Juan** State, Arg
27L1 **San Juan** Trinidad
32D2 **San Juan** Ven
26B2 **San Juan** *Mt* Cuba
8C3 **San Juan** *Mts* USA
34B2 **San Juan** *R* Arg
23B2 **San Juan** *R* Mexico
25D3 **San Juan** *R* Nic/ Costa Rica
23B2 **San Juan Bautista** Mexico
30E4 **San Juan Bautista** Par
22B2 **San Juan Bautista** USA
25D3 **San Juan del Norte** Nic
27D4 **San Juan de los Cayos** Ven
23A1 **San Juan de loz Lagoz** Mexico
23A1 **San Juan del Rio** Mexico
25D3 **San Juan del Sur** Nic
20B1 **San Juan Is** USA
23B2 **San Juan Tepozcolula** Mexico
29C5 **San Julián** Arg
34C2 **San Justo** Arg
60D2 **Sankt-Peterburg** Russian Fed
98C3 **Sankuru** *R* Zaïre
22A2 **San Leandro** USA
93C2 **Şanlıurfa** Turk
32B3 **San Lorenzo** Ecuador
34C2 **San Lorenzo** Arg
22B2 **San Lucas** USA
34B2 **San Luis** Arg
34B2 **San Luis** State, Arg
23A1 **San Luis de la Paz** Mexico
21A2 **San Luis Obispo** USA
23A1 **San Luis Potosi** Mexico
22B2 **San Luis Res** USA
53A3 **Sanluri** Sardegna
33D2 **San Maigualida** *Mts* Ven
34D3 **San Manuel** Arg
34A2 **San Marcos** Chile
23B2 **San Marcos** Mexico
52B2 **San Marino** Republic, Europe
34B2 **San Martin** Mendoza, Arg
112C3 **San Martin** *Base* Ant
47D1 **San Martino di Castroza** Italy
23B2 **San Martin Tuxmelucan** Mexico
22A2 **San Mateo** USA
30E2 **San Matias** Bol
72C3 **Sanmenxia** China
25D3 **San Miguel** El Salvador
22B3 **San Miguel** *I* USA
23A1 **San Miguel del Allende** Mexico
34D3 **San Miguel del Monte** Arg
30C4 **San Miguel de Tucumán** Arg
73D4 **Sanming** China
9B3 **San Nicolas** *I* USA
34C2 **San Nicolás de los Arroyos** Arg
101G1 **Sannieshof** S Africa
97B4 **Sanniquellie** Lib
59C3 **Sanok** Pol
26B5 **San Onofore** Colombia
22D4 **San Onofre** USA
79B3 **San Pablo** Phil
22A1 **San Pablo B** USA
34D2 **San Pedro** Buenos Aires, Arg
97B4 **San Pédro** Ivory Coast
30D3 **San Pedro** Jujuy, Arg
30E3 **San Pedro** Par
22C4 **San Pedro Chan** USA
9C4 **San Pedro de los Colonias** Mexico
25D3 **San Pedro Sula** Honduras
53A3 **San Pietro** *I* Medit S
24A1 **San Quintin** Mexico
34B2 **San Rafael** Arg
22A2 **San Rafael** USA
22C3 **San Rafael Mts** USA
49D3 **San Remo** Italy
34D2 **San Salvador** Arg
26C2 **San Salvador** *I* Caribbean S
32J7 **San Salvador** *I* Ecuador
30C3 **San Salvador de Jujuy** Arg
51B1 **San Sebastian** Spain
53C2 **San Severo** Italy
30C2 **Santa Ana** Bol
25C3 **Santa Ana** Guatemala
22D4 **Santa Ana** USA
22D4 **Santa Ana Mts** USA
34A3 **Santa Bárbara** Chile
24B2 **Santa Barbara** Mexico
22C3 **Santa Barbara** USA
22C4 **Santa Barbara** *I* USA
22B3 **Santa Barbara Chan** USA
22C3 **Santa Barbara Res** USA
22C4 **Santa Catalina** *I* USA
22C4 **Santa Catalina,G of** USA
30F4 **Santa Catarina** State, Brazil
26B2 **Santa Clara** Cuba
22B2 **Santa Clara** USA
22C3 **Santa Clara** *R* USA
29C6 **Santa Cruz** Arg
30D2 **Santa Cruz** Bol
34A2 **Santa Cruz** Chile
79B3 **Santa Cruz** Phil
29B5 **Santa Cruz** State, Arg
22A2 **Santa Cruz** USA
22C4 **Santa Cruz** *I* USA
35D1 **Santa Cruz Cabrália** Brazil
22C3 **Santa Cruz Chan** USA
96A2 **Santa Cruz de la Palma** Canary Is
26B2 **Santa Cruz del Sur** Cuba
96A2 **Santa Cruz de Tenerife** Canary Is
100B2 **Santa Cruz do Cuando** Angola
35B2 **Santa Cruz do Rio Pardo** Brazil
22A2 **Santa Cruz Mts** USA
34D2 **Santa Elena** Arg
33E3 **Santa Elena** Ven
34C2 **Santa Fe** Arg
34C2 **Santa Fe** State, Arg
9C3 **Santa Fe** USA
35A1 **Santa Helena de Goiás** Brazil
73B3 **Santai** China
29B6 **Santa Inés** *I* Chile
34B3 **Santa Isabel** La Pampa, Arg
34C2 **Santa Isabel** Sante Fe, Arg
107E1 **Santa Isabel** *I* Solomon Is
21A2 **Santa Lucia** *Ra* USA
21A2 **Santa Lucia Range** *Mts* USA
97A4 **Santa Luzia** *I* Cape Verde
9B4 **Santa Margarita** *I* Mexico
22D4 **Santa Margarita** *R* USA
30F4 **Santa Maria** Brazil
26C4 **Santa Maria** Colombia
21A3 **Santa Maria** USA
96A1 **Santa Maria** *I* Açores
23B1 **Santa Maria** *R* Queretaro, Mexico
23A1 **Santa Maria del Rio** Mexico
32C1 **Santa Marta** Colombia
22C3 **Santa Monica** USA
22C4 **Santa Monica B** USA
29E2 **Santana do Livramento** Brazil
32B3 **Santander** Colombia
50B1 **Santander** Spain
51C2 **Santañy** Spain
22C3 **Santa Paula** USA
31C2 **Santa Quitéria** Brazil
33G4 **Santarem** Brazil
50A2 **Santarém** Port
22A1 **Santa Rosa** California, USA
25D3 **Santa Rosa** Honduras
34C3 **Santa Rosa** La Pampa, Arg
34B2 **Santa Rosa** Mendoza, Arg
34B2 **Santa Rosa** San Luis, Arg
22B3 **Santa Rosa** *I* USA
24A2 **Santa Rosalía** Mexico
20C2 **Santa Rosa Range** *Mts* USA
31D3 **Santa Talhada** Brazil
35C1 **Santa Teresa** Brazil
53A2 **Santa Teresa di Gallura** Sardegna
22B3 **Santa Ynez** *R* USA
22B3 **Santa Ynez Mts** USA
17C1 **Santee** *R* USA
47C2 **Santhia** Italy
34A2 **Santiago** Chile
27C3 **Santiago** Dom Rep
32A2 **Santiago** Panama
79B2 **Santiago** Phil
32B4 **Santiago** *R* Peru
50A1 **Santiago de Compostela** Spain
26B2 **Santiago de Cuba** Cuba
30D4 **Santiago del Estero** Arg
30D4 **Santiago del Estero** State, Arg
22D4 **Santiago Peak** *Mt* USA
31C5 **Santo** State, Brazil
35A2 **Santo Anastatácio** Brazil
30F4 **Santo Angelo** Brazil
97A4 **Santo Antão** *I* Cape Verde
35A2 **Santo Antonio da Platina** Brazil
27D3 **Santo Domingo** Dom Rep

Santos

35B2 **Santos** Brazil
35C2 **Santos Dumont** Brazil
30E4 **Santo Tomé** Arg
29B5 **San Valentin** *Mt* Chile
34A2 **San Vicente** Chile
98B3 **Sanza Pomba** Angola
30E4 **São Borja** Brazil
35B2 **São Carlos** Brazil
33G5 **São Félix** Mato Grosso, Brazil
35C2 **São Fidélis** Brazil
35C1 **São Francisco** Brazil
31D3 **São Francisco** *R* Brazil
30G4 **São Francisco do Sul** Brazil
35B1 **São Gotardo** Brazil
99D3 **Sao Hill** Tanz
35C2 **São João da Barra** Brazil
35B2 **São João da Boa Vista** Brazil
35C1 **São João da Ponte** Brazil
35C2 **São João del Rei** Brazil
35B2 **São Joaquim da Barra** Brazil
96A1 **São Jorge** *I* Açores
35B2 **São José do Rio Prêto** Brazil
35B2 **São José dos Campos** Brazil
31C2 **São Luis** Brazil
35B1 **São Marcos** *R* Brazil
35C1 **São Maria do Suaçui** Brazil
35D1 **São Mateus** Brazil
35C1 **São Mateus** *R* Brazil
96A1 **São Miguel** *I* Açores
49C2 **Saône** *R* France
97A4 **São Nicolau** *I* Cape Verde
35B2 **São Paulo** Brazil
35A2 **São Paulo** State, Brazil
31C3 **São Raimundo Nonato** Brazil
35B1 **São Romão** Brazil
35B2 **São Sebastia do Paraiso** Brazil
35A1 **São Simão** Goias, Brazil
35B2 **São Simão** Sao Paulo, Brazil
97A4 **São Tiago** *I* Cape Verde
97C4 **São Tomé** *I* W Afriça
97C4 **São Tomé and Principe** Republic, W Africa
96B2 **Saoura** *Watercourse* Alg
35B2 **São Vicente** Brazil
97A4 **São Vincente** *I* Cape Verde
55C2 **Sápai** Greece
78D4 **Sape** Indon
97C4 **Sapele** Nig
74E2 **Sapporo** Japan
53C2 **Sapri** Italy
18A2 **Sapulpa** USA
90A2 **Saqqez** Iran
10C2 **Saquenay** *R* Can
90A2 **Sarāb** Iran
54A2 **Sarajevo** Bosnia-Herzegovina
90D2 **Sarakhs** Iran
61J3 **Saraktash** Russian Fed
63A2 **Sarala** Russian Fed
15D2 **Saranac L** USA
15D2 **Saranac Lake** USA
55B3 **Sarandë** Alb
79C4 **Sarangani Is** Phil
61G3 **Saransk** Russian Fed
61H2 **Sarapul** Russian Fed
17B2 **Sarasota** USA
54C1 **Sarata** Ukraine
15D2 **Saratoga Springs** USA

78C2 **Saratok** Malay
61G3 **Saratov** Russian Fed
61G3 **Saratovskoye Vodokhranilishche** *Res* Russian Fed
67F4 **Sarawak** State, Malay
92A2 **Saraykoy** Turk
90C3 **Sarbisheh** Iran
47D1 **Sarca** *R* Italy
95A2 **Sardalas** Libya
90A2 **Sar Dasht** Iran
52A2 **Sardegna** *I* Medit S
Sardinia = Sardegna
38H5 **Sarektjåkkå** *Mt* Sweden
84C2 **Sargodha** Pak
98B2 **Sarh** Chad
90B2 **Sārī** Iran
94B2 **Sarida** *R* Isreal
93D1 **Sarikamiş** Turk
107D3 **Sarina** Aust
47B1 **Sarine** *R* Switz
84B1 **Sar-i-Pul** Afghan
95B2 **Sarir** Libya
95A2 **Sarir Tibesti** *Desert* Libya
74B3 **Sariwŏn** N Korea
48B2 **Sark** *I* UK
92C2 **Sarkišla** Turk
71E4 **Sarmi** Indon
29C5 **Sarmiento** Arg
39G6 **Särna** Sweden
47C1 **Sarnen** Switz
14B2 **Sarnia** Can
58D2 **Sarny** Ukraine
6E2 **Saroaq** Greenland
84B2 **Sarobi** Afghan
78A3 **Sarolangun** Indon
55B3 **Saronikós Kólpos** *G* Greece
47C2 **Saronno** Italy
55C2 **Saros Körfezi** *B* Turk
39G7 **Sarpsborg** Nor
46D2 **Sarralbe** France
46D2 **Sarrebourg** France
46D2 **Sarreguemines** France
46D2 **Sarre-Union** France
51B1 **Sarrion** Spain
85B3 **Sartanahu** Pak
53A2 **Sartène** Corse
48B2 **Sarthe** *R* France
61H4 **Sarykamys** Kazakhstan
65H5 **Sarysu** *R* Kazakhstan
86A2 **Sasarām** India
74B4 **Sasebo** Japan
5H4 **Saskatchewan** Province, Can
5H4 **Saskatchewan** *R* Can
13F2 **Saskatoon** Can
101G1 **Sasolburg** S Africa
61F3 **Sasovo** Russian Fed
97B4 **Sassandra** Ivory Coast
97B4 **Sassandra** *R* Ivory Coast
53A2 **Sassari** Sardegna
56C2 **Sassnitz** Germany
47D2 **Sassuolo** Italy
34C2 **Sastre** Arg
87A1 **Sātāra** India
4G2 **Satellite B** Can
78D4 **Satengar** *Is* Indon
39H6 **Säter** Sweden
17B1 **Satilla** *R* USA
61J2 **Satka** Russian Fed
84D2 **Satluj** *R* India
86A2 **Satna** India
85C4 **Sätpura Range** *Mts* India
54B1 **Satu Mare** Rom
34D2 **Sauce** Arg
39F7 **Sauda** Nor
80C3 **Saudi Arabia** Kingdom, Arabian Pen
46D2 **Sauer** *R* Germany/Lux
46D1 **Sauerland** Region, Germany
38B1 **Sauðárkrókur** Iceland

14A2 **Saugatuck** USA
16C1 **Saugerties** USA
13B2 **Saugstad,Mt** Can
7B5 **Sault Sainte Marie** Can
14B1 **Sault Ste Marie** Can
14B1 **Sault Ste Marie** USA
71E4 **Saumlaki** Indon
48B2 **Saumur** France
98C3 **Saurimo** Angola
27M2 **Sauteurs** Grenada
54A2 **Sava** *R* Serbia, Yugos
97C4 **Savalou** Benin
17B1 **Savannah** Georgia, USA
17B1 **Savannah** *R* USA
76C2 **Savannakhet** Laos
26B3 **Savanna la Mar** Jamaica
7A4 **Savant Lake** Can
76D2 **Savarane** Laos
97C4 **Savé** Benin
101C3 **Save** *R* Mozam
90B3 **Sāveh** Iran
46D2 **Saverne** France
47B2 **Savigliano** Italy
46B2 **Savigny** France
49D2 **Savoie** *Region* France
49D3 **Savona** Italy
38K6 **Savonlinna** Fin
4A3 **Savoonga** USA
38K5 **Savukoski** Fin
71D4 **Savu S** Indon
76A1 **Saw** Burma
85D3 **Sawai Mādhopur** India
78A2 **Sawang** Indon
76B2 **Sawankhalok** Thai
75C1 **Sawara** Japan
12E1 **Sawtooth Mt** USA
106B2 **Sawu** *I* Indon
97C3 **Say** Niger
84B1 **Sayghan** Afghan
91B5 **Sayhūt** Yemen
61G4 **Saykhin** Kazakhstan
68D2 **Saynshand** Mongolia
61H5 **Say-Utes** Kazakhstan
16C2 **Sayville** USA
13B2 **Sayward** Can
57C3 **Sázava** *R* Czech Republic
51C2 **Sbisseb** *R* Alg
42C2 **Scafell Pike** *Mt* Eng
44E1 **Scalloway** Scot
44C2 **Scapa Flow** *Sd* Scot
15C2 **Scarborough** Can
42D2 **Scarborough** Eng
27E4 **Scarborough** Tobago
44A2 **Scarp** *I* Scot
45B2 **Scarriff** Irish Rep
52A1 **Schaffhausen** Switz
57C3 **Scharding** Austria
46D1 **Scharteberg** *Mt* Germany
7D4 **Schefferville** Can
46B1 **Schelde** *R* Belg
10C2 **Schenectady** USA
47D2 **Schio** Italy
46D1 **Schleiden** Germany
56B2 **Schleswig** Germany
56B2 **Schleswig Holstein** State, Germany
16B1 **Schoharie** USA
71F4 **Schouten** *Is* PNG
7B5 **Schreiber** Can
21B2 **Schurz** USA
16A2 **Schuykill Haven** USA
16B2 **Schuylkill** *R* USA
57B3 **Schwabische Alb** *Upland* Germany
57B3 **Schwarzwald** *Upland* Germany
12C1 **Schwatka Mts** USA
47D1 **Schwaz** Austria
57C2 **Schweinfurt** Germany
101G1 **Schweizer Reneke** S Africa
56C2 **Schwerin** Germany
47C1 **Schwyz** Switz
53B3 **Sciacca** Italy

14B3 **Scioto** *R* USA
109D2 **Scone** Aust
6H2 **Scoresby Sd** Greenland
103F7 **Scotia Ridge** Atlantic O
103F7 **Scotia S** Atlantic O
44B3 **Scotland** Country, UK
112B7 **Scott** *Base* Ant
13B2 **Scott,C** Can
9C2 **Scott City** USA
112C6 **Scott I** Ant
6C2 **Scott Inlet** *B* Can
20B2 **Scott,Mt** USA
106B2 **Scott Reef** Timor S
8C2 **Scottsbluff** USA
17A1 **Scottsboro** USA
109C4 **Scottsdale** Aust
10C2 **Scranton** USA
47D1 **Scuol** Switz
Scutari = Shkodër
5J4 **Seal** *R* Can
108B3 **Sea Lake** Aust
18B2 **Searcy** USA
22B2 **Seaside** California, USA
20B1 **Seaside** Oregon, USA
16B3 **Seaside Park** USA
20B1 **Seattle** USA
22A1 **Sebastopol** USA
58D1 **Sebez** Russian Fed
17B2 **Sebring** USA
111A3 **Secretary I** NZ
18B2 **Sedalia** USA
46C2 **Sedan** France
111B2 **Seddonville** NZ
94B3 **Sede Boqer** Israel
94B3 **Sederot** Israel
97A3 **Sédhiou** Sen
94B3 **Sedom** Israel
100A3 **Seeheim** Namibia
111B2 **Sefton,Mt** NZ
77C5 **Segamat** Malay
51B2 **Segorbe** Spain
97B3 **Ségou** Mali
Segovia = Coco
50B1 **Segovia** Spain
51C1 **Segre** *R* Spain
97B4 **Séguéla** Ivory Coast
96A2 **Seguia el Hamra** *Watercourse* Mor
34C2 **Segundo** *R* Arg
78D2 **Seguntur** Indon
50B2 **Segura** *R* Spain
85B3 **Sehwan** Pak
46D2 **Seille** *R* France
38J6 **Seinäjoki** Fin
48C2 **Seine** *R* France
46B2 **Seine-et-Marne** Department, France
99D3 **Sekenke** Tanz
99D1 **Sek'ot'a** Eth
20B1 **Selah** USA
71E4 **Selaru** *I* Indon
78D4 **Selat Alas** *Str* Indon
78B3 **Selat Bangka** *Str* Indon
78A3 **Selat Berhala** *B* Indon
71E4 **Selat Dampier** *Str* Indon
78B3 **Selat Gaspar** *Str* Indon
78D4 **Selat Lombok** *Str* Indon
78D4 **Selat Sape** *Str* Indon
78A4 **Selat Sunda** *Str* Indon
71D4 **Selat Wetar** *Chan* Indon
12B1 **Selawik** USA
12C1 **Selawik** *R* USA
12B1 **Selawik L** USA
42D3 **Selby** Eng
55C3 **Selçuk** Turk
12D3 **Seldovia** USA
100B3 **Selebi Pikwe** Botswana
6H3 **Selfoss** Iceland
95B2 **Selima Oasis** Sudan
5J4 **Selkirk** Can
42C2 **Selkirk** Scot

13D2 **Selkirk Mts** Can
22C2 **Selma** California, USA
50B2 **Selouane** Mor
12H2 **Selous,Mt** Can
78B3 **Selta Karimata** *Str* Indon
32C5 **Selvas** Region, Brazil
107D3 **Selwyn** Aust
4E3 **Selwyn Mts** Can
78C4 **Semarang** Indon
61E2 **Semenov** Russian Fed
12C3 **Semidi Is** USA
60E3 **Semiluki** Russian Fed
19A2 **Seminole** Oklahoma, USA
17B1 **Seminole,L** USA
65K4 **Semipalatinsk** Kazakhstan
79B3 **Semirara Is** Phil
90B3 **Semirom** Iran
78C2 **Semitau** Indon
90B2 **Semnān** Iran
46C2 **Semois** *R* Belg
23B2 **Sempoala** Hist Site, Mexico
32D5 **Sena Madureira** Brazil
100B2 **Senanga** Zambia
19C3 **Senatobia** USA
74E3 **Sendai** Honshū, Japan
74C4 **Sendai** Kyūshū, Japan
85D4 **Sendwha** India
15C2 **Seneca Falls** USA
97A3 **Senegal** Republic, Africa
97A3 **Sénégal** *R* Maur Sen
101G1 **Senekal** S Africa
31D4 **Senhor do Bonfim** Brazil
52B2 **Senigallia** Italy
52C2 **Senj** Croatia
69E4 **Senkaku Gunto** *Is* Japan
46B2 **Senlis** France
99D1 **Sennar** Sudan
7C5 **Senneterre** Can
49C2 **Sens** France
54A1 **Senta** Serbia, Yugos
98C3 **Sentery** Zaïre
13C2 **Sentinel Peak** *Mt* Can
85D4 **Seoni** India
Seoul = Soul
110B2 **Separation Pt** NZ
76D2 **Sepone** Laos
7D4 **Sept-Iles** Can
95A2 **Séquédine** Niger
21B2 **Sequoia** Nat Pk, USA
71D4 **Seram** *I* Indon
78B4 **Serang** Indon
78B2 **Serasan** *I* Indon
54A2 **Serbia** Republic, Yugos
61F3 **Serdobsk** Russian Fed
77C5 **Seremban** Malay
99D3 **Serengeti Nat Pk** Tanz
100C2 **Serenje** Zambia
59D3 **Seret** *R* Ukraine
61G2 **Sergach** Russian Fed
65H3 **Sergino** Russian Fed
31D4 **Sergipe** State, Brazil
60E2 **Segiyev Posad** Russian Fed
78C2 **Seria** Brunei
78C2 **Serian** Malay
55B3 **Sérifos** *I* Greece
47C2 **Serio** *R* Italy
95B2 **Serir Calanscio** *Desert* Libya
46C2 **Sermaize-les-Bains** France
71D4 **Sermata** *I* Indon
61H3 **Sernovodsk** Russian Fed
65H4 **Serov** Russian Fed
100B3 **Serowe** Botswana
50A2 **Serpa** Port
60E3 **Serpukhov** Russian Fed
35B2 **Serra da Canastra** *Mts* Brazil
50A1 **Serra da Estrela** *Mts* Port
35B2 **Serra da Mantiqueira** *Mts* Brazil
35A1 **Serra da Mombuca** Brazil
35C1 **Serra do Cabral** *Mt* Brazil
33F5 **Serra do Cachimbo** *Mts* Brazil
35A1 **Serra do Caiapó** *Mts* Brazil
35A2 **Serra do Cantu** *Mts* Brazil
35C2 **Serra do Caparaó** *Mts* Brazil
31C5 **Serra do Chifre** Brazil
35C1 **Serra do Espinhaço** *Mts* Brazil
35B2 **Serra do Mar** *Mts* Brazil
35A2 **Serra do Mirante** *Mts* Brazil
33G3 **Serra do Navio** Brazil
35B2 **Serra do Paranapiacaba** *Mts* Brazil
33F6 **Serra dos Caiabis** *Mts* Brazil
35A2 **Serra dos Dourados** *Mts* Brazil
33E6 **Serra dos Parecis** *Mts* Brazil
35B1 **Serra dos Pilões** *Mts* Brazil
35A1 **Serra Dourada** *Mts* Brazil
33F6 **Serra Formosa** *Mts* Brazil
55B2 **Sérrai** Greece
25D3 **Serrana Bank** *Is* Caribbean S
51B1 **Serrana de Cuenca** *Mts* Spain
35A1 **Serranópolis** Brazil
33E3 **Serra Pacaraima** *Mts* Brazil/Ven
33E3 **Serra Parima** *Mts* Brazil
33G3 **Serra Tumucumaque** Brazil
46B2 **Serre** *R* France
34B2 **Serrezuela** Arg
31D4 **Serrinha** Brazil
6G3 **Serrmilik** Greenland
35C1 **Serro** Brazil
35A2 **Sertanópolis** Brazil
72A3 **Sêrtar** China
78C3 **Seruyan** *R* Indon
100A2 **Sesfontein** Namibia
100B2 **Sesheke** Zambia
47B2 **Sestriere** Italy
74D2 **Setana** Japan
49C3 **Sète** France
35C1 **Sete Lagoas** Brazil
96C1 **Sétif** Alg
75B1 **Seto** Japan
75A2 **Seto Naikai** *S* Japan
96B1 **Settat** Mor
42C2 **Settle** Eng
5G4 **Settler** Can
50A2 **Sêtúbal** Port
93E1 **Sevan,Oz** *L* Armenia
60D5 **Sevastopol'** Ukraine
7B4 **Severn** *R* Can
43C3 **Severn** *R* Eng
1B9 **Severnaya Zemlya** *I* Russian Fed
63C2 **Severo-Baykalskoye Nagorye** *Mts* Russian Fed
60E4 **Severo Donets** Ukraine
64E3 **Severodvinsk** Russian Fed
64H3 **Severo Sos'va** *R* Russian Fed
8B3 **Sevier** *R* USA
8B3 **Sevier L** USA
50A2 **Sevilla** Spain
Seville = Sevilla
54C2 **Sevlievo** Bulg
97A4 **Sewa** *R* Sierra Leone
12E2 **Seward** Alaska, USA
18A1 **Seward** Nebraska, USA
12A1 **Seward Pen** USA
13D1 **Sexsmith** Can
89K8 **Seychelles** *Is* Indian O
38C1 **Seyðisfjörður** Iceland
92C2 **Seyhan** Turk
60E3 **Seym** *R* Russian Fed
108C3 **Seymour** Aust
16C2 **Seymour** Connecticut, USA
14A3 **Seymour** Indiana, USA
46B2 **Sézanne** France
96D1 **Sfax** Tunisia
54C1 **Sfînto Gheorghe** Rom
56A2 **'s-Gravenhage** Neth
72B3 **Shaanxi** Province, China
98C3 **Shabunda** Zaïre
82B2 **Shache** China
112C9 **Shackleton Ice Shelf** Ant
85B3 **Shadadkot** Pak
91B3 **Shādhām** *R* Iran
43C4 **Shaftesbury** Eng
29G8 **Shag Rocks** *Is* South Georgia
90A3 **Shāhabād** Iran
94C2 **Shahbā** Syria
91C3 **Shahdap** Iran
86A2 **Shahdol** India
90A2 **Shāhīn Dezh** Iran
90C3 **Shāh Kūh** Iran
91C3 **Shahr-e Bābak** Iran
Shahresa = Qomisheh
90B3 **Shahr Kord** Iran
87B1 **Shājābād** India
84D3 **Shājahānpur** India
85D4 **Shājāpur** India
61F4 **Shakhty** Russian Fed
61G2 **Shakhun'ya** Russian Fed
97C4 **Shaki** Nig
12B2 **Shaktoolik** USA
61J2 **Shamary** Russian Fed
99D2 **Shambe** Sudan
16A2 **Shamokin** USA
16B1 **Shandaken** USA
72D2 **Shandong** Province, China
73C5 **Shangchuan Dao** *I* China
72C1 **Shangdu** China
73E3 **Shanghai** China
72C3 **Shangnan** China
100B2 **Shangombo** Zambia
73D4 **Shangra** China
73B5 **Shangsi** China
72C3 **Shang Xian** China
41B3 **Shannon** *R* Irish Rep
72D3 **Shanqiu** China
74B2 **Shansonggang** China
63F2 **Shantarskiye Ostrova** *I* Russian Fed
73D5 **Shantou** China
72C2 **Shanxi** Province, China
72D3 **Shan Xian** China
73C5 **Shaoguan** China
73E4 **Shaoxing** China
73C4 **Shaoyang** China
44C2 **Shapinsay** *I* Scot
94C2 **Shaqqā** Syria
72A1 **Sharhulsan** Mongolia
90C2 **Sharifābād** Iran
91C4 **Sharjah** UAE
106A3 **Shark B** Aust
90C2 **Sharlauk** Turkmenistan
94B2 **Sharon,Plain of** Israel
61G2 **Sharya** Russian Fed
99D2 **Shashemanē** Eth
73C3 **Shashi** China
20B2 **Shasta L** USA
20B2 **Shasta,Mt** USA
93E3 **Shaţţ al Gharrat** *R* Iraq
94B3 **Shaubak** Jordan
13F3 **Shaunavon** Can
22C2 **Shaver L** USA
16B2 **Shawangunk Mt** USA
15D1 **Shawinigan** Can
19A2 **Shawnee** Oklahoma, USA
73D4 **Sha Xian** China
106B3 **Shay Gap** Aust
94C2 **Shaykh Miskīn** Syria
99E1 **Shaykh 'Uthmān** Yemen
60E3 **Shchekino** Russian Fed
60E3 **Shchigry** Russian Fed
60D3 **Shchors** Ukraine
65J4 **Shchuchinsk** Kazakhstan
99E2 **Shebele** *R* Eth
14A2 **Sheboygan** USA
98B2 **Shebshi** *Mts* Nig
12F1 **Sheenjek** *R* USA
45C1 **Sheep Haven** *Estuary* Irish Rep
43E4 **Sheerness** Eng
94B2 **Shefar'am** Israel
42D3 **Sheffield** Eng
84C2 **Shekhupura** Pak
13B1 **Shelagyote Peak** *Mt* Can
16C1 **Shelburne Falls** USA
14A2 **Shelby** Michigan, USA
8B2 **Shelby** Montana, USA
14A3 **Shelbyville** Indiana, USA
12H2 **Sheldon,Mt** Can
12D3 **Shelikof Str** USA
109D2 **Shellharbour** Aust
111A3 **Shelter Pt** NZ
20B1 **Shelton** USA
93E1 **Shemakha** Azerbaijan
18A1 **Shenandoah** USA
15C3 **Shenandoah** *R* USA
15C3 **Shenandoah Nat Pk** USA
97C4 **Shendam** Nig
95C2 **Shendi** Sudan
72C2 **Shenmu** China
72E1 **Shenyang** China
73C5 **Shenzhen** China
85D3 **Sheopur** India
59D2 **Shepetovka** Ukraine
108C3 **Shepparton** Aust
6B2 **Sherard,C** Can
43C4 **Sherborne** Eng
97A4 **Sherbro I** Sierra Leone
15D1 **Sherbrooke** Can
85C3 **Shergarh** India
19B3 **Sheridan** Arkansas, USA
8C2 **Sheridan** Wyoming, USA
19A3 **Sherman** USA
56B2 **s-Hertogenbosh** Neth
12H3 **Sheslay** Can
40C1 **Shetland** *Is* Scot
Shevchenko = Aktau
91B4 **Sheyk Sho'eyb** *I* Iran
69H2 **Shiashkotan** *I* Russian Fed
84B1 **Shibarghan** Afghan
74D3 **Shibata** Japan
95C1 **Shibin el Kom** Egypt
75B1 **Shibukawa** Japan
72C2 **Shijiazhuang** China
84B3 **Shikarpur** Pak
67G3 **Shikoku** *I* Japan
75A2 **Shikoku-sanchi** *Mts* Japan
86B1 **Shiliguri** India
68D1 **Shilka** Russian Fed
68D1 **Shilka** *R* Russian Fed
16B2 **Shillington** USA
86C1 **Shillong** India
61F3 **Shilovo** Russian Fed
75A2 **Shimabara** Japan

Shimada

76B2 **Sittang** *R* Burma
46C1 **Sittard** Neth
86C2 **Sittwe** Burma
78C4 **Situbondo** Indon
92C2 **Sivas** Turk
93C2 **Siverek** Turk
92B2 **Sivrihisar** Turk
95B2 **Siwa** Egypt
84D2 **Siwalik Range** *Mts* India
86A1 **Siwalik Range** *Mts* Nepal
72D3 **Siyang** China
56C1 **Sjaelland** *I* Den
39G7 **Skagen** Den
39F7 **Skagerrak** *Str* Nor/Den
20B1 **Skagit** *R* USA
20B1 **Skagit Mt** Can
4E4 **Skagway** USA
39G7 **Skara** Sweden
59C2 **Skarzysko-Kamlenna** Pol
5F4 **Skeena** *R* Can
13B1 **Skeena Mts** Can
4D3 **Skeenjek** *R* USA
42E3 **Skegness** Eng
38H5 **Skellefte** *R* Sweden
38J6 **Skellefteå** Sweden
55B3 **Skíathos** *I* Greece
45B3 **Skibbereen** Irish Rep
5E4 **Skidegate** Can
58C2 **Skiemiewice** Pol
39F7 **Skien** Nor
96C1 **Skikda** Alg
74C4 **Skikoku** *I* Japan
42D3 **Skipton** Eng
55B3 **Skíros** *I* Greece
39F7 **Skive** Den
56B1 **Skjern** Den
6F3 **Skjoldungen** Greenland
14A2 **Skokie** USA
55B3 **Skópelos** *I* Greece
54B2 **Skopje** Macedonia
39G7 **Skövde** Sweden
63E2 **Skovorodino** Russian Fed
4C3 **Skwentna** USA
58B2 **Skwierzyna** Pol
40B2 **Skye** *I* Scot
39G7 **Slagelse** Den
45C2 **Slaney** *R* Irish Rep
54B2 **Slatina** Rom
78C4 **Slaung** Indon
5G3 **Slave** *R* Can
13E1 **Slave Lake** Can
65J4 **Slavgorod** Russian Fed
59D2 **Slavuta** Ukraine
60E4 **Slavyansk** Ukraine
44B3 **Sleat,Sound of** *Chan* Scot
12C2 **Sleetmute** USA
45C2 **Sleeve Bloom** *Mts* Irish Rep
19C3 **Slidell** USA
16B2 **Slide Mt** USA
45B1 **Sligo** County, Irish Rep
41B3 **Sligo** Irish Rep
41B3 **Sligo** *B* Irish Rep
54C2 **Sliven** Bulg
54C2 **Slobozia** Rom
13D3 **Slocan** Can
58D2 **Slonim** Belorussia
43D4 **Slough** Eng
22B2 **Slough** *R* USA
59B3 **Slovakia** Republic, Europe
52B1 **Slovenia** Republic, Europe
56C2 **Slubice** Pol
59D2 **Sluch'** *R* Ukraine
58B2 **Słupsk** Pol
58D2 **Slutsk** Belorussia
58D2 **Slutsk** *R* Belorussia
41A3 **Slyne Head** *Pt* Irish Rep
63C2 **Slyudyanka** Russian Fed
7D4 **Smallwood Res** Can
54B2 **Smederevo** Serbia, Yugos
54B2 **Smederevska Palanka** Serbia, Yugos
60D4 **Smela** Ukraine
15C2 **Smethport** USA
13E1 **Smith** Can
4F3 **Smith Arm** *B* Can
13B2 **Smithers** Can
7C3 **Smith I** Can
13B2 **Smith Sd** Can
15C2 **Smiths Falls** Can
109C4 **Smithton** Aust
13D1 **Smoky** *R* Can
109D2 **Smoky C** Aust
13E2 **Smoky Lake** Can
38F6 **Smøla** *I* Nor
60D3 **Smolensk** Russian Fed
55B2 **Smólikas** *Mt* Greece
54B2 **Smolyan** Bulg
58D2 **Smorgon'** Belorussia
16B3 **Smyrna** Delaware, USA
17B1 **Smyrna** Georgia, USA
42B2 **Snaefell** *Mt* Eng
38B2 **Snafell** *Mt* Iceland
8B2 **Snake** *R* USA
8B2 **Snake River Canyon** USA
56B2 **Sneek** Neth
45B3 **Sneem** Irish Rep
22B2 **Snelling** USA
59B2 **Sněžka** *Mt* Pol/Czech Republic
38F6 **Snøhetta** *Mt* Nor
20B1 **Snohomish** USA
20B1 **Snoqualmie P** USA
76D3 **Snoul** Camb
43B3 **Snowdon** *Mt* Wales
43B3 **Snowdonia Nat Pk** Wales
4G3 **Snowdrift** Can
5H4 **Snow Lake** Can
108A2 **Snowtown** Aust
109C3 **Snowy Mts** Aust
9C3 **Snyder** USA
74B4 **Soan-kundo** *I* S Korea
99D2 **Sobat** *R* Sudan
31C2 **Sobral** Brazil
58C2 **Sochaczew** Pol
61E5 **Sochi** Russian Fed
9C3 **Socorro** USA
24A3 **Socorro** *I* Mexico
34A2 **Socos** Chile
81D4 **Socotra** *I* Yemen
38K5 **Sodankylä** Fin
39H6 **Soderhamn** Sweden
39H7 **Södertälje** Sweden
99C1 **Sodiri** Sudan
99D2 **Sodo** Eth
46E1 **Soest** Germany
101C2 **Sofala** Mozam
Sofia = Sofiya
54B2 **Sofiya** Bulg
69G4 **Sofu Gan** *I* Japan
32C2 **Sogamoso** Colombia
39F6 **Sognefjorden** *Inlet* Nor
82D2 **Sog Xian** China
95C2 **Sohâg** Egypt
84D3 **Sohīpat** India
46B1 **Soignies** Belg
46B2 **Soissons** France
85C3 **Sojat** India
74A3 **Söjosön-man** *B* N Korea
92A2 **Söke** Turk
97C4 **Sokodé** Togo
61E2 **Sokol** Russian Fed
58C2 **Sokołka** Pol
97B3 **Sokolo** Mali
6H3 **Søkongens Øy** *I* Greenland
99D1 **Sokota** Eth
97C3 **Sokoto** Nig
97C3 **Sokoto** *R* Nig
111A3 **Solander I** NZ
79B2 **Solano** Phil
87B1 **Solapur** India
47D1 **Solbad Hall** Austria
47D1 **Sölden** Austria
12D2 **Soldotna** USA
26C4 **Soledad** Colombia
43D4 **Solent** *Sd* Eng
46B1 **Solesmes** France
58D2 **Soligorsk** Belorussia
61J2 **Solikamsk** Russian Fed
32C4 **Solimões** *R* Peru
46D1 **Solingen** Germany
38H6 **Sollefteå** Sweden
61H3 **Sol'Iletsk** Russian Fed
70B4 **Solok** Indon
105G4 **Solomon** *Is* Pacific O
47B1 **Solothurn** Switz
39F8 **Soltau** Germany
22B3 **Solvang** USA
42C2 **Solway Firth** *Estuary* Eng/Scot
100B2 **Solwezi** Zambia
75C1 **Sōma** Japan
55C3 **Soma** Turk
81C5 **Somalia** Republic, E Africa
54A1 **Sombor** Serbia, Yugos
107D2 **Somerset** Aust
43C4 **Somerset** County, Eng
16D2 **Somerset** Massachusetts, USA
15C2 **Somerset** Pennsylvania, USA
100B4 **Somerset East** S Africa
6A2 **Somerset I** Can
16B3 **Somers Point** USA
16B2 **Somerville** USA
19A3 **Somerville Res** USA
54B1 **Somes** *R* Rom
46B2 **Somme** Department, France
46B2 **Somme** *R* France
46C2 **Sommesous** France
86A2 **Son** *R* India
74A3 **Sonch'ŏn** N Korea
39F8 **Sønderborg** Den
6E3 **Søndre Strømfjord** Greenland
47C1 **Sondrio** Italy
76D3 **Song Ba** *R* Viet
76D3 **Song Cau** Viet
101C2 **Songea** Tanz
73E3 **Songjiang** China
77C4 **Songkhla** Thai
74B3 **Songnim** N Korea
77C5 **Sông Pahang** *R* Malay
72A3 **Songpan** China
72C1 **Sonid Youqi** China
76C1 **Son La** Viet
85B3 **Sonmiani** Pak
85B3 **Sonmiani Bay** Pak
22A1 **Sonoma** USA
22B2 **Sonora** California, USA
24A2 **Sonora** *R* Mexico
9B3 **Sonoran Desert** USA
22C1 **Sonora P** USA
25D3 **Sonsonate** El Salvador
71E3 **Sonsorol** *I* Pacific O
10B2 **Soo Canals** Can/USA
13C3 **Sooke** Can
58B2 **Sopot** Pol
59B3 **Sopron** Hung
22B2 **Soquel** USA
53B2 **Sora** Italy
94B3 **Sored** *R* Israel
15D1 **Sorel** Can
109C4 **Sorell** Aust
92C2 **Sorgun** Turk
50B1 **Soria** Spain
38J5 **Sørkjosen** Nor
64C2 **Sørksop** *I* Barents S
61H4 **Sor Mertvyy Kultuk** *Plain* Kazakhstan
35B2 **Sorocaba** Brazil
61H3 **Sorochinsk** Russian Fed
71F3 **Soroi** *I* Pacific O
60C4 **Soroki** Moldavia
71E4 **Sorong** Indon
71E4 **Sorong** Province, Indon
99D2 **Soroti** Uganda
38J4 **Sørøya** *I* Nor
53B2 **Sorrento** Italy
38K5 **Sorsatunturi** *Mt* Fin
38H5 **Sorsele** Sweden
79B3 **Sorsogon** Phil
38L6 **Sortavala** Russian Fed
74B3 **Sŏsan** S Korea
59B2 **Sosnowiec** Pol
65H4 **Sos'va** Russian Fed
98B2 **Souanké** Congo
97B4 **Soubré** Ivory Coast
16B2 **Souderton** USA
27P2 **Soufrière** St Lucia
27N2 **Soufrière** *Mt* St Vincent and the Grenadines
48C3 **Souillac** France
96C1 **Souk Ahras** Alg
74B3 **Soul** S Korea
51C2 **Soummam** *R* Alg
Sour = Tyr
101G1 **Sources,Mt aux** Lesotho
31D3 **Sousa** Brazil
96D1 **Sousse** Tunisia
100B4 **South Africa** Republic, Africa
16B2 **South Amboy** USA
14B2 **Southampton** Can
43D4 **Southampton** Eng
16C2 **Southampton** USA
6B3 **Southampton I** Can
28F6 **South Atlantic O**
7D4 **South Aulatsivik I** Can
106C3 **South Australia** State, Aust
104E5 **South Australian Basin** Indian O
19C3 **Southaven** USA
17B2 **South Bay** USA
14B1 **South Baymouth** Can
14A2 **South Bend** Indiana, USA
20B1 **South Bend** Washington, USA
16D1 **Southbridge** USA
South Cape = Ka Lae
11B3 **South Carolina** State, USA
70C2 **South China S** S E Asia
8C2 **South Dakota** State, USA
16C1 **South Deerfield** USA
43D4 **South Downs** Eng
109C4 **South East C** Aust
111A2 **Southen Alps** *Mts* NZ
5H4 **Southend** Can
43E4 **Southend-on-Sea** Eng
111A2 **Southern Alps** *Mts* NZ
106A4 **Southern Cross** Aust
5J4 **Southern Indian L** Can
27H2 **Southfield** Jamaica
105G5 **South Fiji Basin** Pacific O
12D2 **South Fork** *R* Alaska, USA
22B1 **South Fork** *R* California, USA
28F8 **South Georgia** *I* S Atlantic O
43C4 **South Glamorgan** County, Wales
14A2 **South Haven** USA
5J3 **South Henik L** Can
104F3 **South Honshu Ridge** Pacific O
111A2 **South I** NZ
16C2 **Southington** USA
74B3 **South Korea** Republic, S E Asia
21A2 **South Lake Tahoe** USA
112C8 **South Magnetic Pole** Ant
17B2 **South Miami** USA
16A3 **South Mt** USA

6E3 **Sukkertoppen** *L* Greenland
38L6 **Sukkozero** Russian Fed
85B3 **Sukkur** Pak
87C1 **Sukma** India
95A2 **Sŭknah** Libya
100A3 **Sukses** Namibia
75A2 **Sukumo** Japan
13C1 **Sukunka** *R* Can
60E3 **Sula** *R* Russian Fed
84B3 **Sulaiman Range** *Mts* Pak
70C4 **Sulawesi** *I* Indon
54C1 **Sulina** Rom
38H5 **Sulitjelma** Nor
32A4 **Sullana** Peru
18B2 **Sullivan** USA
13B2 **Sullivan Bay** Can
13E2 **Sullivan L** Can
52B2 **Sulmona** Italy
19B3 **Sulphur** Louisiana, USA
19A3 **Sulphur** Oklahoma, USA
19A3 **Sulphur Springs** USA
86A1 **Sultānpur** India
79B4 **Sulu Arch** Phil
70C3 **Sulu S** Philip
30D4 **Sumampa** Arg
70B4 **Sumatera** *I* Indon
70C4 **Sumba** *I* Indon
78D4 **Sumbawa** *I* Indon
78D4 **Sumbawa Besar** Indon
99D3 **Sumbawanga** Tanz
100A2 **Sumbe** Angola
44E2 **Sumburgh Head** *Pt* Scot
78C4 **Sumenep** Indon
69G3 **Sumisu** *I* Japan
13D3 **Summerland** Can
5F4 **Summit Lake** Can
21B2 **Summit Mt** USA
111B2 **Sumner,L** NZ
75A2 **Sumoto** Japan
17B1 **Sumter** USA
60D3 **Sumy** Ukraine
16A2 **Sunbury** USA
34C2 **Sunchales** Arg
74B3 **Sunch'ŏn** N Korea
74B4 **Sunch'ŏn** S Korea
86A2 **Sundargarh** India
86B2 **Sunderbans** *Swamp* India
42D2 **Sunderland** Eng
13E2 **Sundre** Can
15C1 **Sundridge** Can
38H6 **Sundsvall** Sweden
38D3 **Suduroy** Føroyar
78D3 **Sungaianyar** Indon
78A3 **Sungaisalak** Indon
20C1 **Sunnyside** USA
21A2 **Sunnyvale** USA
63D1 **Suntar** Russian Fed
97B4 **Sunyani** Ghana
75A2 **Suō-nada** *B* Japan
38K6 **Suonejoki** Fin
86B1 **Supaul** India
18A1 **Superior** Nebraska, USA
10A2 **Superior** Wisconsin, USA
10B2 **Superior,L** Can/USA
76C3 **Suphan Buri** Thai
93D2 **Süphan Dağ** Turk
71E4 **Supiori** *I* Indon
93E3 **Suq ash Suyukh** Iraq
72D3 **Suqian** China
Suqutra = Socotra
91C5 **Sür** Oman
61G3 **Sura** *R* Russian Fed
78C4 **Surabaya** Indon
75B2 **Suraga-wan** *B* Japan
78C4 **Surakarta** Indon
109C1 **Surat** Aust
85C4 **Sürat** India
84C3 **Süratgarh** India
77B4 **Surat Thani** Thai
85C4 **Surendranagar** India
16B3 **Surf City** USA
64J3 **Surgut** Russian Fed
87B1 **Suriapet** India
49D2 **Sürich** Switz

79C4 **Surigao** Phil
76C3 **Surin** Thai
33F3 **Surinam** Republic, S America
43D4 **Surrey** County, Eng
47C1 **Sursee** Switz
95A1 **Surt** Libya
38A2 **Surtsey** *I* Iceland
78A3 **Surulangan** Indon
47B2 **Susa** Italy
75A2 **Susa** Japan
75A2 **Susaki** Japan
21A1 **Susanville** USA
47D1 **Süsch** Switz
12E2 **Susitna** *R* USA
16A3 **Susquehanna** *R* USA
16B2 **Sussex** USA
43D4 **Sussex West** Eng
13B1 **Sustut Peak** *Mt* Can
100B4 **Sutherland** S Africa
84C2 **Sutlej** *R* Pak
21A2 **Sutter Creek** USA
14B3 **Sutton** USA
12C3 **Sutwik I** USA
74D3 **Suwa** Japan
58C2 **Suwałki** Pol
17B2 **Suwannee** *R* USA
94B2 **Suweilih** Jordan
74B3 **Suwŏn** S Korea
72D3 **Su Xian** China
75B1 **Suzaka** Japan
73E3 **Suzhou** China
74D3 **Suzu** Japan
75B2 **Suzuka** Japan
75B1 **Suzu-misaki** *C* Japan
64C2 **Svalbard** *Is* Barents S
59C3 **Svalyava** Ukraine
38G5 **Svartisen** *Mt* Nor
76D3 **Svay Rieng** Camb
38G6 **Sveg** Sweden
39G7 **Svendborg** Den
Sverdlovsk = Yekaterinburg
6A1 **Sverdrup Chan** Can
69F2 **Svetlaya** Russian Fed
58C2 **Svetlogorsk** Russian Fed
39K6 **Svetogorsk** Russian Fed
54B2 **Svetozarevo** Serbia, Yugos
54C2 **Svilengrad** Bulg
58D2 **Svir'** Belorussia
59B3 **Svitavy** Czech Republic
69E1 **Svobodnyy** Russian Fed
38G5 **Svolvaer** Nor
107E3 **Swain Reefs** Aust
17B1 **Swainsboro** USA
100A3 **Swakopmund** Namibia
42D2 **Swale** *R* Eng
70C3 **Swallow Reef** *I* S E Asia
87B2 **Swāmihalli** India
25D3 **Swan** *I* Honduras
43D4 **Swanage** Eng
108B3 **Swan Hill** Aust
13D2 **Swan Hills** Can
13D2 **Swan Hills** *Mts* Can
26A3 **Swan I** Caribbean S
5H4 **Swan River** Can
43C4 **Swansea** Wales
43C4 **Swansea B** Wales
101G1 **Swartruggens** S Africa
Swatow = Shantou
101H1 **Swaziland** Kingdom, S Africa
39G7 **Sweden** Kingdom, N Europe
20B2 **Sweet Home** USA
9C3 **Sweetwater** USA
100B4 **Swellendam** S Africa
59B2 **Świdnica** Pol
58B2 **Świdwin** Pol
58B2 **Świebodzin** Pol
58B2 **Świecie** Pol
5H4 **Swift Current** Can
43D4 **Swindon** Eng
45B2 **Swinford** Irish Rep

56C2 **Świnoujście** Pol
49D2 **Switzerland** Federal Republic, Europe
45C2 **Swords** Irish Rep
109D2 **Sydney** Aust
7D5 **Sydney** Can
64G3 **Syktyvkar** Russian Fed
17A1 **Sylacauga** USA
38G6 **Sylarna** *Mt* Sweden
86C2 **Sylhet** Bang
56B1 **Sylt** *I* Germany
14B2 **Sylvania** USA
112C11 **Syowa** *Base* Ant
Syracuse = Siracusa
15C2 **Syracuse** USA
65H5 **Syr Darya** *R* Kazakhstan
93C2 **Syria** Republic, S W Asia
61J2 **Sysert'** Russian Fed
61G3 **Syzran'** Russian Fed
56C2 **Szczecin** Pol
58B2 **Szczecinek** Pol
58C2 **Szczytno** Pol
59C3 **Szeged** Hung
59B3 **Székesfehérvár** Hung
59B3 **Szekszard** Hung
59B3 **Szolnok** Hung
59B3 **Szombathely** Hung
58B2 **Szprotawa** Pol

T

90C3 **Tabas** Iran
23A1 **Tabasco** Mexico
32D4 **Tabatinga** Brazil
96B2 **Tabelbala** Alg
76C3 **Tabeng** Camb
13E2 **Taber** Can
79B3 **Tablas** *I* Phil
100A4 **Table Mt** S Africa
12F1 **Table Mt** USA
18B2 **Table Rock Res** USA
78B3 **Taboali** Indon
57C3 **Tábor** Czech Republic
99D3 **Tabora** Tanz
97B4 **Tabou** Ivory Coast
90A2 **Tabrīz** Iran
92C4 **Tabūk** S Arabia
23A2 **Tacámbaro** Mexico
82C1 **Tacheng** China
79C3 **Tacloban** Phil
30B2 **Tacna** Peru
8A2 **Tacoma** USA
99E1 **Tadjoura** Djibouti
87B2 **Tādpatri** India
74B3 **Taebaek Sanmaek** *Mts* S Korea
74B3 **Taegu** S Korea
74B4 **Taehŭksan** *I* S Korea
74B3 **Taejŏn** S Korea
51B1 **Tafalla** Spain
96C2 **Tafasaset** *Watercourse* Alg
43C4 **Taff** *R* Wales
94B3 **Tafila** Jordan
60E4 **Taganrog** Ukraine
97A3 **Tagant** Region, Maur
79B4 **Tagbilaran** Phil
96B2 **Taguenout Hagguerete** *Well* Maur
107E2 **Tagula** *I* Solomon Is
79C4 **Tagum** Phil
Tagus = Tejo
96C2 **Tahat** *Mt* Alg
105J4 **Tahiti** *I* Pacific O
18A2 **Tahlequah** USA
21A2 **Tahoe City** USA
21A2 **Tahoe,L** USA
97C3 **Tahoua** Niger
71D3 **Tahuna** Indon
72D2 **Tai'an** China
72B3 **Taibai Shan** *Mt* China
72D1 **Taibus Qi** China
73E5 **T'ai-chung** Taiwan
111B3 **Taieri** *R* NZ
72C2 **Taihang Shan** China
110C1 **Taihape** NZ
72E3 **Tai Hu** *L* China
108A3 **Tailem Bend** Aust
44B3 **Tain** Scot

73E5 **T'ai-nan** Taiwan
35C1 **Taiobeiras** Brazil
73E5 **T'ai pei** Taiwan
77C5 **Taiping** Malay
75C1 **Taira** Japan
78A3 **Tais** Indon
75A1 **Taisha** Japan
29B5 **Taitao,Pen de** Chile
73E5 **T'ai-tung** Taiwan
38K5 **Taivelkoski** Fin
69E4 **Taiwan** Republic, China
Taiwan Haixia = Formosa Str
72C2 **Taiyuan** China
72D3 **Taizhou** China
81C4 **Ta'izz** Yemen
82A2 **Tajikistan** Republic, Asia
50B1 **Tajo** *R* Spain
76B2 **Tak** Thai
74D3 **Takada** Japan
75A2 **Takahashi** Japan
110B2 **Takaka** NZ
74C4 **Takamatsu** Japan
74D3 **Takaoka** Japan
110B1 **Takapuna** NZ
74D3 **Takasaki** Japan
75B1 **Takayama** Japan
74D3 **Takefu** Japan
70A3 **Takengon** Indon
76C3 **Takeo** Camb
75A2 **Takeo** Japan
Take-shima = Tok-do
90A2 **Takestān** Iran
75A2 **Taketa** Japan
4G3 **Takijvak L** Can
99D1 **Takkaze** *R* Eritrea/Eth
13B1 **Takla L** Can
13B1 **Takla Landing** Can
12B2 **Takslesluk L** USA
12H2 **Taku Arm** *R* Can
23A1 **Tala** Mexico
59B3 **Talabanya** Hung
84C2 **Talagang** Pak
34A2 **Talagante** Chile
87B3 **Talaimannar** Sri Lanka
97C3 **Talak** *Desert* Region, Niger
78A3 **Talangbetutu** Indon
32A4 **Talara** Peru
50B2 **Talavera de la Reina** Spain
34A3 **Talca** Chile
34A3 **Talcahuano** Chile
86B2 **Tālcher** India
82B1 **Taldy Kurgan** Kazakhstan
71D4 **Taliabu** Indon
84B1 **Taligan** Afghan
99D2 **Tali Post** Sudan
78D4 **Taliwang** Indon
12D2 **Talkeetna** USA
12E2 **Talkeetna Mts** USA
17A1 **Talladega** USA
93D2 **Tall 'Afar** Iraq
17B1 **Tallahassee** USA
94C1 **Tall Bīsah** Syria
60B2 **Tallinn** Estonia
92C3 **Tall Kalakh** Syria
19B3 **Tallulah** USA
60D4 **Tal'noye** Ukraine
58C2 **Talpaki** Russian Fed
30B4 **Taltal** Chile
109C1 **Talwood** Aust
78D1 **Tamabo Range** *Mts* Malay
97B4 **Tamale** Ghana
96C2 **Tamanrasset** Alg
96C2 **Tamanrasset** *Watercourse* Alg
16B2 **Tamaqua** USA
Tamatave = Toamasina
23A2 **Tamazula** Jalisco, Mexico
23B2 **Tamazulapán** Mexico
23B1 **Tamazunchale** Mexico
97A3 **Tambacounda** Sen
61F3 **Tambov** Russian Fed
50A1 **Tambre** *R* Spain
98C2 **Tambura** Sudan

97A3 **Tamchaket** Maur
50A1 **Tamega** *R* Port
23B1 **Tamiahua** Mexico
87B2 **Tamil Nādu** State, India
76D2 **Tam Ky** Viet
17B2 **Tampa** USA
17B2 **Tampa B** USA
39J6 **Tampere** Fin
23B1 **Tampico** Mexico
68D2 **Tamsagbulag** Mongolia
86C2 **Tamu** Burma
23B1 **Tamuis** Mexico
109D2 **Tamworth** Aust
43D3 **Tamworth** Eng
38K4 **Tana** Nor
99D1 **Tana** *L* Eth
99E3 **Tana** *R* Kenya
38K5 **Tana** *R* Nor/Fin
75B2 **Tanabe** Japan
38K4 **Tanafjord** *Inlet* Nor
78D3 **Tanahgrogot** Indon
71E4 **Tanahmerah** Indon
12D1 **Tanana** USA
12E2 **Tanana** *R* USA
Tananarive = Antananarivo
47C2 **Tanaro** *R* Italy
74B2 **Tanch'ŏn** N Korea
34D3 **Tandil** Arg
78B2 **Tandjong Datu** *Pt* Indon
71E4 **Tandjung d'Urville** *C* Indon
78D3 **Tandjung Layar** *C* Indon
78B3 **Tandjung Lumut** *C* Indon
78D2 **Tandjung Mangkalihet** *C* Indon
78C3 **Tandjung Sambar** *C* Indon
78C2 **Tandjung Sirik** *C* Malay
71E4 **Tandjung Vals** *C* Indon
85B3 **Tando Adam** Pak
85B3 **Tando Muhammad Khan** Pak
108B2 **Tandou L** Aust
87B1 **Tāndūr** India
110C1 **Taneatua** NZ
76B2 **Tanen Range** *Mts* Burma/Thai
96B2 **Tanezrouft** *Desert Region* Alg
91C4 **Tang** Iran
99D3 **Tanga** Tanz
60E4 **Tanganrog** Russian Fed
99C3 **Tanganyika,L** Tanz/Zaire
96B1 **Tanger** Mor
82C2 **Tanggula Shan** *Mts* China
Tangier = Tanger
78A2 **Tangjungpinang** Indon
82C2 **Tangra Yumco** *L* China
72D2 **Tangshan** China
79B4 **Tangub** Phil
63C2 **Tanguy** Russian Fed
Tanintharyi = Tenasserim
79B4 **Tanjay** Phil
101D3 **Tanjona Ankaboa** *C* Madag
101D2 **Tanjona Babaomby** *C* Madag
101D2 **Tanjona Vilanandro** *C* Madag
101D3 **Tanjona Vohimena** *C* Madag
78C4 **Tanjong Bugel** *C* Indon
78B4 **Tanjong Cangkuang** *C* Indon
78C3 **Tanjong Puting** *C* Indon
78C3 **Tanjong Selatan** *C* Indon
78D3 **Tanjung** Indon

70A3 **Tanjungbalai** Indon
78A3 **Tanjung Jabung** *Pt* Indon
78B3 **Tanjungpandan** Indon
78B4 **Tanjung Priok** Indon
78D2 **Tanjungredeb** Indon
78D2 **Tanjungselor** Indon
84C2 **Tank** Pak
68B1 **Tannu Ola** *Mts* Russian Fed
97B4 **Tano** *R* Ghana
97C3 **Tanout** Niger
23B1 **Tanquián** Mexico
73E4 **Tan-shui** Taiwan
86A1 **Tansing** Nepal
95C1 **Tanta** Egypt
96A2 **Tan-Tan** Mor
4B3 **Tanunak** USA
99D3 **Tanzania** Republic, Africa
72A3 **Tao He** *R* China
72B2 **Taole** China
96B1 **Taourirt** Mor
60C2 **Tapa** Estonia
25C3 **Tapachula** Mexico
33F4 **Tapajós** *R* Brazil
34C3 **Tapalquén** Arg
70B4 **Tapan** Indon
111A3 **Tapanui** NZ
32D5 **Tapauá** *R* Brazil
85D4 **Tapi** *R* India
86B1 **Taplejung** Nepal
111B2 **Tapuaeniku** *Mt* NZ
35B2 **Tapuaritinga** Brazil
79B4 **Tapul Group** *Is* Phil
33E4 **Tapurucuara** Brazil
109D1 **Tara** Aust
65J4 **Tara** Russian Fed
65J4 **Tara** *R* Russian Fed
54A2 **Tara** *R* Bosnia-Herzegovina/Montenegro, Yugos
97D4 **Taraba** *R* Nig
30D2 **Tarabuco** Bol
Tarābulus = Tripoli
50B1 **Taracón** Spain
110C1 **Taradale** NZ
78D2 **Tarakan** Indon
44A3 **Taransay** *I* Scot
53C2 **Taranto** Italy
32B5 **Tarapoto** Peru
49C2 **Tarare** France
110C2 **Tararua Range** *Mts* NZ
96C2 **Tarat** Alg
110C1 **Tarawera** NZ
51B1 **Tarazona** Spain
44C3 **Tarbat Ness** *Pen* Scot
84C2 **Tarbela Res** Pak
42B2 **Tarbert** Strathclyde, Scot
44A3 **Tarbert** Western Isles, Scot
48C3 **Tarbes** France
106C4 **Tarcoola** Aust
109C2 **Tarcoon** Aust
109D2 **Taree** Aust
96A2 **Tarfaya** Mor
95A1 **Tarhūnah** Libya
91B5 **Tarif** UAE
30D3 **Tarija** Bol
87B2 **Tarikere** India
81C4 **Tarim** Yemen
99D3 **Tarime** Tanz
82C1 **Tarim He** *R* China
82C2 **Tarim Pendi** *Basin* China
84B2 **Tarin Kut** Afghan
18A1 **Tarkio** USA
79B2 **Tarlac** Phil
32B6 **Tarma** Peru
49C3 **Tarn** *R* France
59C2 **Tarnobrzeg** Pol
59C3 **Tarnów** Pol
107D3 **Taroom** Aust
51C1 **Tarragona** Spain
109C4 **Tarraleah** Aust
51C1 **Tarrasa** Spain
16C2 **Tarrytown** USA
92B2 **Tarsus** Turk
44D2 **Tartan** *Oilfield* N Sea

47D2 **Tartaro** *R* Italy
60C2 **Tartu** Estonia
92C3 **Tartūs** Syria
35C1 **Tarumirim** Brazil
70A3 **Tarutung** Indon
52B1 **Tarvisio** Italy
80D1 **Tashauz** Turkmenistan
86C1 **Tashigang** Bhutan
82A1 **Tashkent** Uzbekistan
65K4 **Tashtagol** Russian Fed
63A2 **Tashtyp** Russian Fed
78B4 **Tasikmalaya** Indon
94B2 **Tasil** Syria
6E2 **Tasiussaq** Greenland
95A3 **Tasker** *Well* Niger
110B2 **Tasman B** NZ
107D5 **Tasmania** *I* Aust
111B2 **Tasman Mts** NZ
109C4 **Tasman Pen** Aust
107E4 **Tasman S** NZ Aust
92C1 **Taşova** Turk
96C2 **Tassili du Hoggar** *Desert* Region, Alg
96C2 **Tassili N'jjer** *Desert* Region, Alg
96B2 **Tata** Mor
96D1 **Tataouine** Tunisia
65J4 **Tatarsk** Russian Fed
69G2 **Tatarskiy Proliv** *Str* Russian Fed
61G2 **Tatarstan** Russian Fed
75B1 **Tateyama** Japan
5G3 **Tathlina L** Can
12E2 **Tatitlek** USA
13C2 **Tatla Lake** Can
59B3 **Tatry** *Mts* Pol/Slovakia
75A2 **Tatsuno** Japan
85B4 **Tatta** Pak
35B2 **Tatuí** Brazil
93D2 **Tatvan** Turk
31C3 **Tauá** Brazil
35B2 **Taubaté** Brazil
110C1 **Taumarunui** NZ
101F1 **Taung** S Africa
76B2 **Taungdwingyi** Burma
76B1 **Taung-gyi** Burma
76A2 **Taungup** Burma
84C2 **Taunsa** Pak
43C4 **Taunton** Eng
16D2 **Taunton** USA
46E1 **Taunus** Region, Germany
110C1 **Taupo** NZ
110C1 **Taupo,L** NZ
58C1 **Taurage** Lithuania
110C1 **Tauranga** NZ
110C1 **Tauranga Harbour** *B* NZ
110B1 **Tauroa Pt** NZ
7A3 **Tavani** Can
7A3 **Tavani** Can
65H4 **Tavda** *R* Russian Fed
43B4 **Tavistock** Eng
76B3 **Tavoy** Burma
76B3 **Tavoy Pt** Burma
92A2 **Tavsanli** Turk
111B2 **Tawa** NZ
19A3 **Tawakoni,L** USA
14B2 **Tawas City** USA
70C3 **Tawau** Malay
98C1 **Taweisha** Sudan
79B4 **Tawitawi** *I* Phil
79B4 **Tawitawi Group** *Is* Phil
23B2 **Taxco** Mexico
23B2 **Taxcoco** Mexico
44C3 **Tay** *R* Scot
78C3 **Tayan** Indon
12B1 **Taylor** Alaska, USA
13C1 **Taylor** Can
14B2 **Taylor** Michigan, USA
19A3 **Taylor** Texas, USA
18C2 **Taylorville** USA
80B3 **Taymā'** S Arabia
63B1 **Taymura** *R* Russian Fed
76D3 **Tay Ninh** Viet
63B2 **Tayshet** Russian Fed

68B2 **Tayshir** Mongolia
44C3 **Tayside** Region, Scot
79A3 **Taytay** Phil
90D3 **Tayyebāt** Iran
96B1 **Taza** Mor
95B2 **Tazirbu** Libya
12E2 **Tazlina L** USA
64J3 **Tazovskiy** Russian Fed
65F5 **Tbilisi** Georgia
98B3 **Tchibanga** Gabon
95A2 **Tchigai,Plat du** Niger
97C3 **Tchin Tabaradene** Niger
98B2 **Tcholliré** Cam
58B2 **Tczew** Pol
111A3 **Te Anau** NZ
111A3 **Te Anau,L** NZ
110C1 **Te Aroha** NZ
110C1 **Te Awamutu** NZ
96C1 **Tébessa** Alg
23A2 **Teboman** Mexico
23A2 **Tecailtlán** Mexico
21B3 **Tecate** Mexico
61K2 **Techa** *R* Russian Fed
23A1 **Tecolotlán** Mexico
23A2 **Tecpan** Mexico
54C1 **Tecuci** Rom
18A1 **Tecumseh** USA
80E2 **Tedzhen** Turkmenistan
65H6 **Tedzhen** *R* Turkmenistan
42D2 **Tees** *R* Eng
33E4 **Tefé** Brazil
78B4 **Tegal** Indon
78B4 **Tegineneng** Indon
25D3 **Tegucigalpa** Honduras
21B3 **Tehachapi Mts** USA
21B2 **Tehachapi P** USA
4J3 **Tehek L** Can
90B2 **Tehrän** Iran
23B2 **Tehuacán** Mexico
23B2 **Tehuantepec** Mexico
23B2 **Tehuitzingo** Mexico
43B3 **Teifi** *R* Wales
50A2 **Tejo** *R* Port
23A2 **Tejupilco** Mexico
111B2 **Tekapo,L** NZ
82B1 **Tekeli** Kazakhstan
92A1 **Tekirdağ** Turk
55C2 **Tekir Dağlari** *Mts* Turk
86C2 **Teknaf** Bang
110C1 **Te Kuiti** NZ
25D3 **Tela** Honduras
94B2 **Tel Aviv Yafo** Israel
34B3 **Telén** Arg
21B2 **Telescope Peak** *Mt* USA
33F5 **Teles Pires** *R* Brazil
47D1 **Telfs** Austria
63A2 **Teli** Russian Fed
94B3 **Tell el Meise** *Mt* Jordan
12A1 **Teller** USA
87B2 **Tellicherry** India
77C5 **Telok Anson** Malay
78D2 **Telok Darvel** Malay
71E4 **Tělok Flamingo** *B* Indon
78C3 **Tělok Kumai** *B* Indon
78B4 **Tělok Pelabuanratu** *B* Indon
78D4 **Tělok Saleh** *B* Indon
78C3 **Tělok Sampit** *B* Indon
78B3 **Tělok Sukadona** *B* Indon
23B2 **Teloloapán** Mexico
64G3 **Tel'pos-iz** *Mt* Russian Fed
58C1 **Telšiai** Lithuania
71E4 **Teluk Berau** *B* Indon
78B4 **Telukbetung** Indom
70D4 **Teluk Bone** *B* Indon
71E4 **Teluk Cendrawasih** *B* Indon
78D3 **Teluk Mandar** *B* Indon
71D4 **Teluk Tolo** *B* Indon

Tisīyah

94C2 Tisīyah Syria
59C3 Tisza *R* Hung
86A2 Titlagarh India
54B2 Titov Veles
   Macedonia
98C2 Titule Zaïre
17B2 Titusville USA
43C4 Tiverton Eng
52B2 Tivoli Italy
23B2 Tixtla Mexico
99E2 Tiyeglow Somalia
23B2 Tizayuca Mexico
25D2 Tizimin Mexico
96C1 Tizi Ouzou Alg
96B2 Tiznit Mor
23A1 Tizpan el Alto Mexico
23B2 Tlacolula Mexico
23B2 Tlacotalpan Mexico
23A2 Tlalchana Mexico
23B2 Tlalnepantla Mexico
23B2 Tlalpan Mexico
23A1 Tlaltenango Mexico
23B2 Tlancualpicán
   Mexico
23B2 Tlapa Mexico
23B2 Tlapacoyan Mexico
23A1 Tlaquepaque Mexico
23B2 Tlaxcala Mexico
23B2 Tlaxcala State,
   Mexico
23B2 Tlaxiaco Mexico
96B1 Tlemcem Alg
101D2 Toamasina Madag
34C3 Toay Arg
75B2 Toba Japan
84B2 Toba and Kakar
   Ranges *Mts* Pak
27E4 Tobago *I*
   Caribbean S
13C2 Toba Inlet *Sd* Can
71D3 Tobelo Indon
14B1 Tobermory Can
44A3 Tobermory Scot
71E3 Tobi *I* Pacific O
21B1 Tobin,Mt USA
65H4 Tobol *R* Kazakhstan
70D4 Toboli Indon
65H4 Tobol'sk Russian Fed
   Tobruk = Tubruq
31B2 Tocantins *R* Brazil
31B3 Tocantins State,
   Brazil
17B1 Toccoa USA
47C1 Toce *R* Italy
30B3 Tocopilla Chile
30C3 Tocorpuri *Mt* Chile
32D1 Tocuyo *R* Ven
85D3 Toda India
47C1 Tödi *Mt* Switz
75A1 Todong S Korea
9B4 Todos Santos
   Mexico
13E2 Tofield Can
13B3 Tofino Can
12B3 Togiak USA
12B3 Togiak B USA
97C4 Togo Republic, Africa
72C1 Togtoh China
12F2 Tok USA
74E2 Tokachi *R* Japan
75B1 Tokamachi Japan
95C3 Tokar Sudan
69E4 Tokara Retto *Arch*
   Japan
92C1 Tokat Turk
74B3 Tŏkchŏk-kundo *Arch*
   S Korea
75A1 Tok-do *I* S Korea
82B1 Tokmak Kirghizia
110C1 Tokomaru Bay NZ
12H3 Toku *R* Can/USA
78C3 Tokung Indon
69E4 Tokuno *I* Japan
74C4 Tokushima Japan
75A2 Tokuyama Japan
74D3 Tōkyō Japan
110C1 Tolaga Bay NZ
101D3 Tôlañaro Madag
30F3 Toledo Brazil
50B2 Toledo Spain
14B2 Toledo USA
19B3 Toledo Bend Res
   USA
101D3 Toliara Madag

23B1 Toliman Mexico
32B3 Tolina *Mt* Colombia
51B1 Tolosa Spain
29B3 Toltén Chile
23B2 Toluca Mexico
61G3 Tol'yatti Russian Fed
74E2 Tomakomai Japan
78D1 Tomani Malay
58C2 Tomaszów
   Mazowiecka Pol
11B3 Tombigbee *R* USA
98B3 Tomboco Angola
35C2 Tombos Brazil
97B3 Tombouctou Mali
100A2 Tombua Angola
34A3 Tomé Chile
50B2 Tomelloso Spain
50A2 Tomer Port
106B3 Tomkinson Range
   Mts Aust
63E2 Tommot
   Russian Fed
55B2 Tomorrit *Mt* Alb
65K4 Tomsk Russian Fed
16B3 Toms River USA
25C3 Tonalá Mexico
20C1 Tonasket USA
15C2 Tonawanda USA
105H4 Tonga *Is* Pacific O
101H1 Tongaat S Africa
73D3 Tongcheng China
72B2 Tongchuan China
72A2 Tongde China
46C1 Tongeren Belg
76E2 Tonggu Jiao *I* China
73A5 Tonghai China
74B2 Tonghua China
74B3 Tongjosŏn-man
   N Korea
76D1 Tongkin,G of China/
   Viet
72E1 Tonglia China
73D3 Tongling China
108B2 Tongo Aust
34A2 Tongoy Chile
73B4 Tongren Guizhou,
   China
72A2 Tongren Qinghai,
   China
86C1 Tongsa Bhutan
76B1 Tongta Burma
68B3 Tongtian He *R*
   China
44B2 Tongue Eng
72D2 Tong Xian China
72B2 Tongxin China
73B4 Tongzi China
9C4 Tonich Mexico
99C2 Tonj Sudan
85D3 Tonk India
18A2 Tonkawa USA
76C3 Tonle Sap *L* Camb
21B2 Tonopah USA
12E2 Tonsina USA
8B2 Tooele USA
109C1 Toogoolawah Aust
108B1 Toompine Aust
109D1 Toowoomba Aust
22C1 Topaz L USA
18A2 Topeka USA
9C4 Topolobampo
   Mexico
20B1 Toppenish USA
99D2 Tor Eth
55C3 Torbali Turk
90C2 Torbat-e-Heydarīyeh
   Iran
90D2 Torbat-e Jām Iran
12D2 Torbert,Mt USA
50A1 Tordesillas Spain
56C2 Torgau Germany
46B1 Torhout Belg
69G3 Tori *I* Japan
47B2 Torino Italy
99D2 Torit Sudan
35A1 Torixoreu Brazil
50A1 Tormes *R* Spain
13E2 Tornado Mt Can
38J5 Torne L Sweden
38H5 Torneträsk Sweden
7D4 Torngat *Mts* Can
38J5 Tornio Fin
34C3 Tornquist Arg
15C2 Toronto Can

60D2 Toropets
   Russian Fed
99D2 Tororo Uganda
92B2 Toros Dağlari *Mts*
   Turk
43C4 Torquay Eng
22C4 Torrance USA
50A2 Torrão Port
51C1 Torreblanca Spain
53B2 Torre del Greco Italy
50B1 Torrelavega Spain
50B2 Torremolinos Spain
108A2 Torrens,L Aust
24B2 Torreón Mexico
47B2 Torre Pellice Italy
107D2 Torres Str Aust
50A2 Torres Vedras Port
16C2 Torrington
   Connecticut, USA
8C2 Torrington
   Wyoming, USA
9C4 Torrón Mexico
38D3 Tórshavn Føroyar
47C2 Tortona Italy
51C1 Tortosa Spain
90C2 Torūd Iran
58B2 Toruń Pol
40B2 Tory *I* Irish Rep
60D2 Torzhok Russian Fed
75A2 Tosa Japan
74C4 Tosa-shimizu Japan
74C4 Tosa-wan *B* Japan
75B2 To-shima *I* Japan
   Toshkent = Tashkent
60D2 Tosno Russian Fed
75A2 Tosu Japan
92B1 Tosya Turk
61F1 Tot'ma Russian Fed
43C4 Totnes Eng
33F2 Totness Surinam
23B2 Totolapan Mexico
51B2 Totona Spain
109C2 Tottenham Aust
74C3 Tottori Japan
97B4 Touba Ivory Coast
97A3 Touba Sen
96B1 Toubkal *Mt* Mor
97B3 Tougan Burkina
96C1 Touggourt Alg
97A3 Tougué Guinea
46C2 Toul France
49D3 Toulon France
48C3 Toulouse France
97B4 Toumodi Ivory Coast
76B2 Toungoo Burma
46B1 Tourcoing France
96A2 Tourine Maur
46B1 Tournai Belg
48C2 Tours France
74E2 Towada Japan
74E2 Towada-ko *L* Japan
15C2 Towanda USA
107D2 Townsville Aust
16A3 Towson USA
43C4 Towy *R* Wales
74D3 Toyama Japan
75B1 Toyama-wan *B*
   Japan
75B2 Toyohashi Japan
75B2 Toyonaka Japan
75A1 Toyooka Japan
74D3 Toyota Japan
96C1 Tozeur Tunisia
46D2 Traben-Trarbach
   Germany
93C1 Trabzon Turk
22B2 Tracy California,
   USA
34A3 Traiguén Chile
13D3 Trail Can
41B3 Tralee Irish Rep
45B2 Tralee B Irish Rep
45C2 Tramore Irish Rep
39G7 Tranås Sweden
77B4 Trang Thai
71E4 Trangan *I* Indon
109C2 Trangie Aust
12E2 Transalaskan Pipeline
   Transylvanian Alps =
   Muntii Carpaţii
   Meridionali
53B3 Trapani Italy
109C3 Traralgon Aust

97A3 Trarza Region, Maur
76C3 Trat Thai
108B2 Traveller's *L* Aust
56C2 Travemünde
   Germany
14A2 Traverse City USA
12C1 Traverse Peak *Mt*
   USA
111B2 Travers,Mt NZ
47C2 Trebbia *R* Italy
59B3 Třebíč
   Czech Republic
54A2 Trebinje Bosnia-
   Herzegovina
57C3 Trebon
   Czech Republic
29F2 Treinta y Tres Urug
29C4 Trelew Arg
39G7 Trelleborg Sweden
43B3 Tremadog B Wales
15D1 Tremblant,Mt Can
13C2 Trembleur L Can
16A2 Tremont USA
59B3 Trenčin Slovakia
34C3 Trenque Lauquén
   Arg
43D3 Trent *R* Eng
47D1 Trentino Region,
   Italy
47D1 Trento Italy
15C2 Trenton Can
18B1 Trenton Missouri,
   USA
16B2 Trenton New Jersey,
   USA
7E5 Trepassey Can
34C3 Tres Arroyos Arg
35B2 Tres Corações Brazil
30F3 Três Lagoas Brazil
34C3 Tres Lomas Arg
22B2 Três Pinos USA
35C2 Três Rios Brazil
47C2 Treviglio Italy
47E2 Treviso Italy
47C2 Trezzo Italy
87B2 Trichūr India
108C2 Trida Aust
46D2 Trier Germany
52B1 Trieste Italy
45C2 Trim Irish Rep
87C3 Trincomalee
   Sri Lanka
33E6 Trinidad Bol
29E2 Trinidad Urug
9C3 Trinidad USA
34C3 Trinidad *I* Arg
27E4 Trinidad *I*
   Caribbean S
103G6 Trindade *I* Atlantic O
27E4 Trinidad & Tobago
   Republic Caribbean S
19A3 Trinity USA
9D3 Trinity *R* USA
7E5 Trinity B Can
12D3 Trinity Is USA
17A1 Trion USA
94B1 Tripoli Leb
95A1 Tripoli Libya
55B3 Trípolis Greece
86C2 Tripura State, India
103H6 Tristan da Cunha *Is*
   Atlantic O
87B3 Trivandrum India
59B3 Trnava Slovakia
107E1 Trobriand Is PNG
15D1 Trois-Riviéres Can
65H4 Troitsk Russian Fed
39G7 Trollhättan Sweden
38F6 Trollheimen *Mt* Nor
89K9 Tromelin *I* Indian O
38H5 Tromsø Nor
38G6 Trondheim Nor
38G6 Trondheimfjord *Inlet*
   Nor
42B2 Troon Scot
102J3 Tropic of Cancer
103J6 Tropic of Capricorn
96B2 Troudenni Mali
7A4 Trout L Ontario, Can
17A1 Troy Alabama, USA
16C1 Troy New York, USA
14B2 Troy Ohio, USA
54B2 Troyan Bulg
49C2 Troyes France

91B5 **Trucial Coast** Region, UAE	93C3 **Tulūl ash Shāmīyah** *Desert Region* Syria/ S Arabia	18A2 **Turtle Creek Res** USA	34D3 **Udaquoila** Arg
21A2 **Truckee** *R* USA	63C2 **Tulun** Russian Fed	13F2 **Turtle L** Can	39G7 **Uddevalla** Sweden
25D3 **Trujillo** Honduras	78C4 **Tulungagung** Indon	63A1 **Turukhansk** Russian Fed	38H5 **Uddjaur** *L* Sweden
32B5 **Trujillo** Peru	32B3 **Tumaco** Colombia	68C1 **Turuntayevo** Russian Fed	87B1 **Udgir** India
50A2 **Trujillo** Spain	109C3 **Tumbarumba** Aust	35A1 **Turvo** *R* Goias, Brazil	84D2 **Udhampur** India
32C2 **Trujillo** Ven	32A4 **Tumbes** Ecuador	35B2 **Turvo** *R* São Paulo, Brazil	61H2 **Udmurtskaya Respublika,** Russian Fed
109C2 **Trundle** Aust	108A2 **Tumby Bay** Aust	58C2 **Tur'ya** *R* Ukraine	76C2 **Udon Thani** Thai
7D5 **Truro** Can	74B2 **Tumen** China	19C3 **Tuscaloosa** USA	63F2 **Udskaya Guba** *B* Russian Fed
43B4 **Truro** Eng	87B2 **Tumkür** India	18C2 **Tuscola** USA	87A2 **Udupi** India
68B2 **Tsagaan Nuur** *L* Mongolia	77C4 **Tumpat** Malay	90C3 **Tusharik** Iran	75B1 **Ueda** Japan
68B1 **Tsagan-Tologoy** Russian Fed	85D4 **Tumsar** India	**Tutera = Tudela**	99C2 **Uele** *R* Zaïre
101D2 **Tsaratanana** Madag	97B3 **Tumu** Ghana	87B3 **Tuticorin** India	56C2 **Uelzen** Germany
100B3 **Tsau** Botswana	109C3 **Tumut** Aust	54C2 **Tutrakan** Bulg	98C2 **Uere** *R* Zaïre
99D3 **Tsavo** Kenya	109C3 **Tumut** *R* Aust	57B3 **Tuttlingen** Germany	61J3 **Ufa** Russian Fed
99D3 **Tsavo Nat Pk** Kenya	27L1 **Tunapuna** Trinidad	68C2 **Tuul Gol** *R* Mongolia	61J2 **Ufa** *R* Russian Fed
65J4 **Tselinograd** Kazakhstan	93C2 **Tunceli** Turk	105G4 **Tuvalu** *Is* Pacific O	100A3 **Ugab** *R* Namibia
100A3 **Tses** Namibia	99D3 **Tunduma** Zambia	63B2 **Tuvinskaya Respublika,** Russian Fed	99D3 **Ugaila** *R* Tanz
68C2 **Tsetserleg** Mongolia	101C2 **Tunduru** Tanz	23A2 **Tuxpan** Jalisco, Mexico	12D3 **Ugak B** USA
97C4 **Tsévié** Togo	54C2 **Tundzha** *R* Bulg	24B2 **Tuxpan** Nayarit, Mexico	99D2 **Uganda** Republic, Africa
100B3 **Tshabong** Botswana	87B1 **Tungabhadra** *R* India	23B1 **Tuxpan** Veracruz, Mexico	12C3 **Ugashik B** USA
100B3 **Tshane** Botswana	68D4 **Tung-Chiang** Taiwan	23B2 **Tuxtepec** Mexico	12C3 **Ugashik L** USA
98B3 **Tshela** Zaïre	38B2 **Tungnafellsjökull** *Mts* Iceland	25C3 **Tuxtla Gutiérrez** Mexico	47B2 **Ugine** France
98C3 **Tshibala** Zaïre	12J2 **Tungsten** Can	50A1 **Túy** Spain	69G2 **Uglegorsk** Russian Fed
98C3 **Tshikapa** Zaïre	63B1 **Tunguska** *R* Russian Fed	76D3 **Tuy Hoa** Viet	60E2 **Uglich** Russian Fed
98C3 **Tshuapa** *R* Zaïre	87C1 **Tuni** India	92B2 **Tuz Gölü** *Salt L* Turk	60E3 **Ugra** *R* Russian Fed
101D3 **Tsihombe** Madag	96D1 **Tunis** Tunisia	93D3 **Tuz Khurmātū** Iraq	44A3 **Uig** Scot
61F4 **Tsimlyanskoye Vodokhranilishche** *Res* Russian Fed	88E4 **Tunisia** Republic, N Africa	54A2 **Tuzla** Bosnia-Herzegovina	98B3 **Uige** Angola
Tsinan = Jinan	32C2 **Tunja** Colombia	60E2 **Tver'** Russian Fed	61H4 **Uil** Kazakhstan
Tsingtao = Qingdao	12B2 **Tuntutuliak** USA	42C2 **Tweed** *R* Eng/Scot	8B2 **Uinta Mts** USA
101D2 **Tsiroanomandidy** Madag	12B2 **Tununak** USA	109D1 **Tweed Heads** Aust	100B4 **Uitenhage** S Africa
13B2 **Tsitsutl Peak** *Mt* Can	34B2 **Tunuyán** Arg	42C2 **Tweedsmuir Hills** Scot	59C3 **Ujfehértó** Hung
58D2 **Tsna** *R* Belorussia	34B2 **Tunuyán** *R* Arg	7E5 **Twillingate** Can	75B2 **Uji** Japan
72B1 **Tsogt Ovoo** Mongolia	22C2 **Tuolumne Meadows** USA	8B2 **Twin Falls** USA	99C3 **Ujiji** Tanz
68C2 **Tsomog** Mongolia	35A2 **Tupã** Brazil	111B2 **Twins,The** *Mt* NZ	30C3 **Ujina** Chile
75B2 **Tsu** Japan	35B1 **Tupaciguara** Brazil	14A2 **Two Rivers** USA	85D4 **Ujjain** India
75B1 **Tsubata** Japan	19C3 **Tupelo** USA	63E2 **Tygda** Russian Fed	70C4 **Ujung Pandang** Indon
74E3 **Tsuchiura** Japan	30C3 **Tupiza** Bol	19A3 **Tyler** USA	99D3 **Ukerewe** *I* Tanz
74E2 **Tsugaru-kaikyō** *Str* Japan	15D2 **Tupper Lake** USA	65K3 **Tym** *R* Russian Fed	86C1 **Ukhrul** India
100A2 **Tsumeb** Namibia	34B2 **Tupungato** Arg	69G1 **Tymovskoye** Russian Fed	21A2 **Ukiah** California, USA
100A3 **Tsumis** Namibia	29C2 **Tupungato** *Mt* Arg	42D2 **Tyne** *R* Eng	20C1 **Ukiah** Oregon, USA
75B1 **Tsunugi** Japan	86C1 **Tura** India	42D2 **Tyne and Wear** Metropolitan County, Eng	58C1 **Ukmerge** Lithuania
74D3 **Tsuruga** Japan	63C1 **Tura** Russian Fed	42D2 **Tynemouth** Eng	60C4 **Ukraine** Republic, Europe
74D3 **Tsuruoka** Japan	61K2 **Tura** *R* Russian Fed	38G6 **Tynset** Nor	68C2 **Ulaanbaatar** Mongolia
75B1 **Tsushima** Japan	90C2 **Turān** Iran	12D3 **Tyonek** USA	68B2 **Ulaangom** Mongolia
74B4 **Tsushima** *I* Japan	63B2 **Turan** Russian Fed	94B2 **Tyr** Leb	72C1 **Ulaan Uul** Mongolia
74C3 **Tsuyama** Japan	93C3 **Turayf** S Arabia	**Tyre = Tyr**	82C1 **Ulangar Hu** *L* China
50A1 **Tua** *R* Port	80E3 **Turbat** Pak	45C1 **Tyrone** County, N Ire	68C1 **Ulan Ude** Russian Fed
45B2 **Tuam** Irish Rep	32B2 **Turbo** Colombia	108B3 **Tyrrell,L** Aust	68B3 **Ulan Ul Hu** *L* China
60E5 **Tuapse** Russian Fed	54B1 **Turda** Rom	53B2 **Tyrrhenian S** Italy	34B2 **Ulapes** Arg
111A3 **Tuatapere** NZ	63A3 **Turfan Depression** China	65H4 **Tyumen'** Russian Fed	74B3 **Ulchin** S Korea
30G4 **Tubarão** Brazil	65H4 **Turgay** Kazakhstan	43B3 **Tywyn** Wales	54A2 **Ulcinj** Montenegro, Yugos
94B2 **Tubas** Israel	63B3 **Turgen Uul** *Mt* Mongolia	55B3 **Tzoumérka** *Mt* Greece	68D2 **Uldz** Mongolia
79A4 **Tubbataha Reefs** *Is* Phil	54C2 **Turgovishte** Bulg		68B2 **Uliastay** Mongolia
57B3 **Tübingen** Germany	92A2 **Turgutlu** Turk	**U**	58D1 **Ulla** Lithuania
95B1 **Tubruq** Libya	92C1 **Turhal** Turk		109D3 **Ulladulla** Aust
16B3 **Tuckerton** USA	39K7 **Türi** Estonia	99E2 **Uarsciek** Somalia	44B3 **Ullapool** Scot
9B3 **Tucson** USA	51B2 **Turia** *R* Spain	35C2 **Ubá** Brazil	38H5 **Ullsfjorden** *Inlet* Nor
30C4 **Tucumán** State, Arg	**Turin = Torino**	35C1 **Ubaí** Brazil	42C2 **Ullswater** *L* Eng
34B2 **Tucunuco** Arg	61K2 **Turinsk** Russian Fed	98B2 **Ubangi** *R* CAR	74C3 **Ullung-do** *I* S Korea
33E2 **Tucupita** Ven	69F2 **Turiy Rog** Russian Fed	47B2 **Ubaye** *R* France	57C3 **Ulm** Germany
51B1 **Tudela** Spain	99D2 **Turkana,L** Kenya/Eth	75A2 **Ube** Japan	108A1 **Uloowaranie,L** Aust
93C3 **Tudmur** Syria	80E1 **Turkestan** Region, C Asia	50B2 **Ubeda** Spain	74B3 **Ulsan** S Korea
101H1 **Tugela** *R* S Africa	82A1 **Turkestan** Kazakhstan	6E2 **Ubekendt Ejland** *I* Greenland	45C1 **Ulster** Region, N Ire
109D2 **Tuggerah** *L* Aust	92C2 **Turkey** Republic, W Asia	35B1 **Uberaba** Brazil	65K5 **Ulungur He** *R* China
12D3 **Tugidak** *I* USA	80D1 **Turkmenistan** Republic, Asia	35B1 **Uberlândia** Brazil	65K5 **Ulungur Hu** *L* China
79B2 **Tuguegarao** Phil	90B2 **Turkmenskiy Zaliv** *B* Turkmenistan	76C2 **Ubon Ratchathani** Thai	44A3 **Ulva** *I* Scot
63F2 **Tugur** Russian Fed	27C2 **Turks Is** Caribbean S	58D2 **Ubort** *R* Belorussia	42C2 **Ulverston** Eng
72D2 **Tuhai He** *R* China	39J6 **Turku** Fin	98C3 **Ubundi** Zaïre	109C4 **Ulverstone** Aust
4E3 **Tuktoyaktuk** USA	99D2 **Turkwel** *R* Kenya	32C5 **Ucayali** *R* Peru	63G2 **Ulya** *R* Russian Fed
58C1 **Tukums** Latvia	22B2 **Turlock** USA	84C3 **Uch** Pak	60D4 **Uman** Ukraine
99D3 **Tukuyu** Tanz	22B2 **Turlock L** USA	63F2 **Uchar** *R* Russian Fed	6E2 **Umanak** Greenland
84B1 **Tukzar** Afghan	110C2 **Turnagain,C** NZ	74E2 **Uchiura-wan** *B* Japan	86A2 **Umaria** India
60E3 **Tula** Russian Fed	25D3 **Turneffe** *I* Belize	63B2 **Uda** *R* Russian Fed	85B3 **Umarkot** Pak
23B1 **Tulancingo** Mexico	16C1 **Turners Falls** USA	85C4 **Udaipur** India	108A1 **Umaroona,L** Aust
78A3 **Tulangbawang** *R* Indon	46C1 **Turnhout** Belg	86B1 **Udaipur Garhi** Nepal	20C1 **Umatilla** USA
32B3 **Tulcán** Colombia	13F1 **Turnor L** Can		38L5 **Umba** Russian Fed
60C5 **Tulcea** Rom	54B2 **Turnu Măgurele** Rom		99D3 **Umba** *R* Tanz
100B3 **Tuli** Zim	63A3 **Turpan** China		38H6 **Ume** *R* Sweden
94B2 **Tulkarm** Israel	26B2 **Turquino** *Mt* Cuba		38J6 **Umea** Sweden
48C2 **Tulle** France	80E1 **Turtkul'** Uzbekistan		101H1 **Umfolozi** *R* S Africa
19B3 **Tullos** USA			4C3 **Umiat** USA
45C2 **Tullow** Irish Rep			91C4 **Umm al Qaiwain** UAE
18A2 **Tulsa** USA			

Umm as Samīm

61F4 **Volgograd** Russian Fed
61G3 **Volgogradskoye Vodokhranilishche** *Res* Russian Fed
60D2 **Volkhov** Russian Fed
60D2 **Volkhov** *R* Russian Fed
58C2 **Volkovysk** Belorussia
101G1 **Volksrust** S Africa
61F2 **Vologda** Russian Fed
48B2 **Volognes** France
55B3 **Vólos** Greece
61G3 **Vol'sk** Russian Fed
22B2 **Volta** USA
97B3 **Volta Blanche** *R* Burkina
97B4 **Volta,L** Ghana
97B3 **Volta Noire** *R* Burkina
35C2 **Volta Redonda** Brazil
97B3 **Volta Rouge** *R* Burkina
61F4 **Volzhskiy** Russian Fed
12D2 **Von Frank Mt** USA
6J3 **Vopnafjörður** Iceland
47C1 **Voralberg** Province, Austria
47C1 **Vorder Rhein** *R* Switz
56C1 **Vordingborg** Den
64H3 **Vorkuta** Russian Fed
39G6 **Vorma** *R* Nor
60E3 **Voronezh** Russian Fed
38M5 **Voron'ya** *R* Russian Fed
39K7 **Võru** Estonia
49D2 **Vosges** *Mt* France
39F6 **Voss** Nor
63B2 **Vostochnyy Sayan** *Mts* Russian Fed
112B9 **Vostok** *Base* Ant
61H2 **Votkinsk** Russian Fed
46C2 **Vouziers** France
60D4 **Voznesensk** Ukraine
54B2 **Vranje** Serbia, Yugos
54B2 **Vratsa** Bulg
54A1 **Vrbas** Serbia, Yugos
52C2 **Vrbas** *R* Serbia, Yugos
52B1 **Vrbovsko** Bosnia-Herzegovina
101G1 **Vrede** S Africa
33F2 **Vreed en Hoop** Guyana
54B1 **Vršac** Serbia, Yugos
52C2 **Vrtoče** Bosnia-Herzegovina
100B3 **Vryburg** S Africa
101H1 **Vryheid** S Africa
54A1 **Vukovar** Croatia
13E2 **Vulcan** Can
53B3 **Vulcano** *I* Italy
77D3 **Vung Tau** Viet
38J5 **Vuollerim** Sweden
38L6 **Vyartsilya** Russian Fed
61H2 **Vyatka** *R* Russian Fed
69F2 **Vyazemskiy** Russian Fed
60D2 **Vyaz'ma** Russian Fed
61F2 **Vyazniki** Russian Fed
60C1 **Vyborg** Russian Fed
64G3 **Vym'** *R* Russian Fed
43C3 **Vyrnwy** *R* Wales
60D2 **Vyshiy Volochek** Russian Fed
59B3 **Vyškov** Czech Republic
60E1 **Vytegra** Russian Fed

W

97B3 **Wa** Ghana
13E1 **Wabasca** Can
5G4 **Wabasca** *R* Can
13E1 **Wabasca L** Can
14A2 **Wabash** USA
14A3 **Wabash** *R* USA
5J4 **Wabowden** Can
7D4 **Wabush** Can
17B2 **Waccasassa B** USA
16D1 **Wachusett Res** USA
19A3 **Waco** USA
85B3 **Wad** Pak
95A2 **Waddān** Libya
5F4 **Waddington,Mt** Can
93E4 **Wadi al Bātin** *Watercourse* Iraq
93D3 **Wadi al Ghudāf** *Watercourse* Iraq
94C2 **Wadi al Harīr** *V* Syria
93D3 **Wadi al Mirah** *Watercourse* Iraq/ S Arabia
93D3 **Wadi al Ubayyid** *Watercourse* Iraq
93D3 **Wadi Ar'ar** *Watercourse* S Arabia
91A5 **Wadi as Hsabā'** *Watercourse* S Arabia
92C3 **Wadi as Sirhān** *V* Jordan/S Arabia
94C2 **Wadi az Zaydi** *V* Syria
94C3 **Wadi edh Dhab'i** *V* Jordan
94A3 **Wadi el 'Arish** *V* Egypt
94C3 **Wadi el Ghadaf** *V* Jordan
94B3 **Wadi el Hasa** *V* Jordan
94C3 **Wadi el Janab** *V* Jordan
94B3 **Wadi el Jeib** *V* Israel/Jordan
95B3 **Wadi el Milk** *Watercourse* Sudan
92A3 **Wadi el Natrun** *Watercourse* Egypt
94B3 **Wadi es Sir** Jordan
94B3 **Wadi Fidan** *V* Jordan
94B3 **Wadi Hareidin** *V* Egypt
93D3 **Wadi Hawrān** *R* Iraq
95B3 **Wadi Howa** *Watercourse* Sudan
98C1 **Wadi Ibra** *Watercourse* Sudan
94C2 **Wadi Luhfi** *Watercourse* Jordan
94B3 **Wadi Mujib** *V* Jordan
94B3 **Wadi Qītaiya** *V* Egypt
80B3 **Wadi Sha'it** *Watercourse* Egypt
99D1 **Wad Medani** Sudan
93E4 **Wafra** Kuwait
6B3 **Wager B** Can
6A3 **Wager Bay** Can
109C3 **Wagga Wagga** Aust
106A4 **Wagin** Aust
95A2 **Wāḥa** Libya
21C4 **Wahaiwa** Hawaiian Is
18A1 **Wahoo** USA
8D2 **Wahpeton** USA
87A1 **Wai** India
111B2 **Waiau** NZ
111A3 **Waiau** *R* NZ
111B2 **Waiau** *R* NZ
71E3 **Waigeo** *I* Indon
110C1 **Waihi** NZ
110C1 **Waikaremoana,L** NZ
110C1 **Waikato** *R* NZ
108A2 **Waikerie** Aust
111B3 **Waikouaiti** NZ
21C4 **Wailuku** Hawaiian Is
111B2 **Waimakariri** *R* NZ
111B2 **Waimate** NZ
21C4 **Waimea** Hawaiian Is
106B1 **Waingapu** Indon
13E2 **Wainwright** Can
4B2 **Wainwright** USA
111B2 **Waipara** NZ
110C2 **Waipukurau** NZ
111C2 **Wairarapa,L** NZ
111B2 **Wairau** *R* NZ
110C1 **Wairoa** NZ
110C1 **Wairoa** *R* NZ
111B2 **Waitaki** *R* NZ
110B1 **Waitara** NZ
110C1 **Waitomo** NZ
110B1 **Waiuku** NZ
75B1 **Wajima** Japan
99E2 **Wajir** Kenya
75B1 **Wakasa-wan** *B* Japan
111A3 **Wakatipu,L** NZ
74D4 **Wakayama** Japan
42D3 **Wakefield** Eng
27H1 **Wakefield** Jamaica
16D2 **Wakefield** Rhode Island, USA
76B2 **Wakema** Burma
69G2 **Wakkanai** Japan
108B3 **Wakool** *R* Aust
59B2 **Walbrzych** Pol
109D2 **Walcha** Aust
58B2 **Walcz** Pol
46D1 **Waldbröl** Germany
16B2 **Walden** USA
43C3 **Wales** Country, UK
12A1 **Wales** USA
6B3 **Wales I** Can
109C2 **Walgett** Aust
112B4 **Walgreen Coast** Region, Ant
99C3 **Walikale** Zaïre
21B2 **Walker** *L* USA
14B2 **Walkerton** Can
8B2 **Wallace** USA
108A2 **Wallaroo** Aust
109C3 **Walla Walla** Aust
20C1 **Walla Walla** USA
16C2 **Wallingford** USA
105H4 **Wallis and Futuna** *Is* Pacific O
20C1 **Wallowa** USA
20C1 **Wallowa Mts** *Mts* USA
109C1 **Wallumbilla** Aust
18B2 **Walnut Ridge** USA
110C1 **Walouru** NZ
43D3 **Walsall** Eng
9C3 **Walsenburg** USA
9C3 **Walsenburgh** USA
17B1 **Walterboro** USA
17A1 **Walter F George Res** USA
16D1 **Waltham** USA
100A3 **Walvis Bay** Namibia
103J6 **Walvis Ridge** Atlantic O
97C4 **Wamba** Nig
98B3 **Wamba** *R* Zaïre
18A2 **Wamego** USA
84B2 **Wana** Pak
108B1 **Wanaaring** Aust
111A2 **Wanaka** NZ
111A2 **Wanaka,L** NZ
14B1 **Wanapitei L** Can
109C1 **Wandoan** Aust
108B3 **Wanganella** Aust
110C1 **Wanganui** NZ
110C1 **Wanganui** *R* NZ
109C3 **Wangaratta** Aust
99E2 **Wanle Weyne** Somalia
76E2 **Wanning** China
87B1 **Wanparti** India
73B3 **Wanxian** China
73B3 **Wanyuan** China
13D2 **Wapiti** *R* Can
18B2 **Wappapello,L** USA
16C2 **Wappingers Falls** USA
87B1 **Warangal** India
109C4 **Waratah** Aust
108C3 **Waratah B** Aust
108C3 **Warburton** Aust
108A1 **Warburton** *R* Aust
109C1 **Ward** *R* Aust
101G1 **Warden** S Africa
99E2 **Warder** Eth
85D4 **Wardha** India
111A3 **Ware** Can
16C1 **Ware** USA
16D2 **Wareham** USA
109D1 **Warialda** Aust
76C2 **Warin Chamrap** Thai
100B3 **Warmbad** S Africa
16B2 **Warminster** USA
21B2 **Warm Springs** USA
56C2 **Warnemünde** Germany
20B2 **Warner Mts** USA
17B1 **Warner Robins** USA
108B3 **Warracknabeal** Aust
108A1 **Warrandirinna,L** Aust
107D3 **Warrego** *R* Aust
19B3 **Warren** Arkansas, USA
109C2 **Warren** Aust
16D2 **Warren** Massachusetts, USA
14B2 **Warren** Ohio, USA
15C2 **Warren** Pennsylvania, USA
45C1 **Warrenpoint** N Ire
18B2 **Warrensburg** USA
101F1 **Warrenton** S Africa
15C3 **Warrenton** USA
97C4 **Warri** Nig
108A1 **Warrina** Aust
42C3 **Warrington** Eng
108B3 **Warrnambool** Aust
Warsaw = Warszawa
58C2 **Warszawa** Pol
59B2 **Warta** *R* Pol
109D1 **Warwick** Aust
43D3 **Warwick** County, Eng
43D3 **Warwick** Eng
16B2 **Warwick** New York, USA
16D2 **Warwick** Rhode Island, USA
8B3 **Wasatch Range** *Mts* USA
101H1 **Wasbank** S Africa
21B2 **Wasco** USA
4H2 **Washburn L** Can
85D4 **Wāshīm** India
10C3 **Washington** District of Columbia, USA
17B1 **Washington** Georgia, USA
14A3 **Washington** Indiana, USA
18B2 **Washington** Missouri, USA
16B2 **Washington** New Jersey, USA
14B2 **Washington** Pennsylvania, USA
8A2 **Washington** State, USA
14B3 **Washington Court House** USA
6D1 **Washington Land** Can
15D2 **Washington,Mt** USA
43E3 **Wash,The** Eng
85A3 **Washuk** Pak
12E2 **Wasilla** USA
7C4 **Waskaganish** Can
26A4 **Waspán** Nic
70D4 **Watampone** Indon
16C2 **Waterbury** USA
45C2 **Waterford** County, Irish Rep
41B3 **Waterford** Irish Rep
45C2 **Waterford Harbour** Irish Rep
46C1 **Waterloo** Belg
10A2 **Waterloo** USA
15C2 **Watertown** New York, USA
101H1 **Waterval-Boven** S Africa
10D2 **Waterville** Maine, USA
16C1 **Watervliet** USA
5G4 **Waterways** Can
43D4 **Watford** Eng
15C2 **Watkins Glen** USA
8C1 **Watrous** Can
99C2 **Watsa** Zaïre
12J2 **Watson Lake** Can
22B2 **Watsonville** USA
71F4 **Wau** PNG
99C2 **Wau** Sudan
7B5 **Waua** Can
109D2 **Wauchope** Aust
17B2 **Wauchula** USA
14B2 **Waukegan** USA
10B2 **Wausau** USA

Winifreda

19B3 **Yazoo City** USA
76B2 **Ye** Burma
59D3 **Yedintsy** Moldavia
108A2 **Yeelanna** Aust
60E3 **Yefremov** Russian Fed
61F4 **Yegorlyk** *R* Russian Fed
99D2 **Yei** Sudan
65H4 **Yekaterinburg** Russian Fed
60E3 **Yelets** Russian Fed
44E1 **Yell** *I* Scot
87C1 **Yellandu** India
Yellow = Huang He
8B1 **Yellowhead P** Can
4G3 **Yellowknife** Can
5G4 **Yellowmead P** Can
109C2 **Yellow Mt** Aust
69E3 **Yellow Sea** China/ Korea
8C2 **Yellowstone** *R* USA
8B2 **Yellowstone L** USA
6B1 **Yelverton B** Can
97C3 **Yelwa** Nig
81C4 **Yemen** Republic, Arabian Pen
76C1 **Yen Bai** Viet
97B4 **Yendi** Ghana
76B1 **Yengan** Burma
63B2 **Yeniseysk** Russian Fed
63B1 **Yeniseyskiy Kryazh** *Ridge* Russian Fed
64J2 **Yeniseyskiy Zal** *B* Russian Fed
12D2 **Yentna** *R* USA
43C4 **Yeo** *R* Eng
109C2 **Yeoval** Aust
43C4 **Yeovil** Eng
63C1 **Yerbogachen** Russian Fed
65F5 **Yerevan** Armenia
21B2 **Yerington** USA
21B3 **Yermo** USA
69E1 **Yerofey-Pavlovich** Russian Fed
94B3 **Yeroham** Israel
61G3 **Yershov** Russian Fed
Yerushalayim = Jerusalem
92C1 **Yeşil** *R* Turk
94B2 **Yesud Hama'ala** Israel
109D1 **Yetman** Aust
96B2 **Yetti** Maur
93E1 **Yevlakh** Azerbaijan
60D4 **Yevpatoriya** Ukraine
72E2 **Ye Xian** China
60E4 **Yeysk** Russian Fed
55B2 **Yiannitsá** Greece
73A4 **Yibin** China
73C3 **Yichang** China
69E2 **Yichun** China
72B2 **Yijun** China
54C2 **Yildiz Dağlari** *Upland* Turk
92C2 **Yıldızeli** Turk
73A5 **Yiliang** China
72B2 **Yinchuan** China
72D3 **Ying He** *R* China
72E1 **Yingkou** China
73D3 **Yingshan** Hubei, China
72B3 **Yingshan** Sichuan, China
73D4 **Yingtan** China
82C1 **Yining** China
72B1 **Yin Shan** *Upland* China
99D2 **Yirga Alem** Eth
99D2 **Yirol** Sudan
63D3 **Yirshi** China
73B5 **Yishan** China
72D2 **Yishui** China
55B3 **Yíthion** Greece
38J6 **Yivieska** Fin
73C4 **Yiyang** China
38K5 **Yli-Kitka** *L* Fin
38J5 **Ylilornio** Sweden
19A4 **Yoakum** USA
23B2 **Yogope** Mexico
78C4 **Yogyakarta** Indon
13D2 **Yoho Nat Pk** Can
98B2 **Yokadouma** Cam
75B2 **Yokkaichi** Japan
75B1 **Yokohama** Japan
75B1 **Yokosuka** Japan
74C3 **Yonago** Japan
74E3 **Yonezawa** Japan
73D4 **Yong'an** China
72A2 **Yongchang** China
74B3 **Yŏngch'on** S Korea
73B4 **Yongchuan** China
72A2 **Yongdeng** China
73D5 **Yongding** China
72D2 **Yongding He** *R* China
74B3 **Yŏngdŏk** S Korea
74B3 **Yŏnghŭng** N Korea
74B3 **Yongju** S Korea
72B2 **Yongning** China
16C2 **Yonkers** USA
49C2 **Yonne** *R* France
42D3 **York** Eng
18A1 **York** Nebraska, USA
16A3 **York** Pennsylvania, USA
107D2 **York,C** Aust
108A2 **Yorke Pen** Aust
108A3 **Yorketown** Aust
7A4 **York Factory** Can
41C3 **Yorkshire Moors** *Moorland* Eng
42D2 **Yorkshire Wolds** *Upland* Eng
5H4 **Yorkton** Can
22B2 **Yosemite L** USA
22C1 **Yosemite Nat Pk** USA
75A2 **Yoshii** *R* Japan
75A2 **Yoshino** *R* Japan
61G2 **Yoshkar Ola** Russian Fed
74B4 **Yŏsu** S Korea
41B3 **Youghal** Irish Rep
45C3 **Youghal Harb** Irish Rep
73B5 **You Jiang** *R* China
109C2 **Young** Aust
34D2 **Young** Urug
111A2 **Young Range** *Mts* NZ
13E2 **Youngstown** Can
14B2 **Youngstown** Ohio, USA
22A1 **Yountville** USA
73B4 **Youyang** China
92B2 **Yozgat** Turk
20B2 **Yreka** USA
39G7 **Ystad** Sweden
43C3 **Ystwyth** *R* Wales
44C3 **Ythan** *R* Scot
73C4 **Yuan Jiang** *R* Hunan, China
73A5 **Yuan Jiang** *R* Yunnan, China
73A4 **Yuanmu** China
72C2 **Yuanping** China
21A2 **Yuba City** USA
74E2 **Yūbari** Japan
25D3 **Yucatan** *Pen* Mexico
25D2 **Yucatan Chan** Mexico/Cuba
72C2 **Yuci** China
63F2 **Yudoma** *R* Russian Fed
73D4 **Yudu** China
73A4 **Yuexi** China
73C4 **Yueyang** China
54A2 **Yugoslavia** Republic, Europe
73B5 **Yu Jiang** *R* China
12C2 **Yukon** *R* Can/USA
4E3 **Yukon Territory** Can
76E1 **Yulin** Guangdong, China
73C5 **Yulin** Guangxi, China
72B2 **Yulin** Shaanxi, China
9B3 **Yuma** USA
68B3 **Yumen** China
72D2 **Yunan** China
34A3 **Yungay** Chile
73C5 **Yunkai Dashan** *Hills* China
108A2 **Yunta** Aust
72C3 **Yunxi** China
72C3 **Yun Xian** China
73B3 **Yunyang** China
32B5 **Yurimaguas** Peru
73E5 **Yu Shan** *Mt* Taiwan
38L6 **Yushkozero** Russian Fed
82D2 **Yushu** Tibet, China
73A5 **Yuxi** China
74F2 **Yuzhno-Kuril'sk** Russian Fed
69G2 **Yuzhno-Sakhalinsk** Russian Fed
61J3 **Yuzh Ural** *Mts* Russian Fed
46A2 **Yvelines** Department, France
47B1 **Yverdon** Switz

Z

56A2 **Zaandam** Neth
93D2 **Zāb al Babir** *R* Iraq
93D2 **Zāb as Şaghīr** *R* Iraq
68D2 **Zabaykal'sk** Russian Fed
59B3 **Zabreh** Czech Republic
59B2 **Zabrze** Pol
23A2 **Zacapu** Mexico
24B2 **Zacatecas** Mexico
23B2 **Zacatepec** Morelos, Mexico
23B2 **Zacatepec** Oaxaca, Mexico
23B2 **Zacatlan** Mexico
23A1 **Zacoalco** Mexico
23B1 **Zacualtipan** Mexico
52C2 **Zadar** Croatia
76B3 **Zadetkyi** *I* Burma
50A2 **Zafra** Spain
95C1 **Zagazig** Egypt
96B1 **Zagora** Mor
52C1 **Zagreb** Croatia
91D4 **Zāhedān** Iran
94B2 **Zahle** Leb
51C2 **Zahrez Chergui** *Marshland* Alg
61H2 **Zainsk** Russian Fed
98C3 **Zaïre** Republic, Africa
98B3 **Zaïre** *R* Zaïre/Congo
54B2 **Zaječar** Yugos
68C1 **Zakamensk** Russian Fed
93D2 **Zakho** Iraq
55B3 **Zákinthos** *I* Greece
59B3 **Zakopane** Pol
59B3 **Zalaegerszeg** Hung
54B1 **Zalău** Rom
56C2 **Zalew Szczeciński** *Lg* Pol
98C1 **Zalingei** Sudan
63F2 **Zaliv Akademii** *B* Russian Fed
65G5 **Zaliv Kara-Bogaz Gol** *B* Turkmenistan
74C2 **Zaliv Petra Velikogo** *B* Russian Fed
69G2 **Zaliv Turpeniya** *B* Russian Fed
95A2 **Zaltan** Libya
89H9 **Zambesi** *R* Mozam
100B2 **Zambezi** Zambia
100B2 **Zambezi** *R* Zambia
100B2 **Zambia** Republic, Africa
79B4 **Zamboanga** Phil
79B4 **Zamboanga Pen** Phil
58C2 **Zambrów** Pol
32B4 **Zamora** Ecuador
23A2 **Zamora** Mexico
50A1 **Zamora** Spain
59C2 **Zamość** Pol
72A3 **Zamtang** China
98B3 **Zanaga** Congo
50B2 **Záncara** *R* Spain
84D2 **Zanda** China
14B3 **Zanesville** USA
84D2 **Zangla** India
90A2 **Zanjān** Iran
34B2 **Zanjitas** Arg
34B2 **Zanjon** *R* Arg
99D3 **Zanzibar** Tanz
99D3 **Zanzibar** *I* Tanz
96C2 **Zaouatallaz** Alg
72D3 **Zaozhuang** China
93D2 **Zap** *R* Turk
39K7 **Zapadnaja Dvina** *R* Russian Fed
65H3 **Zapadno-Sibirskaya Nizmennost'** *Lowland* Russian Fed
63B2 **Zapadnyy Sayan** *Mts* Russian Fed
34A3 **Zapala** Arg
60E4 **Zaporozh'ye** Ukraine
93C2 **Zara** Turk
23A1 **Zaragoza** Mexico
50B1 **Zaragoza** Spain
90B2 **Zarand** Iran
90C3 **Zarand** Iran
80E2 **Zaranj** Afghan
33D2 **Zarara** Ven
58D1 **Zarasai** Lithuania
34D2 **Zárate** Arg
90B3 **Zard Kuh** *Mt* Iran
12H3 **Zarembo I** USA
84B2 **Zarghun Shahr** Afghan
84B2 **Zargun** *Mt* Pak
97C3 **Zaria** Nig
92C3 **Zarqa** Jordan
94B2 **Zarqa** *R* Jordan
32B4 **Zaruma** Ecuador
58B2 **Zary** Pol
96D1 **Zarzis** Tunisia
84D2 **Zāskār** *Mts* India
84D2 **Zāskār** *R* India
94C2 **Zatara** *R* Jordan
Zatoka Gdańska = Gdańsk,G of
69E1 **Zavitinsk** Russian Fed
59B2 **Zawiercie** Pol
63C2 **Zayarsk** Russian Fed
65K5 **Zaysan** Kazakhstan
82D3 **Zayü** China
68B4 **Zayü** *Mt* China
58B2 **Zduńska Wola** Pol
46B1 **Zeebrugge** Belg
94B3 **Zeelim** Israel
101G1 **Zeerust** S Africa
94B2 **Zefat** Israel
97C3 **Zegueren** *Watercourse* Mali
99E1 **Zeila** Somalia
57C2 **Zeitz** Germany
72A2 **Zekog** China
61G2 **Zelenodol'sk** Russian Fed
39K6 **Zelenogorsk** Russian Fed
47D1 **Zell** Austria
98C2 **Zemio** CAR
64F1 **Zemlya Aleksandry** *I* Barents S
64F2 **Zemlya Frantsa Iosifa** *Is* Barents S
64F1 **Zemlya Georga** *I* Barents S
64H1 **Zemlya Vil'cheka** *I* Barents S
73B4 **Zenning** China
47B1 **Zermatt** Switz
63E2 **Zeya** Russian Fed
63E2 **Zeya** *Res* Russian Fed
50A1 **Zézere** *R* Port
94B1 **Zghorta** Leb
58B2 **Zgierz** Pol
72D1 **Zhangjiakou** China
73D4 **Zhangping** China
72D2 **Zhangwei He** *R* China
72E1 **Zhangwu** China
72A2 **Zhangye** China
73D5 **Zhangzhou** China
73C5 **Zhanjiang** China
73A4 **Zhanyi** China
73C5 **Zhaoqing** China
73A4 **Zhaotong** China
72D2 **Zhaoyang Hu** *L* China
61J4 **Zharkamys** Russian Fed
63E1 **Zhatay** Russian Fed
73D4 **Zhejiang** Province, China
67F3 **Zhengou** China

Zyyi

72C3 **Zhengzhou** China
72D3 **Zhenjiang** China
73A4 **Zhenxiong** China
73B4 **Zhenyuan** China
61F3 **Zherdevka**
Russian Fed
73C3 **Zhicheng** China
68C1 **Zhigalovo**
Russian Fed
73B4 **Zhijin** China
58D2 **Zhitkovichi**
Belorussia
60C3 **Zhitomir** Ukraine
60D3 **Zhlobin** Belorussia
60C4 **Zhmerinka** Ukraine
84B2 **Zhob** Pak
58D2 **Zhodino** Latvia
72B2 **Zhongning** China
112C10 **Zhongshan** Base Ant
73C5 **Zhongshan** China
72B2 **Zhongwei** China
68B4 **Zhougdian** China
73E3 **Zhoushan Quandao**
Arch China
72E2 **Zhuanghe** China
72A3 **Zhugqu** China
73C3 **Zhushan** China

73C4 **Zhuzhou** China
72D2 **Zibo** China
106C3 **Ziel,Mt** Aust
58B2 **Zielona Góra** Pol
76A1 **Zigaing** Burma
73A4 **Zigong** China
97A3 **Ziguinchor** Sen
23A2 **Zihuatanejo** Mexico
94B2 **Zikhron Ya'aqov**
Israel
59B3 **Žilina** Slovakia
95A2 **Zillah** Libya
47D1 **Ziller** R Austria
47D1 **Zillertaler Alpen** Mts
Austria
58D1 **Zilupe** Russian Fed
63C2 **Zima** Russian Fed
23B1 **Zimapan** Mexico
23B2 **Zimatlan** Mexico
100B2 **Zimbabwe** Republic,
Africa
94B3 **Zin** R Israel
23B2 **Zinacatepec** Mexico
23A2 **Zinapécuaro** Mexico
97C3 **Zinder** Niger
73C4 **Zi Shui** China
23A2 **Zitácuaro** Mexico

57C2 **Zittau** Germany
72D2 **Ziya He** R China
72A3 **Ziyang** China
61J2 **Zlatoust**
Russian Fed
59B3 **Zlin** Czech Republic
65K4 **Zmeinogorsk**
Russian Fed
58B2 **Znin** Pol
59B3 **Znoimo**
Czech Republic
100B3 **Zoekmekaar**
S Africa
47B1 **Zofinger** Switz
72A3 **Zoigê** China
59D3 **Zolochev** Ukraine
101C2 **Zomba** Malawi
98B2 **Zongo** Zaïre
92B1 **Zonguldak** Turk
97B4 **Zorzor** Lib
96A2 **Zouerate** Maur
54B1 **Zrenjanin** Serbia,
Yugos
47C1 **Zug** Switz
47D1 **Zugspitze** Mt
Germany
50A2 **Zújar** R Spain

100C2 **Zumbo** Mozam
23B2 **Zumpango** Mexico
97C4 **Zungeru** Nig
73B4 **Zunyi** China
76D1 **Zuo** R China
73B5 **Zuo Jiang** R China
47C1 **Zürich** Switz
47C1 **Zürichsee** L Switz
95A1 **Zuwārah** Libya
95A2 **Zuwaylah** Libya
61H2 **Zuyevka**
Russian Fed
100B4 **Zvishavane** Zim
59B3 **Zvolen** Slovakia
54A2 **Zvornik** Bosnia-
Herzegovina
97B4 **Zwedru** Lib
46D2 **Zweibrücken**
Germany
47B1 **Zweisimmen** Switz
57C2 **Zwickau** Germany
56B2 **Zwolle** Neth
58C2 **Zyrardów** Pol
65K5 **Zyryanovsk**
Kazakhstan
59B3 **Żywiec** Pol
94A1 **Zyyi** Cyprus